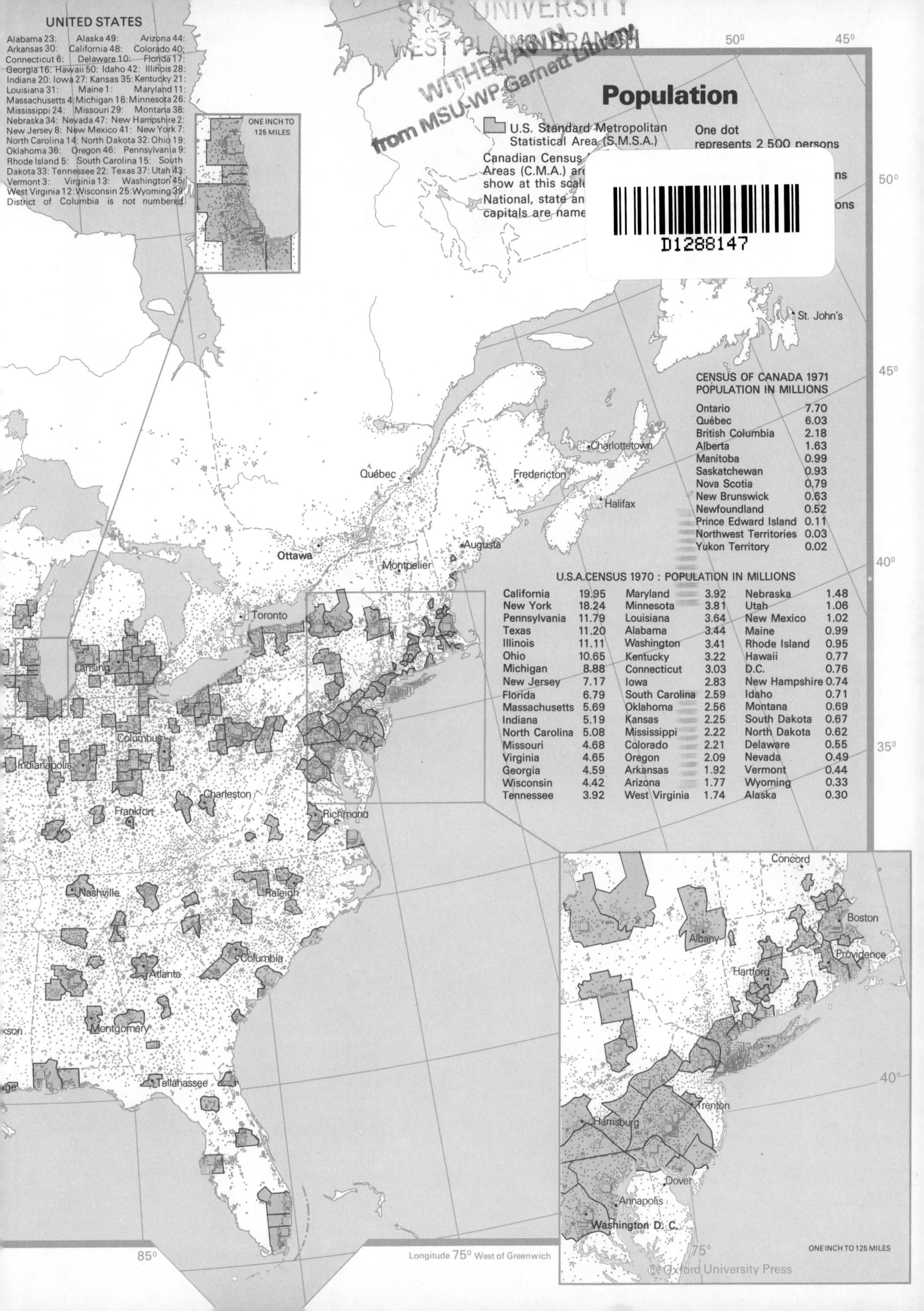

Population

UNITED STATES

Alabama 23: Alaska 49: Arizona 44:
Arkansas 30: California 48: Colorado 40;
Connecticut 6: Delaware 10: Florida 17:
Georgia 16: Hawaii 50: Idaho 42: Illinois 28:
Indiana 20: Iowa 27: Kansas 35: Kentucky 21:
Louisiana 31: Maine 1: Maryland 11:
Massachusetts 4: Michigan 18: Minnesota 26:
Mississippi 24: Missouri 29: Montana 38:
Nebraska 34: Nevada 47: New Hampshire 2:
New Jersey 8: New Mexico 41: New York 7:
North Carolina 14: North Dakota 32: Ohio 19:
Oklahoma 36: Oregon 46: Pennsylvania 9:
Rhode Island 5: South Carolina 15: South
Dakota 33: Tennessee 22: Texas 37: Utah 43:
Vermont 3: Virginia 13: Washington 45:
West Virginia 12: Wisconsin 25: Wyoming 39:
District of Columbia is not numbered

ONE INCH TO 125 MILES

☐ U.S. Standard Metropolitan
Statistical Area (S.M.S.A.)

Canadian Census
Areas (C.M.A.) are
show at this scale

National, state an
capitals are name

One dot
represents 2 500 persons

CENSUS OF CANADA 1971
POPULATION IN MILLIONS

Ontario	7.70
Québec	6.03
British Columbia	2.18
Alberta	1.63
Manitoba	0.99
Saskatchewan	0.93
Nova Scotia	0.79
New Brunswick	0.63
Newfoundland	0.52
Prince Edward Island	0.11
Northwest Territories	0.03
Yukon Territory	0.02

U.S.A. CENSUS 1970 : POPULATION IN MILLIONS

California	19.95	Maryland	3.92	Nebraska	1.48
New York	18.24	Minnesota	3.81	Utah	1.06
Pennsylvania	11.79	Louisiana	3.64	New Mexico	1.02
Texas	11.20	Alabama	3.44	Maine	0.99
Illinois	11.11	Washington	3.41	Rhode Island	0.95
Ohio	10.65	Kentucky	3.22	Hawaii	0.77
Michigan	8.88	Connecticut	3.03	D.C.	0.76
New Jersey	7.17	Iowa	2.83	New Hampshire	0.74
Florida	6.79	South Carolina	2.59	Idaho	0.71
Massachusetts	5.69	Oklahoma	2.56	Montana	0.69
Indiana	5.19	Kansas	2.25	South Dakota	0.67
North Carolina	5.08	Mississippi	2.22	North Dakota	0.62
Missouri	4.68	Colorado	2.21	Delaware	0.55
Virginia	4.65	Oregon	2.09	Nevada	0.49
Georgia	4.59	Arkansas	1.92	Vermont	0.44
Wisconsin	4.42	Arizona	1.77	Wyoming	0.33
Tennessee	3.92	West Virginia	1.74	Alaska	0.30

St. John's

Charlottetown

Québec   Fredericton

Halifax

Ottawa   Augusta

Montpelier

Toronto

Lansing

Columbus

Indianapolis

Charleston

Frankfort

Richmond

Nashville   Raleigh

Columbia

Atlanta

Montgomery

Tallahassee

Concord

Albany   Boston

Hartford   Providence

Harrisburg   Trenton

Dover

Annapolis

Washington D. C.

ONE INCH TO 125 MILES

50°   45°   50°   45°   40°   35°   40°

85°   75°

Oxford Regional
Economic Atlas

The United States
and Canada

Prepared by the Cartographic Department of
Oxford University Press

Advisory Editors

John D. Chapman, University of British Columbia

John C. Sherman, University of Washington

Second Edition

Prepared with the assistance of Quentin H. Stanford
Don Mills Collegiate Institute, Toronto

OXFORD UNIVERSITY PRESS
1975

Oxford University Press, Ely House, London W.1

GLASGOW NEW YORK TORONTO MELBOURNE WELLINGTON
CAPE TOWN IBADAN NAIROBI DAR ES SALAAM LUSAKA ADDIS ABABA
DELHI BOMBAY CALCUTTA MADRAS KARACHI LAHORE DACCA
KUALA LUMPUR SINGAPORE HONG KONG TOKYO

© *Oxford University Press 1975*

Oxford Regional Economic Atlas: The United States and Canada
First edition 1967. Reprinted 1968, 1970, 1973

Cased: ISBN 019 894309 1
Paperback: ISBN 019 894308 3

Compiled, drawn, and processed to film by
The Cartographic Department of Oxford University Press

Printed in Great Britain

Maps: Cook Hammond and Kell Ltd, Mitcham, Surrey

Introductory text and Gazetteer: set by The Church Army Press, Oxford and
printed by J. W. Arrowsmith Ltd, Bristol

Acknowledgements

First Edition 1967

Agent-General for the Alberta Government
Agent-General for the British Columbia Government
Agent-General for the Ontario Government
Agent-General for the Québec Government
Dr. T. Armstrong
Association of American Railroads
E. M. Buxton
Canadian Atlantic Provinces Office
Canadian Government Agencies:
    Department of Energy, Mines and Resources, *formerly* Mines and Technical Surveys
    Department of Indian Affairs and Northern Development, *formerly* Northern Affairs and National Resources
    Dominion Bureau of Statistics
    Geological Survey of Canada
    Ministry of Transport
Canadian National Railways, London Office
Canadian Pacific Railways, London Office
Dr. K. M. Clayton
Dr. A. Coleman
Commissioner General, Canadian Corporation for the 1967 World Exhibition
Dr. A. C. Gerlach
C. F. W. R. Gullick
Dr. F. K. Hare
Hydrographic Department, Admiralty, London, U.K.
Professor G. F. Jenks
Kansas Turnpike Authority
Lovell Johns, Ltd.
Mackay School of Mines, University of Nevada
Maine Turnpike Authority
Manitoba Department of Mines and Natural Resources
Map Room, Bodleian Library, University of Oxford
M. Marsden
Meteorological Office, Bracknell, U.K.
Professor R. E. Murphy
National Institute of Oceanography, Wormley, U.K.
New Jersey Highway Authority
New York State Thruway Authority
Office of the High Commissioner for Canada
Ohio Turnpike Authority
Oklahoma Turnpike Authority
Dr. E. R. Oxburgh
Dr. M. E. D. Poore
Rand McNally & Co.
Dr. A. H. W. Robinson
St. Lawrence Seaway Authority
Saint Lawrence Seaway Development Corporation
Service des Arpentages, Ministère des Terres et Forêts
M. A. Shaw
P. E. Smethurst
The Economist Intelligence Unit
United States Government Agencies:

U.S. Civil Aeronautics Board
U.S. Department of the Army: Army Map Service, Corps of Engineers
U.S. Department of Agriculture: Forest Service, Soil Conservation Service
U.S. Department of Commerce: Bureau of the Census, Coast and Goedeti Survey, Weather Bureau
U.S. Department of the Interior: Bureau of Commercial Fisheries, Bureau of Mines, Geological Survey, National Parks Service
U.S. Department of Labor: Bureau of Labor Statistics
U.S. Federal Power Commission
U.S. Interstate Commerce Commission
U.S. Treasury Department: Internal Revenue Service
U.S. Information Service at the United States Embassy, London, U.K.
Professor J. W. Watson
West Virginia Turnpike Commission

Second Edition 1975

Boston Metropolitan Area Planning Council
Communauté Urban de Montréal
Delaware Valley Regional Planning Commission
Denver Regional Council of Governments
Houston-Galveston Area Council
Los Angeles Regional Planning Commission
Metropolitan Washington Council of Governments
Minneapolis/St. Paul Metropolitan Council
New York Regional Plan Association
Northern Illinois Planning Commission
Orange County Planning Commission
Regional Planning Commission of Jefferson, Orleans, and St. Bernard Parishes
Southeast Michigan Council of Governments
Southwestern Pennsylvania Regional Planning Commission

Aviation Statistics Centre, Ottawa
Joyce Berry
Professor Saul B. Cohen
Canadian Arctic Gas Study, Ltd.
Cox Cartographic, Ltd.
Richard Deily, Institute for Iron and Steel Studies
Economics and Statistics Library, University of Oxford
Environmental—Social Program Northern Pipelines, Ottawa
Indian and Northern Affairs, Ottawa
Newbury Drawing Agency, Ltd.
Miklos Pinther
Joan Stanford
Statistics Canada, *formerly* Dominion Bureau of Statistics
The British Petroleum Company, Ltd.
Robert Wharton
United States Atomic Energy Commission

Topics

Contents

Endpapers Population Distribution

*Maps with an asterisk are on a common base map of the United States and Southern Canada at a scale of 1:15.84M or 1″ to 250 miles. The symbols † & ‡ indicate smaller scale versions of the same map at 1:33.94M or 1″ to 535 miles and 1:46.00M or 1″ to 726 miles respectively.

Projection

All the maps, except the urban plans and Alaska (pp. 42/43) are on the same projection. This is a composite projection: South of 55°N it is conical orthomorphic, with origin at 42° N and standard parallels at 35°N and 49° N. The northern portion has been modified by taking the 90°W meridian as straight, and curving the meridians that lie east and west of it inwards; this has the effect of reducing scale errors in the Arctic (to 10% at most). Alaska is on a Lambert conical orthomorphic projection.

Sources

URBAN PLANS pp. 1–7

Authorities: Prof. J. W. Watson, Edinburgh University.
also
Boston: Saul B. Cohen, Clark University.
Chicago: Douglas B. Cargo, University of Chicago.
Denver: Laurence D. Herold, University of Denver.
Detroit: Byran Thompson, Wayne State University.
Houston: J. E. Coffman, University of Houston.
Los Angeles: Howard Nelson, University of California, Los Angeles.
Minneapolis/St. Paul: John Adams, University of Minnesota.
Montréal: Quentin H. Stanford: Don Mills Collegiate Institute.
New Orleans: Patsy Denton, Regional Planning Commission.
New York: Michael P. Marchioni, Hunter College.
Philadelphia: Roman A. Cybriwsky, Temple University.
Pittsburgh: Louis C. Peltier, University of Pittsburgh.
San Francisco: James E. Vance, University of California, Berkeley.
Seattle: Warren Gill, University of British Columbia.
Toronto: Quentin H. Stanford, Don Mills Collegiate Institute.
Vancouver: Warren Gill, University of British Columbia.
Washington, D.C.: Harold Brodsky, University of Maryland.

Sources: *Base Maps:* U.S. Army Map Service, 1:250 000 series: U.S. Geological Survey, 1:24 000 series.
U.S. Dept of Commerce: Bureau of the Census, PC(1) State reports; National Oceanic & Atmospheric Administration Environmental Data Service, Local Climatological Data, 1971; Sectional Aeronautical Charts, 1:500 000, 1973 *(maps)*.
Regional Planning Councils *see* Acknowledgements.
see also Urban Plan Legend facing page 1.

TOPOGRAPHIC MAPS pp. 8–45, 128

Sources: *Base Maps:* U.S.A.F. 1:1 000 000 Aeronautical Charts and Operational Navigational Charts 1:1 000 000.
U.S. Bureau of the Census: United States Census of Population, 1960 & 1970.
Dominion Bureau of Statistics *now* Statistics Canada: Census of Canada, 1961 & 1971.
U.S. Geological Survey: Map Showing Extent of Glaciations in Alaska, 1:2 500 000, 1965; Alaska Reconnaissance Topographical Series 1:250 000.
U.S. Civil Aeronautics Board: Airport Activity Statistics, 1971.
Statistics Canada: Air Passenger origin and destination, Domestic Report, 1972.
National Atlas of the United States, 1970.
Atlas of Canada, 1957.
Miscellaneous Road maps.

RELIEF pp. 46–47

Sources: U.S. Naval Oceanographic Office: World Charts.
U.S. Geological Survey: Geologic Map of North America, 1965.
International Hydrographic Bureau, Monaco: Carte générale bathymetric des Océans, 1923.
Hydrographic Office, Admiralty, London, U.K.
National Institute of Oceanography, Wormley, Surrey, U.K.
National Atlas of the United States, 1970.

The National Atlas of Canada, 4th edn., 1973.
N. M. Fenneman: Physical Divisions of the United States *(map)*.

SOLID GEOLOGY pp. 48–49

Authorities: U.S. Geological Survey; Dr. E. B. Oxburgh, Oxford University.

Sources: U. S. Geological Survey, Geologic Map of North America, 1965.
Dr. P. King: Evolution of North America, 1959.

PLEISTOCENE GLACIATION AND DRIFT GEOLOGY pp. 50–51

Authority: Prof. K. M. Clayton, East Anglia University.

Sources: Geological Association of Canada: Glacial Map of Canada, 1958.
U.S. Geological Survey: Geologic Map of North America, 1965.
The Geological Society of America: Glacial Map of North America, 1945; Glacial Map of the United States East of the Rocky Mountains, 1959; Pleistocene Eolian Deposits in the United States, Alaska and parts of Canada, 1952 *(map)*.
J. L. Hough: Geology of the Great Lakes, 1958.
Science, February 1965: G. Falconer, J. T. Andrews and J. D. Ives, Late Wisconsin End Moraines in Northern Canada.
Geographical Bulletin, Ottawa, May 1962: W. R. Ferrard and R. T. Gujda, Isobases of the Wisconsin Marine Limits in Canada.
U.S.G.S. Professional Papers, 1961: J. H. Feth, Glacial Lakes.
Geological Survey of Canada: Geology and Economic Minerals of Canada, Edit. R. J. W. Douglas, 1970.

SOILS pp. 52–53

Authority: Prof. K. M. Clayton, East Anglia University.

Sources: Atlas Mira, 1965.
U.S. Soil Conservation Service, General Soil Map of the United States (experimental), 1964.
Atlas of Canada, 1957.

POTENTIAL VEGETATION pp. 54–55

Authority: Dr. F. K. Hare, Toronto University.

Sources: A. W. Küchler; Potential Natural Vegetation of the Conterminous United States, 1964 *(map)*.
Atlas of Canada, 1957.
World Forestry Atlas, 1951.
Dr. F. K. Hare: A Photo-reconnaissance Survey of Labrador-Ungava *(map)*.
B. V. Gutsell: Newfoundland (Modified) *(map)*.
Department of Northern Affairs and National Resources: Forestry Regions of Canada *(map)*.

RIVER FLOW pp. 56–57

Authority: Prof. J. D. Chapman, University of British Columbia.

Sources: 86th Congress, 1960: Senate Resolution No. 48, Surface Water Resources of the United States.
United States Geological Survey: Circular No. 676, Estimated Use of Water in the United States in 1970.
The National Atlas of Canada, 1970.

SOURCES

LAND USE pp. 58–59

Sources: The National Atlas of the United States, 1970.
International Association of Agricultural Economists: Instituto Geografico De Agostini S.p.A., World Atlas of Agriculture, 1971.

THE NORTH pp. 60–61

Authority: Q. H. Stanford, Don Mills Collegiate Institute, Toronto.

Sources: The Sub-Committee on Science and Technology, Advisory Committee on Northern Development: Science and the North, A Seminar on Guidelines for Scientific Activities in Northern Canada, 1972.
Department of Indian and Northern Affairs: Oil and Gas Activities, edn. 8, 1971; Mines and Mineral Activities, edn. 8, 1971; Canada Showing Location of Indian Bands with Linguistic Affiliations, 1968 (*map*).
Department of Energy, Mines and Resources: North West Canada Transportation Facilities, 1972 (*map*).
Yukon and Northwest Territories Roads and Tracts, 1973 (*map*).
U.S. Bureau of the Census: United States Census of Population, 1970.
Statistics Canada: Census of Canada, 1971.
Mackenzie Valley Pipe Line Research Ltd.: Arctic Oil Pipe Line Feasibility Study, 1974.
Canadian Arctic Gas Study Ltd.: Arctic Gas System Route Map 1974.
U.S. Bureau of Mines: Minerals Yearbook, 1971.
National Atlas of the United States, 1970.
National Atlas of Canada, 4th edn., 1970.

CLIMATIC MAPS pp. 62–71

Authorities: Dr. F. K. Hare, Toronto University; M. Marsden, Sir George Williams University, Montréal.

Sources: U.S. Weather Bureau: Maps and published normals; Mean Daily Solar Radiation, Monthly and Annual, 1964 (*map*); Climatology of the United States, No. 81, Monthly Normals of Temperature, Precipitation, and Heating Degree Days, 1931–1960.
Ministry of Transport, Ottawa: MSS data.
Meteorological Office, Bracknell, U.K.: R.A.F. Form 2215A.
WMO/OMM: No. 117, TP52, Climatological Normals (Clino) for Climat and Climat Ship stations for the period 1931–60.
Canadian Meteorological Memoirs: No. 17, 1964, C. C. Brughner, Distribution of Growing Degree Days in Canada.
M. Marsden: MSS data.
National Atlas of the United States, 1955.
Atlas of Canada, 1957.

DEMOGRAPHIC MAPS pp. 72–77

Authority: Q. H. Stanford, Don Mills Collegiate Institute, Toronto.

Sources: United States Bureau of the Census: Census of Population 1960 & 1970; Census of Population and Housing, 1970; Negro Population in Selected Places and Selected Counties, 1970; General Social and Economic Characteristics, 1970; County and City Data Book, 1972.
United States Department of Health, Education and Welfare: Monthly Vital Statistics Report, Annual Summary for the United States, 1972.

United States Department of Labor: United States Employment and Earnings, Vol. 18, No. 11, May 1972.
United States Statistical Abstract, 1973.
Statistics Canada: Census of Canada, 1966 & 1971; Number of Inhabitants, Population by Ethnic Groups, 1971; Income Distribution by Size in Canada, 1971; Vital Statistics, 1972; The Labour Force, April & October, 1973.
M. V. George, Census Monograph: Internal Migration in Canada, 1961.
The National Atlas of the United States, 1970.

AGRICULTURAL MAPS pp. 78–85

Authorities: Prof. J. C. Sherman, University of Washington; Prof. J. D. Chapman, University of British Columbia.

Sources: United States Department of Agriculture; various statistics.
United States Bureau of the Census: Cotton Production in the United States—Crop of 1963.
Dominion Bureau of Statistics: various statistics.
Prof. G. F. Jenks: Livestock and Livestock Products Sold in the United States, 1959 (*map*).
Pineapple Growers' Association: Pineapple Fact Book, Hawaii, 1965; MSS data.
Department of the Treasury, Bureau of Alcohol, Tobacco and Firearms, ATF PB23.1(4–74): Alcohol, Tobacco and Firearms, Summary Statistics, 1973.
Statistics Canada: Tobacco and Tobacco Products Statistics, 1973.
National Atlas of the United States, 1955.
Atlas of Canada, 1957.

WOOD PROCESSING pp. 86–87

Authority: Q. H. Stanford, Don Mills Collegiate Institute, Toronto.

Sources: Post's Pulp and Paper Directory, 1974.
Directory of Forest Products Industry 1973.
Dept. of the Environment, Canadian Forestry Service: J. S. Rowe, Forest Regions of Canada, Public. No. 1300, 1972.
The National Atlas of the United States, 1970.

COMMERCIAL FISHERIES pp. 88–89

Authority: Q. H. Stanford, Don Mills Collegiate Institute, Toronto.

Sources: F.A.O.: Atlas of Living Resources of the Sea, 1972.
Department of Mines and Technical Surveys, Ottawa: Natural Resources, 1958 (*map*).
U.S. Department of Commerce: Current Fisheries Statistics, No. 5900, 1971; Fishery Statistics of the United States, Statistical Digest No. 64, 1970.
Statistics Canada: Fishery Statistics, New Brunswick, Newfoundland, Northwest Territories, Nova Scotia, Ontario, Prairie Provinces, Prince Edward Island, Québec, 1971; Shipping Reports, Pts. II & III, 1971.
Department of the Army, Corps of Engineers: Waterborne Commerce of the United States, 1972.

FUELS MAPS pp. 90–97

Authorities: Prof. J. D. Chapman, University of British Columbia; Q. H. Stanford, Don Mills Collegiate Institute, Toronto.

SOURCES

Sources: Oxford Regional Economic Atlas: The United States and Canada, 1st. edn., 1967.
United States Department of the Interior: Bituminous Coal and Lignite Distribution, 1969.
United States Bureau of Mines: Preprint from Minerals Yearbook; Coal—Bituminous and Lignite, 1971; Coal—Pennsylvanite Anthracite, 1971; Crude Petroleum and Petroleum Products, 1970; Natural Gas, 1971.
Department of Energy, Mines and Resources, Minerals Branch, Ottawa: Operators List No. 4, Coal Mines in Canada, Jan. 1973; Operator List No. 5, Petroleum Refineries in Canada, 1973; Canadian Minerals Yearbook, 1971; Offshore Exploration, 1973; Electrical Power in Canada, 1971; Main Electrical Transmission Systems and Principal Power Generating Developments, 1971 (*map*).
National Coal Association, Washington: Bituminous Coal Facts, 1972.
Exxon Corpn.: Oil and Gas Atlas, 1972.
The Petroleum Publishing Co.: Oil and Gas Journal, 1970; Oil and Gas Journal Atlas.
Federal Power Commission: Electric Utility Listing by State, Dec., 1969; Steam-Electric Plant Construction Cost and Annual Production Expenses, 1971; Hydroelectric Plant Construction Cost and Annual Production Expenses, 1971; Principal Electrical Facilities, 1971 (*national and regional maps*).
Nuclear Energy International, Washington: Atomic Power, Jan., 1971.
Acres Ltd.: Mid Canada Development Corridor . . . a concept, 1967.
National Atlas of the United States, 1970.
Atlas of Canada, 1957.

MINING AND MINERAL PROCESSING MAPS pp. 98–105

Authorities: Prof. J. D. Chapman, University of British Columbia; Q. H. Stanford, Don Mills Collegiate Institute, Toronto.

Sources: United States Bureau of Mines: Minerals Yearbook, 1970 & 1971; Preprints from Minerals Yearbook, 1971.
United States Atomic Energy Commission: The Nuclear Industry, 1971.
Department of Energy, Mines and Resources, Minerals Resources Division, Ottawa: Minerals Yearbook, 1971; Operators List, No. 1, Primary Iron and Steel, Jan. 1971, No. 2 Metal and Industrial Mineral Mines and processing Plant, 1971.
Engineering and Mining Journal: International Directory of Mining and Mineral Processing Operations, 1973.
Geological Survey of Canada: Mineral Deposits of Canada, 1969 (*map*).
Pit and Quarry Publications Inc.: Portland Cement Plant in the United States, Canada and Mexico, 1973 (*map*).

IRON AND STEEL pp. 106–107

Authority: Q. H. Stanford, Don Mills Collegiate Institute, Toronto.

Sources: Institute for Iron and Steel Studies, Greenbrook, N.J.: Commentaries January, February, March 1973, January–February, 1974; Directory of Iron & Steel Works of the United States & Canada, 1971.
American Iron and Steel Institute: Iron and Steel Producing and Finishing Works of the United States and Canada, 1970.

Engineering and Mining Journal: International Directory of Mining and Mineral Processing Operations, 1973.
Department of Energy, Mines and Resources, Minerals Resources Branch, Ottawa: Operators List No. 1, Primary Iron and Steel, January 1971.
Statistics Canada: Shipping Reports Pts. I and II, 1971.
The St. Lawrence Seaway Authority: Traffic Report of the St. Lawrence Seaway, 1971.

FABRICATED METALS AND MACHINERY pp. 108–109

Authority: Prof. J. D. Chapman, University of British Columbia.

Sources: United States Department of Commerce: County Business Patterns, 1970.
Dominion Bureau of Statistics: Manufacturing Industries in Canada, Section G, Geographical Distribution, 1967.

TRANSPORT EQUIPMENT pp. 110–111

Authorities: Prof. J. D. Chapman, University of British Columbia: Economist Intelligence Unit, London.

Sources: Oxford Regional Economic Atlas: The United States and Canada, 1st. edn., 1967.
Interavia World Directory of Aviation and Astronautics, 1974.
Jane's World Railways, 1974.
Moodie's Industrial Manual, 1973.
' Automotive News ' 1973 Review and Reference Edition.
International Shipping and Shipbuilding Directory, 1973.
Scott's Industrial Directories: Ontario Manufacturers, 1972–73; Québec, 1971–72.
Directories of: British Columbia, Trade, 1971; California Manufacturers, 1969; Illinois Manufacturers, 1972; Manitoba Trade, 1974; Michigan Manufacturers, 1971; New England Manufacturers, 1974; Nova Scotia, Manufacturing, 1970–71; Texas Manufacturers, 1970.

CHEMICALS pp. 112–113

Sources: European Chemical News, London, U.K.: Chemical Plant Data, 1970.

TEXTILES pp. 114–115

Authorities: Prof. J. D. Chapman, University of British Columbia; Q. H. Stanford, Don Mills Collegiate Institute, Toronto.

Sources: Oxford Regional Economic Atlas: United States and Canada, 1st. edn., 1967.
Davidson's Blue Books, 1973.

MANUFACTURING pp. 116–117

Authority: Prof. J. D. Chapman, University of British Columbia.

Sources: *see* Fabricated Metals and Machinery.

TOURISM pp. 118–119

Authority: Q. H. Stanford, Don Mills Collegiate Institute, Toronto.

Sources: U.S. Department of the Interior, National Park Service: Number of Tourist Visits and Overnight stays in Areas under the Auspices of the National Park Service during 1973.

SOURCES

U.S. Department of Commerce, 1972 Census of Transportation: Travel during 1972.

U.S. Travel Data Center: 1972 National Travel Expenditure Study.

U.S. Bureau of the Census: Annual Survey of Manufactures 1971.

Statistics Canada: Advance Information, Canada Travel Survey, 1971: Travel, Tourism & Outdoor Recreation—A Statistical Digest, 1972.

Dept. of Trade, Industry and Commerce, Travel Industry Board: The Canadian Tourism Facts Book, 1972.

The National Geographic Society: National Geographic, Feb. 1970, June 1971, Feb. 1974.

The National Atlas of the United States, 1970.

Miscellaneous Road maps.

WATERBORNE COMMERCE pp. 120–121

Sources: Department of the Army, Corps of Engineers: Waterborne Commerce of the United States, Parts I–IV, 1972.

Statistics Canada: Shipping Report, Parts II & III, 1971.

St. Lawrence Seaway Authority: Traffic Report of St. Lawrence Seaway, 1971.

SURFACE COMMUNICATIONS pp. 122–123

Sources: Amtrak Marketing Department: Amtrak Routes, 1973 (*map*).

National Railway Publication Company: The Official Guide of the Railways, Aug. 1972.

Canadian National Railways: Timetable, Oct. 1973–April 1974; Across Canada (*map*).

Canadian Pacific Rail: Timetable, Oct. 1973–April 1974; C.P. Services, 1974 (*map*).

United States Department of Transportation; Federal Highways Administration 1972, Average Daily Traffic on Rural Mileage of the Interstate system of the Travelled-Way (*map*).

Mobil Oil Corpn.: Travel Maps, 1971.

DATES OF RAILROAD CONSTRUCTION pp. 124–125

Authorities: C. F. W. R. Gullick, *formerly* Oxford University; Prof. Saul B. Cohen, Clark University.

Sources: Rand McNally: Handy Railroad Atlas of the United States, 1965.

C. L. Lord and E. H. Lord: Historical Atlas of the United States, 1953.

C. O. Paullin: Atlas of the Historical Geography of the United States, 1932.

Hammond's American History Atlas, 1964.

L. J. Burpee: Historical Atlas of Canada, 1927.

Canadian National Railways: MSS data.

AIR COMMUNICATIONS pp. 126–127

Sources: International Civil Aeronautical Organization, Montréal: Digest of Statistics, No. 166 TF. 1971.

United States Department of Transportation, Federal Aviation Administration, Civil Aeronautics Board: Airport Statistics of Certified Route Air Carriers, June 1971; Handbook of Airline Statistics, 1972; Airman's Information Manual, Airport Directory, 1972.

Statistics Canada: Air Passenger origin and destination, Domestic Report, 1972; Aviation Statistics Centre, Airport Activity Statistics, 1971–1972.

United States Department of Transportation and Canadian Surveys and Mapping Branch: Standard Time Zones of North America, 1971 (*map*).

Abbreviations
used on maps and in the gazeteer

Ala.	Alabama	Ind.	Indiana	Oreg.	Oregon
Alta.	Alberta	Junc(t)., Jnc.	Junction	P.	Pass
Aq.	Aqueduct	Ky.	Kentucky	Pa.	Pennsylvania
Arch.	Archipelago	L.	Lake	P.E.I.	Prince Edward Island
Ariz.	Arizona	La.	Louisiana	Pen., penin.	Peninsula
Ark.	Arkansas	Ldg.	Landing	Pk.	Park, peak
B.	Bay	Man.	Manitoba	Plat.	Plateau
B.C.	British Columbia	Mass.	Massachusetts	Prov. Park	Provincial Park
Br.*br.*	Bridge, branch	Md.	Maryland	Pt(e).	Point(e)
C.	Cape	Mich.	Michigan	Qué.	Québec
Calif.	California	Minn.	Minnesota	R., *r.*	River
Can.	Canada	Miss.	Mississippi	Ra(s).	Range(s)
Cen.	Center, centre	Mo.	Missouri	Res.	Reservoir
Ch., chan.	Channel	Mont.	Montana	R.I.	Rhode Island
Colo.	Colorado	Mt(s)., mtn(s).	Mount(s), mountain(s)	S.	South
Conn.	Connecticut	N.	North	Sask.	Saskatchewan
Cors.	Corners	Nat'l Hist. Park	National Historical Park	S.C.	South Carolina
Cr., *cr.*	Creek	Nat. Mon., N.M.	National Monument	Sd.	Sound
D.C.	District of Columbia	Nat. Park., N.P.	National Park	S.D.	South Dakota
Del.	Delaware	Nat. Rec. Area	National Recreation Area	*Sett.*	Settlement
Des.	Desert	N.B.	New Brunswick	Sprs.	Springs
E.	East	N.C.	North Carolina	St(e).	Saint(e)
Fd.	Fiord	N.D.	North Dakota	Stn.	Station
Fk.	Fork	Nebr.	Nebraska	St. Park	State Park
Fla.	Florida	Nev.	Nevada	Str.	Strait
Ft.	Fort	Nfld.	Newfoundland	Tenn.	Tennessee
G.	Gulf	N.H.	New Hampshire	Tpk.	Turnpike
Ga.	Georgia	N.J.	New Jersey	Va.	Virginia
Gdn.	Garden	N. Mex.	New Mexico	Vt.	Vermont
Harb.	Harbor, Harbour	N.S.	Nova Scotia	W.	West
Hd.	Head	N.W.T.	Northwest Territories	Wash.	Washington
Hts.	Heights	N.Y.	New York	Wis.	Wisconsin
I(s)., *i(s)*.	Island(s)	Okla.	Oklahoma	W. Va.	West Virginia
Ill.	Illinois	Ont.	Ontario	Wyo.	Wyoming

Foreword

J. H. Paterson, Professor of Geography, in the University of Leicester

During the hundred years that preceded the ending of World War II in 1945, the peoples of the United States and Canada had broken all previous statistical records for speed and scale of economic development. Never before had there been so rapid an enlargement of the sown area over against the wild, or so immense a movement of settlers from overseas, first to the inhabited core areas and then on to the frontiers; never so great an expansion of railroad mileage against such physical odds. And when the figures for steel production in Carnegie's Pittsburgh were received in steel-making Sheffield in England, they were greeted with sheer disbelief: such was their scale that it seemed as if only Vulcan himself could have matched them.

Even after 1945, with development in full swing over the continental vastness of the Soviet Union, Western Europe achieving new levels of production, and Japan set upon its meteoric rise, Anglo-America still contrived to set fresh records. Its farmers fed the hungry in other lands. It supplied much of the world with farm machinery and commercial aircraft, and to this day leads all other countries in the production of petroleum and bituminous coal. As its railroad services began to atrophy, it developed instead the world's largest network of superhighways. Inevitably, the question has arisen: how has all this been achieved? Was it because of a super-endowment with natural resources? Or was it done by draining off human skills from the rest of the world? Or by some magic of organization or virtue of democracy? And from those questions one is irresistibly drawn on to another: is this primacy permanent or passing? How long is it all likely to last?

In the middle 1800s, when our hundred-year period began, most of the answers to questions like these would have focussed on two things, the political system and the natural endowment. While the system gave rise to such legislative landmarks as the Homestead Acts and the idealistic concept of land granted free to the " actual cultivator," the natural endowment in its turn gave rise to phrases like " limitless resources "; phrases which expressed a confidence that development and the increase of individual wealth could continue indefinitely, because there was enough and to spare for all.

Today we know better. We know that " the system " was abused and that it crushed some and ruined others, ideals notwithstanding. We know that while average wealth has increased and is increasing, averages also imply minima—in this case, the poverty of a minority. And one good reason why the increase of wealth is slow is that resources are in reality far from limitless; that even common resources like water are in short supply; that space itself is a resource; and that the United States (if not, for the present, Canada) is running out of space in the midst of 9 million square kilometres of it.

It is therefore appropriate that, early on in the *Oxford Regional Economic Atlas of the United States and Canada*, there is a section of topographic maps. They remind us of the dimensions of the stage on which the remarkable Anglo-American drama has been played: it has happened on these plains and mountains, which are no different from those of other lands, and beside these rivers and seas. They also remind us that space for future development is limited. Whatever Anglo-Americans may require or demand in the century ahead must be provided from this natural base—from these lands and no others. Even those limited ventures into imperialism which gave the United States access to resources beyond its shores, in the Philippines and the Caribbean, are now effectively over and cannot be repeated. Today, as never before, Anglo-America must look to its own resources.

So an accurate stock-taking becomes of the utmost importance. What resources do these lands possess: what soils, what minerals, what potential for cultivation? For the answers to these questions, we move into the main body of the Atlas, where patterns of natural conditions and economic development are mapped. And bearing in mind the times, and the population explosion, and the political realities, we shall be particularly concerned to examine those areas which may be thought of as the " reserves," empty now, but holding a potential for future development— northern Canada and Alaska. It is no coincidence that Alaska and the Northwest figure with much greater prominence in this second edition of the Atlas than they did in the first, of 1967. Since that date there have been changes affecting Alaska through, so to speak, both supply and demand. On the supply side, there has been the discovery of the great oil fields of the Arctic Shore and the long arguments among technicians and conservationists about how to get the oil out. On the demand side, there has been the swiftly mounting ecological crisis, the pollution of eastern rivers and lakes, the sprawl of the cities, and the consequent upward revision of the value to the nation of a million and a half square kilometres of Alaska's clean water and untouched land.

Largely empty at present, these " reserves " may well appear to offer ample space and resources for the next generation, and the next after that. But what is their real capacity? Will, for example, the widespread belief that the Canadian North is full of natural wealth merely waiting to be tapped when needed bear detailed examination? Can we take it for granted that there are resources still undiscovered, that capital will be attracted to their exploitation, and labour be provided by Canadians and others eager and willing to work at remote northern sites? On the basis of past experience we can, perhaps, allow ourselves the first of these assumptions; the second and third we cannot. But the first step is to be clear what, so far, is where, and this is a task which the Atlas sets out to fulfil.

It quickly becomes apparent that some part, at least, of Anglo-America's primacy is founded on genuine natural advantages. As examples of these we may take at random the accessibility of the huge Appalachian coal measures, the fertile glacial drifts which give a smooth, cultivable surface to the Agricultural Interior, and the fortuitous penetration of the chain of Great Lakes across the heart of the continent. But none of these of itself created or guaranteed wealth; that depended on the efforts of the inhabitants in organizing coal production and use, in criss-crossing the agricultural areas with railroad tracks, and in linking the Great Lakes by canals.

It therefore becomes important to examine more closely, as the Atlas does, the characteristics of this population, broadly termed Anglo-American because 95 per cent of its 230 million members speak English. To it, Europe has contributed the most numerically, Africa the most tragically (through the shipment of slaves), Asia significantly, Latin America increasingly. The mixture has proved resourceful, hardy (for it has taken hardiness to survive, whether on a cotton plantation, or on a prairie homestead, or in a city ghetto), and successful. But the unmixed elements have also made their contributions—the French of Québec, the Chicanos of the Southwest, and now the blacks and the Indians, asserting ever more emphatically their own cultural distinctiveness. Most of these groups the present Atlas maps; it is safe to predict that the third edition, as and when it is called for, will need to devote even more space to them.

With the second edition of this work in hand, the reader may well find two questions forming in his mind. Firstly, what evidence does it provide that Anglo-American development is still continuing; between 1967 and 1975, how great have the changes been? The answer must be: considerable. To give expression to them, the editors of the Atlas have introduced a range of new maps, as well as updating the others. Consider, as examples, the implications of the map of tourism (pp. 118–9), the greatest "growth industry" of the decade; or the fresh presentation of the chemical industry, with its range of new products; or the map of internal migration from country to town (p. 77), reminding us that, at the last census, over 73 per cent of the population of both countries was classified as urban (and, incidentally, that the Atlas's city maps gain in importance from this fact). These developments may not, as in previous decades, represent the conquest of virgin lands, but they do represent no less significant shifts in the internal economic balance of the continent.

Secondly, however, it may be asked: can a hundred, or a thousand, symbols on a page really tell us anything about these countries? Does it matter that the symbols may, for this second edition, have been moved or enlarged, often by quantities so small as to be invisible to the naked eye?

Clearly, it matters to the cartographer; it is his task and his satisfaction to portray reality as accurately as possible. But the general reader may still need reassuring, and that reassurance can perhaps be offered in the terms of an old geographical axiom, that what concerns us in geography is *the discontinuity of distribution*. We may begin with the impression that we have before us nothing but a page covered with dots. But the dots do not, of course, blanket the *whole* page, and that is precisely the point—it is their uneven distribution on the page that interests us. It raises the question: if here, why not there? And with the asking of that question, we are fairly launched on geographical investigation. Why were all the main railroads except one in the United States (pp. 124–5) built before 1913 while, across the border in Canada, considerable portions of the network were added after that date, and where are these portions? Why is the growing of sorghums so intensive in Kansas and Texas (p. 80), but cut off almost as by a wall at the Colorado and New Mexico state lines? And so on.

On the pages of the second—or, for that matter, the twenty-second edition of this Atlas, a host of similar questions will arouse the curiosity of the reader.

Urban Plans

J. W. Watson, formerly Professor of Geography, in the University of Edinburgh

Scale: Each urban area is shown on the same scale— 1 inch to 6 miles. Each is divided up in the same way to indicate:—

Black: a central business core of multiple stores, office blocks, hotels and passenger stations which, in the case of a metropolitan complex of communities, may be deemed to be the principal commercial centre;

Red: lesser, but significant, business centres, often of secondary cities within the central metropolitan area, or of former towns amalgamated with a city;

Blue: industrial districts, mainly of groups of large-scale plants serving the region or nation as a whole, and excluding service industries related to the city needs only. Isolated industries are shown by conventional squares and areas of industrial wasteland and spoil tips by triangles;

Brown: the built-up area, where urban uses of land predominate; these are chiefly houses, institutions, and streets, but they include playgrounds, cemeteries, transportation yards, and other open spaces used for urban purposes;

Green: major city parks and wooded wastes such as ravines;

Yellow: major military and naval installations.

The data for mapping are based upon reports of city planning boards and industrial commissions; on the U.S. and Canadian Censuses; on the U.S. Army Map Service series, United States 1:250 000 and the U.S. Geological Survey 1:24 000 map series and the Atlas of Canada city maps 1:100 000; on road maps of various oil companies; on aerial photographs; and on personal submissions to the editor. It was not possible to work from a single datum line, although each city has been scrutinized by a local authority in 1974.
The symbols cannot be given identical interpretation on each map. Thus

the central business districts of great urban complexes, based on functions central to the whole metropolitan area, are smaller by comparison through the exclusion of services used principally by the central city itself, than business cores of single large cities. Similarly, in the latter, the subsidiary commercial centres may be smaller than those not shown at all in the larger urban complexes. This is seen, too, in district names. In places like Los Angeles and New York, such names have to be kept for what are themselves big communities—often separate cities—whereas in lesser cities they are used for neighbourhoods or suburbs.
This inclusion of slightly differing categories under the same symbol is true of roads, where the names, Freeways, Thruways, Parkways, Turnpikes, Trunk Roads, National Roads, State or Provincial Highways, or major urban thoroughfares, often apply to different classes in different States and Counties. The major roads shown are limited access ones of at least four lanes meant for fast through traffic. They include however, roads with as many as eight lanes. Moreover, some of them have only partially separated, others completely separated junctions, lead-ins and exits. The point is that, for their region and their particular city, they are the rapid-transit thoroughfares.
Still other complications are found in the important institutions; colleges in many a large city are larger than universities in smaller cities. Some cities are built round famous institutions; others may have institutions which are equal in size and repute, but owe their standing as cities to commerce or industry; in the one case the institution has been shown, in the other, it has not. Similarly, differences occur in showing major airports, transportation yards, and fuel depots. Some ports may have oil-storage depots larger than cities which refine oil; in the latter oil-storage is shown as part of the industrial area, but not necessarily so in the former. Thus although every city is mapped by use of the same categories, these categories have to be interpreted in terms of the city itself, its region, and the state or province or country it belongs to. A very important feature of cities is that, although they share much in common, they are essentially unique entities, reflecting unique factors in geography and history.

Black	Boundaries	Red	Highways
▬▬▬▬	International	▬▬▬▬	Limited access and rapid transit
– – – –	State or Province	– – – –	Other main highways
- - - -	County	= = = =	Tunnels

Red
Railroads and transportation yards

⊕ Airports and airfields

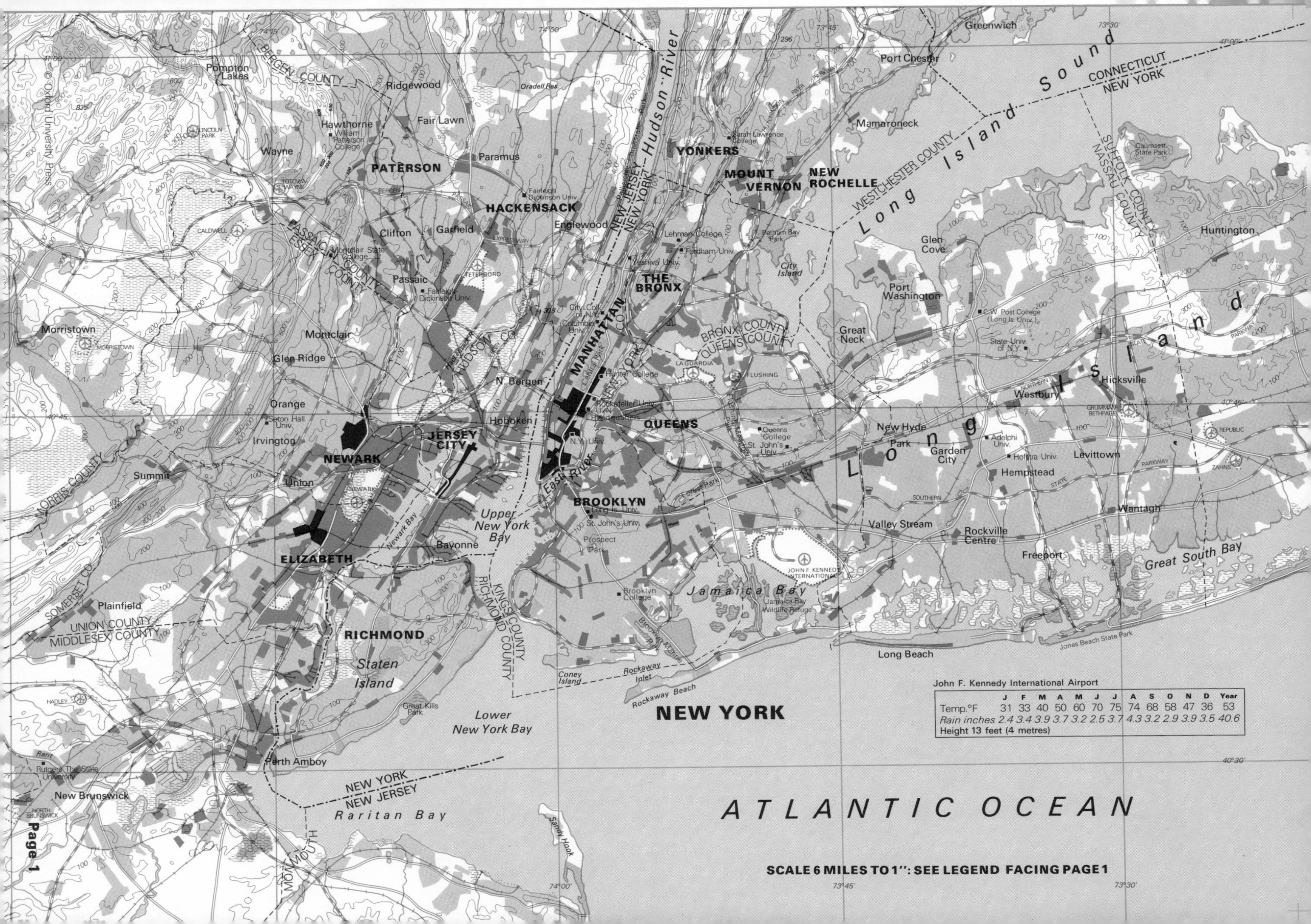

Sound

Long

Island

CONNECTICUT
NEW YORK

Greenwich

Port Chester

Mamaroneck

WESTCHESTER COUNTY

Rye

New Rochelle

MOUNT
VERNON

NEW
ROCHELLE

YONKERS

THE BRONX

MANHATTAN

Hudson River

NEW JERSEY
NEW YORK

PATERSON

HACKENSACK

Fair Lawn

Ridgewood

Clifton

Passaic

Garfield

Montclair

Glen Ridge

Orange

Irvington

Union

NEWARK

ELIZABETH

JERSEY
CITY

Bayonne

Hoboken

N. Bergen

BERGEN COUNTY

ESSEX COUNTY

UNION COUNTY

Wayne

Pompton Lakes

Morristown

Plainfield

Summit

New Brunswick

MIDDLESEX COUNTY

SOMERSET CO.

MORRIS CO.

Huntington

SUFFOLK COUNTY
NEW YORK

NASSAU COUNTY

Hicksville

Westbury

Levittown

Hempstead

Garden City

Great Neck

Glen Cove

Port Washington

New Hyde Park

Valley Stream

Rockville Centre

Freeport

Wantagh

Bethpage

Long Beach

Great South Bay

Jones Beach State Park

QUEENS

BROOKLYN

East River

Coney Island

Rockaway Beach

Jamaica Bay

JOHN F. KENNEDY INTERNATIONAL

John F. Kennedy Wildlife Refuge

Jamaica Bay

KINGS COUNTY
RICHMOND COUNTY

Upper New York Bay

Lower New York Bay

Great Kills Park

RICHMOND

Staten Island

Perth Amboy

Sandy Hook

Raritan Bay

NEW YORK
NEW JERSEY

NEW YORK

ATLANTIC OCEAN

John F. Kennedy International Airport													
	J	F	M	A	M	J	J	A	S	O	N	D	Year
Temp.°F	31	33	40	50	60	70	75	74	68	58	47	36	53
Rain inches	2.4	3.4	3.9	3.7	3.2	2.5	3.7	4.3	3.2	2.9	3.5	40.6

Height 13 feet (4 metres)

SCALE 6 MILES TO 1": SEE LEGEND FACING PAGE 1

© Oxford University Press

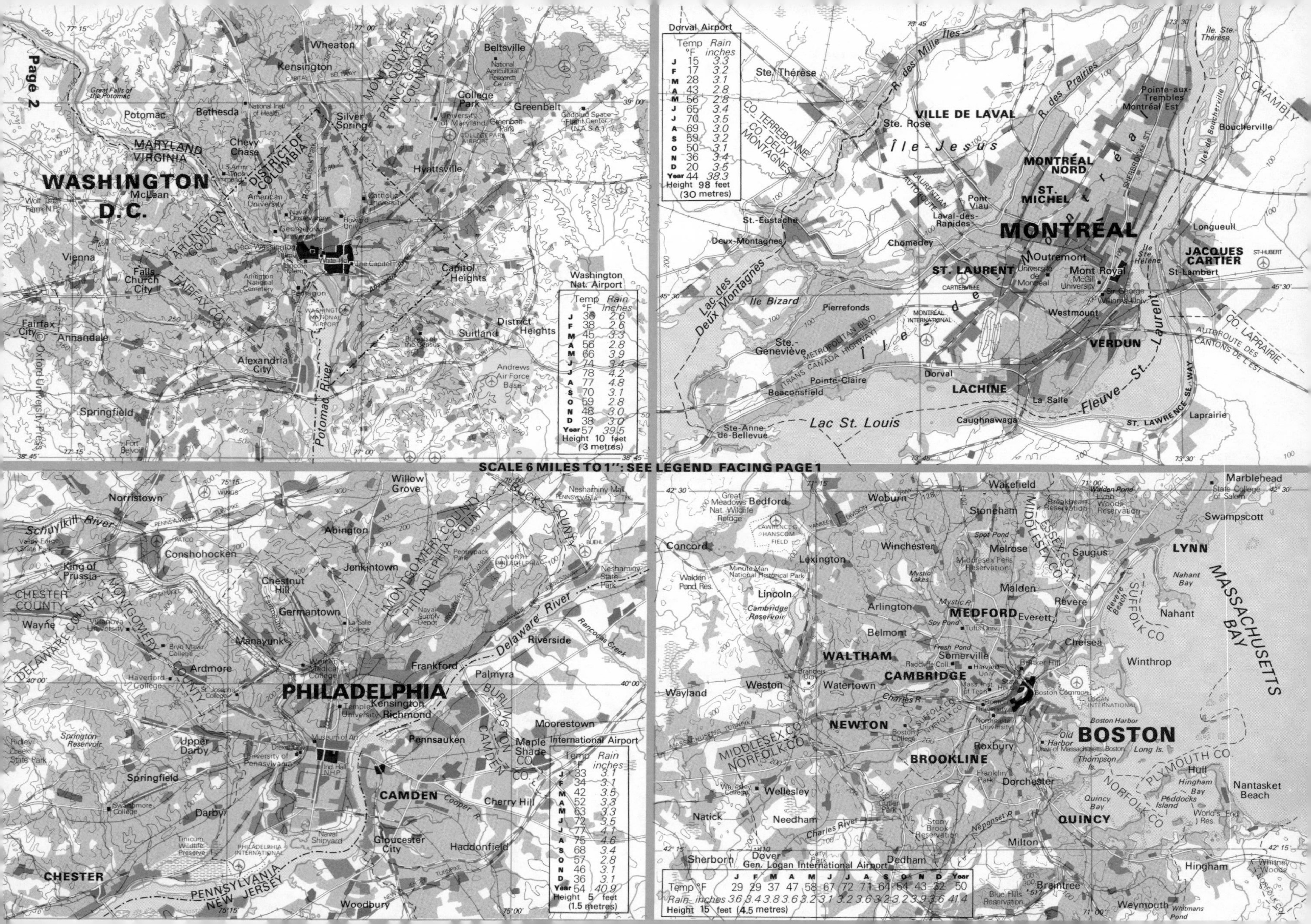

Washington Nat. Airport

	Temp °F	Rain inches
J	36	2.6
F	38	2.6
M	45	3.3
A	56	2.8
M	66	3.9
J	74	3.4
J	78	4.2
A	77	4.8
S	70	3.1
O	59	2.8
N	48	3.0
D	38	3.0
Year	57	39.5

Height 10 feet (3 metres)

Dorval Airport

	Temp °F	Rain inches
J	15	3.3
F	17	3.2
M	28	3.1
A	43	2.8
M	56	2.8
J	65	3.4
J	70	3.5
A	69	3.0
S	59	3.2
O	50	3.1
N	36	3.4
D	20	3.5
Year	44	38.3

Height 98 feet (30 metres)

International Airport

	Temp °F	Rain inches
J	33	3.1
F	34	3.1
M	42	3.5
A	52	3.3
M	63	3.3
J	72	3.5
J	77	4.1
A	75	4.6
S	68	3.4
O	57	2.8
N	46	3.1
D	36	3.1
Year	54	40.9

Height 5 feet (1.5 metres)

Gen. Logan International Airport

	J	F	M	A	M	J	J	A	S	O	N	D	Year
Temp °F	29	29	37	47	58	67	72	71	64	54	43	32	50
Rain inches	3.6	3.4	3.8	3.6	3.2	3.1	3.2	3.6	3.2	3.2	3.9	3.6	41.4

Height 15 feet (4.5 metres)

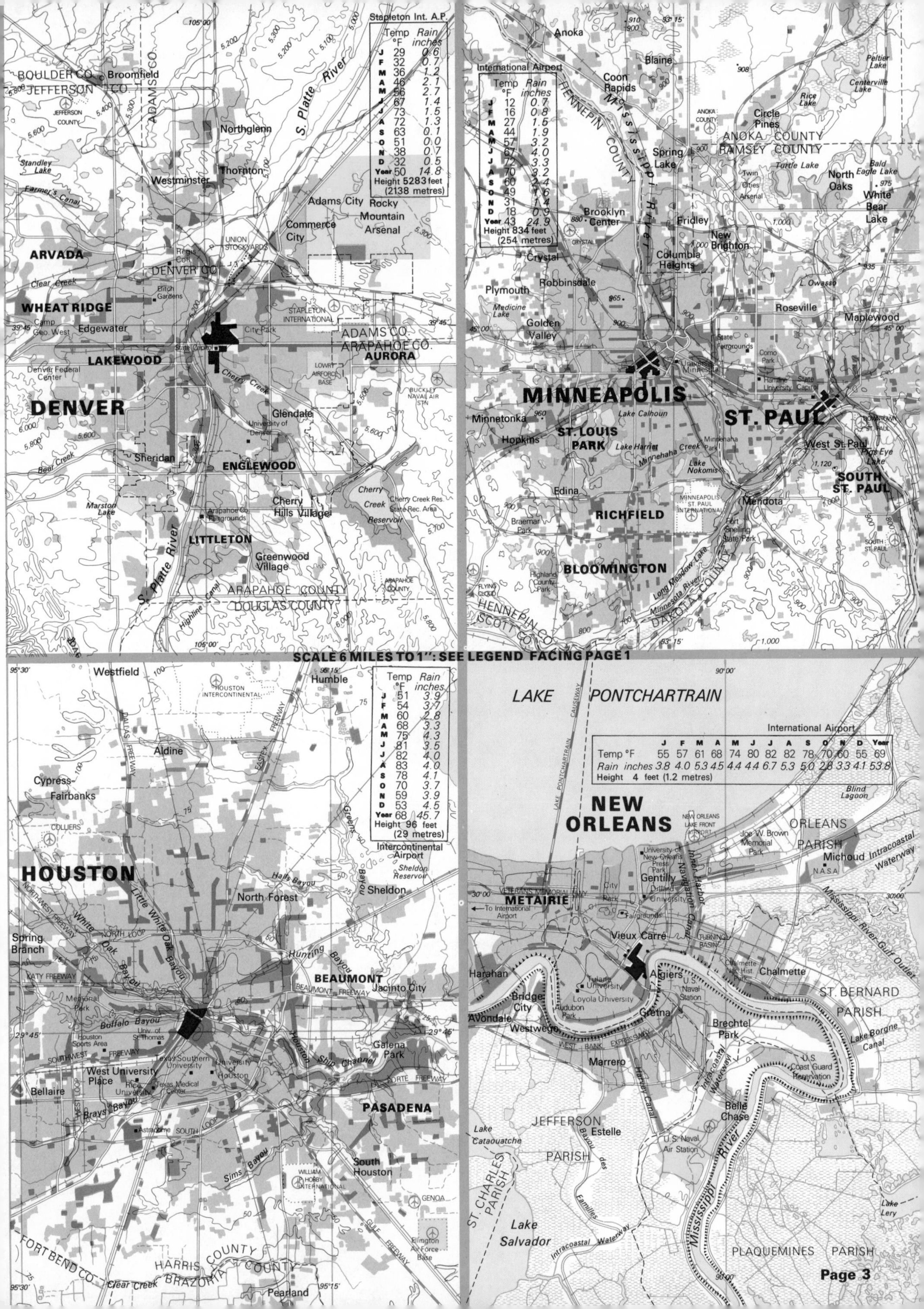

Stapleton Int. A.P.
Temp °F Rain inches
J 29 0.6
F 32 0.7
M 36 1.2
A 46 2.1
M 56 2.7
J 67 1.4
J 73 1.5
A 72 1.3
S 63 0.1
O 51 0.0
N 38 0.7
D 32 0.5
Year 50 14.8
Height 5283 feet (2138 metres)
DENVER
ARVADA
WHEAT RIDGE
LAKEWOOD
ENGLEWOOD
LITTLETON
AURORA
Broomfield
Northglenn
Thornton
Westminster
Adams City
Commerce City
Rocky Mountain Arsenal
Edgewater
Glendale
Sheridan
Cherry Hills Village
Greenwood Village
S. Platte River
BOULDER CO.
JEFFERSON CO.
ADAMS CO.
DENVER CO.
ARAPAHOE CO.
ARAPAHOE COUNTY
DOUGLAS COUNTY
Cherry Creek Reservoir
International Airport
Temp °F Rain inches
J 12 0.7
F 16 0.8
M 27 1.5
A 44 1.9
M 57 3.2
J 67 4.0
J 72 3.3
A 70 3.2
S 60 2.4
O 49 1.6
N 31 1.4
D 18 0.9
Year 43 24.9
Height 834 feet (254 metres)
MINNEAPOLIS
ST. PAUL
ST. LOUIS PARK
RICHFIELD
BLOOMINGTON
SOUTH ST. PAUL
Anoka
Blaine
Coon Rapids
Circle Pines
Spring Lake
Brooklyn Center
Fridley
New Brighton
Columbia Heights
Crystal
Robbinsdale
Plymouth
Golden Valley
Roseville
Maplewood
North Oaks
White Bear Lake
Minnetonka
Hopkins
Edina
West St. Paul
Mendota
Mississippi River
ANOKA COUNTY
RAMSEY COUNTY
HENNEPIN COUNTY
DAKOTA COUNTY
SCOTT CO.
Temp °F Rain inches
J 51 3.9
F 54 3.7
M 60 2.8
A 68 3.3
M 75 4.3
J 81 3.5
J 82 4.0
A 83 4.0
S 78 4.1
O 70 3.7
N 59 3.9
D 53 4.5
Year 68 45.7
Height 96 feet (29 metres)
Intercontinental Airport
HOUSTON
BEAUMONT
PASADENA
Westfield
Humble
Aldine
Cypress-Fairbanks
North Forest
Sheldon
Spring Branch
Jacinto City
Galena Park
West University Place
Bellaire
South Houston
Pearland
HARRIS COUNTY
FORT BEND CO.
BRAZORIA COUNTY
Houston Ship Channel
LAKE PONTCHARTRAIN
International Airport
	J	F	M	A	M	J	J	A	S	O	N	D	Year
Temp °F	55	57	61	68	74	80	82	82	78	70	60	55	69
Rain inches	3.8	4.0	5.3	4.5	4.4	4.4	6.7	5.3	5.0	2.8	3.3	4.1	53.8
Height 4 feet (1.2 metres)
NEW ORLEANS
METAIRIE
Gentilly
Vieux Carré
Algiers
Harahan
Bridge City
Avondale
Westwego
Gretna
Marrero
Chalmette
Brechtel Park
Belle Chase
Estelle
Lake Salvador
Lake Cataouatche
ORLEANS PARISH
JEFFERSON PARISH
ST. CHARLES PARISH
ST. BERNARD PARISH
PLAQUEMINES PARISH
Mississippi River
Mississippi River-Gulf Outlet

SCALE 6 MILES TO 1": SEE LEGEND FACING PAGE 1

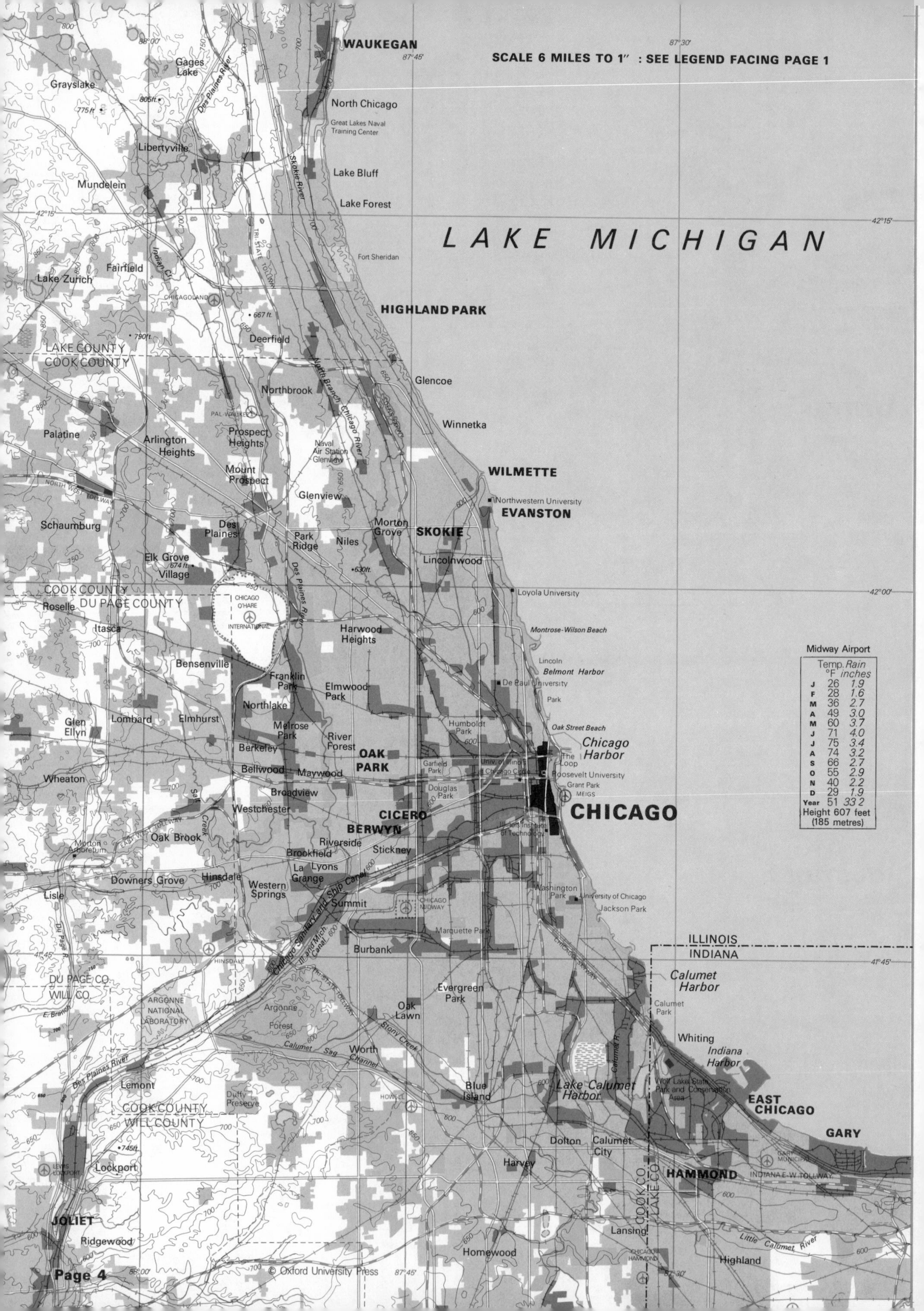

SCALE 6 MILES TO 1" : SEE LEGEND FACING PAGE 1

WAUKEGAN

LAKE MICHIGAN

North Chicago
Great Lakes Naval
Training Center

Lake Bluff

Lake Forest

Fort Sheridan

Grayslake

Gages
Lake

Libertyville

Mundelein

HIGHLAND PARK

Deerfield

Glencoe

Winnetka

WILMETTE

Northwestern University
EVANSTON

SKOKIE

Lincolnwood

Loyola University

Fairfield

Lake Zurich

Palatine

Arlington
Heights

Prospect
Heights

Mount
Prospect

Schaumburg

Des
Plaines

Park
Ridge

Niles

Morton
Grove

Elk Grove
Village

Naval
Air Station
Glenview

Glenview

LAKE COUNTY
COOK COUNTY

Northbrook

Roselle

Itasca

Bensenville

COOK COUNTY
DU PAGE COUNTY

CHICAGO
O'HARE
INTERNATIONAL

Harwood
Heights

Montrose-Wilson Beach

Lincoln

Belmont Harbor

De Paul University

Lincoln
Park

Glen
Ellyn

Lombard

Elmhurst

Franklin
Park

Elmwood
Park

Northlake

Melrose
Park

River
Forest

OAK
PARK

Humboldt
Park

Garfield
Park

Univ. of Illinois
at Chicago Circle

Berkeley

Wheaton

Bellwood

Broadview

Maywood

Westchester

Oak Brook

Riverside

Stickney

Brookfield

La
Grange

Lyons

Western
Springs

Summit

Douglas
Park

The
Loop

Chicago
Harbor

Oak Street Beach

Roosevelt University

Grant Park

MEIGS

CHICAGO

Illinois Institute
of Technology

Morton
Arboretum

Downers Grove

Hinsdale

Lisle

DU PAGE CO.
WILL CO.

Lemont

ARGONNE
NATIONAL
LABORATORY

Argonne
Forest

Oak
Lawn

Burbank

Evergreen
Park

Worth

Marquette Park

CHICAGO
MIDWAY

Washington
Park

University of Chicago

Jackson Park

ILLINOIS
INDIANA

Calumet
Harbor

Calumet
Park

Whiting

Indiana
Harbor

Wolf Lake State
Park and Conservation
Area

EAST
CHICAGO

GARY

Duffy
Preserve

Blue
Island

Lake Calumet
Harbor

COOK COUNTY
WILL COUNTY

Lockport

JOLIET

Ridgewood

Dolton

Calumet
City

Harvey

HAMMOND

Lansing

Homewood

Highland

INDIANA E-W TOLLWAY

Little Calumet River

© Oxford University Press

	Temp.	Rain
	°F	inches
J	26	1.9
F	28	1.6
M	36	2.7
A	49	3.0
M	60	3.7
J	71	4.0
J	75	3.4
A	74	3.2
S	66	2.7
O	55	2.9
N	40	2.2
D	29	1.9
Year	51	33.2

Midway Airport

Height 607 feet
(185 metres)

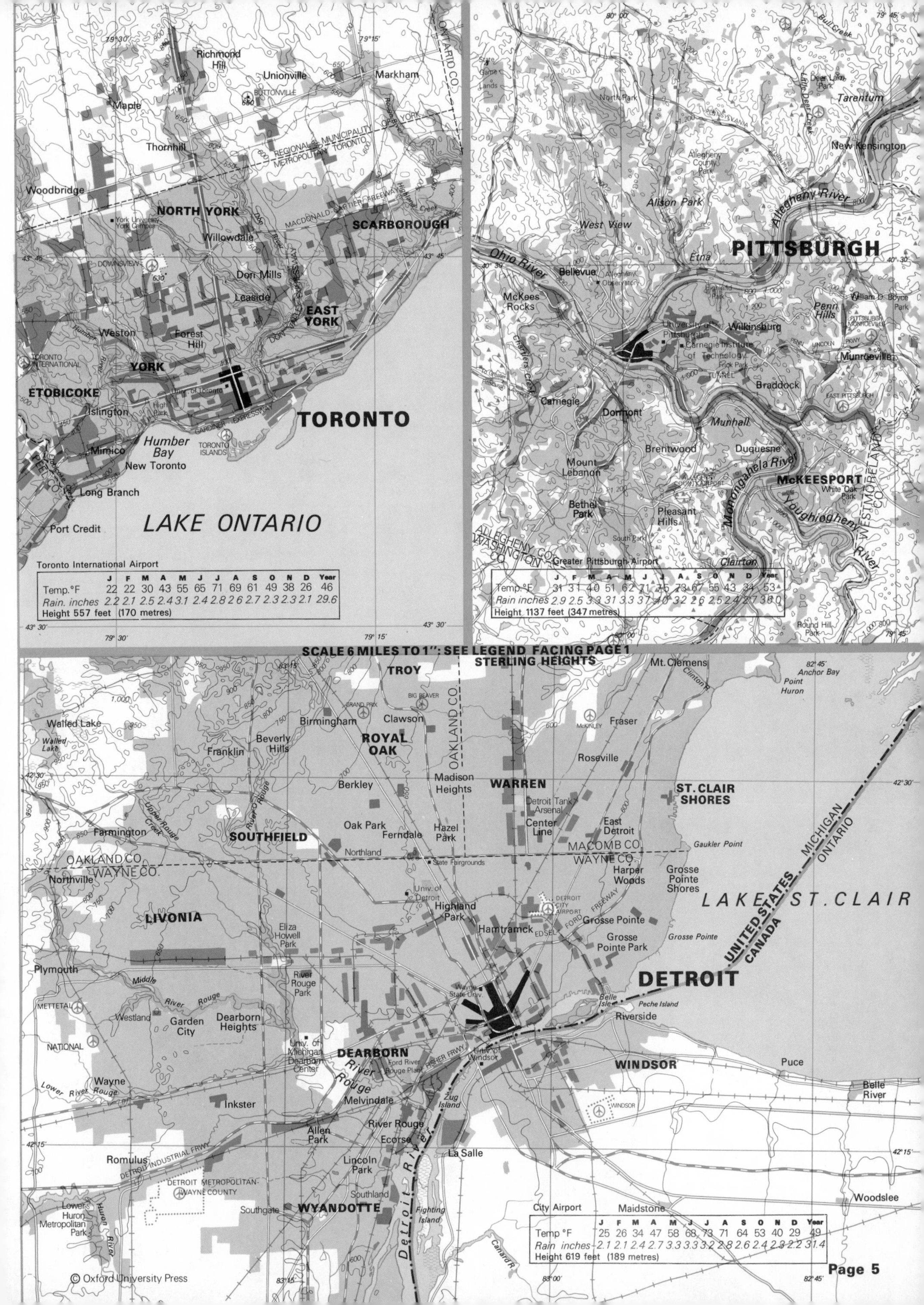

Toronto International Airport

	J	F	M	A	M	J	J	A	S	O	N	D	Year
Temp. °F	22	22	30	43	55	65	71	69	61	49	38	26	46
Rain. inches	2.2	2.1	2.5	2.4	3.1	2.4	2.8	2.6	2.7	2.3	2.3	2.1	29.6

Height 557 feet (170 metres)

Greater Pittsburgh Airport

	J	F	M	A	M	J	J	A	S	O	N	D	Year
Temp. °F	31	31	40	51	62	71	75	73	67	55	43	34	53
Rain inches	2.9	2.5	3.3	3.1	3.3	3.7	4.0	3.2	2.6	2.5	2.4	2.7	36.0

Height 1137 feet (347 metres)

City Airport

	J	F	M	A	M	J	J	A	S	O	N	D	Year
Temp °F	25	26	34	47	58	68	73	71	64	53	40	29	49
Rain inches	2.1	2.1	2.4	2.7	3.3	3.3	3.2	2.8	2.6	2.4	2.3	2.2	31.4

Height 619 feet (189 metres)

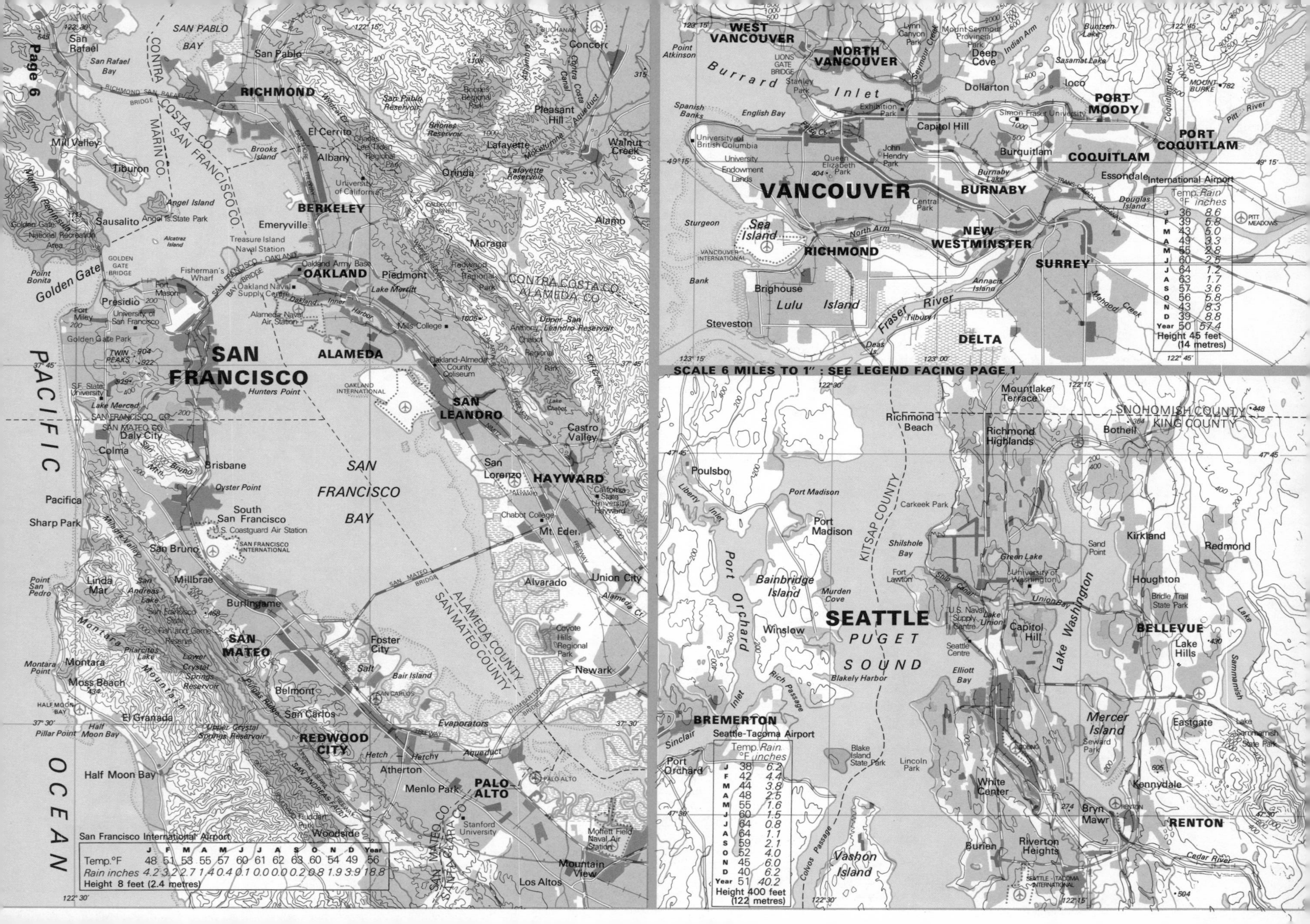

San Francisco International Airport

	J	F	M	A	M	J	J	A	S	O	N	D	Year
Temp.°F	48	51	53	55	57	60	61	62	63	60	54	49	56
Rain inches	4.2	3.2	2.7	1.4	0.4	0.1	0.0	0.0	0.2	0.8	1.9	3.9	18.8

Height 8 feet (2.4 metres)

International Airport (Vancouver)

	Temp. °F	Rain inches
J	36	8.6
F	39	5.8
M	43	5.0
A	49	3.3
M	55	2.8
J	60	2.5
J	64	1.2
A	63	1.7
S	57	3.6
O	56	5.8
N	43	8.3
D	39	8.8
Year	50	57.4

Height 45 feet (14 metres)

SCALE 6 MILES TO 1" : SEE LEGEND FACING PAGE 1

Seattle-Tacoma Airport

	Temp. °F	Rain. inches
J	38	6.2
F	42	4.4
M	44	3.8
A	48	2.5
M	55	1.6
J	60	1.5
J	64	0.8
A	64	1.1
S	59	2.1
O	52	4.0
N	45	6.0
D	40	6.2
Year	51	40.2

Height 400 feet (122 metres)

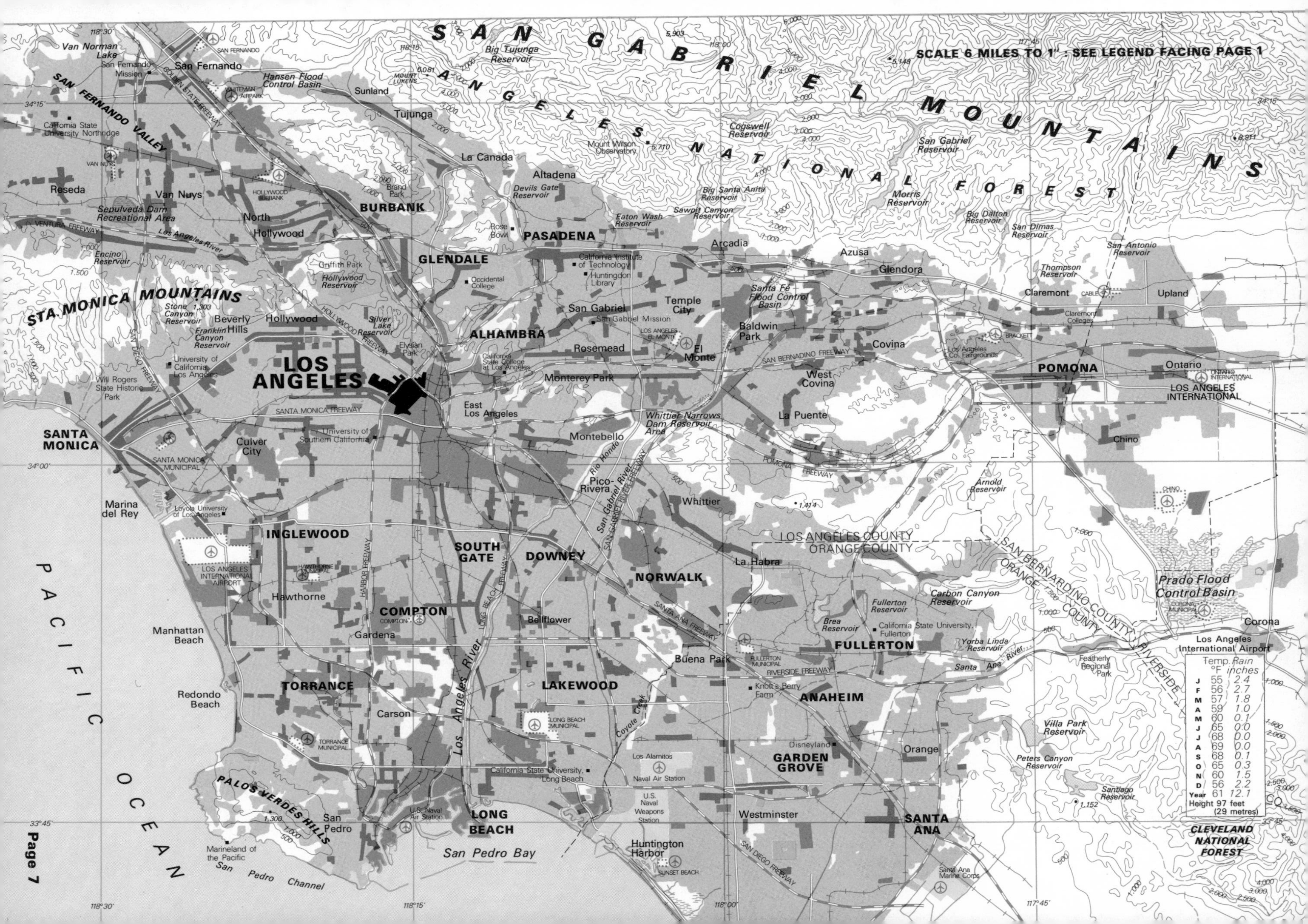

SCALE 6 MILES TO 1" : SEE LEGEND FACING PAGE 1
SAN GABRIEL MOUNTAINS
ANGELES NATIONAL FOREST
SAN FERNANDO VALLEY
STA. MONICA MOUNTAINS
PACIFIC OCEAN
San Pedro Bay
San Pedro Channel
PALOS VERDES HILLS
CLEVELAND NATIONAL FOREST
LOS ANGELES
LONG BEACH
SANTA MONICA
GLENDALE
BURBANK
PASADENA
ALHAMBRA
POMONA
INGLEWOOD
TORRANCE
COMPTON
SOUTH GATE
DOWNEY
NORWALK
LAKEWOOD
ANAHEIM
FULLERTON
GARDEN GROVE
SANTA ANA
Van Norman Lake
San Fernando Mission
San Fernando
Hansen Flood Control Basin
Sunland
Tujunga
La Canada
Altadena
Big Tujunga Reservoir
Mount Wilson Observatory
Cogswell Reservoir
San Gabriel Reservoir
Big Santa Anita Reservoir
Sawpit Canyon Reservoir
Morris Reservoir
Big Dalton Reservoir
San Dimas Reservoir
San Antonio Reservoir
Thompson Reservoir
Devils Gate Reservoir
Eaton Wash Reservoir
California State University Northridge
Reseda
Van Nuys
Sepulveda Dam Recreational Area
North Hollywood
Encino Reservoir
Griffith Park
Hollywood Reservoir
Stone Canyon Reservoir
Franklin Canyon Reservoir
Beverly Hills
Hollywood
Silver Lake Reservoir
Elysian Park
University of California Los Angeles
Will Rogers State Historic Park
Rose Bowl
California Institute of Technology
Huntingdon Library
Occidental College
San Gabriel
San Gabriel Mission
California State College at Los Angeles
Rosemead
Monterey Park
East Los Angeles
Arcadia
Temple City
El Monte
Santa Fe Flood Control Basin
Baldwin Park
Azusa
Glendora
Covina
West Covina
La Puente
Claremont
Claremont Colleges
Upland
Ontario
Los Angeles Co. Fairgrounds
LOS ANGELES INTERNATIONAL
Chino
Whittier Narrows Dam Reservoir Area
Montebello
Rio Hondo
San Gabriel River
Pico-Rivera
Whittier
Arnold Reservoir
LOS ANGELES COUNTY
ORANGE COUNTY
SAN BERNARDINO COUNTY
RIVERSIDE
La Habra
Prado Flood Control Basin
Corona
Carbon Canyon Reservoir
Fullerton Reservoir
Brea Reservoir
California State University, Fullerton
Yorba Linda Reservoir
Santa Ana River
Featherly Regional Park
Villa Park Reservoir
Peters Canyon Reservoir
Santiago Reservoir
Orange
Disneyland
Knott's Berry Farm
Buena Park
Bellflower
Coyote Creek
Los Alamitos Naval Air Station
U.S. Naval Weapons Station
Westminster
Huntington Harbor
Santa Ana Marine Corps
Culver City
University of Southern California
Marina del Rey
Loyola University of Los Angeles
LOS ANGELES INTERNATIONAL AIRPORT
Hawthorne
Gardena
Manhattan Beach
Redondo Beach
Carson
Los Angeles River
California State University, Long Beach
LONG BEACH MUNICIPAL
TORRANCE MUNICIPAL
U.S. Naval Air Station
San Pedro
Marineland of the Pacific
GOLDEN STATE FREEWAY
VENTURA FREEWAY
SAN DIEGO FREEWAY
HOLLYWOOD FREEWAY
SANTA MONICA FREEWAY
HARBOR FREEWAY
LONG BEACH FREEWAY
SAN GABRIEL RIVER FREEWAY
SANTA ANA FREEWAY
SAN BERNARDINO FREEWAY
POMONA FREEWAY
RIVERSIDE FREEWAY
Los Angeles International Airport
Temp. °F Rain inches
J 55 2.4
F 56 2.7
M 57 1.8
A 59 1.0
M 60 0.1
J 65 0.0
J 68 0.0
A 69 0.0
S 68 0.1
O 65 0.3
N 60 1.5
D 56 2.2
Year 61 12.1
Height 97 feet (29 metres)

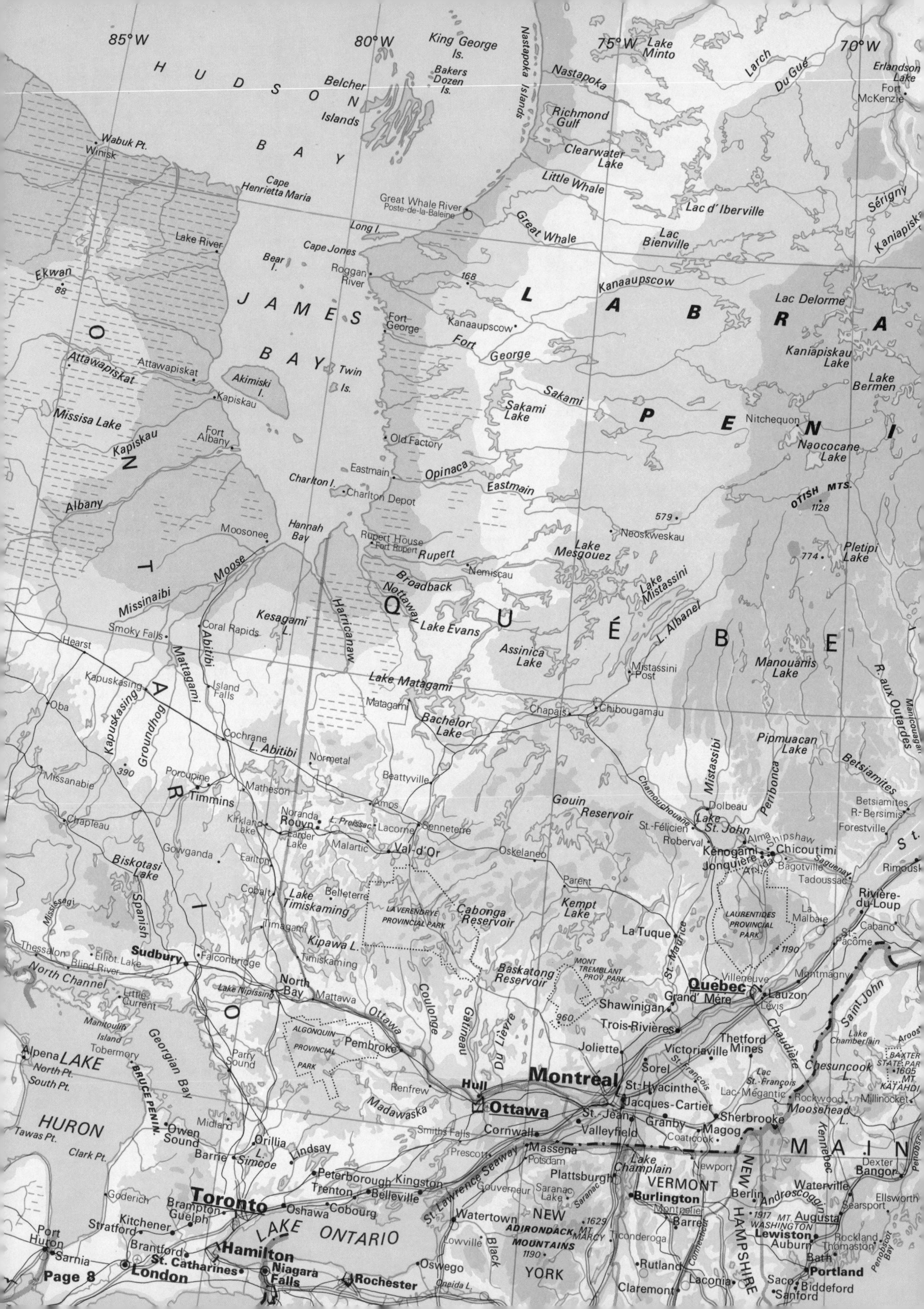

85°W
80°W
75°W
70°W
HUDSON BAY
JAMES BAY
LAKE HURON
LAKE ONTARIO
ONTARIO
QUÉBEC
LABRADOR PENINSULA
VERMONT
NEW HAMPSHIRE
NEW YORK
MAINE
King George Is.
Belcher Islands
Bakers Dozen Is.
Nastapoka Islands
Lake Minto
Nastapoka
Richmond Gulf
Clearwater Lake
Little Whale
Great Whale River
Poste-de-la-Baleine
Great Whale
Lac d' Iberville
Lac Bienville
Larch
Du Gué
Erlandson Lake
Fort McKenzie
Sérigny
Kaniapiskau
Wabuk Pt.
Winisk
Cape Henrietta Maria
Lake River
Long I.
Cape Jones
Bear I.
Roggan River
Ekwan
88
168
Kanaaupscow
Lac Delorme
Fort George
Kaniapiskau Lake
Lake Bermen
Sakami
Sakami Lake
Attawapiskat
Akimiski I.
Twin Is.
Kapiskau
Missisa Lake
Fort Albany
Old Factory
Nitchequon
Naococane Lake
Eastmain
Opinaca
Charlton I.
Charlton Depot
OTISH MTS.
1128
579
Albany
Moosonee
Hannah Bay
Rupert House
Fort Rupert
Rupert
Neoskweskau
Lake Mesgouez
Pletipi Lake
774
Nemiscau
Broadback
Nottaway
Moose
Missinaibi
Lake Mistassini
Coral Rapids
Kesagami L.
Lake Evans
Smoky Falls
Abitibi
Harricanaw
Assinica Lake
L. Albanel
Hearst
Mattagami
Manouanis Lake
R. aux Outardes
Mistassini Post
Lake Matagami
Kapuskasing
Island Falls
Matagami
Chapais
Chibougamau
Oba
Groundhog
Bachelor Lake
Manicouagan
Cochrane
L. Abitibi
Pipmuacan Lake
Normetal
Mistassibi
Betsiamites
390
Porcupine
Missanabie
Timmins
Matheson
Beattyville
Amos
Chamouchouane
Gouin Reservoir
Dolbeau
Peribonca
Betsiamites
R.-Bersimis
Chapleau
Kirkland Lake
Noranda
Rouyn
L. Preissac
Lacorne
Senneterre
Larder Lake
Malartic
Val-d'Or
Lake St. John
St.-Félicien
Roberval
Alma
Shipshaw
Forestville
Kenogami
Jonquière
Arvida
Chicoutimi
Bagotville
Saguenay
Tadoussac
Rimouski
Gowganda
Earlton
Oskelaneo
Biskotasi Lake
Cobalt
Belleterre
Parent
Rivière-du-Loup
Lake Timiskaming
LA VERENDRYE PROVINCIAL PARK
Cabonga Reservoir
Kempt Lake
LAURENTIDES PROVINCIAL PARK
La Malbaie
Mississagi
Spanish
Timagami
Cabano
La Tuque
Kipawa L.
1190
St.-Pacôme
Thessalon
Elliot Lake
Sudbury
Falconbridge
Timiskaming
Blind River
MONT TREMBLANT PROV. PARK
Baskatong Reservoir
Montmagny
North Channel
Lake Nipissing
North Bay
Villeneuve
Québec
Lauzon
Little Current
Mattawa
St.-Maurice
Grand' Mère
Lévis
Manitoulin Island
Coulonge
Gatineau
Du Lièvre
Shawinigan
960
Saint John
Ottawa
Trois-Rivières
Chaudière
Georgian Bay
ALGONQUIN PROVINCIAL PARK
Tobermory
Pembroke
Thetford Mines
Lake Chamberlain
Aroostook
Alpena
North Pt.
South Pt.
Parry Sound
Joliette
Victoriaville
Chesuncook L.
BRUCE PENIN.
Sorel
St. François
Montreal
BAXTER STATE PARK
1605
MT. KATAHDI
Hull
St.-Hyacinthe
Lac St.-François
Renfrew
Ottawa
Jacques-Cartier
Lac-Mégantic
Rockwood
Millinocket
Madawaska
Moosehead L.
St.-Jean
Sherbrooke
Owen Sound
Midland
Cornwall
Valleyfield
Granby
Magog
Kennebec
Tawas Pt.
Smiths Falls
Coaticook
Clark Pt.
Orillia
Massena
Prescott
Potsdam
Lake Champlain
Newport
Dexter
Barrie
Simcoe L.
Lindsay
Plattsburgh
Bangor
Peterborough
Kingston
St. Lawrence Seaway
Waterville
Goderich
Trenton
Belleville
Saranac Lake
Saranac
Burlington
Berlin
Androscoggin
Ellsworth
Toronto
Gouverneur
Brampton
Guelph
Oshawa
Cobourg
Montpelier
1917
MT. WASHINGTON
Augusta
Searsport
Kitchener
Watertown
ADIRONDACK MTS.
1629
MT. MARCY
Barre
Stratford
Port Huron
Lowville
Black
Ticonderoga
Lewiston
Auburn
Rockland
Thomaston
Penobscot Bay
Brantford
Hamilton
MOUNTAINS
Bath
Sarnia
St. Catharines
Niagara Falls
1190
Oswego
Rutland
Connecticut
Portland
Page 8
London
Rochester
Oneida L.
Claremont
Laconia
Saco
Biddeford
Sanford

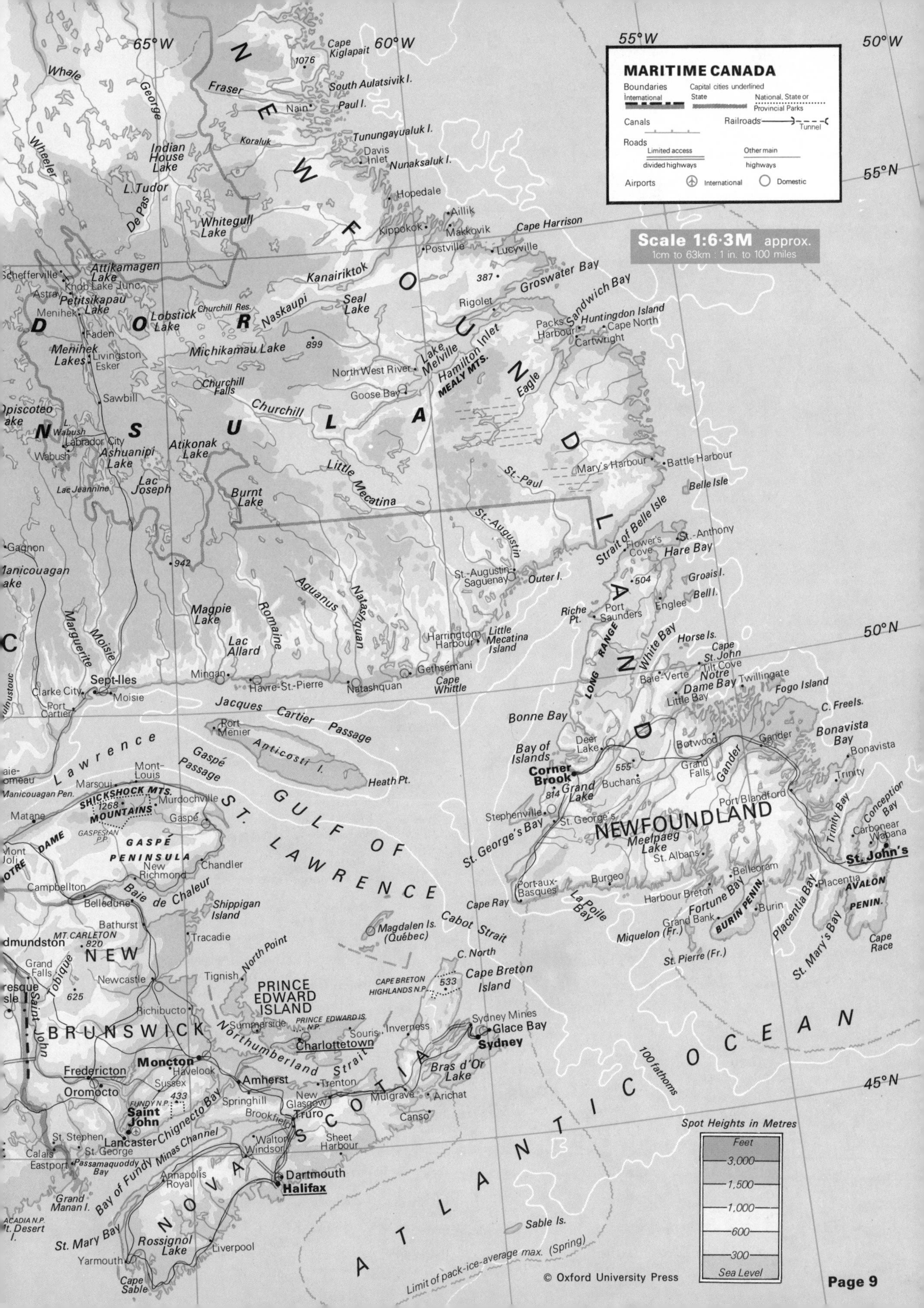

MARITIME CANADA
Boundaries
International
State
Capital cities underlined
National, State or Provincial Parks
Canals
Railroads
Tunnel
Roads
Limited access divided highways
Other main highways
Airports
International
Domestic
Scale 1:6·3M approx.
1cm to 63km : 1 in. to 100 miles
Spot Heights in Metres
Feet
3,000
1,500
1,000
600
300
Sea Level
65°W
60°W
55°W
50°W
55°N
50°N
45°N
NEWFOUNDLAND
LABRADOR
PENINSULA
GULF OF ST. LAWRENCE
ATLANTIC OCEAN
NEW BRUNSWICK
NOVA SCOTIA
PRINCE EDWARD ISLAND
GASPÉ PENINSULA
Cape Kiglapait
1076
South Aulatsivik I.
Fraser
Nain
Paul I.
Whale
George
Koraluk
Tunungayualuk I.
Davis Inlet
Nunaksaluk I.
Indian House Lake
Wheeler
L. Tudor
De Pas
Hopedale
Whitegull Lake
Aillik
Kippokok
Makkovik
Cape Harrison
Postville
Lucyville
Attikamagen Lake
Schefferville
Knob Lake Junc.
Astray
Petitsikapau Lake
Kanairiktok
387
Groswater Bay
Sandwich Bay
Rigolet
Seal Lake
Naskaupi
Churchill Res.
Lobstick Lake
Menihek
Faden
Packs Harbour
Huntingdon Island
Cape North
Cartwright
Michikamau Lake
899
Menihek Lakes
Livingston
Esker
Lake Melville
Hamilton Inlet
North West River
MEALY MTS.
Eagle
Churchill Falls
Goose Bay
Sawbill
Churchill
L. Wabush
Labrador City
Wabush
Ashuanipi Lake
Atikonak Lake
Mary's Harbour
Battle Harbour
St.-Paul
Little Mecatina
Belle Isle
Lac Jeannine
Lac Joseph
Burnt Lake
St.-Augustin
Strait of Belle Isle
Flower's Cove
St.-Anthony
Hare Bay
Gagnon
942
St.-Augustin Saguenay
Outer I.
504
Groais I.
Aguanus
Natashquan
Bell I.
Riche Pt.
Port Saunders
Englee
Magpie Lake
Romaine
Marguerite
Moisie
Lac Allard
Harrington Harbour
Little Mecatina Island
Horse Is.
White Bay
Cape St. John
LONG RANGE
Tilt Cove
Baie-Verte
Notre Dame Bay
Twillingate
Fogo Island
Mingan
Havre-St.-Pierre
Natashquan
Gethsémani
Cape Whittle
Sept-Iles
Moisie
Clarke City
Port Cartier
Little Bay
C. Freels
Jacques Cartier Passage
Bonne Bay
Port Menier
Anticosti I.
Deer Lake
Botwood
Gander
Bonavista Bay
Bonavista
Bay of Islands
555
Grand Falls
Lawrence
Mont-Louis
Gaspé Passage
Heath Pt.
Corner Brook
Buchans
Trinity
Marsoui
Manicouagan Pen.
SHICKSHOCK MTS.
1268
MOUNTAINS
Murdochville
814
Grand Lake
Port Blandford
Matane
Gaspé
Stephenville
St. George's
NEWFOUNDLAND
Trinity Bay
Conception Bay
Carbonear
Wabana
GASPESIAN P.P.
DAME
St. George's Bay
Meelpaeg Lake
St. Albans
St. John's
Chandler
New Richmond
Belleoram
Campbellton
Baie de Chaleur
Port-aux-Basques
La Poile Bay
Burgeo
Harbour Breton
Fortune Bay
Placentia
AVALON PENIN.
Belledune
Shippigan Island
Cape Ray
BURIN PENIN.
Burin
Placentia Bay
Bathurst
Magdalen Is. (Québec)
Cabot Strait
Grand Bank
MT. CARLETON
820
Tracadie
Miquelon (Fr.)
St. Mary's Bay
Cape Race
St. Pierre (Fr.)
Grand Falls
Tobique
North Point
C. North
Cape Breton Island
Newcastle
Tignish
CAPE BRETON HIGHLANDS N.P.
533
625
Saint John
Richibucto
Sydney Mines
Glace Bay
Summerside
PRINCE EDWARD IS. N.P.
Souris
Inverness
Sydney
Charlottetown
Northumberland Strait
Bras d'Or Lake
100 fathoms
Fredericton
Moncton
Havelock
Amherst
Trenton
Sussex
Oromocto
433
FUNDY N.P.
Springhill
New Glasgow
Mulgrave
Arichat
Saint John
Chignecto Bay
Brookfield
Truro
Canso
St. Stephen
St. George
Lancaster
Minas Channel
Walton
Windsor
Sheet Harbour
Calais
Eastport
Passamaquoddy Bay
Bay of Fundy
Annapolis Royal
Dartmouth
Halifax
Grand Manan I.
ACADIA N.P.
St. Mary Bay
Sable Is.
Rossignol Lake
Liverpool
Yarmouth
Limit of pack-ice-average max. (Spring)
Cape Sable

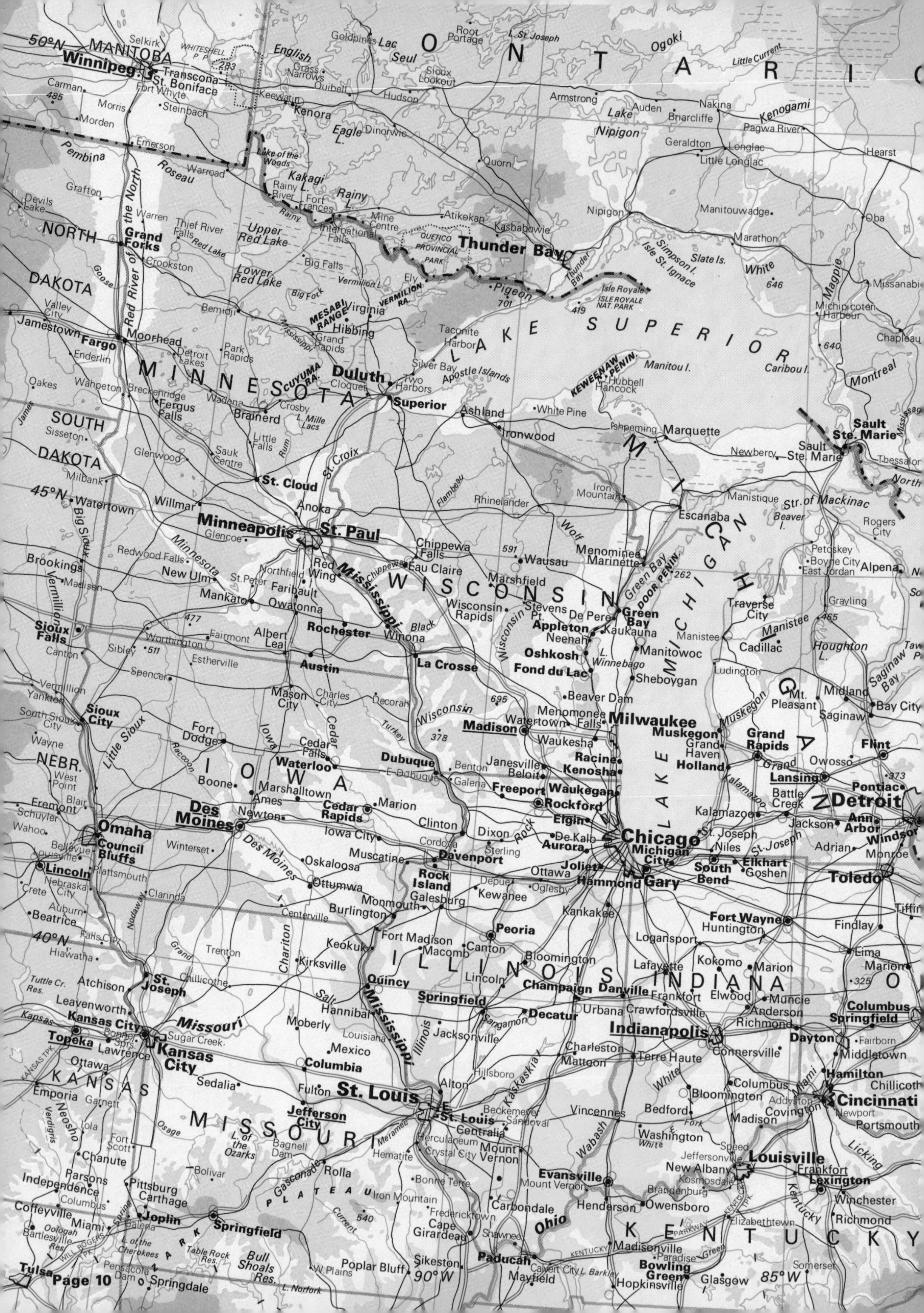
50°N
MANITOBA
Selkirk
WHITESHELL P. P.
Winnipeg
Transcona
St. Boniface
Fort Whyte
Carman
Morris
Steinbach
Morden
Emerson
Pembina
Roseau
Warroad
Grafton
Devils Lake
NORTH
DAKOTA
Warren
Thief River Falls
Red Lake
Grand Forks
Crookston
Red River of the North
Goose
Valley City
Jamestown
Fargo
Moorhead
Enderlin
Detroit Lakes
Oakes
Wahpeton
Breckenridge
Fergus Falls
James
SOUTH
DAKOTA
Sisseton
Milbank
45°N
Watertown
Big Sioux
Brookings
Madison
Vermillion
Sioux Falls
Canton
Vermillion
Yankton
South Sioux City
Sioux City
Wayne
NEBR.
West Point
Blair
Fremont
Schuyler
Wahoo
Omaha
Council Bluffs
Bellevue
Louisville
Lincoln
Plattsmouth
Nebraska City
Crete
Auburn
Beatrice
40°N
Falls City
Hiawatha
Tuttle Cr. Res.
Atchison
Leavenworth
Kansas
Kansas City
Topeka
Bonner Sprs.
Lawrence
Ottawa
KANSAS
KANSAS TPK.
Emporia
Garnett
Verdigris
Neosho
Iola
Fort Scott
Chanute
Parsons
Independence
Columbus
Coffeyville
Oologah
Bartlesville Res.
WILL ROGERS TPK.
Miami
Tulsa
Page 10
Lac Seul
English
Grass Narrows
Goldpines
Root Portage
St. Joseph
ONTARIO
Ogoki
Little Current
Sioux Lookout
Quibell
Hudson
Keewatin
Kenora
Eagle L.
Dinorwic
Armstrong
Auden
Lake Nipigon
Nakina
Briarcliffe
Kenogami
Pagwa River
Geraldton
Longlac
Little Longlac
Hearst
Lake of the Woods
Kakagi L.
Rainy River
Fort Frances
Rainy L.
Rainy
Quorn
Nipigon
Manitouwadge
Oba
Mine Centre
Atikokan
International Falls
Kashabowie
QUETICO PROVINCIAL PARK
Thunder Bay
Marathon
Simpson I.
Isle St. Ignace
Slate Is.
White
646
Magpie
Missanabie
Upper Red Lake
Lower Red Lake
Big Falls
Vermilion L.
Ely
VERMILION RA.
Pigeon
701
Isle Royale
ISLE ROYALE NAT. PARK
419
Michipicoten Harbour
Chapleau
Big Fork
Bemidji
MESABI RANGE
Virginia
Hibbing
Mississippi
Grand Rapids
Taconite Harbor
LAKE SUPERIOR
640
Park Rapids
CUYUNA RA.
Duluth
Silver Bay
Two Harbors
Apostle Islands
Cloquet
Superior
KEWEENAW PENIN.
Manitou I.
Hubbell
Hancock
Caribou I.
Montreal
MINNESOTA
Wadena
Crosby
Brainerd
L. Mille Lacs
Ashland
Ironwood
White Pine
Ishpeming
Marquette
Sault Ste. Marie
Newberry
Thessalon
Glenwood
Little Falls
Rum
Sauk Centre
St. Croix
St. Cloud
Flambeau
Iron Mountain
Rhinelander
Manistique
Str. of Mackinac
North
Beaver I.
Rogers City
Willmar
Anoka
Minneapolis
St. Paul
Glencoe
Minnesota
Escanaba
Wolf
Chippewa Falls
591
Wausau
Menominee
Marinette
Petoskey
Boyne City
East Jordan
Alpena
Redwood Falls
New Ulm
Northfield
Red Wing
Eau Claire
Chippewa
Mississippi
Marshfield
Green Bay
DOOR PENIN.
262
St. Peter
Faribault
WISCONSIN
Mankato
Owatonna
Wisconsin Rapids
Stevens Pt.
De Pere
Green Bay
Traverse City
Grayling
465
477
Fairmont
Albert Lea
Rochester
Winona
Black
Appleton
Neenah
Kaukauna
Manistee
Manistee
Cadillac
Houghton L.
Saginaw Bay
Worthington
Sibley
511
Estherville
Austin
La Crosse
Oshkosh
L. Winnebago
Manitowoc
Fond du Lac
Sheboygan
Ludington
Spencer
Mason City
Charles City
Decorah
Beaver Dam
Mt. Pleasant
Midland
Bay City
Little Sioux
Fort Dodge
Iowa
Cedar
Turkey
Wisconsin
695
Madison
Watertown
Menomonee Falls
Milwaukee
Muskegon
Muskegon
Grand Haven
Saginaw
378
Waukesha
Grand Rapids
Flint
Raccoon
Cedar Falls
Waterloo
IOWA
Dubuque
Benton
E. Dubuque
Galena
Janesville
Beloit
Racine
Kenosha
Holland
Grand
Owosso
Lansing
Boone
Marshalltown
Ames
Freeport
Rockford
Waukegan
Kalamazoo
Battle Creek
Pontiac
373
Detroit
Des Moines
Newton
Cedar Rapids
Marion
Clinton
Dixon
Rock
Elgin
Chicago
Kalamazoo
St. Joseph
Jackson
Ann Arbor
Windsor
Winterset
Des Moines
Iowa City
Cordova
Sterling
De Kalb
Aurora
Michigan City
Niles
St. Joseph
Adrian
Monroe
Muscatine
Davenport
Joliet
South Bend
Elkhart
Goshen
Toledo
Oskaloosa
Rock Island
Depue
Ottawa
Oglesby
Hammond
Gary
Ottumwa
Galesburg
Kewanee
Clarinda
Nodaway
Monmouth
Burlington
Kankakee
Tiffin
Centerville
Fort Wayne
Huntington
Findlay
Chariton
Keokuk
Fort Madison
Macomb
Peoria
Canton
Logansport
Trenton
Grand
Kirksville
ILLINOIS
Bloomington
Lafayette
Kokomo
Marion
Lima
Chillicothe
Quincy
Lincoln
Champaign
Danville
INDIANA
Elwood
325
Salt
Mississippi
Springfield
Urbana
Frankfort
Muncie
Anderson
Columbus
Missouri
Hannibal
Decatur
Crawfordsville
Richmond
Springfield
Moberly
Illinois
Sangamon
Indianapolis
Dayton
Fairborn
Sugar Creek
Kansas City
Louisiana
Jacksonville
Charleston
Terre Haute
Middletown
Mexico
Mattoon
Connersville
Columbia
Hillsboro
Hamilton
Chillicoth
Sedalia
Alton
Kaskaskia
White
Columbus
Bloomington
Miami
Cincinnati
Fulton
St. Louis
E. St. Louis
Beckemeyer
Vincennes
Addyston
Covington
Newport
Osage
MISSOURI
Jefferson City
Meramec
Sandoval
Centralia
Bedford
Madison
Portsmouth
L. of the Ozarks
Bagnell Dam
Herculaneum
Crystal City
Mount Vernon
Wabash
Washington
White
Fork
Licking
Hematite
Jeffersonville
Speed
Louisville
Bolivar
Gasconade
Rolla
Bonne Terre
Evansville
New Albany
Kosmosdale
Frankfort
Lexington
PLATEAU
Iron Mountain
Mount Vernon
Brandenburg
Winchester
Pittsburg
Carthage
540
Fredericktown
Carbondale
Henderson
Owensboro
Kentucky
Joplin
Springfield
Current
Cape Girardeau
Ohio
Elizabethtown
Richmond
Galena
Spring
L. of the Cherokees
OZARK
Table Rock Res.
Bull Shoals Res.
Shawnee
KENTUCKY
KENTUCKY PKWY.
Madisonville
Green
Pensacola Dam
Springdale
Poplar Bluff
Sikeston
Paducah
Calvert City
L. Barkley
Paradise
Bowling Green
Somerset
W. Plains
90°W
Mayfield
Hopkinsville
Glasgow
85°W
L. Norfork

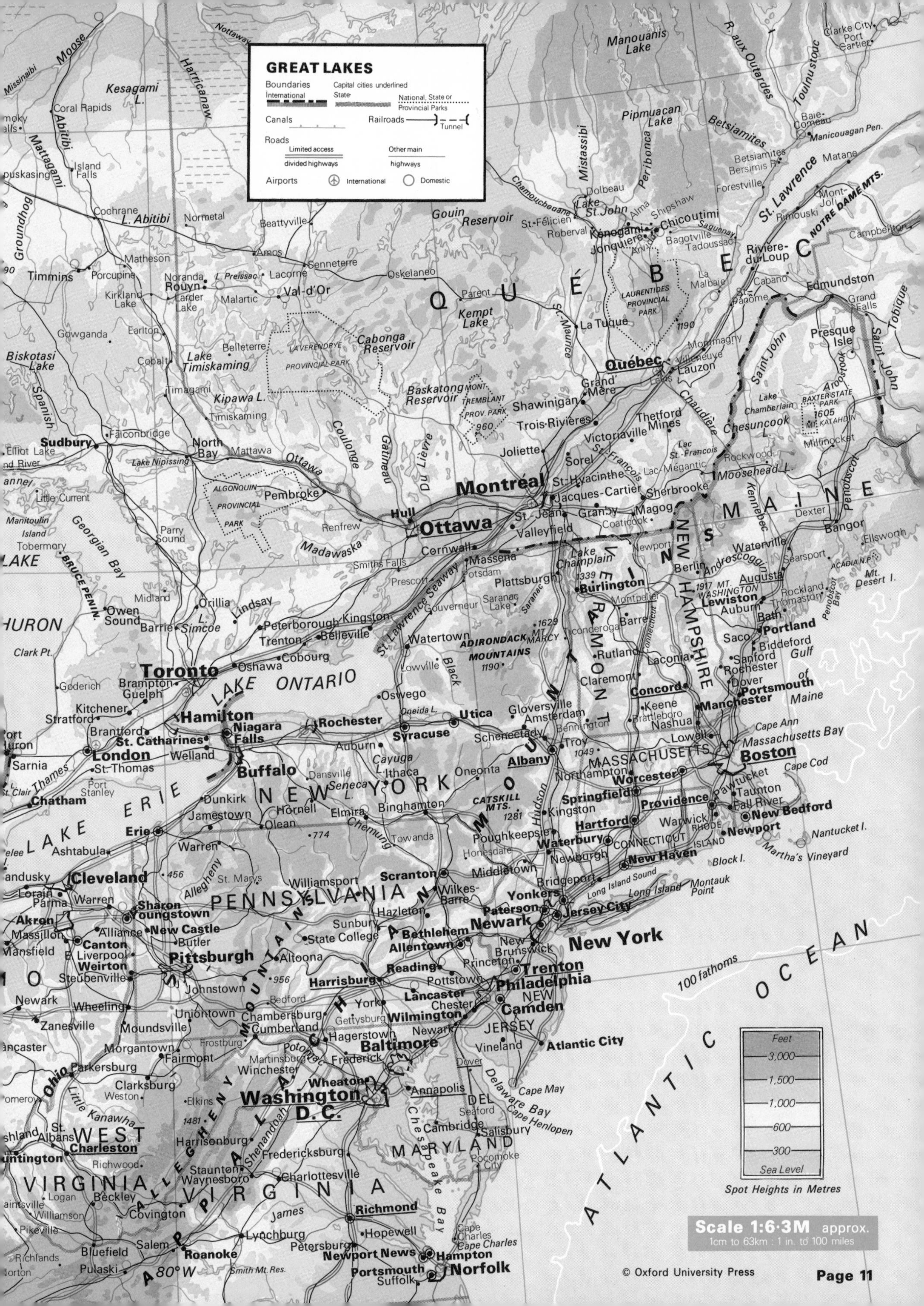
GREAT LAKES
Boundaries
International
Capital cities underlined
State
National, State or Provincial Parks
Canals
Railroads
Tunnel
Roads
Limited access divided highways
Other main highways
Airports
International
Domestic
Feet
3,000
1,500
1,000
600
300
Sea Level
Spot Heights in Metres
Scale 1:6·3M approx.
1cm to 63km : 1 in. to 100 miles
QUÉBEC
MAINE
NEW HAMPSHIRE
VERMONT
MASSACHUSETTS
CONNECTICUT
RHODE ISLAND
NEW YORK
PENNSYLVANIA
NEW JERSEY
DEL
MARYLAND
VIRGINIA
WEST VIRGINIA
ATLANTIC OCEAN
100 fathoms
LAKE ONTARIO
LAKE ERIE
HURON
Georgian Bay
Manouanis Lake
Pipmuacan Lake
Gouin Reservoir
Cabonga Reservoir
Baskatong Reservoir
Kempt Lake
Lake Timiskaming
Kipawa L.
Lake Nipissing
L. Abitibi
Kesagami L.
Lake St. John
Lake Champlain
Moosehead L.
Chesuncook L.
Lake Chamberlain
Oneida L.
Cayuga L.
Seneca L.
L. Simcoe
Massachusetts Bay
Cape Cod
Nantucket I.
Martha's Vineyard
Block I.
Long Island Sound
Long Island
Montauk Point
Delaware Bay
Cape May
Cape Henlopen
Chesapeake Bay
Cape Charles
Gulf of Maine
Cape Ann
Manicouagan Pen.
NOTRE DAME MTS.
ADIRONDACK MOUNTAINS
CATSKILL MTS.
APPALACHIAN MOUNTAINS
ALLEGHENY MOUNTAINS
BRUCE PENIN.
LAURENTIDES PROVINCIAL PARK
LA VERENDRYE PROVINCIAL PARK
MONT TREMBLANT PROV. PARK
ALGONQUIN PROVINCIAL PARK
BAXTER STATE PARK
ACADIA N.P.
1917 MT. WASHINGTON
1629 MT. MARCY
1605 MT. KATAHDIN
St. Lawrence
St. Lawrence Seaway
Ottawa
Hudson
Mohawk
Susquehanna
Potomac
Shenandoah
James
Ohio
Allegheny
Little Kanawha
Chemung
Connecticut
Kennebec
Penobscot
Androscoggin
Saint John
Chaudière
St. Maurice
Saguenay
Moose
Abitibi
Mattagami
Harricanaw
Nottaway
Spanish
Thames
Montréal
Ottawa
Québec
Toronto
Boston
New York
Philadelphia
Washington D.C.
Baltimore
Pittsburgh
Cleveland
Buffalo
Rochester
Syracuse
Albany
Hartford
Providence
Concord
Augusta
Montpelier
Harrisburg
Trenton
Richmond
Charleston
Hamilton
London
Niagara Falls
Erie
Akron
Youngstown
Newark
Jersey City
Paterson
Camden
Wilmington
Norfolk
Portsmouth
Newport News
Hampton
Roanoke
Lynchburg
Charlottesville
Annapolis
Atlantic City
Scranton
Allentown
Bethlehem
Reading
Lancaster
Worcester
Springfield
New Haven
Waterbury
Bridgeport
Portland
Bangor
Burlington
Sherbrooke
Trois-Rivières
Chicoutimi
Sudbury
North Bay
Timmins
Kingston
Peterborough
Oshawa
Brantford
Kitchener
St. Catharines
Windsor
Sarnia
Chatham
Utica
Binghamton
Elmira
Ithaca
Watertown
Oswego
Plattsburgh
Schenectady
Troy
Poughkeepsie
Newburgh
Yonkers
Manchester
Nashua
Lowell
Lewiston
Fall River
New Bedford
Newport
Pawtucket
Taunton
Warwick
Dover
Wheeling
Steubenville
Canton
Morgantown
Parkersburg
Fairmont
Clarksburg
Hagerstown
Frederick
Cumberland
Altoona
Johnstown
State College
Williamsport
Wilkes-Barre
Hazleton
York
Gettysburg
Chester
Vineland
Salisbury
Fredericksburg
Staunton
Waynesboro
Harrisonburg
Petersburg
Bluefield
Beckley
Huntington
Pulaski
Salem
Hopewell
Suffolk
Smith Mt. Res.
80°W

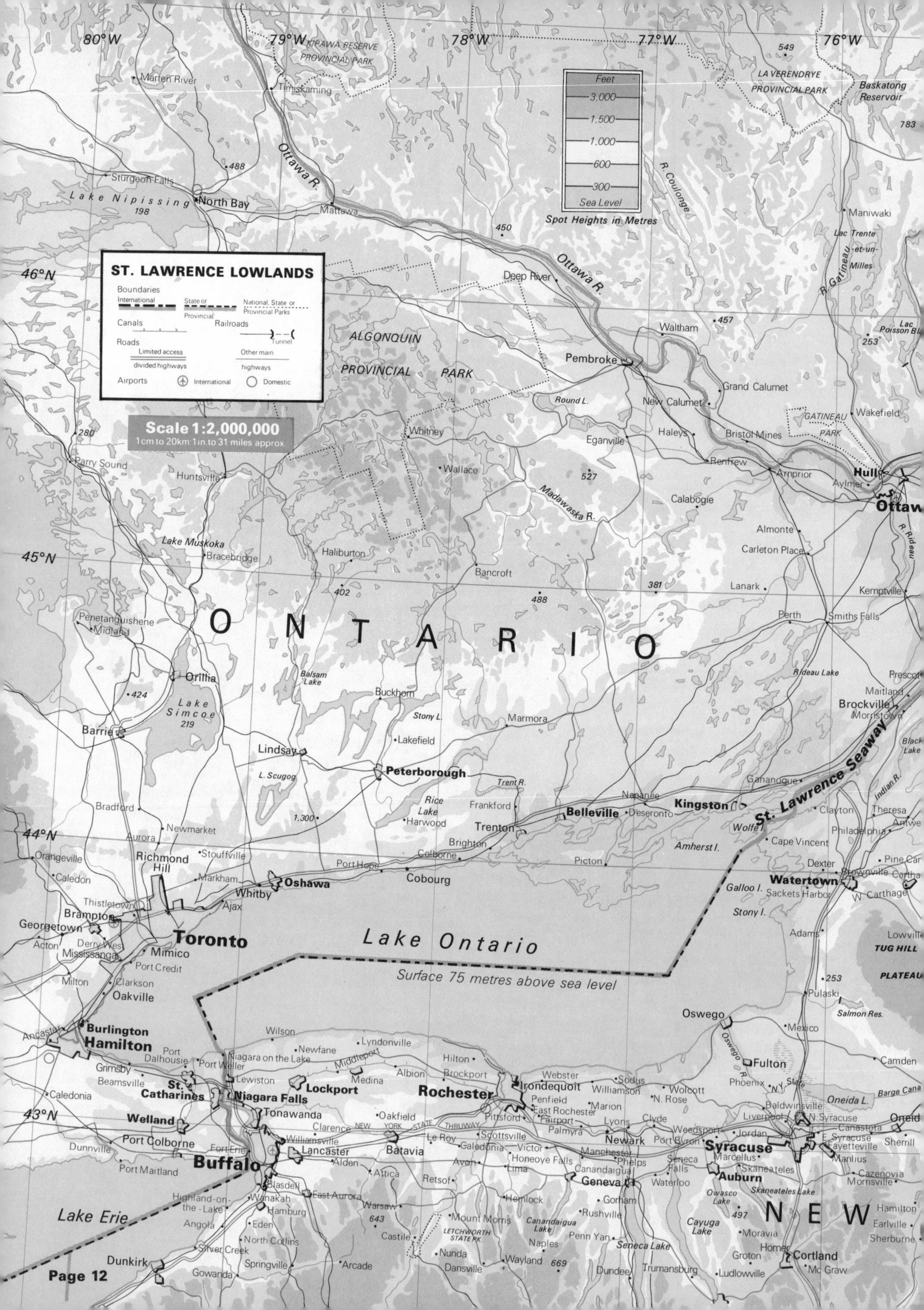
ST. LAWRENCE LOWLANDS
Boundaries
International
State or Provincial
National, State or Provincial Parks
Canals
Railroads
Tunnel
Roads
Limited access divided highways
Other main highways
Airports
International
Domestic
Scale 1:2,000,000
1cm to 20km:1in to 31 miles approx.
Feet
3,000
1,500
1,000
600
300
Sea Level
Spot Heights in Metres
80°W
79°W
78°W
77°W
76°W
46°N
45°N
44°N
43°N
ONTARIO
NEW
Lake Ontario
Surface 75 metres above sea level
Lake Erie
KIPAWA RESERVE PROVINCIAL PARK
LA VERENDRYE PROVINCIAL PARK
ALGONQUIN PROVINCIAL PARK
GATINEAU PARK
LETCHWORTH STATE PK
TUG HILL PLATEAU
St. Lawrence Seaway
Ottawa R.
R. Coulonge
R. Gatineau
Madawaska R.
R. Rideau
Trent R.
Oswego R.
Indian R.
Lake Nipissing
198
Lake Muskoka
Lake Simcoe
219
Balsam Lake
Stony L.
L. Scugog
Rice Lake
Round L.
Rideau Lake
Baskatong Reservoir
Lac Trente-et-un-Milles
Lac Poisson Bl
Wolfe I.
Amherst I.
Galloo I.
Stony I.
Salmon Res.
Oneida L.
Black Lake
Owasco Lake
Skaneateles Lake
Cayuga Lake
Seneca Lake
Canandaigua Lake
Marten River
Timiskaming
Sturgeon Falls
North Bay
Mattawa
Deep River
Waltham
Pembroke
Grand Calumet
New Calumet
Wakefield
Maniwaki
Haleys
Bristol Mines
Eganville
Renfrew
Arnprior
Hull
Aylmer
Ottaw
Calabogie
Whitney
Wallace
Parry Sound
Huntsville
Bracebridge
Haliburton
Bancroft
Almonte
Carleton Place
Lanark
Kemptville
Perth
Smiths Falls
Penetanguishene
Midland
Orillia
Barrie
Buckhorn
Marmora
Lakefield
Lindsay
Peterborough
Frankford
Harwood
Trenton
Belleville
Deseronto
Napanee
Kingston
Gananoque
Brockville
Maitland
Prescott
Morristown
Clayton
Theresa
Philadelphia
Antwe
Cape Vincent
Bradford
Newmarket
Aurora
Stouffville
Orangeville
Richmond Hill
Caledon
Markham
Whitby
Oshawa
Ajax
Port Hope
Cobourg
Colborne
Brighton
Picton
Dexter
Brownville
Watertown
Sackets Harbor
W. Carthage
Pine Car
Adams
Lowvill
Thistletown
Brampton
Georgetown
Acton
Derry West
Mississauga
Toronto
Mimico
Port Credit
Milton
Clarkson
Oakville
Ancaster
Burlington
Hamilton
Port Dalhousie
Grimsby
Beamsville
St. Catharines
Caledonia
Welland
Port Colborne
Dunnville
Port Maitland
Fort Erie
Buffalo
Wilson
Newfane
Lyndonville
Niagara on the Lake
Port Weller
Lewiston
Niagara Falls
Lockport
Middleport
Medina
Albion
Hilton
Brockport
Rochester
Irondequoit
Webster
Sodus
Williamson
Wolcott
N. Rose
Oswego
Fulton
Phoenix
Mexico
Pulaski
Camden
Penfield
East Rochester
Fairport
Pittsford
Marion
Lyons
Clyde
Palmyra
Newark
Tonawanda
Oakfield
Clarence
Williamsville
Lancaster
Alden
Batavia
Le Roy
Scottsville
Caledonia
Victor
Avon
Honeoye Falls
Lima
Manchester
Phelps
Geneva
Seneca Falls
Waterloo
Weedsport
Port Byron
Jordan
Baldwinsville
Liverpool
N. Syracuse
Syracuse
E. Syracuse
Canastota
Oneid
Fayetteville
Manlius
Sherrill
Marcellus
Skaneateles
Auburn
Cazenovia
Morrisville
Hamilton
Earlville
Sherburne
Moravia
Homer
Cortland
Mc Graw
Groton
Ludlowville
Trumansburg
Dundee
Penn Yan
Rushville
Gorham
Canandaigua
Hemlock
Naples
Wayland
Dansville
Nunda
Mount Morris
Castile
Warsaw
Attica
Retsof
Arcade
East Aurora
Blasdell
Wanakah
Hamburg
Highland-on-the-Lake
Eden
Angola
North Collins
Silver Creek
Springville
Dunkirk
Gowanda
NEW YORK STATE THRUWAY
N.Y. State Barge Canal
549
783
488
450
457
253
527
381
488
402
424
1,300
280
253
497
643
669

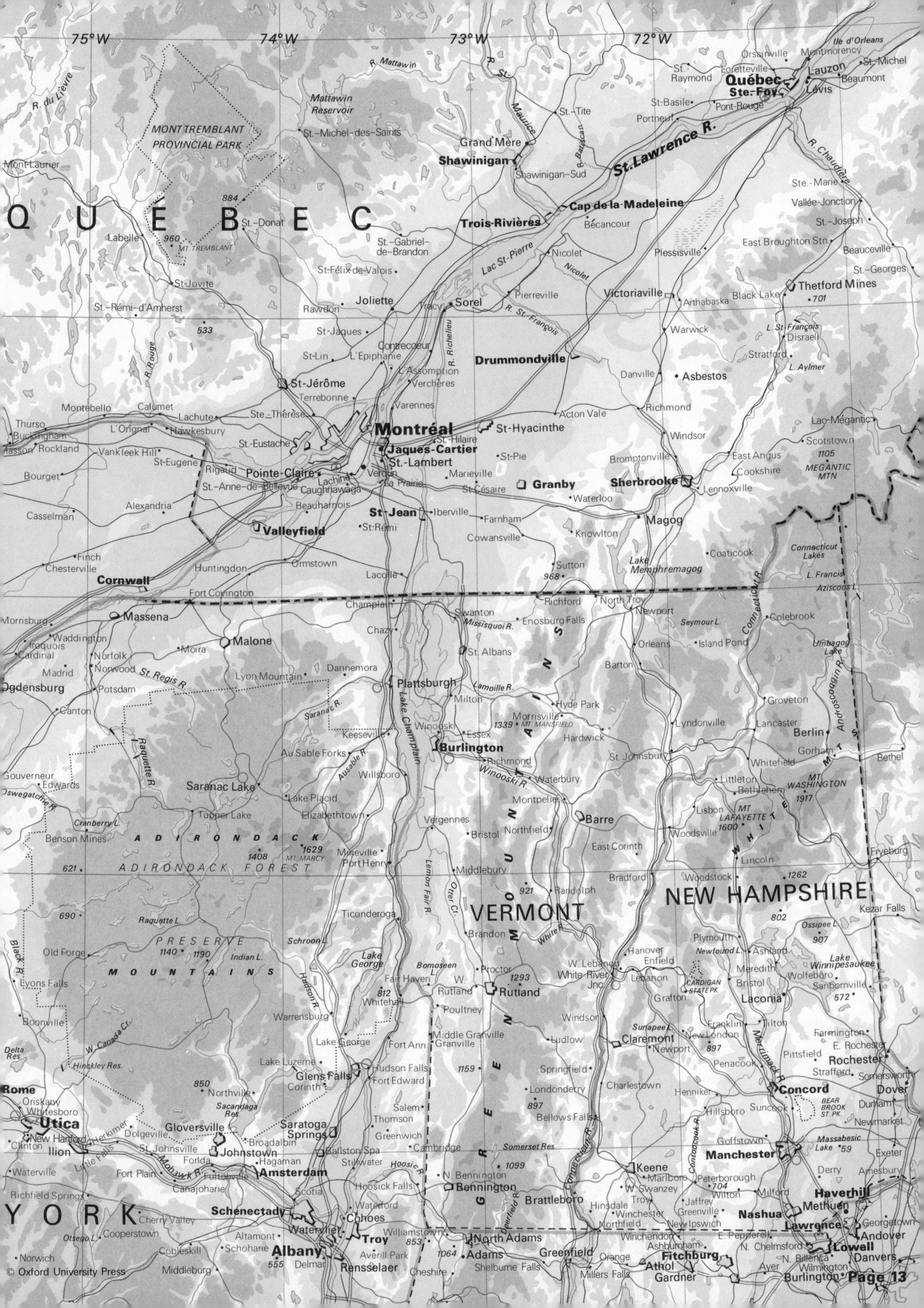
75°W
74°W
73°W
72°W
R. du Lièvre
R. Mattawin
Mattawin Reservoir
MONT TREMBLANT PROVINCIAL PARK
St.-Michel-des-Saints
Ile d'Orleans
Orsainville
Montmorency
St.-Michel
Lauzon
Beaumont
St.-Raymond
Loretteville
Québec
Ste.-Foy
Lévis
St.-Basile
Pont-Rouge
Portneuf
St.-Tite
R. St.-Maurice
R. Batiscan
Grand Mère
Shawinigan
Shawinigan-Sud
St. Lawrence R.
R. Chaudière
Mont-Laurier
Ste.-Marie
Vallée-Jonction
884
QUÉBEC
Cap de la Madeleine
Trois-Rivières
Bécancour
St.-Joseph
St.-Donat
Labelle
960
MT. TREMBLANT
St.-Gabriel-de-Brandon
Lac St-Pierre
Nicolet
Plessisville
East Broughton Stn.
Beauceville
St-Félix-de-Valois
Nicolet
St.-Georges
St-Jovite
Joliette
Pierreville
Victoriaville
Arthabaska
Black Lake
Thetford Mines
701
St.-Rémi-d'Amherst
Rawdon
Tracy
Sorel
R. St.-François
533
St-Jaques
R. Richelieu
Warwick
L. St-François
Disraeli
Contrecoeur
St-Lin
L'Epiphanie
Drummondville
Stratford
R. Rouge
L'Assomption
L. Aylmer
Danville
Asbestos
St-Jérôme
Verchères
Terrebonne
Montebello
Calumet
Lachute
Ste.-Thérèse
Varennes
Richmond
Acton Vale
Lac-Mégantic
Thurso
Buckingham
L'Orignal
Hawkesbury
Montréal
St-Hyacinthe
Windsor
Scotstown
Masson
Rockland
St.-Eustache
St.-Hilaire
Jacques-Cartier
Vankleek Hill
St-Eugene
St.-Lambert
St-Pie
Bromptonville
East Angus
1105
MEGANTIC MTN
Bourget
Rigaud
Pointe-Claire
Lachine
Verdun
Marieville
Cookshire
St.-Anne-de-Bellevue
Caughnawaga
La Prairie
St-Césaire
Granby
Sherbrooke
Lennoxville
Alexandria
Beauharnois
Waterloo
Casselman
St-Jean
Iberville
Farnham
Magog
Valleyfield
St-Rémi
Cowansville
Knowlton
Coaticook
Finch
Connecticut Lakes
Chesterville
Huntingdon
Ormstown
Lake Memphremagog
Lacolle
Sutton
L. Francis
968
Aziscoos L.
Cornwall
Fort Covington
Richford
North Troy
Connecticut R.
Champlain
Morrisburg
Massena
Swanton
Newport
Colebrook
Missisquoi R.
Enosburg Falls
Seymour L.
Waddington
Iroquois
Chazy
Norfolk
Moira
Malone
St. Albans
Orleans
Island Pond
Umbagog Lake
Cardinal
Madrid
Norwood
St. Regis R.
Dannemora
Barton
Androscoggin R.
Ogdensburg
Potsdam
Lyon Mountain
Plattsburgh
Lamoille R.
Milton
Hyde Park
Groveton
Canton
Saranac R.
Morrisville
1339
MT. MANSFIELD
Lyndonville
Lancaster
Berlin
Winooski
Essex
Keeseville
Lake Champlain
Hardwick
Gorham
Raquette R.
Burlington
Au Sable Forks
St. Johnsbury
Whitefield
Bethel
Ausable R.
Richmond
Gouverneur
Willsboro
Winooski R.
Waterbury
Littleton
Edwards
Saranac Lake
Bethlehem
MT. WASHINGTON
Oswegatchie R.
Lake Placid
Montpelier
1917
Tupper Lake
Elizabethtown
Lisbon
MT. LAFAYETTE
Barre
Cranberry L.
Vergennes
1600
Benson Mines
ADIRONDACK
Bristol
Northfield
Woodsville
1629
1408
MT. MARCY
Mineville
Port Henry
East Corinth
Fryeburg
621
ADIRONDACK FOREST
Lemon Fair R.
Lincoln
Middlebury
Otter Cr.
WHITE MTS.
Bradford
Woodstock
1262
Randolph
921
NEW HAMPSHIRE
690
Raquette L.
Ticonderoga
VERMONT
Kezar Falls
802
Ossipee L.
PRESERVE
Schroon L.
Brandon
White R.
Plymouth
907
Black R.
Old Forge
1140
1190
Indian L.
Lake George
Hanover
Newfound L.
Ashland
Bomoseen L.
Enfield
Lake Winnipesaukee
MOUNTAINS
Hudson R.
Proctor
W. Lebanon
Meredith
Wolfeboro
Fair Haven
1293
White River Jnc.
Lebanon
CARDIGAN STATE PK.
Sanbornville
Lyons Falls
W. Rutland
Bristol
812
Whitehall
Rutland
Grafton
Laconia
572
Warrensburg
Poultney
Windsor
Tilton
Boonville
Franklin
Farmington
Middle Granville
Sunapee L.
New London
Merrimack R.
W. Canada Cr.
Lake George
Fort Ann
Granville
Ludlow
Claremont
897
E. Rochester
Delta Res.
Newport
Pittsfield
Hinckley Res.
Lake Luzerne
Hudson Falls
Penacook
Rochester
1159
Springfield
Strafford
Somersworth
Glens Falls
Fort Edward
850
Rome
Corinth
Charlestown
Henniker
Concord
Dover
Oriskany
Northville
Londonderry
BEAR BROOK ST. PK.
Whitesboro
Sacandaga Res.
Salem
897
Hillsboro
Suncook
Durham
Utica
Thomson
Bellows Falls
Gloversville
Saratoga Springs
Newmarket
New Hartford
Herkimer
Dolgeville
Greenwich
Contoocook R.
Goffstown
Massabesic Lake
Clinton
St. Johnsville
Broadalbin
Ballston Spa
Cambridge
Somerset Res.
59
Ilion
Little Falls
Johnstown
Manchester
Exeter
Fonda
Hagaman
Stillwater
Hoosic R.
1099
Waterville
Fort Plain
Mohawk R.
Fultonville
Amsterdam
N. Bennington
Keene
Derry
Amesbury
Canajoharie
Scotia
Hoosick Falls
Marlboro
Peterborough
Richfield Springs
Bennington
Deerfield R.
Connecticut R.
704
Milford
Haverhill
W. Swanzey
Wilton
YORK
Schenectady
Cherry Valley
Waterford
Brattleboro
Jaffrey
Hinsdale
Troy
Methuen
Cohoes
Winchester
Greenville
Nashua
Georgetown
Watervliet
Northfield
New Ipswich
Otsego L.
Cooperstown
Lawrence
Altamont
Troy
Williamstown
North Adams
Winchendon
E. Pepperell
Andover
Cobleskill
Schoharie
853
Ashburnham
Lowell
Albany
Averill Park
1064
Adams
Greenfield
Orange
Fitchburg
N. Chelmsford
N. Billerica
Danvers
Norwich
555
Delmar
Athol
Wilmington
Middleburg
Rensselaer
Cheshire
Shelburne Falls
Millers Falls
Gardner
Ayer
Burlington

Page 13

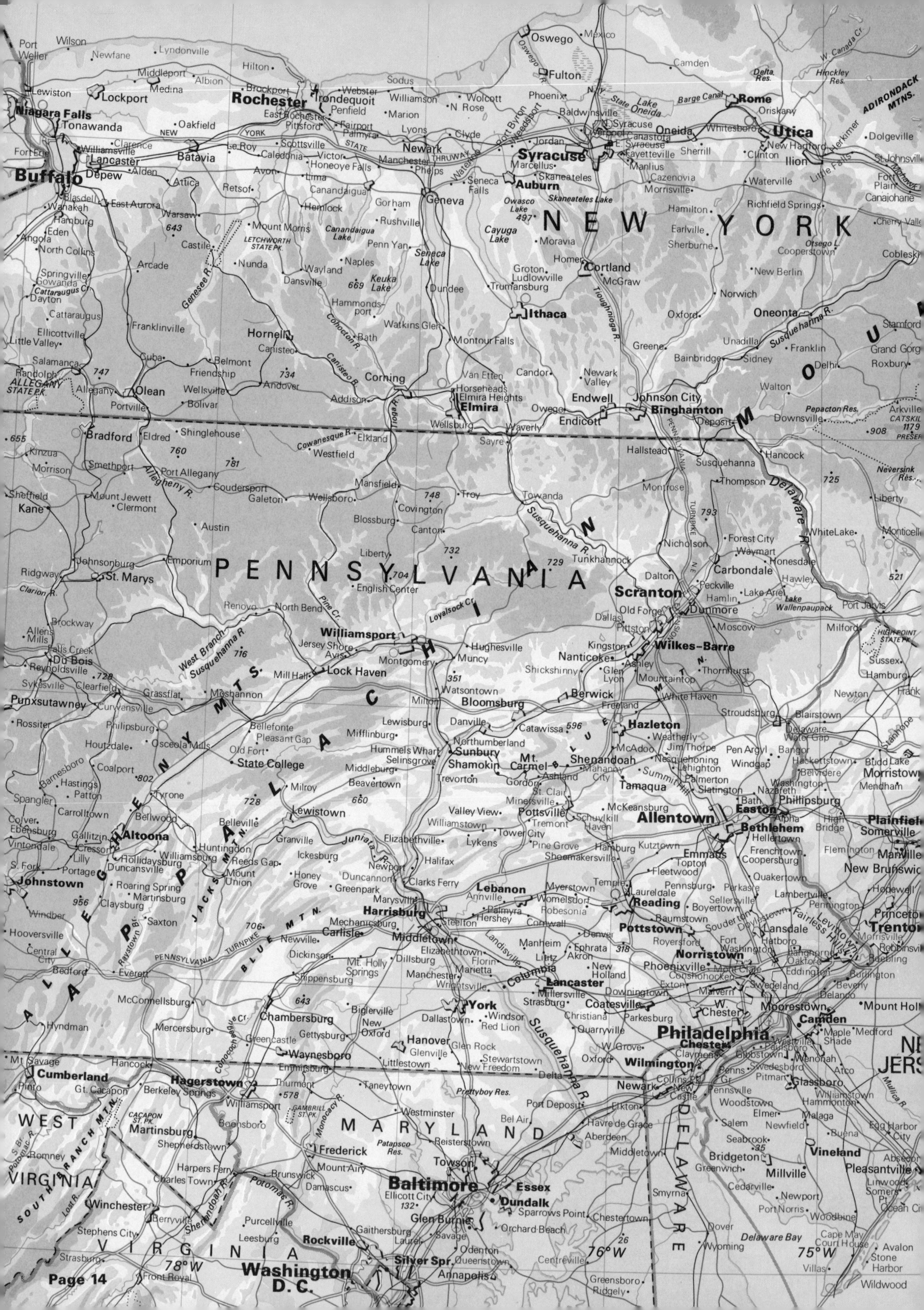
NEW YORK
PENNSYLVANIA
MARYLAND
DELAWARE
WEST VIRGINIA
VIRGINIA
NEW JERS
APPALACHIAN MOUNTAINS
ALLEGHENY MTS.
ADIRONDACK MTNS.
BLUE MTN.
Buffalo
Niagara Falls
Lockport
Rochester
Irondequoit
Oswego
Fulton
Syracuse
Auburn
Geneva
Rome
Utica
Oneida
Ithaca
Cortland
Elmira
Corning
Hornell
Olean
Binghamton
Johnson City
Endicott
Endwell
Batavia
Lancaster
Tonawanda
Oneonta
Bradford
St. Marys
Williamsport
Lock Haven
State College
Altoona
Johnstown
Scranton
Wilkes-Barre
Hazleton
Allentown
Bethlehem
Easton
Reading
Lancaster
York
Harrisburg
Carlisle
Chambersburg
Hagerstown
Cumberland
Frederick
Baltimore
Washington D.C.
Rockville
Silver Spr.
Philadelphia
Camden
Trenton
Wilmington
Chester
Vineland
Millville
Bridgeton
Lake Ontario
Lake Erie
Seneca Lake
Cayuga Lake
Keuka Lake
Canandaigua Lake
Owasco Lake
Skaneateles Lake
Oneida Lake
Barge Canal
NEW YORK STATE THRUWAY
PENNSYLVANIA TURNPIKE
Susquehanna R.
West Branch Susquehanna R.
Delaware R.
Allegheny R.
Genesee R.
Juniata R.
Potomac R.
Shenandoah R.
Delaware Bay
Chesapeake Bay
LETCHWORTH STATE PK.
ALLEGANY STATE PK.
HIGH POINT STATE PK.
CATSKILL
78°W
76°W
75°W

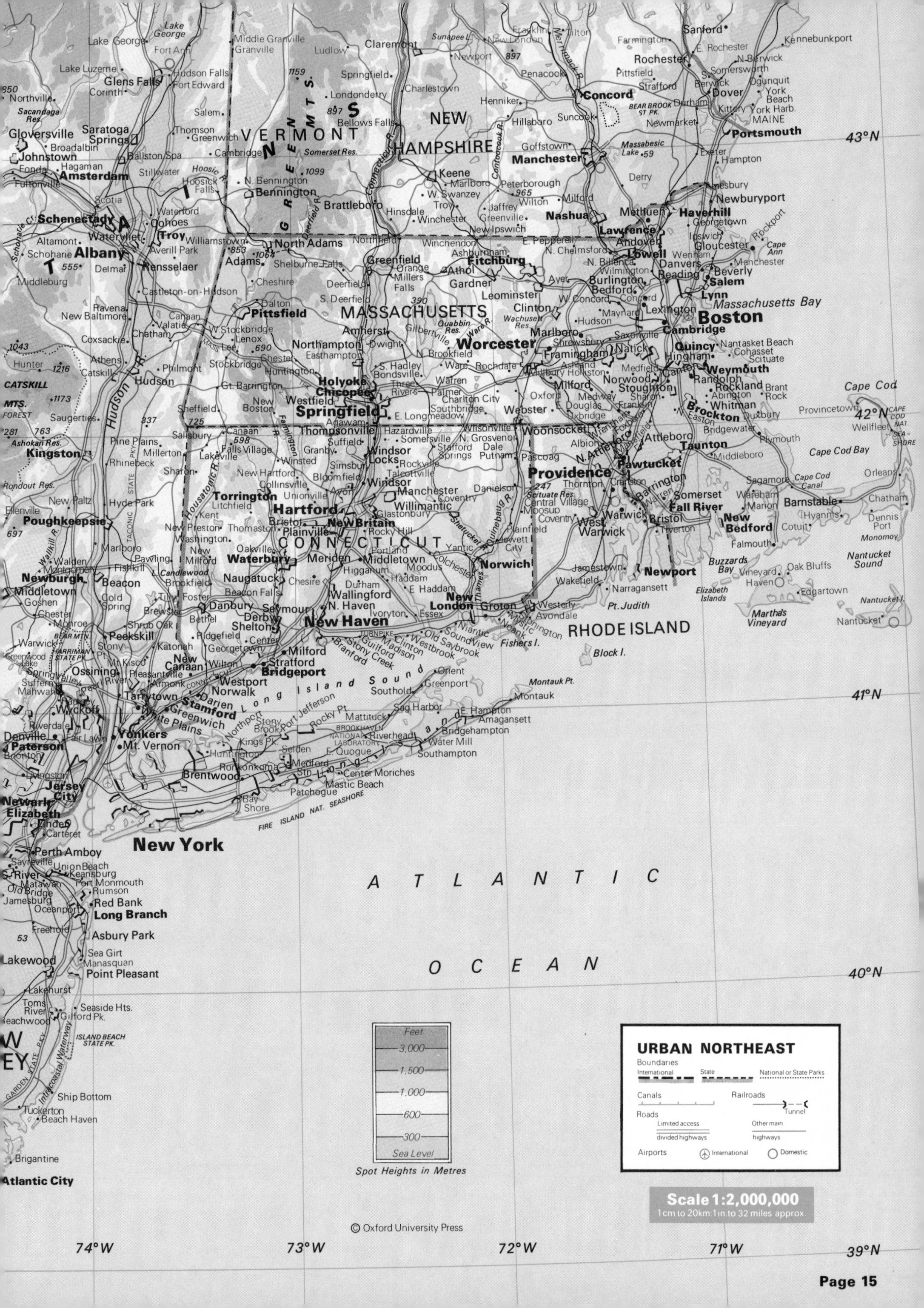
URBAN NORTHEAST
Boundaries
International
State
National or State Parks
Canals
Railroads
Tunnel
Roads
Limited access divided highways
Other main highways
Airports
International
Domestic
Feet
3,000
1,500
1,000
600
300
Sea Level
Spot Heights in Metres
Scale 1:2,000,000
1cm to 20km 1in to 32 miles approx.
© Oxford University Press
74°W
73°W
72°W
71°W
43°N
42°N
41°N
40°N
39°N
ATLANTIC
OCEAN
VERMONT
NEW HAMPSHIRE
MAINE
MASSACHUSETTS
CONNECTICUT
RHODE ISLAND
GREEN MTS.
CATSKILL MTS.
Long Island Sound
Long Island
Massachusetts Bay
Cape Cod Bay
Cape Cod
Nantucket Sound
Block I.
Fishers I.
Martha's Vineyard
Nantucket I.
Elizabeth Islands
Buzzards Bay
Montauk Pt.
Pt. Judith
FIRE ISLAND NAT. SEASHORE
CAPE COD NAT. SEA-SHORE
BEAR BROOK ST. PK.
HARRIMAN STATE PK.
ISLAND BEACH STATE PK.
BROOKHAVEN NATIONAL LABORATORY
Quabbin Res.
Wachusett Res.
Scituate Res.
Ashokan Res.
Sacandaga Res.
Hudson R.
Connecticut R.
Merrimack R.
Housatonic R.
Thames
Albany
Schenectady
Troy
Saratoga Springs
Glens Falls
Lake George
Amsterdam
Kingston
Poughkeepsie
Newburgh
Yonkers
Paterson
Jersey City
Newark
Elizabeth
New York
Perth Amboy
Red Bank
Long Branch
Asbury Park
Lakewood
Point Pleasant
Atlantic City
Concord
Manchester
Nashua
Portsmouth
Dover
Rochester
Sanford
Keene
Brattleboro
Bennington
North Adams
Pittsfield
Greenfield
Fitchburg
Worcester
Springfield
Holyoke
Chicopee
Boston
Cambridge
Quincy
Lowell
Lawrence
Haverhill
Salem
Lynn
Brockton
Taunton
Fall River
New Bedford
Providence
Pawtucket
Woonsocket
Warwick
Newport
Hartford
New Britain
Waterbury
New Haven
Bridgeport
Stamford
Norwich
New London
Danbury
Middletown
Meriden
Torrington

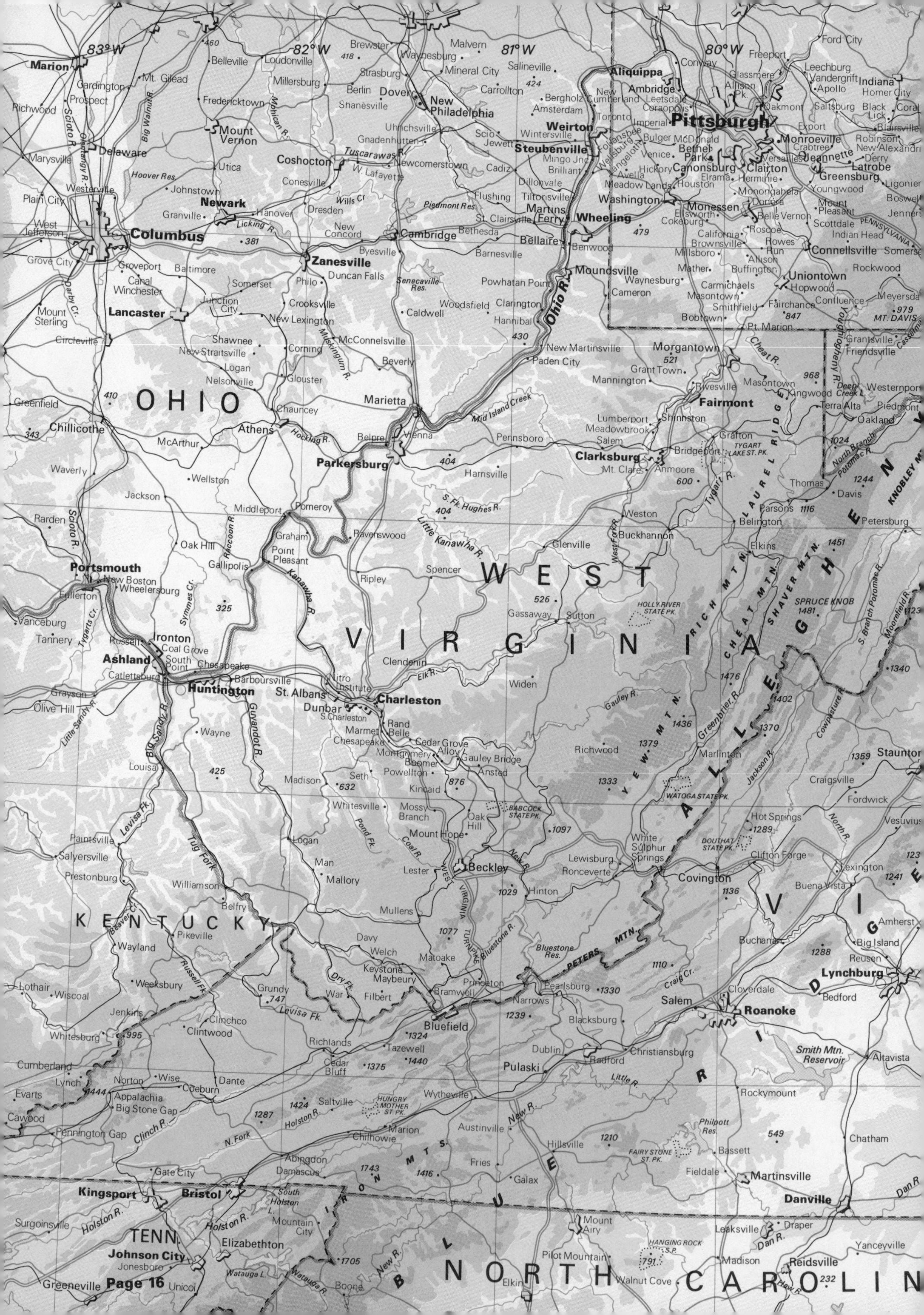

83°W
82°W
81°W
80°W
Marion
460
Belleville
Loudonville
Brewster
418
Waynesburg
Malvern
Salineville
424
Conway
Freeport
Ford City
Mt. Gilead
Gardington
Prospect
Richwood
Scioto R.
Big Walnut R.
Millersburg
Strasburg
Mineral City
Carrollton
Aliquippa
Ambridge
Glassmere
Allison Pk.
Leechburg
Vandergrift
Apollo
Indiana
Homer City
Fredericktown
Mohican R.
Berlin
Dover
Shanesville
New Philadelphia
Bergholz
Amsterdam
New Cumberland
Leetsdale
Coraopolis
Oakmont
Saltsburg
Black Lick
Coral
Blairsville
Mount Vernon
Uhrichsville
Gnadenhutten
Scio
Jewett
Wintersville
Weirton
Toronto
Imperial
Pittsburgh
Export
Delaware
Olentangy R.
Marysville
Tuscarawas R.
Coshocton
W. Lafayette
Newcomerstown
Steubenville
Mingo Jct.
Brilliant
Follansbee
Wellsburg
Bethany
Bulger
McDonald
Bethel Park
Venice
Hickory
Canonsburg
Clairton
Monroeville
Crabtree
Versailles
Jeannette
Robinson
New Alexandria
Derry
Latrobe
Greensburg
Hoover Res.
Utica
Westerville
Johnstown
Conesville
Cadiz
Dillonvale
Avella
Meadow Lands
Houston
Elrama
Herminie
Youngwood
Ligonier
Plain City
Newark
Granville
Hanover
Dresden
Wills Cr.
Piedmont Res.
Flushing
Tiltonsville
Washington
Monessen
Monongahela
Donora
Mount Pleasant
Boswell
Jenners
West Jefferson
Columbus
Licking R.
381
New Concord
Cambridge
Bethesda
St. Clairsville
Martins Ferry
Wheeling
Ellsworth
Cokeburg
Belle Vernon
Scottdale
Pennsylvania
Indian Head
Bellaire
Benwood
479
California
Brownsville
Roscoe
Rowes Run
Connellsville
Somerset
Grove City
Groveport
Baltimore
Zanesville
Byesville
Barnesville
Millsboro
Allison
Canal Winchester
Somerset
Philo
Duncan Falls
Senecaville Res.
Powhatan Point
Moundsville
Waynesburg
Mather
Buffington
Uniontown
Hopwood
Rockwood
Darby Cr.
Mount Sterling
Lancaster
Junction City
Crooksville
New Lexington
Caldwell
Woodsfield
Clarington
Hannibal
Ohio R.
Cameron
Carmichaels
Masontown
Smithfield
Fairchance
Confluence
Meyersdale
979
MT. DAVIS
847
Bobtown
Pt. Marion
Youghiogheny R.
Circleville
Shawnee
New Straitsville
Corning
Muskingum R.
McConnelsville
430
New Martinsville
Paden City
Morgantown
521
Grant Town
Cheat R.
Grantsville
Friendsville
Casselman
Logan
Beverly
Mannington
Masontown
968
Kingwood
Deep Creek L.
Westernport
Nelsonville
Glouster
OHIO
410
Greenfield
Chauncey
Marietta
Mid Island Creek
Rivesville
Fairmont
Terra Alta
Piedmont
Oakland
Chillicothe
343
Athens
Hocking R.
Belpre
Vienna
Lumberport
Shinnston
Meadowbrook
Salem
LAUREL RIDGE
McArthur
Parkersburg
Pennsboro
Grafton
TYGART LAKE ST. PK.
Clarksburg
Bridgeport
1024
North Branch Potomac R.
Waverly
404
Harrisville
Mt. Clare
Anmoore
600
Tygart R.
Thomas
Davis
1244
KNOBLEY MTN.
Wellston
Jackson
Middleport
Pomeroy
S. Fk. Hughes R.
404
Parsons
1116
Petersburg
Scioto R.
Rarden
Raccoon R.
Little Kanawha R.
Weston
Belington
Oak Hill
Graham
Ravenswood
West Fork R.
Buckhannon
Glenville
Elkins
1451
Portsmouth
Gallipolis
Point Pleasant
Kanawha R.
Ripley
Spencer
WEST
Rich Mtn.
Cheat Mtn.
Shaver Mtn.
New Boston
Wheelersburg
Fullerton
Symmes Cr.
325
526
Gassaway
Sutton
HOLLY RIVER STATE PK.
SPRUCE KNOB 1481
S. Branch Potomac R.
Moorefield R.
Vanceburg
Tannery
Tygarts Cr.
Russell
Ironton
Coal Grove
South Point
VIRGINIA
Ashland
Chesapeake
Catlettsburg
Huntington
Barboursville
Nitro
Institute
Clendenin
Elk R.
Widen
1476
1340
Grayson
Olive Hill
Little Sandy R.
Big Sandy R.
Guyandot R.
St. Albans
Dunbar
S. Charleston
Charleston
Gauley R.
1436
Greenbrier R.
1402
Cowpasture R.
Wayne
Marmet
Rand
Belle
Chesapeake
Cedar Grove
Montgomery
Alloy
Boomer
Gauley Bridge
Richwood
1379
Yew Mtn.
1370
Marlinton
Staunton
1359
Louisa
425
Madison
Seth
632
Powellton
Ansted
Kincaid
876
1333
WATOGA STATE PK.
Jackson R.
Craigsville
Fordwick
Whitesville
Mossy Branch
Oak Hill
BABCOCK STATE PK.
Levisa Fk.
Pond Fk.
Mount Hope
1097
Hot Springs
1289
DOUTHAT STATE PK.
North R.
Vesuvius
Paintsville
Salyersville
Logan
Coal R.
Tug Fork
New R.
White Sulphur Springs
Lewisburg
Ronceverte
Clifton Forge
Lexington
Prestonburg
Man
Mallory
Lester
Beckley
West Virginia Turnpike
Hinton
Covington
1136
Buena Vista
1241
Williamson
1029
Belfry
KENTUCKY
Mullens
ALLEGHENY
Beaver Cr.
Pikeville
Wayland
1077
Bluestone R.
Davy
Welch
Matoake
Bluestone Res.
Peters Mtn.
Buchanan
1288
Amherst
Big Island
Reusen
Keystone
Maybeury
Rand
Dry Fk.
Weeksbury
Russell Fk.
Lothair
Wiscoal
Grundy
747
War
Filbert
Bramwell
Princeton
Pearisburg
1330
Narrows
1110
Craig Cr.
Cloverdale
Lynchburg
Bedford
Salem
Roanoke
Jenkins
Clinchco
Clintwood
Levisa Fk.
Bluefield
1239
Blacksburg
Whitesburg
995
Richlands
1324
Tazewell
1440
Christiansburg
Smith Mtn. Reservoir
Altavista
Cumberland
Cedar Bluff
1375
Dublin
Radford
Pulaski
Little R.
Lynch
Norton
Wise
Dante
Coeburn
Evarts
1444
Appalachia
Big Stone Gap
1424
Saltville
HUNGRY MOTHER ST. PK.
Wytheville
Rockymount
Cawood
1287
Holston R.
Clinch R.
Pennington Gap
N. Fork
Marion
Chilhowie
Austinville
New R.
Philpott Res.
1210
549
Chatham
Abingdon
Damascus
Iron Mts.
1743
1416
Fries
Hillsville
FAIRY STONE ST. PK.
Bassett
Gate City
Galax
Fieldale
Martinsville
Kingsport
Bristol
South Holston L.
BLUE RIDGE
Danville
Dan R.
Surgoinsville
Holston R.
Holston R.
Mountain City
Mount Airy
Leaksville
Draper
TENN.
Elizabethton
Dan R.
HANGING ROCK S.P.
Yanceyville
Johnson City
Jonesboro
1705
New R.
Pilot Mountain
791
Madison
Reidsville
Greeneville
Page 16
Unicoi
Watauga L.
Watauga R.
Boone
Elkin
NORTH
Walnut Cove
CAROLIN
232
Haw R.

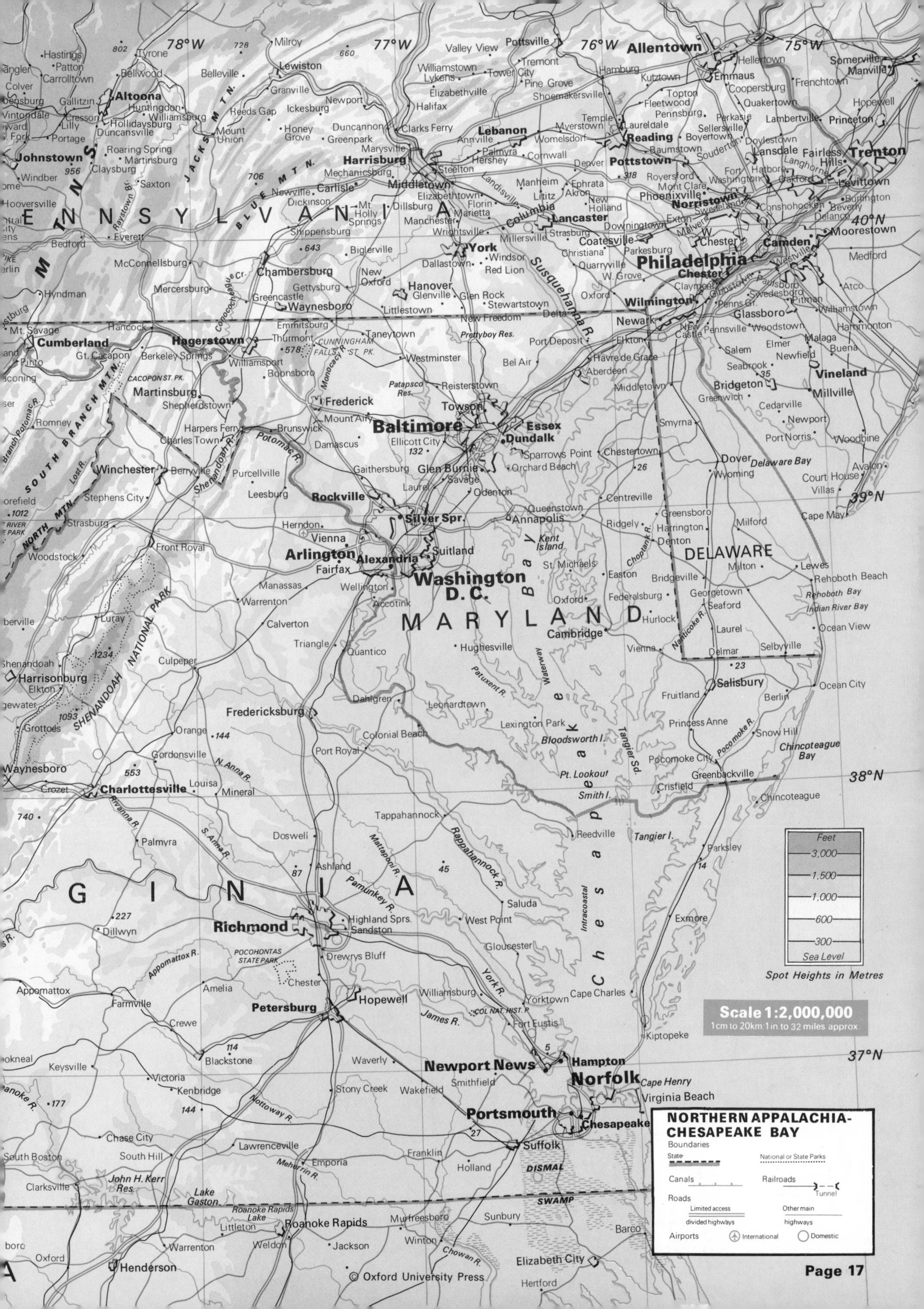

NORTHERN APPALACHIA-
CHESAPEAKE BAY

Boundaries
State
National or State Parks

Canals
Railroads
Tunnel

Roads
Limited access
Other main

divided highways
highways

Airports ⊕ International ◯ Domestic

Scale 1:2,000,000
1cm to 20km:1 in.to 32 miles approx

Feet
3,000
1,500
1,000
600
300
Sea Level

Spot Heights in Metres

Page 17

© Oxford University Press

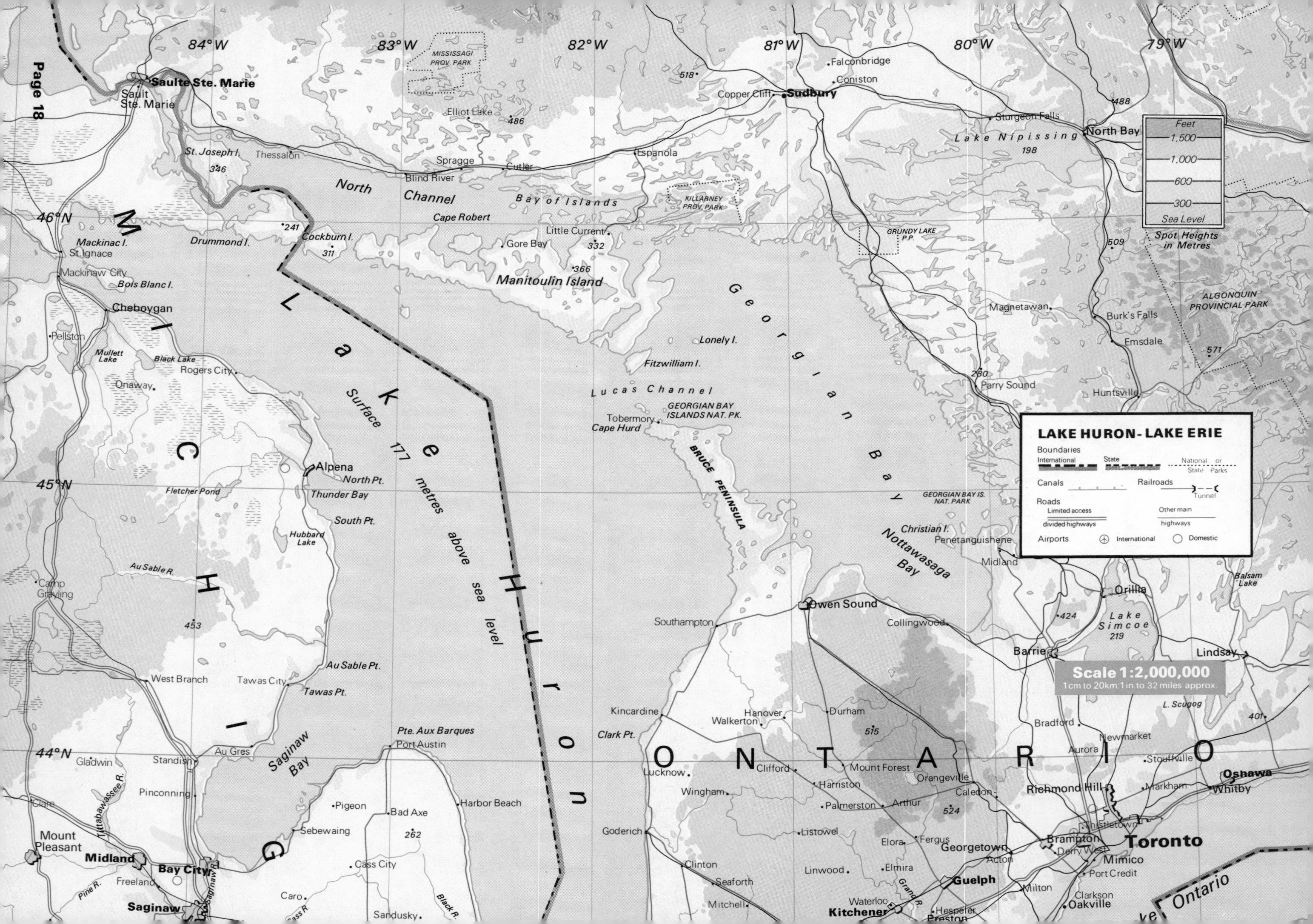

LAKE HURON - LAKE ERIE

Boundaries
International
State

Canals   Railroads

Roads
Limited access
divided highways

Airports   ⊕ International   ○ Domestic

National or
State - Parks

Other main
highways

Tunnel

Scale 1:2,000,000
1cm to 20km 1in to 32 miles approx

Spot Heights
in Metres

Feet
1,500
1,000
600
300
Sea Level

ONTARIO

ver Ontario

Toronto
Oshawa
Whitby

Lindsay
L. Scugog
Stouffville
Markham
Aurora
Newmarket
Port Credit
Richmond Hill
Brampton
Clarkson
Oakville
Mimico
Dixie
Milton

Balsam
Lake

Lake
Simcoe   219

Orillia

Barrie
Bradford
Caledon
Acton
Georgetown   Guelph
524
Orangeville
Fergus   Hespeler
Mount Forest   Elora   Grand R.
424   Durham   Arthur   Elmira   Waterloo R.
515   Palmerston   Linwood   Kitchener
Collingwood   Hanover   Harriston   Preston
Owen Sound   Walkerton   Listowel   Clifford   Wingham
Southampton   Lucknow   Clinton   Seaforth
Kincardine   Wingham   Mitchell
Clark Pt.   Goderich

Midland
Penetanguishene
Christian I.
Nottawasaga   Bay
Georgian Bay
GEORGIAN BAY IS.
NAT. PARK

Parry Sound
280
Magnetawan

ALGONQUIN
PROVINCIAL PARK
571

North Bay
488
509
Burk's Falls
Emsdale
Huntsville
Sturgeon Falls
198
Lake Nipissing

Sudbury
Coniston
Falconbridge
Copper Cliff
518

80°W
81°W
79°W

Espanola
KILLARNEY
PROV. PARK

GRUNDY LAKE
P.P.

Georgian   Bay

Lonely I.
Fitzwilliam I.
GEORGIAN BAY
ISLANDS NAT. PK.

BRUCE PENINSULA

Lucas Channel
Tobermory
Cape Hurd

82°W

MISSISSAGI
PROV PARK

Elliot Lake
486
Sprague
Blind River
Cutler
Cape Robert

Bay of Islands
Little Current
Gore Bay
332
366
Manitoulin Island

North   Channel

83°W

Thessalon
St. Joseph I.
336
Drummond I.
241
Cockburn I.
311

Lake   Huron

Surface   177   metres   above   sea   level

Harbor Beach
Black R.
262
Bad Axe
Sandusky
Cass City
Pigeon
Sebewaing
Caro.
Vassar
Saginaw   Bay
Pte. Aux Barques
Port Austin
Au Gres

North Pt.
Alpena
Thunder Bay
South Pt.
Hubbard
Lake
AuSable Pt.
Tawas Pt.
Tawas City
East Tawas

Fletcher Pond
453
AuSable R.
West Branch
Standish
Pinconning
Au Gres

MICHIGAN

84°W

Sault Ste. Marie
Sault
Ste. Marie

Mackinac I.
St. Ignace
Bois Blanc I.
Mackinaw City
Cheboygan
Onaway
Mullet Lake
Black Lake
Rogers City
Pellston
Gaylord

Standish
Camp
Grayling
Mount
Pleasant   Midland
Gladwin
Freeland
Bay City
Saginaw
Pine R.
Tittabawassee R.

46°N
45°N
44°N

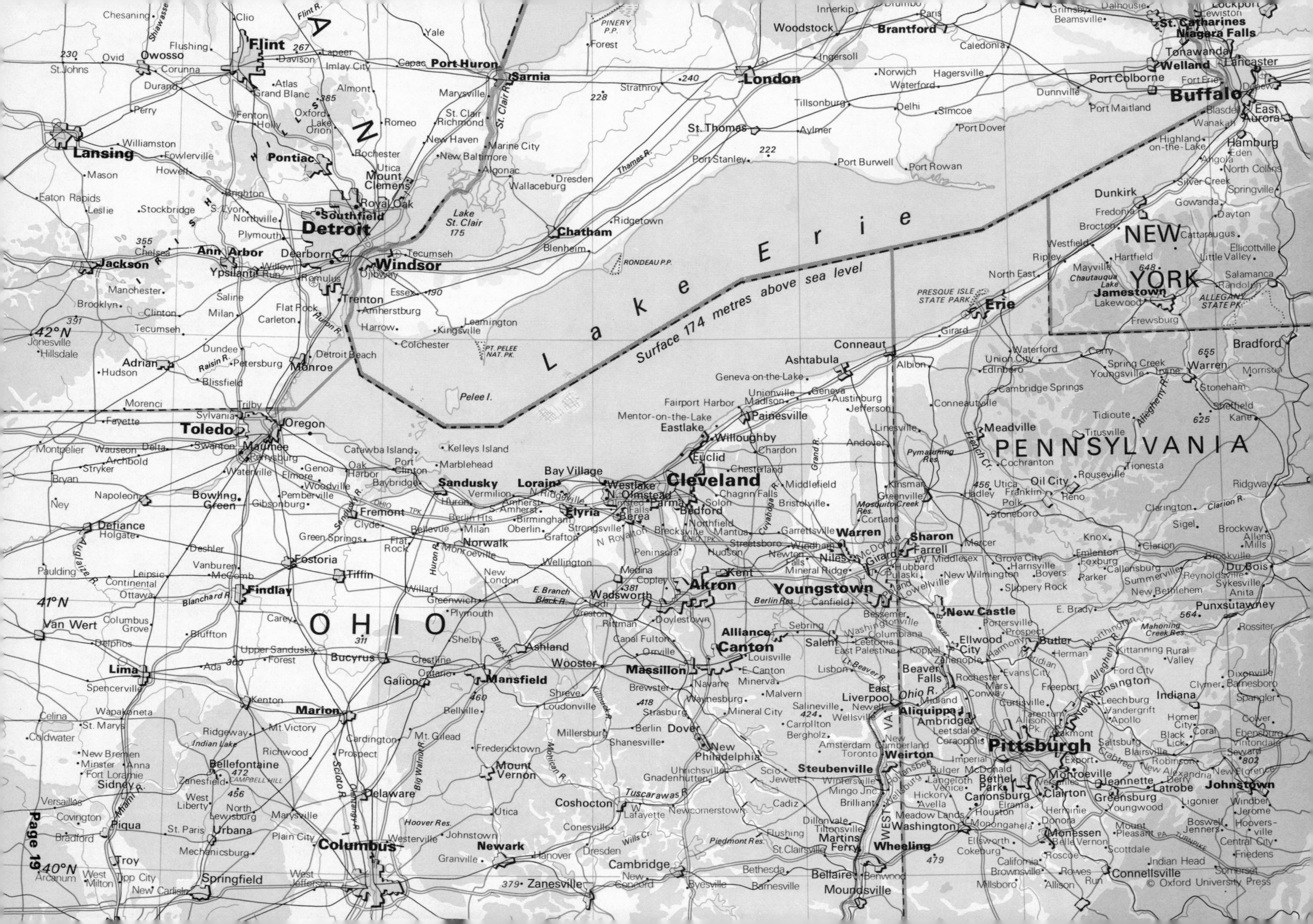
Lake Erie
Surface 174 metres above sea level
OHIO
PENNSYLVANIA
NEW YORK
Flint
Lansing
Pontiac
Detroit
Southfield
Ann Arbor
Jackson
Windsor
Port Huron
Sarnia
Chatham
London
Brantford
Woodstock
St. Thomas
St. Catharines
Niagara Falls
Welland
Buffalo
Toledo
Sandusky
Lorain
Elyria
Cleveland
Akron
Canton
Youngstown
Warren
Erie
Jamestown
Pittsburgh
Johnstown
Columbus
Mansfield
Findlay
Lima
Springfield
Newark
Zanesville
Steubenville
Wheeling
Weirton
New Castle
Sharon
Lake St. Clair 175
42°N
41°N
40°N
© Oxford University Press

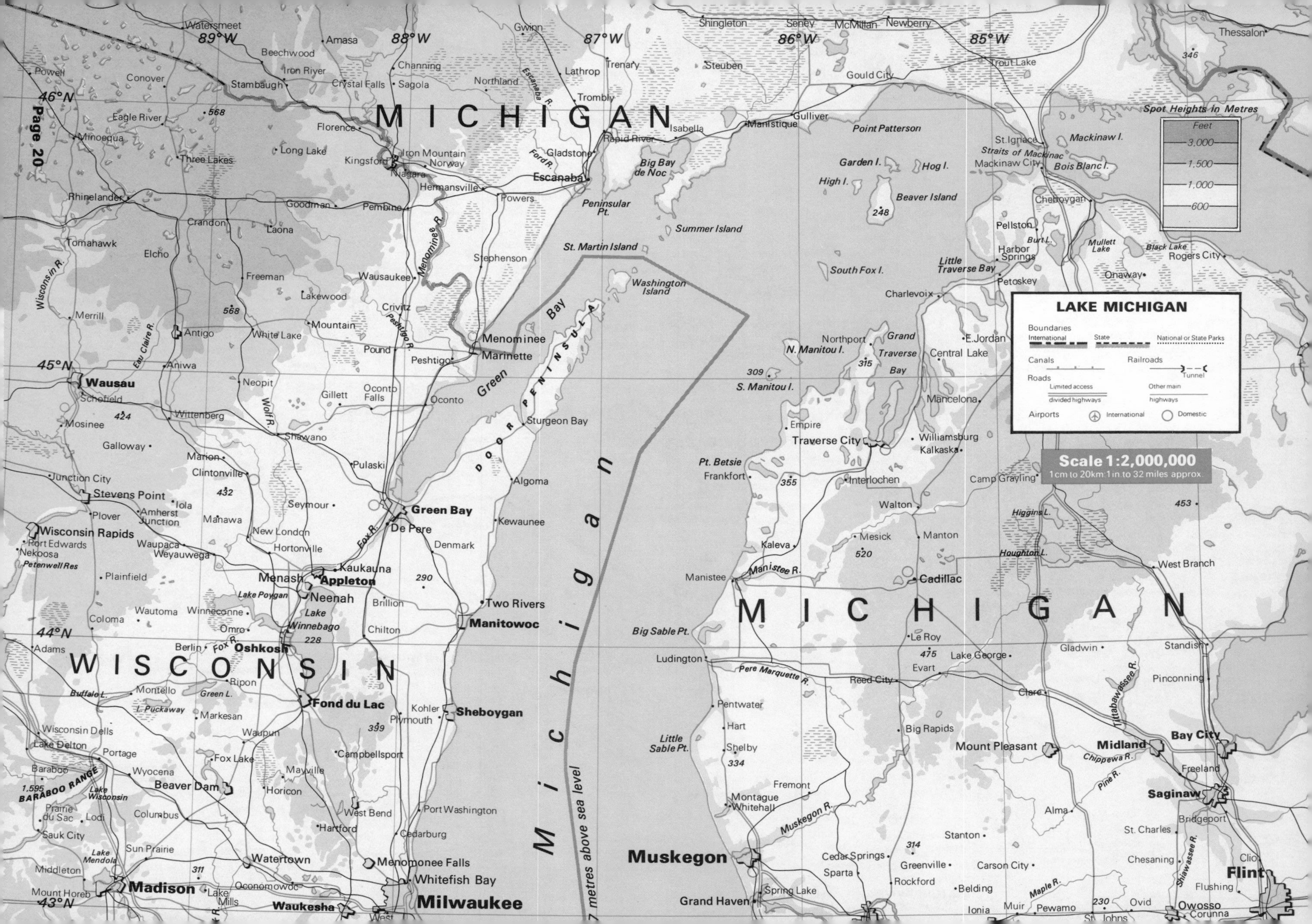

Page 20
LAKE MICHIGAN
Boundaries
International
State
National or State Parks
Canals
Railroads
Tunnel
Roads
Limited access divided highways
Other main highways
Airports
International
Domestic
Scale 1:2,000,000
1cm to 20km:1in.to 32 miles approx.
Spot Heights in Metres
Feet
3,000
1,500
1,000
600
MICHIGAN
MICHIGAN
WISCONSIN
Michigan
7 metres above sea level
89°W
88°W
87°W
86°W
85°W
46°N
45°N
44°N
43°N
Green Bay
DOOR PENINSULA
Big Bay de Noc
Straits of Mackinac
Little Traverse Bay
Grand Traverse Bay
Lake Winnebago
Lake Poygan
BARABOO RANGE
Milwaukee
Green Bay
Muskegon
Madison
Wausau
Oshkosh
Appleton
Fond du Lac
Sheboygan
Manitowoc
Escanaba
Menominee
Marinette
Traverse City
Cadillac
Midland
Bay City
Saginaw
Flint
Mount Pleasant
Stevens Point
Wisconsin Rapids
Waukesha
Beaver Dam
Grand Haven
Ludington
Manistee
Manistique
Cheboygan
Petoskey
Charlevoix
Two Rivers
Sturgeon Bay
Beaver Island
Washington Island
St. Martin Island
Summer Island
South Fox I.
N. Manitou I.
S. Manitou I.
Mackinaw I.
Bois Blanc I.
Big Sable Pt.
Little Sable Pt.
Pt. Betsie
Peninsular Pt.
Point Patterson
Wisconsin R.
Menominee R.
Wolf R.
Fox R.
Muskegon R.
Manistee R.
Pere Marquette R.
Tittabawassee R.

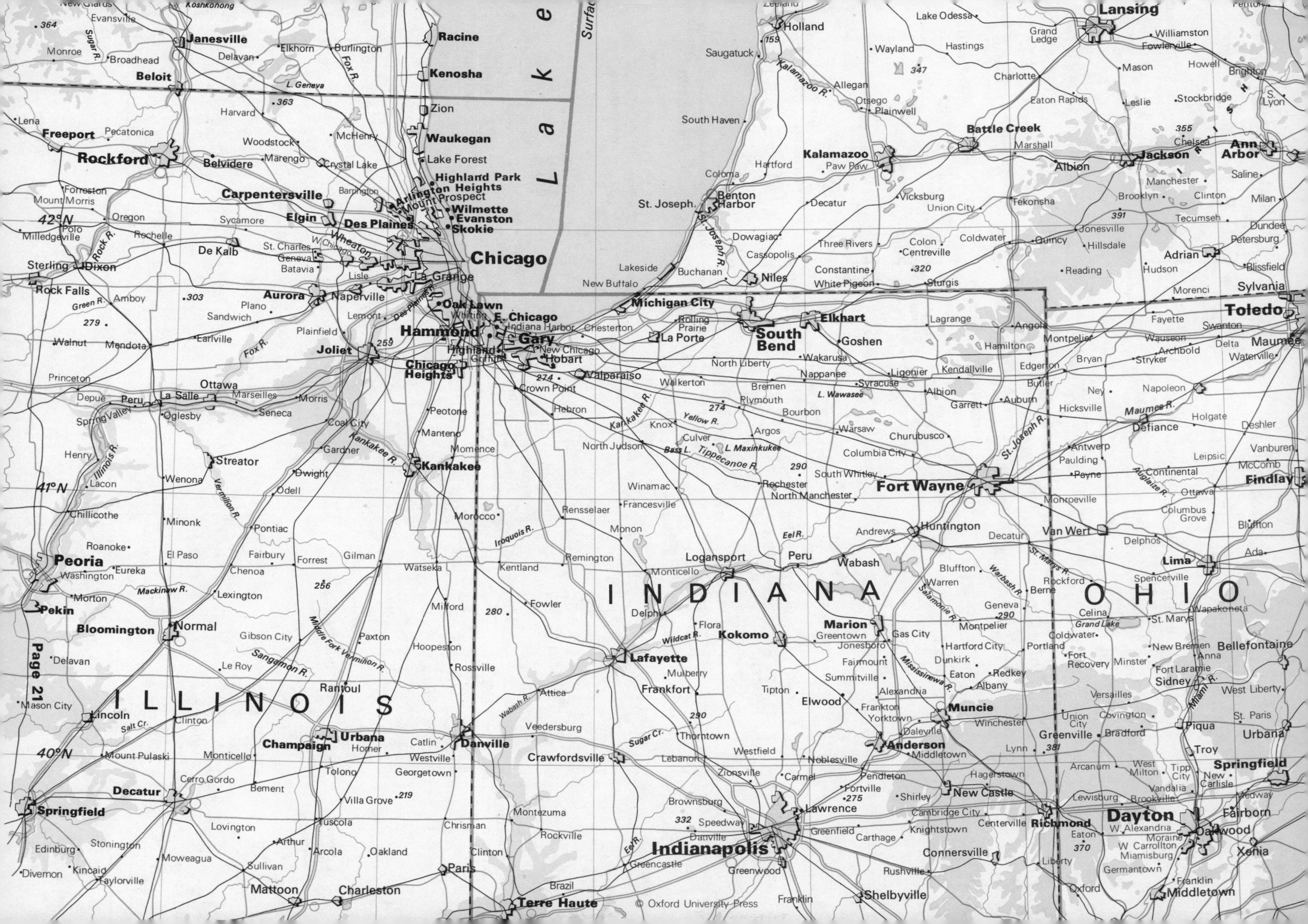

ILLINOIS
INDIANA
OHIO
Lake
Chicago
Rockford
Peoria
Bloomington
Normal
Springfield
Decatur
Champaign
Urbana
Danville
Kankakee
Joliet
Aurora
Elgin
Des Plaines
Carpentersville
Waukegan
Kenosha
Racine
Janesville
Beloit
Freeport
Belvidere
De Kalb
Dixon
Sterling
Rock Falls
Streator
Ottawa
La Salle
Peru
Pekin
Lincoln
Mattoon
Charleston
Paris
Zion
Lake Forest
Highland Park
Arlington Heights
Mount Prospect
Wilmette
Evanston
Skokie
La Grange
Oak Lawn
Naperville
Wheaton
W. Chicago
St. Charles
Geneva
Batavia
Lisle
Lemont
Plainfield
Hammond
Chicago Heights
E. Chicago
Whiting
Indiana Harbor
Gary
Highland
Griffith
Hobart
New Chicago
Valparaiso
Crown Point
Michigan City
La Porte
South Bend
Elkhart
Goshen
Fort Wayne
Huntington
Wabash
Peru
Logansport
Kokomo
Marion
Lafayette
Frankfort
Muncie
Anderson
New Castle
Richmond
Indianapolis
Lawrence
Crawfordsville
Terre Haute
Shelbyville
Connersville
Lansing
Jackson
Ann Arbor
Battle Creek
Kalamazoo
Holland
Benton Harbor
St. Joseph
Niles
Adrian
Toledo
Sylvania
Maumee
Findlay
Lima
Van Wert
Defiance
Dayton
Springfield
Xenia
Fairborn
Oakwood
Middletown
Sidney
Piqua
Troy
Urbana
Bellefontaine
42°N
41°N
40°N
Page 21
© Oxford University Press

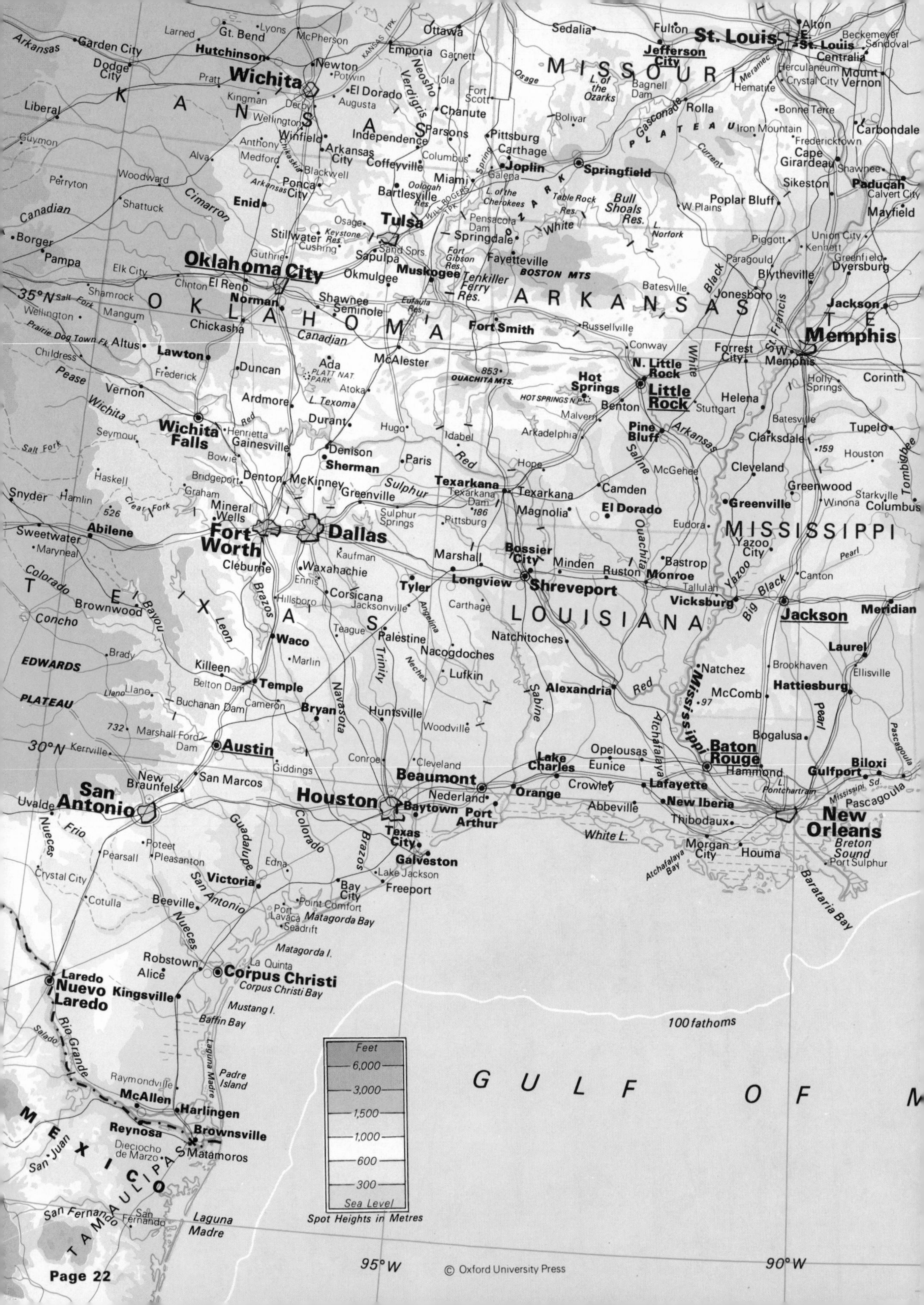

KANSAS
MISSOURI
OKLAHOMA
ARKANSAS
TENNESSEE
MISSISSIPPI
LOUISIANA
TEXAS
MEXICO
TAMAULIPAS
GULF OF M
OZARK PLATEAU
BOSTON MTS
OUACHITA MTS.
EDWARDS PLATEAU
35°N
30°N
95°W
90°W
100 fathoms
Feet
6,000
3,000
1,500
1,000
600
300
Sea Level
Spot Heights in Metres
Larned
Gt. Bend
Lyons
McPherson
Garden City
Dodge City
Hutchinson
Newton
Potwin
Wichita
Pratt
Kingman
El Dorado
Augusta
Derby
Wellington
Winfield
Arkansas City
Liberal
Guymon
Anthony
Medford
Alva
Blackwell
Ponca City
Woodward
Perryton
Shattuck
Enid
Canadian
Borger
Pampa
Cimarron
Arkansas
Stillwater
Cushing
Keystone Res.
Guthrie
Oklahoma City
El Reno
Clinton
Elk City
Shamrock
Salt Fork
Wellington
Mangum
Prairie Dog Town Fk.
Norman
Chickasha
Shawnee
Seminole
Altus
Childress
Lawton
Duncan
Frederick
Pease
Vernon
Wichita
Ardmore
Ada
PLATT NAT. PARK
Wichita Falls
Henrietta
Seymour
Salt Fork
Gainesville
Bowie
Haskell
Bridgeport
Graham
Denton
McKinney
Snyder
Hamlin
Clear Fork
526
Mineral Wells
Sweetwater
Abilene
Maryneal
Fort Worth
Dallas
Colorado
Brownwood
Concho
Bayou
Brady
Cleburne
Waxahachie
Ennis
Hillsboro
Brazos
Leon
Waco
Marlin
Killeen
Belton Dam
Temple
Llano
Buchanan Dam
Cameron
732
Marshall Ford Dam
Kerrville
Austin
Bryan
Navasota
San Marcos
New Braunfels
Giddings
San Antonio
Uvalde
Nueces
Frio
Poteet
Pearsall
Pleasanton
Crystal City
Cotulla
Guadalupe
Beeville
Victoria
Edna
Port Lavaca
Seadrift
Matagorda Bay
Matagorda I.
Point Comfort
Bay City
Robstown
Alice
Corpus Christi
Corpus Christi Bay
La Quinta
Mustang I.
Laredo
Nuevo Laredo
Kingsville
Baffin Bay
Salado
Rio Grande
Laguna Madre
Padre Island
Raymondville
McAllen
Harlingen
Reynosa
Brownsville
Dieciocho de Marzo
Matamoros
San Juan
San Fernando
Laguna Madre
Emporia
Ottawa
Garnett
Iola
Neosho
Verdigris
Chanute
Fort Scott
Parsons
Independence
Columbus
Coffeyville
Pittsburg
Carthage
Joplin
Miami
Galena
Bartlesville
Oologah Res.
Will Rogers Tpk.
Tulsa
Osage
Sand Sprs.
Sapulpa
Okmulgee
Muskogee
Eufaula Res.
Fort Gibson Res.
Tenkiller Ferry Res.
Pensacola Dam
L. of the Cherokees
Springdale
Fayetteville
Fort Smith
McAlester
Canadian
Atoka
L. Texoma
Durant
Denison
Sherman
Hugo
Idabel
Red
Paris
Sulphur
Greenville
Sulphur Springs
Pittsburg
Texarkana
Texarkana Dam
186
Kaufman
Corsicana
Tyler
Jacksonville
Marshall
Longview
Carthage
Angelina
Palestine
Teague
Trinity
Neches
Nacogdoches
Lufkin
Huntsville
Woodville
Conroe
Cleveland
Beaumont
Houston
Baytown
Nederland
Port Arthur
Orange
Texas City
Galveston
Lake Jackson
Freeport
Colorado
Sedalia
Fulton
Jefferson City
St. Louis
E. St. Louis
Alton
Beckemeyer
Sandoval
Centralia
Herculaneum
Hematite
Meramec
Crystal City
Mount Vernon
Osage
L. of the Ozarks
Bagnell Dam
Gasconade
Rolla
Bonne Terre
Bolivar
Iron Mountain
Carbondale
Fredericktown
Cape Girardeau
Current
Springfield
Table Rock Res.
White
Bull Shoals Res.
L. Norfork
W. Plains
Poplar Bluff
Sikeston
Shawnee
Paducah
Calvert City
Mayfield
Piggott
Union City
Kennett
Greenfield
Dyersburg
Paragould
Blytheville
Black
Batesville
Jonesboro
St. Francis
Jackson
Russellville
Conway
Forrest City
Memphis
W. Memphis
White
853
N. Little Rock
Little Rock
Hot Springs
HOT SPRINGS N.P.
Benton
Malvern
Arkadelphia
Helena
Stuttgart
Holly Springs
Corinth
Pine Bluff
Arkansas
Batesville
Tupelo
Clarksdale
159
Houston
Tombigbee
Hope
Saline
McGehee
Cleveland
Camden
Magnolia
El Dorado
Greenwood
Starkville
Winona
Columbus
Greenville
Eudora
Yazoo City
Ouachita
Bossier City
Minden
Ruston
Monroe
Bastrop
Shreveport
Tallulah
Yazoo
Big Black
Pearl
Canton
Vicksburg
Jackson
Meridian
Natchitoches
Laurel
Natchez
Brookhaven
Ellisville
Alexandria
Red
Sabine
McComb
97
Hattiesburg
Mississippi
Atchafalaya
Pearl
Bogalusa
Pascagoula
Opelousas
Lake Charles
Eunice
Baton Rouge
Hammond
Biloxi
Gulfport
Crowley
Lafayette
L. Pontchartrain
Mississippi Sd.
Pascagoula
Abbeville
New Iberia
Thibodaux
New Orleans
White L.
Morgan City
Houma
Breton Sound
Port Sulphur
Atchafalaya Bay
Barataria Bay
© Oxford University Press

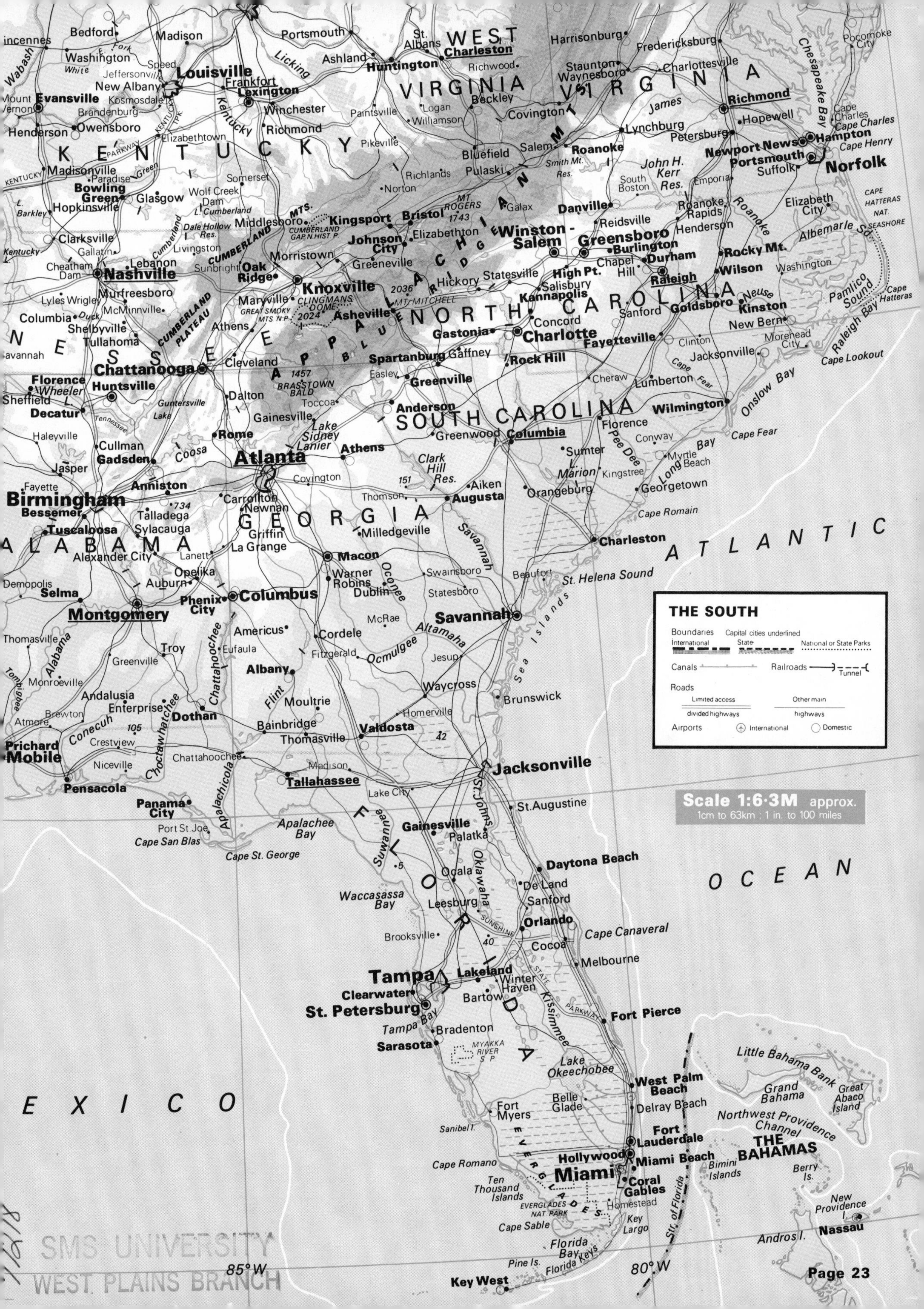

THE SOUTH

Boundaries   Capital cities underlined
International ▪▪▪▪ State ▪▪▪▪ National or State Parks ▪▪▪▪

Canals ━━━━   Railroads ━━━━
                              Tunnel)━━━(
Roads
  Limited access   Other main
  ━━━━ divided highways   ━━━━ highways
Airports ⊕ International ○ Domestic

Scale 1:6·3M approx.
1cm to 63km : 1 in. to 100 miles

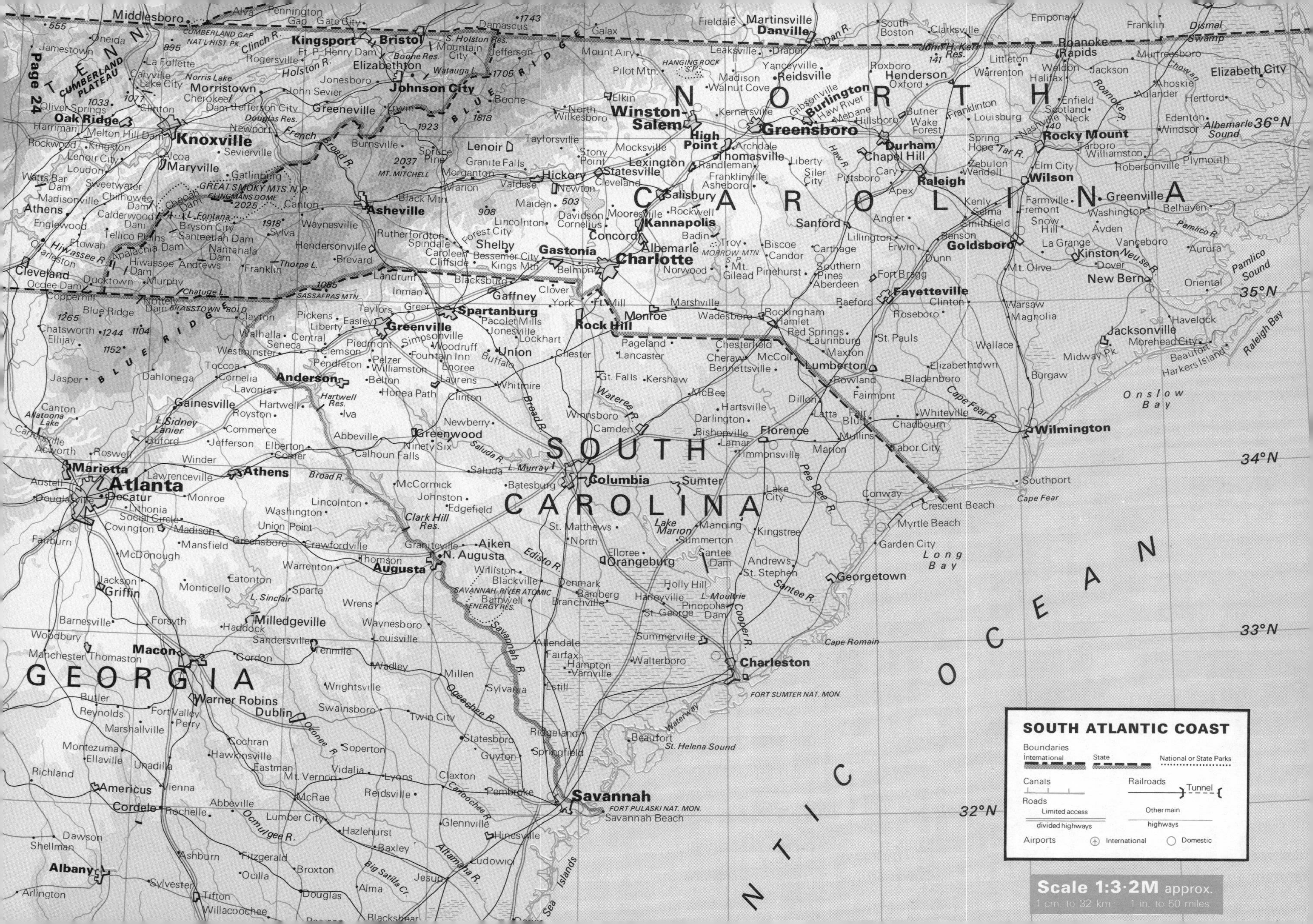

SOUTH ATLANTIC COAST

Scale 1:3·2M approx.
1 cm to 32 km   1 in. to 50 miles

Boundaries
International ───
State ─·─·─
National or State Parks
Canals
Roads
Limited access
Other main highways
divided highways
Tunnel)─(
Airports ⊕ International ○ Domestic
Railroads ┼┼┼

OCEAN
ATLANTIC

NORTH CAROLINA

SOUTH CAROLINA

GEORGIA

TENNESSEE

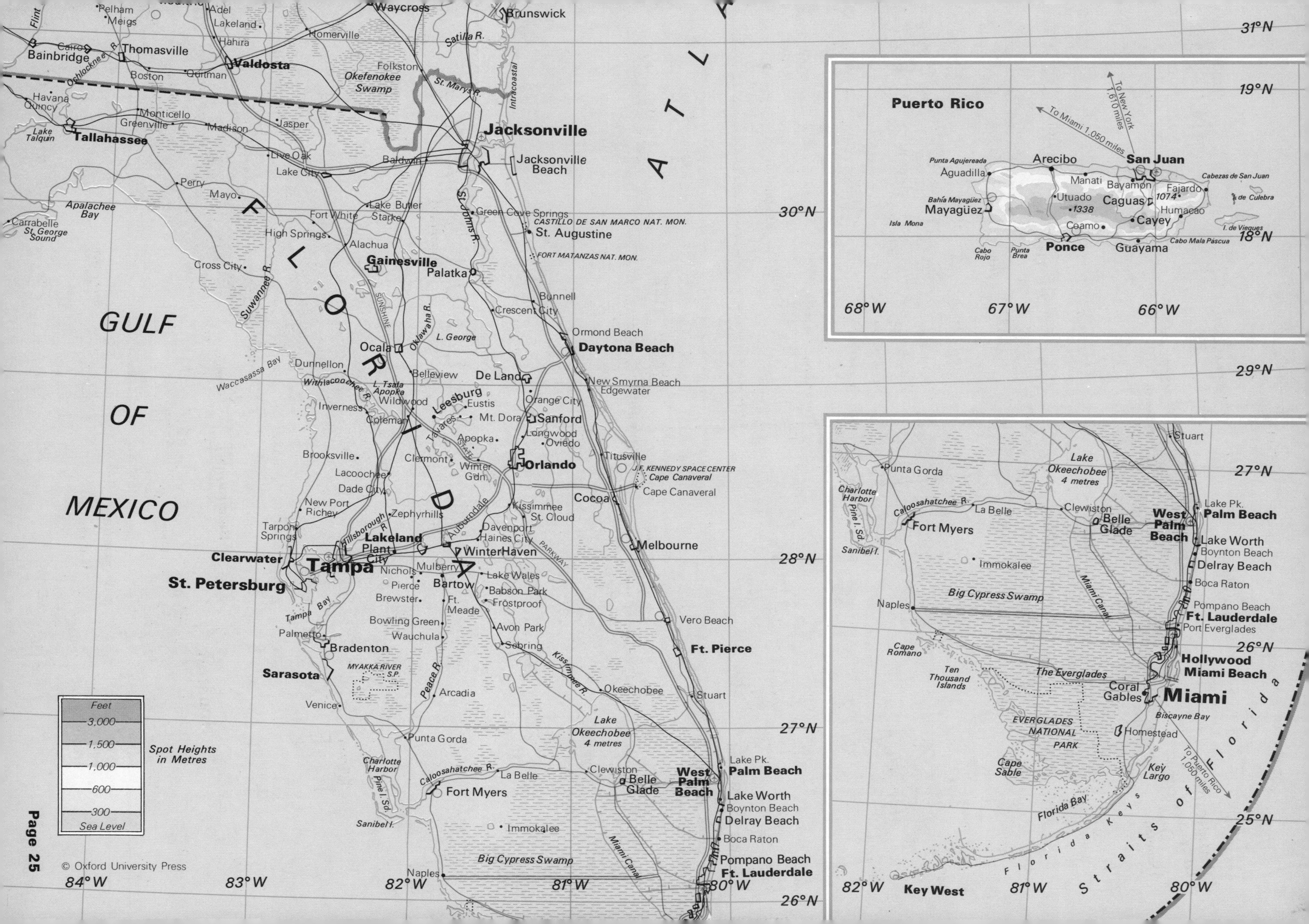

Puerto Rico

31°N
19°N
18°N
29°N
27°N
26°N
25°N
30°N
28°N
27°N
26°N

Cabezas de San Juan
San Juan
To New York
1,610 miles
Bayamón
Arecibo
Manati
Caguas
Humacao
Cayey
Utuado
1338
Guayama
Ponce
Coamo
To Miami 1,050 miles
Fajardo
I. de Culebra
1074
I. de Vieques
Punta Aguijereada
Aguadilla
Mayagüez
Bahía Mayagüez
Punta Brea
Cabo Mala Pascua
Cabo Rojo
Isla Mona

66°W
67°W
68°W

Stuart
Lake Pk.
Palm Beach
Lake Worth
Boynton Beach
Delray Beach
Boca Raton
Pompano Beach
Ft. Lauderdale
Port Everglades
Hollywood
Miami Beach
Miami
West Palm Beach
Belle Glade
Clewiston
Lake Okeechobee
4 metres
Miami Canal
Biscayne Bay
Coral Gables
Homestead
Key Largo
To Puerto Rico
1,050 miles
La Belle
Immokalee
The Everglades
EVERGLADES NATIONAL PARK
Big Cypress Swamp
Fort Myers
Cape Sable
Florida Bay
Caloosahatchee R.
Ten Thousand Islands
Cape Romano
Naples
Punta Gorda
Charlotte Harbor
Pine I. Sd.
Sanibel I.
Key West
Florida Keys
Florida Straits
© Oxford University Press

80°W
81°W
82°W

Brunswick
Intracoastal
Jacksonville
Jacksonville Beach
Green Cove Springs
St. Augustine
FORT MATANZAS NAT. MON.
CASTILLO DE SAN MARCO NAT. MON.
Bunnell
Ormond Beach
Daytona Beach
New Smyrna Beach
Edgewater
Crescent City
Orange City
Sanford
Longwood
Oviedo
Orlando
Titusville
Cocoa
Cape Canaveral
J.F. KENNEDY SPACE CENTER
Melbourne
Vero Beach
Ft. Pierce
Stuart
Lake Pk.
Palm Beach
Lake Worth
Boynton Beach
Delray Beach
Boca Raton
Pompano Beach
Ft. Lauderdale
West Palm Beach
a Belle Glade
Clewiston
Lake Okeechobee
4 metres
Miami Canal
Kissimmee R.
Okeechobee
Immokalee
Big Cypress Swamp
Fort Myers
Caloosahatchee R.
Naples
Punta Gorda
Charlotte Harbor
Pine I. Sd.
Sanibel I.
MYAKKA RIVER S.P.

De Land
St. Cloud
Kissimmee
PARKWAY
Davenport
Haines City
Lake Wales
Winter Gdn.
Apopka
Mt. Dora
Eustis
L. George
Leesburg
Wildwood
L. Tsala Apopka
Coleman
Clermont
Zephyrhills
Dade City
Lakeland
Plant City
Nichols
Mulberry
Pierce
Bartow
Brewster
Frostproof
Avon Park
Babson Park
Sebring
Arcadia
Bowling Green
Wauchula
Bradenton
Palmetto
Venice
Peace R.
Sarasota
Clearwater
St. Petersburg
Tampa
Tampa Bay
Tarpon Springs
New Port Richey
Brooksville
Inverness
Lacoochee
Dade City
Hillsborough R.
Withlacoochee R.

Waycross
Satilla R.
St. Marys R.
Baxter
Folkston
Okefenokee Swamp
Homerville
Jasper
Live Oak
Lake City
Fort White
St. Johns R.
Green Cove Springs
Palatka
Ocklawaha R.
Gainesville
SUNSHINE
Alachua
High Springs
Lake Butler
Starke
Suwannee R.
Cross City
Mayo
Perry
Waccasassa Bay
Chiefland
Dunnellon
Ocala
Belleview
Inverness

Valdosta
Lakeland
Hahira
Adel
Thomasville
Boston
Meigs
Pelham
Cairo
Havana
Monticello
Greenville
Madison
Tallahassee
Lake Talquin
Apalachee Bay
Carrabelle
St. George Sound
St. George I.
Flint
Bainbridge

F L O R I D A
GULF OF MEXICO
A T L A

Feet
3,000
1,500
1,000
600
300
Sea Level
Spot Heights
in Metres

83°W
84°W
81°W
82°W

Page 25

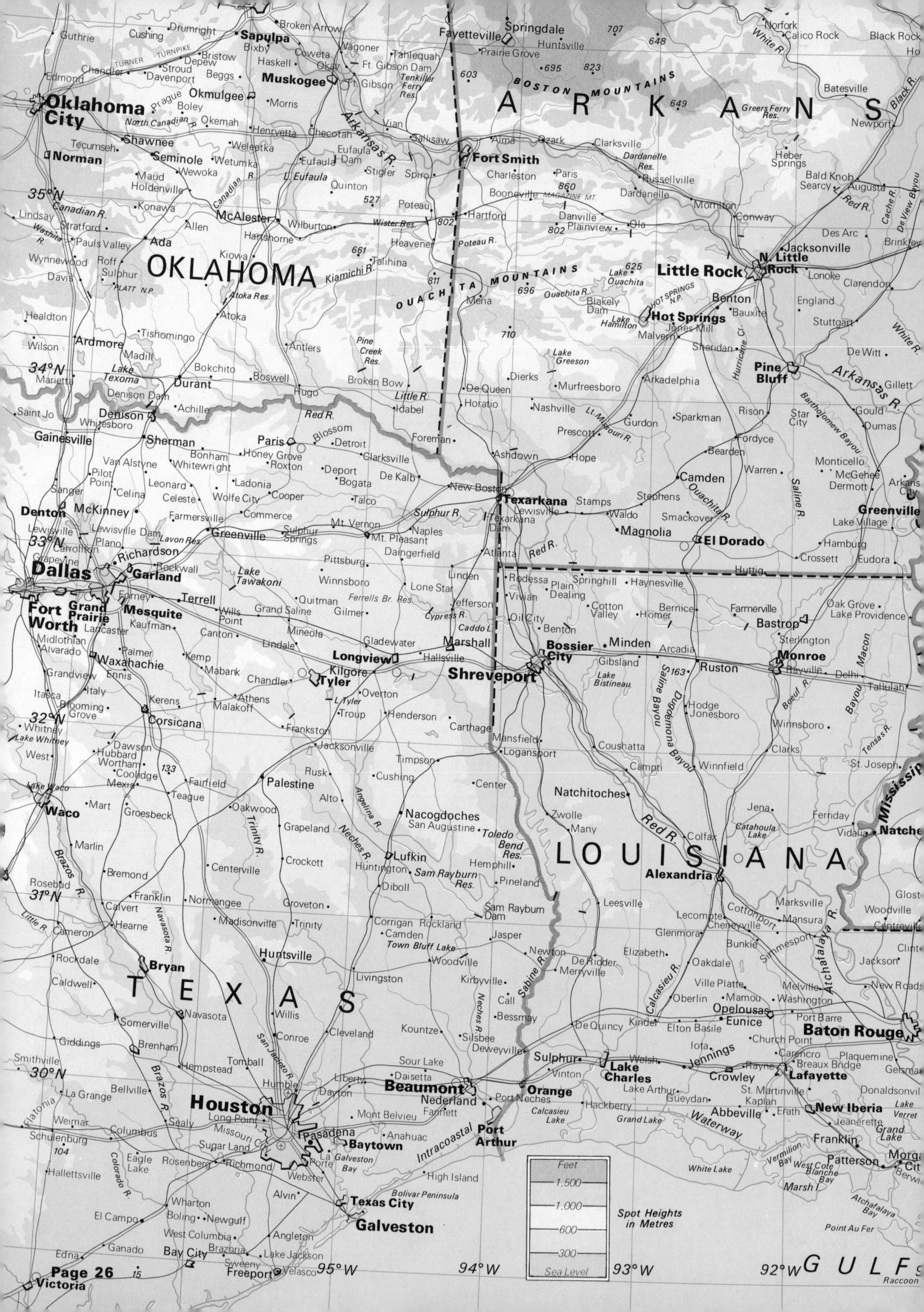

Guthrie
Cushing
Drumright
Sapulpa
Broken Arrow
Fayetteville
Springdale
707
648
Norfork
Calico Rock
Black Rock
Bixby
Wagoner
Huntsville
White R.
TURNER
TURNPIKE
Bristow
Depew
Haskell
Coweta
Tahlequah
Prairie Grove
Chandler
Stroud
Okay
Ft. Gibson Dam
695
823
Edmond
Davenport
Beggs
Muskogee
Ft. Gibson
Tenkiller Ferry Res.
603
BOSTON MOUNTAINS
Batesville
Black R.
Prague
Okmulgee
Oklahoma City
Boley
Morris
ARKANSAS
649
Greers Ferry Res.
Newport
North Canadian R.
Okemah
Arkansas R.
Vian
Henryetta
Checotah
Sallisaw
Alma
Ozark
Clarksville
Tecumseh
Shawnee
Weleetka
Eufaula Dam
Fort Smith
Dardanelle Res.
Heber Springs
Norman
Seminole
Wetumka
Eufaula
Stigler
Spiro
Charleston
Paris
Russellville
Bald Knob
Searcy
Augusta
Maud
Wewoka
L. Eufaula
Quinton
860
Holdenville
Canadian R.
Booneville
MAGAZINE MT.
Dardanelle
Morrilton
L. Red R.
Cache R.
De View Bayou
35°N
Canadian R.
Konawa
527
Poteau
Lindsay
Stratford
McAlester
Wilburton
Wister Res.
802
Hartford
Danville
802
Plainview
Ola
Conway
Washita R.
Allen
Pauls Valley
Ada
Hartshorne
Heavener
Poteau R.
Des Arc
Brinkley
Jacksonville
661
Kiowa
N. Little Rock
Wynnewood
Roff
OKLAHOMA
Talihina
Kiamichi R.
625
Little Rock
Lonoke
Davis
Sulphur
811
OUACHITA MOUNTAINS
Lake Ouachita
Clarendon
PLATT N.P.
696
Ouachita R.
HOT SPRINGS N.P.
Benton
Atoka Res.
Mena
Blakely Dam
England
Healdton
Atoka
Lake Hamilton
Hot Springs
Bauxite
Jones Mill
Stuttgart
Tishomingo
710
Malvern
White R.
Wilson
Ardmore
Antlers
Pine Creek Res.
Sheridan
Hurricane Cr.
De Witt
Madill
Lake Greeson
34°N
Bokchito
Pine Bluff
Marietta
Lake Texoma
Boswell
Dierks
Broken Bow
Arkadelphia
Arkansas R.
Gillett
Durant
Hugo
Murfreesboro
Denison Dam
Little R.
De Queen
Saint Jo
Achille
Idabel
Horatio
Nashville
Lt. Missouri R.
Rison
Gould
Denison
Red R.
Gurdon
Sparkman
Star City
Dumas
Whitesboro
Bartholomew Bayou
Blossom
Prescott
Gainesville
Sherman
Paris
Detroit
Foreman
Fordyce
Bonham
Honey Grove
Ashdown
Hope
Bearden
Van Alstyne
Roxton
Clarksville
Monticello
Whitewright
Deport
Warren
Pilot Point
Camden
McGehee
Ladonia
Bogata
De Kalb
Dermott
Leonard
New Boston
Saline R.
Sanger
Celina
Celeste
Wolfe City
Cooper
Stephens
Ouachita R.
Arkansas City
Texarkana
Stamps
Talco
Denton
McKinney
Lewisville
Waldo
Smackover
Greenville
Farmersville
Commerce
Sulphur R.
Texarkana Dam
Lake Village
Lewisville
Mt Vernon
Lewisville Dam
Sulphur Springs
Naples
Magnolia
El Dorado
33°N
Plano
Lavon Res.
Greenville
Mt. Pleasant
Red R.
Hamburg
Carrollton
Grapevine
Richardson
Daingerfield
Atlanta
Crossett
Eudora
Pittsburg
Dallas
Rockwall
Lake Tawakoni
Linden
Huttig
Garland
Winnsboro
Lone Star
Rodessa
Springhill
Haynesville
Plain Dealing
Forney
Quitman
Ferrells Br. Res.
Vivian
Bernice
Farmerville
Oak Grove
Fort Worth
Grand Prairie
Terrell
Wills Point
Grand Saline
Gilmer
Jefferson
Cotton Valley
Lake Providence
Mesquite
Cypress R.
Homer
Bastrop
Kaufman
Oil City
Lancaster
Mineola
Caddo L.
Canton
Benton
Sterlington
Midlothian
Gladewater
Marshall
Minden
Macon
Alvarado
Lindale
Bossier City
Arcadia
Palmer
Longview
Hallsville
Monroe
Waxahachie
Kemp
Gibsland
Rayville
Delhi
Mabank
Shreveport
163
Ruston
Kilgore
Tallulah
Grandview
Ennis
Chandler
Tyler
Lake Bistineau
Boeuf R.
Italy
Overton
Saline Bayou
Bayou
Itasca
L. Tyler
Hodge
Kerens
Athens
Dugdemona Bayou
Jonesboro
Blooming Grove
Malakoff
Troup
Henderson
32°N
Corsicana
Carthage
Winnsboro
Whitney
Frankston
Lake Whitney
Mansfield
Tensas R.
Dawson
Coushatta
Clarks
Hubbard
Jacksonville
Logansport
Wortham
Timpson
West
133
Winnfield
St. Joseph
Coolidge
Rusk
Campti
Fairfield
Palestine
Cushing
Mexia
Center
Lake Waco
Teague
Natchitoches
Alto
Angelina R.
Waco
Mart
Groesbeck
Oakwood
Nacogdoches
Zwolle
Jena
Ferriday
San Augustine
Toledo Bend Res.
Many
Red R.
Vidalia
Natchez
Grapeland
Colfax
Catahoula Lake
Marlin
Neches R.
Trinity R.
LOUISIANA
Brazos R.
Crockett
Lufkin
Hemphill
Centerville
Huntington
Sam Rayburn Res.
Alexandria
Rosebud
Bremond
Pineland
Diboll
31°N
Franklin
Leesville
Marksville
Calvert
Normangee
Groveton
Sam Rayburn Dam
Woodville
Cottonport
Navasota R.
Little R.
Hearne
Madisonville
Trinity
Corrigan
Rockland
Lecompte
Mansura
Atchafalaya R.
Cameron
Camden
Cheneyville
Town Bluff Lake
Jasper
Glenmora
Bunkie
Simmesport
Rockdale
Huntsville
Newton
De Ridder
Elizabeth
Jackson
Bryan
Woodville
Merryville
Oakdale
Caldwell
Livingston
Kirbyville
Sabine R.
TEXAS
Calcasieu R.
Ville Platte
Melville
New Roads
Neches R.
Call
Oberlin
Mamou
Washington
Somerville
Navasota
Willis
Bessmay
Opelousas
Eunice
Port Barre
Cleveland
Kountze
Kinder
San Jacinto R.
Giddings
Conroe
Silsbee
De Quincy
Elton
Basile
Baton Rouge
Brenham
Deweyville
Church Point
Smithville
Iota
Sour Lake
Jennings
Carencro
Plaquemine
Tomball
Sulphur
Welsh
30°N
Brazos R.
Hempstead
Lake Charles
Rayne
Breaux Bridge
Daisetta
Vinton
Crowley
Lafayette
Gonzales
Liberty
Humble
Beaumont
Orange
Lake Arthur
St. Martinville
Bellville
Dayton
Donaldsonville
La Grange
Houston
Nederland
Port Neches
Gueydan
Kaplan
Lake Verret
Flatonia
Long Point
Hackberry
Abbeville
Erath
New Iberia
Mont Belvieu
Fannett
Calcasieu Lake
Weimar
Sealy
Missouri C.
Grand Lake
Jeanerette
Columbus
Pasadena
Anahuac
Port Arthur
Waterway
Grand Lake
Schulenburg
Baytown
Intracoastal
Franklin
104
Sugar Land
La Porte
Galveston Bay
Morgan City
Colorado R.
Eagle Lake
Rosenberg
Richmond
Feet
Vermilion Bay
Patterson
Berwick
White Lake
West Cote Blanche Bay
Hallettsville
Webster
High Island
1,500
Marsh I.
Wharton
Alvin
Bolivar Peninsula
1,000
Texas City
Atchafalaya Bay
El Campo
Boling
Newgulf
600
Spot Heights in Metres
Galveston
Point Au Fer
West Columbia
Angleton
300
Ganado
Brazoria
Edna
Bay City
Lake Jackson
Sweeny
95°W
94°W
Sea Level
93°W
92°W
GULF
Page 26
15
Freeport
Velasco
Victoria
Raccoon

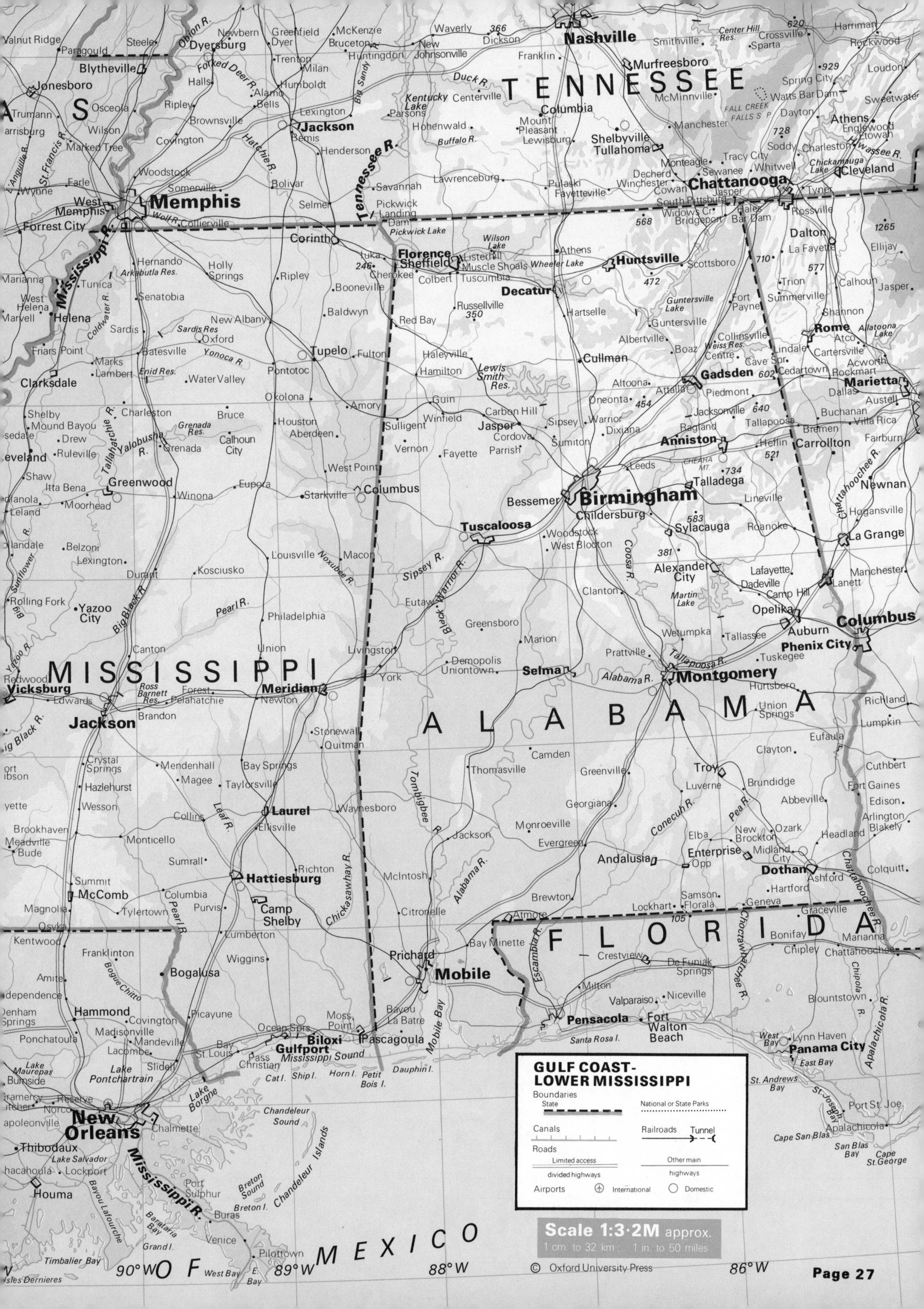
TENNESSEE
MISSISSIPPI
ALABAMA
FLORIDA
OF MEXICO
Nashville
Memphis
Jackson
Chattanooga
Murfreesboro
Huntsville
Birmingham
Montgomery
Mobile
Tuscaloosa
Columbus
Meridian
Vicksburg
Hattiesburg
Laurel
Gulfport
Biloxi
Pascagoula
New Orleans
Pensacola
Panama City
Dothan
Tupelo
Corinth
Greenwood
Clarksdale
Gadsden
Anniston
Decatur
Florence
Sheffield
Selma
Rome
Marietta
Cleveland
Dalton
Columbia
Shelbyville
Tullahoma
Dyersburg
Blytheville
Jonesboro
West Memphis
Helena
Yazoo City
McComb
Bogalusa
Hammond
Houma
Thibodaux
Prichard
Camp Shelby
Auburn
Opelika
Phenix City
Troy
Enterprise
Andalusia
Alexander City
Talladega
Sylacauga
Jasper
Cullman
La Grange
Carrollton
Newnan
Fort Walton Beach
Mississippi R.
Tennessee R.
Tombigbee R.
Alabama R.
Black Warrior R.
Coosa R.
Tallapoosa R.
Chattahoochee R.
Pearl R.
Big Black R.
Yazoo R.
Sunflower R.
Tallahatchie R.
Yalobusha R.
Noxubee R.
Chickasawhay R.
Leaf R.
Conecuh R.
Pea R.
Choctawhatchee R.
Escambia R.
Apalachicola R.
Chipola R.
Duck R.
Buffalo R.
Hatchie R.
Forked Deer R.
Obion R.
St. Francis R.
Wolf R.
Coldwater R.
Yocona R.
Sipsey R.
Kentucky Lake
Pickwick Lake
Wilson Lake
Wheeler Lake
Guntersville Lake
Weiss Res.
Allatoona Lake
Martin Lake
Lewis Smith Res.
Sardis Res.
Enid Res.
Grenada Res.
Arkabutla Res.
Ross Barnett Res.
Lake Pontchartrain
Lake Maurepas
Lake Borgne
Lake Salvador
Mississippi Sound
Chandeleur Sound
Chandeleur Islands
Breton Sound
Mobile Bay
Santa Rosa I.
St. Andrews Bay
St. Joseph Bay
Apalachicola
Cape San Blas
Cape St. George
Dauphin I.
Petit Bois I.
Horn I.
Ship I.
Cat I.
Barataria Bay
Timbalier Bay
Isles Dernieres
Grand I.
Venice
Pilottown
West Bay
E. Bay
90° W
89° W
88° W
86° W
GULF COAST-
LOWER MISSISSIPPI
Boundaries
State
National or State Parks
Canals
Railroads
Tunnel
Roads
Limited access divided highways
Other main highways
Airports
International
Domestic
Scale 1:3·2M approx.
1 cm. to 32 km.
1 in. to 50 miles

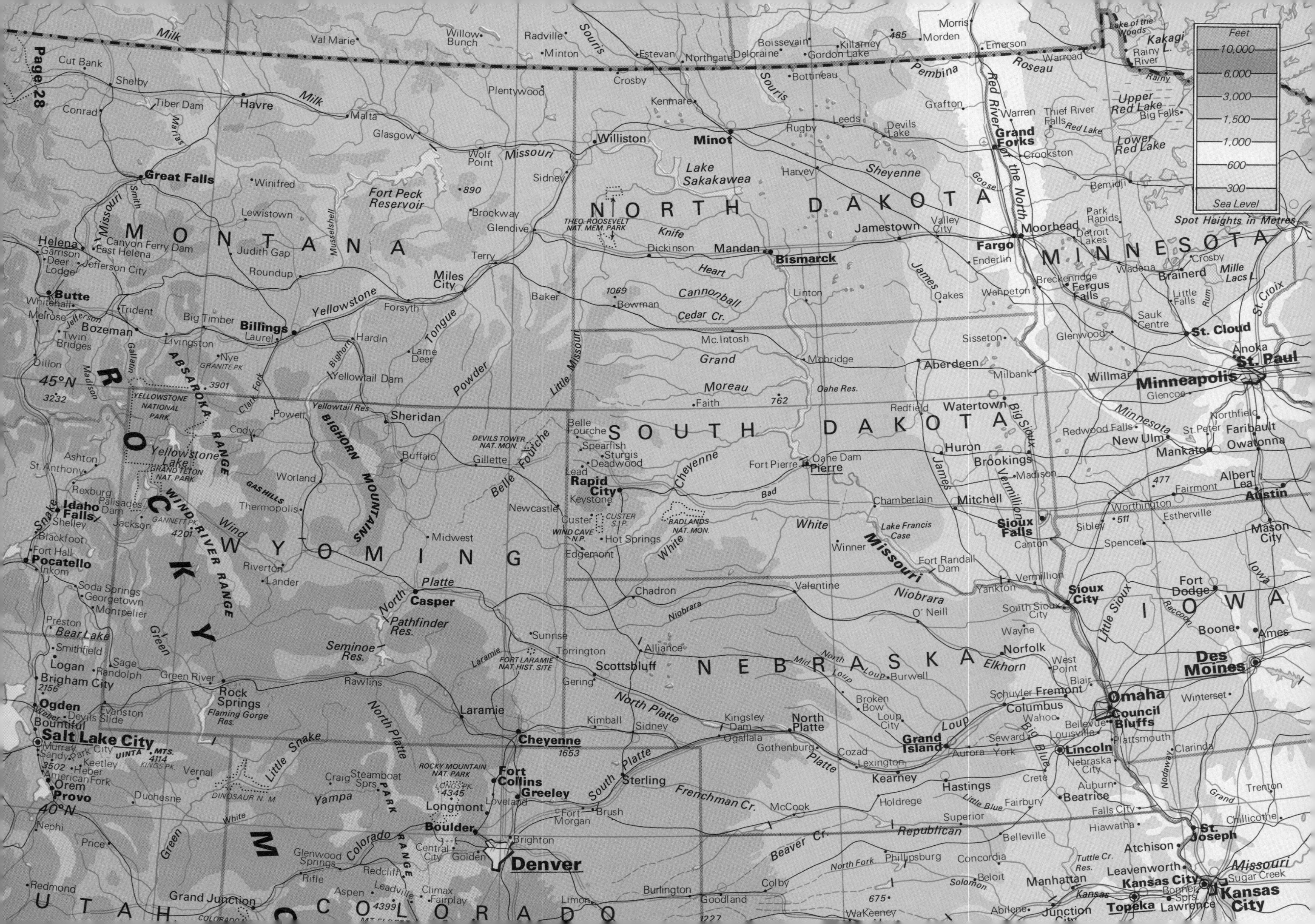

Feet
10,000
6,000
3,000
1,500
1,000
600
300
Sea Level
Spot Heights in Metres
MONTANA
NORTH DAKOTA
SOUTH DAKOTA
MINNESOTA
WYOMING
NEBRASKA
IOWA
UTAH
COLORADO
ROCKY MTS.
Great Falls
Helena
Butte
Bozeman
Billings
Havre
Shelby
Cut Bank
Conrad
Malta
Glasgow
Wolf Point
Lewistown
Miles City
Glendive
Sidney
Williston
Minot
Bismarck
Mandan
Dickinson
Jamestown
Fargo
Moorhead
Grand Forks
Devils Lake
Rugby
Lake Sakakawea
Fort Peck Reservoir
THEO. ROOSEVELT NAT. MEM. PARK
Aberdeen
Watertown
Huron
Brookings
Mitchell
Sioux Falls
Pierre
Fort Pierre
Oahe Dam
Oahe Res.
Rapid City
Lead
Deadwood
Sturgis
Spearfish
Belle Fourche
BADLANDS NAT. MON.
DEVILS TOWER NAT. MON.
WIND CAVE N.P.
CUSTER S.P.
Lake Francis Case
Fort Randall Dam
Yankton
Sioux City
St. Cloud
Minneapolis
St. Paul
Anoka
Mankato
New Ulm
Owatonna
Faribault
Albert Lea
Austin
Mason City
Fort Dodge
Des Moines
Ames
Boone
Omaha
Council Bluffs
Lincoln
Grand Island
North Platte
Kearney
Hastings
Norfolk
Columbus
Fremont
Valentine
Chadron
Alliance
Scottsbluff
Sidney
Kimball
Cheyenne
Laramie
Casper
Sheridan
Gillette
Buffalo
Cody
Powell
Worland
Thermopolis
Riverton
Lander
Rawlins
Rock Springs
Green River
Evanston
YELLOWSTONE NATIONAL PARK
Yellowstone Lake
GRAND TETON NAT. PARK
ABSAROKA RANGE
BIGHORN MOUNTAINS
WIND RIVER RANGE
GANNETT PK. 4201
Pathfinder Res.
Seminoe Res.
Flaming Gorge Res.
FORT LARAMIE NAT. HIST. SITE
Idaho Falls
Pocatello
Ogden
Salt Lake City
Provo
Orem
Logan
Brigham City
UINTA MTS.
KINGS PK. 4114
DINOSAUR N. M.
Vernal
Fort Collins
Greeley
Boulder
Longmont
Denver
ROCKY MOUNTAIN NAT. PARK
LONGS PK. 4345
Sterling
Fort Morgan
Grand Junction
Glenwood Springs
Steamboat Sprs.
Aspen
Leadville
Kansas City
St. Joseph
Topeka
Lawrence
Leavenworth
Atchison
Manhattan
Junction City
45°N
40°N
Missouri
Yellowstone
Milk
Platte
North Platte
South Platte
Niobrara
Cheyenne
White
James
Red River of the North
Big Sioux
Little Missouri
Powder
Tongue
Bighorn
Snake
Green
Colorado
Republican

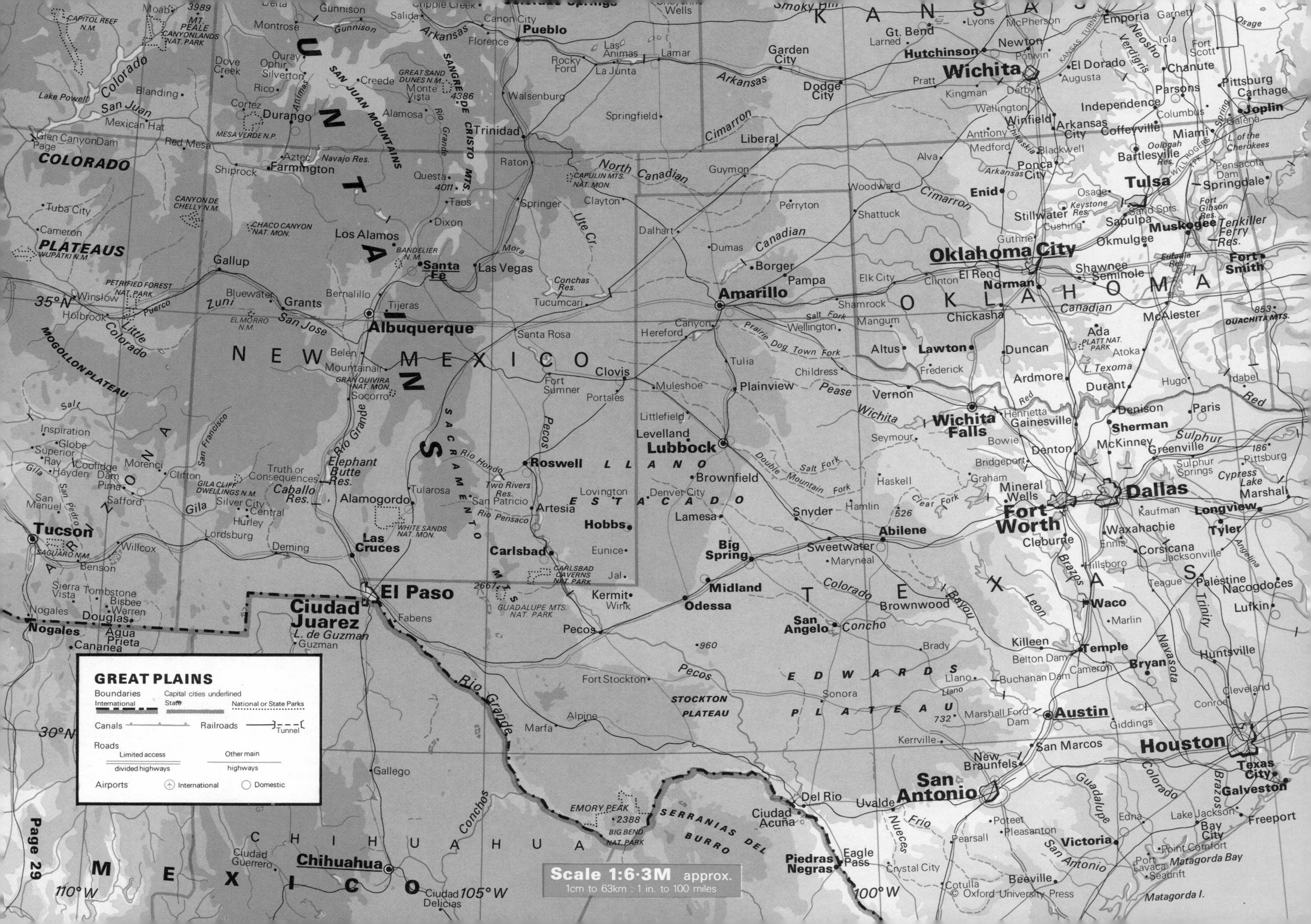

GREAT PLAINS
Boundaries
International
State
Capital cities underlined
National or State Parks
Canals
Railroads
Tunnel
Roads
Limited access divided highways
Other main highways
Airports
International
Domestic
Scale 1:6·3M approx.
1cm to 63km : 1 in. to 100 miles
© Oxford University Press
KANSAS
OKLAHOMA
TEXAS
NEW MEXICO
ARIZONA
UTAH
MEXICO
CHIHUAHUA
COLORADO PLATEAUS
MOGOLLON PLATEAU
SAN JUAN MOUNTAINS
SANGRE DE CRISTO MTS.
SACRAMENTO MTS.
LLANO ESTACADO
EDWARDS PLATEAU
STOCKTON PLATEAU
SERRANIAS DEL BURRO
OUACHITA MTS.
Wichita
Oklahoma City
Tulsa
Amarillo
Lubbock
Albuquerque
Santa Fe
El Paso
Ciudad Juarez
Tucson
Dallas
Fort Worth
Austin
Houston
San Antonio
Chihuahua
Rio Grande
Pecos
Red
Canadian
Arkansas
Colorado
35°N
30°N
110°W
105°W
100°W

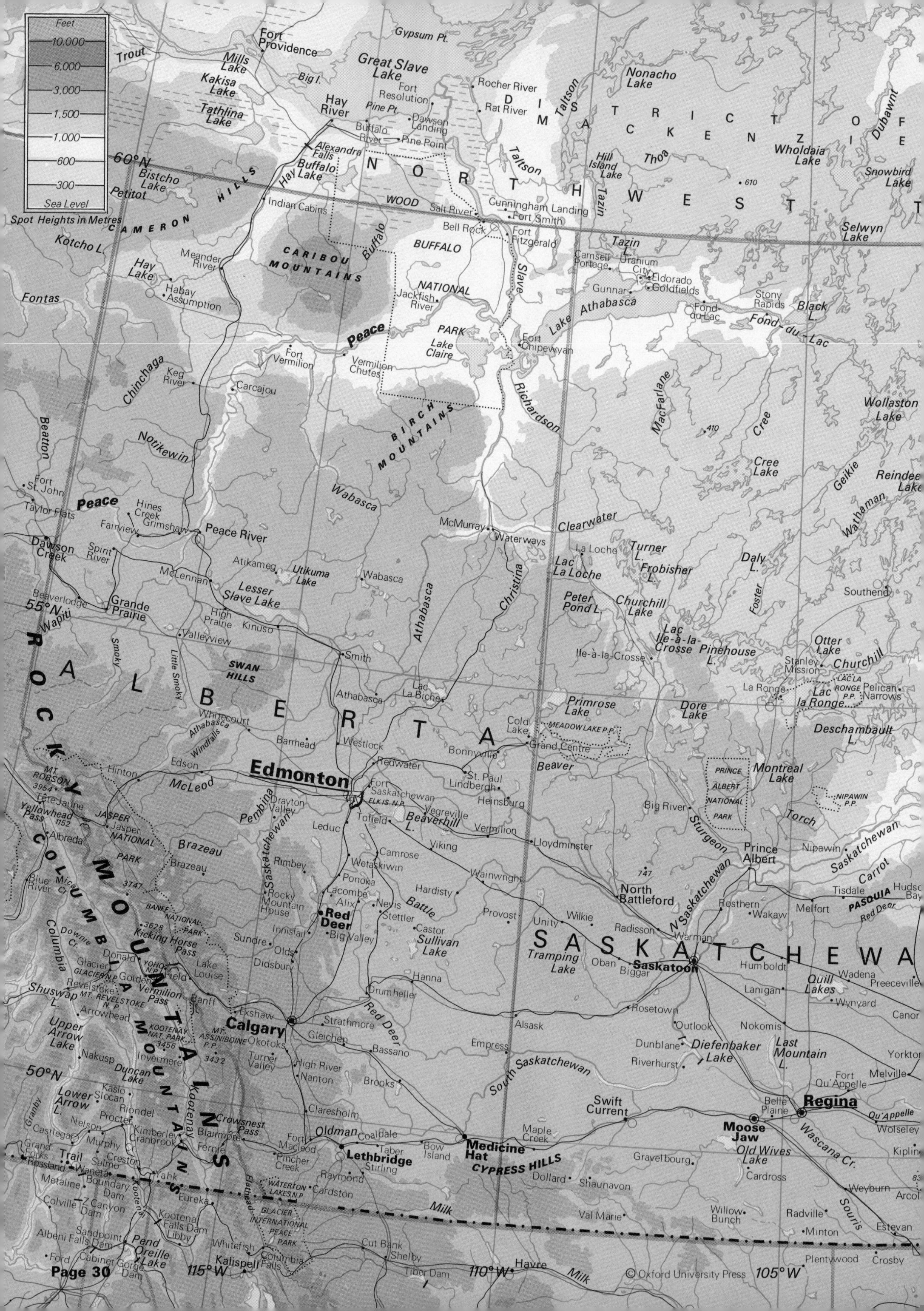

Feet
10,000
6,000
3,000
1,500
1,000
600
300
Sea Level

Spot Heights in Metres

Trout

Gypsum Pt.

Fort
Providence

Mills
Lake

Kakisa
Lake

Big I.

Great Slave
Lake

Fort
Resolution

Rocher River

Rat River

Nonacho
Lake

D I S T R I C T   O F

Tathlina
Lake

Hay
River

Pine Lake

Dawson
Landing

Buffalo
River

Pine Point

Taltson

Hill
Island
Lake

Thoa

Wholdaia
Lake

Snowbird
Lake

M A C K E N Z I E

Bistcho
Lake

60°N

HILLS

Alexandra
Falls

Buffalo
Lake

N O R T H

WOOD

Salt River

Cunningham Landing

Fort Smith

Tazin

Uranium
City

Eldorado

Selwyn
Lake

W E S T

Dubawnt

Petitot

CAMERON

Indian Cabins

Buffalo

BUFFALO

Bell Rock

Fort
Fitzgerald

Camsell
Portage

Goldfields

Stony
Rapids

Fond-
du-Lac

Black
L.

Kotcho L.

Hay
Lake

Meander
River

Habay
Assumption

CARIBOU
MOUNTAINS

NATIONAL

Jackfish
River

Gunnar

610

Fond-du-Lac

Wollaston
Lake

Fontas

Chinchaga

Keg
River

Fort
Vermilion

Carcajou

Vermilion
Chutes

Peace

PARK

Lake
Claire

Fort
Chipewyan

Lake   Athabasca

MacFarlane

410

Cree

Cree
Lake

Geikie
L.

Reindee
Lake

Beatton

Fort
St. John

Taylor Flats

Peace

Notikewin

Wabasca

BIRCH
MOUNTAINS

McMurray

Waterways

Richardson

Clearwater

La Loche

Turner
L.

Frobisher
L.

Daly
L.

Southend

Watharman

55°N

Wapiti

Hines
Creek

Grimshaw

Fairview

Spirit
River

Peace River

Atikameg

McLennan

Lesser
Slave Lake

Utikuma
Lake

Wabasca

Athabasca

Christina

Lac
La Loche

Peter
Pond L.

Churchill
Lake

Lac
Ile-à-la-
Crosse Pinehouse
L.

Otter
Lake

Stanley
Mission

Churchill

Dawson
Creek

Beaverlodge

Grande
Prairie

Smoky

High
Prairie

Kinuso

Valleyview

SWAN
HILLS

Smith

Ile-à-la-Crosse

Primrose
Lake

Dore
Lake

La Ronge

LAC LA
RONGE
P.P.

Pelican
Narrows

ROCKY

MT.
ROBSON
3954

A

L

Whitecourt

Athabasca
Windfalls

Edson

Barrhead

Westlock

Lac
La Biche

Bonnyville

MEADOW LAKE P.P.

Grand Centre

Beaver

Cold
Lake

B

E

R

T

A

Big River

Deschambault
L.

NIPAWIN
P.P.

Yellowhead
Pass

Tete Jaune

1152

JASPER

Jasper

NATIONAL

Hinton

McLeod

Edmonton

Fort
Saskatchewan

ELK IS. N.P.

Drayton
Valley

Pembina

Leduc

Tofield

Beaverhill
L.

Vegreville

Heinsburg

St. Paul
Lindbergh

Vermilion

Lloydminster

North
Battleford

PRINCE
ALBERT
NATIONAL
PARK

Montreal
Lake

Sturgeon

Torch

Prince
Albert

Nipawin

N Saskatchewan

Saskatchewan

Carrot

Hudso
Bay

PASQUIA

Red Deer

Albreda

PARK

Blue
River

Columbia

Miette

3747

Brazeau

Brazeau

Rocky
Mountain
House

Rimbey

Ponoka
Lacombe
Alix

Camrose

Wetaskiwin

Viking

Nevis
Stettler

Hardisty

Battle

Wainwright

Provost

Unity

Wilkie

Radisson

Warman

Rosthern

Wakaw

Tisdale

Melfort

Red Deer

COLUMBIA

Downie

Donald

3628

BANFF

NATIONAL

PARK

Red
Deer

Innisfail

Big Valley

Castor

Sullivan
Lake

Tramping
Lake

Oban
Biggar

747

SASKATCHEWA

Saskatoon

Humboldt

Wadena

Quill
Lakes

Preeceville

Glacier

Golden

Kicking Horse
Pass

YOHO
N.P.

Lake
Louise

Banff

Sundre

Olds

Didsbury

Hanna

Drumheller

Rosetown

Lanigan

Wynyard

Canor

Revelstoke

MT. REVELSTOKE
N.P.

Shuswap
L.

Arrowhead

MT.
ASSINIBOINE
P.P.
3456

Vermilion
Pass

GLACIER
NAT. PARK

3432

KOOTENAY
NAT. PARK

Exshaw

Calgary

Okotoks

Turner
Valley

Gleichen

Strathmore

High
River

Red Deer

Bassano

Brooks

Alsask

Empress

South Saskatchewan

Dunblane

Diefenbaker
Lake

Riverhurst

Outlook

Nokomis

Last
Mountain
L.

Yorkton

Melville

Upper
Arrow
Lake

Nakusp

Duncan
Lake

Invermere

Kootenay

Nanton

Claresholm

Swift
Current

Maple
Creek

Belle
Plaine

50°N

Lower
Arrow
L.

Kaslo

Slocan

Riondel

Procter

Crowsnest
Pass

Fort
Macleod

Oldman

Coaldale

Taber

Bow
Island

Medicine
Hat

Gravelbourg

Moose
Jaw

Old Wives
Lake

Regina

Qu'Appelle

Fort
Qu'Appelle

Wolseley

Castlegar

Nelson

Murphy

Kimberley

Blairmore

Fernie

Pincher
Creek

Raymond

Stirling

Lethbridge

Cardston

CYPRESS HILLS

Dollard

Shaunavon

Val Marie

Cardross

Kipling

Weyburn

Grand

Trail

Rossland

Salmo

Creston

Yahk

WATERTON
LAKES N.P.

GLACIER
INTERNATIONAL
PEACE
PARK

Milk

Willow
Bunch

Radville

Minton

Souris

Estevan

Arco

83

Metaline

Boundary
Dam

Eureka

Kootenai
Falls Dam

Libby

Whitefish

Cut Bank
Shelby

Columbia
Falls

Milk

Plentywood

Crosby

Colville

Z Canyon
Dam

Sandpoint

Albeni Falls
Dam

Pend
Oreille
Lake

Ford

Cabinet
Gorge Dam

Kalispell

Tiber Dam

Havre

© Oxford University Press

Page 30

115°W

110°W

105°W

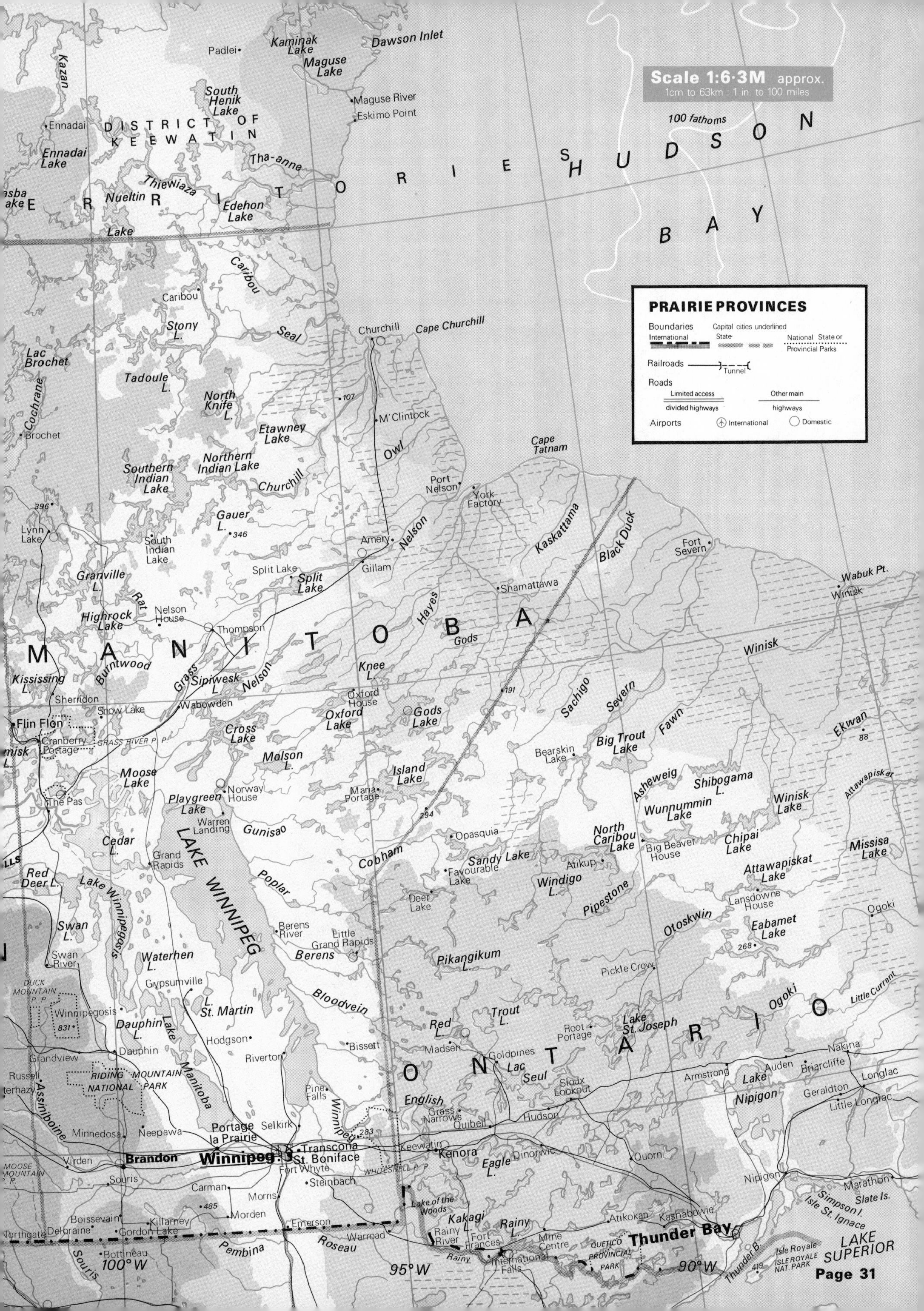

Scale 1:6·3M approx.
1cm to 63km : 1 in. to 100 miles

100 fathoms

DISTRICT OF KEEWATIN

TERRITORIES

HUDSON BAY

Kazan

Padlei
Kaminak Lake
Maguse Lake
Dawson Inlet

Maguse River
Eskimo Point

Ennadai
Ennadai Lake
Tha-anne
Thlewiaza
Nueltin Lake
Edehon Lake

asba Lake E

Caribou
Caribou
Stony L.
North Knife L.
Seal
Churchill
Cape Churchill

Lac Brochet
Tadoule L.
Etawney Lake
Northern Indian Lake
Churchill
M'Clintock
Owl
107

Cochrane
Brochet

Cape Tatnam
Port Nelson
York Factory

Southern Indian Lake
Gauer L.
346
Nelson
Amery
Gillam
Hayes
Shamattawa
Kaskattama
Black Duck
Fort Severn

Wabuk Pt.
Winisk

396
Lynn Lake
Granville L.
South Indian Lake
Split Lake
Split Lake
Nelson House
Rat
Highrock Lake
Thompson
Gods

Winisk
Ekwan
88

MANITOBA
Kississing L.
Burntwood
Grass
Sipiwesk L.
Nelson
Knee L.
Oxford House
Oxford Lake
Gods Lake
191
Sachigo
Severn
Fawn
Attawapiskat

Sherridon
Snow Lake
Wabowden
Cross Lake
Molson L.
Island Lake
Gods Lake
Bearskin Lake
Big Trout Lake
Asheweig
Shibogama
Winisk Lake
Missisa Lake

Flin Flon
Cranberry Portage
GRASS RIVER P.P.
Mana Portage
294
Opasquia
North Caribou Lake
Big Beaver House
Chipai Lake
Lansdowne House
268

misk
The Pas
Moose Lake
Playgreen Lake
Norway House
Cobham
Favourable Lake
Sandy Lake
Atikup
Windigo L.
Pipestone
Attawapiskat Lake
Eabamet Lake
Ogoki

Red Deer L.
Cedar L.
Warren Landing
Gunisao
Deer Lake
Pikangikum
Otoskwin

LLS
Grand Rapids

Swan L.
Swan River
Berens River
Little Grand Rapids
Berens
Pickle Crow

J
DUCK MOUNTAIN P.P.
Winnipegosis
831
Waterhen L.
Gypsumville
Poplar
Bloodvein
Red L.
Trout L.
Root Portage
Lake St. Joseph
Ogoki
Little Current

LAKE WINNIPEG
L. St. Martin
Lake Manitoba

Grandview
Russell
terhazy
Dauphin L.
Dauphin
Hodgson
Riverton
Bissett
Madsen
Goldpines
Sioux Lookout
Armstrong
Lake Nipigon
Auden
Briarcliffe
Nakina
Longlac
Geraldton
Little Longlac

RIDING MOUNTAIN NATIONAL PARK
Minnedosa
Neepawa
Portage la Prairie
Selkirk
Pine Falls
English
Grass Narrows
Quibell
Hudson
Quorn
Nipigon

MOOSE MOUNTAIN
Virden
Brandon
Winnipeg
Transcona
St. Boniface
Fort Whyte
283
Keewatin
Kenora
Eagle L.
Dinorwic
Thunder Bay

Souris
Carman
Morris
Steinbach
WHITESHELL P.P.
Lake of the Woods
Kakagi L.
Rainy L.
Fort Frances
Mine Centre
QUETICO PROVINCIAL PARK
Atikokan
Kashabowie
Thunder B.
Simpson I.
Slate Is.
Isle St. Ignace

485
Boissevain
Deloraine
Killarney
Gordon Lake
Morden
Emerson
Warroad
Rainy River
Rainy
International Falls
419
ISLE ROYALE NAT. PARK
Isle Royale

Northgate
Pembina
Roseau

100°W
95°W
90°W
LAKE SUPERIOR

ONTARIO

PRAIRIE PROVINCES

Boundaries
International · · · · · ·   State ─ ─ ─   National State or Provincial Parks

Capital cities underlined

Railroads ──── Tunnel

Roads

Limited access ══════   Other main ──────
divided highways   highways

Airports ⊕ International ○ Domestic

Page 31

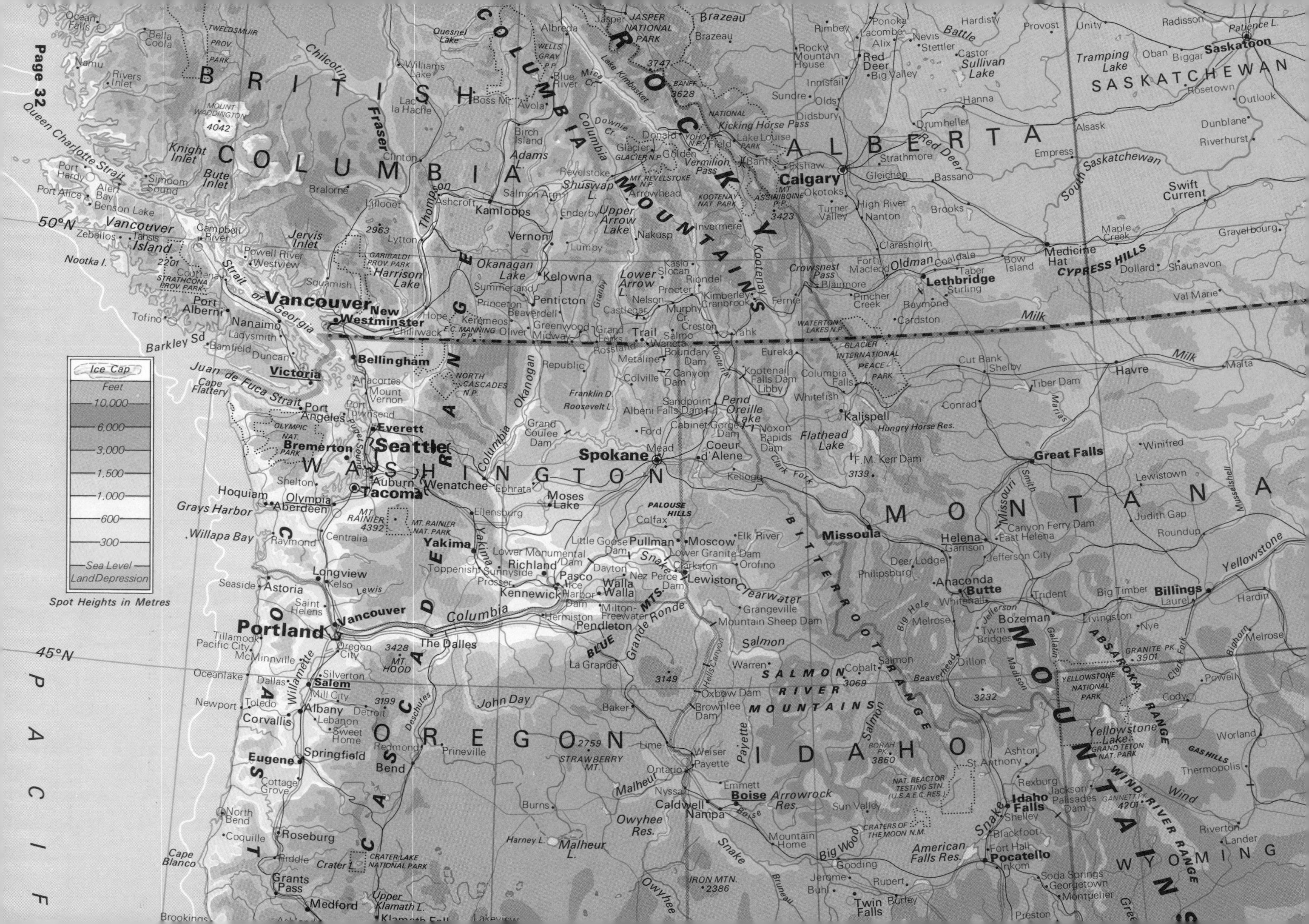

Page 32
BRITISH COLUMBIA
ALBERTA
SASKATCHEWAN
MONTANA
WASHINGTON
OREGON
IDAHO
WYOMING
ROCKY MOUNTAINS
COLUMBIA MOUNTAINS
CASCADE RANGE
COAST
BITTERROOT RANGE
SALMON RIVER MOUNTAINS
ABSAROKA RANGE
WIND RIVER RANGE
BLUE MTS
CYPRESS HILLS
PALOUSE HILLS
PACIF
Vancouver
New Westminster
Victoria
Bellingham
Everett
Seattle
Tacoma
Bremerton
Olympia
Portland
Salem
Eugene
Spokane
Yakima
Kamloops
Kelowna
Calgary
Lethbridge
Medicine Hat
Saskatoon
Great Falls
Billings
Helena
Missoula
Butte
Boise
Pocatello
Idaho Falls
Juan de Fuca Strait
Strait of Georgia
Puget Sound
Queen Charlotte Strait
Vancouver Island
Columbia
Snake
Fraser
Kootenay
Yellowstone
Missouri
50°N
45°N
Ice Cap
Feet
10,000
6,000
3,000
1,500
1,000
600
300
Sea Level
Land Depression
Spot Heights in Metres

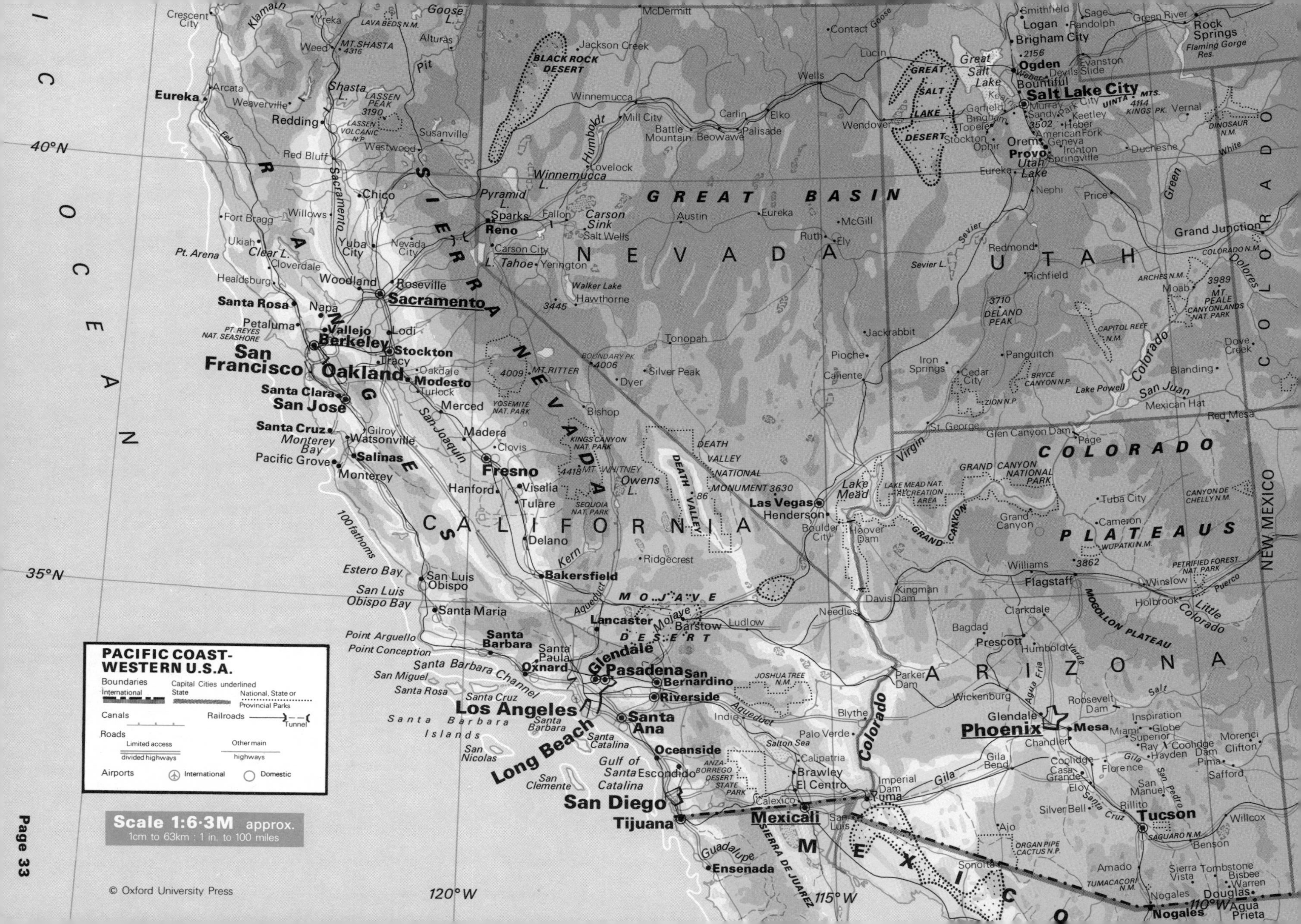

PACIFIC COAST-WESTERN U.S.A.
Boundaries
International
State
Capital Cities underlined
National, State or Provincial Parks
Canals
Railroads
Tunnel
Roads
Limited access divided highways
Other main highways
Airports
International
Domestic
Scale 1:6·3M approx.
1cm to 63km : 1 in. to 100 miles
© Oxford University Press
PACIFIC OCEAN
40°N
35°N
120°W
115°W
110°W
NEVADA
UTAH
COLORADO
NEW MEXICO
ARIZONA
CALIFORNIA
MEXICO
SIERRA NEVADA
GREAT BASIN
COLORADO PLATEAUS
MOJAVE DESERT
GREAT SALT LAKE DESERT
BLACK ROCK DESERT
DEATH VALLEY
GRAND CANYON
Sacramento
Salt Lake City
Phoenix
Mexicali
San Francisco
Oakland
San Jose
Los Angeles
Long Beach
San Diego
Tijuana
Las Vegas
Reno
Fresno
Tucson

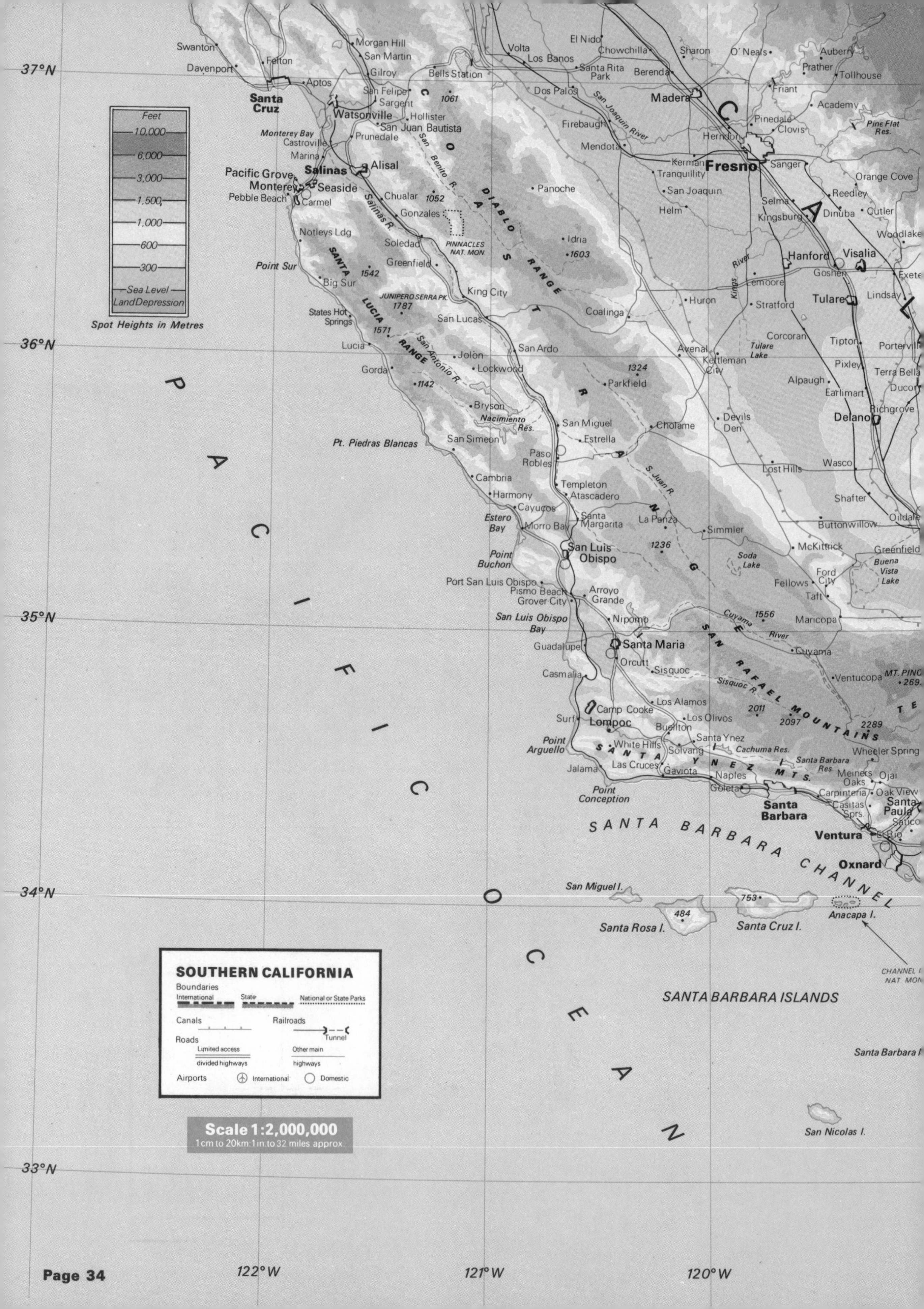

37°N

Swanton Morgan Hill El Nido
Davenport Felton San Martin Volta Los Banos Chowchilla Sharon O'Neals Auberry Prather Tollhouse
Santa Cruz Aptos Gilroy Bells Station Santa Rita Park Berenda Madera Friant Academy
Watsonville San Felipe Sargent Dos Palos San Joaquin River Pinedale Clovis Pine Flat Res.
Monterey Bay Castroville Hollister San Juan Bautista Firebaugh Mendota Herndon Fresno Sanger
Marina Prunedale Kerman Tranquillity
Pacific Grove Salinas Alisal Orange Cove Reedley
Monterey Seaside Chualar 1052 Panoche San Joaquin Selma Dinuba Cutler
Pebble Beach Carmel Gonzales Helm Kingsburg Woodlake
Notleys Ldg Soledad PINNACLES NAT. MON Idria Hanford Visalia Exeter
Point Sur Greenfield 1603 Goshen
Big Sur 1542 King City Huron Stratford Tulare Lindsay
JUNIPERO SERRA PK. 1787 Coalinga Corcoran Tipton Porterville
States Hot Springs San Lucas Avenal Tulare Lake Pixley Terra Bella Ducor

36°N

Lucia 1571 Kettleman City Alpaugh Earlimart Richgrove
Gorda Jolon San Ardo 1324 Delano
1142 Lockwood Parkfield Devils Den Lost Hills Wasco
Bryson San Miguel Cholame Shafter
Pt. Piedras Blancas Nacimiento Res. Estrella McKittrick Oildale
San Simeon Paso Robles La Panza 1236 Simmler Soda Lake Fellows Ford City Buena Vista Lake Greenfield
Cambria Templeton Santa Margarita Buttonwillow
Harmony Atascadero Taft
Cayucos Morro Bay Maricopa
Estero Bay San Luis Obispo 1556 Cuyama
Point Buchon Cuyama River Cuyama
Port San Luis Obispo Arroyo Grande 2011 2097 2289 MT. PINO 269.
Pismo Beach Nipomo SAN RAFAEL MOUNTAINS
Grover City

35°N

San Luis Obispo Bay Santa Maria Ventucopa
Guadalupe Orcutt Sisquoc Sisquoc R.
Casmalia Los Alamos Wheeler Spring
Surf Camp Cooke Los Olivos Santa Barbara Res.
Lompoc Buellton Santa Ynez Cachuma Res. Meiners Oaks Ojai
Point Arguello White Hills Solvang SANTA YNEZ MTS. Casitas Res. Oak View
Jalama Las Cruces Gaviota Naples Carpinteria Santa Paula
Point Conception Goleta Casitas Sprs. Satico
Santa Barbara Ventura
SANTA BARBARA CHANNEL Oxnard El Rio

34°N

San Miguel I. 753
484
Santa Rosa I. Santa Cruz I. Anacapa I. CHANNEL I. NAT. MON

SANTA BARBARA ISLANDS

Santa Barbara I.

San Nicolas I.

SOUTHERN CALIFORNIA
Boundaries
International State National or State Parks
Canals Railroads
Roads Tunnel
Limited access
divided highways Other main highways
Airports International Domestic

Scale 1:2,000,000
1cm to 20km:1 in. to 32 miles approx.

PACIFIC OCEAN

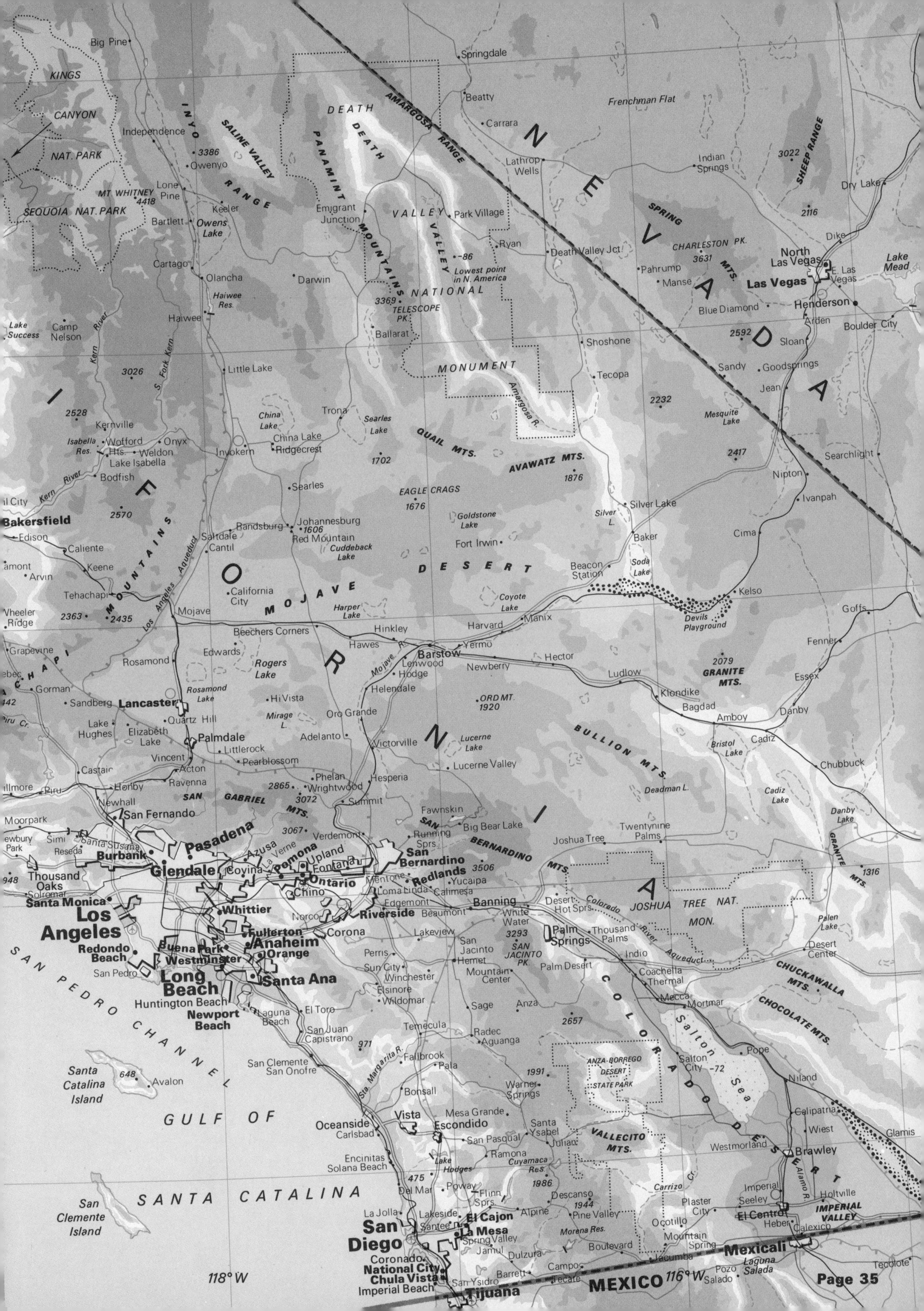

KINGS
CANYON
NAT. PARK

SEQUOIA NAT. PARK

Big Pine

Independence

MT. WHITNEY
4418

Owenyo
3386

Lone Pine

Keeler

Bartlett

Owens
Lake

Cartago

Olancha

Haiwee
Res.

Darwin

Camp
Nelson

Lake
Success

Isabella
Res.

Kernville

Wofford
Hts.
Lake Isabella

Onyx
Weldon

Bodfish

Bakersfield

Edison

Caliente

Arvin

Keene

Tehachapi

Wheeler
Ridge

Gorman

Sandberg

Lancaster

Quartz Hill

Palmdale

Littlerock

Pearblossom

Lake
Hughes

Elizabeth
Lake

Vincent

Acton

Ravenna

Castaic

Hornby

Newhall

San Fernando

Pasadena

Burbank

Glendale

Santa Susana
Reseda

Thousand
Oaks

Santa Monica

Los
Angeles

Redondo
Beach

San Pedro

Long
Beach

Huntington Beach

Newport
Beach

Santa
Catalina
Island

Avalon

San
Clemente
Island

SANTA CATALINA

GULF OF

SAN PEDRO CHANNEL

INYO RANGE

SALINE VALLEY

PANAMINT RANGE

DEATH

DEATH VALLEY

VALLEY

Emigrant
Junction

TELESCOPE
PK.
3369

Ballarat

PANAMINT MOUNTAINS

NATIONAL

MONUMENT

Springdale

Beatty

Carrara

Frenchman Flat

Lathrop
Wells

Ryan

Park Village

-86
Lowest point
in N. America

Death Valley Jct

AMARGOSA RANGE

NEVADA

Indian
Springs

3022

2116

Dry Lake

North
Las Vegas

E. Las
Vegas

Las Vegas

Henderson

Arden

Boulder City

Lake
Mead

SPRING

CHARLESTON PK.
3631

MTS.

Pahrump

Manse

Blue Diamond

2592

Sloan

Sandy

Goodsprings

Jean

Mesquite
Lake

Dike

Shoshone

Tecopa

2232

2417

Searchlight

Nipton

Ivanpah

Silver Lake

Silver
L.

Cima

Goffs

Fenner

Little Lake

China
Lake

China Lake

Searles
Lake

Trona

1702

QUAIL MTS.

Amargosa R.

AVAWATZ MTS.
1876

EAGLE CRAGS
1676

Goldstone
Lake

Fort Irwin

Coyote
Lake

DESERT

Beacon
Station

Soda
Lake

Baker

Devils
Playground

Kelso

GRANITE
MTS.
2079

Essex

Bagdad

Amboy

Danby

Klondike

Ludlow

Hector

Newberry

Barstow

Lenwood

Hodge

Helendale

Oro Grande

Victorville

Adelanto

Hesperia

Phelan

Wrightwood

Summit

ORD MT.
1920

Lucerne
Lake

Lucerne Valley

Deadman L.

BULLION MTS.

Bristol
Lake

Cadiz

Cadiz
Lake

Chubbuck

Danby
Lake

1316

GRANITE MTS.

Isabella
2528

3026

2570

2363

2435

Mojave

Rosamond

Edwards

Rogers
Lake

Rosamond
Lake

Hi Vista

Mirage
L.

TEHACHAPI MOUNTAINS

Randsburg

Saltdale

Cantil

Red Mountain
1606

Cuddeback
Lake

Johannesburg

California
City

Harper
Lake

Hawes

Hinkley

Harvard

Manix

Yermo

MOJAVE

Mojave R.

CALIFORNIA

Beechers Corners

Fawnskin

Big Bear Lake

Running
Sprs.

Verdemont

SAN

BERNARDINO

MTS.

Joshua Tree

Twentynine
Palms

2657

JOSHUA TREE NAT.

MON.

Colorado

Aqueduct

1316

Palen
Lake

Desert
Center

CHUCKAWALLA MTS.

CHOCOLATE MTS.

SAN GABRIEL MTS.
3072

3067

Azusa

La Verne

Upland

Fontana

Pomona

Covina

Ontario

Chino

Mentone
Loma Linda

San
Bernardino
3506

Redlands

Yucaipa

Calimesa

Edgemont

Norco

Whittier

Riverside

Beaumont

Banning

White
Water

Desert
Hot Sprs.

Thousand
Palms

Palm
Springs

Indio

Coachella

Mecca

Thermal

Palm Desert

SAN
JACINTO
PK.
3293

San
Jacinto

Hemet

Mountain
Center

Anza

COLORADO

Salton
Sea

Salton
City -72

Pope

Mortmar

Niland

Calipatria

Wiest

Glamis

Fullerton

Anaheim

Orange

Buena Park

Westminster

Santa Ana

El Toro

Perris

Sun City

Winchester

Elsinore

Wildomar

Lakeview

Corona

Sage

2865

Laguna
Beach

San Juan
Capistrano

971

San Clemente

San Onofre

Fallbrook

Pala

Temecula

Radec

Aguanga

Warner
Springs

1991

ANZA-BORREGO

DESERT

STATE PARK

Bonsall

Vista

Sta. Margarita R.

Oceanside

Carlsbad

Encinitas

Solana Beach

Del Mar

475

La Jolla

San
Diego

Coronado

National City

Chula Vista

Imperial Beach

Tijuana

648

Escondido

Mesa Grande

San Pasqual

Ramona

Santa
Ysabel

Julian

Lake
Hodges

Cuyamaca
Res.
1986

Poway

Flinn
Sprs.

Lakeside

Santee

El Cajon

La Mesa

Spring Valley

Jamul

Dulzura

Campo

San Ysidro

Barrett

Tecate

Descanso
1944

Pine Valley

Morena Res.

Boulevard

Alpine

VALLECITO
MTS.

Carrizo

Westmorland

Brawley

Imperial

Seeley

El Centro

Heber

Calexico

Mexicali

IMPERIAL
VALLEY

Holtville

Mountain
Spring

Ocotillo

Plaster
City

Jacumba

Tecomba

Pozo
Salado

Laguna
Salada

Tecolote

MEXICO

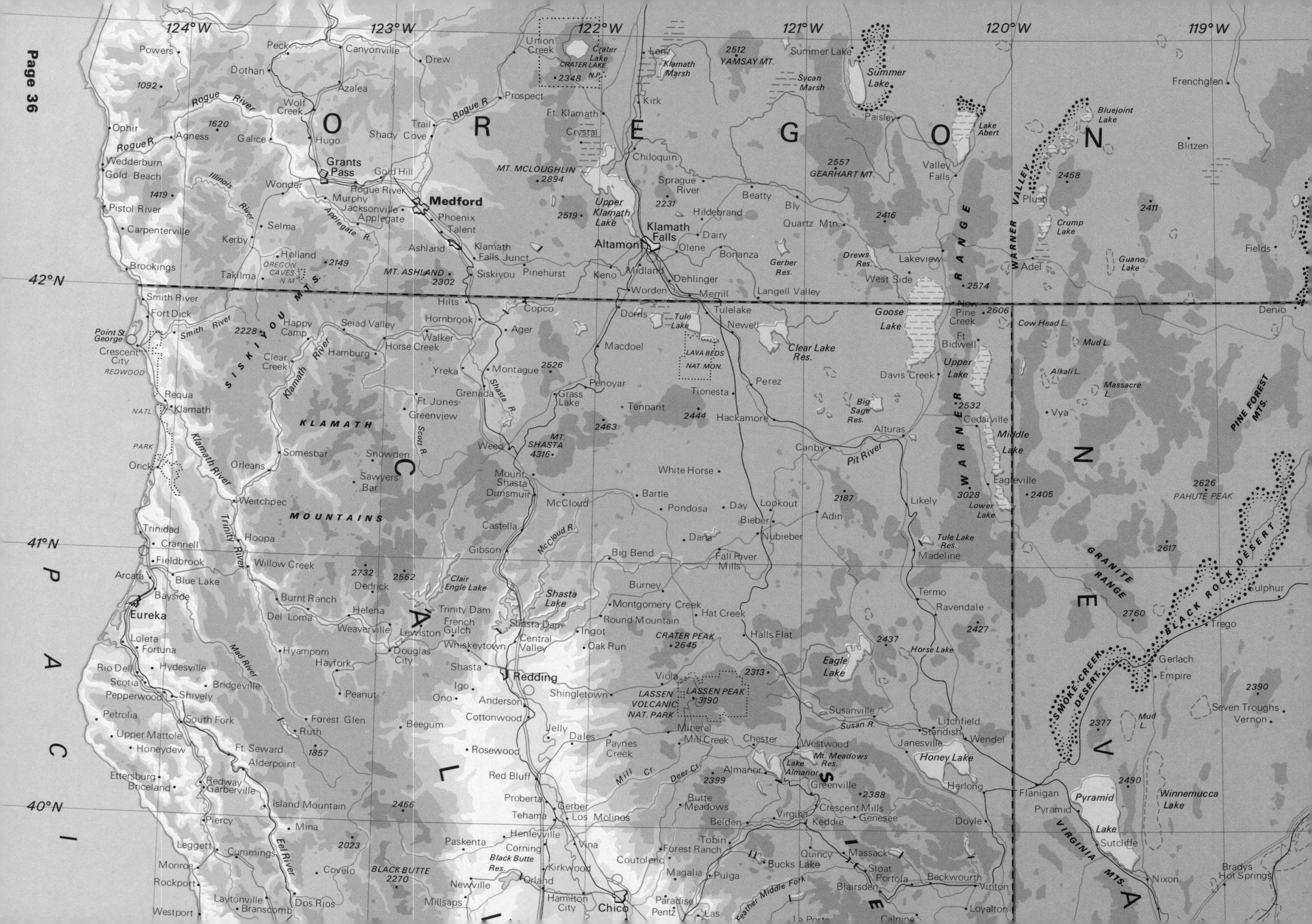
O R E G O N
N E V A D A
C A L I F
P A C I
119° W
120° W
121° W
122° W
123° W
124° W
42° N
41° N
40° N
Medford
Grants Pass
Klamath Falls
Altamont
Eureka
Redding
Chico
Crescent City
Lakeview
Alturas
Susanville
Yreka
Weed
Mount Shasta
Arcata
Ashland
Brookings
Gold Beach
Crater Lake
CRATER LAKE N.P.
MT. MCLOUGHLIN 2894
MT. ASHLAND 2302
YAMSAY MT.
GEARHART MT.
MT. SHASTA 4316
CRATER PEAK 2645
LASSEN PEAK 3190
LASSEN VOLCANIC NAT. PARK
LAVA BEDS NAT. MON.
OREGON CAVES N.M.
KLAMATH MOUNTAINS
SISKIYOU MTS.
WARNER RANGE
WARNER VALLEY
GRANITE RANGE
BLACK ROCK DESERT
SMOKE CREEK DESERT
PINE FOREST MTS.
VIRGINIA MTS.
PAHUTE PEAK
BLACK BUTTE 2270
Goose Lake
Honey Lake
Pyramid Lake
Eagle Lake
Summer Lake
Lake Abert
Upper Klamath Lake
Tule Lake
Clear Lake Res.
Shasta Lake
Clair Engle Lake
Winnemucca Lake
Klamath River
Trinity River
Rogue River
Eel River
Pit River
Mad River
Scott R.
Shasta R.
McCloud R.
Denio
Fields
Frenchglen
Blitzen
Paisley
Adel
Plush
Gerlach
Empire
Sulphur
Trego
Vya
Cedarville
Eagleville
Ft. Bidwell
Tulelake
Canby
Adin
Bieber
McCloud
Dunsmuir
Weaverville
Hoopa
Orick
Fortuna
Quincy
Greenville
Chester
Westwood
Red Bluff
Corning
Orland
Laytonville
Garberville
Westport

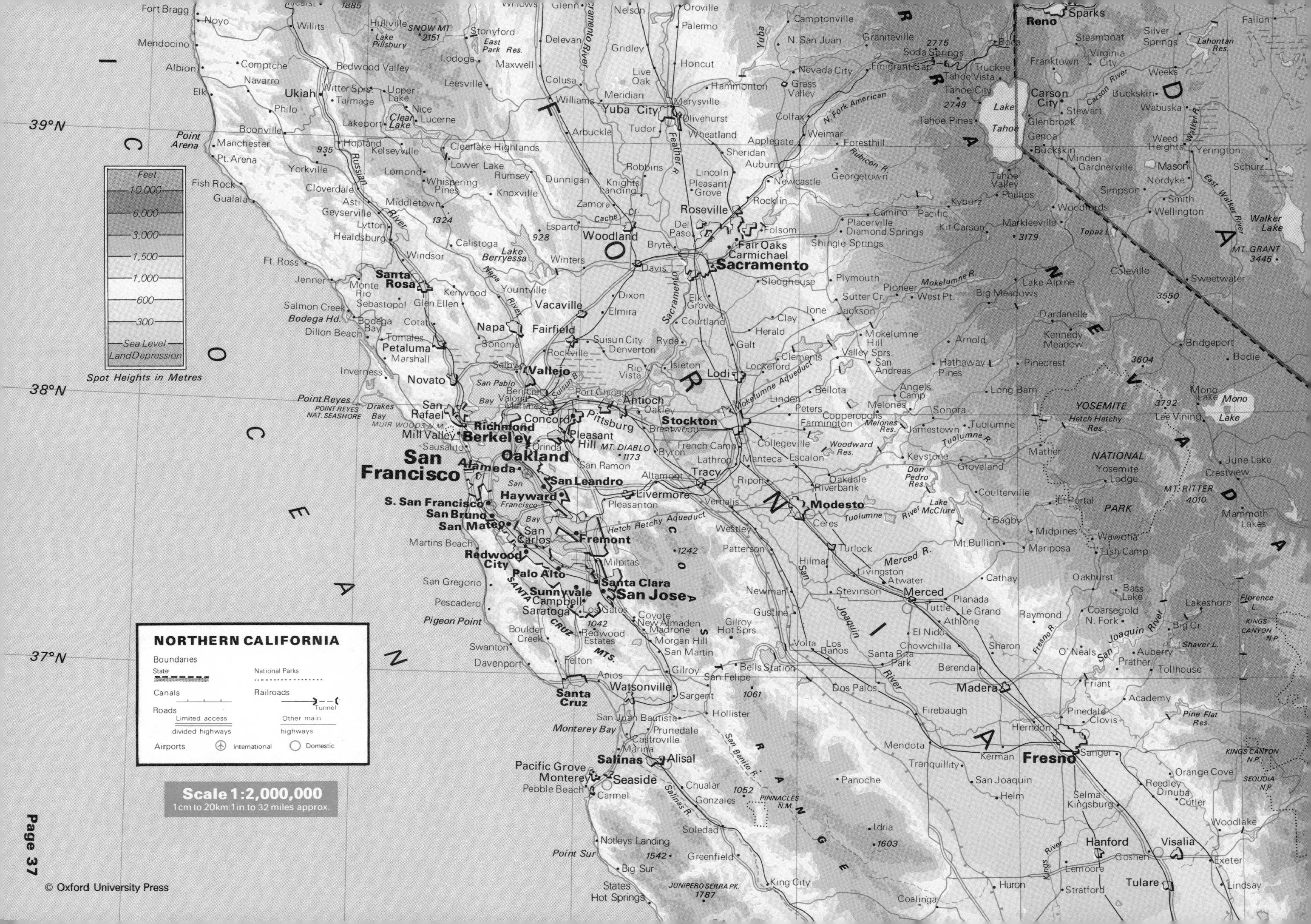

NEVADA

CALIFORNIA

Reno
Sparks

Carson City

Lake Tahoe

Sacramento

Stockton

San Francisco
Oakland
San Jose

Fresno

Hanford
Tulare
Visalia

YOSEMITE NATIONAL PARK

KINGS CANYON N.P.

SEQUOIA N.P.

PACIFIC OCEAN

39°N
38°N
37°N

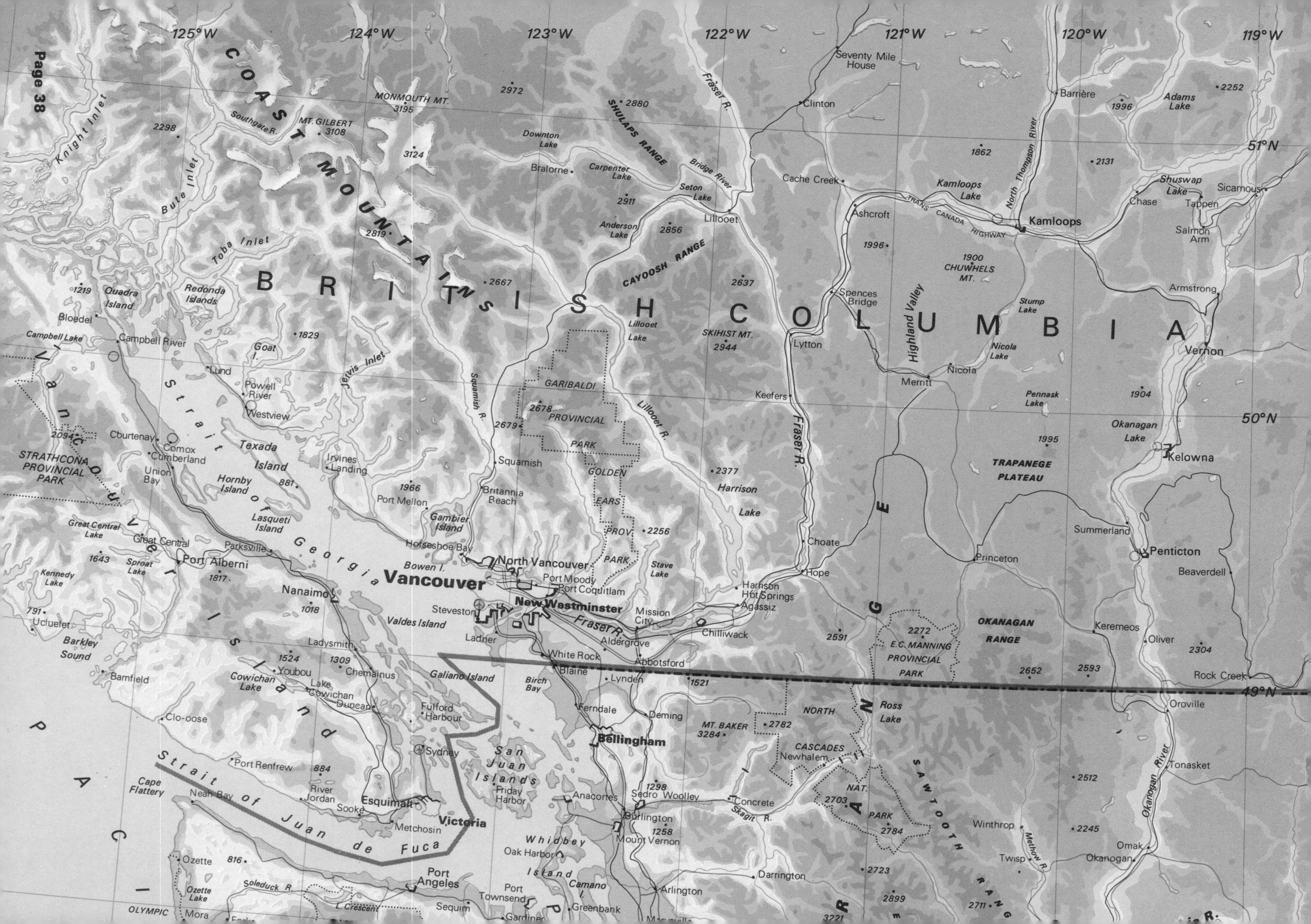

Page 38
125°W
124°W
123°W
122°W
121°W
120°W
119°W
51°N
50°N
49°N
BRITISH COLUMBIA
COAST MOUNTAINS
Vancouver Island
Strait of Georgia
Strait of Juan de Fuca
PACIFIC
Knight Inlet
Bute Inlet
Toba Inlet
Southgate R.
MONMOUTH MT. 3195
MT. GILBERT 3108
Quadra Island
Redonda Islands
Bloedel
Campbell Lake
Campbell River
Goat I.
Lund
Powell River
Westview
Jervis Inlet
Courtenay
Comox
Cumberland
Union Bay
STRATHCONA PROVINCIAL PARK
Texada Island
Hornby Island
Lasqueti Island
Irvines Landing
Port Mellon
Gambier Island
Horseshoe Bay
Bowen I.
Great Central Lake
Great Central
Sproat Lake
Kennedy Lake
Port Alberni
Parksville
Nanaimo
Valdes Island
Ucluelet
Barkley Sound
Bamfield
Ladysmith
Youbou
Chemainus
Cowichan Lake
Lake Cowichan
Duncan
Galiano Island
Fulford Harbour
Sydney
Clo-oose
Port Renfrew
River Jordan
Sooke
Esquimalt
Metchosin
Victoria
Cape Flattery
Neah Bay
Ozette
Ozette Lake
Soleduck R.
L. Crescent
OLYMPIC
Mora
Port Angeles
Sequim
Port Townsend
Gardiner
San Juan Islands
Friday Harbor
Whidbey Island
Oak Harbor
Camano I.
Greenbank
Anacortes
Burlington
Mount Vernon
Sedro Woolley
Arlington
Darrington
Concrete
Skagit R.
Bellingham
Ferndale
Deming
Lynden
Birch Bay
Blaine
White Rock
Ladner
Steveston
Vancouver
North Vancouver
Port Moody
Port Coquitlam
New Westminster
Fraser R.
Aldergrove
Abbotsford
Mission City
Chilliwack
Harrison Hot Springs
Agassiz
Stave Lake
GOLDEN EARS PROV. PARK
GARIBALDI PROVINCIAL PARK
Squamish
Squamish R.
Britannia Beach
Lillooet R.
Lillooet Lake
Harrison Lake
SKIHIST MT. 2944
CAYOOSH RANGE
Anderson Lake
Carpenter Lake
Bralorne
Downton Lake
SHULAPS RANGE
Seton Lake
Bridge River
Lillooet
Clinton
Seventy Mile House
Cache Creek
Ashcroft
Spences Bridge
Lytton
Keefers
Choate
Hope
Highland Valley
Merritt
Nicola
Nicola Lake
Stump Lake
1900 CHUWHELS MT.
Kamloops Lake
TRANS CANADA HIGHWAY
Kamloops
North Thompson River
Barrière
Adams Lake
Shuswap Lake
Chase
Tappen
Salmon Arm
Sicamous
Armstrong
Vernon
Pennask Lake
Okanagan Lake
Kelowna
TRAPANEGE PLATEAU
Summerland
Penticton
Beaverdell
Princeton
OKANAGAN RANGE
Keremeos
Oliver
Rock Creek
E.C. MANNING PROVINCIAL PARK
NORTH CASCADES NAT. PARK
Ross Lake
Newhalem
MT. BAKER 3284
SAWTOOTH RANGE
Oroville
Tonasket
Okanogan River
Omak
Okanogan
Winthrop
Twisp
Methow R.

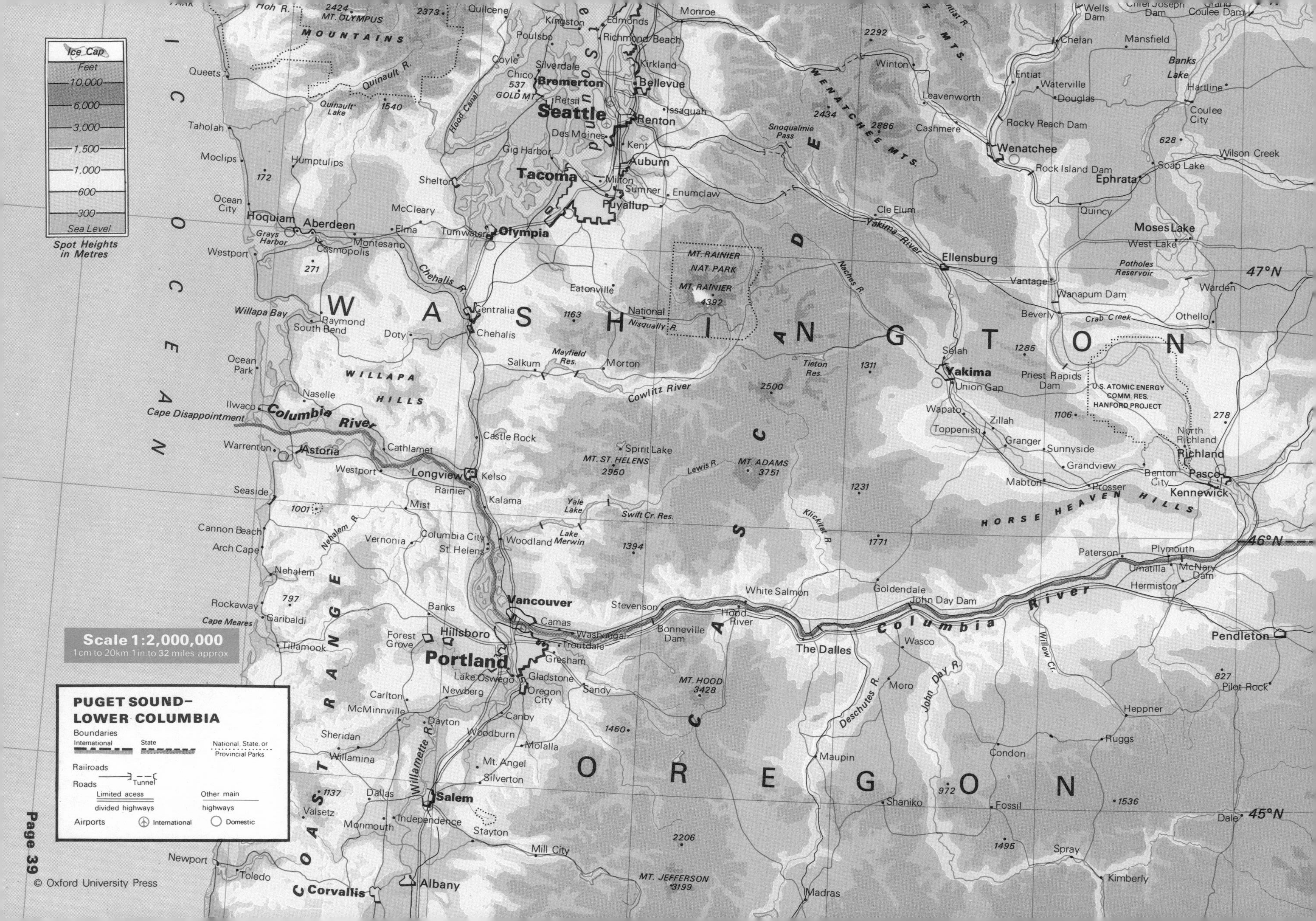

PUGET SOUND–
LOWER COLUMBIA

Scale 1:2,000,000
1cm to 20km 1in to 32 miles approx

Boundaries
International
State
National, State, or
Provincial Parks

Roads
Other main
Limited acess
divided highways
highways

Railroads

Tunnel

Airports
International
Domestic

© Oxford University Press

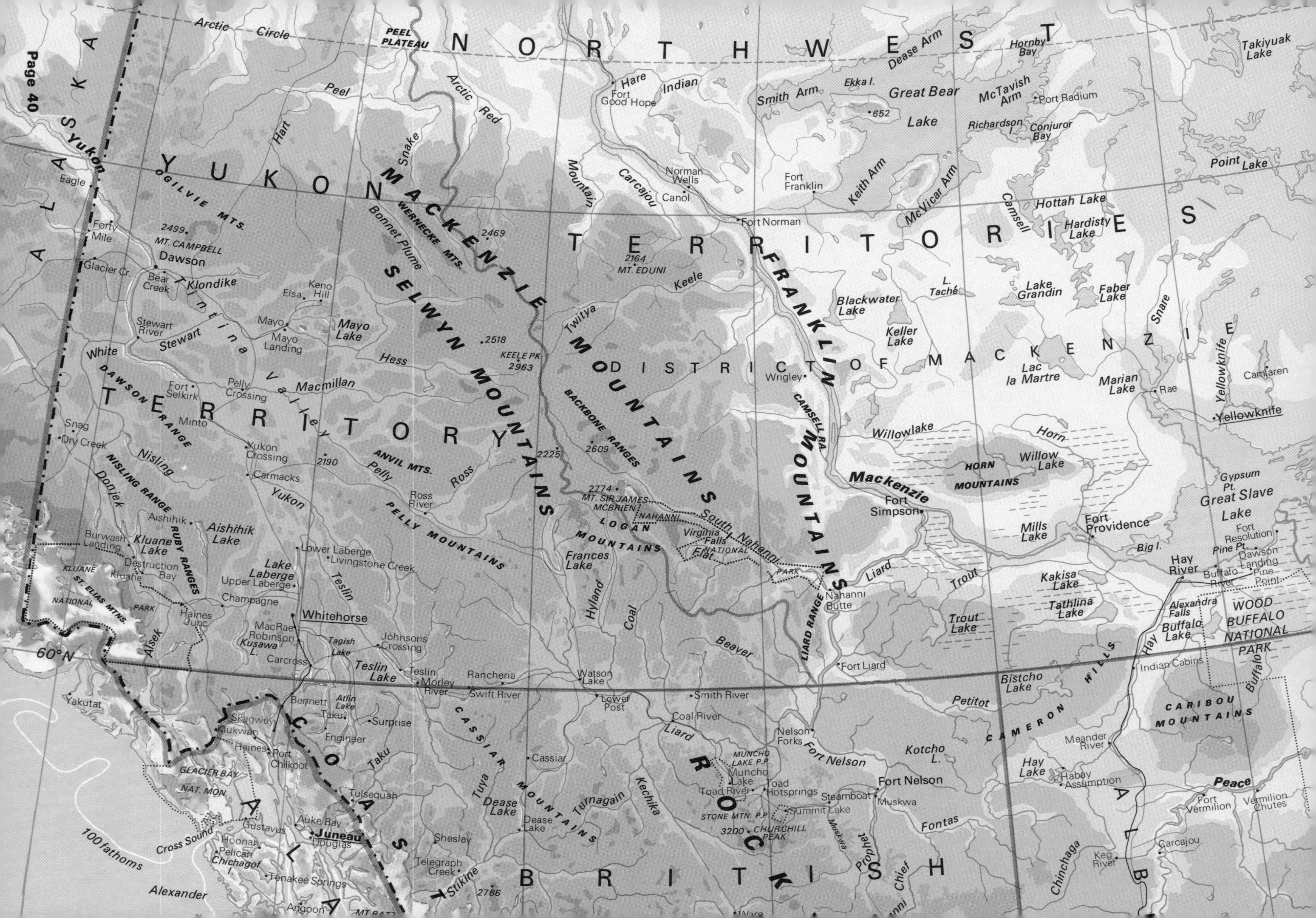
NORTHWEST TERRITORIES
DISTRICT OF MACKENZIE
YUKON TERRITORY
ALASKA
BRITISH COLUMBIA
ALBERTA
MACKENZIE MOUNTAINS
FRANKLIN MOUNTAINS
SELWYN MOUNTAINS
OGILVIE MTS.
WERNECKE MTS.
BACKBONE RANGES
LOGAN MOUNTAINS
PELLY MOUNTAINS
ANVIL MTS.
CASSIAR MOUNTAINS
ROCKY
COAST
ST. ELIAS MTS.
RUBY RANGES
NISLING RANGE
DAWSON RANGE
HORN MOUNTAINS
CARIBOU MOUNTAINS
CAMERON HILLS
CAMSELL RA.
LIARD RANGE
STONE MTN. P.P.
MUNCHO LAKE P.P.
CHURCHILL PEAK
WOOD BUFFALO NATIONAL PARK
NAHANNI NATIONAL PARK
KLUANE NATIONAL PARK
GLACIER BAY NAT. MON.
PEEL PLATEAU
Great Bear Lake
Great Slave Lake
Smith Arm
McTavish Arm
Keith Arm
McVicar Arm
Dease Arm
Hornby Bay
Conjuror Bay
Takiyuak Lake
Point Lake
Hottah Lake
Hardisty Lake
Faber Lake
Marian Lake
Lac la Martre
Lake Grandin
Willow Lake
Mills Lake
Kakisa Lake
Tathlina Lake
Trout Lake
Bistcho Lake
Hay Lake
Buffalo Lake
Blackwater Lake
Keller Lake
L. Taché
Kotcho L.
Muncho Lake
Frances Lake
Dease Lake
Teslin Lake
Atlin Lake
Tagish Lake
Kusawa L.
Lake Laberge
Aishihik Lake
Kluane Lake
Mayo Lake
Yellowknife
Rae
Fort Resolution
Hay River
Fort Providence
Fort Simpson
Fort Liard
Fort Nelson
Nelson Forks
Wrigley
Fort Norman
Norman Wells
Canol
Fort Good Hope
Fort Franklin
Port Radium
Nahanni Butte
Virginia Falls
Watson Lake
Lower Post
Cassiar
Whitehorse
Carcross
Dawson
Mayo
Elsa
Keno Hill
Carmacks
Ross River
Teslin
Johnsons Crossing
Skagway
Haines
Juneau
Douglas
Yakutat
Eagle
Forty Mile
Burwash Landing
Destruction Bay
Haines Junc.
Telegraph Creek
Mackenzie
Liard
Yukon
Peel
Pelly
Stewart
White
Macmillan
Hess
Ross
Snake
Arctic Red
Hart
Donjek
Alsek
Taku
Stikine
Kechika
Hyland
Coal
Beaver
Keele
Twitya
Carcajou
Mountain
Hare Indian
Camsell
Horn
Willowlake
Petitot
Fontas
Muskwa
Prophet
Chinchaga
Peace
Snare
Yellowknife
Tintina Valley
Arctic Circle
60°N
100 fathoms
Alexander
Cross Sound
2469
2518
2963
2225
2609
2774
2164
2190
2499
2786
3200
652

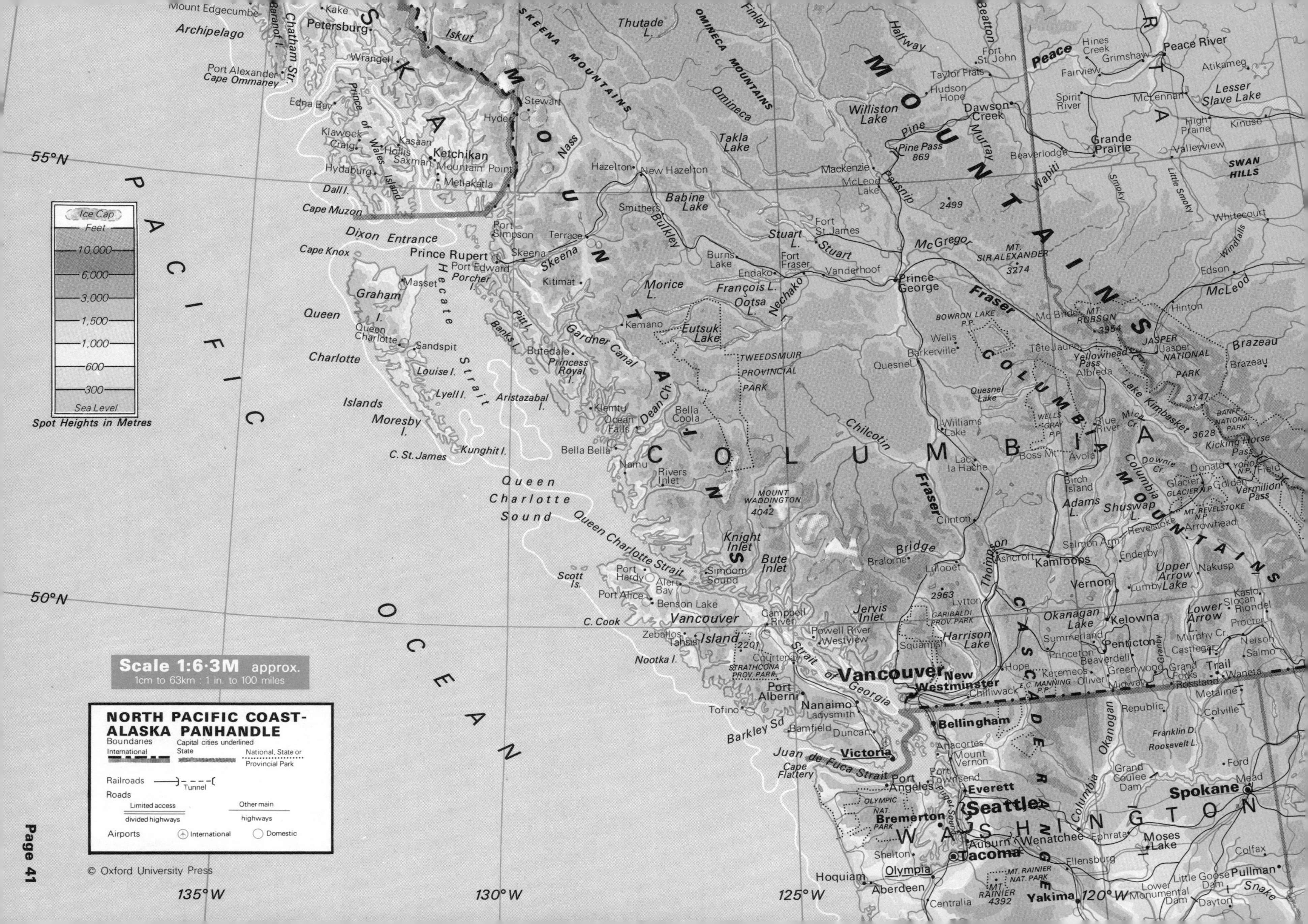

NORTH PACIFIC COAST-
ALASKA PANHANDLE
Boundaries
International
State
Capital cities underlined
National, State or Provincial Park
Railroads
Tunnel
Roads
Limited access divided highways
Other main highways
Airports
International
Domestic
Scale 1:6·3M approx.
1cm to 63km : 1 in. to 100 miles
Ice Cap
Feet
10,000
6,000
3,000
1,500
1,000
600
300
Sea Level
Spot Heights in Metres
P A C I F I C
O C E A N
M O U N T A I N S
C O A S T
M O U N T A I N S
C O L U M B I A
C A S C A D E R
W A S H I N G T O N
SKEENA MOUNTAINS
OMINECA MOUNTAINS
Queen Charlotte Islands
Graham I.
Moresby I.
Queen Charlotte Sound
Hecate Strait
Dixon Entrance
Prince of Wales Island
Vancouver Island
Strait of Georgia
Juan de Fuca Strait
Queen Charlotte Strait
TWEEDSMUIR PROVINCIAL PARK
JASPER NATIONAL PARK
MOUNT WADDINGTON 4042
MT. ROBSON 3954
Vancouver
New Westminster
Victoria
Seattle
Tacoma
Olympia
Spokane
Bellingham
Everett
Yakima
Prince Rupert
Prince George
Kamloops
Kelowna
Vernon
Penticton
Nanaimo
Ketchikan
Petersburg
Wrangell
Peace River
Dawson Creek
Grande Prairie
Fraser
Columbia
Peace
55°N
50°N
135°W
130°W
125°W
120°W
© Oxford University Press

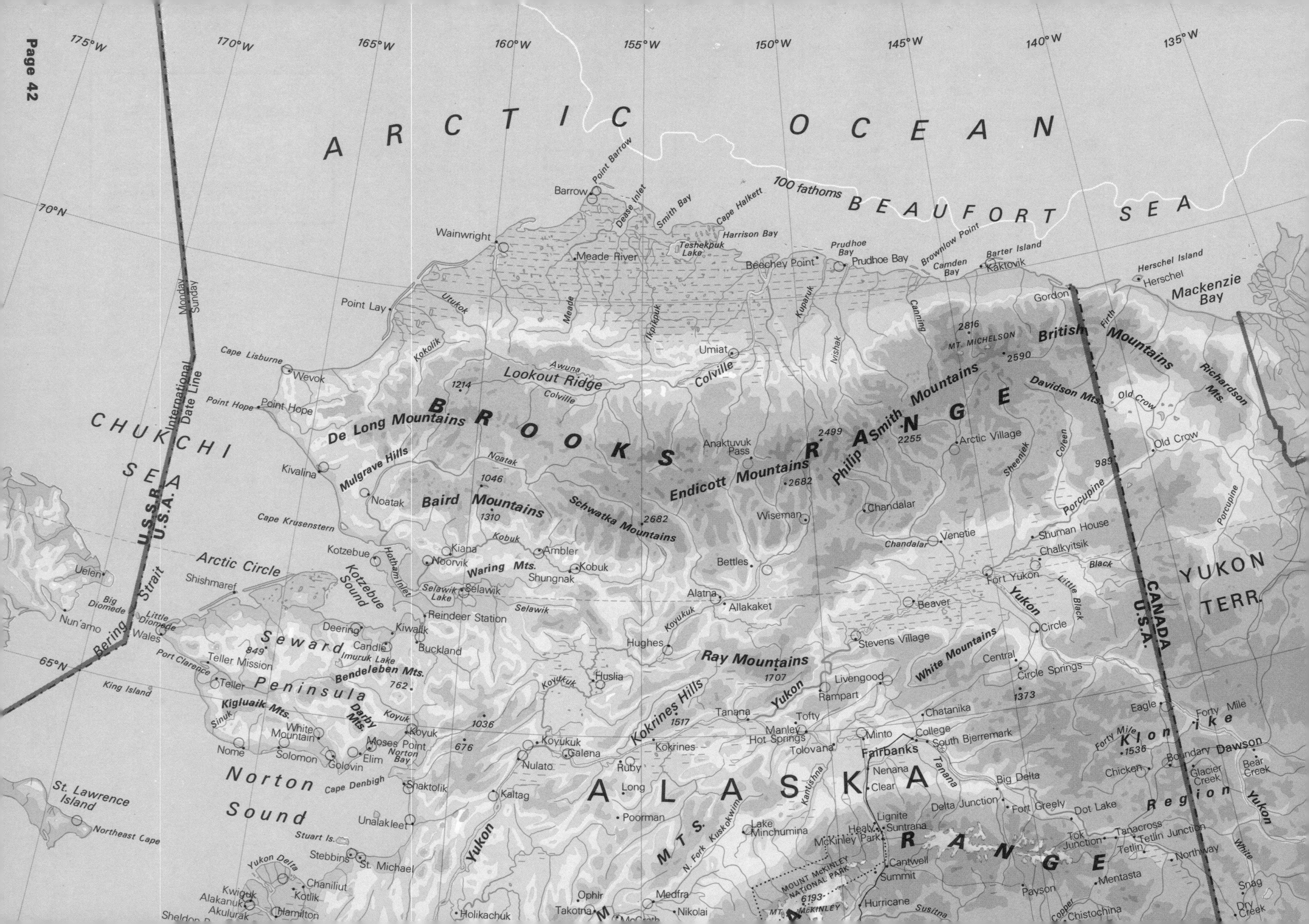

ARCTIC OCEAN
BEAUFORT SEA
CHUKCHI SEA
100 fathoms
175°W
170°W
165°W
160°W
155°W
150°W
145°W
140°W
135°W
70°N
65°N
International Date Line
Monday
Sunday
U.S.S.R.
U.S.A.
CANADA
U.S.A.
YUKON TERR.
BROOKS RANGE
ALASKA
ALASKA RANGE
Arctic Circle
Point Barrow
Barrow
Dease Inlet
Smith Bay
Cape Halkett
Harrison Bay
Teshekpuk Lake
Wainwright
Meade River
Meade
Beechey Point
Prudhoe Bay
Brownlow Point
Camden Bay
Barter Island
Kaktovik
Herschel Island
Herschel
Mackenzie Bay
Gordon
Point Lay
Utukok
Ikpikpuk
Kuparuk
Ivishak
Canning
Umiat
Colville
Cape Lisburne
Wevok
Kokolik
Awuna
Lookout Ridge
1214
Point Hope
De Long Mountains
Mulgrave Hills
Kivalina
Noatak
1046
Baird Mountains
1310
Schwatka Mountains
2682
Anaktuvuk Pass
2499
Endicott Mountains
Philip Smith Mountains
2255
Mt. Michelson
2816
2590
British Mountains
Firth
Richardson Mts.
Davidson Mts.
Old Crow
989
Arctic Village
Sheenjek
Coleen
Porcupine
Chandalar
Wiseman
Cape Krusenstern
Kotzebue
Kotzebue Sound
Hotham Inlet
Kiana
Noorvik
Kobuk
Ambler
Waring Mts.
Shungnak
Selawik Lake
Selawik
Reindeer Station
Bettles
Alatna
Allakaket
Koyukuk
Venetie
Shuman House
Chalkyitsik
Black
Little Black
Fort Yukon
Yukon
Beaver
Circle
Stevens Village
White Mountains
Central
Circle Springs
1373
Uelen
Big Diomede
Little Diomede
Nun'amo
Bering Strait
Wales
Shishmaref
Deering
Kiwalik
Candle
Imuruk Lake
Buckland
Seward Peninsula
849
Teller Mission
Port Clarence
Teller
Bendeleben Mts.
762
King Island
Kigluaik Mts.
Sinuk
Darby Mts.
Koyuk
White Mountain
Nome
Solomon
Golovin
Moses Point
Elim
Norton Bay
1036
676
Hughes
Huslia
Ray Mountains
1707
Kokrines Hills
1517
Tanana
Livengood
Rampart
Tofty
Manley Hot Springs
Tolovana
Chatanika
Minto
College
Fairbanks
South Bjerremark
Nenana
Clear
Koyukuk
Nulato
Galena
Kokrines
Ruby
Long
Poorman
Kaltag
Norton Sound
Cape Denbigh
Shaktolik
Unalakleet
St. Lawrence Island
Northeast Cape
Stuart Is.
Stebbins
St. Michael
Yukon Delta
Chaniliut
Kotlik
Kwiguk
Alakanuk
Akulurak
Hamilton
Ophir
Takotna
Medfra
Nikolai
Holikachuk
Kuskokwim Mts.
N. Fork Kuskokwim
Kantishna
Lake Minchumina
McKinley Park
Healy
Suntrana
Lignite
Cantwell
Summit
Hurricane
Susitna
Mount McKinley National Park
6193
Mt. McKinley
Big Delta
Delta Junction
Fort Greely
Dot Lake
Tok Junction
Tanacross
Tetlin Junction
Tetlin
Northway
Mentasta
Chistochina
Copper
Payson
Eagle
Forty Mile
Klondike Region
1536
Chicken
Boundary
Dawson
Glacier Creek
Bear Creek
Dry Creek
Snag
White

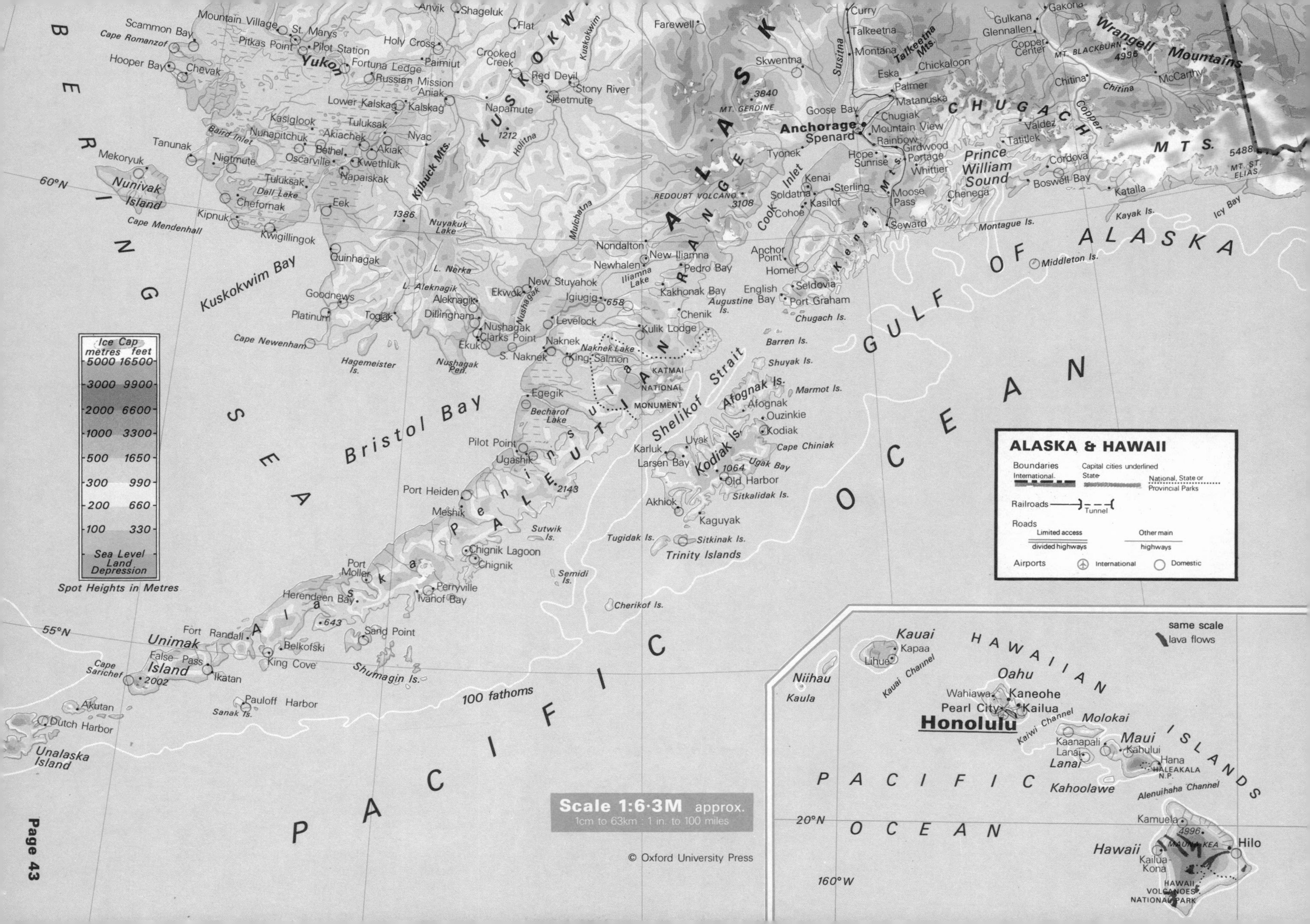

ALASKA & HAWAII
Boundaries
International.
Capital cities underlined
State
National, State or Provincial Parks
Railroads
Tunnel
Roads
Limited access divided highways
Other main highways
Airports
International
Domestic
Ice Cap
metres feet
5000 16500
3000 9900
2000 6600
1000 3300
500 1650
300 990
200 660
100 330
Sea Level Land Depression
Spot Heights in Metres
Scale 1:6·3M approx.
1cm to 63km : 1 in. to 100 miles
© Oxford University Press
B E R I N G
S E A
Bristol Bay
Kuskokwim Bay
G U L F O F A L A S K A
P A C I F I C
O C E A N
KUSKOKW
Kuskokwim
ALASKA RANGE
CHUGACH MTS.
Wrangell Mountains
Talkeetna Mts.
Kilbuck Mts.
Kenai Mts
ALEUTIAN
Alaska Peninsula
MT. BLACKBURN 4996
MT. ST. ELIAS 5488
MT. GERDINE 3840
REDOUBT VOLCANO 3108
KATMAI NATIONAL MONUMENT
Yukon
Susitna
Chitina
Copper
Holitna
Mulchatna
Nushagak
Mountain Village
St. Marys
Pitkas Point
Pilot Station
Anvik
Shageluk
Flat
Holy Cross
Paimiut
Crooked Creek
Red Devil
Stony River
Sleetmute
Fortuna Ledge
Russian Mission
Aniak
Lower Kalskag
Kalskag
Napamute
Scammon Bay
Cape Romanzof
Hooper Bay
Chevak
Kasigluk
Tuluksak
Nunapitchuk
Akiachek
Nyac
Baird Inlet
Bethel
Akiak
Oscarville
Kwethluk
Napaiskak
Tanunak
Nigtmute
Mekoryuk
Nunivak Island
60°N
Tuluksak
Dall Lake
Chefornak
Eek
Kipnuk
Cape Mendenhall
Kwigillingok
1212
1386
Nuyakuk Lake
Quinhagak
L. Nerka
L. Aleknagik
Aleknagik
Dillingham
Goodnews
Platinum
Togiak
Cape Newenham
Hagemeister Is.
Nushagak
Clarks Point
Ekuk
Nushagak Pen.
Ekwok
New Stuyahok
Igiugig
658
Levelock
Naknek
S. Naknek
King Salmon
Naknek Lake
Kulik Lodge
Egegik
Becharof Lake
Pilot Point
Ugashik
2143
Port Heiden
Meshik
Chignik Lagoon
Chignik
Sutwik Is.
Semidi Is.
Port Moller
Perryville
Ivanof Bay
Herendeen Bay
643
Sand Point
Shumagin Is.
Fort Randall
Belkofski
King Cove
55°N
Unimak Island
False Pass
Cape Sarichef
2002
Ikatan
Pauloff Harbor
Sanak Is.
Akutan
Dutch Harbor
Unalaska Island
100 fathoms
Cherikof Is.
Farewell
Skwentna
Curry
Talkeetna
Montana
Eska
Palmer
Chickaloon
Matanuska
Chugiak
Goose Bay
Anchorage
Spenard
Mountain View
Rainbow
Girdwood
Portage
Whittier
Hope
Sunrise
Tyonek
Cook Inlet
Kenai
Soldatna
Kasilof
Sterling
Cohoe
Moose Pass
Seward
Nondalton
New Iliamna
Newhalen
Iliamna Lake
Pedro Bay
Kakhonak Bay
Augustine Is.
Chenik
Anchor Point
Homer
English Bay
Seldovia
Port Graham
Chugach Is.
Barren Is.
Shuyak Is.
Marmot Is.
Shelikof Strait
Afognak Is.
Afognak
Ouzinkie
Kodiak
Cape Chiniak
Uyak
Karluk
Larsen Bay
Kodiak Is.
1064
Ugak Bay
Old Harbor
Sitkalidak Is.
Akhiok
Kaguyak
Tugidak Is.
Sitkinak Is.
Trinity Islands
Gulkana
Gakona
Glennallen
Copper Center
Chitina
McCarthy
Valdez
Tatitlek
Prince William Sound
Chenega
Cordova
Boswell Bay
Katalla
Montague Is.
Kayak Is.
Icy Bay
Middleton Is.
same scale
lava flows
Kauai
Kapaa
Lihue
Kauai Channel
Niihau
Kaula
HAWAIIAN ISLANDS
Oahu
Wahiawa
Kaneohe
Pearl City
Kailua
Honolulu
Kaiwi Channel
Molokai
Kaanapali
Lanai
Maui
Kahului
Hana
HALEAKALA N.P.
Kahoolawe
Alenuihaha Channel
P A C I F I C
O C E A N
20°N
160°W
Kamuela
4996
MAUNA KEA
Hilo
Hawaii
Kailua Kona
HAWAII VOLCANOES NATIONAL PARK

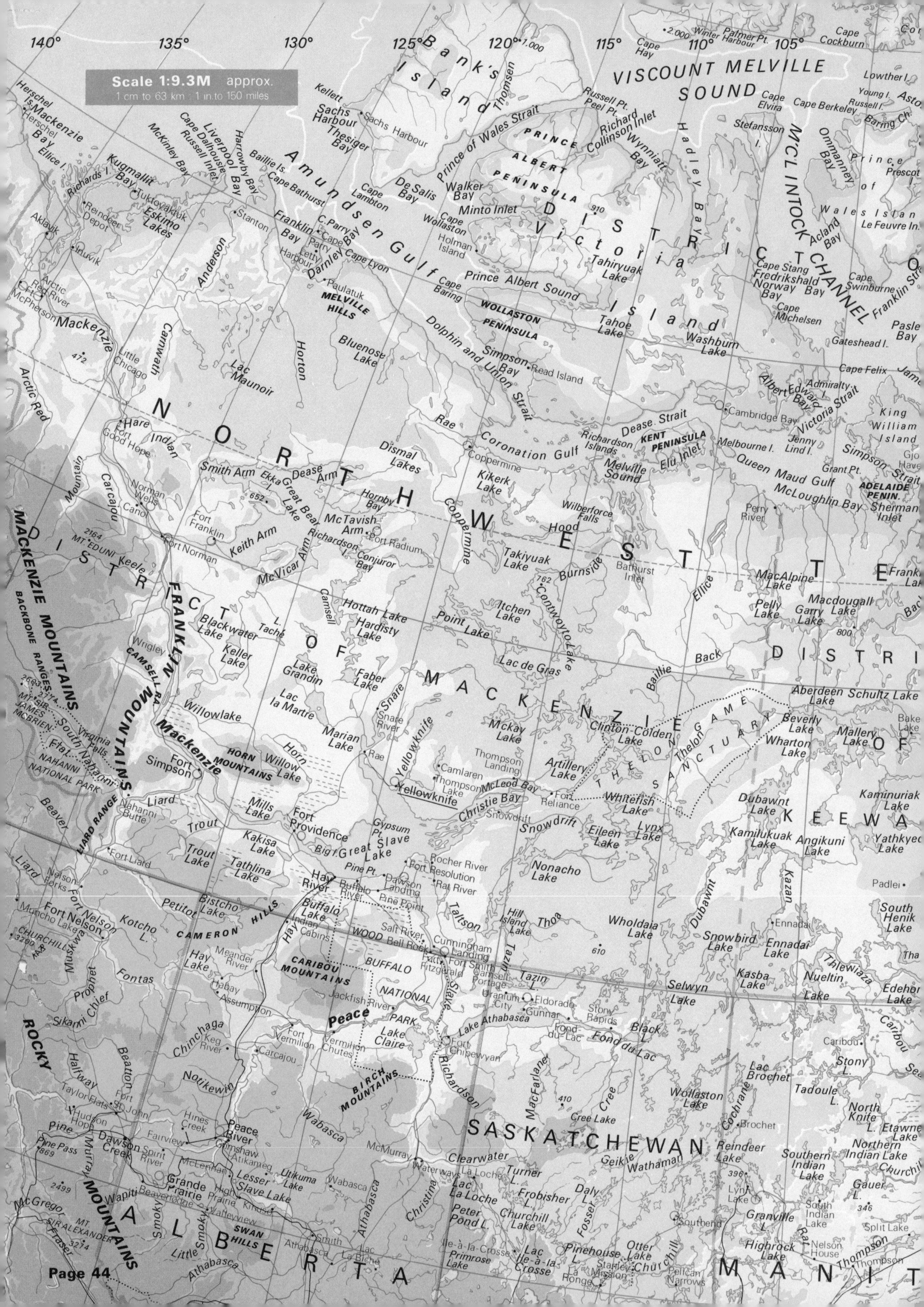
140°
135°
130°
125°
120°
115°
110°
105°
Scale 1:9.3M approx.
1 cm to 63 km : 1 in. to 150 miles
Bank's Island
Thomsen
Kellett
Sachs Harbour
Thesiger Bay
VISCOUNT MELVILLE SOUND
Cape Hay
Winter Harbour
Palmer Pt.
Cape Cockburn
Lowther I.
Young I.
Russell I.
Cape Elvira
Cape Berkeley
Baring Ch.
Stefansson I.
Russell Pt.
Peel Pt.
Prince of Wales Strait
Richard Collinson Inlet
Wynniatt Bay
Hadley Bay
M'CLINTOCK CHANNEL
Ommanney Bay
Prince of Wales Island
Prescot I.
Le Feuvre In.
Acland Bay
PRINCE ALBERT PENINSULA
Herschel Is.
Herschel
Mackenzie Bay
Ellice I.
Richards I.
Kugmallit Bay
Tuktoyaktuk
Reindeer Depot
Eskimo Lakes
Aklavik
Inuvik
Arctic Red River
Fort McPherson
Liverpool Bay
Cape Dalhousie
Russell Inlet
McKinley Bay
Harrowby Bay
Baillie Is.
Cape Bathurst
Amundsen Gulf
Stanton
Franklin Bay
Cape Parry
Letty Harbour
Darnley Bay
Cape Lyon
Cape Lambton
De Salis Bay
Walker Bay
Minto Inlet
Cape Wollaston
Holman Island
DISTRICT
Victoria Island
Tahiryuak Lake
Cape Stang
Fredrikshald Bay
Norway Bay
Cape Swinburne
Franklin Str.
Cape Michelsen
Pasle Bay
Gateshead I.
Cape Felix
Paulatuk
MELVILLE HILLS
Cape Baring
Prince Albert Sound
WOLLASTON PENINSULA
Tahoe Lake
Washburn Lake
Anderson
Mackenzie
Little Chicago
Carnwath
Horton
Bluenose Lake
Dolphin and Union Strait
Simpson Bay
Read Island
Lac Maunoir
Arctic Red
NORTH WEST TERRITORIES
Albert Edward Bay
Admiralty I.
Victoria Strait
King William Island
Cambridge Bay
Hare Indian
Fort Good Hope
Rae
Coronation Gulf
Coppermine
Dease Strait
KENT PENINSULA
Richardson Islands
Melville Sound
Elu Inlet
Melbourne I.
Jenny Lind I.
Queen Maud Gulf
Grant Pt.
Simpson Strait
Dismal Lakes
Kikerk Lake
ADELAIDE PENIN.
McLoughlin Bay
Sherman Inlet
Mountain
Carcajou
Norman Wells
Canol
Smith Arm
Ekka I.
Dease Arm
Great Bear Lake
Hornby Bay
McTavish Arm
Port Radium
Coppermine
Wilberforce Falls
Hood
Perry River
2164 MT. EDUNI
Fort Franklin
Keith Arm
Fort Norman
Keele
Richardson I.
Conjuror Bay
McVicar Arm
Takiyuak Lake
762
Burnside
Bathurst Inlet
MacAlpine Lake
MACKENZIE MOUNTAINS
BACKBONE RANGES
DISTRICT OF MACKENZIE
FRANKLIN MOUNTAINS
Camsell
Hottah Lake
Hardisty Lake
Point Lake
Itchen Lake
Contwoyto Lake
Ellice
Pelly Lake
Garry Lake
Macdougall Lake
Blackwater Lake
L. Taché
Keller Lake
Wrigley
CAMSELL RA.
Lake Grandin
Faber Lake
Lac de Gras
Baillie
Back
800
DISTRICT
2774
MT. SIR JAMES MCBRIEN
South Nahanni
Virginia Falls
NAHANNI NATIONAL PARK
Willowlake
Lac la Martre
Snare
Snare River
MACKENZIE
Clinton-Colden Lake
THELON GAME SANCTUARY
Aberdeen Lake
Schultz Lake
Beverly Lake
Mallery Lake
Baker Lake
Wharton Lake
Mackenzie
Fort Simpson
HORN MOUNTAINS
Willow Lake
Horn
Marian Lake
Rae
Yellowknife
Mckay Lake
Thompson Landing
Artillery Lake
Camlaren
Thompson Lake
McLeod Bay
Fort Reliance
Whitefish Lake
Dubawnt Lake
Kaminuriak Lake
KEEWATIN
Beaver
LIARD RANGE
Liard
Nahanni Butte
Trout
Mills Lake
Fort Providence
Christie Bay
Snowdrift
Eileen Lake
Lynx Lake
Kamilukuak Lake
Angikuni Lake
Yathkyed Lake
Fort Liard
Kakisa Lake
Trout Lake
Tathlina Lake
Gypsum Pt.
Big I.
Great Slave Lake
Rocher River
Fort Resolution
Rat River
Pine Pt.
Nonacho Lake
Kazan
Padlei
Liard
Nelson Forks
Fort Nelson
Muncho Lake
CHURCHILL 3200
Muskwa
Hay River
Buffalo River
Dawson Landing
Pine Point
Petitot
Bistcho Lake
CAMERON HILLS
Buffalo Lake
Indian Cabins
Taltson
Hill Island Lake
Thoa
Wholdaia Lake
Dubawnt
Snowbird Lake
Ennadai
Ennadai Lake
South Henik Lake
Kotcho L.
Hay
Salt River
WOOD BUFFALO NATIONAL PARK
Bell Rock
Cunningham Landing
Fitzgerald
Fort Smith
Tazin
610
Prophet
Hay Lake
Meander River
Fontas
CARIBOU MOUNTAINS
Camsell Portage
Slave
Tazin L.
Selwyn Lake
Kasba Lake
Nueltin Lake
Thlewiaza
Edehon Lake
Habay
Assumption
Jackfish River
Uranium City
Eldorado
Gunnar
Stony Rapids
Sikanni Chief
ROCKY MOUNTAINS
Chinchaga
Keg River
Peace
Fort Vermilion
Vermilion Chutes
Lake Claire
Lake Athabasca
Fond-du-Lac
Fond du Lac
Black L.
Caribou
Caribou
Carcajou
Fort Chipewyan
Stony L.
Beatton
Halfway
Notikewin
Richardson
MacFarlane
410
Cree
Lac Brochet
Wollaston Lake
Cochrane
Tadoule L.
North Knife L.
Etawney Lake
Taylor Flats
Fort St. John
Hudson Hope
BIRCH MOUNTAINS
Wabasca
Hines Creek
Peace River
Cree Lake
Brochet
Pine
Pine Pass
869
Dawson Creek
Fairview
Spirit River
Grimshaw
SASKATCHEWAN
Reindeer Lake
Northern Indian Lake
Southern Indian Lake
Churchill
Murray
Atikameg
McLennan
Utikuma Lake
McMurray
Clearwater
Turner L.
Geikie
Wathaman
2499
Wapiti
Grande Prairie
Lesser Slave Lake
High Prairie
Beaverlodge
Valleyview
Kinuso
Wabasca
Waterways
La Loche
Lac La Loche
Frobisher L.
Daly L.
396
Lynn Lake
Gauer L.
346
McGregor
MOUNTAINS
Smoky
Athabasca
Christina
Peter Pond L.
Churchill Lake
Fossel
Southend
Granville L.
South Indian Lake
Split Lake
MT. SIR ALEXANDER 3214
Fraser
ALBERTA
Little Smoky
SWAN HILLS
Smith
Athabasca
La Biche
Lac La Biche
Ile-à-la-Crosse
Primrose Lake
Lac Ile-à-la Crosse
Pinehouse L.
Otter Lake
Churchill
Stanley Mission
La Ronge
Pelican Narrows
Highrock Lake
Rat
Nelson House
Thompson
Thompson
MANITOBA
Athabasca

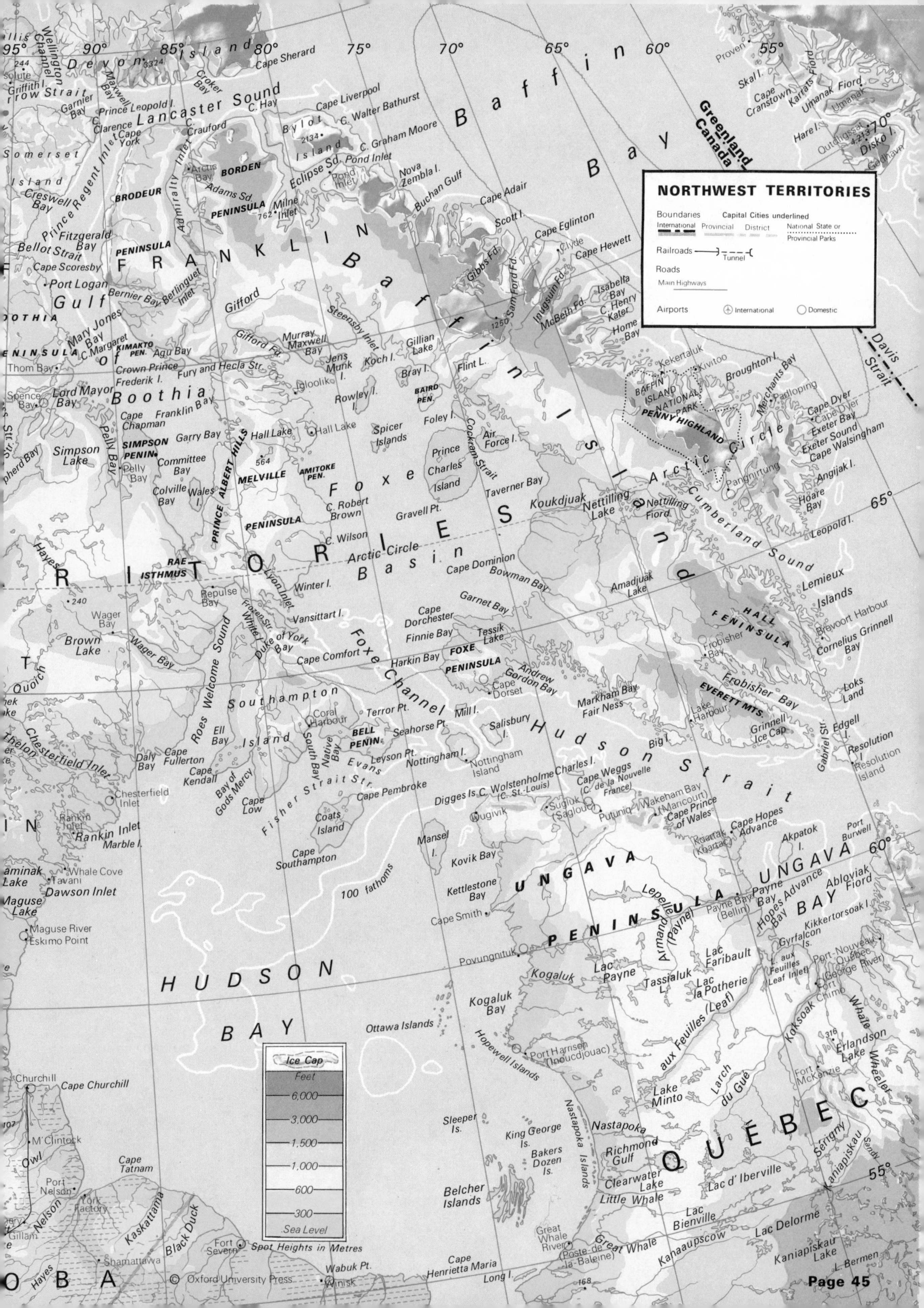

NORTHWEST TERRITORIES

Boundaries   Capital Cities underlined
International Provincial District   National State or Provincial Parks

Railroads ———┤ ├——— Tunnel ———┤ ├———

Roads
Main Highways

Airports ✈ International ○ Domestic

95°   90°   85°   80°   75°   70°   65°   60°   55°

Wellington Channel
Devon Island
Griffith I.
Garner Bay
Maxwell Bay
Cape Sherard
Proven
Skal I.
Cape Cranstown Kartats
Umanak Fiord
Umanak
Cape Hay
Cape Liverpool
Prince Leopold Inlet
Clarence Head Cape York
Crauford
C. Walter Bathurst
Hare I.
Disko I.
70°

Lancaster Sound
Somerset
Island
Creswell Bay
BORDEN
Bylot Island
2134
C. Graham Moore
Pond Inlet
Eclipse Sd. Pond Inlet
Nova Zembla I.
Buchan Gulf
Cape Adair
Greenland
Canada

Fitzgerald Bay
Bellot Strait
Cape Scoresby
Port Logan
BRODEUR
PENINSULA
Berlinguet Inlet
Bernier Bay
Gifford
Milne Inlet
762
Admiralty Inlet
Arctic Bay
Adams Sd.
Scott I.
Cape Eglinton
Clyde
Cape Hewett
Isabella Bay
C. Henry Kater
Home Bay

Gulf
OF
BOOTHIA
Mary Jones Bay
C. Margaret
KIMAKTO PEN.
Agu Bay
Gifford Fd.
Murray Maxwell Bay
Steensby Inlet
1250
Iougguin Fd.
McBeth Fd.
Davis Strait

PENINSULA
OF
Thom Bay
Crown Prince Frederik I.
Fury and Hecla Str.
Jens Munk I.
Koch I.
Gillian Lake
Bray I.
Flint L.
Kekertaluk
Kivitoo
Broughton I.
Merchants Bay
Padloping
Cape Dyer
Exeter Sound
Cape Walsingham

Boothia
Spence Bay
Lord Mayor Bay
Cape Franklin
Garry Bay
Hall Lake
Hall Lake
Rowley I.
BAIRD PEN.
Foley I.
Spicer Islands
Prince Charles Island
Air Force I.
BAFFIN ISLAND NATIONAL PARK
PENNY HIGHLAND
Pangnirtung
Angiak I.
Hoare Bay

shepherd Bay
Simpson Lake
SIMPSON PENIN.
564
MELVILLE PEN.
AMITOKE PEN.
Foxe
C. Robert Brown
Gravell Pt.
Taverner Bay
Cumberland Sound
Leopold I.
65°

Pelly Bay
Colville Bay
Committee Bay
PRINCE ALBERT HILLS
Wales I.
C. Wilson
Koukdjuak
Nettilling Lake
Nettilling Fiord

240
RAE ISTHMUS
Lyon Inlet
Winter I.
Arctic Circle
Basin
Cape Dominion
Bowman Bay
Amadjuak Lake
HALL PENINSULA
Lemieux Islands

Wager Bay
Brown Lake
Repulse Bay
Frozen Strait
Vansittart I.
Cape Dorchester
Garnet Bay
Brevoort Harbour
Cornelius Grinnell Bay

Hayes
Quoich
Wager Bay
Roes Welcome Sound
Duke of York Bay
Finnie Bay
Harkin Bay
Tessik Lake
Andrew Gordon Bay
Markham Bay
Fair Ness
Frobisher Bay
EVERETT MTS.
Lake Harbour
Loks Land

Thelon
Southampton
Coral Harbour
Terror Pt.
FOXE PENINSULA
Cape Dorset
Grinnell Ice Cap
Gabriel Str.
Edgell I.
Resolution Island

Chesterfield Inlet
Daly Bay
Ell Bay
Cape Fullerton
Island
South Bay
Native Bay
Evans
Seahorse Pt.
Leyson Pt.
Mill I.
Salisbury
Big I.

Chesterfield Inlet
Cape Kendall
Bay of Gods Mercy
Cape Low
Coats Island
Nottingham I.
Digges Is.
C. Wolstenholme
Charles I.
Cape Weggs
(C. de la Nouvelle France)

Rankin Inlet
Marble I.
Fisher Strait Str.
Cape Pembroke
Dugivik
Sugluk (Saglouc)
Putuniq
Wakeham Bay
Cape Prince of Wales
Akpatok I.
Port Burwell

aminak Lake
Tavani
Whale Cove
Dawson Inlet
Cape Southampton
Mansel I.
Kovik Bay
UNGAVA
Koartak (Kcartac)
Cape Hopes Advance
Hopes Advance Bay
UNGAVA BAY
Port Nouveau
60°

Maguse Lake
Maguse River
Eskimo Point
100 fathoms
Kettlestone Bay
Cape Smith
PENINSULA
Armand River (Bellin) (Payne)
Payne Bay (Payne)
Kikkertorsoak I.
Gyrfalcon I.
Ablaviak Fiord

HUDSON
BAY
Ottawa Islands
Povungnituk
Kogaluk
Lac Payne
Lac Faribault
Tassialuk
L. aux Feuilles
Leaf Inlet
Port-Nouveau-Québec (George River)

Churchill
Cape Churchill
Sleeper Is.
Hopewell Islands
Port Harrison (Inoucdjouac)
Kogaluk Bay
Nastapoka
King George Is.
Bakers Dozen Is.
Nastapoka Islands
aux Feuilles (Leaf)
Lac la Potherie (Leaf)
Lac Minto
Larch
Koksoak Chimo
Fort McKenzie
Erlandson Lake
316
Whale River

M'Clintock
Owl
Port Nelson
Cape Tatnam
Belcher Islands
Richmond Gulf
Clearwater Lake
Lake Minto
Lac d' Iberville
QUÉBEC
Serigny
Kaniapiskau
55°

107
Kaskattama
Fort Severn
Spot Heights in Metres
Sleeper Is.
Great Whale River (Poste-de-la-Baleine)
Little Whale
Lac Bienville
Lac Delorme
L. Bermen
Kaniapiskau Lake

BA
Shamattawa
Wabuk Pt.
Winisk
Cape Henrietta Maria
Long I.
168
Kanaaupscow

Gillam
Hayes
York Factory
Black Duck
© Oxford University Press

Ice Cap
Feet
6,000
3,000
1,500
1,000
600
300
Sea Level

Page 45

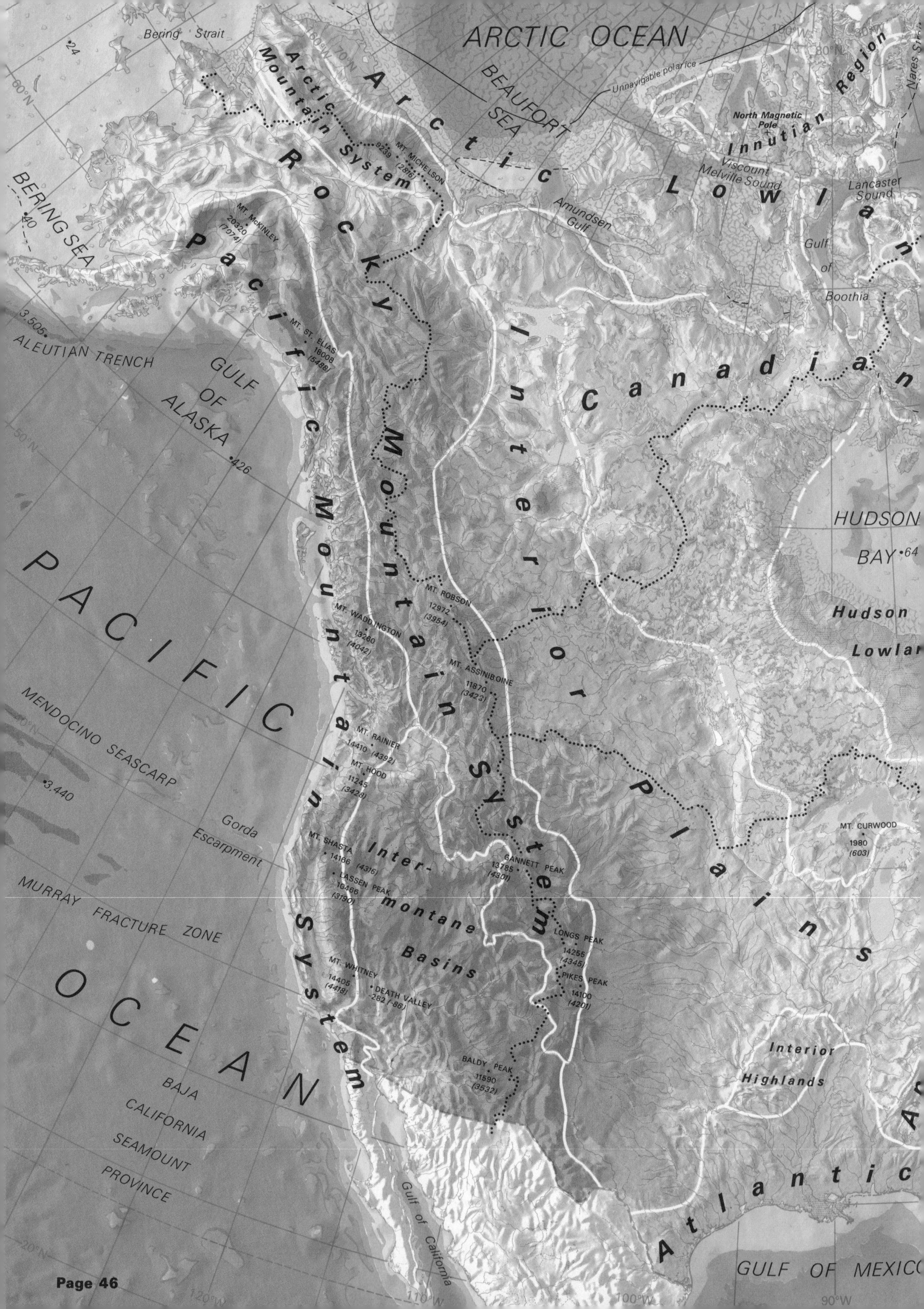

ARCTIC OCEAN

BEAUFORT SEA

Unnavigable polar ice

Innuitian Region

North Magnetic Pole

Viscount Melville Sound

Lancaster Sound

Amundsen Gulf

Gulf of Boothia

Arctic Lowlan

Bering Strait

•24

Arctic Mountain System

MT. MICHELSON 9239 (2816)

Rocky

MT. MCKINLEY 20320 (7074)

Canadian

BERING SEA

•40

3,505•

ALEUTIAN TRENCH

Pacific

MT. ST. ELIAS 18008 (5489)

GULF OF ALASKA

•426

Mountain

Interior

HUDSON BAY •64

Hudson Lowlan

PACIFIC

MENDOCINO SEASCARP

Mountain

MT. ROBSON 12972 (3954)

MT. ASSINIBOINE 11870 (3423)

Plains

•3,440

Gorda Escarpment

System

MT. WADDINGTON 13260 (4042)

MT. RAINIER 14410 (4392)

MT. HOOD 11245 (3428)

System

MT. CURWOOD 1980 (603)

MURRAY FRACTURE ZONE

Inter-

MT. SHASTA 14166 (4316)

LASSEN PEAK 10466 (3190)

montane

GANNETT PEAK 13785 (4301)

OCEAN

Basins

MT. WHITNEY 14405 (4418)

•DEATH VALLEY -282 (-86)

LONGS PEAK 14255 (4345)

•PIKES PEAK 14100 (4201)

BAJA CALIFORNIA SEAMOUNT PROVINCE

System

BALDY PEAK 11590 (3532)

Interior Highlands

Atlantic

Gulf of California

GULF OF MEXICO

Atlantic C

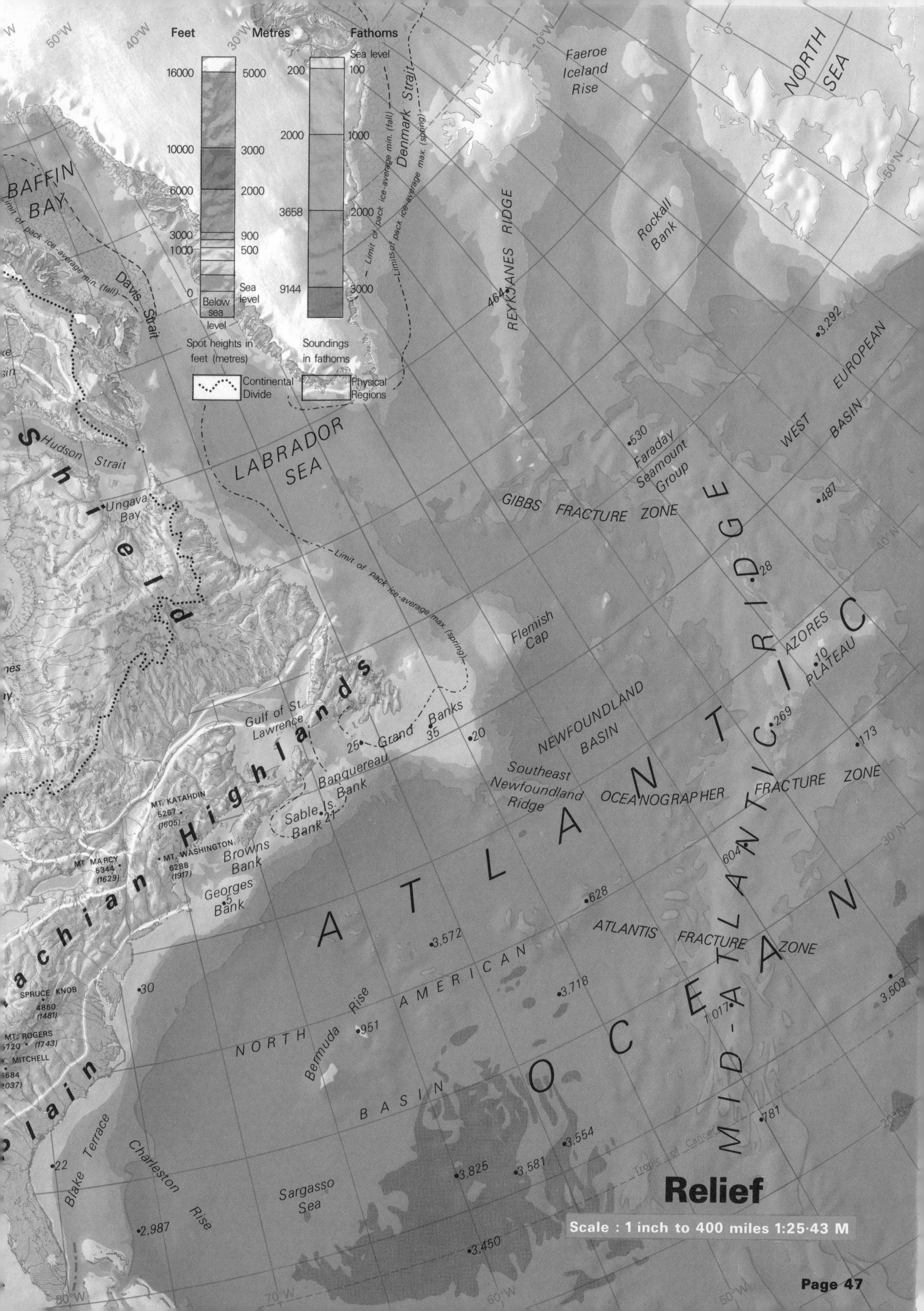

50°W 50°W 40°W 30°W 20°W 10°W 0° 10°E

Feet **Metres** **Fathoms**

16000	5000	200	100	Sea level
10000	3000	2000	1000	
6000	2000	3658	2000	
3000	900			
1000	500	9144	3000	
0	Sea level			

Below sea level

Spot heights in feet (metres)

Soundings in fathoms

Continental Divide

Physical Regions

BAFFIN BAY

Limit of pack ice average min. (fall)

Davis Strait

S h i e l d

Hudson Strait

Ungava Bay

LABRADOR SEA

Denmark Strait

Faeroe Iceland Rise

NORTH SEA

Limit of pack ice-average min. (fall)

Limits of pack ice-average max. (spring)

REYKJANES RIDGE

Rockall Bank

•464

WEST EUROPEAN BASIN

•3.292

•487

Limit of pack ice-average max (spring)

GIBBS FRACTURE ZONE

•530

Faraday Seamount Group

Flemish Cap

Gulf of St Lawrence

Grand Banks

25• •35 •20

Banquereau Bank

Sable Is. Bank •21

MT. KATAHDIN 5267 (1605)

A p p a l a c h i a n   H i g h l a n d s

MT. WASHINGTON 6288 (1917)

Browns Bank

Georges •5 Bank

MT. MARCY 5344 (1629)

SPRUCE KNOB 4860 (1481)

•30

MT. ROGERS 5720 (1743)

MITCHELL 6684 (2037)

P l a i n

NEWFOUNDLAND BASIN

Southeast Newfoundland Ridge

OCEANOGRAPHER FRACTURE ZONE

•269

•173

•28

AZORES PLATEAU •10

A T L A N T I C   R I D G E

M I D - A T L A N T I C

•604

•628

ATLANTIS FRACTURE ZONE

•3.503

A T L A N T I C

•3.572

NORTH AMERICAN BASIN

Bermuda Rise

•3.718

•951

1.017•

•781

O C E A N

Blake Terrace

Charleston Rise

•22

•2.987

Sargasso Sea

•3.825

•3.581

•3.554

Tropic of Cancer

•3.450

Relief

Scale : 1 inch to 400 miles 1:25·43 M

70°W 60°W 50°W 60°N 50°N 40°N 30°N

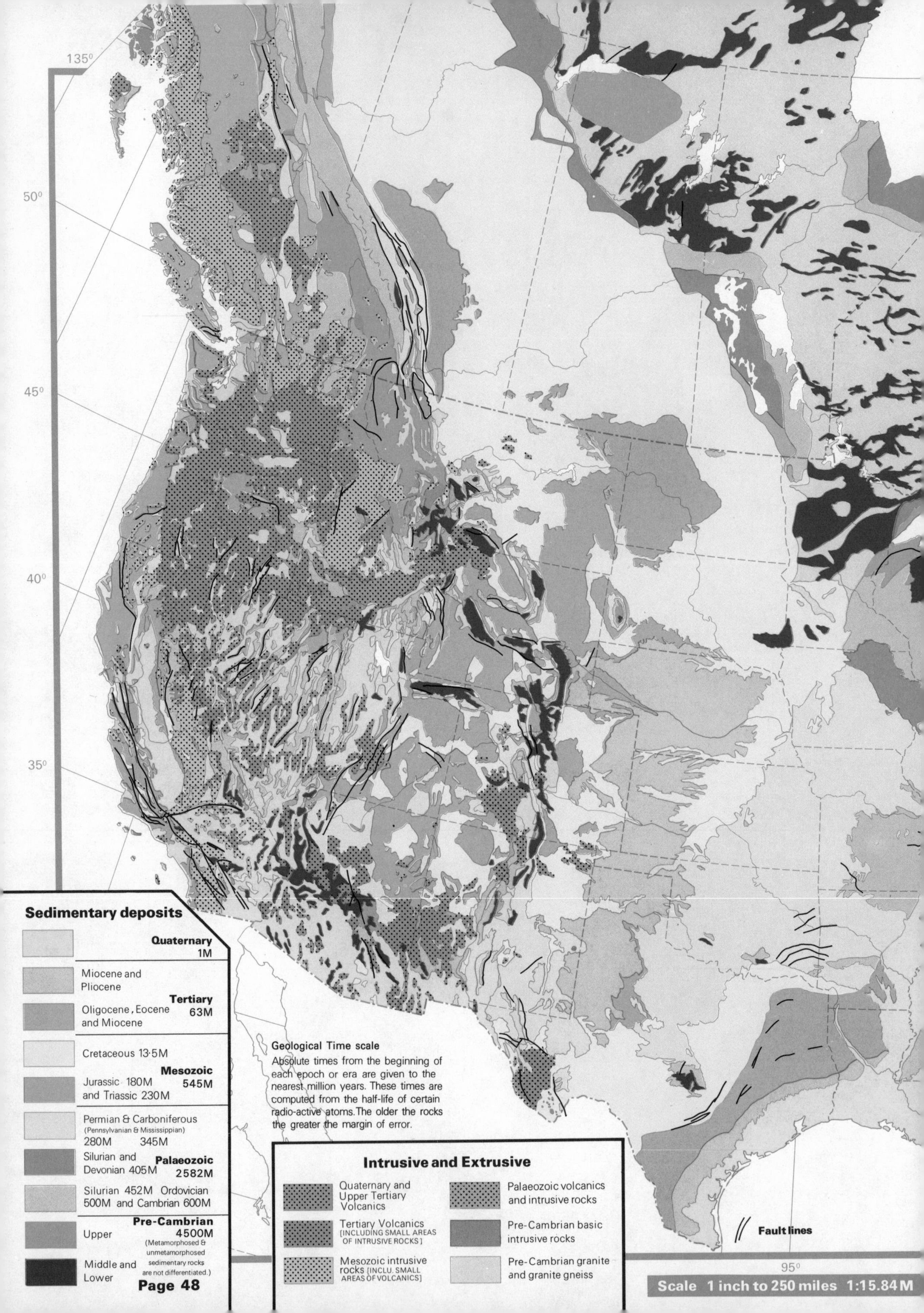

135°

50°

45°

40°

35°

Sedimentary deposits

	Quaternary 1M
	Miocene and Pliocene
	Oligocene, Eocene and Miocene **Tertiary** 63M
	Cretaceous 13·5M
	Jurassic 180M and Triassic 230M **Mesozoic** 545M
	Permian & Carboniferous (Pennsylvanian & Mississippian) 280M 345M
	Silurian and Devonian 405M **Palaeozoic** 2582M
	Silurian 452M Ordovician 500M and Cambrian 600M
	Upper **Pre-Cambrian** 4500M
	Middle and Lower (Metamorphosed & unmetamorphosed sedimentary rocks are not differentiated.)

Page 48

Geological Time scale
Absolute times from the beginning of each epoch or era are given to the nearest million years. These times are computed from the half-life of certain radio-active atoms. The older the rocks the greater the margin of error.

Intrusive and Extrusive

	Quaternary and Upper Tertiary Volcanics		Palaeozoic volcanics and intrusive rocks
	Tertiary Volcanics [INCLUDING SMALL AREAS OF INTRUSIVE ROCKS]		Pre-Cambrian basic intrusive rocks
	Mesozoic intrusive rocks [INCLU. SMALL AREAS OF VOLCANICS]		Pre-Cambrian granite and granite gneiss

// **Fault lines**

95°

Scale   1 inch to 250 miles   1:15.84M

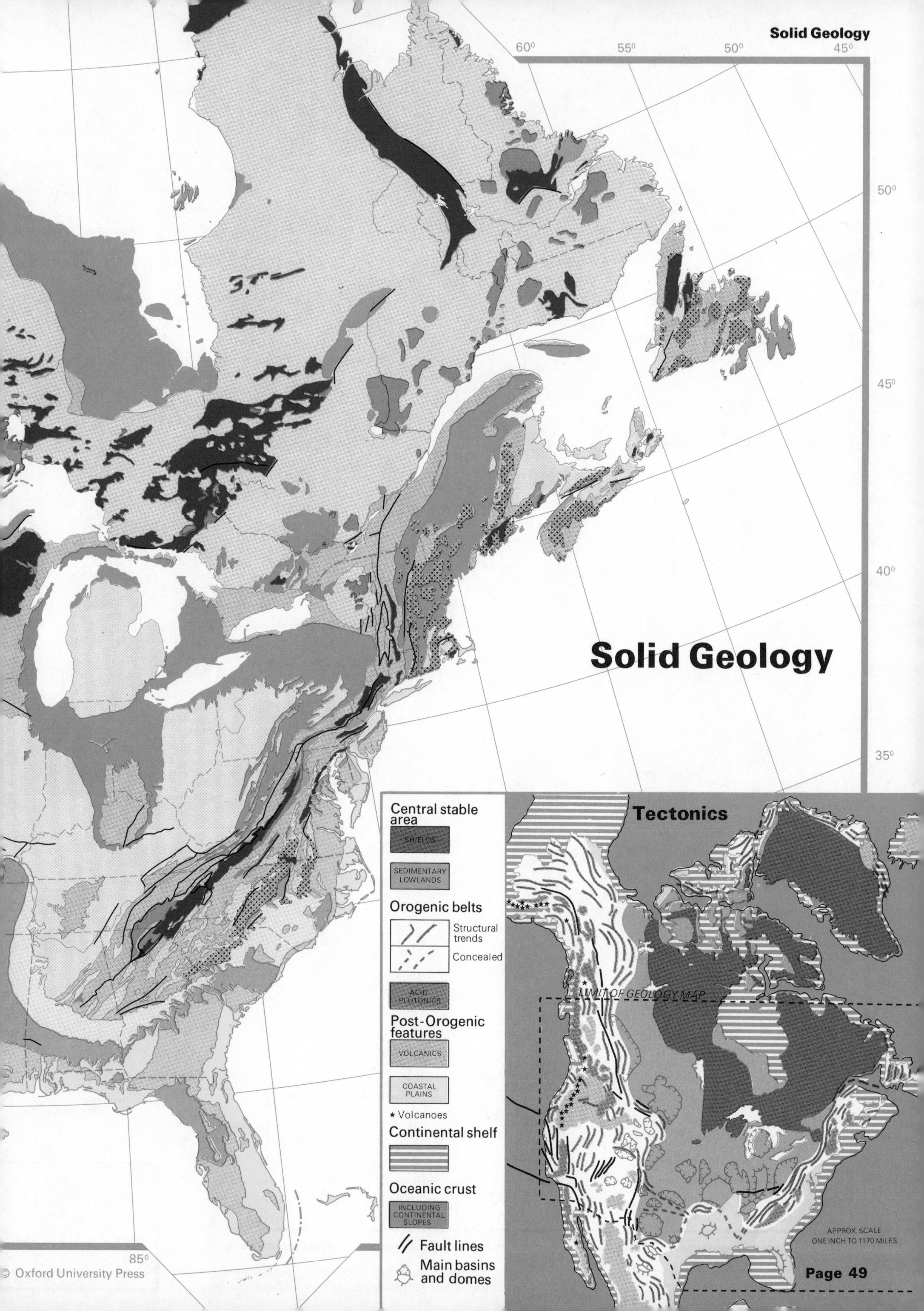

60° 55° 50° 45°

50°

45°

40°

35°

Solid Geology

Central stable area
- SHIELDS
- SEDIMENTARY LOWLANDS

Orogenic belts
- Structural trends
- Concealed
- ACID PLUTONICS

Post-Orogenic features
- VOLCANICS
- COASTAL PLAINS
- ★ Volcanoes

Continental shelf

Oceanic crust
- INCLUDING CONTINENTAL SLOPES
- // Fault lines
- Main basins and domes

Tectonics

LIMIT OF GEOLOGY MAP

APPROX SCALE
ONE INCH TO 1170 MILES

85°

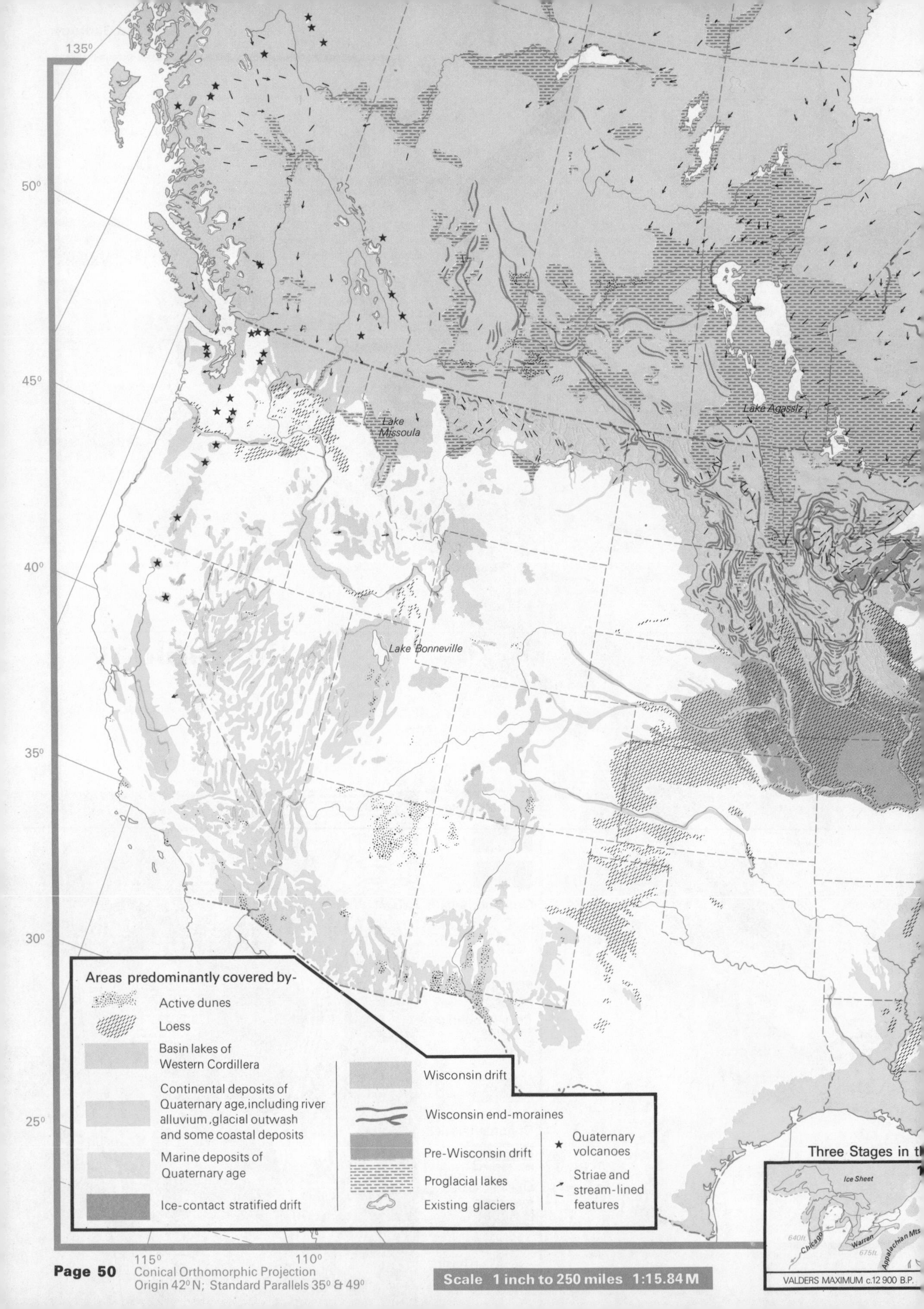

135°

50°

45°

40°

35°

30°

25°

Lake
Missoula

Lake Bonneville

Lake Agassiz

Areas predominantly covered by-

Active dunes

Loess

Basin lakes of
Western Cordillera

Continental deposits of
Quaternary age, including river
alluvium, glacial outwash
and some coastal deposits

Marine deposits of
Quaternary age

Ice-contact stratified drift

Wisconsin drift

Wisconsin end-moraines

Pre-Wisconsin drift

Proglacial lakes

Existing glaciers

Quaternary
volcanoes

Striae and
stream-lined
features

Three Stages in th

Ice Sheet

640ft

Chicago

Warren

675ft

Applachian Mts

VALDERS MAXIMUM c.12 900 B.P.

115°   110°

Conical Orthomorphic Projection
Origin 42° N; Standard Parallels 35° & 49°

Scale 1 inch to 250 miles   1:15.84 M

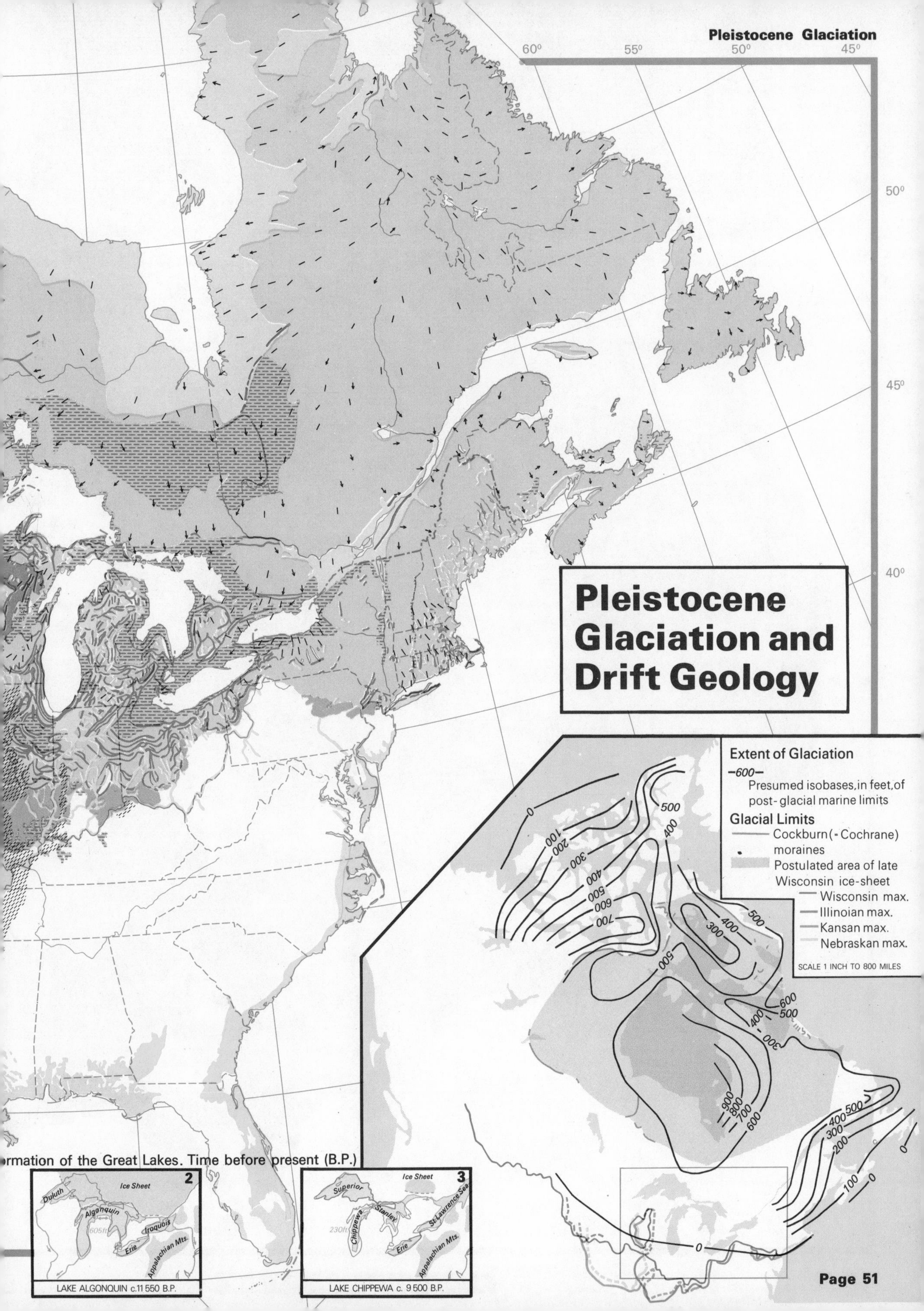

60° 55° 50° 45°

50°

45°

40°

Pleistocene Glaciation and Drift Geology

Extent of Glaciation

—600— Presumed isobases, in feet, of post-glacial marine limits

Glacial Limits

Cockburn (- Cochrane) moraines

Postulated area of late Wisconsin ice-sheet

Wisconsin max.

Illinoian max.

Kansan max.

Nebraskan max.

SCALE 1 INCH TO 800 MILES

...rmation of the Great Lakes. Time before present (B.P.)

Duluth Ice Sheet **2**
Algonquin
605ft. Iroquois
Erie Appalachian Mts.

LAKE ALGONQUIN c.11 550 B.P.

Superior Ice Sheet **3**
Chippewa Stanley St Lawrence Sea
230ft. Erie Appalachian Mts.

LAKE CHIPPEWA c. 9 500 B.P.

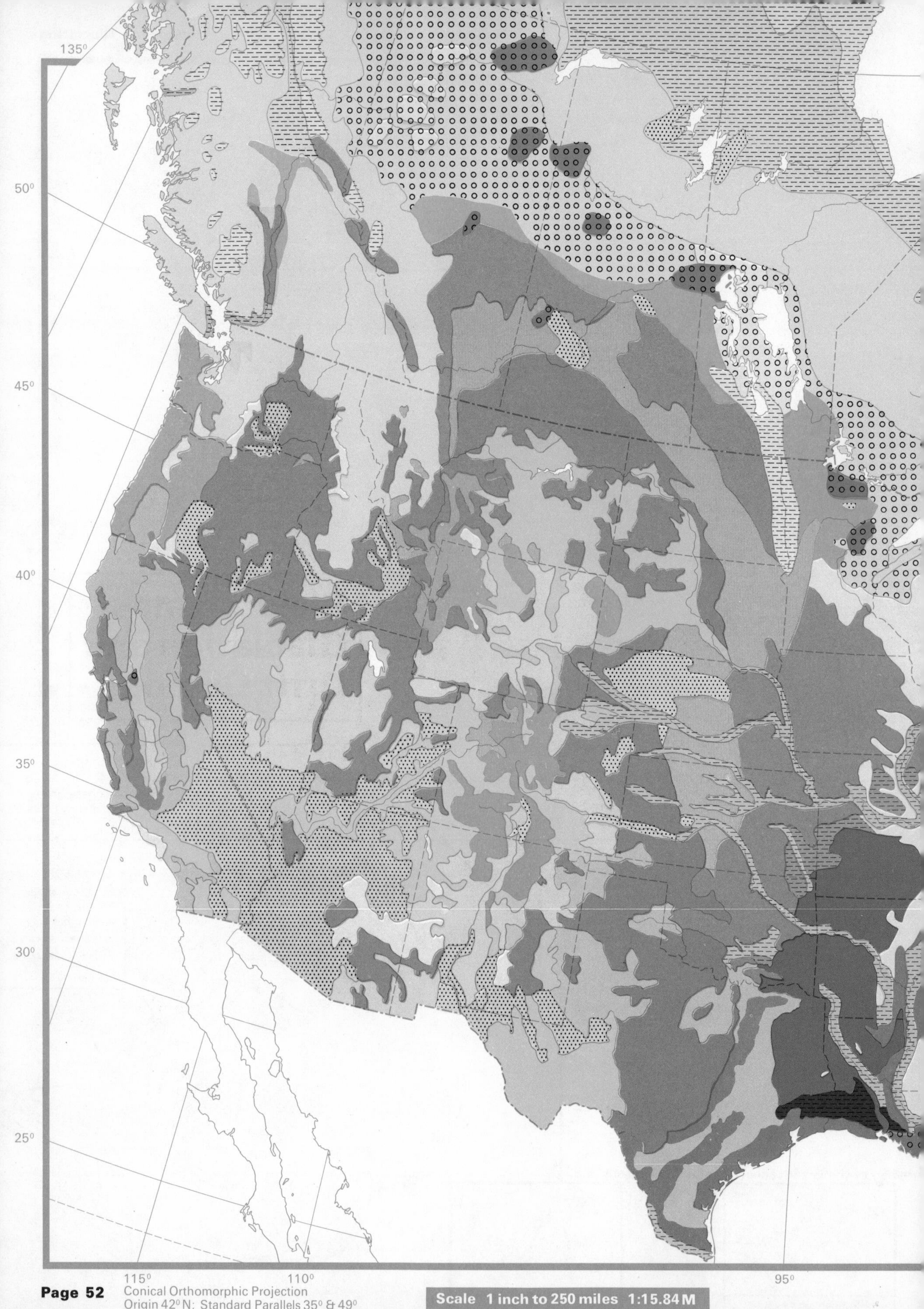

Conical Orthomorphic Projection
Origin 42° N; Standard Parallels 35° & 49°

Scale 1 inch to 250 miles 1:15.84 M

135°

115°   110°   95°

50°

45°

40°

35°

30°

25°

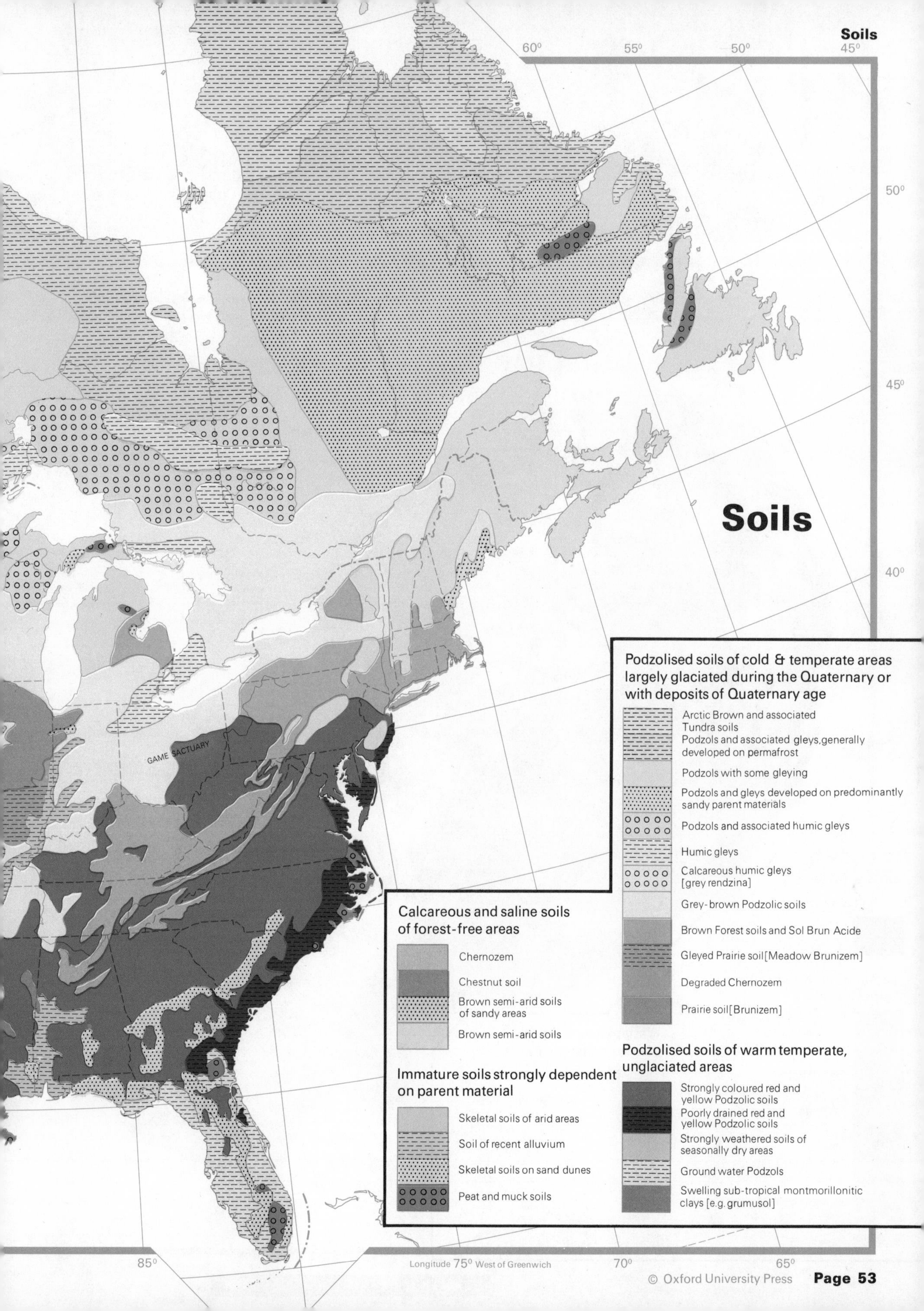

Soils

Podzolised soils of cold & temperate areas largely glaciated during the Quaternary or with deposits of Quaternary age

Arctic Brown and associated Tundra soils

Podzols and associated gleys, generally developed on permafrost

Podzols with some gleying

Podzols and gleys developed on predominantly sandy parent materials

Podzols and associated humic gleys

Humic gleys

Calcareous humic gleys [grey rendzina]

Grey-brown Podzolic soils

Brown Forest soils and Sol Brun Acide

Gleyed Prairie soil [Meadow Brunizem]

Degraded Chernozem

Prairie soil [Brunizem]

Calcareous and saline soils of forest-free areas

Chernozem

Chestnut soil

Brown semi-arid soils of sandy areas

Brown semi-arid soils

Immature soils strongly dependent on parent material

Skeletal soils of arid areas

Soil of recent alluvium

Skeletal soils on sand dunes

Peat and muck soils

Podzolised soils of warm temperate, unglaciated areas

Strongly coloured red and yellow Podzolic soils

Poorly drained red and yellow Podzolic soils

Strongly weathered soils of seasonally dry areas

Ground water Podzols

Swelling sub-tropical montmorillonitic clays [e.g. grumusol]

GAME SANCTUARY

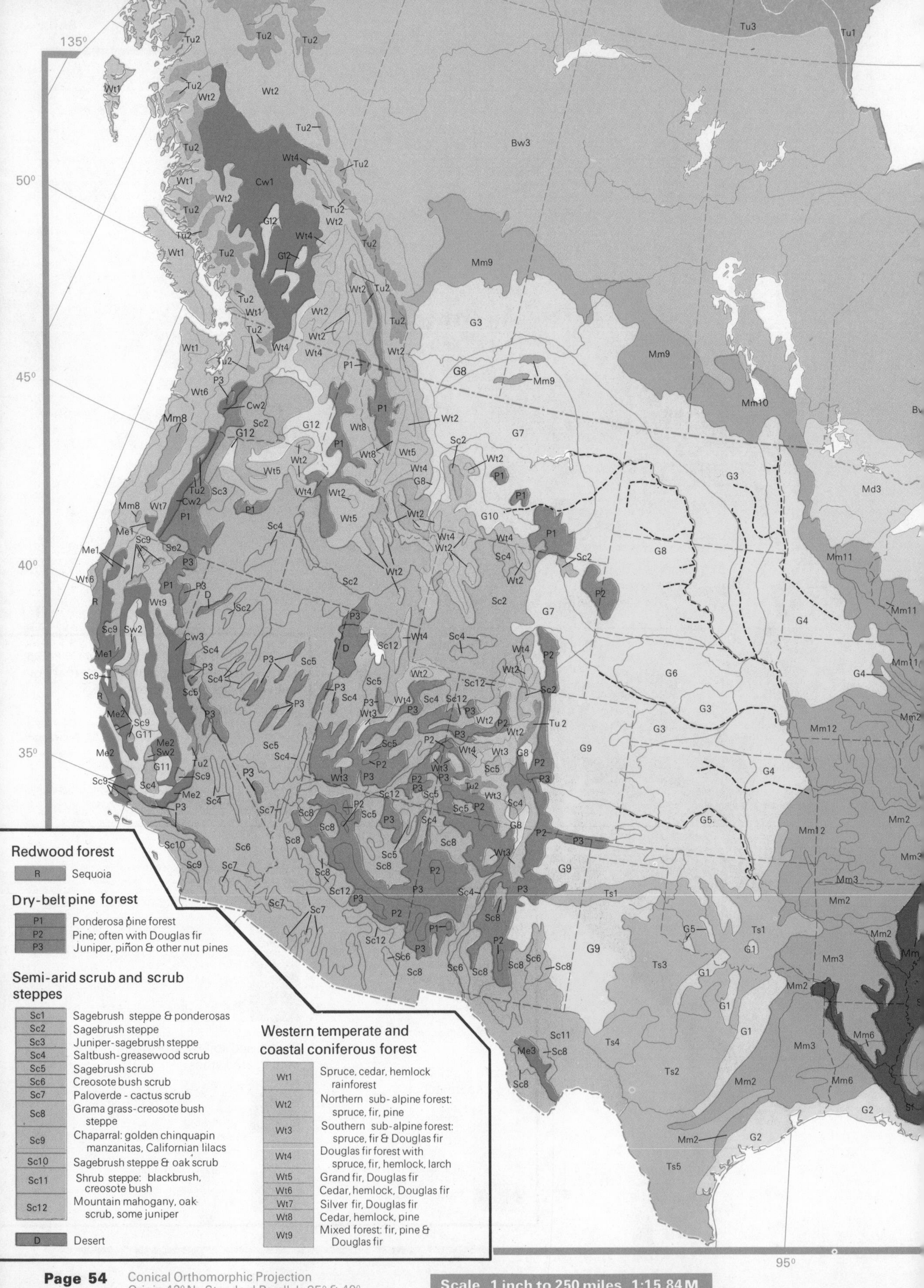

Redwood forest

R	Sequoia

Dry-belt pine forest

P1	Ponderosa pine forest
P2	Pine; often with Douglas fir
P3	Juniper, piñon & other nut pines

Semi-arid scrub and scrub steppes

Sc1	Sagebrush steppe & ponderosas
Sc2	Sagebrush steppe
Sc3	Juniper-sagebrush steppe
Sc4	Saltbush-greasewood scrub
Sc5	Sagebrush scrub
Sc6	Creosote bush scrub
Sc7	Paloverde - cactus scrub
Sc8	Grama grass-creosote bush steppe
Sc9	Chaparral: golden chinquapin manzanitas, Californian lilacs
Sc10	Sagebrush steppe & oak scrub
Sc11	Shrub steppe: blackbrush, creosote bush
Sc12	Mountain mahogany, oak-scrub, some juniper
D	Desert

Western temperate and coastal coniferous forest

Wt1	Spruce, cedar, hemlock rainforest
Wt2	Northern sub-alpine forest: spruce, fir, pine
Wt3	Southern sub-alpine forest: spruce, fir & Douglas fir
Wt4	Douglas fir forest with spruce, fir, hemlock, larch
Wt5	Grand fir, Douglas fir
Wt6	Cedar, hemlock, Douglas fir
Wt7	Silver fir, Douglas fir
Wt8	Cedar, hemlock, pine
Wt9	Mixed forest: fir, pine & Douglas fir

Conical Orthomorphic Projection
Origin 42° N; Standard Parallels 35° & 49°

Scale 1 inch to 250 miles 1:15.84 M

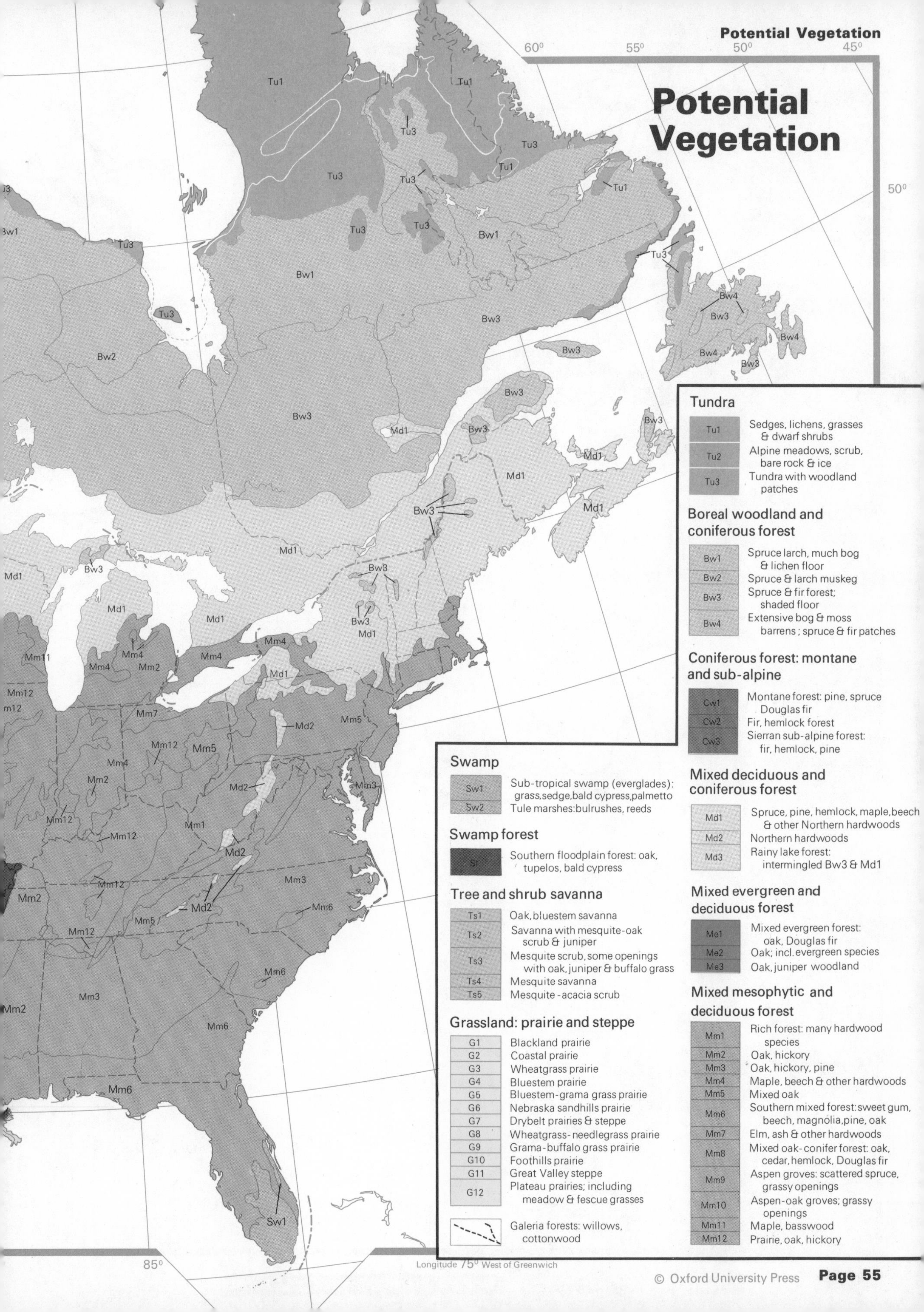

Potential Vegetation

Tundra

Tu1	Sedges, lichens, grasses & dwarf shrubs
Tu2	Alpine meadows, scrub, bare rock & ice
Tu3	Tundra with woodland patches

Boreal woodland and coniferous forest

Bw1	Spruce larch, much bog & lichen floor
Bw2	Spruce & larch muskeg
Bw3	Spruce & fir forest; shaded floor
Bw4	Extensive bog & moss barrens; spruce & fir patches

Coniferous forest: montane and sub-alpine

Cw1	Montane forest: pine, spruce Douglas fir
Cw2	Fir, hemlock forest
Cw3	Sierran sub-alpine forest: fir, hemlock, pine

Mixed deciduous and coniferous forest

Md1	Spruce, pine, hemlock, maple, beech & other Northern hardwoods
Md2	Northern hardwoods
Md3	Rainy lake forest: intermingled Bw3 & Md1

Mixed evergreen and deciduous forest

Me1	Mixed evergreen forest: oak, Douglas fir
Me2	Oak; incl. evergreen species
Me3	Oak, juniper woodland

Mixed mesophytic and deciduous forest

Mm1	Rich forest: many hardwood species
Mm2	Oak, hickory
Mm3	Oak, hickory, pine
Mm4	Maple, beech & other hardwoods
Mm5	Mixed oak
Mm6	Southern mixed forest: sweet gum, beech, magnolia, pine, oak
Mm7	Elm, ash & other hardwoods
Mm8	Mixed oak-conifer forest: oak, cedar, hemlock, Douglas fir
Mm9	Aspen groves: scattered spruce, grassy openings
Mm10	Aspen-oak groves; grassy openings
Mm11	Maple, basswood
Mm12	Prairie, oak, hickory

Swamp

Sw1	Sub-tropical swamp (everglades): grass, sedge, bald cypress, palmetto
Sw2	Tule marshes: bulrushes, reeds

Swamp forest

Sf	Southern floodplain forest: oak, tupelos, bald cypress

Tree and shrub savanna

Ts1	Oak, bluestem savanna
Ts2	Savanna with mesquite-oak scrub & juniper
Ts3	Mesquite scrub, some openings with oak, juniper & buffalo grass
Ts4	Mesquite savanna
Ts5	Mesquite-acacia scrub

Grassland: prairie and steppe

G1	Blackland prairie
G2	Coastal prairie
G3	Wheatgrass prairie
G4	Bluestem prairie
G5	Bluestem-grama grass prairie
G6	Nebraska sandhills prairie
G7	Drybelt prairies & steppe
G8	Wheatgrass-needlegrass prairie
G9	Grama-buffalo grass prairie
G10	Foothills prairie
G11	Great Valley steppe
G12	Plateau prairies; including meadow & fescue grasses

Galeria forests: willows, cottonwood

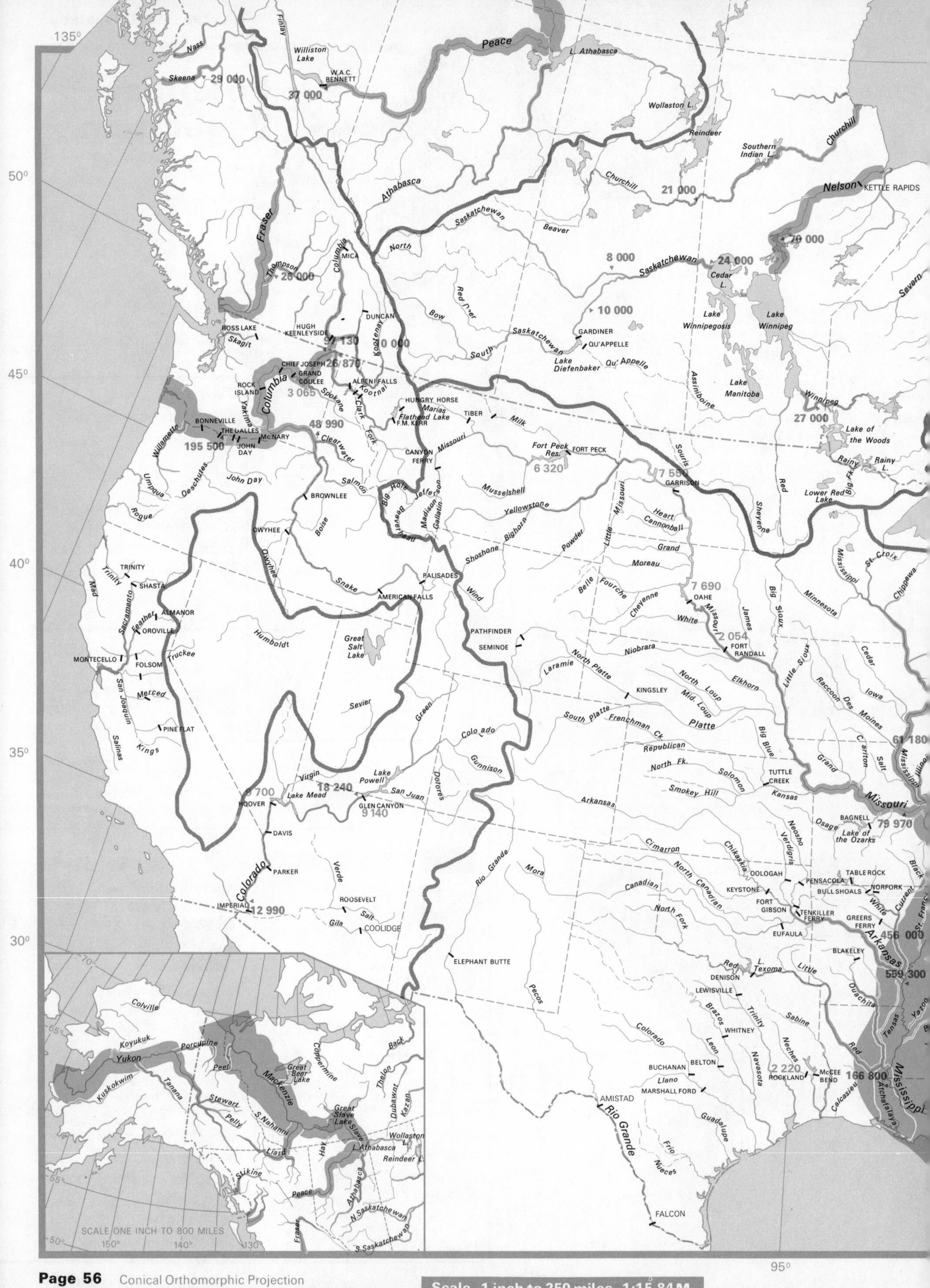

Conical Orthomorphic Projection
Origin 42° N; Standard Parallels 35° & 49°

Scale 1 inch to 250 miles 1:15.84 M

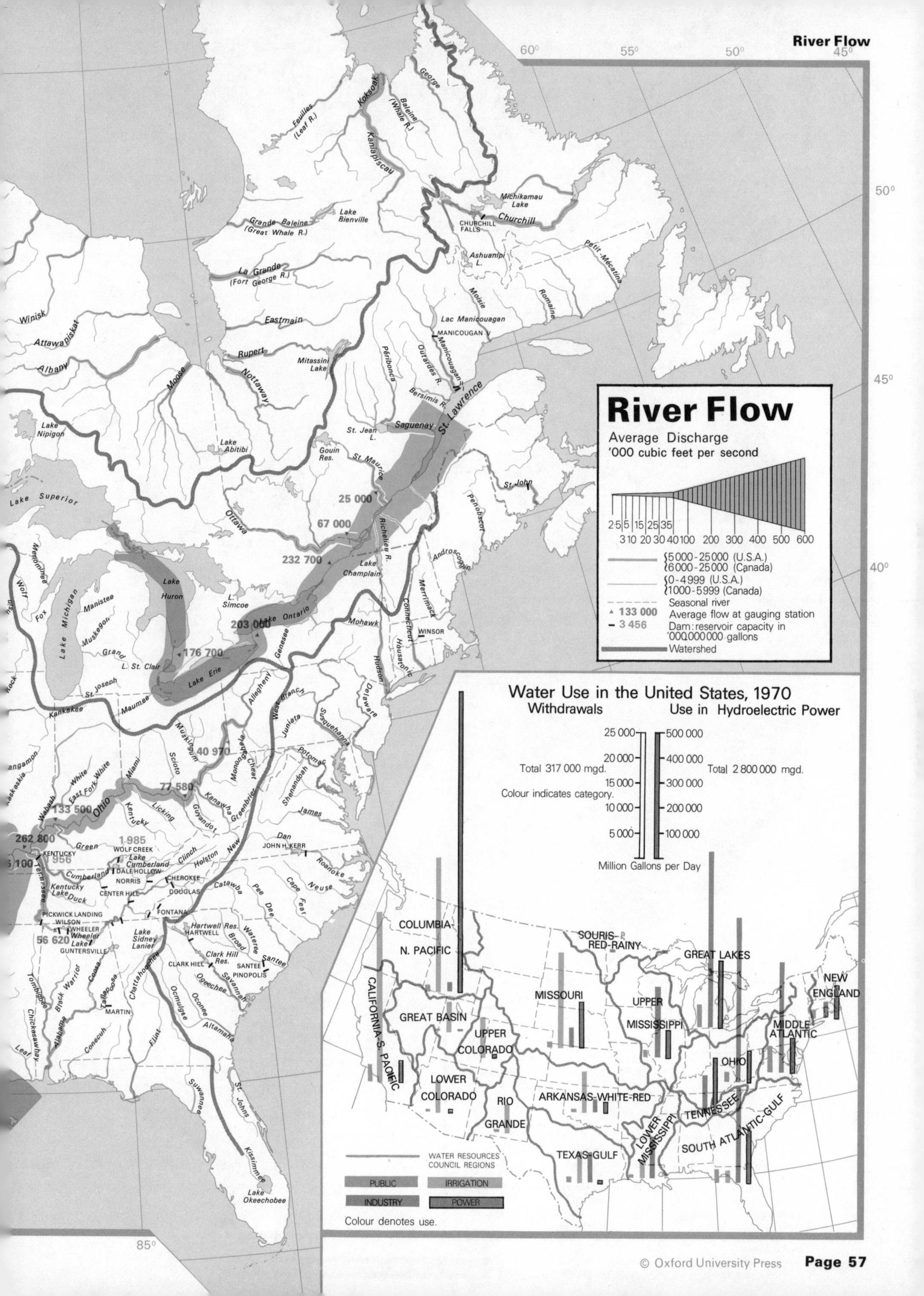

River Flow

Average Discharge
'000 cubic feet per second

| 5000-25000 (U.S.A.) |
| 6000-25000 (Canada) |
| 0-4999 (U.S.A.) |
| 1000-5999 (Canada) |

Seasonal river
▲ 133 000 — Average flow at gauging station
— 3 456 — Dam: reservoir capacity in '000 000 000 gallons
Watershed

Water Use in the United States, 1970
Withdrawals   Use in Hydroelectric Power

Total 317 000 mgd.   Total 2 800 000 mgd.
Colour indicates category.

Million Gallons per Day

WATER RESOURCES COUNCIL REGIONS

PUBLIC   IRRIGATION
INDUSTRY   POWER

Colour denotes use.

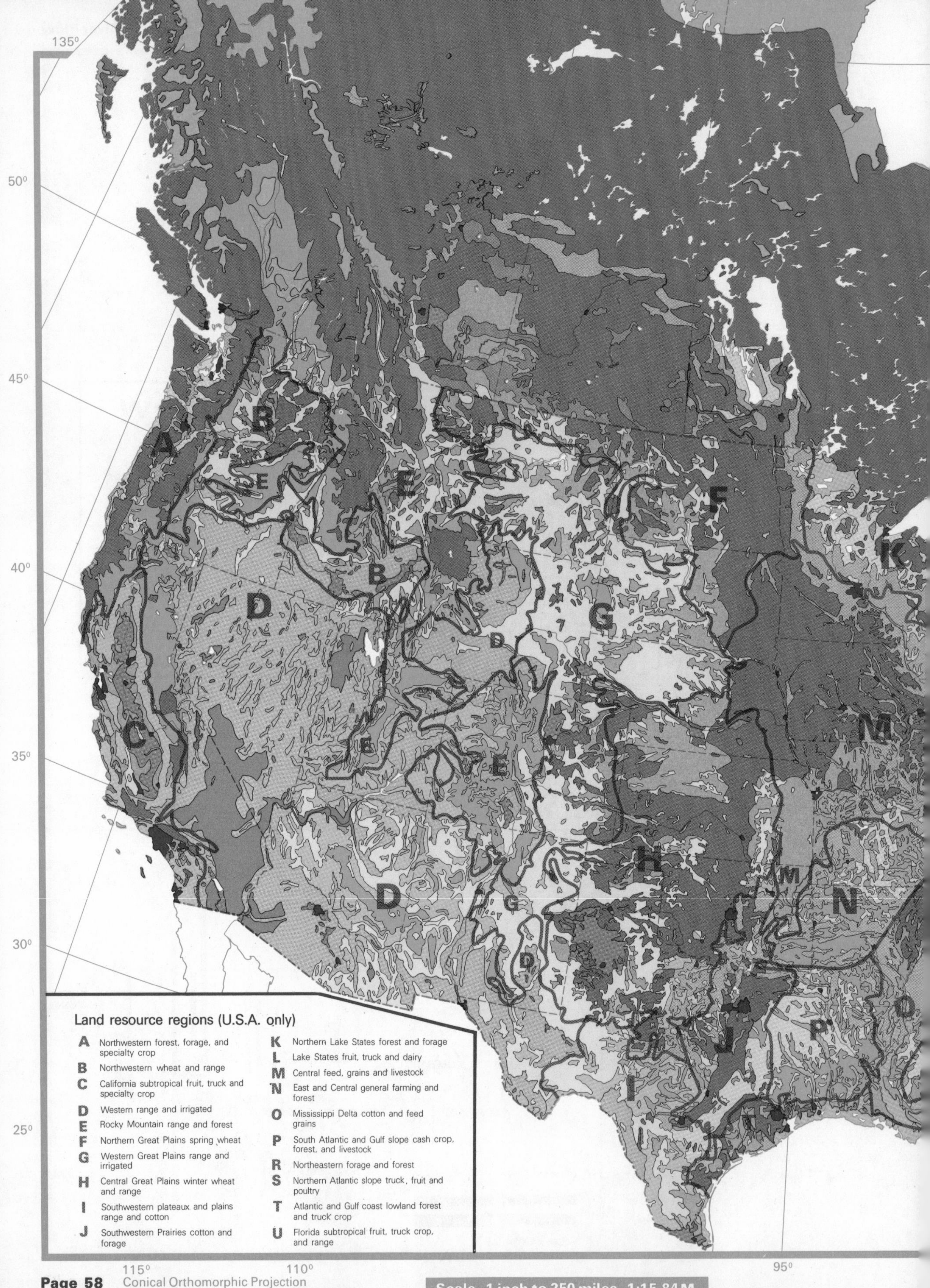

50°

45°

40°

35°

30°

25°

Land resource regions (U.S.A. only)

A Northwestern forest, forage, and specialty crop

B Northwestern wheat and range

C California subtropical fruit, truck and specialty crop

D Western range and irrigated

E Rocky Mountain range and forest

F Northern Great Plains spring wheat

G Western Great Plains range and irrigated

H Central Great Plains winter wheat and range

I Southwestern plateaux and plains range and cotton

J Southwestern Prairies cotton and forage

K Northern Lake States forest and forage

L Lake States fruit, truck and dairy

M Central feed, grains and livestock

N East and Central general farming and forest

O Mississippi Delta cotton and feed grains

P South Atlantic and Gulf slope cash crop, forest, and livestock

R Northeastern forage and forest

S Northern Atlantic slope truck, fruit and poultry

T Atlantic and Gulf coast lowland forest and truck crop

U Florida subtropical fruit, truck crop, and range

115°   110°   95°

Scale 1 inch to 250 miles 1:15.84 M

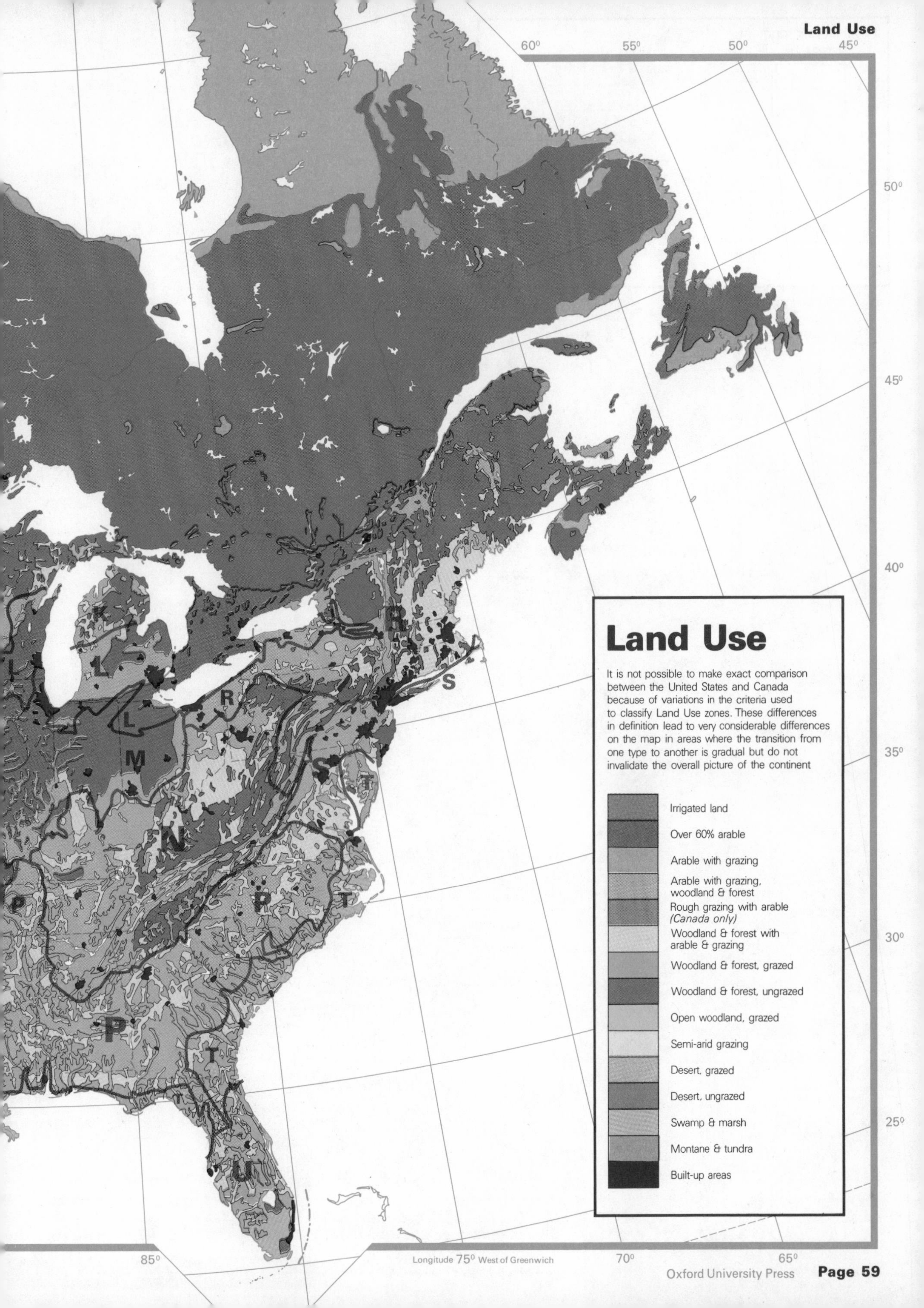

Land Use

It is not possible to make exact comparison between the United States and Canada because of variations in the criteria used to classify Land Use zones. These differences in definition lead to very considerable differences on the map in areas where the transition from one type to another is gradual but do not invalidate the overall picture of the continent

Irrigated land

Over 60% arable

Arable with grazing

Arable with grazing, woodland & forest

Rough grazing with arable *(Canada only)*

Woodland & forest with arable & grazing

Woodland & forest, grazed

Woodland & forest, ungrazed

Open woodland, grazed

Semi-arid grazing

Desert, grazed

Desert, ungrazed

Swamp & marsh

Montane & tundra

Built-up areas

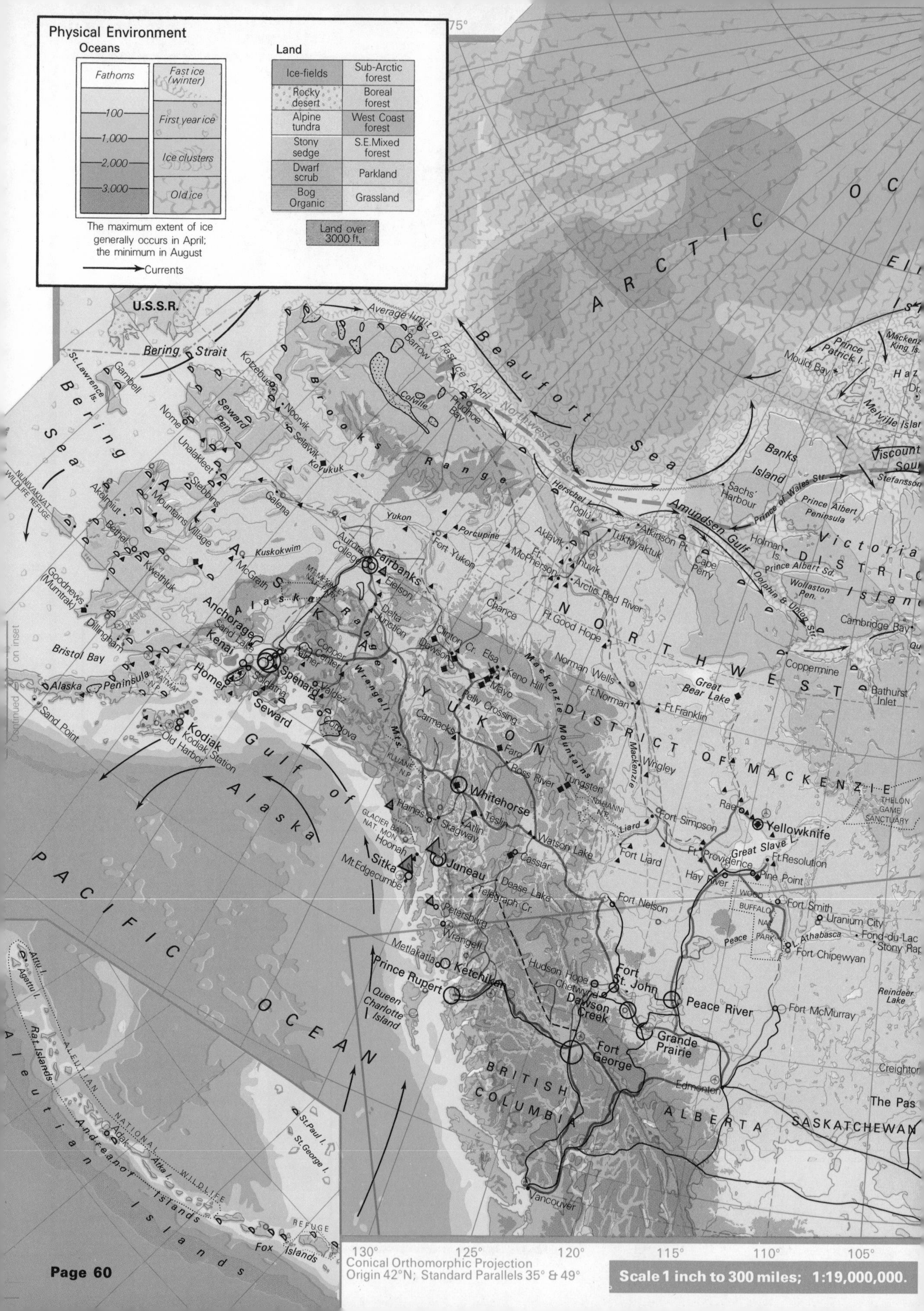

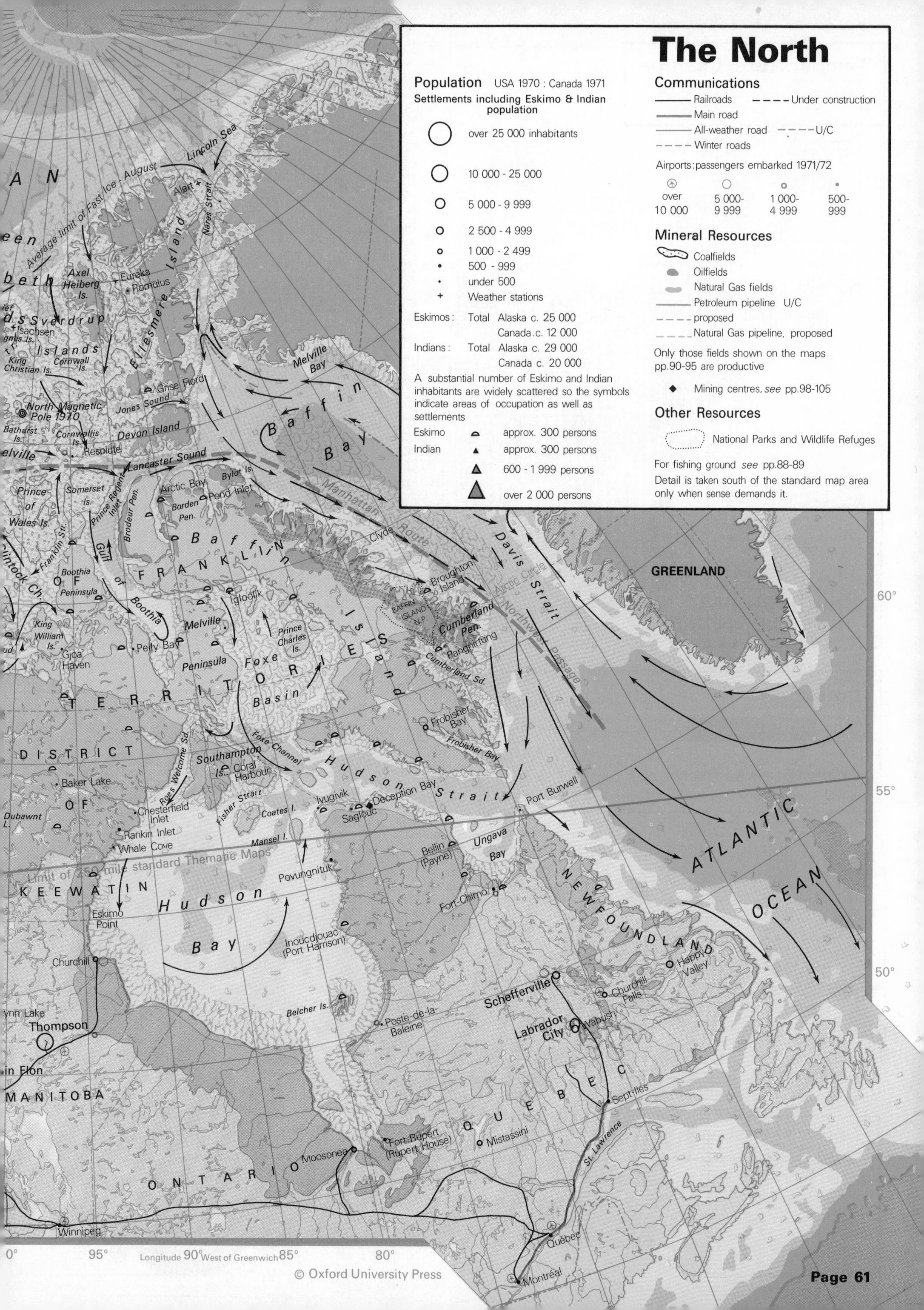

The North

Population USA 1970 : Canada 1971
Settlements including Eskimo & Indian population

○ over 25 000 inhabitants
○ 10 000 - 25 000
○ 5 000 - 9 999
○ 2 500 - 4 999
○ 1 000 - 2 499
• 500 - 999
· under 500
+ Weather stations

Eskimos : Total Alaska c. 25 000
                          Canada c. 12 000

Indians : Total Alaska c. 29 000
                         Canada c. 20 000

A substantial number of Eskimo and Indian inhabitants are widely scattered so the symbols indicate areas of occupation as well as settlements

Eskimo   ◖   approx. 300 persons
Indian   ▲   approx. 300 persons
               ▲   600 - 1 999 persons
               ▲   over 2 000 persons

Communications

— Railroads   ----- Under construction
— Main road
— All-weather road   ----- U/C
---- Winter roads

Airports : passengers embarked 1971/72

⊕ over 10 000   ○ 5 000- 9 999   ○ 1 000- 4 999   · 500- 999

Mineral Resources

▭ Coalfields
◖ Oilfields
◖ Natural Gas fields
— Petroleum pipeline U/C
---- proposed
---- Natural Gas pipeline, proposed

Only those fields shown on the maps pp.90-95 are productive

◆ Mining centres, *see* pp.98-105

Other Resources

⬭ National Parks and Wildlife Refuges

For fishing ground *see* pp.88-89
Detail is taken south of the standard map area only when sense demands it.

GREENLAND

ATLANTIC

OCEAN

NEWFOUNDLAND

QUEBEC

ONTARIO

MANITOBA

KEEWATIN

DISTRICT OF

TERRITORIES

FRANKLIN

Baffin Island

Baffin Bay

Davis Strait

Hudson Bay

Hudson Strait

Foxe Basin

Foxe Channel

Lincoln Sea

Nares Strait

Melville Bay

Jones Sound

Lancaster Sound

Devon Island

Ellesmere Island

Axel Heiberg Is.

Sverdrup Islands

King Christian Is.

Cornwall Is.

Isachsen

Eureka

Alert

Romulus

Grise Fiord

North Magnetic Pole 1970

Cornwallis Is.

Resolute

Bathurst Is.

Prince of Wales Is.

Somerset Is.

Boothia Peninsula

Gulf of Boothia

King William Is.

Gjoa Haven

Pelly Bay

Melville Peninsula

Prince Charles Is.

Igloolik

Arctic Bay

Borden Pen.

Brodeur Pen.

Bylot Is.

Pond Inlet

Clyde

Broughton Island

BAFFIN ISLAND N.P

Cumberland Pen.

Pangnirtung

Cumberland Sd.

Frobisher Bay

Southampton Is.

Coral Harbour

Fisher Strait

Coates I.

Mansel I.

Baker Lake

Chesterfield Inlet

Rankin Inlet

Whale Cove

Dubawnt L.

Eskimo Point

Churchill

Thompson

nn Lake

in Flon

Belcher Is.

Ivugivik

Sugluk

Deception Bay

Port Burwell

Bellin (Payne)

Ungava Bay

Fort Chimo

Povungnituk

Inoucdjouac (Port Harrison)

Poste-de-la-Baleine

Fort Rupert (Rupert House)

Mistassini

Moosonee

Schefferville

Labrador City

Wabush

Churchill Falls

Happy Valley

Septiles

St. Lawrence

Québec

Montréal

Winnipeg

Average limit of Fast-ice August

Arctic Circle

North-West passage

Manhattan Route

Prince Regent

Franklin Str.

Clintock Ch.

Ross Welcome Sd.

Rae

Limit of 2 : 50 mile standard Thematic Maps

60°
55°
50°

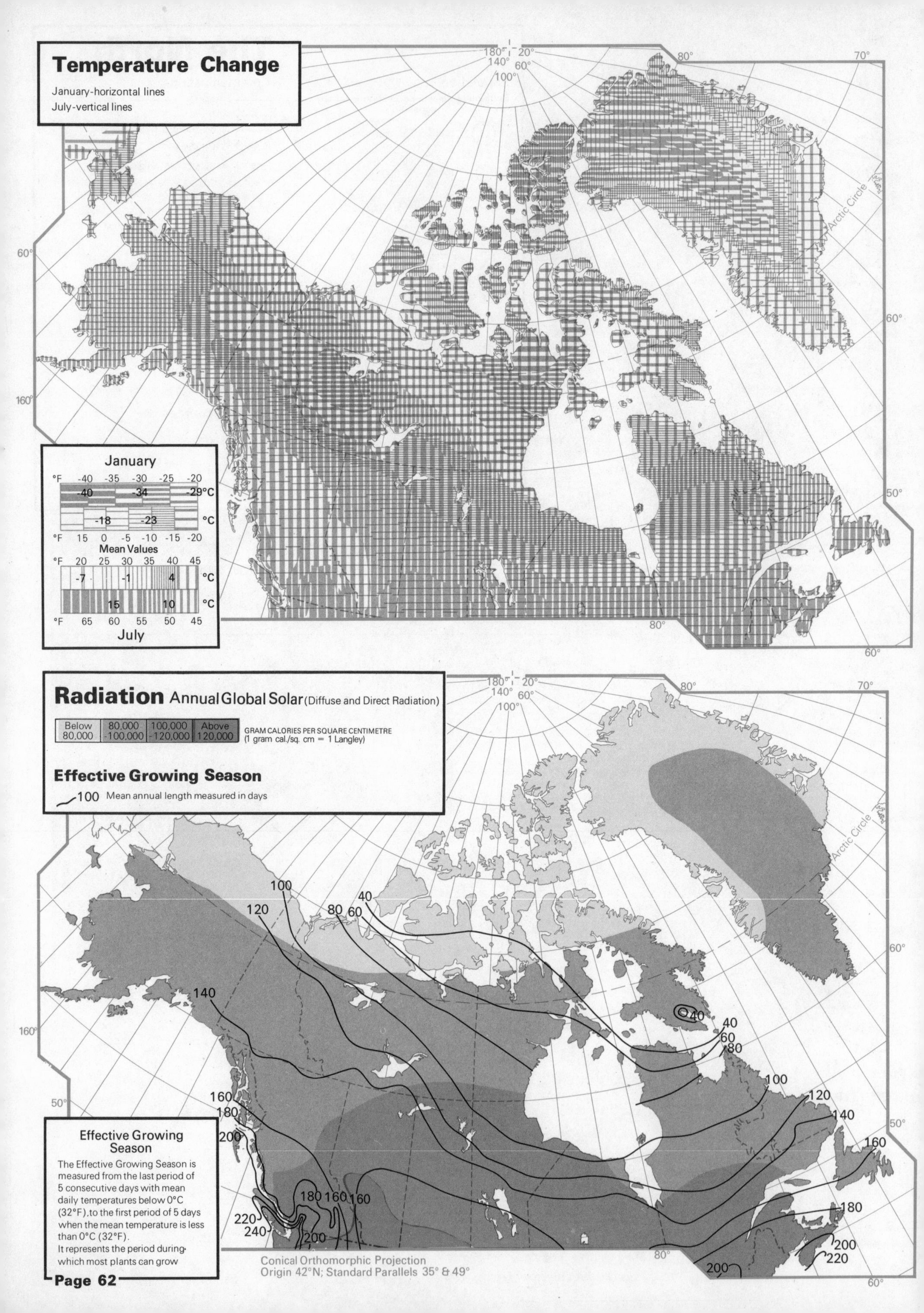

Temperature Change

January-horizontal lines
July-vertical lines

January

°F	-40	-35	-30	-25	-20
	-40		**-34**		**-29**°C
		-18		**-23**	°C

| °F | 15 | 10 | 5 | 0 | -5 | -10 | -15 | -20 |

Mean Values

°F	20	25	30	35	40	45
	-7		**-1**		**4**	°C
		15			**10**	°C

| °F | 65 | 60 | 55 | 50 | 45 |

July

Radiation Annual Global Solar (Diffuse and Direct Radiation)

Below 80,000	80,000 -100,000	100,000 -120,000	Above 120,000

GRAM CALORIES PER SQUARE CENTIMETRE
(1 gram cal./sq. cm = 1 Langley)

Effective Growing Season

⌒100 Mean annual length measured in days

Effective Growing Season

The Effective Growing Season is measured from the last period of 5 consecutive days with mean daily temperatures below 0°C (32°F), to the first period of 5 days when the mean temperature is less than 0°C (32°F).
It represents the period during which most plants can grow

Conical Orthomorphic Projection
Origin 42°N; Standard Parallels 35° & 49°

Page 62

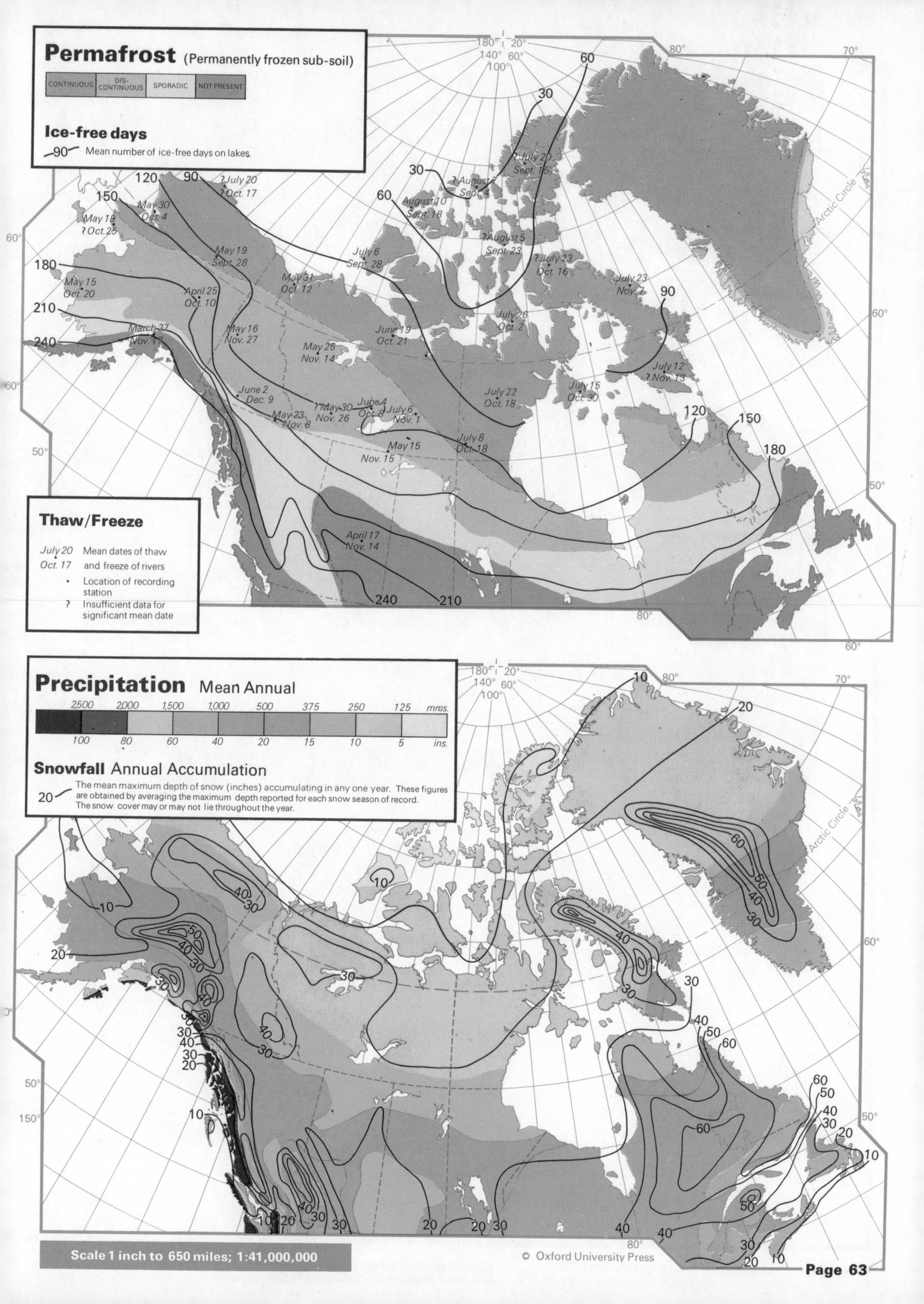

Permafrost (Permanently frozen sub-soil)

CONTINUOUS	DIS-CONTINUOUS	SPORADIC	NOT PRESENT

Ice-free days

—90— Mean number of ice-free days on lakes.

Thaw/Freeze

July 20   Mean dates of thaw
Oct. 17   and freeze of rivers

•   Location of recording station

?   Insufficient data for significant mean date

Precipitation   Mean Annual

2500	2000	1,500	1,000	500	375	250	125	mms.
100	80	60	40	20	15	10	5	ins.

Snowfall   Annual Accumulation

—20— The mean maximum depth of snow (inches) accumulating in any one year. These figures are obtained by averaging the maximum depth reported for each snow season of record. The snow cover may or may not lie throughout the year.

Scale 1 inch to 650 miles; 1:41,000,000

© Oxford University Press

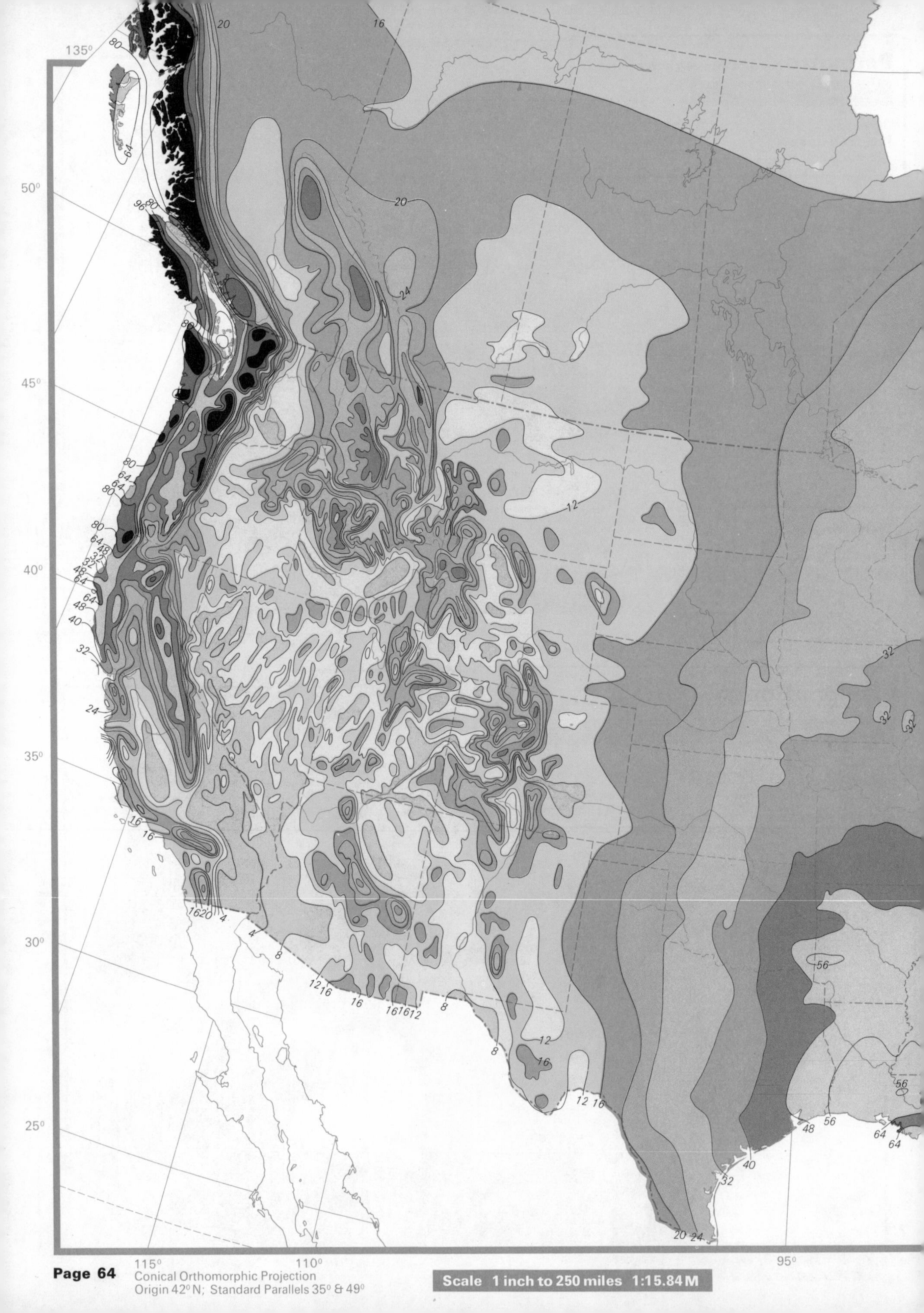

Conical Orthomorphic Projection
Origin 42° N; Standard Parallels 35° & 49°

Scale 1 inch to 250 miles 1:15.84 M

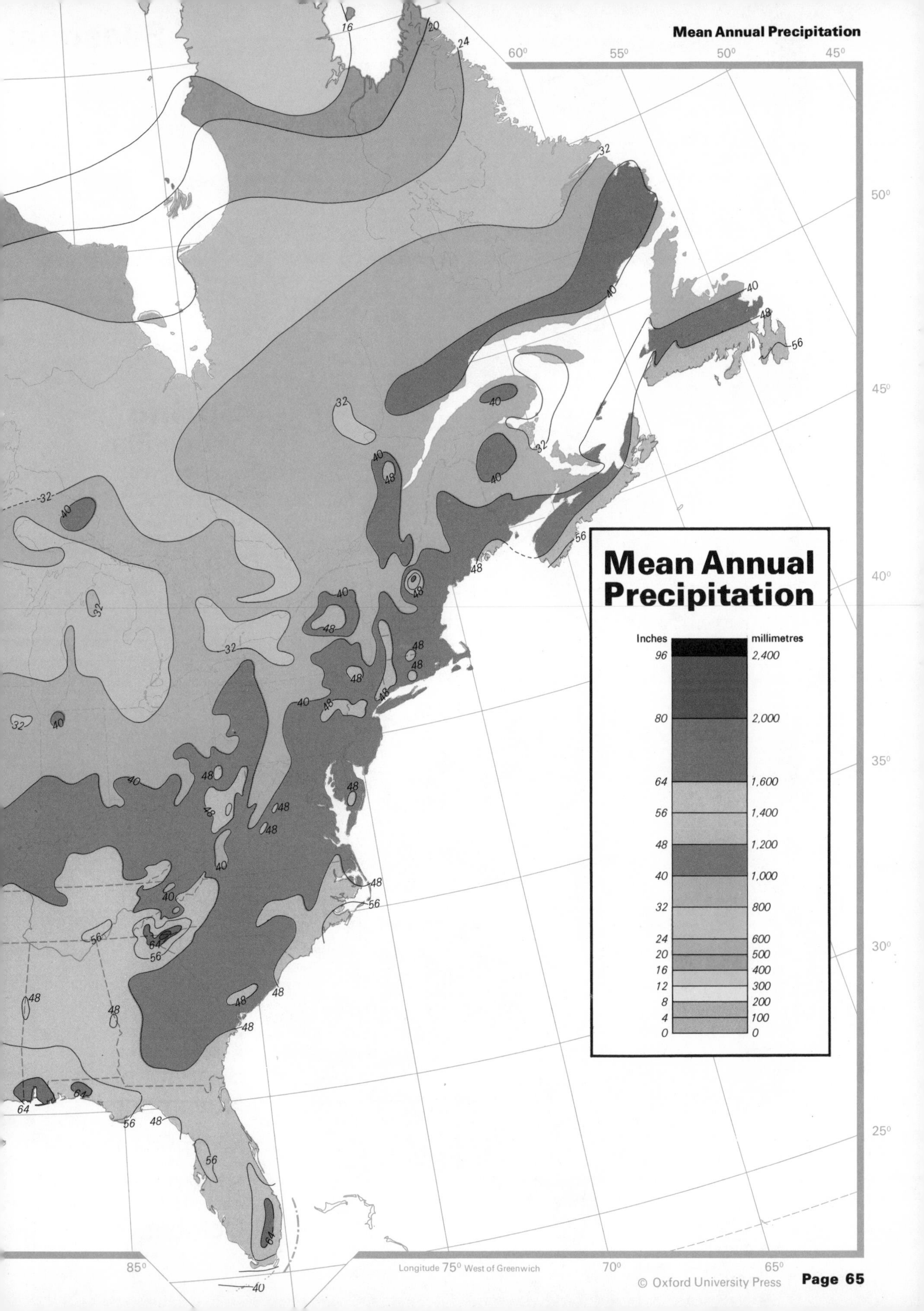

Mean Annual Precipitation

Inches		millimetres
96		2,400
80		2,000
64		1,600
56		1,400
48		1,200
40		1,000
32		800
24		600
20		500
16		400
12		300
8		200
4		100
0		0

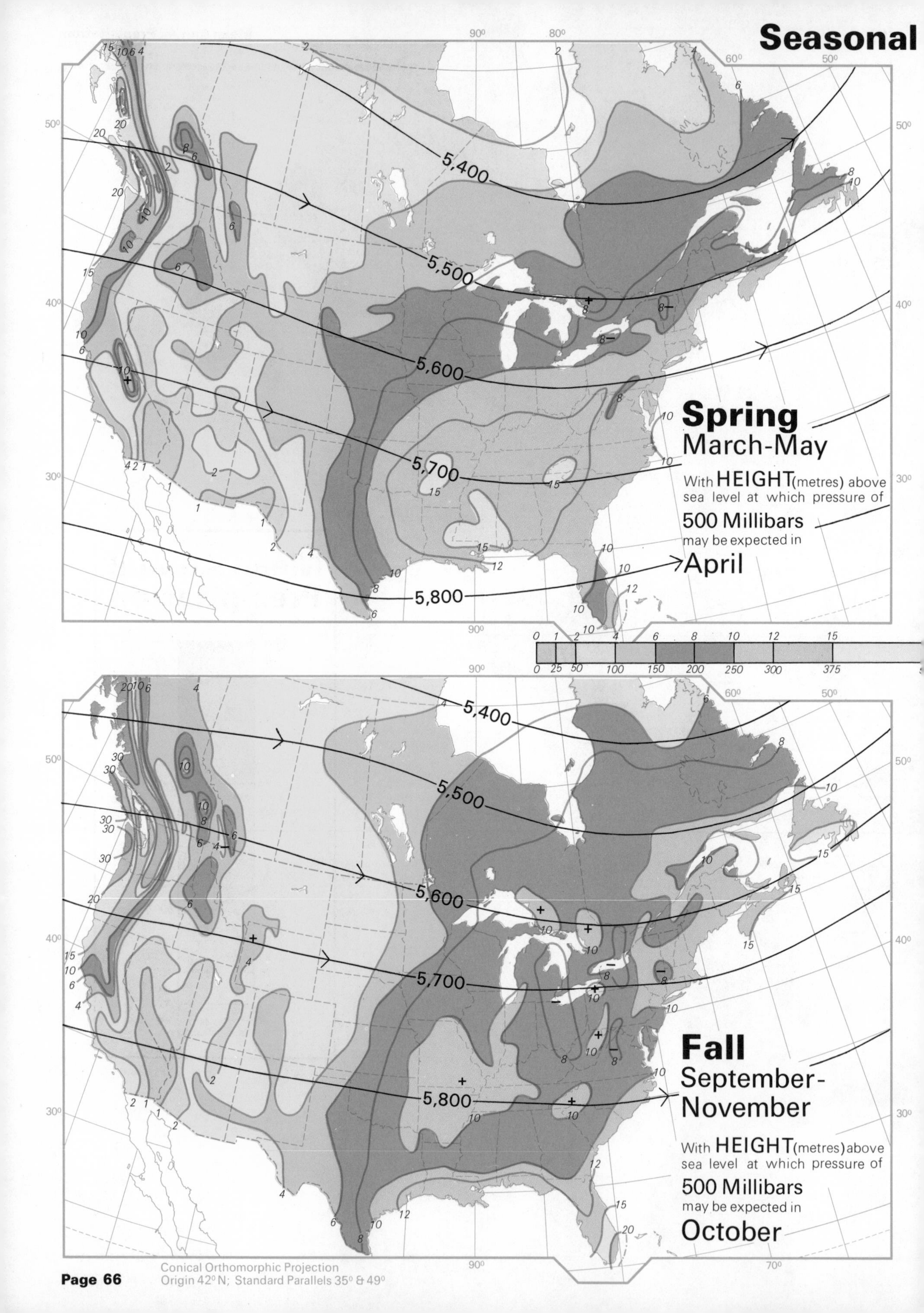

Spring
March-May

With HEIGHT(metres) above
sea level at which pressure of

500 Millibars
may be expected in
→April

5,400

5,500

5,600

5,700

5,800

0	1	2	4	6	8	10	12	15
0	25	50	100	150	200	250	300	375

5,400

5,500

5,600

5,700

5,800

Fall
September-
November

With HEIGHT(metres)above
sea level at which pressure of

500 Millibars
may be expected in
October

Conical Orthomorphic Projection
Origin 42° N; Standard Parallels 35° & 49°

Precipitation

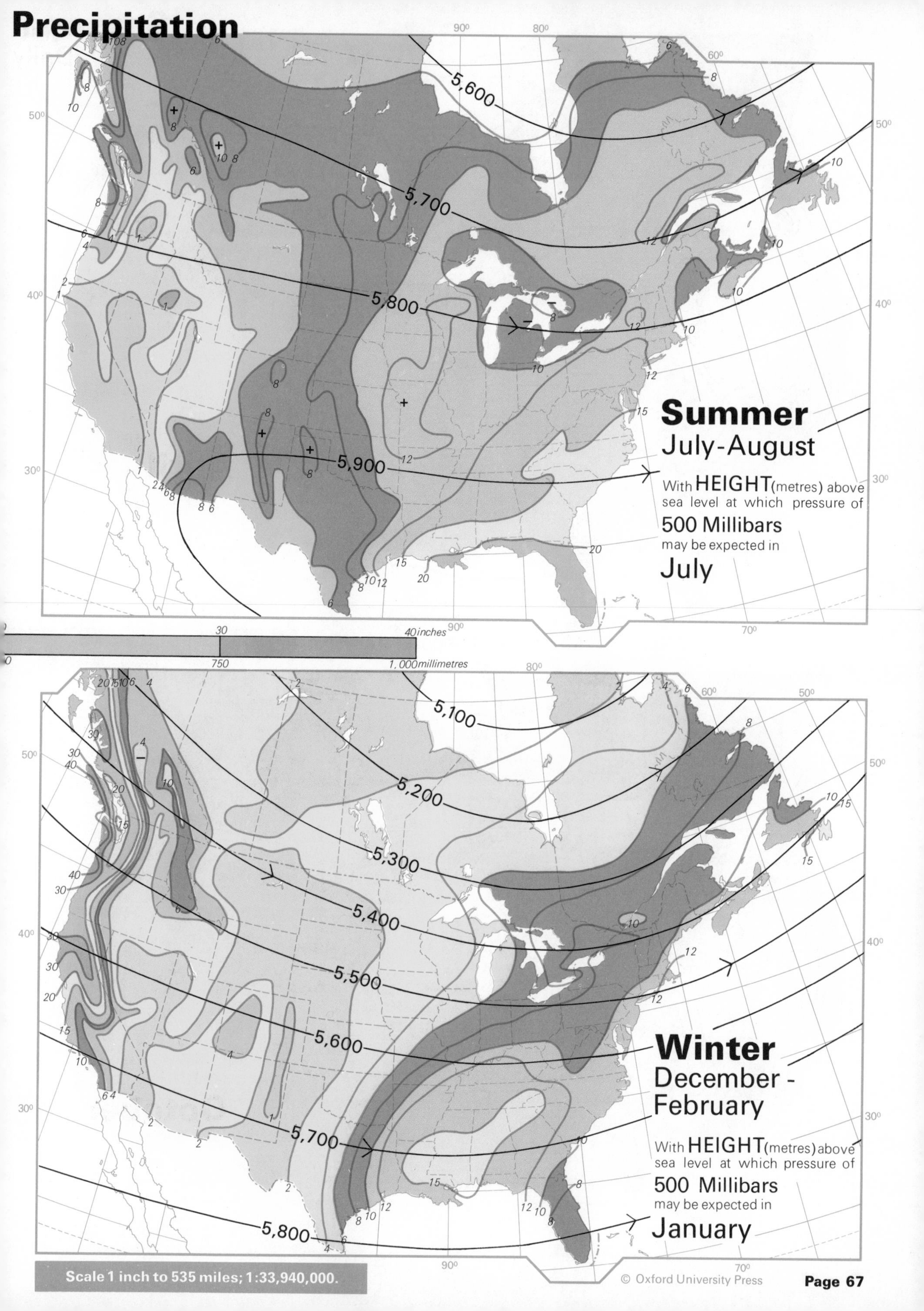

Summer
July-August

With HEIGHT (metres) above sea level at which pressure of **500 Millibars** may be expected in July

Winter
December - February

With HEIGHT (metres) above sea level at which pressure of **500 Millibars** may be expected in January

Scale 1 inch to 535 miles; 1:33,940,000.

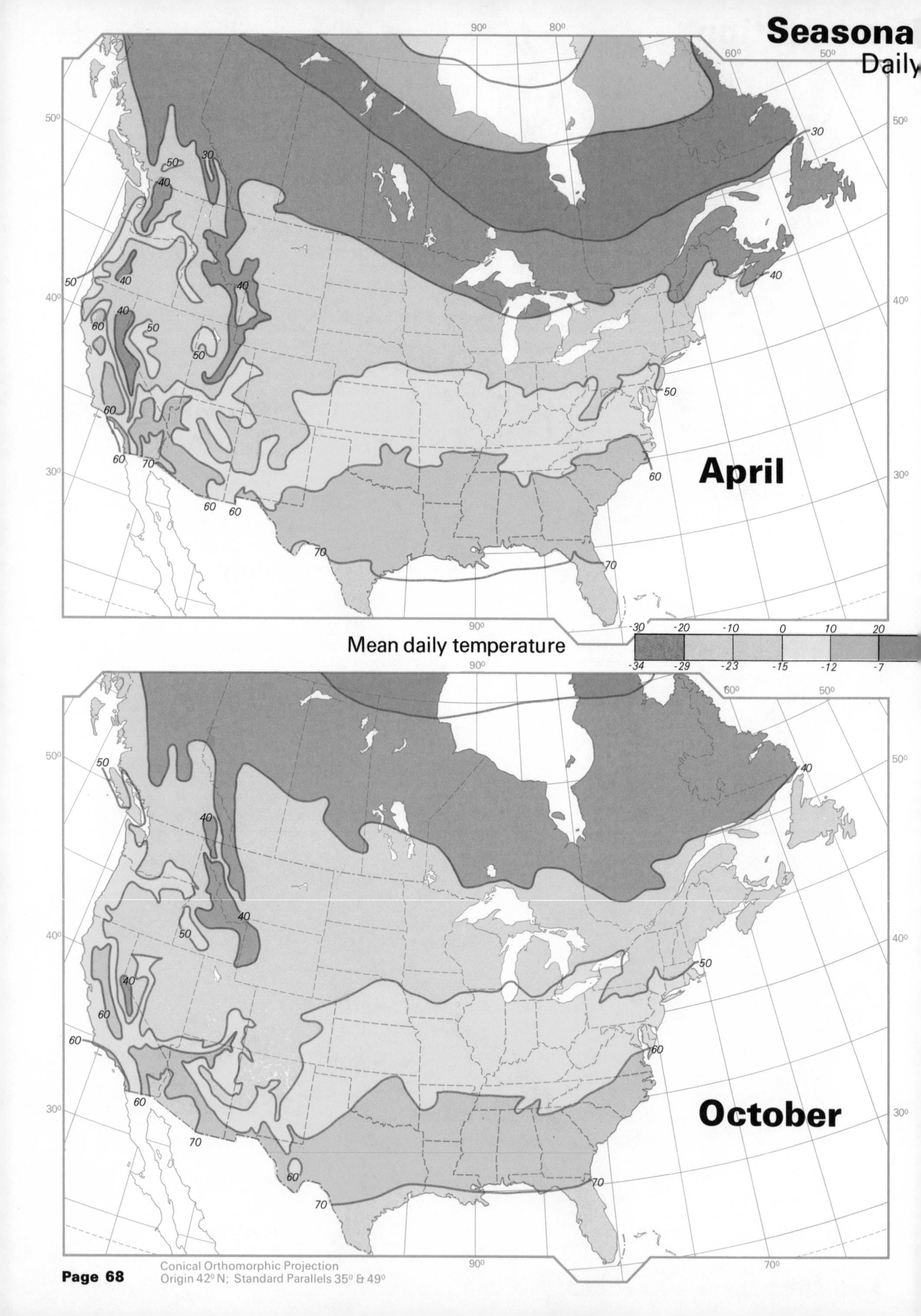

April

Mean daily temperature

-30	-20	-10	0	10	20
-34	-29	-23	-15	-12	-7

October

Conical Orthomorphic Projection
Origin 42° N; Standard Parallels 35° & 49°

Temperature
Mean °F

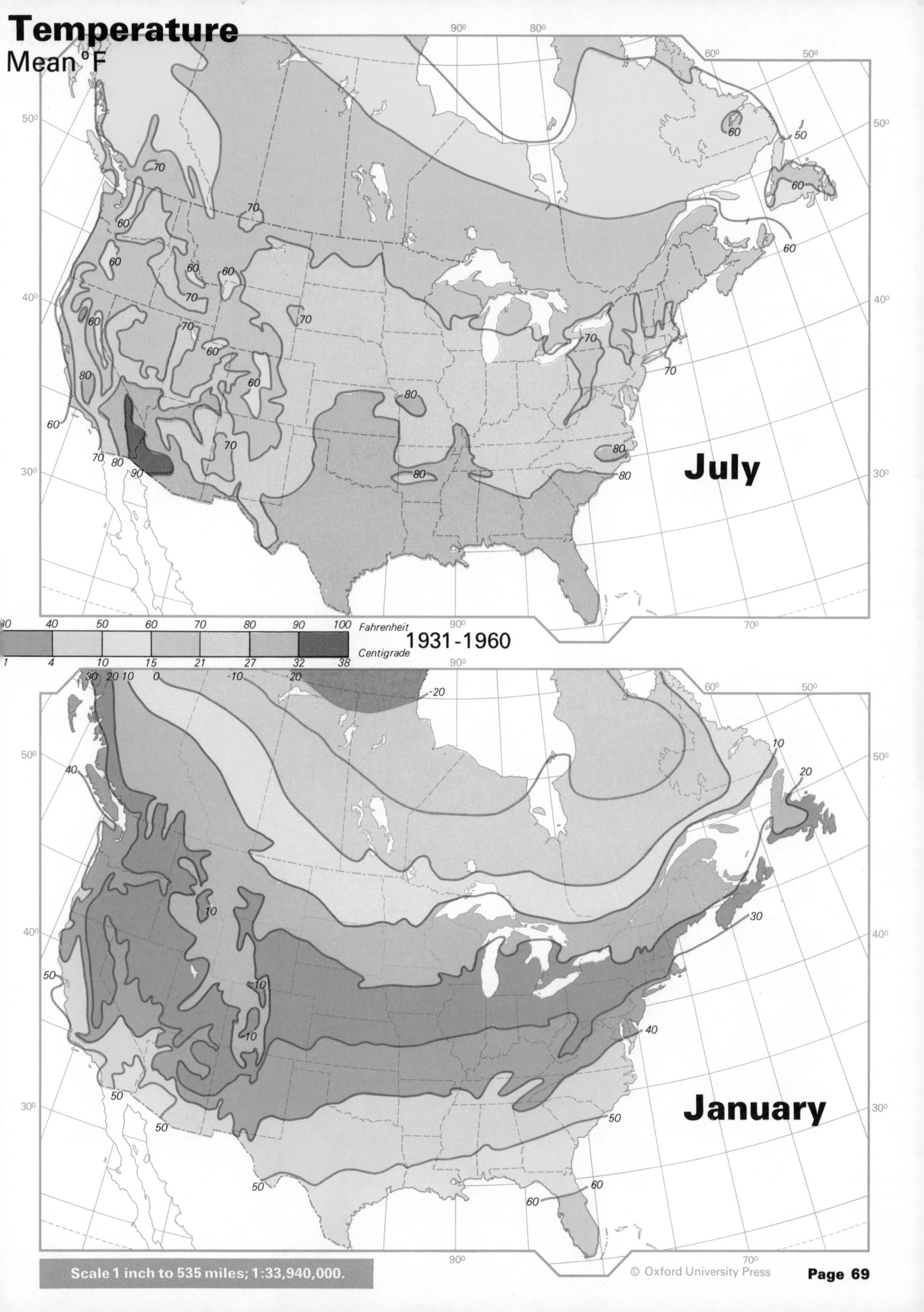

July

30	40	50	60	70	80	90	100	*Fahrenheit*
1	4	10	15	21	27	32	38	*Centigrade*

1931-1960

January

© Oxford University Press

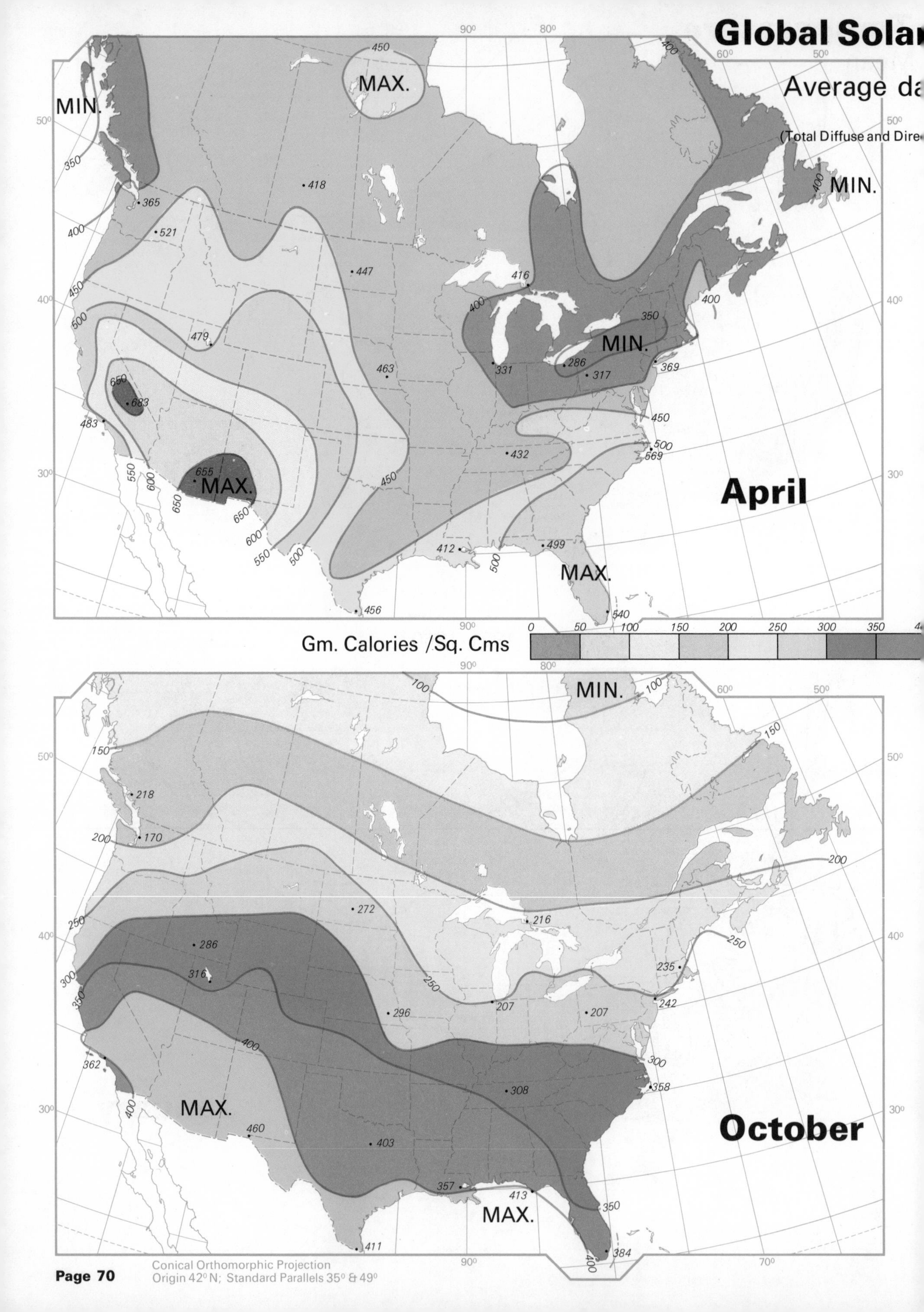

Global Solar

Average da

(Total Diffuse and Dire

April

MIN.
450
MAX.
MIN.
• 418
• 365
• 521
• 447
416
MIN.
400
350
MIN.
479
286 • 317
331 • 369
463
650
• 683
483
450
• 432
500
569
550
600
655
MAX.
650
650
600
550 500
• 456
412 • 499
MAX.
540

Gm. Calories /Sq. Cms

0	50	100	150	200	250	300	350	4

October

100 MIN. 100
150
150
• 218
200
200 • 170
250
• 272
250
216 •
250
• 286
235 •
316 •
250
• 296
207 242 •
207 • 207
400
300
362 •
• 308
• 358
400
MAX.
460
300
• 403
350
357 •
413 •
350
MAX.
• 411
400 • 384

Conical Orthomorphic Projection
Origin 42° N; Standard Parallels 35° & 49°

Radiation

totals

(radiation)

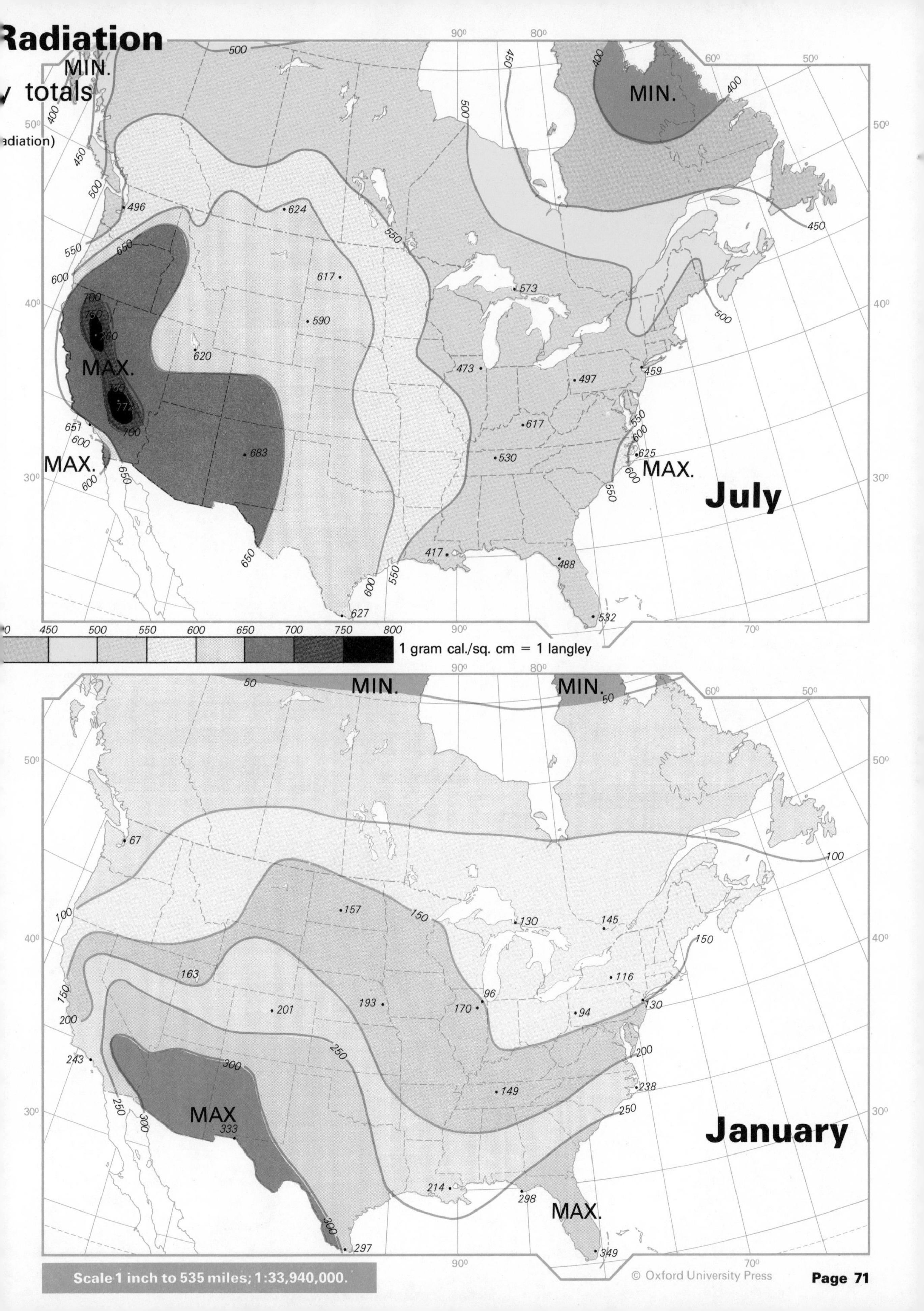

July

MIN.				

MIN.

MAX.

MAX.

MAX.

496 · 624

617 ·

590 ·

620

750
760

MAX.

750
772

651
700

683 ·

500

550

600

650

700

573 ·

473 ·

530 ·

617 ·

497 ·

459 ·

625 ·
600
650

417 ·

488 ·

532 ·

627 ·

450 500 550 600 650 700 750 800   1 gram cal./sq. cm = 1 langley

---

January

MIN.   MIN.   50

67 ·

157 ·   150   130 ·   145 ·

150

163

193 ·   96 ·   116 ·

201 ·   170 ·   94 ·   130

243 ·   250   200

300   149 ·   238 ·

MAX   250
333

214 ·   298 ·   250

MAX.

300

297 ·   349 ·

Scale 1 inch to 535 miles; 1:33,940,000.

© Oxford University Press   **Page 71**

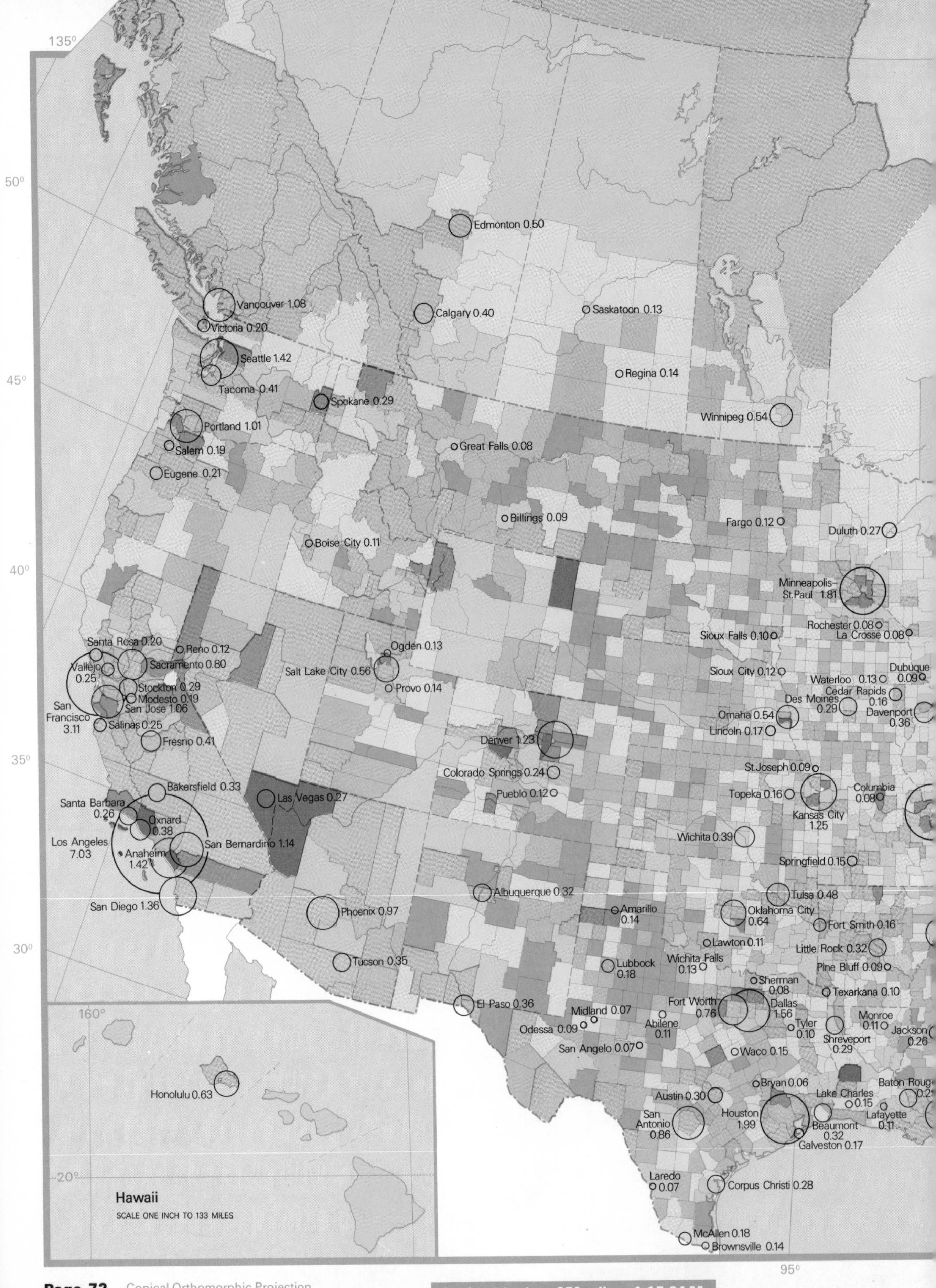

135°

50°

45°

40°

35°

30°

Edmonton 0.50

Calgary 0.40

Saskatoon 0.13

Regina 0.14

Winnipeg 0.54

Vancouver 1.08
Victoria 0.20
Seattle 1.42
Tacoma 0.41
Spokane 0.29
Portland 1.01
Salem 0.19
Eugene 0.21

Great Falls 0.08

Billings 0.09

Boise City 0.11

Fargo 0.12
Duluth 0.27

Minneapolis-St.Paul 1.81

Rochester 0.08
La Crosse 0.08

Santa Rosa 0.20
Reno 0.12
Sacramento 0.80
Vallejo 0.25
Stockton 0.29
Modesto 0.19
San Jose 1.06
San Francisco 3.11
Salinas 0.25
Fresno 0.41

Salt Lake City 0.56
Ogden 0.13
Provo 0.14

Denver 1.23

Colorado Springs 0.24
Pueblo 0.12

Sioux Falls 0.10

Sioux City 0.12
Waterloo 0.13
Dubuque 0.09
Cedar Rapids 0.16
Des Moines 0.29
Davenport 0.36
Omaha 0.54
Lincoln 0.17

St.Joseph 0.09
Columbia 0.08
Topeka 0.16
Kansas City 1.25

Wichita 0.39

Springfield 0.15

Bakersfield 0.33
Las Vegas 0.27
Santa Barbara 0.26
Oxnard 0.38
Los Angeles 7.03
Anaheim 1.42
San Bernardino 1.14
San Diego 1.36

Albuquerque 0.32

Phoenix 0.97

Tucson 0.35

Amarillo 0.14

Lawton 0.11
Lubbock 0.18
Wichita Falls 0.13

Tulsa 0.48
Oklahoma City 0.64
Fort Smith 0.16
Little Rock 0.32
Pine Bluff 0.09
Texarkana 0.10

El Paso 0.36
Midland 0.07
Odessa 0.09
Abilene 0.11
San Angelo 0.07

Sherman 0.08
Fort Worth 0.76
Dallas 1.56
Tyler 0.10
Monroe 0.11
Shreveport 0.29
Jackson 0.26
Waco 0.15

Honolulu 0.63

Bryan 0.06
Austin 0.30
San Antonio 0.86
Houston 1.99
Lake Charles 0.15
Beaumont 0.32
Galveston 0.17
Baton Roug 0.2
Lafayette 0.11

Laredo 0.07
Corpus Christi 0.28

McAllen 0.18
Brownsville 0.14

160°

20°

Hawaii
SCALE ONE INCH TO 133 MILES

95°

Page 72 Conical Orthomorphic Projection
Origin 42°N; Standard Parallels 35° & 49°

Scale 1 inch to 250 miles 1:15·84 M

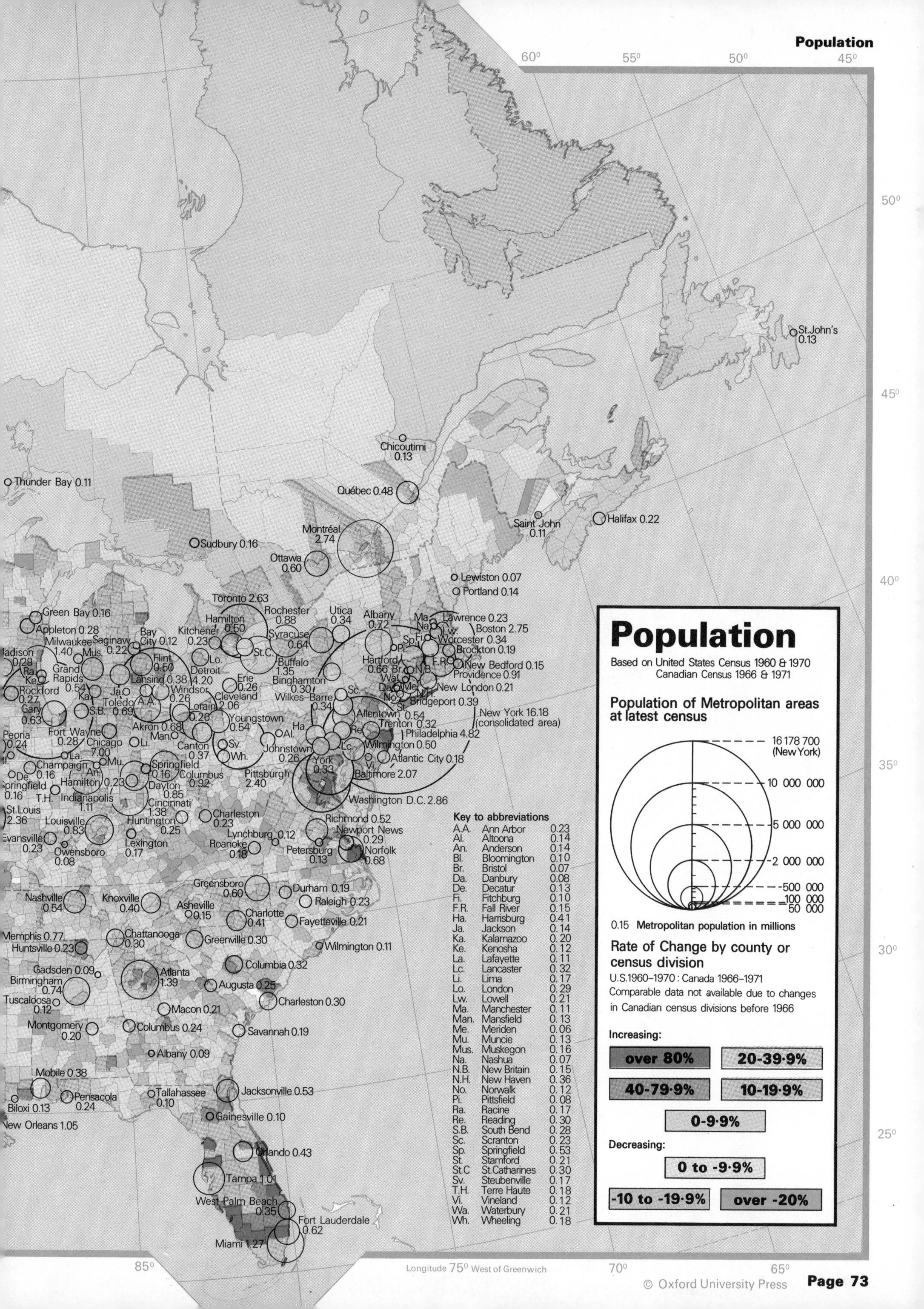

Population

Based on United States Census 1960 & 1970
Canadian Census 1966 & 1971

Population of Metropolitan areas at latest census

16 178 700 (New York)
10 000 000
5 000 000
2 000 000
500 000
100 000
50 000

0.15 Metropolitan population in millions

Rate of Change by county or census division

U.S.1960–1970 : Canada 1966–1971
Comparable data not available due to changes in Canadian census divisions before 1966

Increasing:
over 80%
40-79·9%
20-39·9%
10-19·9%
0-9·9%

Decreasing:
0 to -9·9%
-10 to -19·9%
over -20%

Key to abbreviations

A.A.	Ann Arbor	0.23
Al.	Altoona	0.14
An.	Anderson	0.14
Bl.	Bloomington	0.10
Br.	Bristol	0.07
Da.	Danbury	0.08
De.	Decatur	0.13
Fi.	Fitchburg	0.10
F.R.	Fall River	0.15
Ha.	Harrisburg	0.41
Ja.	Jackson	0.14
Ka.	Kalamazoo	0.20
Ke.	Kenosha	0.12
La.	Lafayette	0.11
Lc.	Lancaster	0.32
Li.	Lima	0.17
Lo.	London	0.29
Lw.	Lowell	0.21
Ma.	Manchester	0.11
Man.	Mansfield	0.13
Me.	Meriden	0.06
Mu.	Muncie	0.13
Mus.	Muskegon	0.16
Na.	Nashua	0.07
N.B.	New Britain	0.15
N.H.	New Haven	0.36
No.	Norwalk	0.12
Pi.	Pittsfield	0.08
Ra.	Racine	0.17
Re.	Reading	0.30
S.B.	South Bend	0.28
Sc.	Scranton	0.23
Sp.	Springfield	0.53
St.	Stamford	0.21
St.C	St.Catharines	0.30
Sv.	Steubenville	0.17
T.H.	Terre Haute	0.18
Vi.	Vineland	0.12
Wa.	Waterbury	0.21
Wh.	Wheeling	0.18

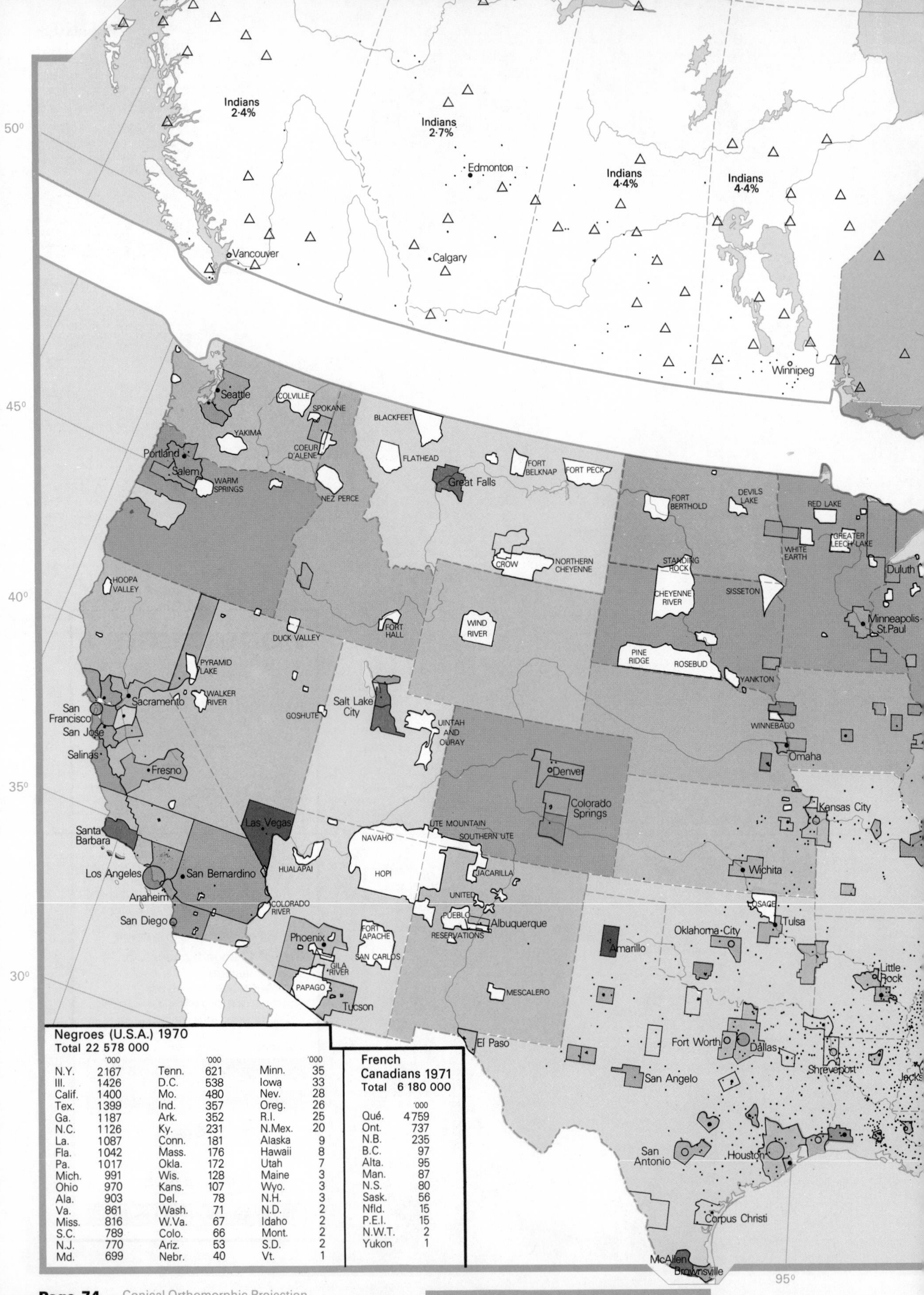

Negroes (U.S.A.) 1970
Total 22 578 000

	'000		'000		'000
N.Y.	2167	Tenn.	621	Minn.	35
Ill.	1426	D.C.	538	Iowa	33
Calif.	1400	Mo.	480	Nev.	28
Tex.	1399	Ind.	357	Oreg.	26
Ga.	1187	Ark.	352	R.I.	25
N.C.	1126	Ky.	231	N.Mex.	20
La.	1087	Conn.	181	Alaska	9
Fla.	1042	Mass.	176	Hawaii	8
Pa.	1017	Okla.	172	Utah	7
Mich.	991	Wis.	128	Maine	3
Ohio	970	Kans.	107	Wyo.	3
Ala.	903	Del.	78	N.H.	3
Va.	861	Wash.	71	N.D.	2
Miss.	816	W.Va.	67	Idaho	2
S.C.	789	Colo.	66	Mont.	2
N.J.	770	Ariz.	53	S.D.	2
Md.	699	Nebr.	40	Vt.	1

French Canadians 1971
Total 6 180 000

	'000
Qué.	4759
Ont.	737
N.B.	235
B.C.	97
Alta.	95
Man.	87
N.S.	80
Sask.	56
Nfld.	15
P.E.I.	15
N.W.T.	2
Yukon	1

Conical Orthomorphic Projection
Origin 42°N; Standard Parallels 35° & 49°

Scale 1 inch to 250 miles 1:15.84 M

60° 55° 50° 45°

French Canadians

Rate of Change by Census Division, 1961-1971 (For provinces in which French Canadians comprise over 9% of the population)

Population, 1971

• One dot represents 2 500 French Canadians

Population in Census Metropolitan Areas (C.M.A.'s)
see U.S. Negro Central City legend

□ Cities, other than C.M.A.'s with over 25 000 French Canadians

Increasing:

100-220%	30-49·9%
50-99·9%	10-29·9%
	0-9·9%

Decreasing:

	0--9·9%
-10--29·9%	over -30%

	1961 & 1971 data not comparable

Native Indians

△ Principal areas of settlement

2·4% Indian population as a percentage
etc. of province population

Indians 0·2%

Indians 0·8%

Indians 0·5%

Indians 0·6%

Indians 0·3%

Indians 0·6%

Chicoutimi

Québec

Montréal

Ottawa

Sudbury

Toronto

Hamilton

Windsor

Principal Ethnic Groups

Manchester

Rochester
Utica
Albany
Boston
Buffalo
Springfield
Providence
Binghamton
Meriden

Milwaukee
Flint
Chicago
Detroit
Wilkes-Barre
New York
Toledo
Cleveland
Pittsburgh
Harrisburg
Philadelphia
Baltimore
Indianapolis
Dayton
Columbus
Terre Haute
Cincinnati
Washington D.C.
ouis

Richmond

Nashville
Knoxville
Norfolk

Hurtsville
Charlotte
Greensboro

Columbia
Wilmington
mphis
Atlanta
Augusta

Birmingham
Charleston
Tusdaloosa
Columbus
Savannah
Montgomery

Jacksonville
Mobile
ew Orleans

Orlando
Tampa

West Palm Beach
BIG CYPRESS
Miami

Negroes (U.S.A.)

Population, 1970

• One dot represents 2 500 Negroes

Central City Population

- — — — — 2 000 000
- — — — — 500 000
- — — — 100 000
- — — 50 000
- ○ 40-50 000
- • 20-40 000
- • 10-20 000

Boundary of Standard Metropolitan Statistical Area (S.M.S.A.)

Rate of Change in Central Cities,[1] S.M.S.A.'s outside Central Cities and Nonmetropolitan Areas, 1960-1970

[1] with 40 000 or more Negroes

Increasing:

500-1000%	50-99·9%
250-499·9%	20-49·9%
100-249·9%	0-19·9%

Decreasing:

	0- -19·9%
-20--49·9%	over -50%

Native Indians

OSAGE	Reservation

85° Longitude 75° West of Greenwich 70° 65°

© Oxford University Press **Page 75**

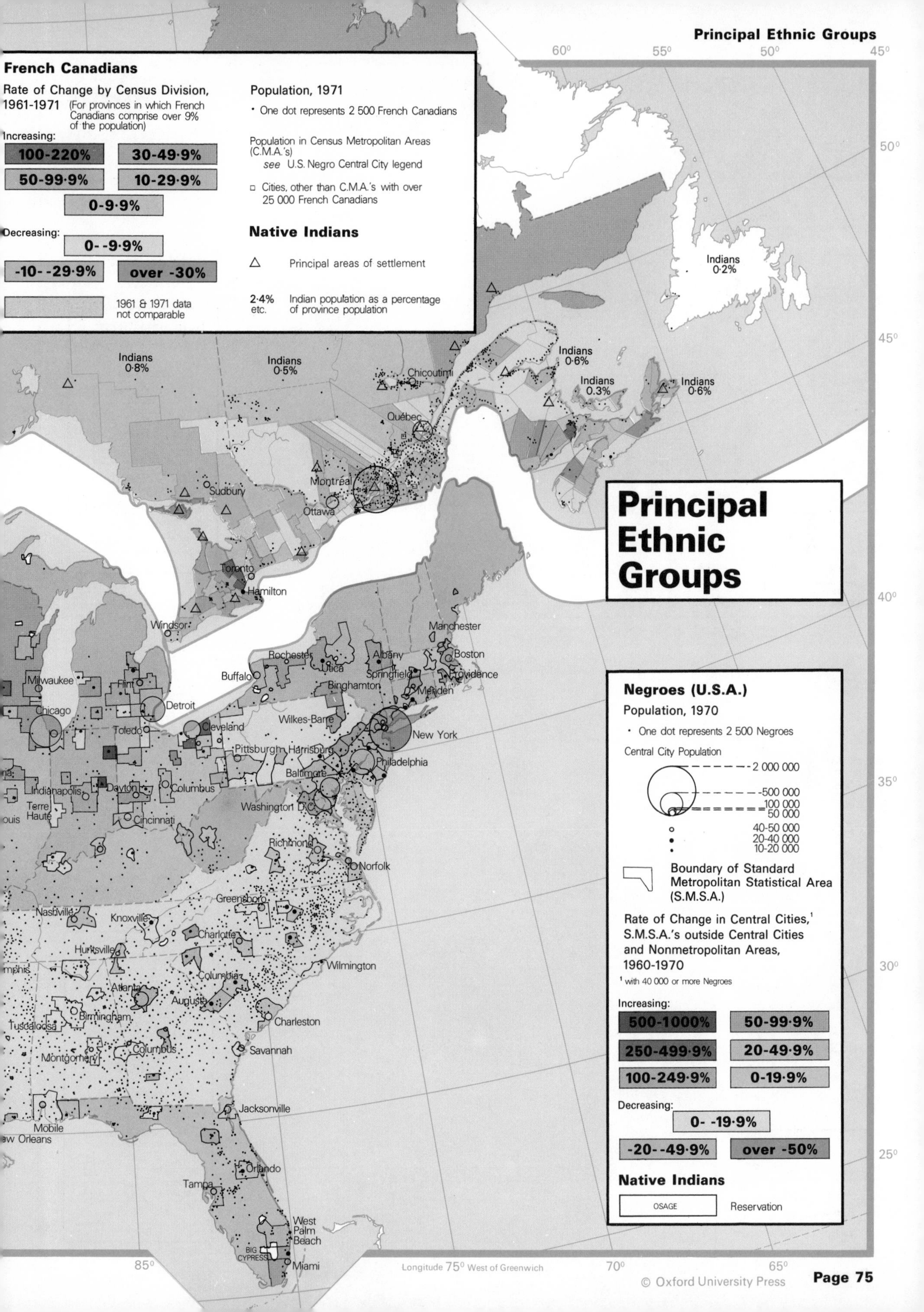

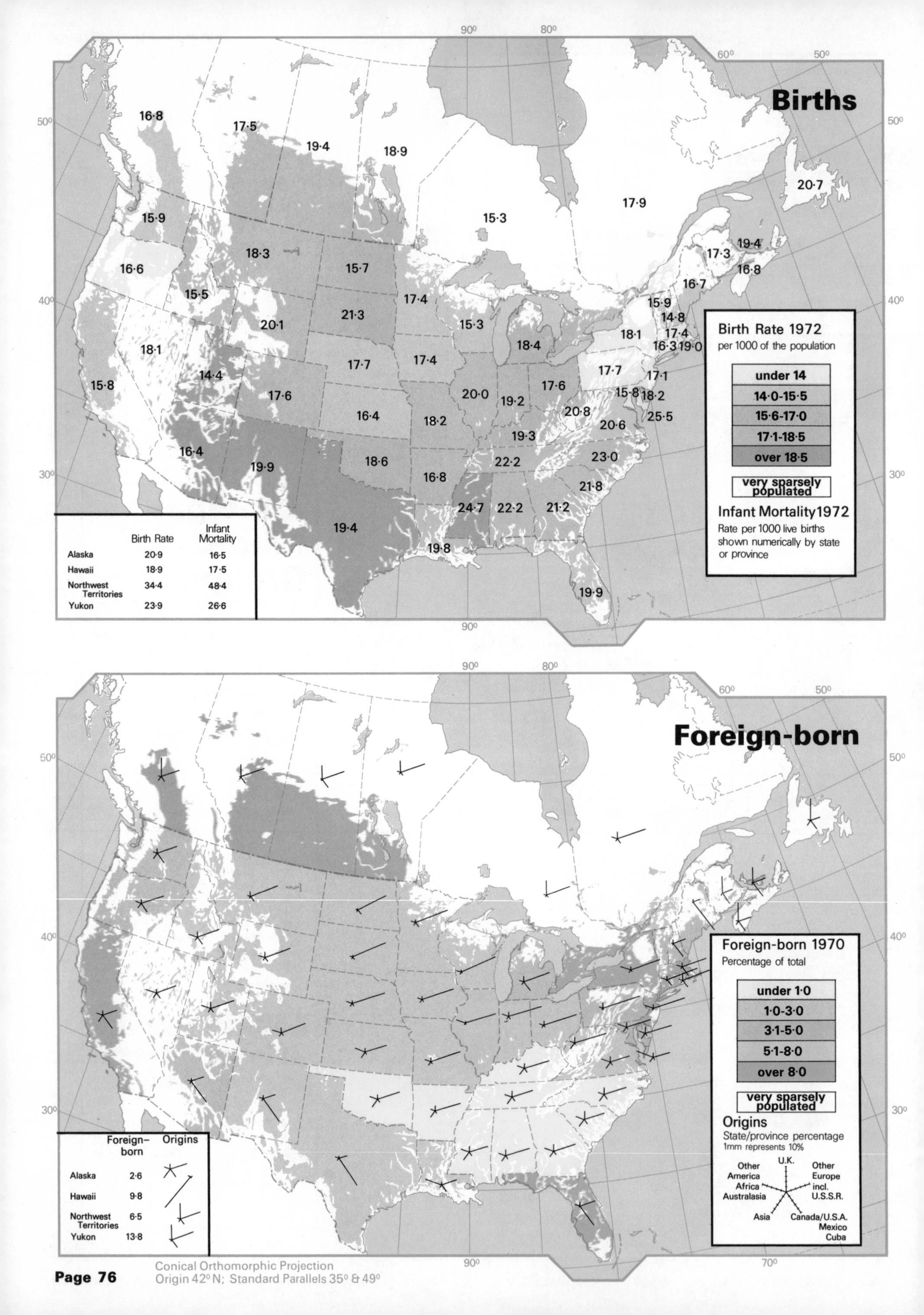

Births

Birth Rate 1972
per 1000 of the population

| under 14 |
| 14·0-15·5 |
| 15·6-17·0 |
| 17·1-18·5 |
| over 18·5 |

very sparsely populated

Infant Mortality 1972
Rate per 1000 live births shown numerically by state or province

	Birth Rate	Infant Mortality
Alaska	20·9	16·5
Hawaii	18·9	17·5
Northwest Territories	34·4	48·4
Yukon	23·9	26·6

Foreign-born

Foreign-born 1970
Percentage of total

| under 1·0 |
| 1·0-3·0 |
| 3·1-5·0 |
| 5·1-8·0 |
| over 8·0 |

very sparsely populated

Origins
State/province percentage
1mm represents 10%

Other America
Africa
Australasia
U.K.
Other Europe incl. U.S.S.R.
Asia
Canada/U.S.A. Mexico Cuba

	Foreign-born	Origins
Alaska	2·6	
Hawaii	9·8	
Northwest Territories	6·5	
Yukon	13·8	

Conical Orthomorphic Projection
Origin 42° N; Standard Parallels 35° & 49°

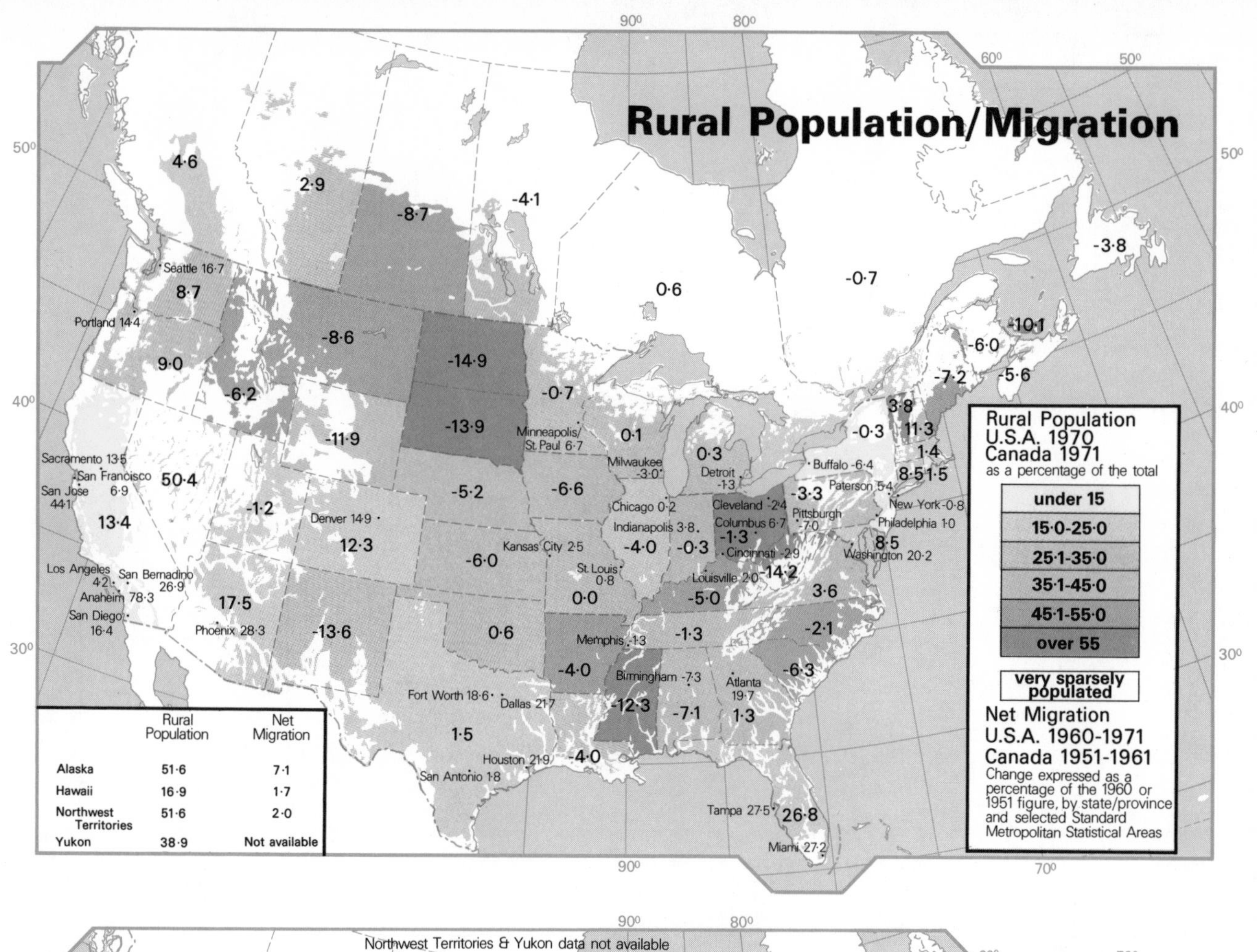

Rural Population/Migration

	Rural Population	Net Migration
Alaska	51·6	7·1
Hawaii	16·9	1·7
Northwest Territories	51·6	2·0
Yukon	38·9	Not available

**Rural Population
U.S.A. 1970
Canada 1971**
as a percentage of the total

under 15
15·0-25·0
25·1-35·0
35·1-45·0
45·1-55·0
over 55

very sparsely populated

**Net Migration
U.S.A. 1960-1971
Canada 1951-1961**
Change expressed as a percentage of the 1960 or 1951 figure, by state/province and selected Standard Metropolitan Statistical Areas

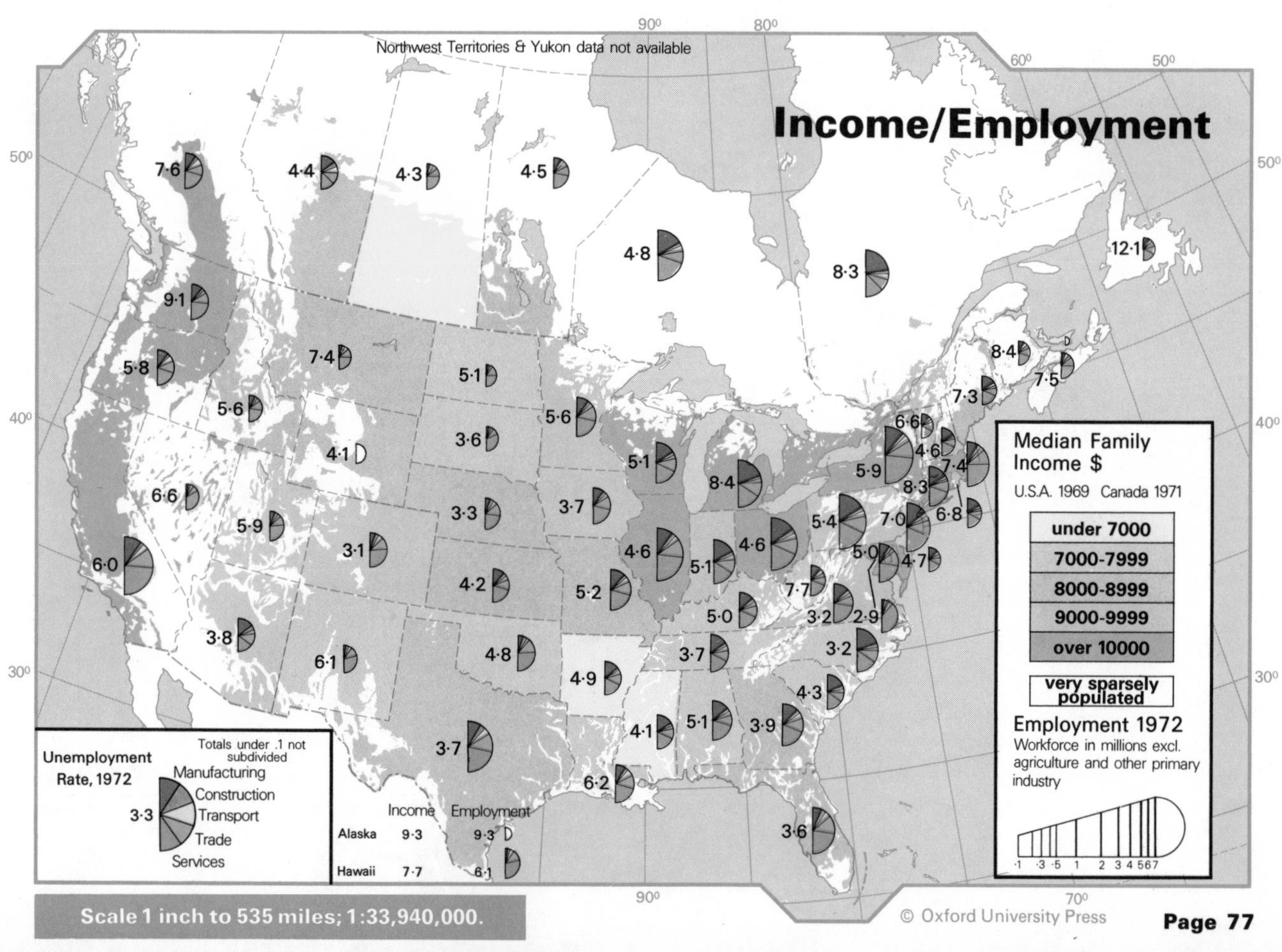

Northwest Territories & Yukon data not available

Income/Employment

Median Family Income $

U.S.A. 1969 Canada 1971

under 7000
7000-7999
8000-8999
9000-9999
over 10000

very sparsely populated

Employment 1972
Workforce in millions excl. agriculture and other primary industry

·1 ·3 ·5 1 2 3 4 5 6 7

Unemployment Rate, 1972

Totals under ·1 not subdivided
Manufacturing
Construction
Transport
Trade
Services

3·3

	Income	Employment
Alaska	9·3	9·3
Hawaii	7·7	6·1

© Oxford University Press

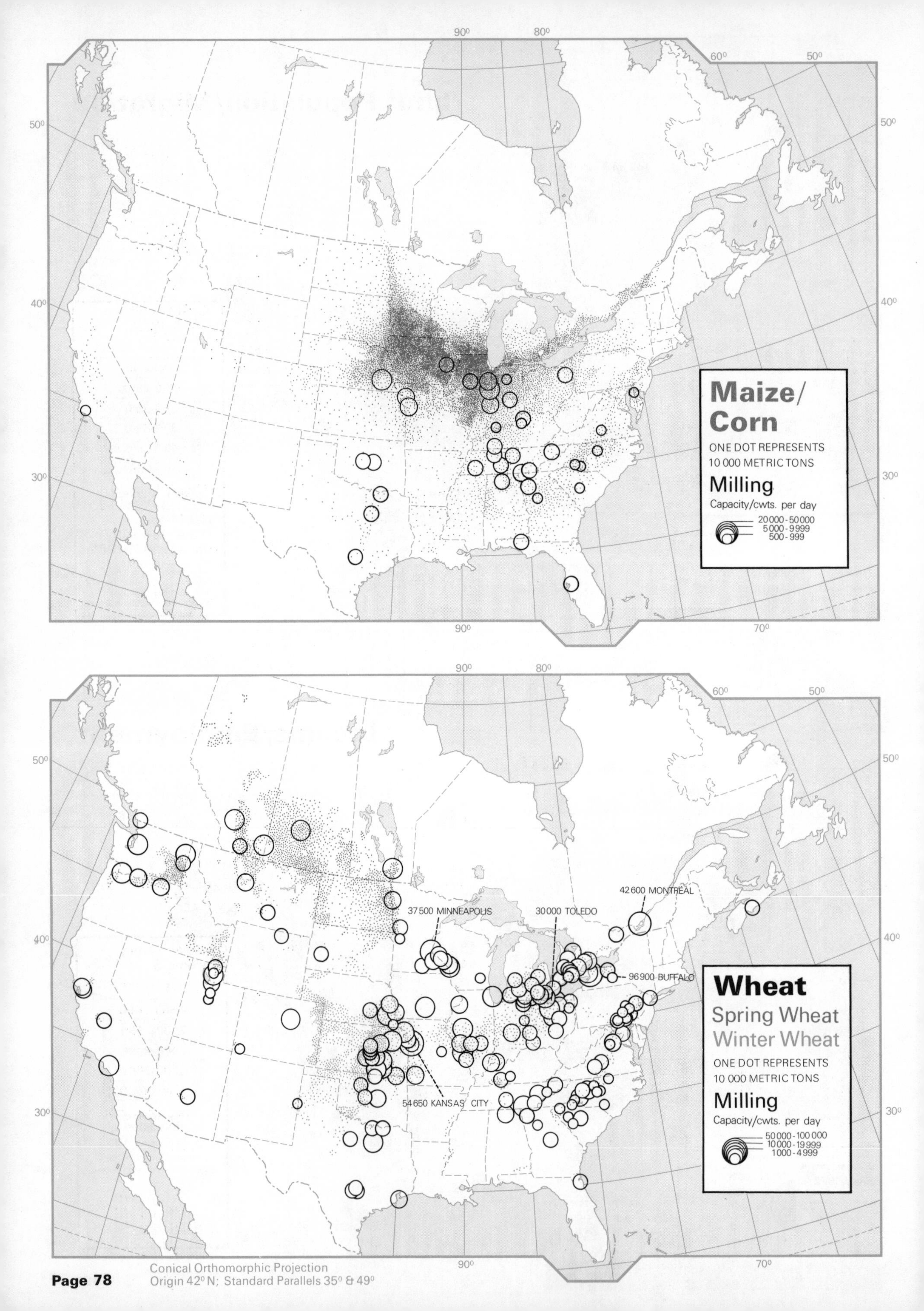

Maize/Corn

ONE DOT REPRESENTS
10 000 METRIC TONS

Milling
Capacity/cwts. per day

20 000 - 50 000
5 000 - 9 999
500 - 999

42 600 MONTREAL

37 500 MINNEAPOLIS

30 000 TOLEDO

96 900 BUFFALO

54 650 KANSAS CITY

Wheat

Spring Wheat
Winter Wheat

ONE DOT REPRESENTS
10 000 METRIC TONS

Milling
Capacity/cwts. per day

50 000 - 100 000
10 000 - 19 999
1 000 - 4 999

Conical Orthomorphic Projection
Origin 42° N; Standard Parallels 35° & 49°

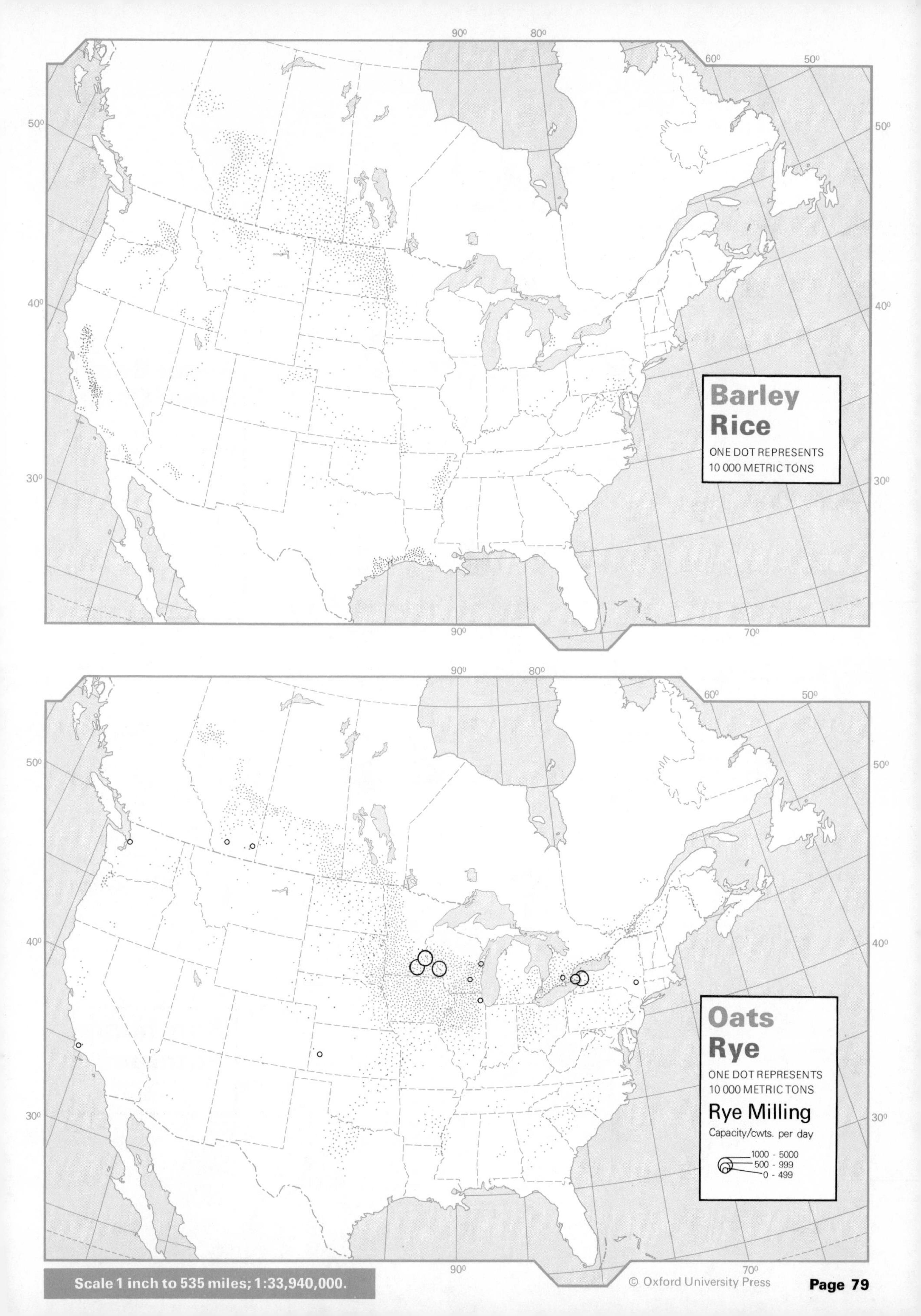

Barley
Rice

ONE DOT REPRESENTS
10 000 METRIC TONS

Oats
Rye

ONE DOT REPRESENTS
10 000 METRIC TONS

Rye Milling

Capacity/cwts. per day

1000 - 5000
500 - 999
0 - 499

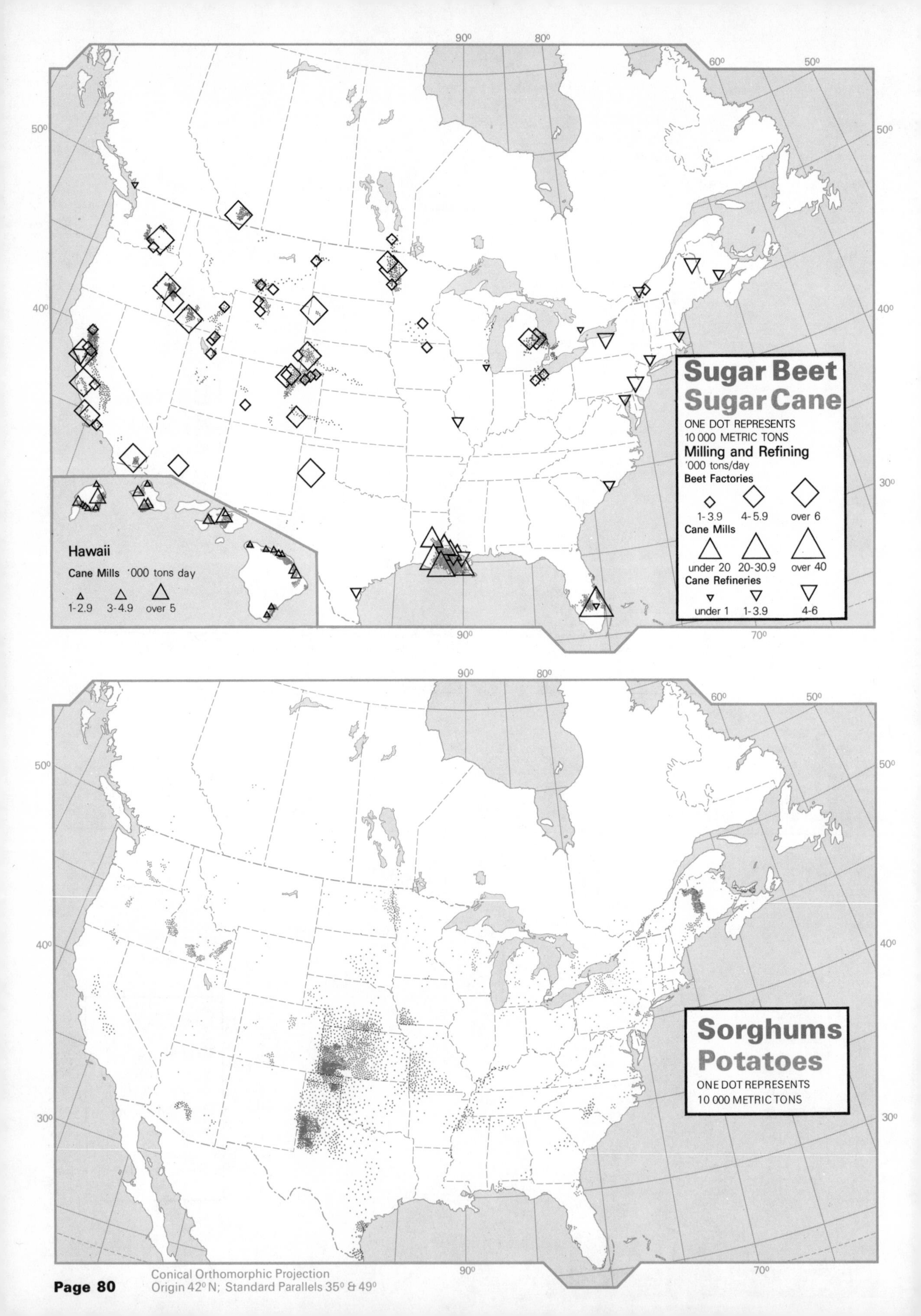

Sugar Beet
Sugar Cane

ONE DOT REPRESENTS
10 000 METRIC TONS
Milling and Refining
'000 tons/day
Beet Factories

1- 3.9   4- 5.9   over 6

Cane Mills

under 20   20-30.9   over 40

Cane Refineries

under 1   1- 3.9   4-6

Hawaii

Cane Mills '000 tons day

1-2.9   3- 4.9   over 5

Sorghums
Potatoes

ONE DOT REPRESENTS
10 000 METRIC TONS

Conical Orthomorphic Projection
Origin 42º N; Standard Parallels 35º & 49º

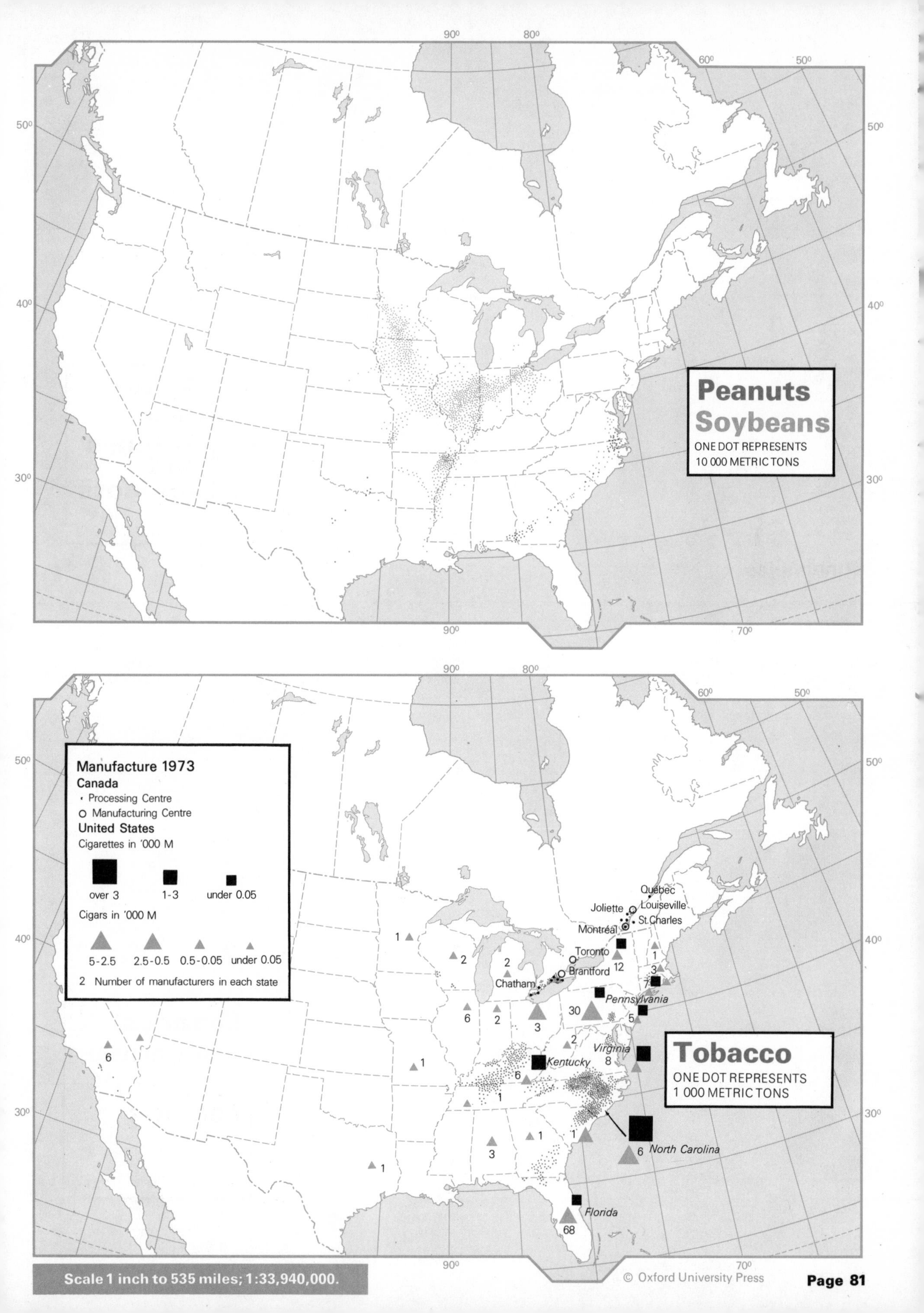

Peanuts
Soybeans
ONE DOT REPRESENTS
10 000 METRIC TONS

Manufacture 1973
Canada
- Processing Centre
○ Manufacturing Centre

United States
Cigarettes in '000 M

■ over 3   ■ 1-3   ■ under 0.05

Cigars in '000 M

▲ 5-2.5   ▲ 2.5-0.5   ▲ 0.5-0.05   ▲ under 0.05

2 Number of manufacturers in each state

Québec
Joliette   Louiseville
Montréal   St Charles
Toronto
Brantford   12
Chatham
Pennsylvania   30
Kentucky
Virginia   8
North Carolina   6
Florida   68

1   2   2   1   3   1   7
6   2   3   5
6   2
6   1   2
1   6
1   1   1
3
1

Tobacco
ONE DOT REPRESENTS
1 000 METRIC TONS

Scale 1 inch to 535 miles; 1:33,940,000.

© Oxford University Press   **Page 81**

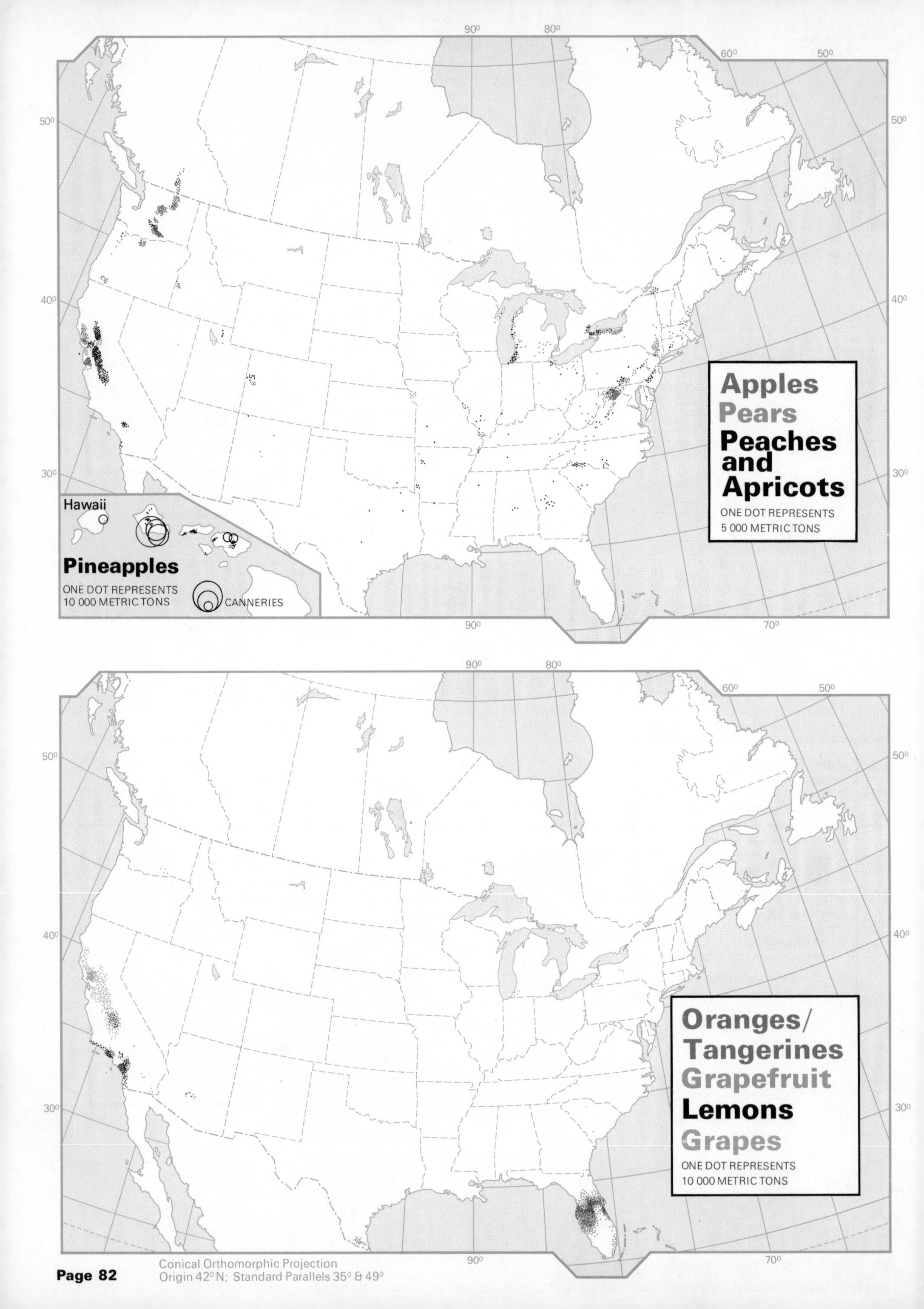

Apples
Pears
**Peaches
and
Apricots**
ONE DOT REPRESENTS
5 000 METRIC TONS

Hawaii

Pineapples
ONE DOT REPRESENTS
10 000 METRIC TONS   CANNERIES

**Oranges/
Tangerines
Grapefruit
Lemons
Grapes**
ONE DOT REPRESENTS
10 000 METRIC TONS

Conical Orthomorphic Projection
Origin 42° N; Standard Parallels 35° & 49°

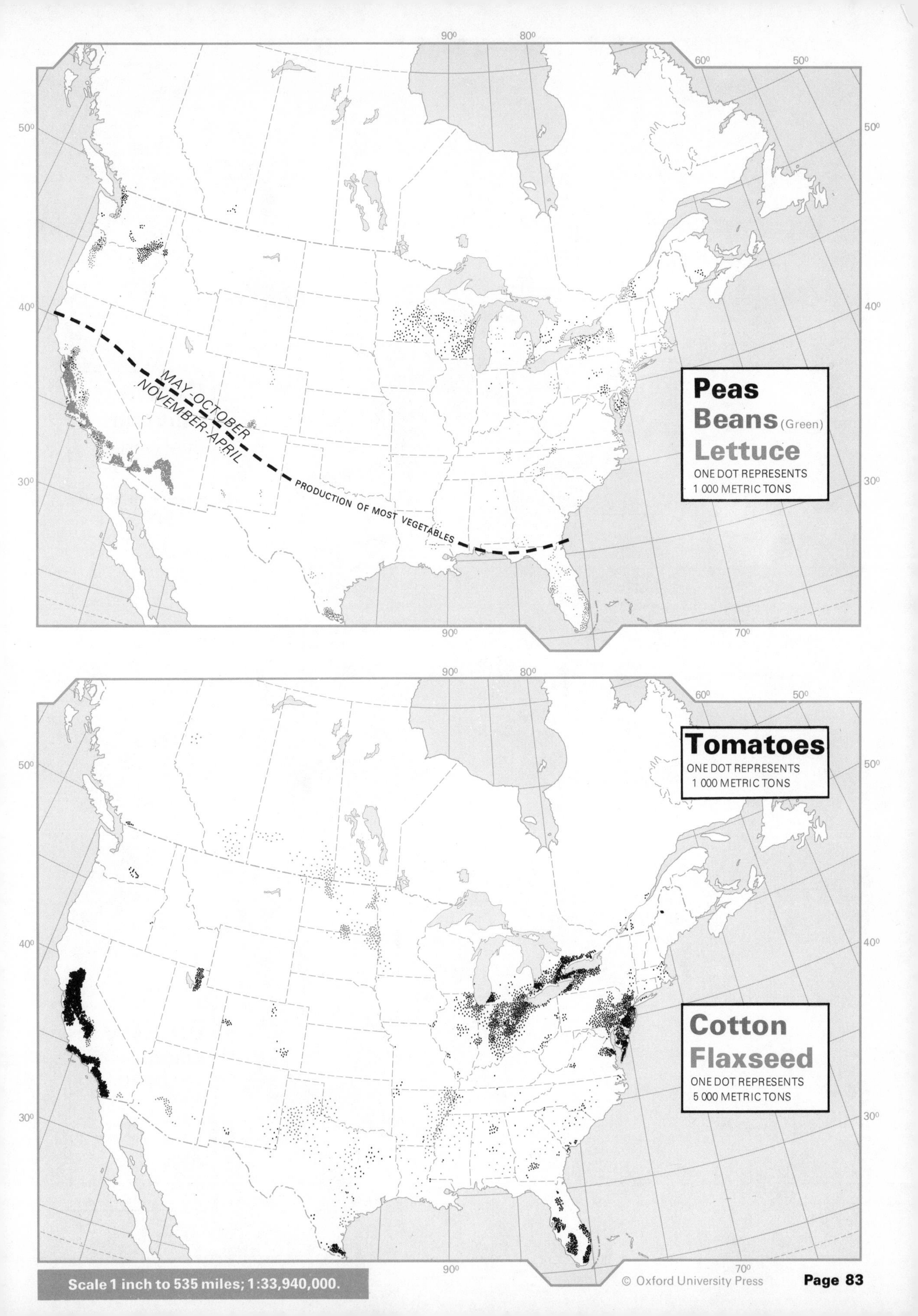

Peas
Beans (Green)
Lettuce
ONE DOT REPRESENTS
1 000 METRIC TONS

MAY-OCTOBER
NOVEMBER-APRIL
PRODUCTION OF MOST VEGETABLES

Tomatoes
ONE DOT REPRESENTS
1 000 METRIC TONS

Cotton
Flaxseed
ONE DOT REPRESENTS
5 000 METRIC TONS

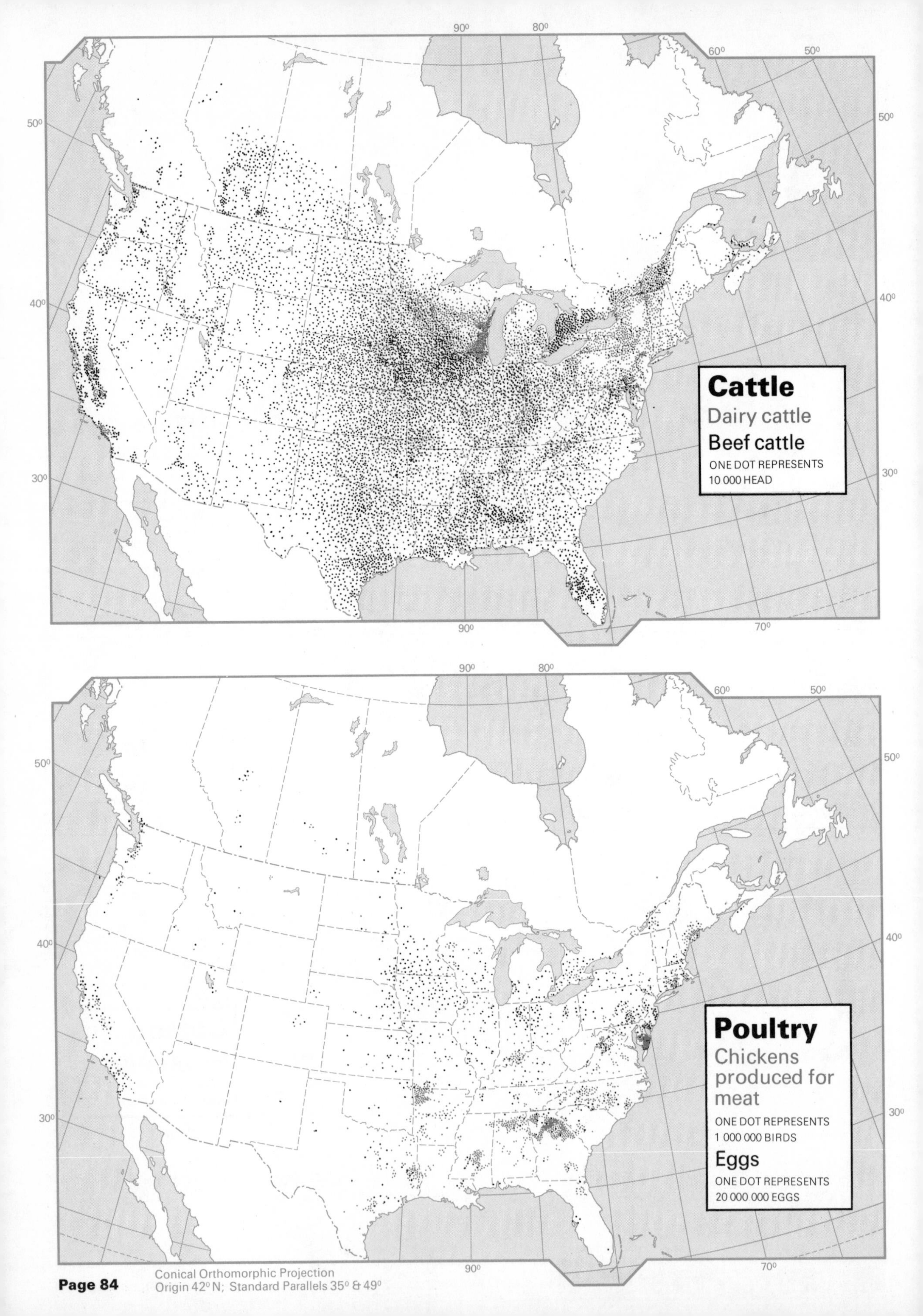

Cattle
Dairy cattle
Beef cattle
ONE DOT REPRESENTS
10 000 HEAD

Poultry
Chickens
produced for
meat
ONE DOT REPRESENTS
1 000 000 BIRDS
Eggs
ONE DOT REPRESENTS
20 000 000 EGGS

Conical Orthomorphic Projection
Origin 42° N; Standard Parallels 35° & 49°

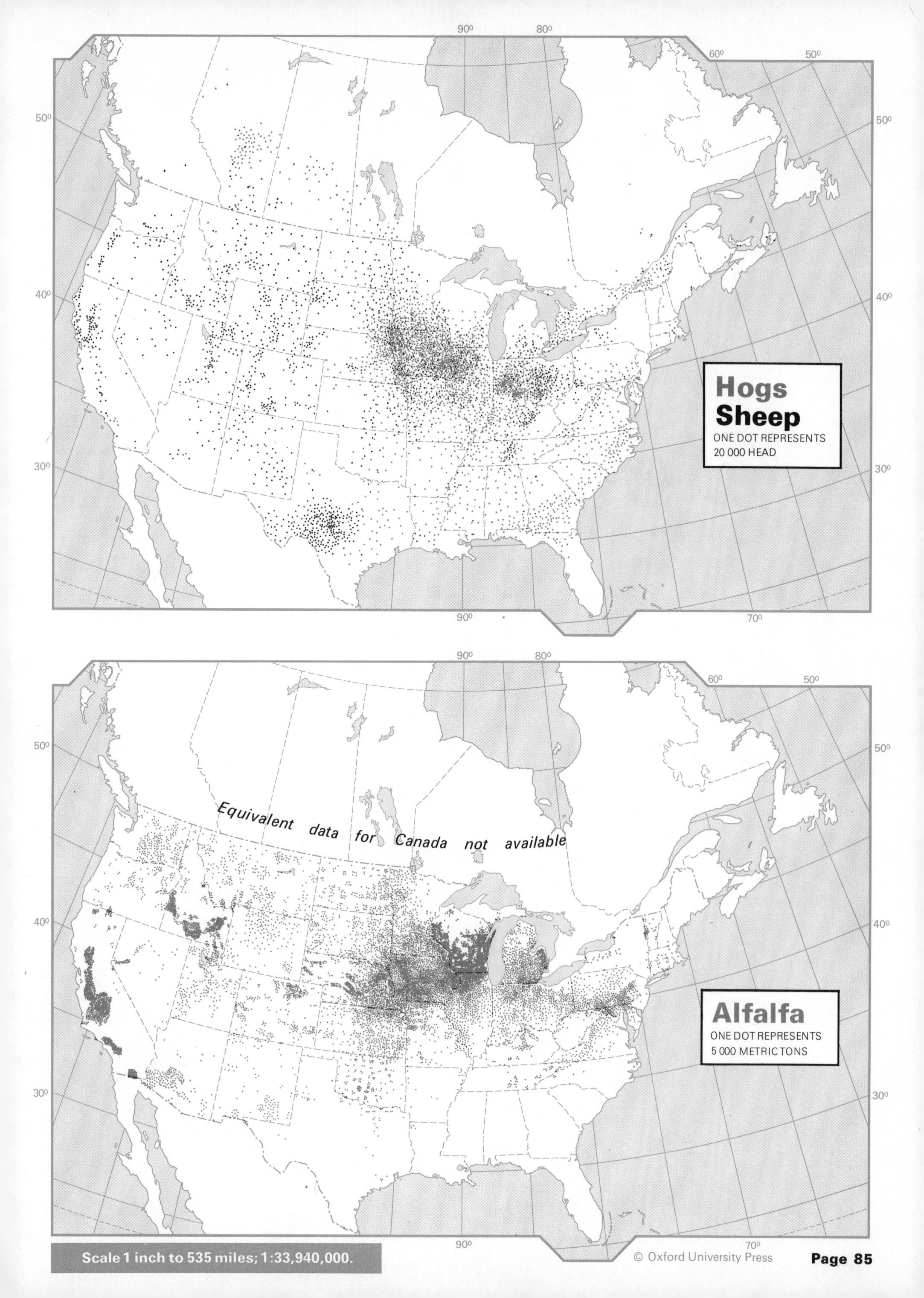

Hogs
Sheep
ONE DOT REPRESENTS
20 000 HEAD

Equivalent data for Canada not available

Alfalfa
ONE DOT REPRESENTS
5 000 METRIC TONS

Scale 1 inch to 535 miles; 1:33,940,000.

© Oxford University Press   **Page 85**

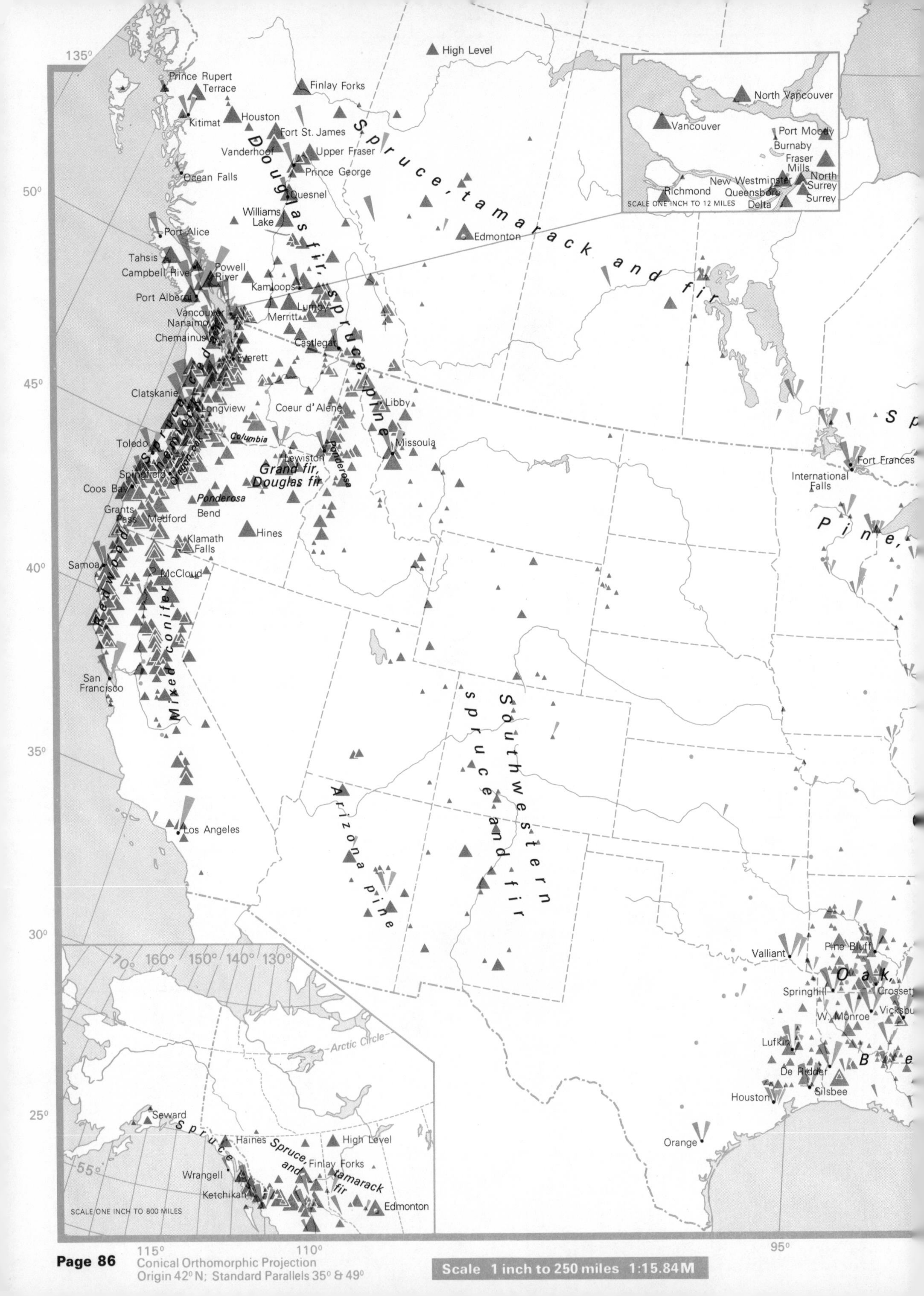

Conical Orthomorphic Projection
Origin 42° N; Standard Parallels 35° & 49°

Scale 1 inch to 250 miles 1:15.84M

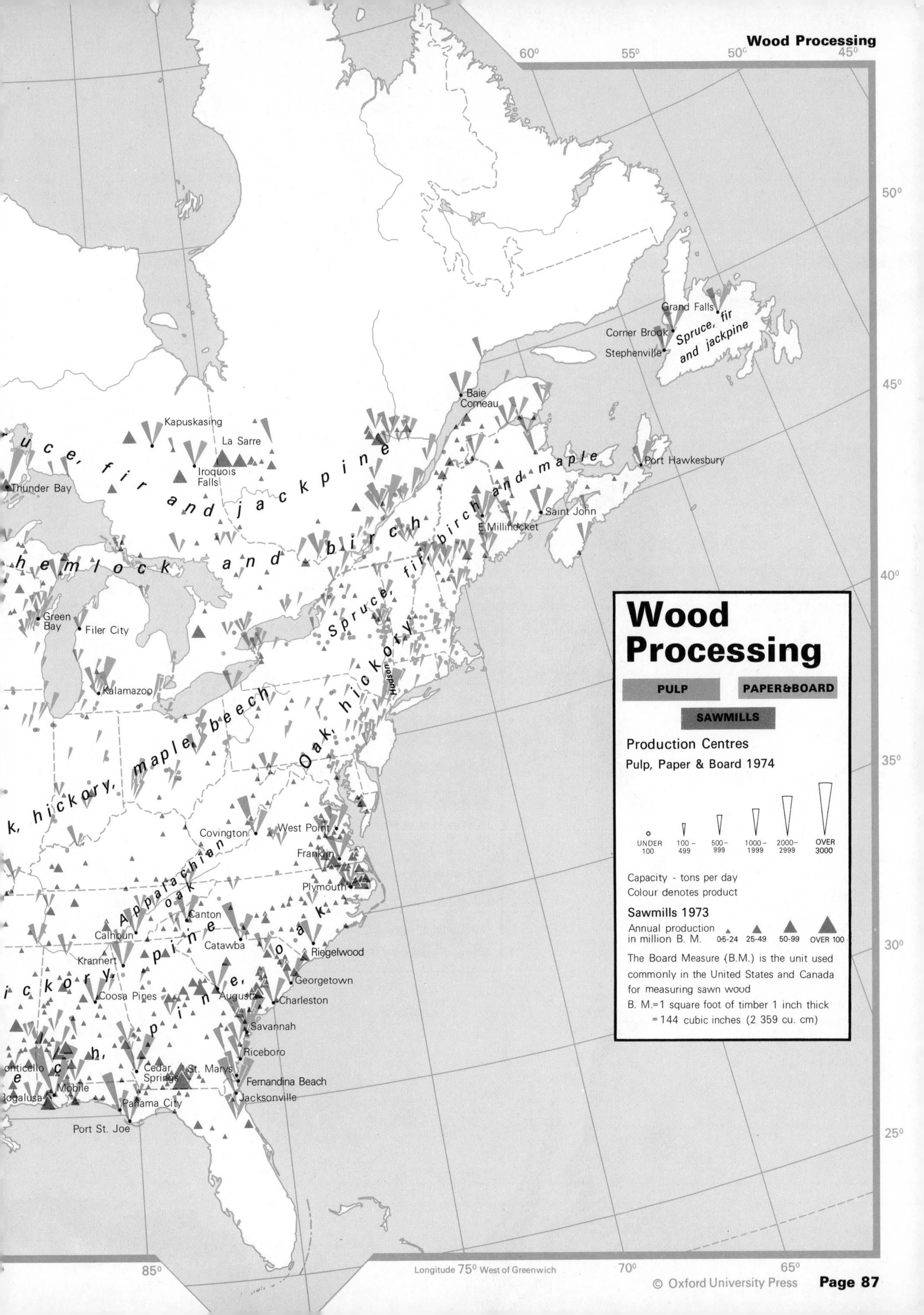

Grand Falls

Corner Brook

Stephenville

Spruce, fir and jackpine

Baie Comeau

Port Hawkesbury

Kapuskasing

La Sarre

Iroquois Falls

Thunder Bay

uce, fir and jackpine

hemlock and birch and maple

Saint John

E. Millinocket

Spruce, fir, birch and maple

Hudson

Green Bay

Filer City

Kalamazoo

k, hickory, maple, beech

Oak, hickory

Covington

West Point

Franklin

Plymouth

Appalachian oak

Canton

Calhoun

Catawba

Krannert

Coosa Pines

Augusta

Charleston

pine, oak

Riegelwood

Georgetown

Savannah

Riceboro

ickory

pine,

h,

c

e

onticello

Mobile

ogalusa

Cedar Springs

St. Marys

Fernandina Beach

Panama City

Jacksonville

Port St. Joe

Wood Processing

PULP	PAPER&BOARD
SAWMILLS	

Production Centres
Pulp, Paper & Board 1974

○	▽	▽	▽	▽	▽
UNDER 100	100 – 499	500 – 999	1000 – 1999	2000 – 2999	OVER 3000

Capacity - tons per day
Colour denotes product

Sawmills 1973
Annual production
in million B. M.   ▴ 06-24   ▲ 25-49   ▲ 50-99   ▲ OVER 100

The Board Measure (B.M.) is the unit used
commonly in the United States and Canada
for measuring sawn wood
B. M.=1 square foot of timber 1 inch thick
= 144 cubic inches (2 359 cu. cm)

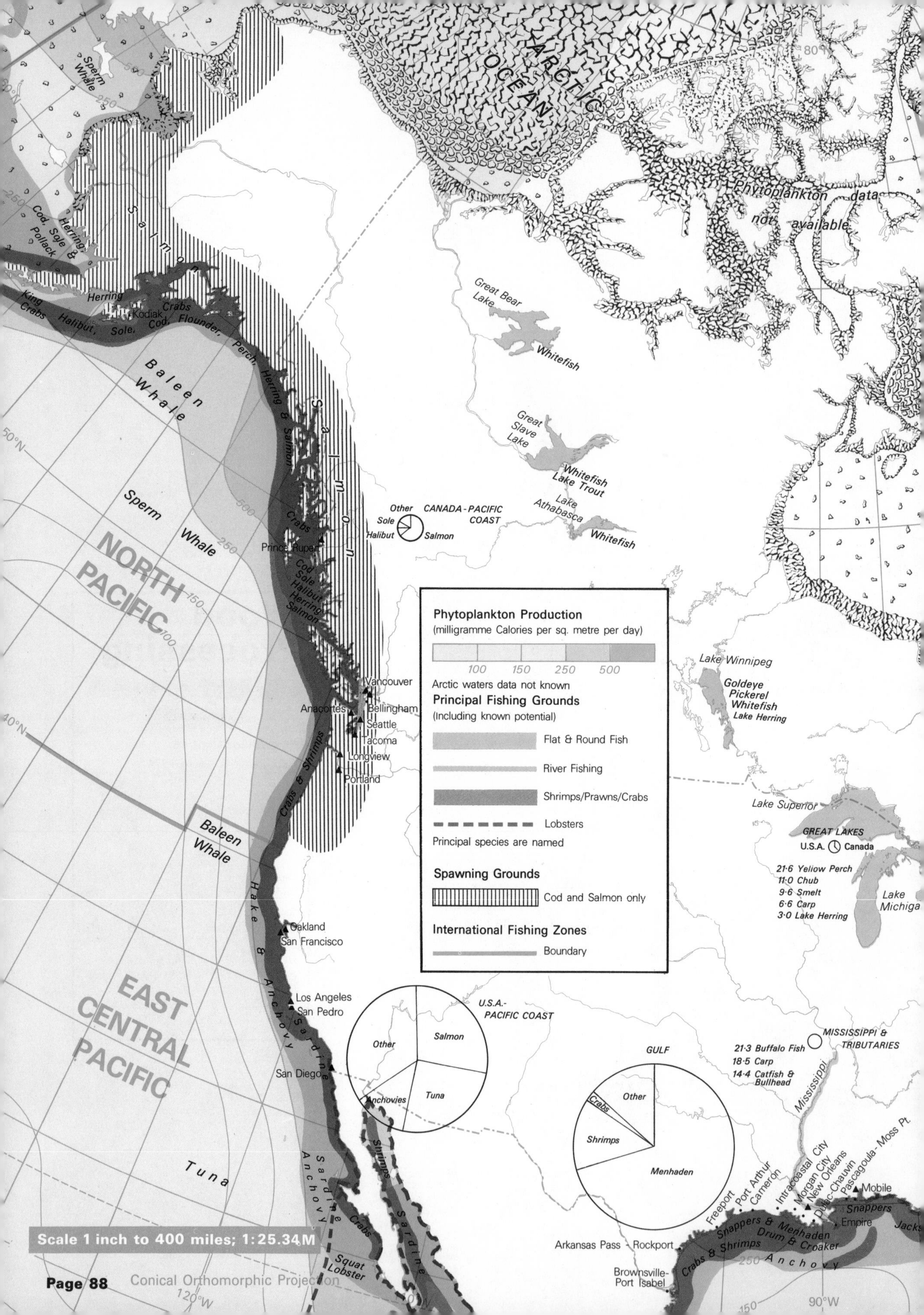

ARCTIC OCEAN

Phytoplankton data not available

Sperm Whale

Cod Sole & Pollack

King Crabs

Halibut

Herring

Kodiak

Sole, Cod, Flounder, Perch

Crabs

Salmon

Baleen Whale

Great Bear Lake

Whitefish

Great Slave Lake

Whitefish Lake Trout

Lake Athabasca

Whitefish

Sperm Whale

NORTH PACIFIC

Prince Rupert

Cod, Sole, Halibut, Herring, Salmon

CANADA - PACIFIC COAST

Other
Sole
Halibut   Salmon

50°N

Crabs

Salmon

Vancouver

Anacortes

Bellingham

Seattle

Tacoma

40°N

Longview

Portland

Cod & Shrimps

Baleen Whale

Hake & Anchovy

Oakland
San Francisco

Los Angeles
San Pedro

San Diego

EAST CENTRAL PACIFIC

Tuna

Sardine · Anchovy

Shrimps

Crabs

Sardine

Squat Lobster

Lake Winnipeg

Goldeye
Pickerel
Whitefish
Lake Herring

Lake Superior

GREAT LAKES
U.S.A. ◷ Canada

21·6 Yellow Perch
11·0 Chub
9·6 Smelt
6·6 Carp
3·0 Lake Herring

Lake Michiga

U.S.A.- PACIFIC COAST

Other   Salmon

Anchovies   Tuna

GULF

21·3 Buffalo Fish
18·5 Carp
14·4 Catfish & Bullhead

MISSISSIPPI & TRIBUTARIES

Crabs

Shrimps

Other

Menhaden

Mississippi

Freeport
Port Arthur
Cameron

Intracoastal City
Morgan City
New Orleans

Buras
Chauvin
Pascagoula - Moss Pt.

Mobile

Snappers

Empire

Jack

Arkansas Pass - Rockport

Brownsville - Port Isabel

Snappers & Menhaden
Drum & Croaker

Crabs & Shrimps

Anchovy

Phytoplankton Production
(milligramme Calories per sq. metre per day)

100   150   250   500

Arctic waters data not known

Principal Fishing Grounds
(Including known potential)

Flat & Round Fish

River Fishing

Shrimps/Prawns/Crabs

- - - Lobsters

Principal species are named

Spawning Grounds

Cod and Salmon only

International Fishing Zones

Boundary

Conical Orthomorphic Projection

Scale 1 inch to 400 miles; 1:25.34M

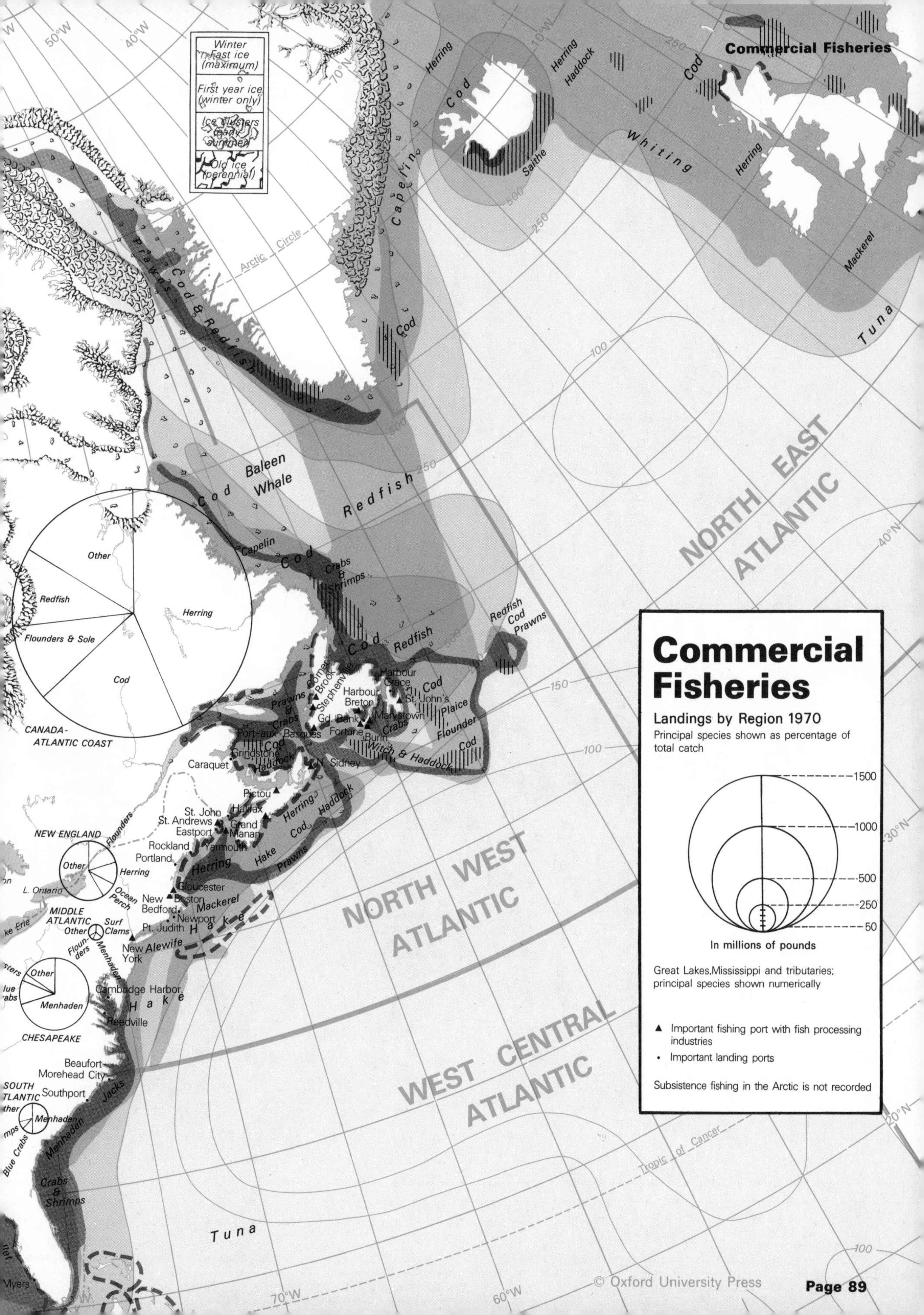

Winter
Fast ice
(maximum)

First year ice
(winter only)

Ice glaciers
(early summer)

Old ice
(perennial)

Herring

Cod

Capelin

Herring

Haddock

Cod

Whiting

Herring

Mackerel

Saithe

Tuna

Cod

Prawns

Cod & Redfish

Baleen
Whale

Cod

Redfish

Capelin

Cod

Crabs
&
Shrimps

Cod

Redfish

Cod

Redfish
Cod
Prawns

Gomer
Brook
Stephen Brook

Prawns
&
Crabs

Harbour
Grace

Harbour
Breton

Cod

St. John's

Plaice

Other

Redfish

Flounders & Sole

Cod

Herring

CANADA-
ATLANTIC COAST

Gd. Bank
Fortune Burin
Port-aux-Basques

Marystown
Crabs

Flounder

Witch & Haddock

Cod

Grindstone

Cod

Caraquet

Haddock

N. Sidney

Pictou

Herring

Haddock

NEW ENGLAND

St. John
St. Andrews
Eastport

Halifax
Grand
Manan
Yarmouth

Cod

Flounders

Rockland
Portland

Herring

Hake

Prawns

Other

Herring

L. Ontario

Ocean
Perch

Herring

MIDDLE
ATLANTIC

Other

Surf
Clams

New
Bedford
Newport

Gloucester
Boston

Mackerel

Hake

ke Erie

Floun-
ders

Menhaden

Pt. Judith
New
York

Alewife

Hake

sters

Other

Crabs

Menhaden

Cambridge Harbor

Hake

lue
abs

CHESAPEAKE

Reedville

Beaufort
Morehead City

SOUTH
TLANTIC
ther

Southport

Jacks

Menhaden

mps

Menhaden

Blue Crabs

Crabs
&
Shrimps

Myers

Tuna

NORTH EAST
ATLANTIC

NORTH WEST
ATLANTIC

WEST CENTRAL
ATLANTIC

Arctic Circle

Tropic of Cancer

Commercial
Fisheries

Landings by Region 1970
Principal species shown as percentage of
total catch

1500

1000

500

250

50

In millions of pounds

Great Lakes, Mississippi and tributaries;
principal species shown numerically

▲ Important fishing port with fish processing
industries

• Important landing ports

Subsistence fishing in the Arctic is not recorded

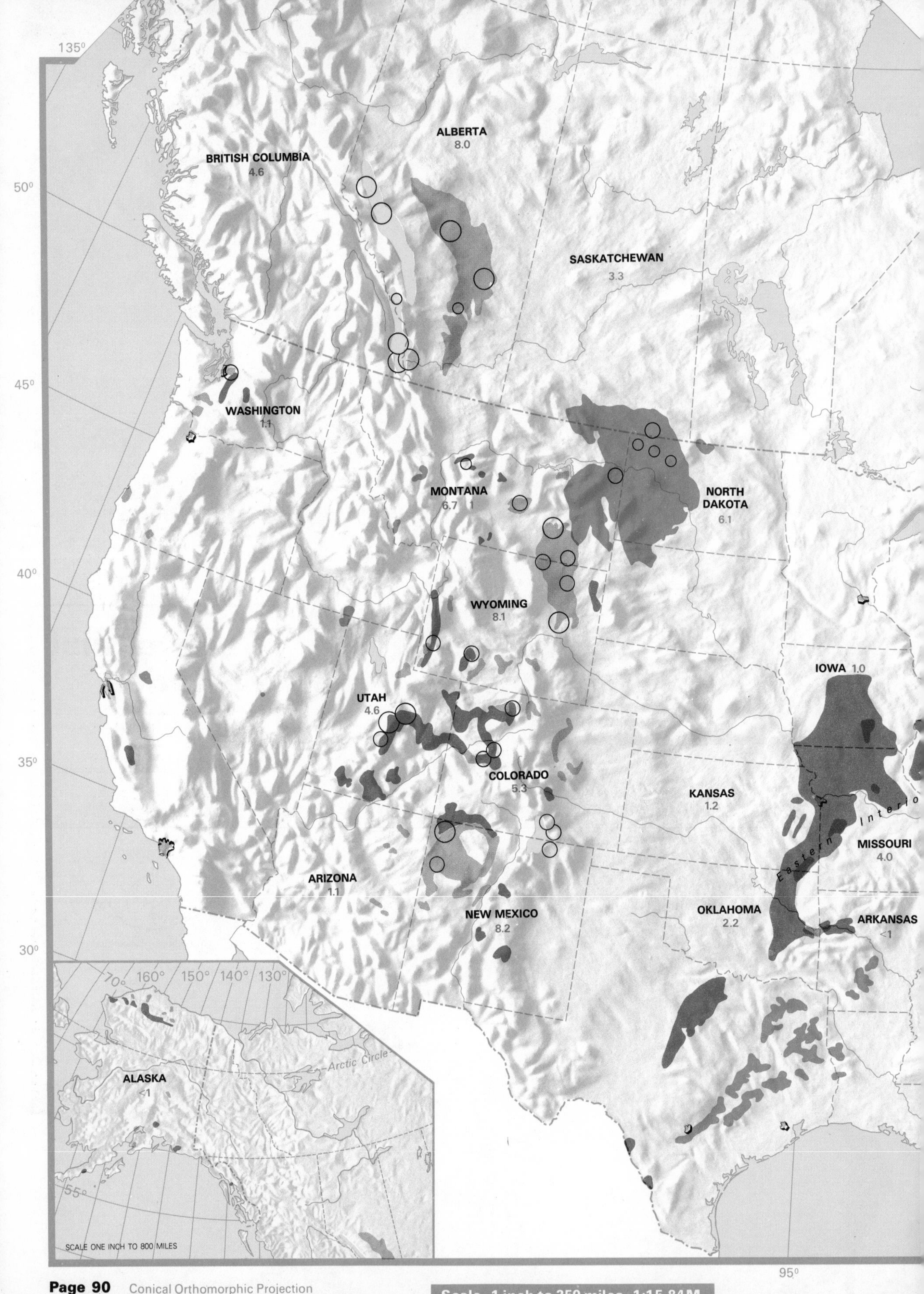

BRITISH COLUMBIA
4.6

ALBERTA
8.0

SASKATCHEWAN
3.3

WASHINGTON
1.1

MONTANA
6.7 1

NORTH
DAKOTA
6.1

WYOMING
8.1

IOWA 1.0

UTAH
4.6

COLORADO
5.3

KANSAS
1.2

MISSOURI
4.0

ARKANSAS
<1

ARIZONA
1.1

NEW MEXICO
8.2

OKLAHOMA
2.2

Eastern Interio

Arctic Circle

ALASKA
<1

SCALE ONE INCH TO 800 MILES

Conical Orthomorphic Projection
Origin 42° N; Standard Parallels 35° & 49°

Scale   1 inch to 250 miles   1:15.84 M

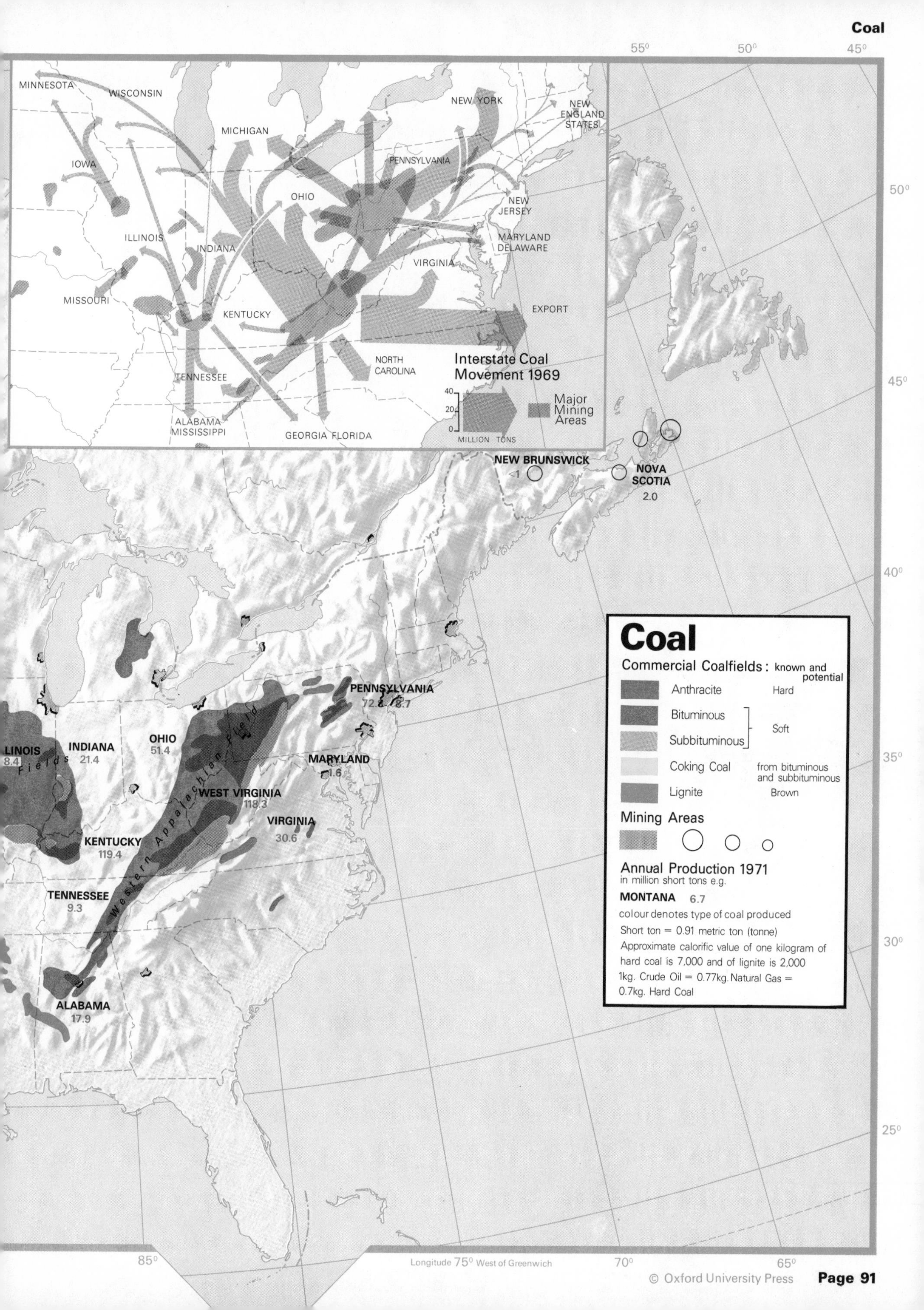

55° 50° 45°

MINNESOTA WISCONSIN

IOWA MICHIGAN NEW YORK NEW ENGLAND STATES

ILLINOIS INDIANA OHIO PENNSYLVANIA

MISSOURI NEW JERSEY

KENTUCKY VIRGINIA MARYLAND DELAWARE

TENNESSEE NORTH CAROLINA EXPORT

ALABAMA MISSISSIPPI GEORGIA FLORIDA

Interstate Coal Movement 1969

40
20
0
MILLION TONS

Major Mining Areas

50°

45°

NEW BRUNSWICK
<1

NOVA SCOTIA
2.0

40°

Coal

Commercial Coalfields : known and potential

Anthracite   Hard

Bituminous   ⎫
                ⎬ Soft
Subbituminous ⎭

Coking Coal   from bituminous and subbituminous

Lignite   Brown

Mining Areas

○ ○ ○

Annual Production 1971
in million short tons e.g.

MONTANA 6.7

colour denotes type of coal produced

Short ton = 0.91 metric ton (tonne)

Approximate calorific value of one kilogram of hard coal is 7,000 and of lignite is 2,000

1kg. Crude Oil = 0.77kg. Natural Gas = 0.7kg. Hard Coal

35°

PENNSYLVANIA
72.8 18.7

LINOIS
8.4

INDIANA
21.4

OHIO
51.4

MARYLAND
1.6

WEST VIRGINIA
118.3

VIRGINIA
30.6

KENTUCKY
119.4

TENNESSEE
9.3

30°

ALABAMA
17.9

Western Appalachian field

25°

85°

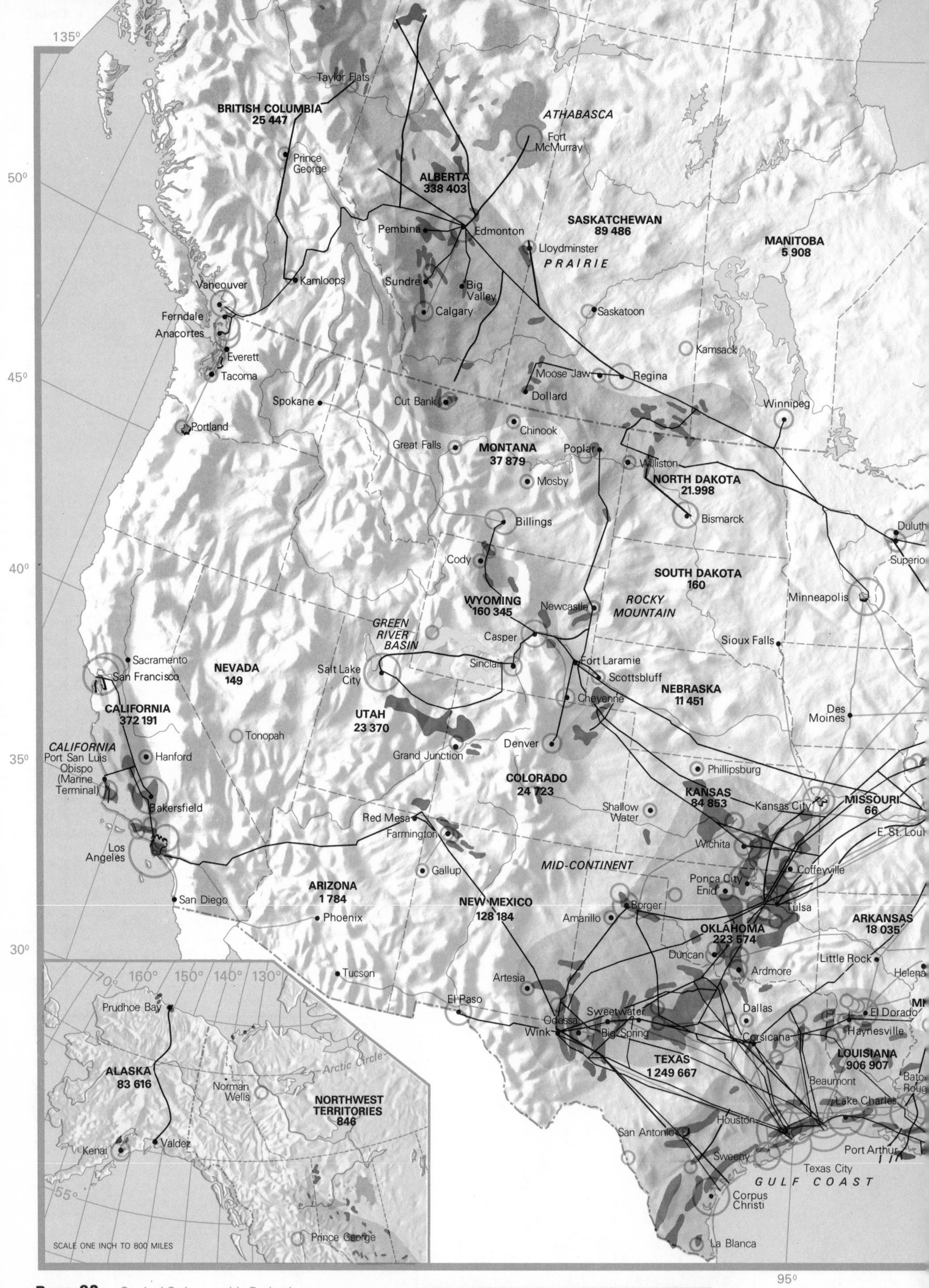

BRITISH COLUMBIA
25 447

Taylor Flats

ATHABASCA

Fort
McMurray

Prince
George

ALBERTA
338 403

SASKATCHEWAN
89 486

MANITOBA
5.908

Pembina

Edmonton

Lloydminster

PRAIRIE

Vancouver

Kamloops

Sundre

Big
Valley

Saskatoon

Kamsack

Ferndale
Anacortes

Calgary

Everett
Tacoma

Moose Jaw

Regina

Winnipeg

Spokane

Cut Bank

Dollard

Portland

Chinook

Great Falls

MONTANA
37 879

Poplar

Williston

Duluth

Mosby

NORTH DAKOTA
21.998

Superior

Billings

Bismarck

Cody

SOUTH DAKOTA
160

Minneapolis

Newcastle

ROCKY
MOUNTAIN

WYOMING
160 345

Casper

Sioux Falls

GREEN
RIVER
BASIN

Sinclair

Fort Laramie

Sacramento

Salt Lake
City

Scottsbluff

Des
Moines

San Francisco

NEVADA
149

Cheyenne

NEBRASKA
11 451

CALIFORNIA
372 191

Tonopah

UTAH
23 370

Denver

Phillipsburg

KANSAS
84 853

MISSOURI
66

CALIFORNIA
Port San Luis
Obispo
(Marine
Terminal)

Hanford

Grand Junction

COLORADO
24 723

Kansas City

Bakersfield

Shallow
Water

Wichita

E. St. Louis

Red Mesa

Farmington

MID-CONTINENT

Ponca City
Enid

Coffeyville

Los
Angeles

Gallup

Tulsa

ARKANSAS
18 035

San Diego

ARIZONA
1 784

NEW MEXICO
128 184

Amarillo

Borger

OKLAHOMA
223 574

Little Rock

Helena

Phoenix

Duncan

Ardmore

Tucson

Artesia

El Paso

Odessa
Wink

Sweetwater

Big Spring

Dallas

Corsicana

El Dorado

Haynesville

LOUISIANA
906 907

Prudhoe Bay

Arctic Circle

TEXAS
1 249 667

Beaumont

Lake Charles

Bato
Rou

Norman
Wells

NORTHWEST
TERRITORIES
846

San Antonio

Houston

Port Arthur

ALASKA
83 616

Sweeny

Texas City

Kenai

Valdez

GULF COAST

Corpus
Christi

La Blanca

Prince George

SCALE ONE INCH TO 800 MILES

Page 92   Conical Orthomorphic Projection
Origin 42° N; Standard Parallels 35° & 49°

Scale 1 inch to 250 miles 1:15.84M

Inset Map

BR. COLUMBIA

ALASKA

ALBERTA

SASKATCHEWAN

MANITOBA

WASHINGTON

MONTANA

QUEBEC

MIDDLE EAST VENEZUELA AFRICA

MAINE

WYOMING

MINNESOTA

ONTARIO

NEW YORK

MIDDLE EAST VENEZUELA NORTH AFRICA NIGERIA

C A L I F O R N I A

UTAH

COLORADO

MICHIGAN

ILLINOIS

INDIANA

OHIO

PENNSYLVANIA

MARYLAND

KANSAS

MISSOURI

KENTUCKY

TENNESSEE

Come-by-Chance

VENEZUELA SUMATRA MIDDLE EAST

NEW MEXICO

OKLAHOMA

ALABAMA

Holyrood

TEXAS

LOUISIANA

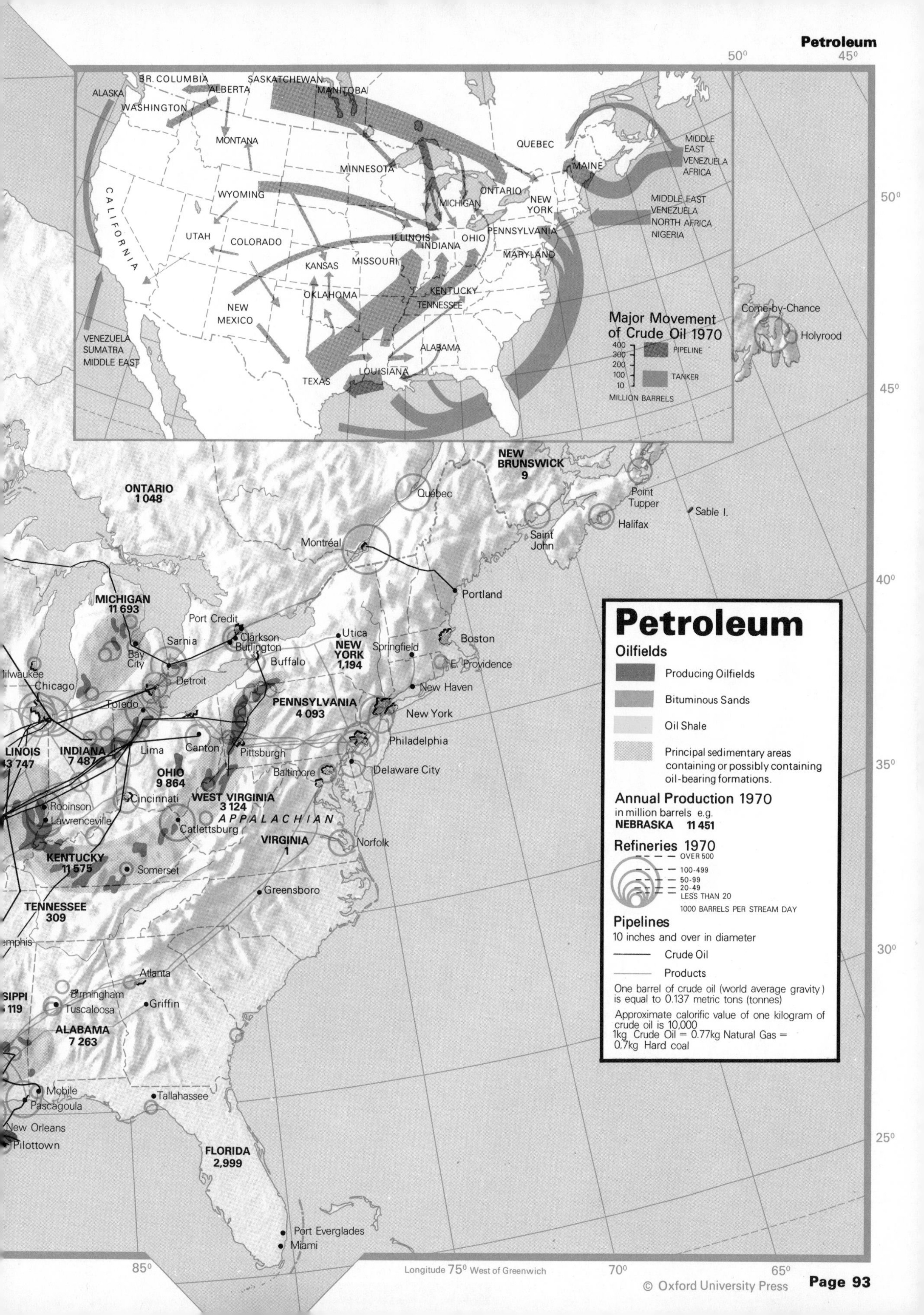

Major Movement of Crude Oil 1970

400	
300	PIPELINE
200	
100	TANKER
10	

MILLION BARRELS

Main Map

ONTARIO 1 048

Québec

NEW BRUNSWICK 9

Point Tupper

Sable I.

Montréal

Portland

Saint John

Halifax

MICHIGAN 11 693

Port Credit

Clarkson Burlington

Sarnia

Utica

NEW YORK 1,194

Springfield

Boston

Bay City

Detroit

Buffalo

E. Providence

Milwaukee

Chicago

New Haven

Toledo

PENNSYLVANIA 4 093

New York

ILLINOIS 43 747

INDIANA 7 487

Lima

Canton

Pittsburgh

Philadelphia

Delaware City

OHIO 9 864

Baltimore

Cincinnati

Robinson

Lawrenceville

WEST VIRGINIA 3 124

APPALACHIAN

Catlettsburg

VIRGINIA 1

Norfolk

KENTUCKY 11 575

Somerset

Greensboro

TENNESSEE 309

Memphis

Atlanta

MISSISSIPPI 119

Birmingham

Tuscaloosa

Griffin

ALABAMA 7 263

Mobile

Pascagoula

Tallahassee

New Orleans

Pilottown

FLORIDA 2,999

Port Everglades

Miami

Legend

Petroleum

Oilfields

Producing Oilfields

Bituminous Sands

Oil Shale

Principal sedimentary areas containing or possibly containing oil-bearing formations.

Annual Production 1970

in million barrels e.g.

NEBRASKA   11 451

Refineries 1970

OVER 500

100-499

50-99

20-49

LESS THAN 20

1000 BARRELS PER STREAM DAY

Pipelines

10 inches and over in diameter

—— Crude Oil

---- Products

One barrel of crude oil (world average gravity) is equal to 0.137 metric tons (tonnes)

Approximate calorific value of one kilogram of crude oil is 10,000
1kg Crude Oil = 0.77kg Natural Gas = 0.7kg Hard coal

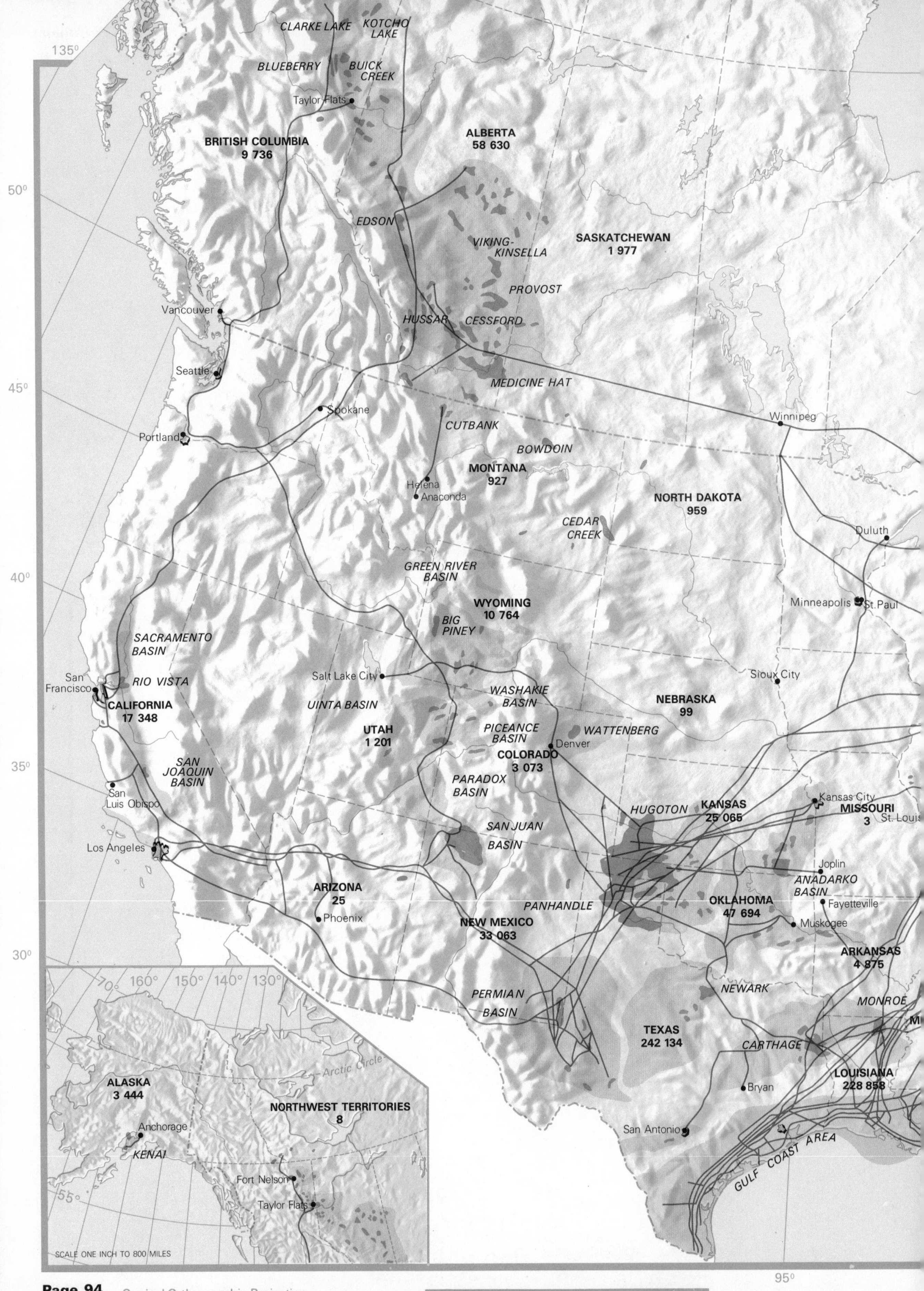

CLARKE LAKE
KOTCHO LAKE
BLUEBERRY
BUICK CREEK
Taylor Flats

BRITISH COLUMBIA
9 736

ALBERTA
58 630

EDSON

VIKING-KINSELLA

SASKATCHEWAN
1 977

PROVOST

Vancouver

HUSSAR
CESSFORD

Seattle

MEDICINE HAT

Spokane

Winnipeg

CUTBANK

Portland

BOWDOIN

MONTANA
927

Helena
Anaconda

NORTH DAKOTA
959

Duluth

CEDAR CREEK

GREEN RIVER BASIN

Minneapolis   St. Paul

WYOMING
10 764

BIG PINEY

SACRAMENTO BASIN

Sioux City

RIO VISTA

Salt Lake City

San Francisco

WASHAKIE BASIN

CALIFORNIA
17 348

NEBRASKA
99

UINTA BASIN

PICEANCE BASIN

UTAH
1 201

WATTENBERG

Denver

COLORADO
3 073

San Luis Obispo

SAN JOAQUIN BASIN

PARADOX BASIN

Kansas City

HUGOTON   KANSAS
25 065

MISSOURI
3   St. Louis

SAN JUAN BASIN

Joplin

Los Angeles

ANADARKO BASIN

Fayetteville

ARIZONA
25

PANHANDLE

OKLAHOMA
47 694

Muskogee

Phoenix

NEW MEXICO
33 063

ARKANSAS
4 875

NEWARK

MONROE
M

PERMIAN BASIN

TEXAS
242 134

CARTHAGE

LOUISIANA
228 858

Bryan

ALASKA
3 444

NORTHWEST TERRITORIES
8

Arctic Circle

San Antonio

GULF COAST AREA

Anchorage

KENAI

Fort Nelson

Taylor Flats

SCALE ONE INCH TO 800 MILES

Scale 1 inch to 250 miles   1:15.84M

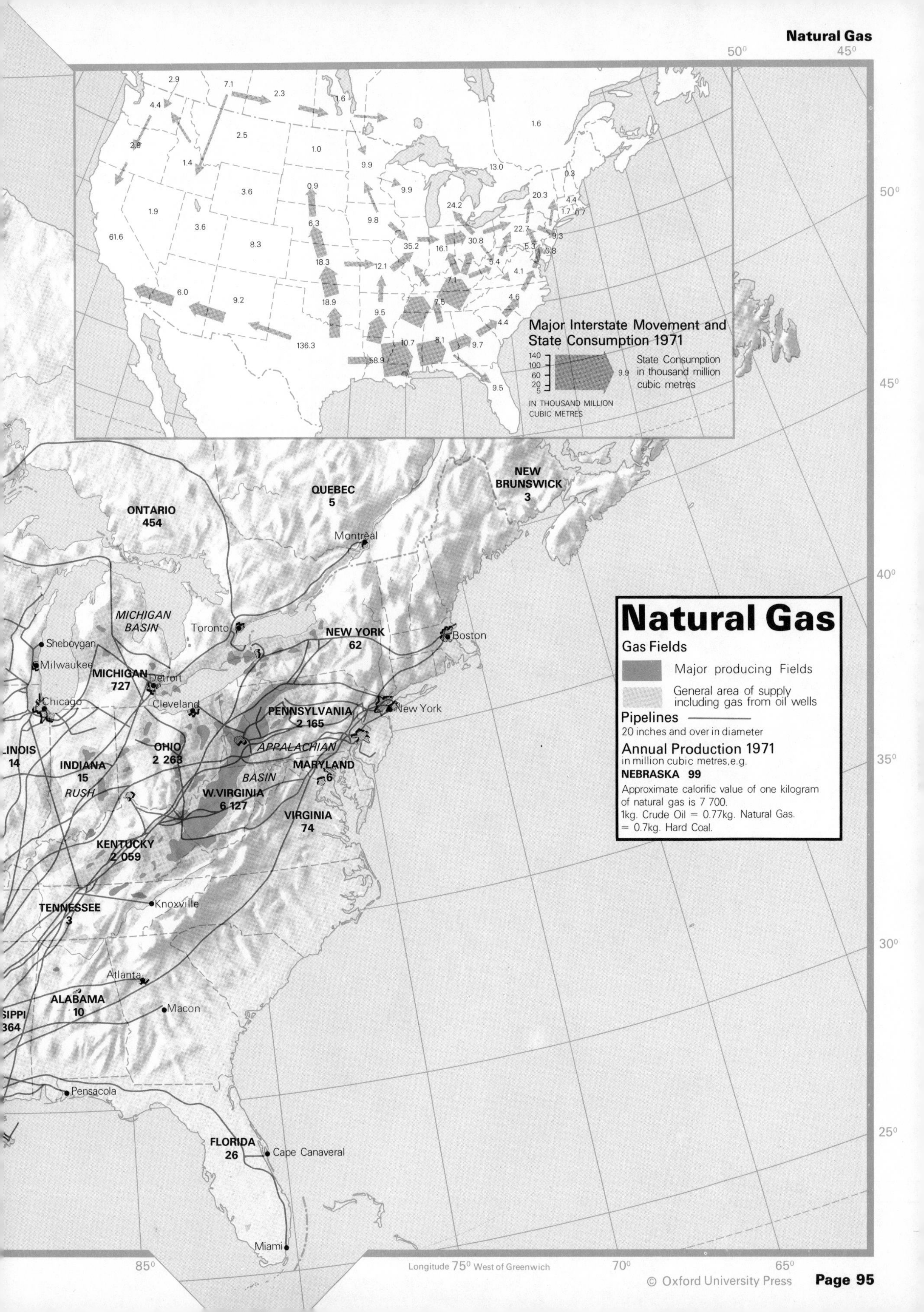

Major Interstate Movement and
State Consumption 1971

140
100
60
20
5

IN THOUSAND MILLION
CUBIC METRES

State Consumption
in thousand million
cubic metres

9.9

2.9   7.1   2.3   1.6
4.4
2.9   1.6
2.5   1.0
1.4   9.9   13.0   0.3
3.6   0.9   9.9   20.3   4.4
6.3   9.8   24.2   22.7   1.7 0.7
1.9   8.3   35.2   16.1   30.8   5.5 9.3
61.6   3.6   18.3   12.1   5.4   4.1
6.0   9.2   18.9   7.5   4.6
136.3   9.5   7.5   4.4
58.9   10.7   8.1   9.7
9.5

QUEBEC
5

NEW
BRUNSWICK
3

ONTARIO
454

Montréal

MICHIGAN
BASIN

Sheboygan

Milwaukee

Toronto

NEW YORK
62

Boston

MICHIGAN
727

Detroit

Chicago

Cleveland

PENNSYLVANIA
2 165

New York

APPALACHIAN

OHIO
2 268

LINOIS
14

INDIANA
15

MARYLAND
6

RUSH

BASIN

W.VIRGINIA
6 127

VIRGINIA
74

KENTUCKY
2 059

TENNESSEE
3

Knoxville

Atlanta

ALABAMA
10

Macon

SIPPI
364

Pensacola

FLORIDA
26

Cape Canaveral

Miami

Natural Gas

Gas Fields

Major producing Fields

General area of supply
including gas from oil wells

Pipelines ———
20 inches and over in diameter

Annual Production 1971
in million cubic metres, e.g.

NEBRASKA   99

Approximate calorific value of one kilogram
of natural gas is 7 700.

1kg. Crude Oil = 0.77kg. Natural Gas.
= 0.7kg. Hard Coal.

50°   45°

50°

45°

40°

35°

30°

25°

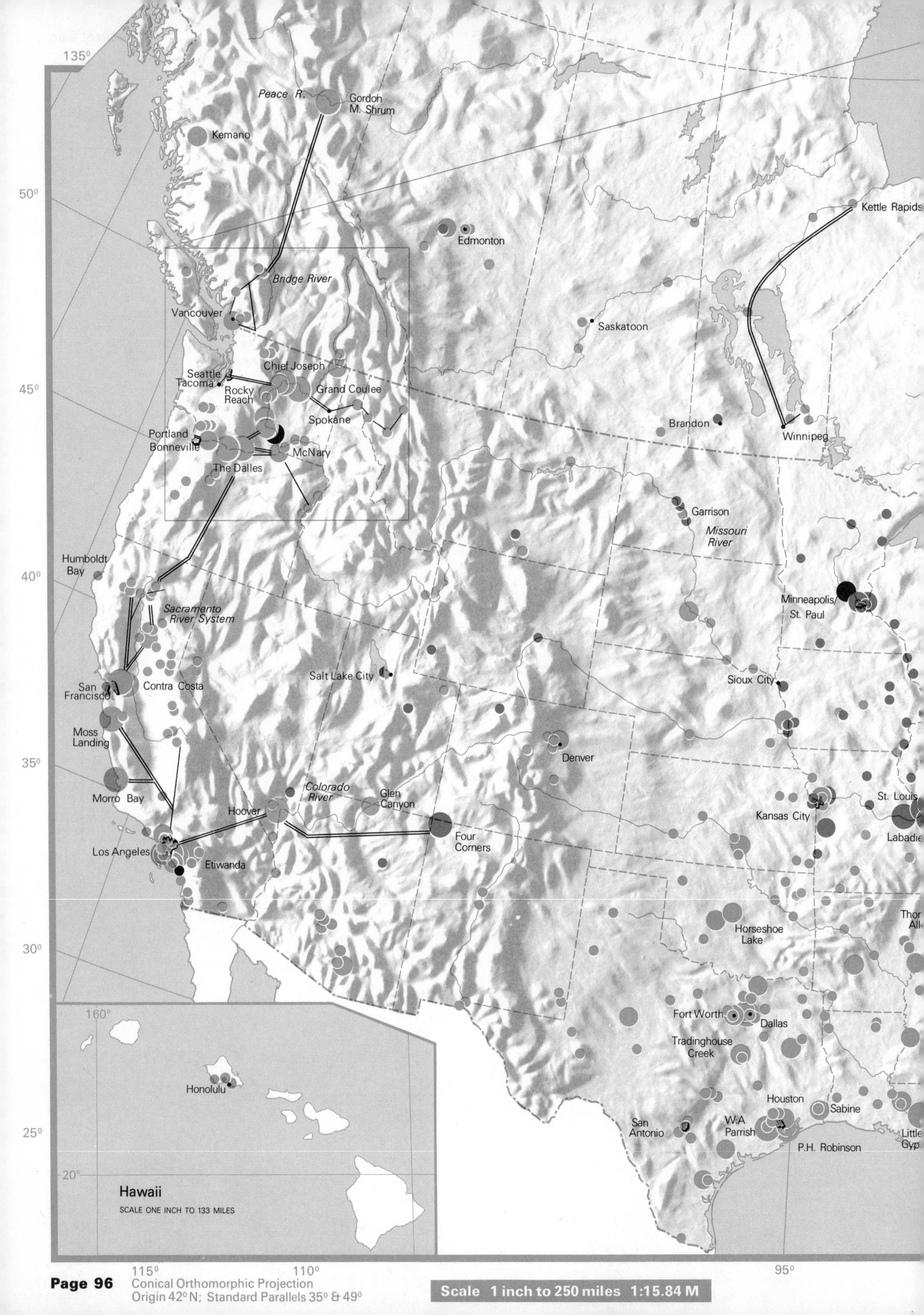

135°

50°

Peace R.   Gordon
          M. Shrum
Kemano

Edmonton

Bridge River

Kettle Rapids

Vancouver

Saskatoon

45°

Seattle   Chief Joseph
Tacoma   Grand Coulee
Rocky
Reach   Spokane
Portland
Bonneville
The Dalles   McNary

Brandon

Winnipeg

Garrison

_Missouri
River_

40°

Humboldt
Bay

_Sacramento
River System_

Minneapolis/
St. Paul

Salt Lake City

Sioux City

San
Francisco   Contra Costa

Denver

St. Louis

35°

Moss
Landing

Kansas City

Labadie

Morro Bay

_Colorado
River_   Glen
         Canyon

Hoover

Four
Corners

Los Angeles

Etiwanda

Thor
Alle

30°

Horseshoe
Lake

160°

Fort Worth
Dallas

Tradinghouse
Creek

Honolulu

Houston
Sabine

25°

San
Antonio   W.A
          Parrish

Little
Gyp

P.H. Robinson

20°

Hawaii

SCALE ONE INCH TO 133 MILES

Conical Orthomorphic Projection
Origin 42° N; Standard Parallels 35° & 49°

115°   110°   95°

Scale 1 inch to 250 miles 1:15.84 M

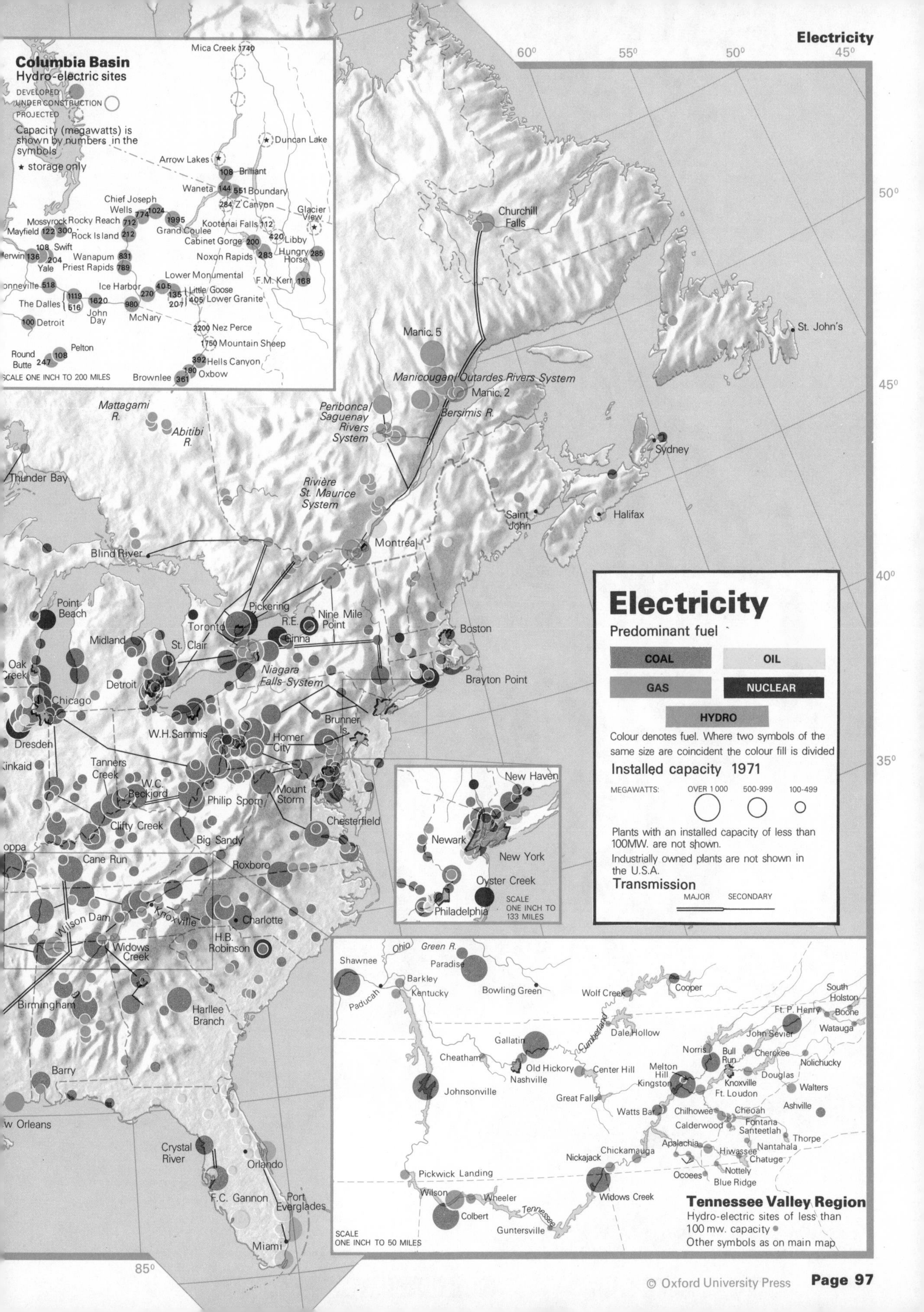
Electricity
Predominant fuel
COAL
OIL
GAS
NUCLEAR
HYDRO
Colour denotes fuel. Where two symbols of the same size are coincident the colour fill is divided
Installed capacity 1971
MEGAWATTS:
OVER 1 000
500-999
100-499
Plants with an installed capacity of less than 100MW. are not shown.
Industrially owned plants are not shown in the U.S.A.
Transmission
MAJOR
SECONDARY
Columbia Basin
Hydro-electric sites
DEVELOPED
UNDER CONSTRUCTION
PROJECTED
Capacity (megawatts) is shown by numbers in the symbols
★ storage only
Mica Creek 1740
Duncan Lake
Arrow Lakes
108 Brilliant
Waneta 144
551 Boundary
284 Z Canyon
Chief Joseph 1024
Wells 774
Rocky Reach 712
Mossyrock
Mayfield 122
300
Rock Island 212
Grand Coulee 1995
Kootenai Falls 112
Glacier View
420 Libby
Cabinet Gorge 200
Noxon Rapids 283
Hungry Horse 285
108 Swift
136
204 Yale
Wanapum 831
Priest Rapids 789
Lower Monumental
F.M. Kerr 168
518
Ice Harbor
405
270
135 Little Goose
207
405 Lower Granite
The Dalles 1119
516
1620 John Day
980 McNary
100 Detroit
3200 Nez Perce
1750 Mountain Sheep
Round Butte 247
108 Pelton
392 Hells Canyon
190 Oxbow
Brownlee 361
SCALE ONE INCH TO 200 MILES
Churchill Falls
Manic. 5
Manicougan/Outardes Rivers System
Manic. 2
Bersimis R.
Peribonca/Saguenay Rivers System
Mattagami R.
Abitibi R.
Rivière St. Maurice System
Thunder Bay
St. John's
Sydney
Saint John
Halifax
Montréal
Blind River
Point Beach
Pickering
Toronto
R.E. Ginna
Nine Mile Point
Boston
Midland
St. Clair
Oak Creek
Detroit
Niagara Falls System
Brayton Point
Chicago
Dresden
W.H.Sammis
Brunner Is.
Homer City
Kinkaid
Tanners Creek
W.C. Beckjord
Mount Storm
Philip Sporn
Clifty Creek
Chesterfield
Big Sandy
Cane Run
Roxboro
Knoxville
Wilson Dam
Charlotte
Widows Creek
H.B. Robinson
Birmingham
Harllee Branch
Barry
New Orleans
Crystal River
Orlando
F.C. Gannon
Port Everglades
Miami
New Haven
Newark
New York
Oyster Creek
Philadelphia
SCALE ONE INCH TO 133 MILES
Tennessee Valley Region
Hydro-electric sites of less than 100 mw. capacity
Other symbols as on main map
Ohio
Green R.
Shawnee
Paradise
Paducah
Barkley
Kentucky
Bowling Green
Wolf Creek
Cooper
South Holston
Ft. P. Henry
Boone
Watauga
Cumberland
Dale Hollow
John Sevier
Gallatin
Norris
Bull Run
Cherokee
Nolichucky
Cheatham
Old Hickory
Nashville
Center Hill
Melton Hill
Kingston
Knoxville
Douglas
Walters
Johnsonville
Great Falls
Ft. Loudon
Watts Bar
Chilhowee
Cheoah
Ashville
Calderwood
Fontana
Santeetlah
Thorpe
Apalachia
Hiwassee
Nantahala
Nickajack
Chickamauga
Chatuge
Nottely
Ocoees
Blue Ridge
Pickwick Landing
Wilson
Wheeler
Tennessee
Widows Creek
Colbert
Guntersville
SCALE ONE INCH TO 50 MILES
60°
55°
50°
45°
40°
35°
85°

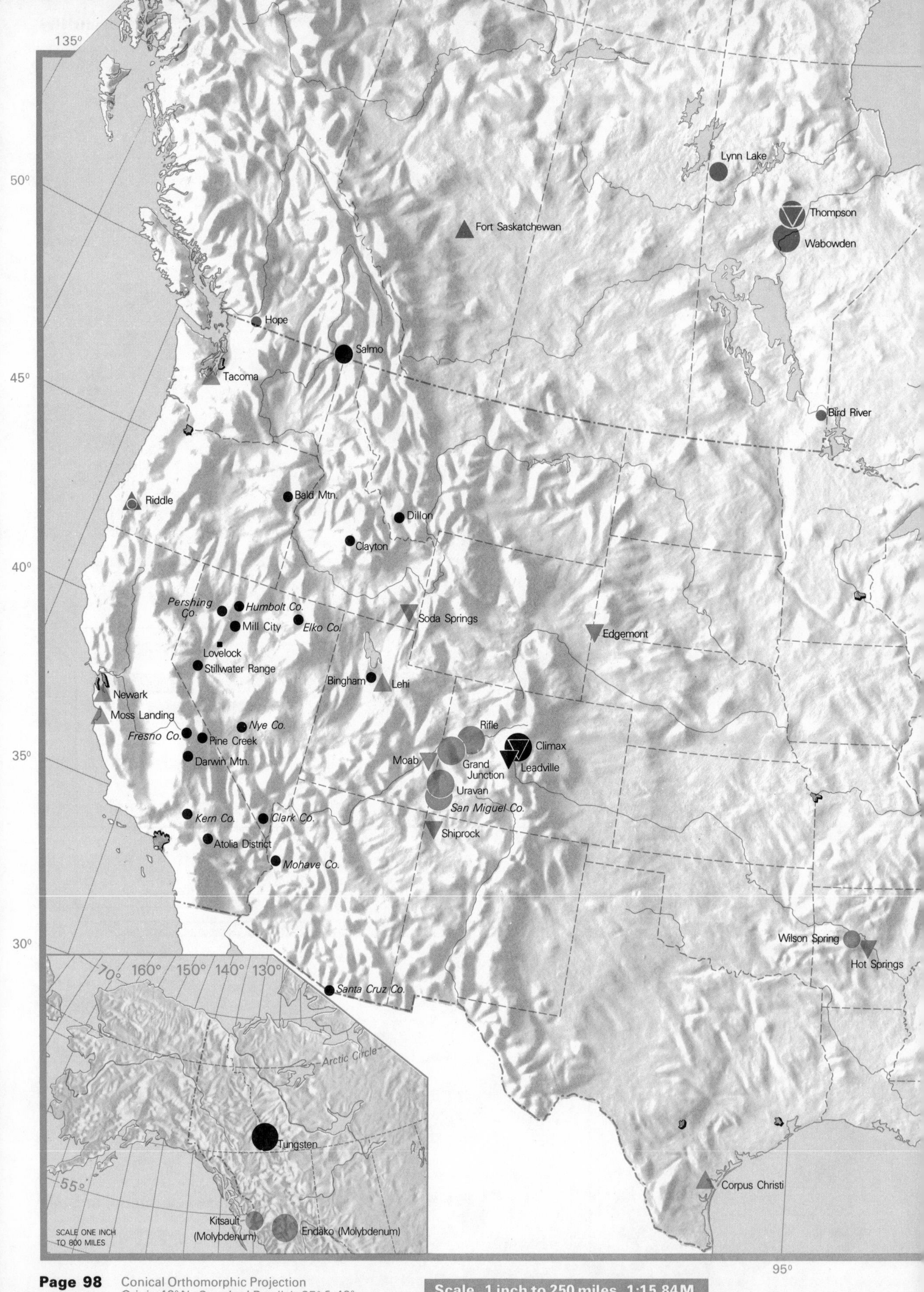

Conical Orthomorphic Projection
Origin 42⁰ N; Standard Parallels 35⁰ & 49⁰

Scale 1 inch to 250 miles 1:15.84M

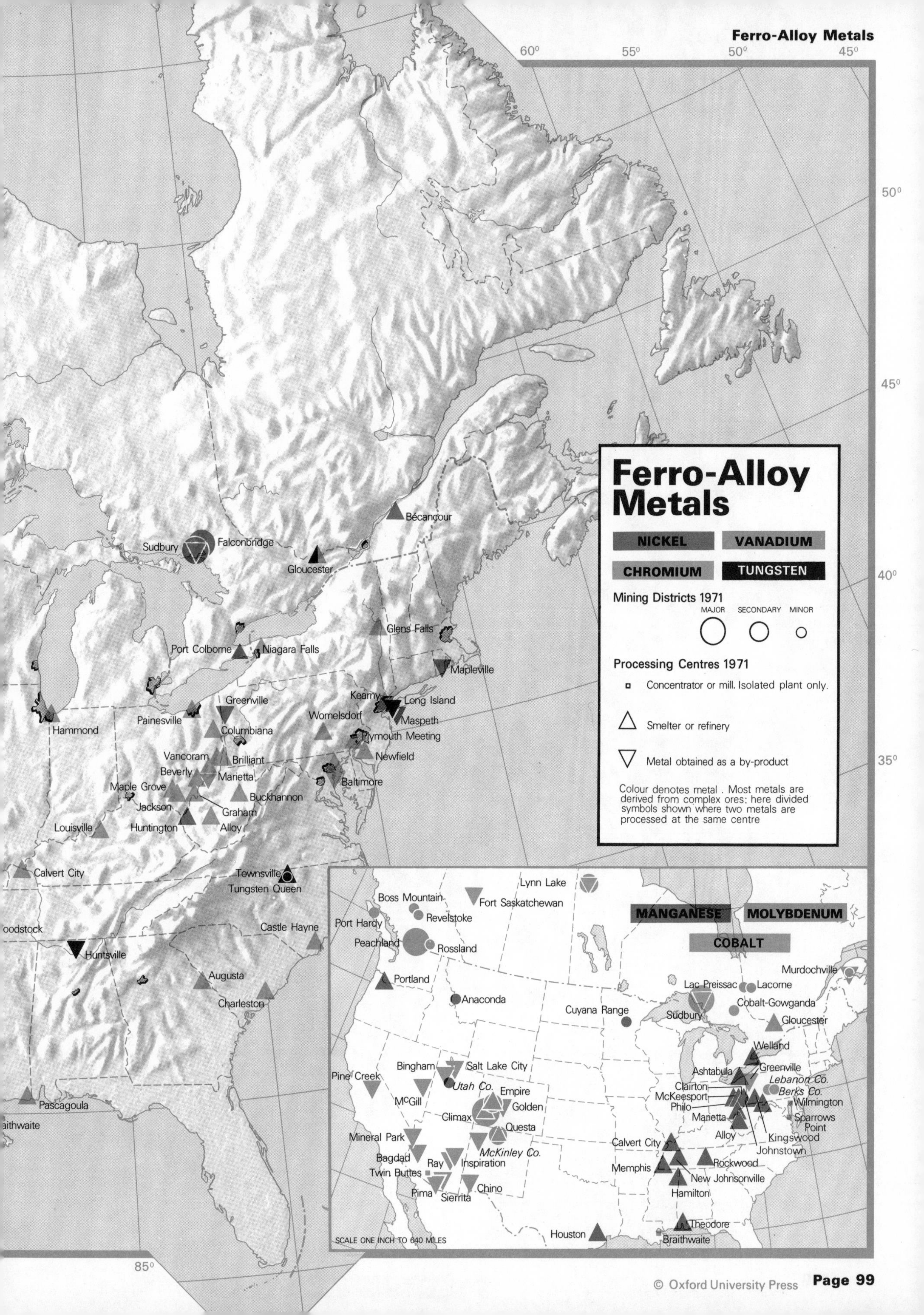
Ferro-Alloy Metals
NICKEL
VANADIUM
CHROMIUM
TUNGSTEN
Mining Districts 1971
MAJOR
SECONDARY
MINOR
Processing Centres 1971
Concentrator or mill. Isolated plant only.
Smelter or refinery
Metal obtained as a by-product
Colour denotes metal . Most metals are derived from complex ores: here divided symbols shown where two metals are processed at the same centre
60°
55°
50°
45°
50°
45°
40°
35°
85°
Bécancour
Sudbury
Falconbridge
Gloucester
Glens Falls
Port Colborne
Niagara Falls
Mapleville
Kearny
Long Island
Maspeth
Greenville
Painesville
Hammond
Womelsdorf
Columbiana
Plymouth Meeting
Newfield
Vancoram
Brilliant
Beverly
Marietta
Baltimore
Maple Grove
Buckhannon
Jackson
Graham
Louisville
Huntington
Alloy
Calvert City
Townsville
Tungsten Queen
oodstock
Castle Hayne
Huntsville
Augusta
Charleston
Pascagoula
aithwaite
MANGANESE
MOLYBDENUM
COBALT
Lynn Lake
Boss Mountain
Fort Saskatchewan
Revelstoke
Port Hardy
Peachland
Rossland
Portland
Anaconda
Murdochville
Lac Preissac
Lacorne
Cobalt-Gowganda
Cuyana Range
Sudbury
Gloucester
Welland
Greenville
Ashtabula
Lebanon Co.
Berks Co.
Clairton
McKeesport
Philo
Wilmington
Marietta
Sparrows Point
Alloy
Kingswood
Johnstown
Bingham
Salt Lake City
Pine Creek
Utah Co.
Empire
McGill
Golden
Climax
Questa
Mineral Park
McKinley Co.
Bagdad
Ray
Inspiration
Twin Buttes
Pima
Sierrita
Chino
Calvert City
Memphis
Rockwood
New Johnsonville
Hamilton
Theodore
Braithwaite
Houston
SCALE ONE INCH TO 640 MILES

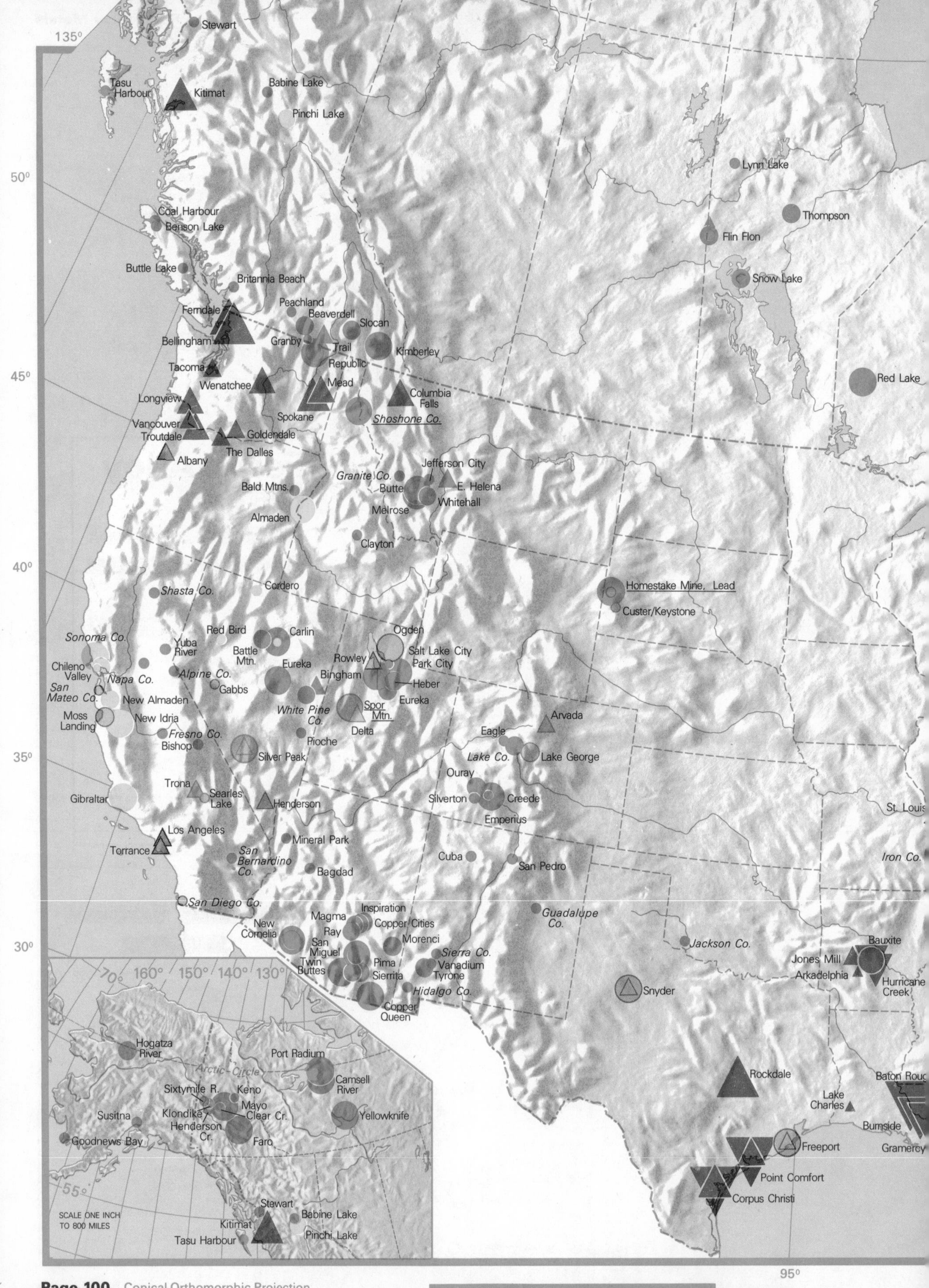

135°

50°

45°

40°

35°

30°

Stewart

Tasu
Harbour

Kitimat

Babine Lake

Pinchi Lake

Lynn Lake

Thompson

Coal Harbour
Benson Lake

Flin Flon

Snow Lake

Buttle Lake

Britannia Beach

Red Lake

Peachland
Beaverdell

Ferndale

Slocan

Granby

Bellingham

Trail

Kimberley

Republic

Tacoma

Mead

Wenatchee

Columbia
Falls

Longview

Spokane

Shoshone Co.

Vancouver
Troutdale

Goldendale

Albany

The Dalles

Granite Co.

Jefferson City

Bald Mtns.

Butte

E. Helena

Almaden

Melrose

Whitehall

Clayton

Cordero

Homestake Mine, Lead

Shasta Co.

Custer/Keystone

Sonoma Co.

Red Bird

Carlin

Yuba
River

Battle
Mtn.

Ogden

Chileno
Valley

Eureka

Rowley

Salt Lake City
Park City

Napa Co.

Alpine Co.

Bingham

Heber

San Mateo Co.

Gabbs

Eureka

New Almaden

White Pine
Co.

Spor
Mtn.

Moss
Landing

New Idria

Delta

Arvada

Fresno Co.

Pioche

Eagle

Bishop

Silver Peak

Lake Co.

Lake George

Trona

Ouray

Gibraltar

Searles
Lake

Henderson

Silverton

Creede

Emperius

Los Angeles

Mineral Park

Cuba

Torrance

San
Bernardino
Co.

Bagdad

San Pedro

Iron Co.

St. Louis

San Diego Co.

Magma

Inspiration

Guadalupe
Co.

New
Cornelia

Ray

Copper Cities

San
Miguel

Morenci

Jackson Co.

Bauxite

Twin
Buttes

Pima

Sierra Co.

Jones Mill

Sierrita

Vanadium
Tyrone

Arkadelphia

Hurricane
Creek

Copper
Queen

Hidalgo Co.

Snyder

Rockdale

Lake
Charles

Baton Rouge

Burnside

Freeport

Gramercy

Point Comfort

Corpus Christi

Hogatza
River

Port Radium

Arctic Circle

Camsell
River

Sixtymile R.

Keno

Klondika
Henderson
Cr.

Mayo
Clear Cr.

Yellowknife

Susitna

Faro

Goodnews Bay

55°

SCALE ONE INCH
TO 800 MILES

70°

160°

150°

140°

130°

Stewart

Babine Lake

Kitimat

Pinchi Lake

Tasu Harbour

Page 100 Conical Orthomorphic Projection
Origin 42° N; Standard Parallels 35° & 49°

Scale 1 inch to 250 miles 1:15.84M

95°

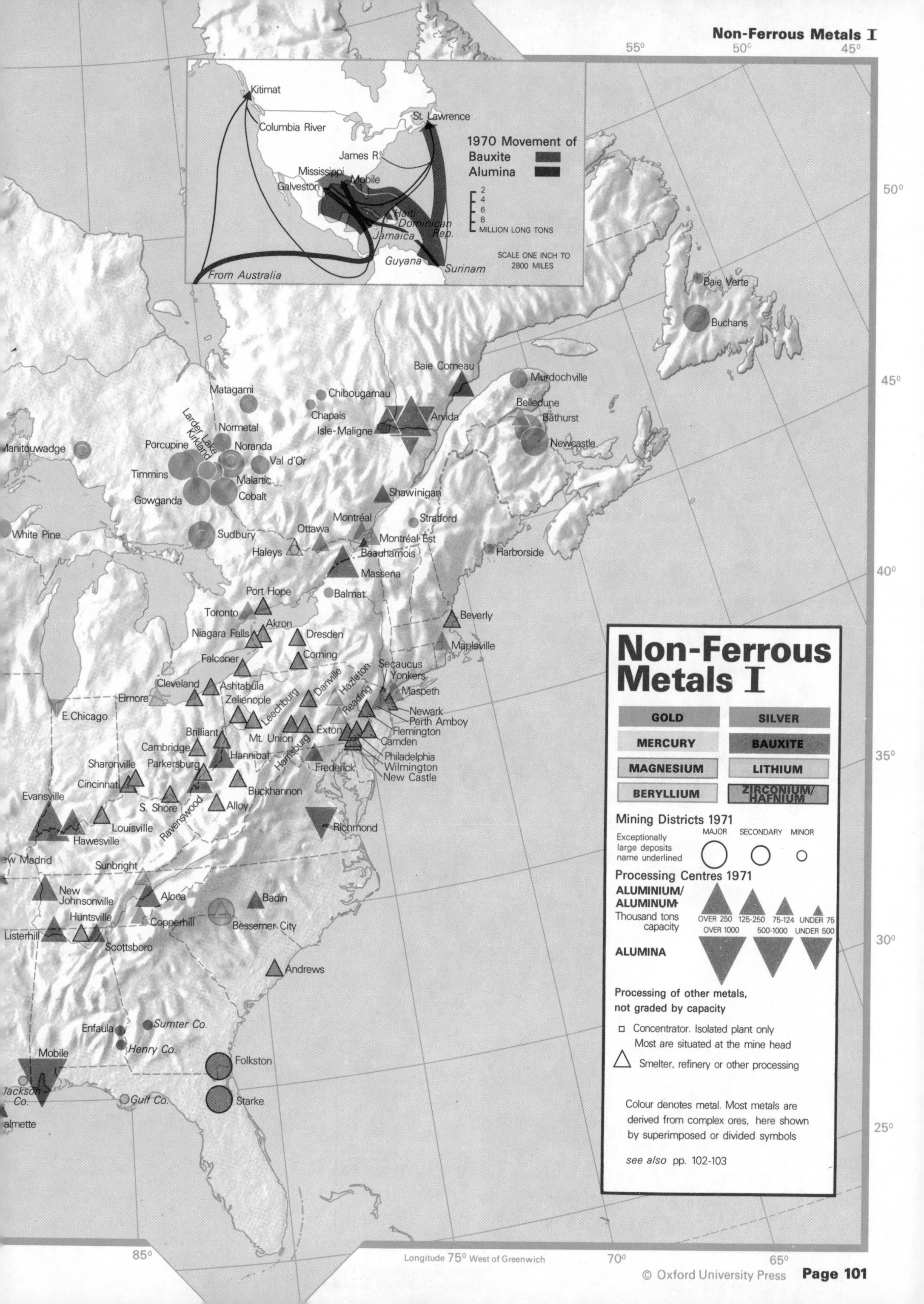

55°   50°   45°

Kitimat

Columbia River

St. Lawrence

James R.

Mississippi
Galveston   Mobile

1970 Movement of
Bauxite
Alumina

2
4
6
8
MILLION LONG TONS

Haiti
Dominican Rep.
Jamaica

Guyana   Surinam

SCALE ONE INCH TO
2800 MILES

From Australia

Baie Verte

Buchans

50°

Manitouwadge

Matagami

Baie Comeau

Murdochville

45°

Chibougamau

Normetal

Chapais
Isle-Maligne   Arvida

Belledune
Bathurst

Larder Lake
Porcupine   Kirkland

Normanda

Noranda

Newcastle

Timmins
Gowganda

Val d'Or

Malartic
Cobalt

Shawinigan

White Pine

Sudbury

Haleys

Ottawa

Montréal
Montréal Est
Beauharnois

Stratford

Harborside

40°

Port Hope

Massena

Toronto

Balmat

Akron

Beverly

Niagara Falls

Dresden

Mapleville

Falconer

Corning

Secaucus
Yonkers
Maspeth

Cleveland

Ashtabula
Zelienople

Danville
Leechburg

Hazleton
Reading

Newark
Perth Amboy
Flemington

35°

Elmore

E.Chicago

Brilliant

Mt. Union

Exton

Camden
Philadelphia
Wilmington
New Castle

Sharonville
Cambridge
Parkersburg

Cincinnati

Hannibal

Harrisburg

Frederick

Buckhannon

Evansville

S. Shore

Ravenswood

Alloy

Richmond

Louisville
Hawesville

New Madrid

Sunbright

Non-Ferrous
Metals I

GOLD	SILVER
MERCURY	BAUXITE
MAGNESIUM	LITHIUM
BERYLLIUM	ZIRCONIUM/ HAFNIUM

Mining Districts 1971

Exceptionally
large deposits
name underlined

MAJOR   SECONDARY   MINOR

Processing Centres 1971
ALUMINIUM/
ALUMINUM
Thousand tons
capacity

OVER 250   125-250   75-124   UNDER 75
OVER 1000   500-1000   UNDER 500

ALUMINA

Processing of other metals,
not graded by capacity

☐   Concentrator. Isolated plant only
Most are situated at the mine head

△   Smelter, refinery or other processing

Colour denotes metal. Most metals are
derived from complex ores, here shown
by superimposed or divided symbols

see also pp. 102-103

New
Johnsonville

Alcoa

Badin

Huntsville

Copperhill

Bessemer City

30°

Listerhill

Scottsboro

Andrews

Enfaula

Sumter Co.

Henry Co.

Mobile

Folkston

Jackson
Co.

Gulf Co.

Starke

25°

almette

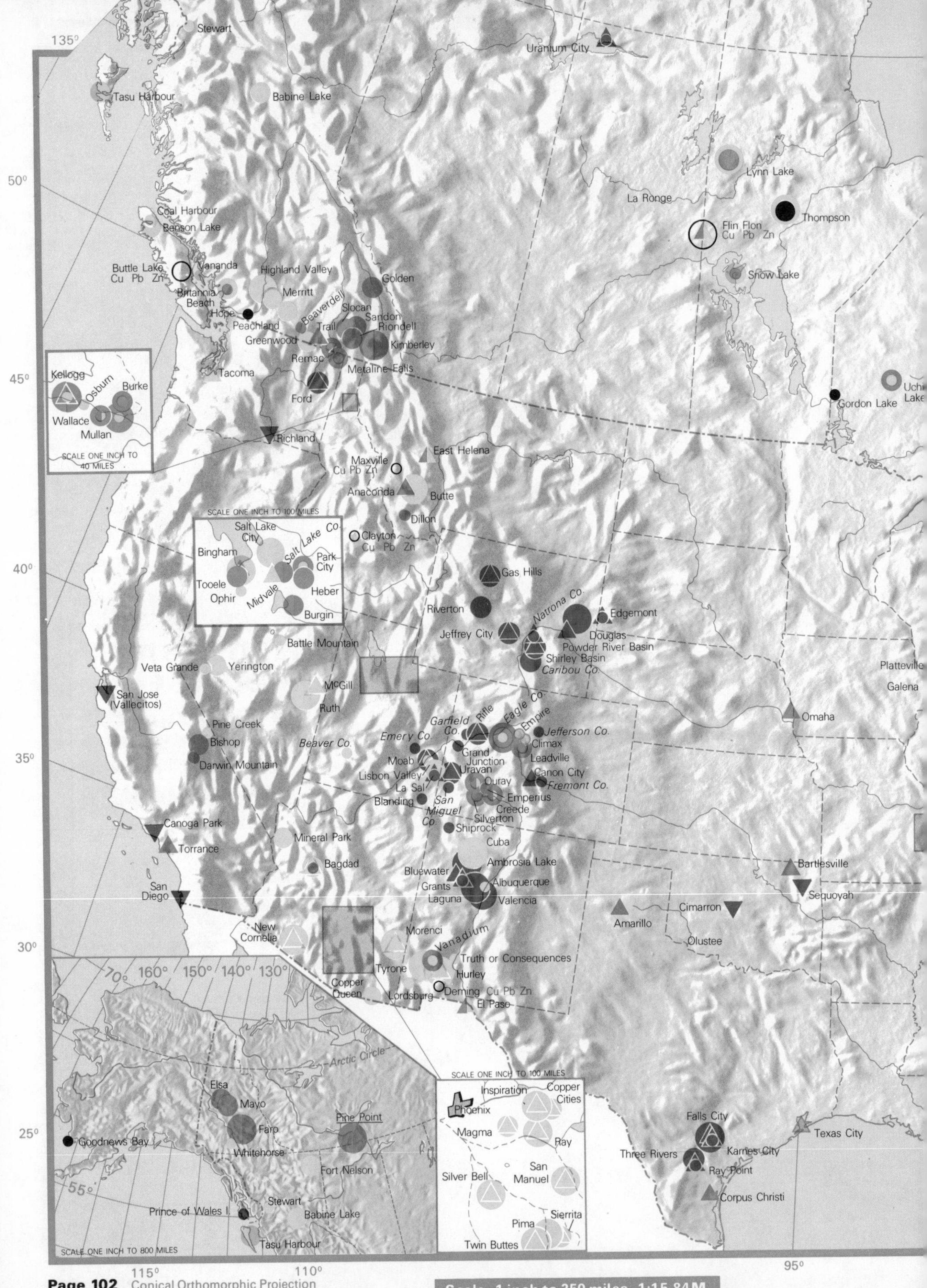

Stewart

Tasu Harbour

Babine Lake

Uranium City

50°

Coal Harbour
Benson Lake

La Ronge

Lynn Lake

Flin Flon
Cu Pb Zn

Thompson

Butte Lake
Cu Pb Zn

Vananda

Highland Valley

Golden

Snow Lake

Britannia
Beach

Hope

Merritt

Beaverdell

Slocan
Sandon
Riondell

Gordon Lake

Uchi
Lake

45°

Peachland

Greenwood

Trail

Kimberley

Kellogg
Osburn
Wallace
Mullan

Burke

Remac

Ford

Metaline Falls

Tacoma

SCALE ONE INCH TO
40 MILES

Richland

East Helena

Maxville
Cu Pb Zn

Anaconda

Butte

SCALE ONE INCH TO 100 MILES

Dillon

40°

Salt Lake
City

Salt Lake Co.

Bingham

Park
City

Clayton
Cu Pb Zn

Gas Hills

Tooele
Ophir

Midvale

Heber

Riverton

Natrona Co.

Edgemont

Battle Mountain

Burgin

Jeffrey City

Douglas
Powder River Basin

Veta Grande

Yerington

McGill

Shirley Basin

Caribou Co.

Platteville
Galena

35°

San Jose
(Vallecitos)

Ruth

Pine Creek
Bishop

Beaver Co.

Garfield
Co.

Rifle

Eagle
Co.

Empire

Jefferson Co.

Omaha

Darwin Mountain

Emery Co.

Moab

Grand
Junction
Uravan

Climax

Leadville

Canon City
Fremont Co.

Lisbon Valley

Ouray

Emperius

Canoga Park

La Sal
Blanding

San
Miguel
Co.

Creede
Silverton

Bartlesville

Torrance

Mineral Park

Shiprock

Cuba

Sequoyah

San
Diego

Bagdad

Bluewater

Ambrosia Lake

30°

New
Cornelia

Grants
Laguna

Albuquerque
Valencia

Cimarron

Amarillo

Olustee

Morenci

Vanadium

Truth or Consequences

Tyrone

Hurley

Copper
Queen

Lordsburg

Deming Cu Pb Zn

El Paso

SCALE ONE INCH TO 100 MILES

Elsa

Inspiration

Copper
Cities

Falls City

25°

Mayo

Phoenix

Magma

Ray

Three Rivers

Karnes City

Farp

Pine Point

Silver Bell

San
Manuel

Ray Point

Whitehorse

Texas City

Goodnews Bay

Fort Nelson

Corpus Christi

Prince of Wales I.

Stewart

Sierrita

Babine Lake

Pima

Twin Buttes

Tasu Harbour

SCALE ONE INCH TO 800 MILES

Arctic Circle

135°

70°

160°

150°

140°

130°

55°

115°

110°

95°

Conical Orthomorphic Projection
Origin 42° N; Standard Parallels 35° & 49°

Scale 1 inch to 250 miles 1:15.84 M

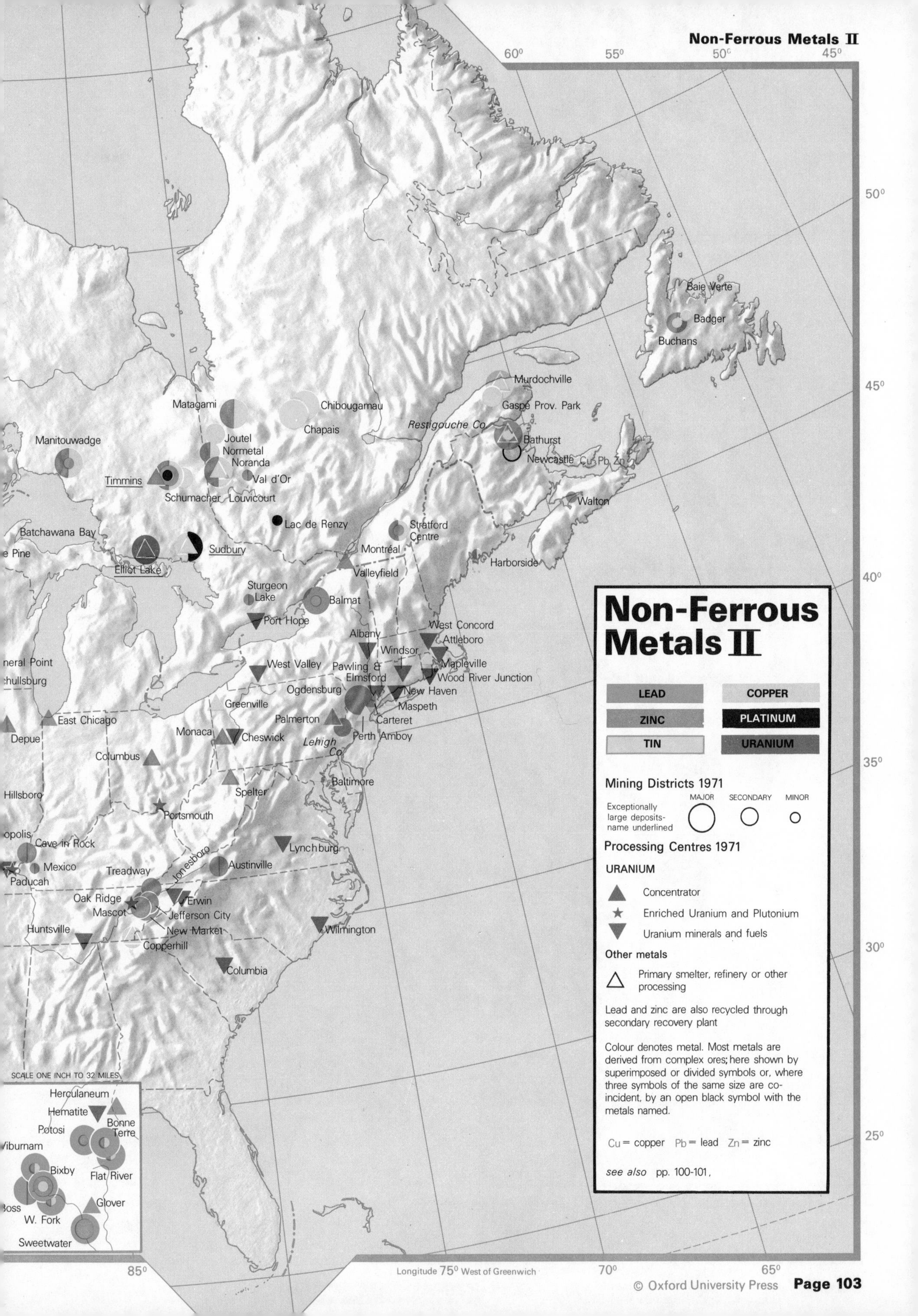

60° 55° 50° 45°

Baie Verte
Badger
Buchans

Murdochville
Gaspé Prov. Park
Restigouche Co.
Bathurst
Newcastle Cu Pb Zn

Walton

Matagami
Chibougamau
Chapais
Joutel
Normetal
Noranda
Val d'Or
Timmins
Schumacher Louvicourt
Manitouwadge

Lac de Renzy

Stratford
Centre
Montréal
Harborside

Batchawana Bay
e Pine
Elliot Lake
Sudbury

Valleyfield

Sturgeon
Lake
Balmat
Port Hope

West Concord
Albany
Attleboro
Windsor
Mapleville
Pawling &
Wood River Junction
Elmsford
New Haven
Maspeth
Carteret
Perth Amboy

West Valley
Ogdensburg
Greenville
Palmerton

neral Point
chullsburg

East Chicago
Monaca
Cheswick
*Lehigh
Co.*

Depue

Columbus

Hillsboro
Spelter

opolis
Portsmouth

Cave in Rock
Baltimore

Mexico
Treadway
Jonesboro
Austinville
Lynchburg
Paducah

Oak Ridge
Mascot
Erwin
Jefferson City
Huntsville
New Market
Copperhill
Wilmington

Columbia

SCALE ONE INCH TO 32 MILES

Herculaneum
Hematite
Bonne
Terre
Potosi
viburnam
Bixby
Flat River
Boss
Glover
W. Fork
Sweetwater

Non-Ferrous
Metals II

LEAD	COPPER
ZINC	PLATINUM
TIN	URANIUM

Mining Districts 1971

Exceptionally
large deposits-
name underlined

MAJOR   SECONDARY   MINOR

Processing Centres 1971

URANIUM

▲ Concentrator

★ Enriched Uranium and Plutonium

▼ Uranium minerals and fuels

Other metals

△ Primary smelter, refinery or other
processing

Lead and zinc are also recycled through
secondary recovery plant

Colour denotes metal. Most metals are
derived from complex ores; here shown by
superimposed or divided symbols or, where
three symbols of the same size are coincident, by an open black symbol with the
metals named.

Cu = copper   Pb = lead   Zn = zinc

see also   pp. 100-101,

50°

45°

40°

35°

30°

25°

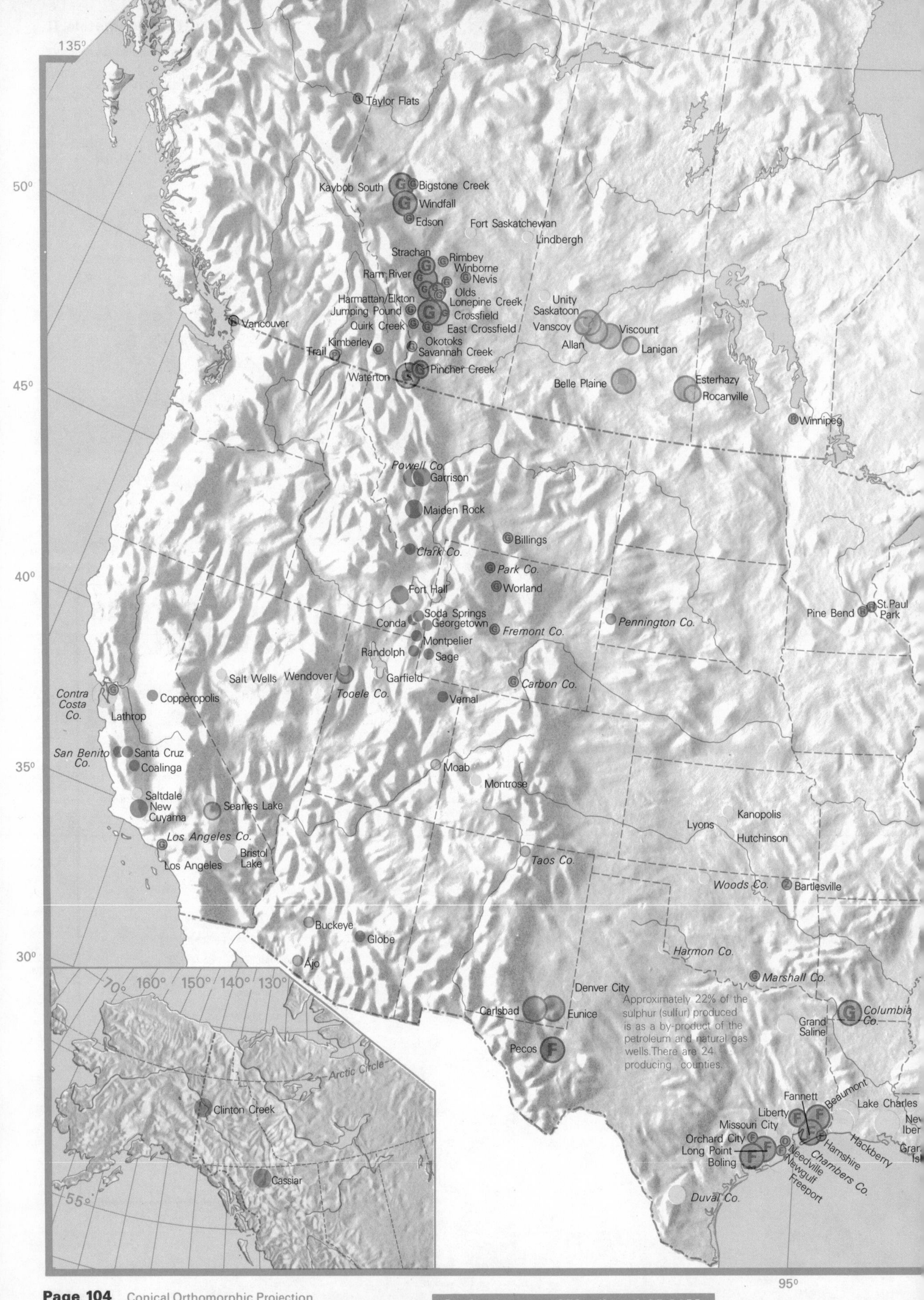

Taylor Flats

Kaybob South G G Bigstone Creek
G Windfall
Edson
Fort Saskatchewan
Lindbergh
Strachan Rimbey
Ram River G Winborne
G Nevis
Harmattan/Elkton Olds
Jumping Pound G Lonepine Creek
Quirk Creek Crossfield
Kimberley East Crossfield
Trail Okotoks
Vancouver Savannah Creek
Waterton S G Pincher Creek

Unity
Saskatoon
Vanscoy Viscount
Allan Lanigan

Belle Plaine
Esterhazy
Rocanville

Winnipeg

Powell Co.
Garrison
Maiden Rock
Billings
Clark Co.
Park Co.
Worland
Fort Hall
Soda Springs
Conda Georgetown Fremont Co.
Montpelier Pennington Co.
Randolph Sage
Pine Bend St. Paul Park
Salt Wells Wendover Garfield
Tooele Co. Carbon Co.
Copperopolis Vernal

Contra
Costa
Co.
Lathrop
San Benito
Co. Santa Cruz
Coalinga Moab
Montrose
Saltdale Lyons Kanopolis
New Cuyama Searles Lake Hutchinson
Los Angeles Co.
Los Angeles Bristol Taos Co.
Lake
Woods Co. Bartlesville

Buckeye
Globe Harmon Co.
Ajo Marshall Co.

Denver City
Carlsbad Eunice Approximately 22% of the Grand Columbia
sulphur (sulfur) produced Saline Co.
Pecos F is as a by-product of the
petroleum and natural gas
wells. There are 24
producing counties.

Fannett Beaumont
Liberty F F Lake Charles
Missouri City Nev
Iber
Orchard City F Hamshire Hackberry Gran
Long Point F Chambers Co. Isl
Boling F Needville
Newgulf
Freeport
Duval Co.

Alaska inset

70° 160° 150° 140° 130°

Arctic Circle

Clinton Creek

Cassiar

55°

Conical Orthomorphic Projection
Origin 42° N; Standard Parallels 35° & 49°

Scale 1 inch to 250 miles 1:15.84 M

135° 50° 45° 40° 35° 30° 95°

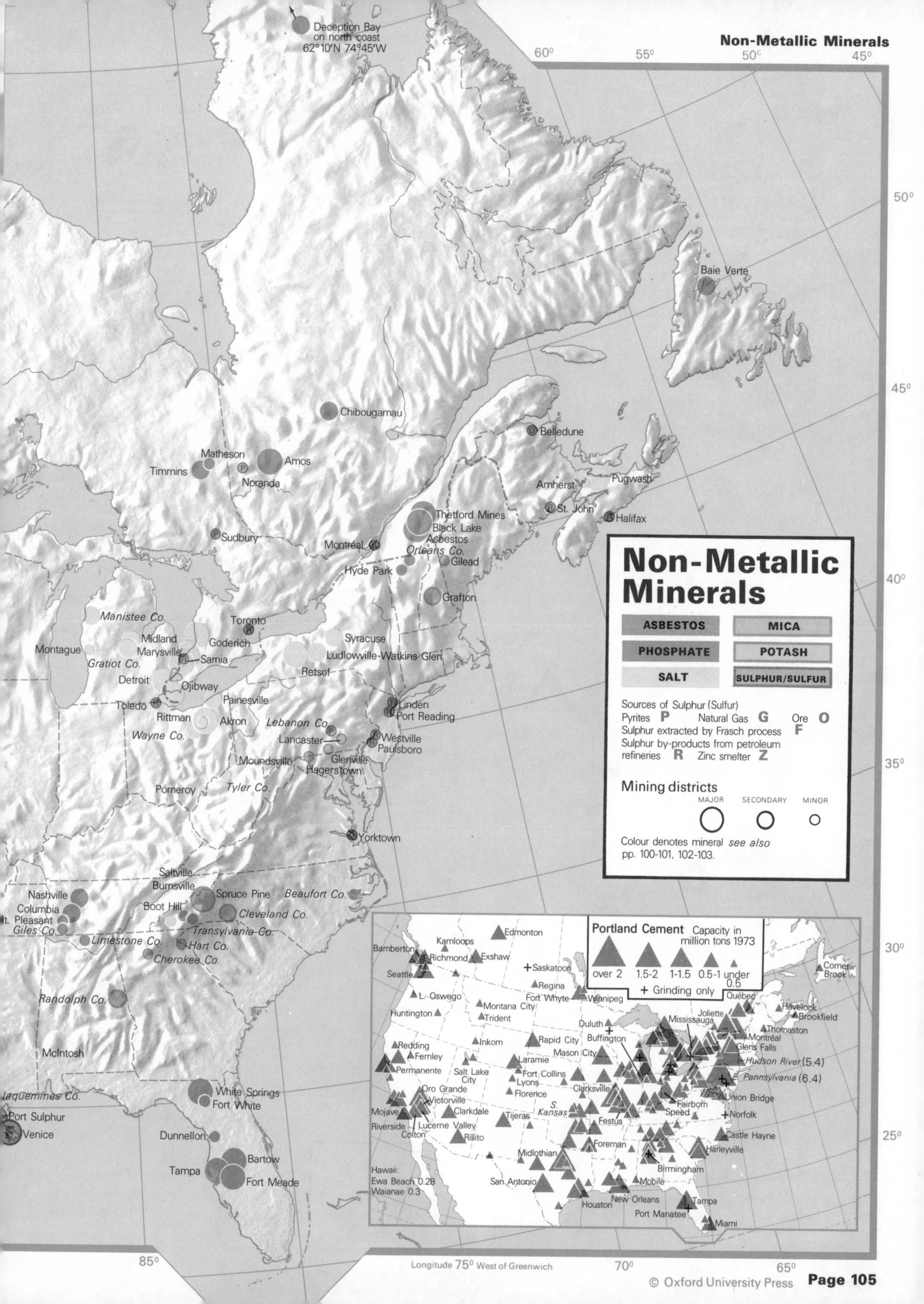
Non-Metallic Minerals
ASBESTOS
MICA
PHOSPHATE
POTASH
SALT
SULPHUR/SULFUR
Sources of Sulphur (Sulfur)
Pyrites P
Natural Gas G
Ore O
Sulphur extracted by Frasch process F
Sulphur by-products from petroleum refineries R
Zinc smelter Z
Mining districts
MAJOR
SECONDARY
MINOR
Colour denotes mineral see also pp. 100-101, 102-103.
Deception Bay on north coast 62°10′N 74°45′W
Baie Verte
Chibougamau
Belledune
Matheson
Timmins
Amos
Noranda
Pugwash
Amherst
St. John
Halifax
Thetford Mines
Black Lake
Asbestos
Sudbury
Montréal
Orleans Co.
Hyde Park
Gilead
Grafton
Manistee Co.
Toronto
Midland
Goderich
Syracuse
Montague
Marysville
Sarnia
Ludlowville-Watkins Glen
Gratiot Co.
Retsof
Detroit
Ojibway
Painesville
Toledo
Linden
Port Reading
Rittman
Akron
Lebanon Co.
Wayne Co.
Lancaster
Westville
Paulsboro
Moundsville
Glenville
Hagerstown
Pomeroy
Tyler Co.
Yorktown
Saltville
Burnsville
Nashville
Spruce Pine
Beaufort Co.
Columbia
Boot Hill
Cleveland Co.
Mt. Pleasant
Giles Co.
Transylvania Co.
Limestone Co.
Hart Co.
Cherokee Co.
Randolph Co.
McIntosh
Plaquemines Co.
White Springs
Fort White
Port Sulphur
Venice
Dunnellon
Bartow
Tampa
Fort Meade
Portland Cement Capacity in million tons 1973
over 2
1.5-2
1-1.5
0.5-1
under 0.5
+ Grinding only
Edmonton
Kamloops
Bamberton
Richmond
Exshaw
Saskatoon
Seattle
Regina
Corner Brook
L. Oswego
Fort Whyte
Winnipeg
Québec
Montana City
Havelock
Huntington
Trident
Joliette
Brookfield
Duluth
Mississauga
Thomaston
Buffington
Montréal
Redding
Inkom
Rapid City
Glens Falls
Mason City
Fernley
Laramie
Hudson River (5.4)
Permanente
Salt Lake City
Fort Collins
E. Pennsylvania (6.4)
Oro Grande
Lyons
Clarksville
Florence
Union Bridge
Victorville
Fairborn
Mojave
Clarkdale
S. Kansas
Speed
Tijeras
Norfolk
Riverside
Lucerne Valley
Festus
Colton
Rillito
Castle Hayne
Foreman
Harleyville
Midlothian
Birmingham
Hawaii: Ewa Beach 0.28 Waianae 0.3
San Antonio
Mobile
Houston
New Orleans
Tampa
Port Manatee
Miami
60°
55°
50°
45°
50°
45°
40°
35°
30°
25°
85°
Longitude 75° West of Greenwich
70°
65°

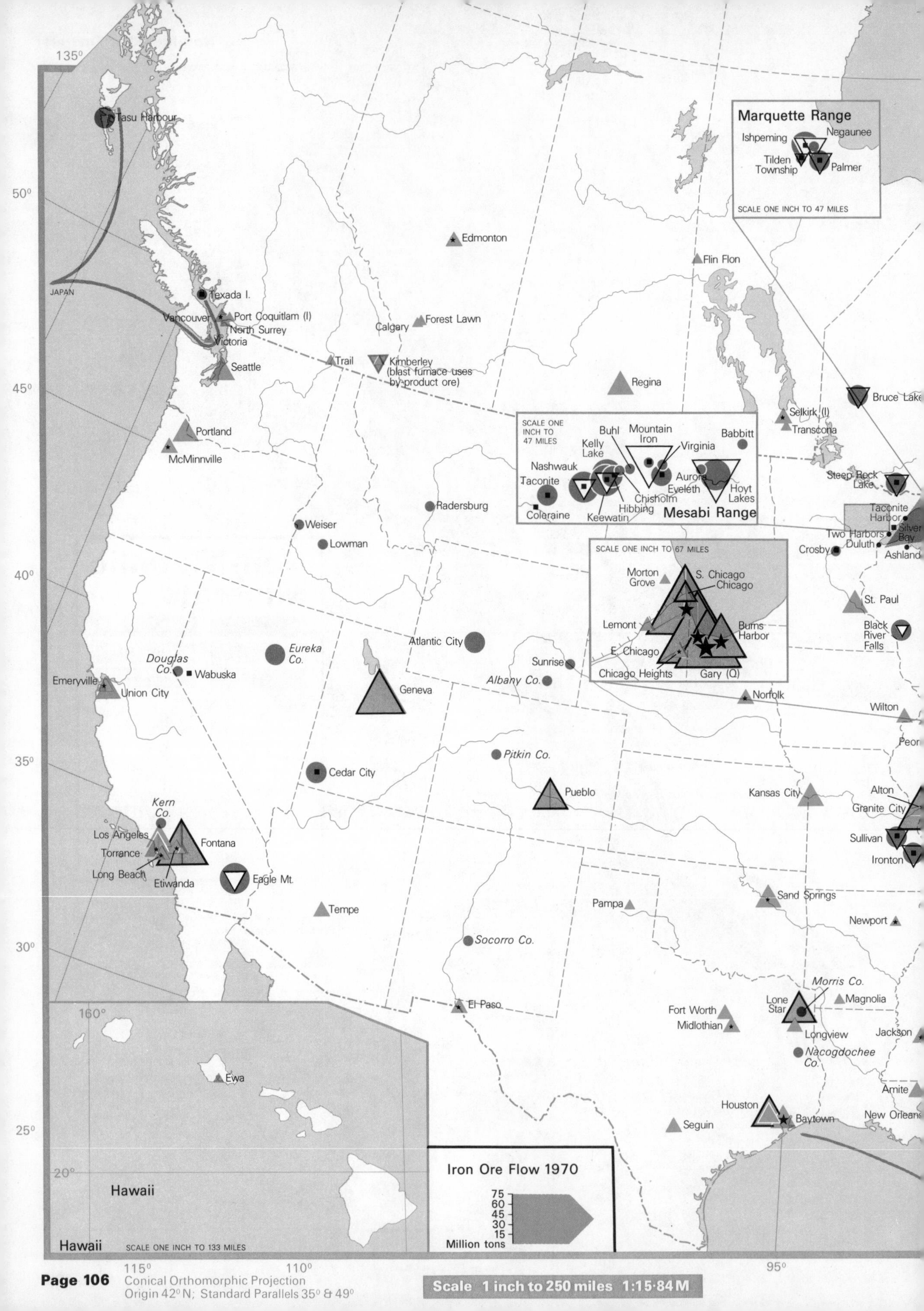

Marquette Range

Ishpeming · Negaunee
Tilden Township · Palmer

SCALE ONE INCH TO 47 MILES

JAPAN

Tasu Harbour

Texada I.
Vancouver
Port Coquitlam (I)
North Surrey
Victoria
Seattle

Edmonton

Flin Flon

Calgary · Forest Lawn

Trail
Kimberley
(blast furnace uses
by-product ore)

Regina

Selkirk (I)
Transcona

Bruce Lake

Steep Rock
Lake

Portland
McMinnville

SCALE ONE
INCH TO
47 MILES

Buhl · Mountain Iron
Kelly Lake · Virginia · Babbitt
Nashwauk · Aurora
Taconite · Eveleth
Coleraine · Chisholm · Hoyt Lakes
Hibbing
Keewatin · **Mesabi Range**

Taconite Harbor
Two Harbors · Silver Bay
Crosby · Duluth
Ashland

Weiser
Lowman

Radersburg

SCALE ONE INCH TO 67 MILES

Morton Grove · S. Chicago · Chicago
Lemont · Burns Harbor
E. Chicago
Chicago Heights · Gary (Q)

St. Paul

Black River Falls

Atlantic City

Sunrise

Albany Co.

Norfolk

Wilton

Peor

Emeryville
Union City

Douglas Co.
Wabuska

Eureka Co.

Geneva

Alton
Granite City

Kansas City

Sullivan
Ironton

Cedar City

Pitkin Co.

Pueblo

Kern Co.
Los Angeles
Torrance
Long Beach
Etiwanda

Fontana

Eagle Mt.

Tempe

Socorro Co.

El Paso

Pampa

Sand Springs

Newport

Fort Worth
Midlothian

Morris Co.
Lone Star
Longview

Magnolia

Jackson

Nacogdoches Co.

Amite

New Orleans

Hawaii

160°

Ewa

Houston
Seguin
Baytown

20°

Hawaii

SCALE ONE INCH TO 133 MILES

Iron Ore Flow 1970

75
60
45
30
15

Million tons

Conical Orthomorphic Projection
Origin 42° N; Standard Parallels 35° & 49°

Scale 1 inch to 250 miles 1:15·84 M

135°

50°

45°

40°

35°

30°

25°

115°
110°
95°

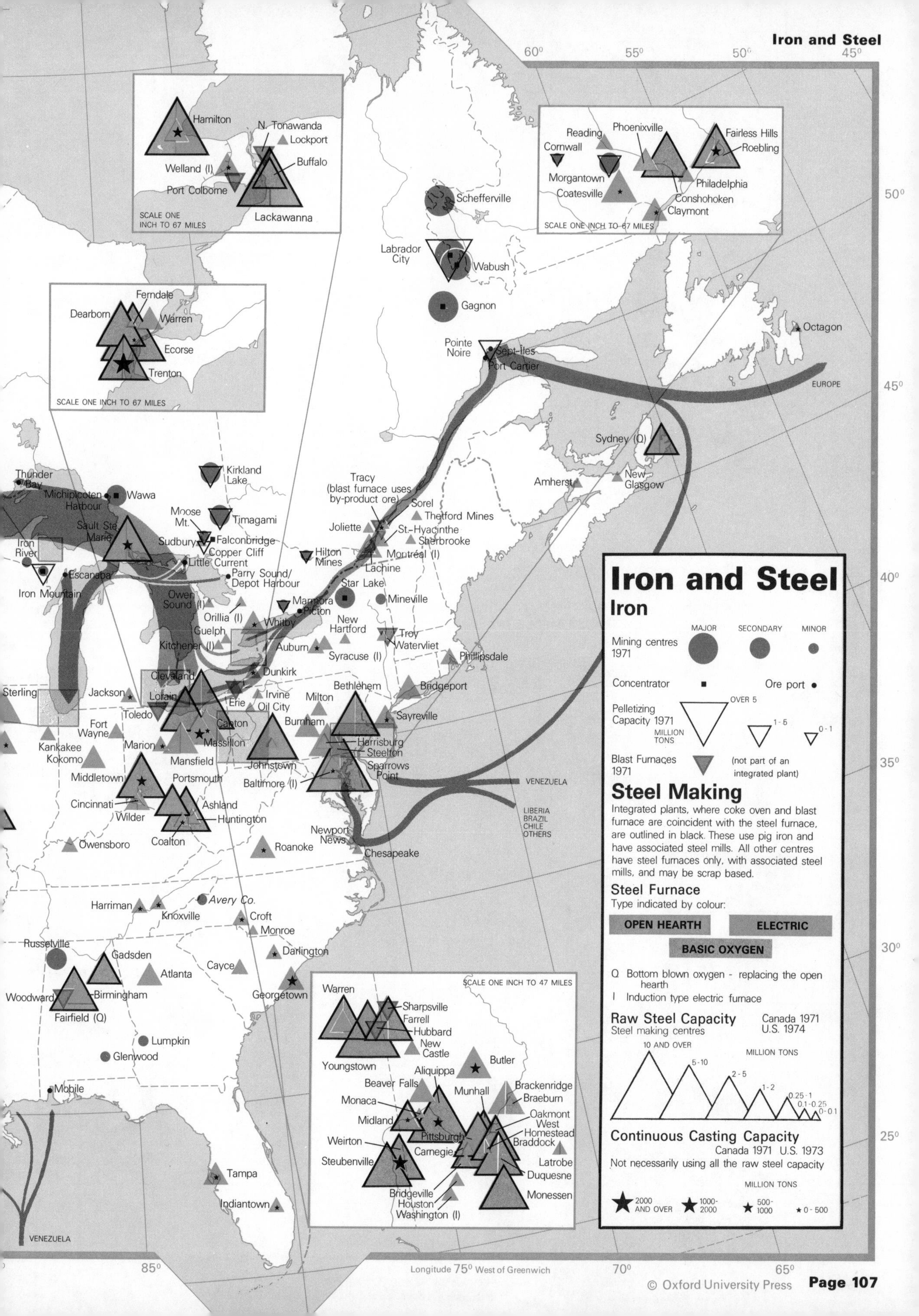

Iron and Steel

Iron

Mining centres 1971 — MAJOR, SECONDARY, MINOR

Concentrator ■   Ore port ●

Pelletizing Capacity 1971 — OVER 5, 1-5, 0-1 MILLION TONS

Blast Furnaces 1971 — (not part of an integrated plant)

Steel Making

Integrated plants, where coke oven and blast furnace are coincident with the steel furnace, are outlined in black. These use pig iron and have associated steel mills. All other centres have steel furnaces only, with associated steel mills, and may be scrap based.

Steel Furnace
Type indicated by colour:

OPEN HEARTH   ELECTRIC

BASIC OXYGEN

Q Bottom blown oxygen - replacing the open hearth
I Induction type electric furnace

Raw Steel Capacity   Canada 1971
Steel making centres   U.S. 1974
10 AND OVER, 5-10, 2-5, 1-2, 0.25-1, 0.1-0.25, 0-0.1 MILLION TONS

Continuous Casting Capacity
Canada 1971 U.S. 1973
Not necessarily using all the raw steel capacity
MILLION TONS
★ 2000 AND OVER   ★ 1000-2000   ★ 500-1000   ★ 0-500

SCALE ONE INCH TO 67 MILES

SCALE ONE INCH TO 67 MILES

SCALE ONE INCH TO 67 MILES

SCALE ONE INCH TO 47 MILES

Hamilton, N. Tonawanda, Lockport, Welland (I), Port Colborne, Buffalo, Lackawanna

Reading, Cornwall, Phoenixville, Fairless Hills, Roebling, Morgantown, Coatesville, Philadelphia, Conshohocken, Claymont

Ferndale, Dearborn, Warren, Ecorse, Trenton

Schefferville, Labrador City, Wabush, Gagnon

Pointe Noire, Sept-Iles, Port Cartier, Octagon

EUROPE

Thunder Bay, Michipicoten Harbour, Wawa, Sault Ste. Marie, Iron River, Escanaba, Iron Mountain

Kirkland Lake, Moose Mt., Timagami, Sudbury, Falconbridge, Copper Cliff, Little Current, Parry Sound/Depot Harbour, Owen Sound (I), Orillia (I), Guelph, Kitchener (I), Whitby

Tracy (blast furnace uses by-product ore), Sorel, Joliette, Thetford Mines, St-Hyacinthe, Sherbrooke, Montréal (I), Lachine

Hilton Mines, Star Lake, Marmora, Picton, New Hartford, Mineville, Troy, Watervliet, Auburn, Syracuse (I), Phillipsdale

Sydney (Q), Amherst, New Glasgow

Sterling, Jackson, Fort Wayne, Kankakee, Kokomo, Middletown, Cincinnati, Wilder, Coalton, Owensboro

Cleveland, Lorain, Toledo, Marion, Mansfield, Massillon, Canton, Portsmouth, Ashland, Huntington

Erie, Irvine Oil City, Milton, Burnham, Johnstown, Harrisburg, Steelton, Bethlehem, Sayreville, Sparrows Point, Baltimore (I), Dunkirk, Bridgeport

Newport News, Chesapeake, Roanoke

VENEZUELA
LIBERIA BRAZIL CHILE OTHERS

Harriman, Knoxville, Croft, Monroe, Darlington, Cayce

Russelville, Gadsden, Atlanta, Woodward, Birmingham, Fairfield (Q), Lumpkin, Glenwood, Mobile, Georgetown

Tampa, Indiantown

Warren, Sharpsville, Farrell, Hubbard, New Castle, Butler, Youngstown, Aliquippa, Beaver Falls, Monaca, Brackenridge, Braeburn, Munhall, Midland, Oakmont, West Homestead, Braddock, Weirton, Pittsburgh, Carnegie, Latrobe, Duquesne, Steubenville, Monessen, Bridgeville, Houston, Washington (I)

Avery Co.

VENEZUELA

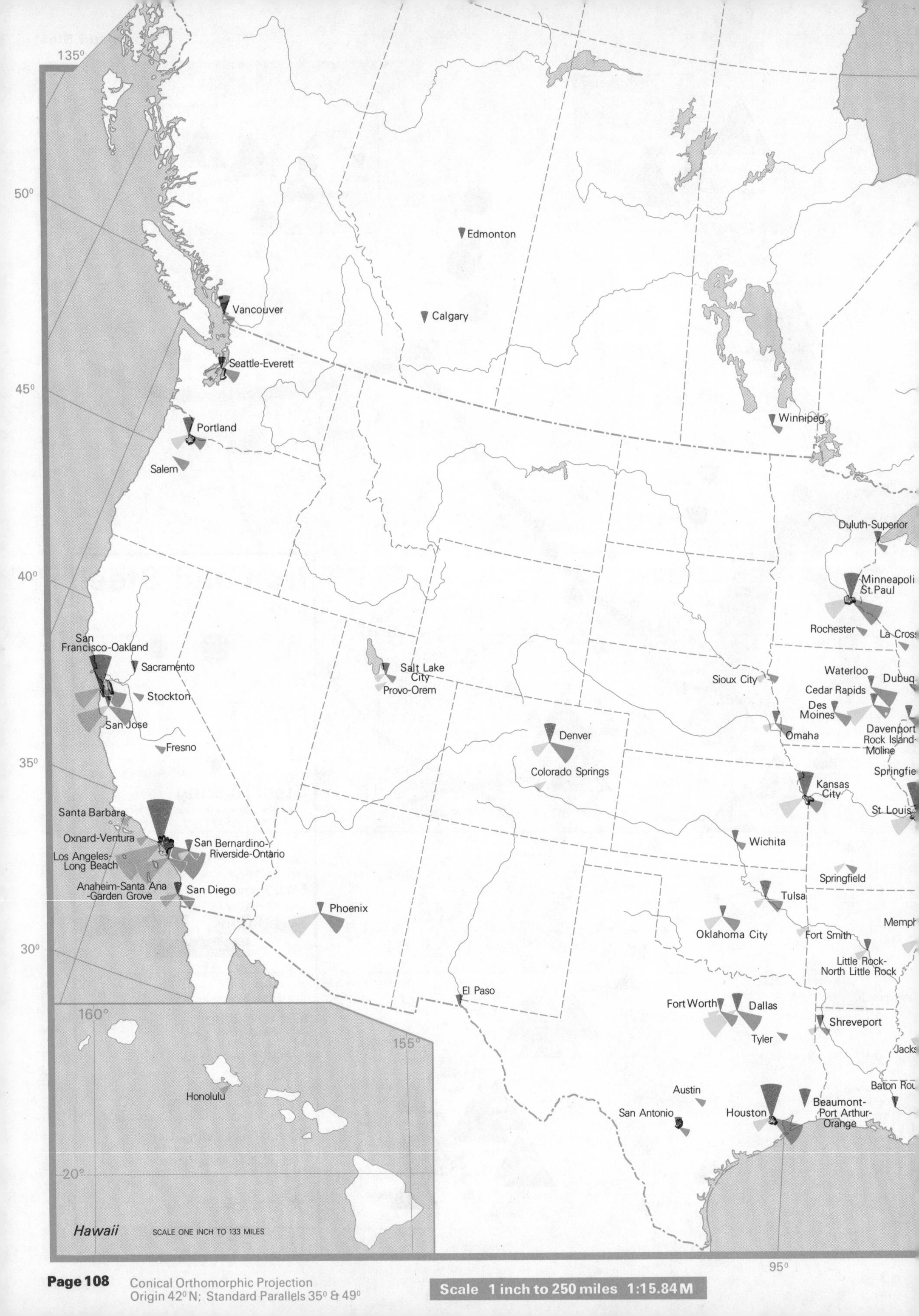

Edmonton

Calgary

Vancouver

Seattle-Everett

Portland

Salem

Winnipeg

Duluth-Superior

Minneapoli
St.Paul

Rochester

La Cross

Sioux City

Waterloo

Dubuq

Cedar Rapids

Des
Moines

Davenport
Rock Island
Moline

San
Francisco-Oakland

Sacramento

Stockton

San Jose

Fresno

Salt Lake
City
Provo-Orem

Denver

Colorado Springs

Omaha

Springfie

Kansas
City

St. Louis

Wichita

Springfield

Santa Barbara

Oxnard-Ventura

Los Angeles-
Long Beach

Anaheim-Santa Ana
-Garden Grove

San Bernardino-
Riverside-Ontario

San Diego

Phoenix

Tulsa

Oklahoma City

Fort Smith

Memph

Little Rock-
North Little Rock

El Paso

Fort Worth

Dallas

Tyler

Shreveport

Jacks

Baton Rou

Austin

San Antonio

Houston

Beaumont-
Port Arthur-
Orange

Honolulu

Hawaii SCALE ONE INCH TO 133 MILES

Scale 1 inch to 250 miles 1:15.84 M

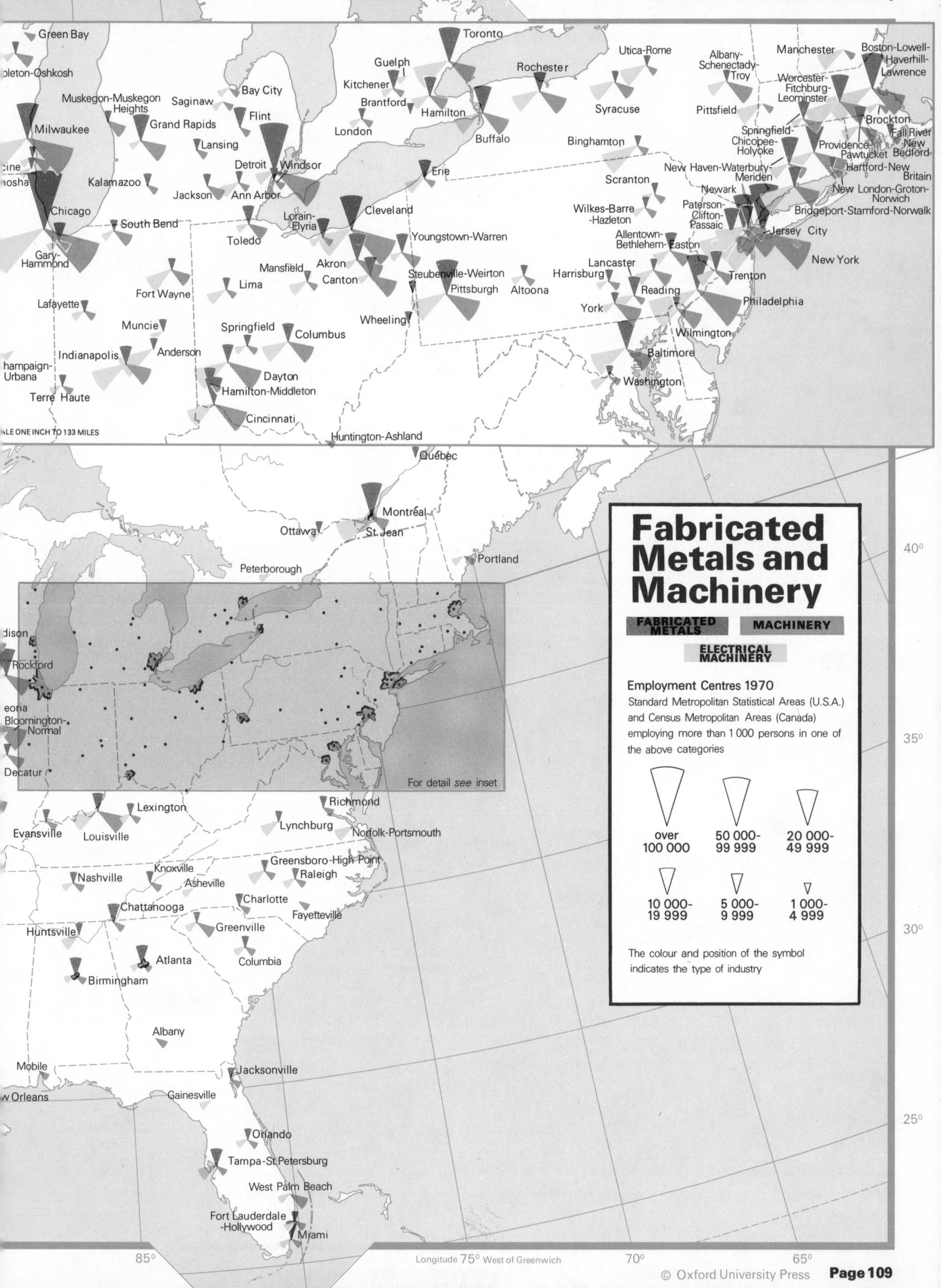

Fabricated Metals and Machinery

FABRICATED METALS   MACHINERY

ELECTRICAL MACHINERY

Employment Centres 1970
Standard Metropolitan Statistical Areas (U.S.A.)
and Census Metropolitan Areas (Canada)
employing more than 1 000 persons in one of
the above categories

over 100 000   50 000– 99 999   20 000– 49 999

10 000– 19 999   5 000– 9 999   1 000– 4 999

The colour and position of the symbol
indicates the type of industry

Green Bay
pleton-Oshkosh
Muskegon-Muskegon Heights
Saginaw
Bay City
Milwaukee
Grand Rapids
Flint
cine
Kalamazoo
Lansing
nosha
Jackson
Detroit
Windsor
Chicago
Ann Arbor
South Bend
Lorain-Elyria
Toledo
Gary-Hammond
Mansfield
Akron
Lima
Canton
Lafayette
Fort Wayne
Muncie
Springfield
Columbus
hampaign-Urbana
Indianapolis
Anderson
Terre Haute
Dayton
Hamilton-Middleton
Cincinnati
Huntington-Ashland

Toronto
Guelph
Kitchener
Brantford
Hamilton
London
Buffalo
Erie
Cleveland
Youngstown-Warren
Steubenville-Weirton
Pittsburgh
Wheeling
Altoona

Rochester
Utica-Rome
Syracuse
Binghamton
Scranton
Wilkes-Barre-Hazleton
Harrisburg
Lancaster
York
Reading
Altoona

Albany-Schenectady-Troy
Pittsfield
Springfield-Chicopee-Holyoke
New Haven-Waterbury-Meriden
Newark
Paterson-Clifton-Passaic
Allentown-Bethlehem-Easton
Trenton
Philadelphia
Wilmington
Baltimore
Washington

Manchester
Worcester-Fitchburg-Leominster
Providence-Pawtucket
Hartford-New Britain
New London-Groton-Norwich
Bridgeport-Stamford-Norwalk
Jersey City
New York

Boston-Lowell-Haverhill-Lawrence
Brockton
Fall River
New Bedford

SCALE ONE INCH TO 133 MILES

Québec
Montréal
Ottawa
St.Jean
Peterborough
Portland

dison
Rockford
eoria
Bloomington-Normal
Decatur

For detail *see* inset

Evansville
Lexington
Louisville
Lynchburg
Richmond
Norfolk-Portsmouth
Nashville
Knoxville
Asheville
Greensboro-High Point
Raleigh
Chattanooga
Charlotte
Fayetteville
Huntsville
Greenville
Atlanta
Columbia
Birmingham
Albany
Mobile
Jacksonville
w Orleans
Gainesville
Orlando
Tampa-St.Petersburg
West Palm Beach
Fort Lauderdale-Hollywood
Miami

40°
35°
30°
25°

85°   Longitude 75° West of Greenwich   70°   65°

© Oxford University Press   **Page 109**

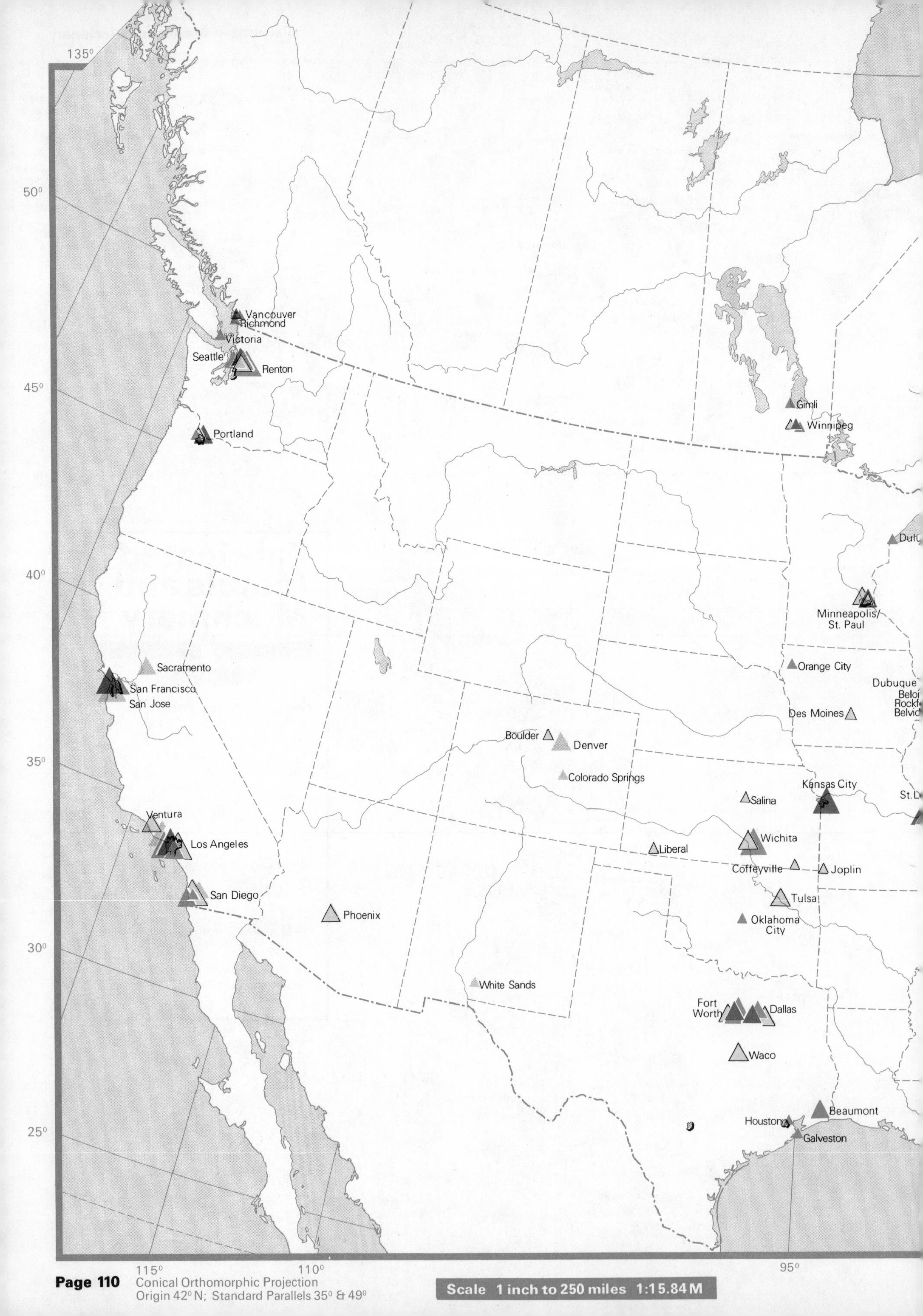

135°

50°

45°

40°

35°

30°

25°

115°   110°   95°

Vancouver
Richmond
Victoria
Seattle
Renton
Portland

Gimli
Winnipeg

Dul

Sacramento
San Francisco
San Jose

Minneapolis/
St. Paul

Orange City

Dubuque
Belo
Rockf
Des Moines   Belvi

Boulder   Denver

Kansas City
St. L

Colorado Springs

Salina

Ventura
Los Angeles

Wichita
Liberal   Joplin
Coffeyville
Tulsa

San Diego

Phoenix

Oklahoma
City

White Sands

Fort   Dallas
Worth

Waco

Beaumont
Houston
Galveston

Conical Orthomorphic Projection
Origin 42° N; Standard Parallels 35° & 49°

Scale 1 inch to 250 miles 1:15.84 M

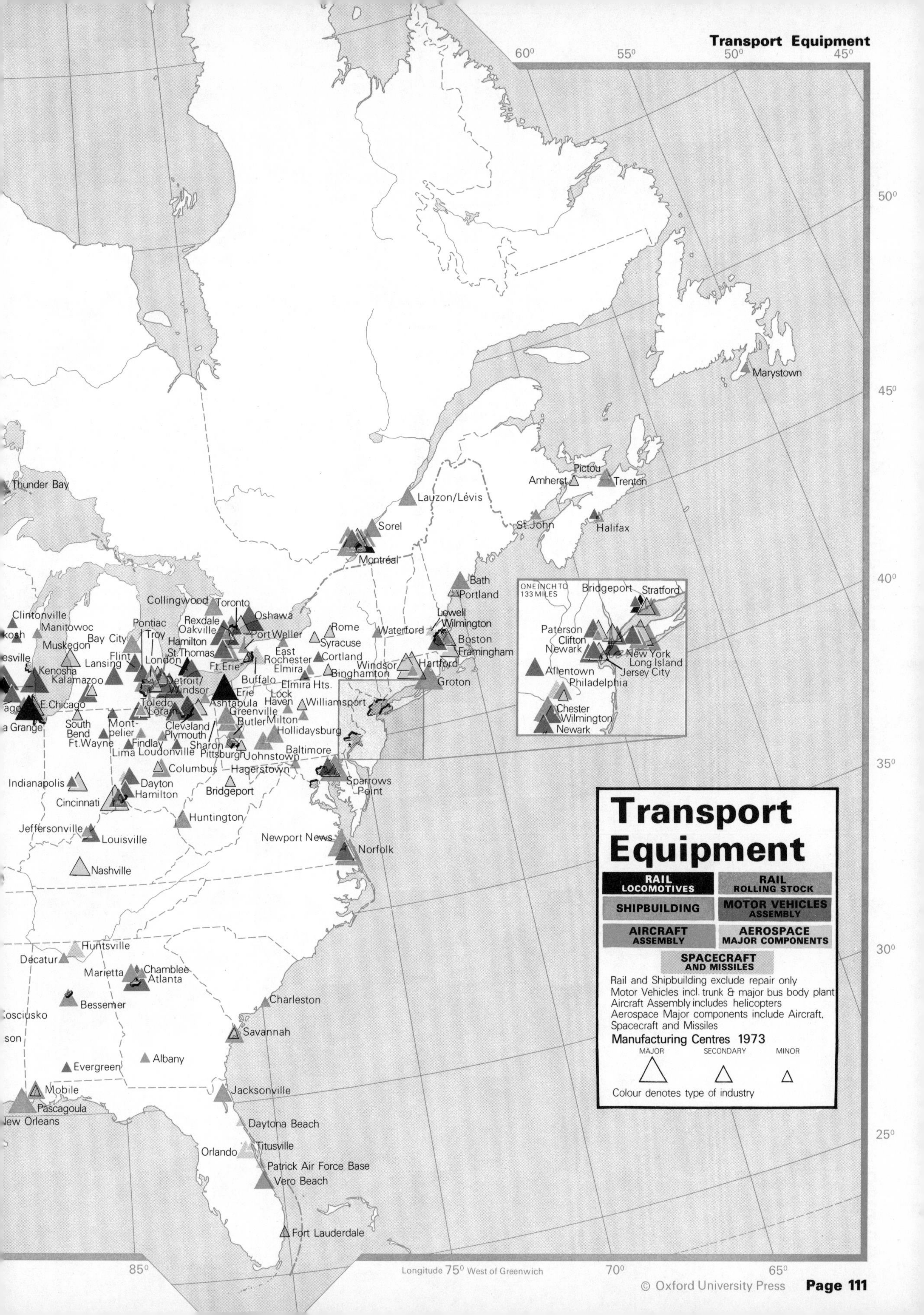

Transport Equipment

RAIL LOCOMOTIVES	RAIL ROLLING STOCK
SHIPBUILDING	MOTOR VEHICLES ASSEMBLY
AIRCRAFT ASSEMBLY	AEROSPACE MAJOR COMPONENTS
SPACECRAFT AND MISSILES	

Rail and Shipbuilding exclude repair only
Motor Vehicles incl. trunk & major bus body plant
Aircraft Assembly includes helicopters
Aerospace Major components include Aircraft,
Spacecraft and Missiles

Manufacturing Centres 1973

MAJOR   SECONDARY   MINOR

Colour denotes type of industry

Longitude 75° West of Greenwich

© Oxford University Press   **Page 111**

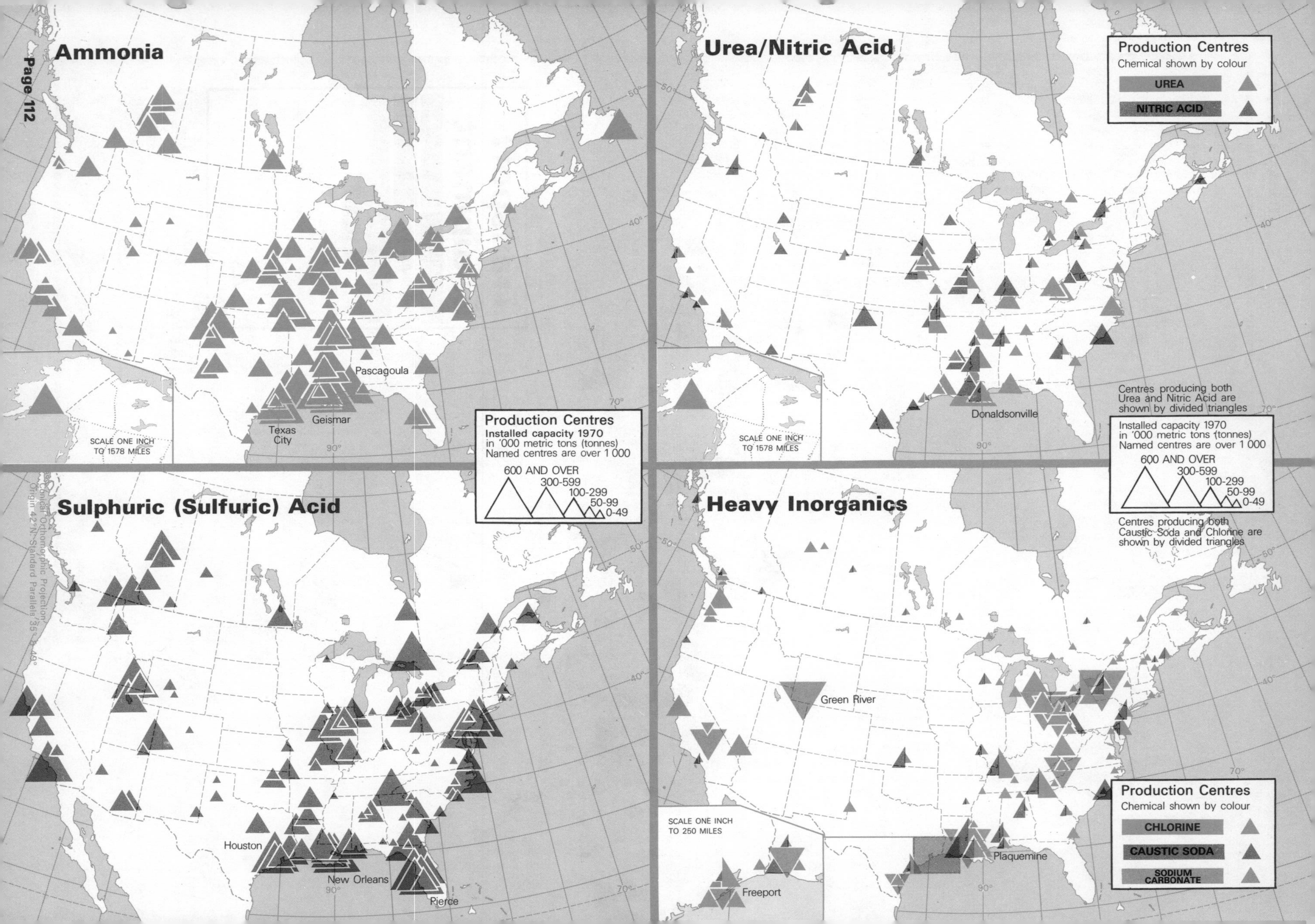

Ammonia

Production Centres
Installed capacity 1970
in '000 metric tons (tonnes)
Named centres are over 1 000

600 AND OVER
300-599
100-299
50-99
0-49

Pascagoula
Geismar
Texas City

SCALE ONE INCH
TO 1578 MILES

Urea/Nitric Acid

Production Centres
Chemical shown by colour

UREA
NITRIC ACID

Centres producing both
Urea and Nitric Acid are
shown by divided triangles

Installed capacity 1970
in '000 metric tons (tonnes)
Named centres are over 1 000

600 AND OVER
300-599
100-299
50-99
0-49

Donaldsonville

SCALE ONE INCH
TO 1578 MILES

Sulphuric (Sulfuric) Acid

New Orleans
Houston
Pierce

Heavy Inorganics

Production Centres
Chemical shown by colour

CHLORINE
CAUSTIC SODA
SODIUM CARBONATE

Centres producing both
Caustic Soda and Chlorine are
shown by divided triangles

Plaquemine
Green River
Freeport

SCALE ONE INCH
TO 250 MILES

Conical Orthomorphic Projection
Origin 42°N Standard Parallels 35° & 49°

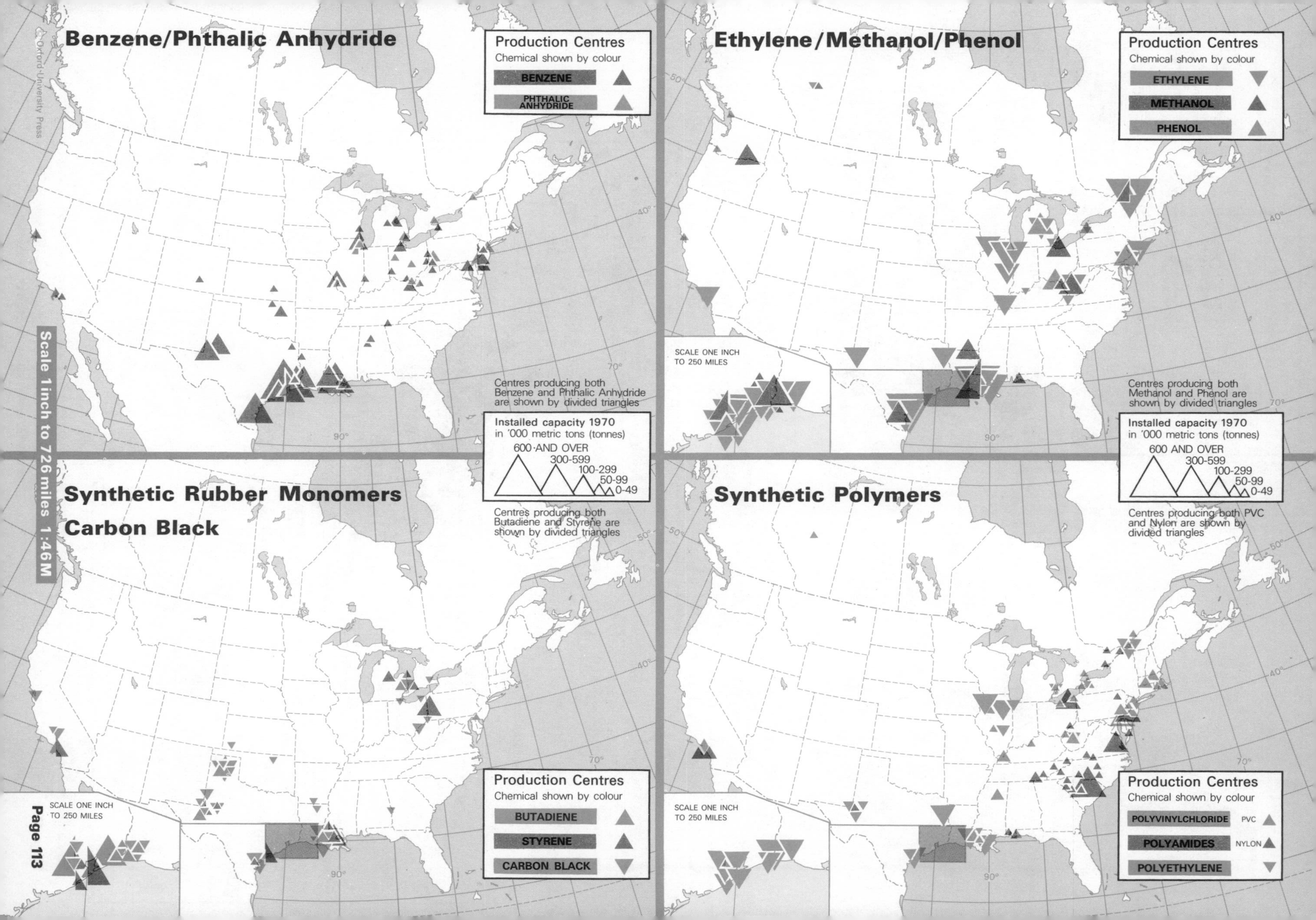

Ethylene/Methanol/Phenol

Production Centres
Chemical shown by colour

| ETHYLENE |
| METHANOL |
| PHENOL |

Centres producing both Methanol and Phenol are shown by divided triangles

Installed capacity 1970 in '000 metric tons (tonnes)

600 AND OVER
300-599
100-299
50-99
0-49

Centres producing both PVC and Nylon are shown by divided triangles

SCALE ONE INCH TO 250 MILES

Synthetic Polymers

Production Centres
Chemical shown by colour

| POLYVINYLCHLORIDE | PVC |
| POLYAMIDES | NYLON |
| POLYETHYLENE |

SCALE ONE INCH TO 250 MILES

Benzene/Phthalic Anhydride

Production Centres
Chemical shown by colour

| BENZENE |
| PHTHALIC ANHYDRIDE |

Centres producing both Benzene and Phthalic Anhydride are shown by divided triangles

Installed capacity 1970 in '000 metric tons (tonnes)

600 AND OVER
300-599
100-299
50-99
0-49

Centres producing both Butadiene and Styrene are shown by divided triangles

Synthetic Rubber Monomers Carbon Black

Production Centres
Chemical shown by colour

| BUTADIENE |
| STYRENE |
| CARBON BLACK |

SCALE ONE INCH TO 250 MILES

Scale 1 inch to 726 miles 1:46 M

© Oxford University Press

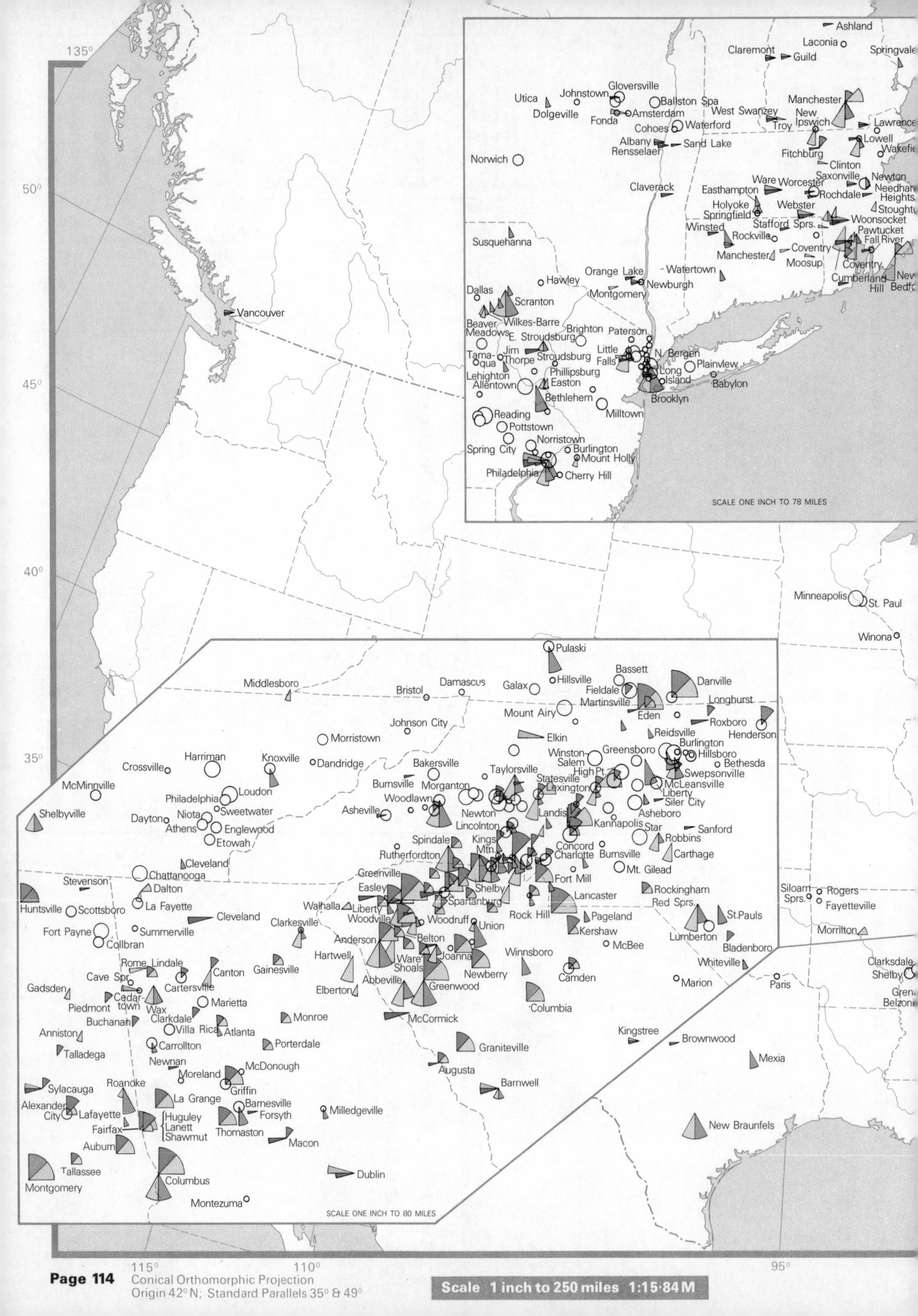

Conical Orthomorphic Projection
Origin 42° N; Standard Parallels 35° & 49°

Scale 1 inch to 250 miles 1:15·84 M

60° 55° 50° 45°

50°

45°

Mont Joli

Stellarton
Truro
Sussex
Windsor

Grand'Mère Montmorency
Plessisville St. Georges
Montréal Drummond- Guilford
St.-Jérôme ville Dexter
Lachute Clinton Corinna
Hawkesbury Sherbrooke Ellsworth
Valleyfield Granby Augusta
St.-Jean Waterville Lewiston
Perth St.-Hyacinthe Westbrook

Biddeford

Midland
Listowel Toronto Lindsay
Two Rivers Scarborough
Hespeler Hamilton Rochester
rlin Sheboygan London Auburn
Milwaukee Woodstock Depew Seneca Falls
Kenosha Jackson Five Corners Canisteo
ockford Willoughby Jamestown Troy
chelle Chicago Salamanca Bloomsburg
Cleveland Solon Williamsport Hazleton
Chicago Heights Lock Haven Berwick
Altoona New Holland
Greenville Bellefontaine McConnellsburg Dover
Columbus Grantsville Hagerstown
Hamilton Winchester Front Royal
Cincinnati Charlottesville
Louisville Waynesboro Scottsville Tappahannock
Covington Petersburg
Rockfield Lynchburg Emporia
Springfield Franklin Burnt Mills
yersburg Lebanon Rocky Ahoskie
mis Nashville Mount Tarboro
Greenville
rinth Decatur Delway
atesville West Point Wilmington
Fayette
Beatty Northport
Koskiusko Prattville
idian Demopolis
Butler Albany West Green
Jackson Elba
Monroeville Dothan

35°

30°

25°

40°

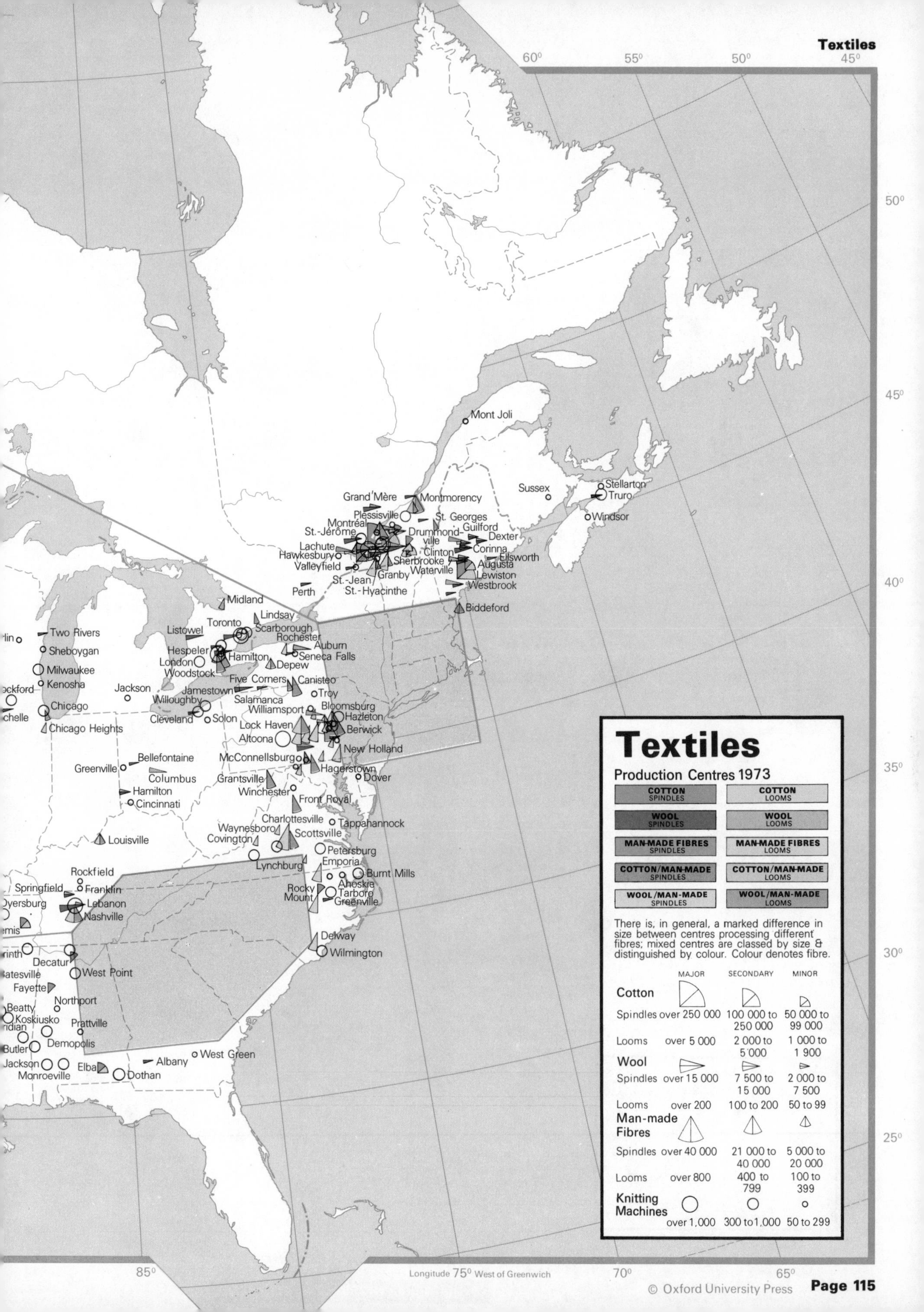

Textiles
Production Centres 1973

COTTON SPINDLES	COTTON LOOMS
WOOL SPINDLES	WOOL LOOMS
MAN-MADE FIBRES SPINDLES	MAN-MADE FIBRES LOOMS
COTTON/MAN-MADE SPINDLES	COTTON/MAN-MADE LOOMS
WOOL/MAN-MADE SPINDLES	WOOL/MAN-MADE LOOMS

There is, in general, a marked difference in size between centres processing different fibres; mixed centres are classed by size & distinguished by colour. Colour denotes fibre.

	MAJOR	SECONDARY	MINOR
Cotton			
Spindles	over 250 000	100 000 to 250 000	50 000 to 99 000
Looms	over 5 000	2 000 to 5 000	1 000 to 1 900
Wool			
Spindles	over 15 000	7 500 to 15 000	2 000 to 7 500
Looms	over 200	100 to 200	50 to 99
Man-made Fibres			
Spindles	over 40 000	21 000 to 40 000	5 000 to 20 000
Looms	over 800	400 to 799	100 to 399
Knitting Machines	over 1,000	300 to 1,000	50 to 299

Longitude 75° West of Greenwich

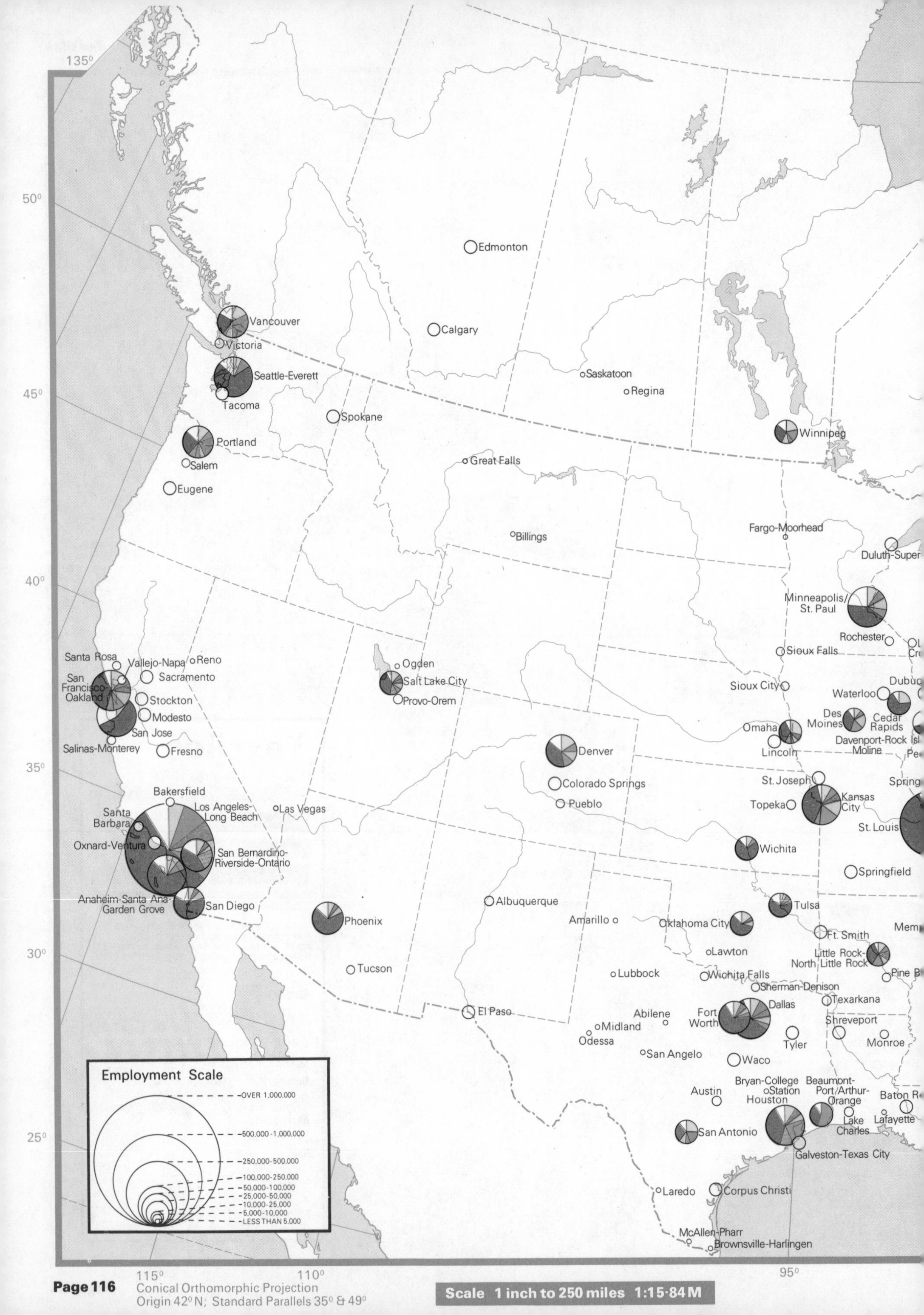

Edmonton

Calgary

Saskatoon

Regina

Vancouver

Victoria

Seattle-Everett

Tacoma

Spokane

Portland

Salem

Eugene

Great Falls

Winnipeg

Billings

Fargo-Moorhead

Duluth-Super

Minneapolis/
St. Paul

Rochester

Santa Rosa

Vallejo-Napa

Reno

Sacramento

Sioux Falls

Cr

San Francisco-
Oakland

Stockton

Modesto

San Jose

Salinas-Monterey

Fresno

Ogden

Salt Lake City

Provo-Orem

Sioux City

Dubu

Waterloo

Des
Moines

Cedar
Rapids

Davenport-Rock Isl
Moline

Pe

Lincoln

Omaha

Denver

Colorado Springs

Pueblo

St. Joseph

Kansas
City

Topeka

Spring

St. Louis

Bakersfield

Santa
Barbara

Los Angeles-
Long Beach

Las Vegas

Oxnard-Ventura

San Bernardino-
Riverside-Ontario

Anaheim-Santa Ana-
Garden Grove

San Diego

Phoenix

Tucson

Albuquerque

Amarillo

Oklahoma City

Lawton

Wichita

Springfield

Tulsa

Ft. Smith

Little Rock-
North Little Rock

Mem

Pine B

El Paso

Lubbock

Wichita Falls

Sherman-Denison

Dallas

Texarkana

Shreveport

Monroe

Abilene

Ft.
Worth

Midland

Odessa

San Angelo

Tyler

Waco

Austin

Bryan-College
Station

Houston

Beaumont-
Port Arthur-
Orange

Baton R

Lafayette

Lake
Charles

San Antonio

Galveston-Texas City

Laredo

Corpus Christi

McAllen-Pharr

Brownsville-Harlingen

Employment Scale

OVER 1,000,000

500,000–1,000,000

250,000–500,000

100,000–250,000

50,000–100,000

25,000–50,000

10,000–25,000

5,000–10,000

LESS THAN 5,000

Conical Orthomorphic Projection
Origin 42° N; Standard Parallels 35° & 49°

Scale 1 inch to 250 miles 1:15·84 M

135°

50°

45°

40°

35°

30°

25°

115°

110°

95°

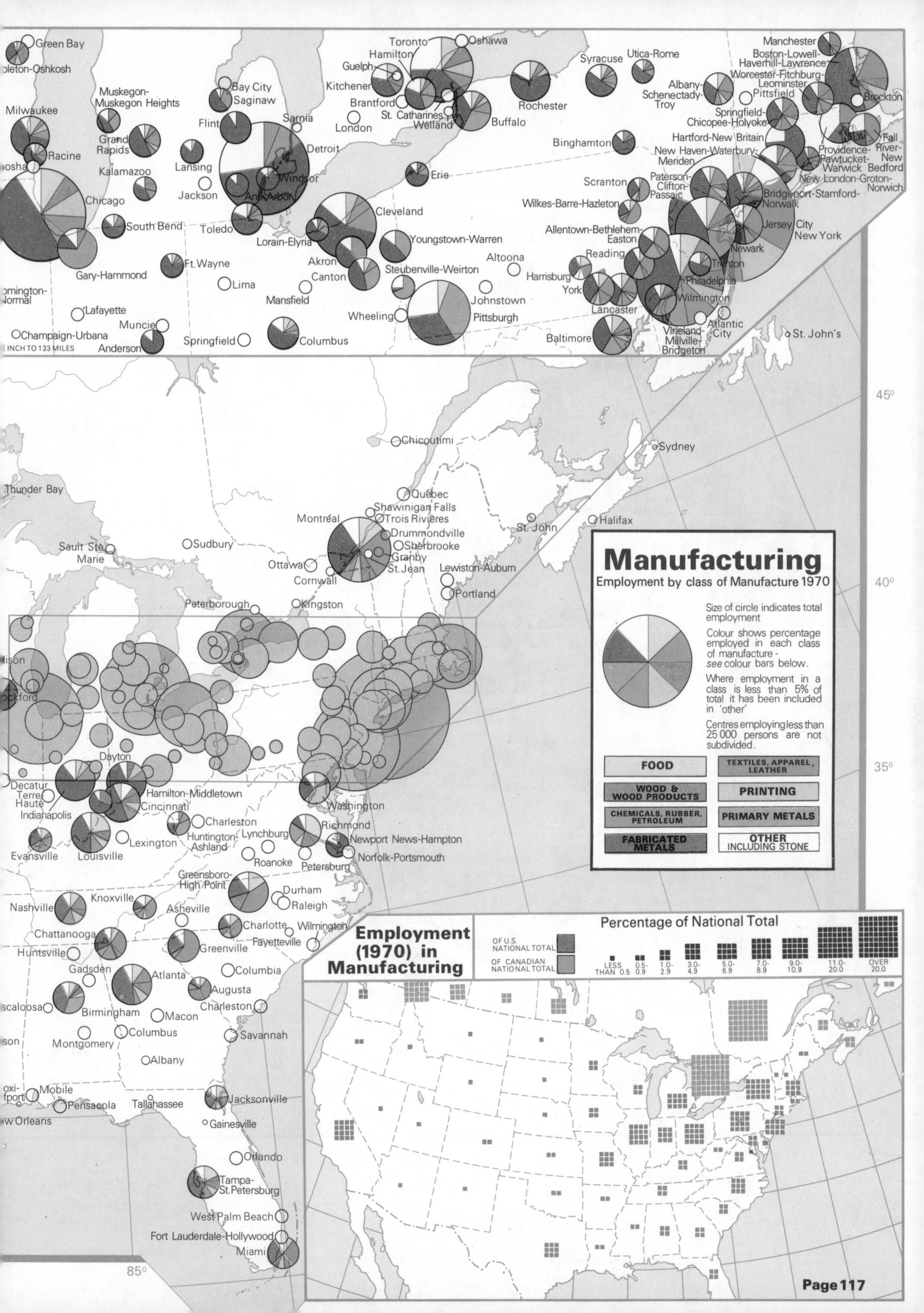

Manufacturing
Employment by class of Manufacture 1970
Size of circle indicates total employment
Colour shows percentage employed in each class of manufacture - see colour bars below.
Where employment in a class is less than 5% of total it has been included in 'other'
Centres employing less than 25 000 persons are not subdivided.
FOOD
TEXTILES, APPAREL, LEATHER
WOOD & WOOD PRODUCTS
PRINTING
CHEMICALS, RUBBER, PETROLEUM
PRIMARY METALS
FABRICATED METALS
OTHER INCLUDING STONE
Employment (1970) in Manufacturing
Percentage of National Total
OF U.S. NATIONAL TOTAL
OF CANADIAN NATIONAL TOTAL
LESS THAN 0.5
0.5-0.9
1.0-2.9
3.0-4.9
5.0-6.9
7.0-8.9
9.0-10.9
11.0-20.0
OVER 20.0
Green Bay
Milwaukee
Racine
Chicago
Gary-Hammond
Muskegon-Muskegon Heights
Grand Rapids
Kalamazoo
South Bend
Lansing
Jackson
Flint
Bay City
Saginaw
Sarnia
Detroit
Windsor
Ann Arbor
Toledo
Ft. Wayne
Lima
Lafayette
Muncie
Anderson
Champaign-Urbana
Springfield
Columbus
Mansfield
Canton
Akron
Lorain-Elyria
Cleveland
Youngstown-Warren
Steubenville-Weirton
Wheeling
Pittsburgh
Johnstown
Altoona
Erie
London
Toronto
Hamilton
Oshawa
Guelph
Kitchener
Brantford
St. Catharines
Welland
Buffalo
Rochester
Syracuse
Utica-Rome
Binghamton
Albany-Schenectady-Troy
Pittsfield
Manchester
Boston-Lowell-Haverhill-Lawrence
Worcester-Fitchburg-Leominster
Brockton
Springfield-Chicopee-Holyoke
Hartford-New Britain
New Haven-Waterbury-Meriden
Providence-Pawtucket-Warwick
Fall River-New Bedford
New London-Groton-Norwich
Bridgeport-Stamford-Norwalk
Scranton
Wilkes-Barre-Hazleton
Paterson-Clifton-Passaic
Jersey City
New York
Newark
Allentown-Bethlehem-Easton
Reading
Harrisburg
York
Lancaster
Trenton
Philadelphia
Wilmington
Baltimore
Vineland-Millville-Bridgeton
Atlantic City
St. John's
1 INCH TO 133 MILES
Chicoutimi
Sydney
Thunder Bay
Québec
Shawinigan Falls
Trois Rivières
Montréal
Drummondville
Sherbrooke
Granby
St. Jean
St. John
Halifax
Sault Ste. Marie
Sudbury
Ottawa
Cornwall
Lewiston-Auburn
Portland
Peterborough
Kingston
45°
40°
35°
Dayton
Decatur
Terre Haute
Indianapolis
Hamilton-Middletown
Cincinnati
Charleston
Huntington-Ashland
Lexington
Louisville
Evansville
Lynchburg
Roanoke
Richmond
Washington
Petersburg
Newport News-Hampton
Norfolk-Portsmouth
Greensboro-High Point
Durham
Raleigh
Knoxville
Nashville
Asheville
Chattanooga
Charlotte
Wilmington
Fayetteville
Huntsville
Greenville
Gadsden
Atlanta
Columbia
Augusta
Birmingham
Charleston
Macon
Columbus
Savannah
Montgomery
Albany
Mobile
Pensacola
Tallahassee
Jacksonville
Gainesville
Orlando
Tampa-St. Petersburg
West Palm Beach
Fort Lauderdale-Hollywood
Miami
85°

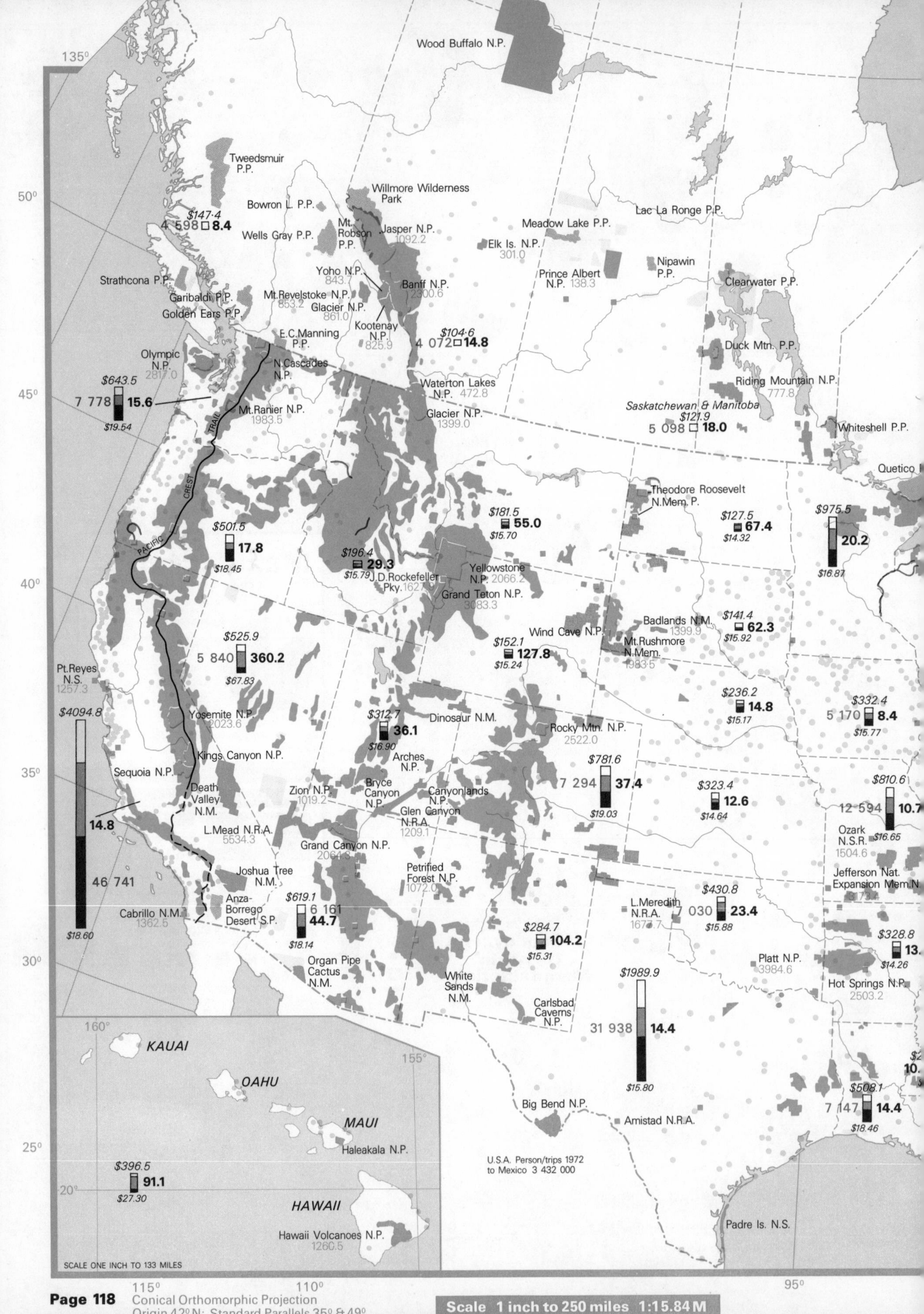

Conical Orthomorphic Projection
Origin 42° N; Standard Parallels 35° & 49°

Scale 1 inch to 250 miles   1:15.84 M

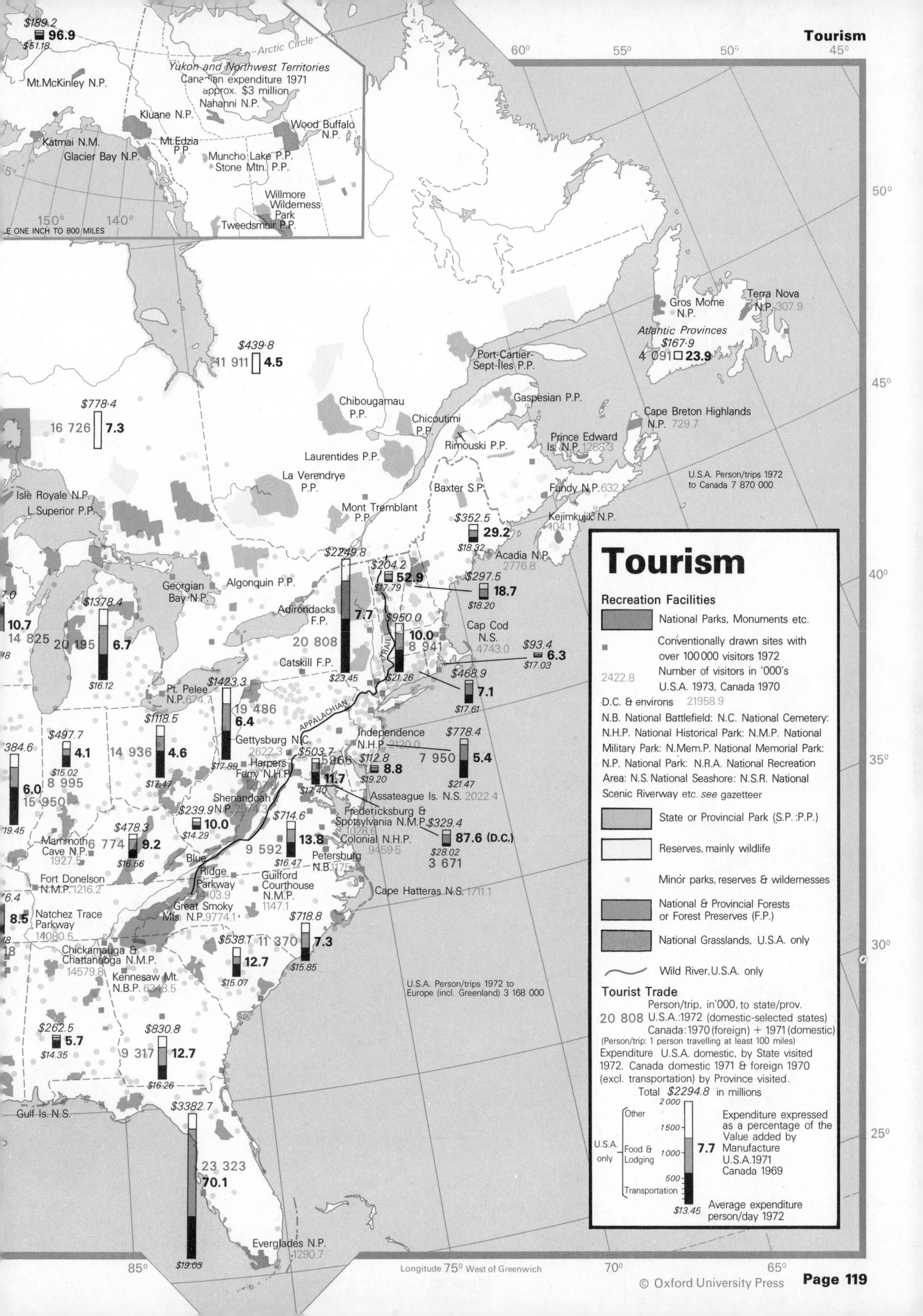
Tourism
Recreation Facilities
National Parks, Monuments etc.
Conventionally drawn sites with over 100 000 visitors 1972
2422.8 Number of visitors in '000's U.S.A. 1973, Canada 1970
D.C. & environs 21958.9
N.B. National Battlefield: N.C. National Cemetery: N.H.P. National Historical Park: N.M.P. National Military Park: N.Mem.P. National Memorial Park: N.P. National Park: N.R.A. National Recreation Area: N.S. National Seashore: N.S.R. National Scenic Riverway etc. see gazetteer
State or Provincial Park (S.P.:P.P.)
Reserves, mainly wildlife
Minor parks, reserves & wildernesses
National & Provincial Forests or Forest Preserves (F.P.)
National Grasslands, U.S.A. only
Wild River, U.S.A. only
Tourist Trade
20 808 Person/trip, in'000, to state/prov. U.S.A.:1972 (domestic-selected states) Canada: 1970 (foreign) + 1971 (domestic)
(Person/trip: 1 person travelling at least 100 miles)
Expenditure U.S.A. domestic, by State visited 1972. Canada domestic 1971 & foreign 1970 (excl. transportation) by Province visited.
Total $2294.8 in millions
Other
Food & Lodging
Transportation
U.S.A. only
7.7 Expenditure expressed as a percentage of the Value added by Manufacture U.S.A.1971 Canada 1969
$13.45 Average expenditure person/day 1972
Yukon and Northwest Territories
Canadian expenditure 1971 approx. $3 million
Arctic Circle
Mt.McKinley N.P.
Kluane N.P.
Nahanni N.P.
Wood Buffalo N.P.
Katmai N.M.
Glacier Bay N.P.
Mt.Edzia P.P.
Muncho Lake P.P.
Stone Mtn. P.P.
Willmore Wilderness Park
Tweedsmuir P.P.
ONE INCH TO 800 MILES
U.S.A. Person/trips 1972 to Canada 7 870 000
U.S.A. Person/trips 1972 to Europe (incl. Greenland) 3 168 000
Gros Morne N.P.
Terra Nova N.P. 307.9
Atlantic Provinces
Port-Cartier-Sept-Îles P.P.
Gaspesian P.P.
Cape Breton Highlands N.P. 729.7
Prince Edward Is. N.P. 1288.3
Chibougamau P.P.
Chicoutimi P.P.
Rimouski P.P.
Laurentides P.P.
La Verendrye P.P.
Baxter S.P.
Fundy N.P. 632.1
Mont Tremblant P.P.
Kejimkujik N.P. 104.1
Acadia N.P. 2776.8
Isle Royale N.P.
L.Superior P.P.
Georgian Bay N.P.
Algonquin P.P.
Adirondacks F.P.
Catskill F.P.
Cap Cod N.S. 4743.0
Pt. Pelee N.P. 674.7
Gettysburg N.C. 2622.3
Harpers Ferry N.H.P.
Independence N.H.P. 2120.0
APPALACHIAN TRAIL
Shenandoah N.P. 2574.3
Assateague Is. N.S. 2022.4
Fredericksburg & Spotsylvania N.M.P. 1028.6
Colonial N.H.P. 9459.5
87.6 (D.C.)
Mammoth Cave N.P. 1927.5
Petersburg N.B. 1175
Blue Ridge Parkway 14103.9
Guilford Courthouse N.M.P. 1147.1
Cape Hatteras N.S. 1711.1
Fort Donelson N.M.P. 1216.2
Natchez Trace Parkway 14080.5
Great Smoky Mts. N.P. 9774.1
Chickamauga & Chattanooga N.M.P. 14579.8
Kennesaw Mt. N.B.P. 6348.5
Gulf Is. N.S.
Everglades N.P. 1290.7
Longitude 75° West of Greenwich

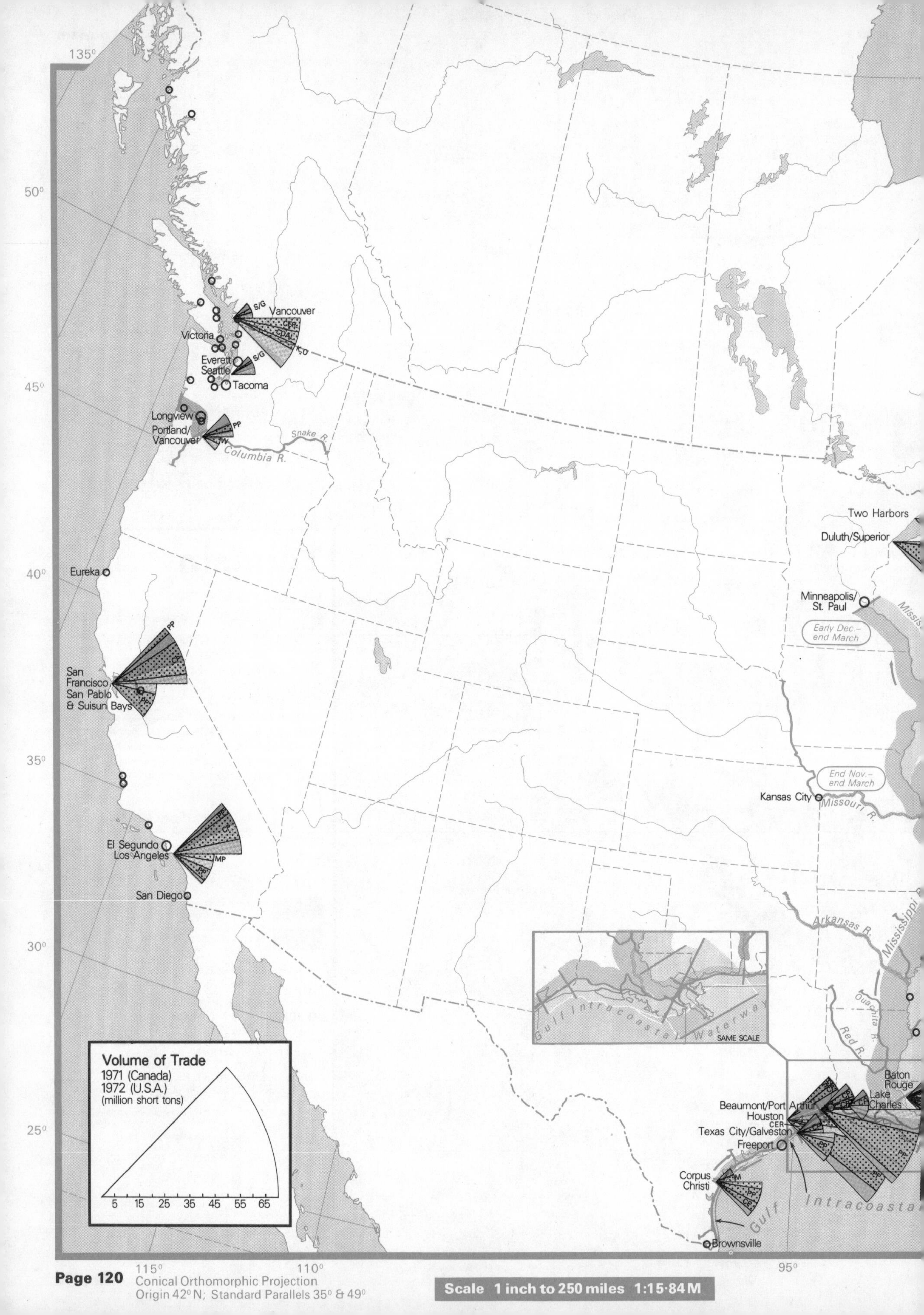

S/G Vancouver
CER
CDAL
K/O
Victoria
S/G
Everett
Seattle
Tacoma

Longview
PP
Portland/
Vancouver
W
Snake R.
Columbia R.

Two Harbors
Duluth/Superior

Eureka
Minneapolis/
St. Paul
Missis

Early Dec.–
end March

San
Francisco,
San Pablo
& Suisun Bays
PP
CP

Kansas City
Missouri R.

Arkansas R.

End Nov–
end March

Mississippi

El Segundo
Los Angeles
CP
MP

San Diego

Gulf Intracoastal
Waterway
SAME SCALE

Ouachita R.

Red R.

Baton
Rouge
Lake
Charles
Beaumont/Port Arthur
Houston
CER
Texas City/Galveston
Freeport

Corpus
Christi

Gulf Intracoastal

Brownsville

Volume of Trade
1971 (Canada)
1972 (U.S.A.)
(million short tons)

5   15   25   35   45   55   65

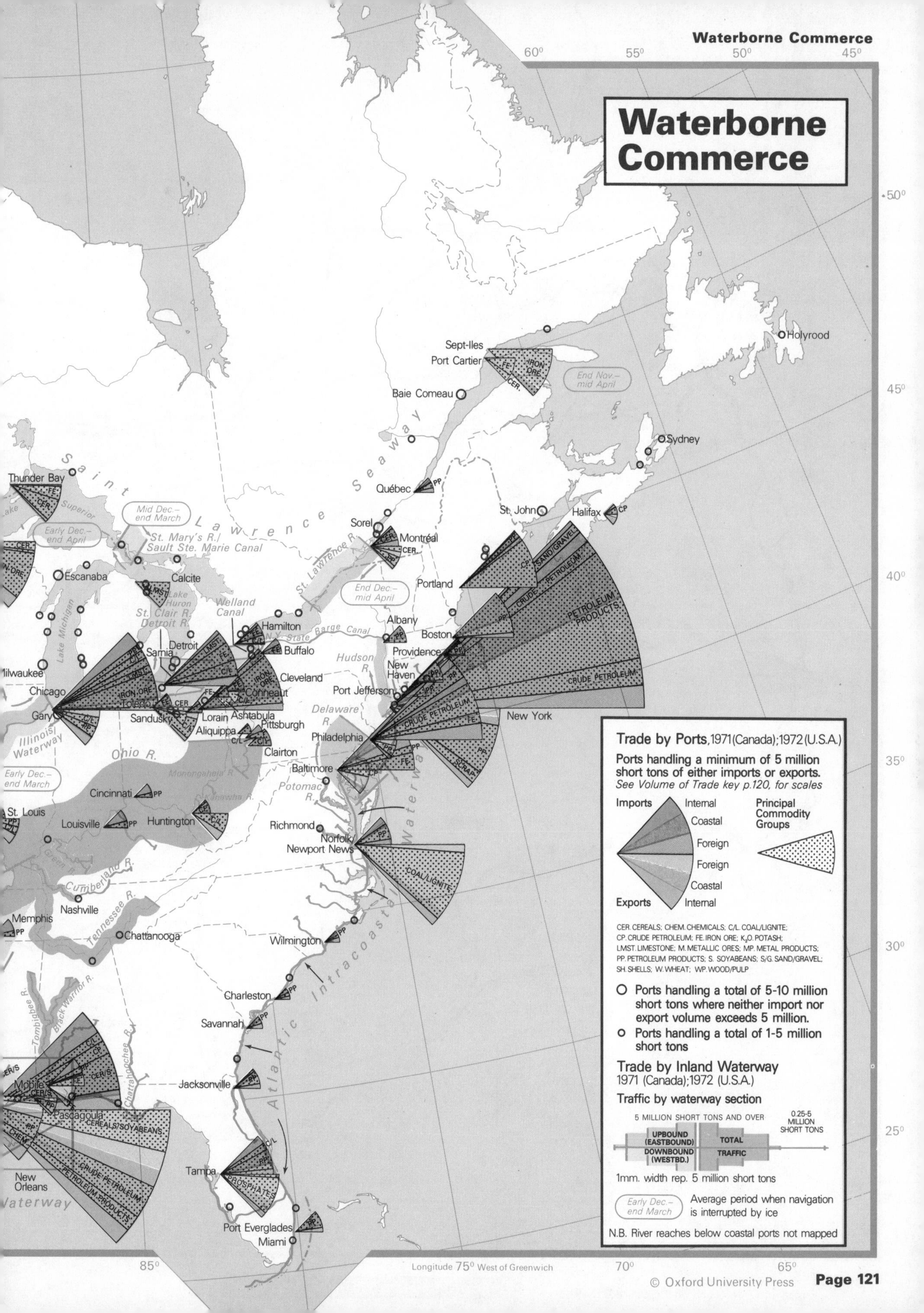
Waterborne Commerce
Trade by Ports, 1971 (Canada); 1972 (U.S.A.)
Ports handling a minimum of 5 million short tons of either imports or exports.
See Volume of Trade key p.120, for scales
Imports
Internal
Coastal
Foreign
Foreign
Coastal
Exports
Internal
Principal Commodity Groups
CER. CEREALS; CHEM. CHEMICALS; C/L. COAL/LIGNITE; CP. CRUDE PETROLEUM; FE. IRON ORE; K2O. POTASH; LMST. LIMESTONE; M. METALLIC ORES; MP. METAL PRODUCTS; PP. PETROLEUM PRODUCTS; S. SOYABEANS; S/G. SAND/GRAVEL; SH. SHELLS; W. WHEAT; WP. WOOD/PULP
Ports handling a total of 5-10 million short tons where neither import nor export volume exceeds 5 million.
Ports handling a total of 1-5 million short tons
Trade by Inland Waterway
1971 (Canada); 1972 (U.S.A.)
Traffic by waterway section
5 MILLION SHORT TONS AND OVER
0.25-5 MILLION SHORT TONS
UPBOUND (EASTBOUND)
DOWNBOUND (WESTBD.)
TOTAL TRAFFIC
1mm. width rep. 5 million short tons
Early Dec.– end March
Average period when navigation is interrupted by ice
N.B. River reaches below coastal ports not mapped
Holyrood
Sept-Iles
Port Cartier
Baie Comeau
End Nov.– mid April
Sydney
Halifax
St. John
Québec
Sorel
Montréal
Saint Lawrence Seaway
St. Lawrence R.
End Dec.– mid April
Portland
Boston
Albany
Providence
New Haven
Port Jefferson
New York
PETROLEUM PRODUCTS
CRUDE PETROLEUM
SAND/GRAVEL
Hudson R.
Delaware R.
Philadelphia
Baltimore
Potomac R.
Richmond
Norfolk/Newport News
COAL/LIGNITE
Atlantic Intracoastal Waterway
Wilmington
Charleston
Savannah
Jacksonville
Tampa
PHOSPHATES
Port Everglades
Miami
Thunder Bay
Superior
Mid Dec.– end March
Early Dec.– end April
St. Mary's R./ Sault Ste. Marie Canal
Escanaba
Calcite
Lake Huron
St. Clair R. Detroit R.
Welland Canal
Hamilton
N.Y. State Barge Canal
Buffalo
Lake Michigan
Milwaukee
Sarnia
Detroit
Chicago
Gary
Toledo
Sandusky
Lorain
Cleveland
Conneaut
Ashtabula
Aliquippa
Pittsburgh
Clairton
Illinois Waterway
Ohio R.
Monongahela R.
Early Dec.– end March
Cincinnati
St. Louis
Louisville
Huntington
Kanawha R.
Green R.
Cumberland R.
Nashville
Tennessee R.
Memphis
Chattanooga
Tombigbee R.
Black Warrior R.
Chattahoochee R.
Mobile
Pascagoula
CEREALS/SOYABEANS
New Orleans
CRUDE PETROLEUM
PETROLEUM PRODUCTS
Waterway
60°
55°
50°
45°
85°
Longitude 75° West of Greenwich
70°
65°

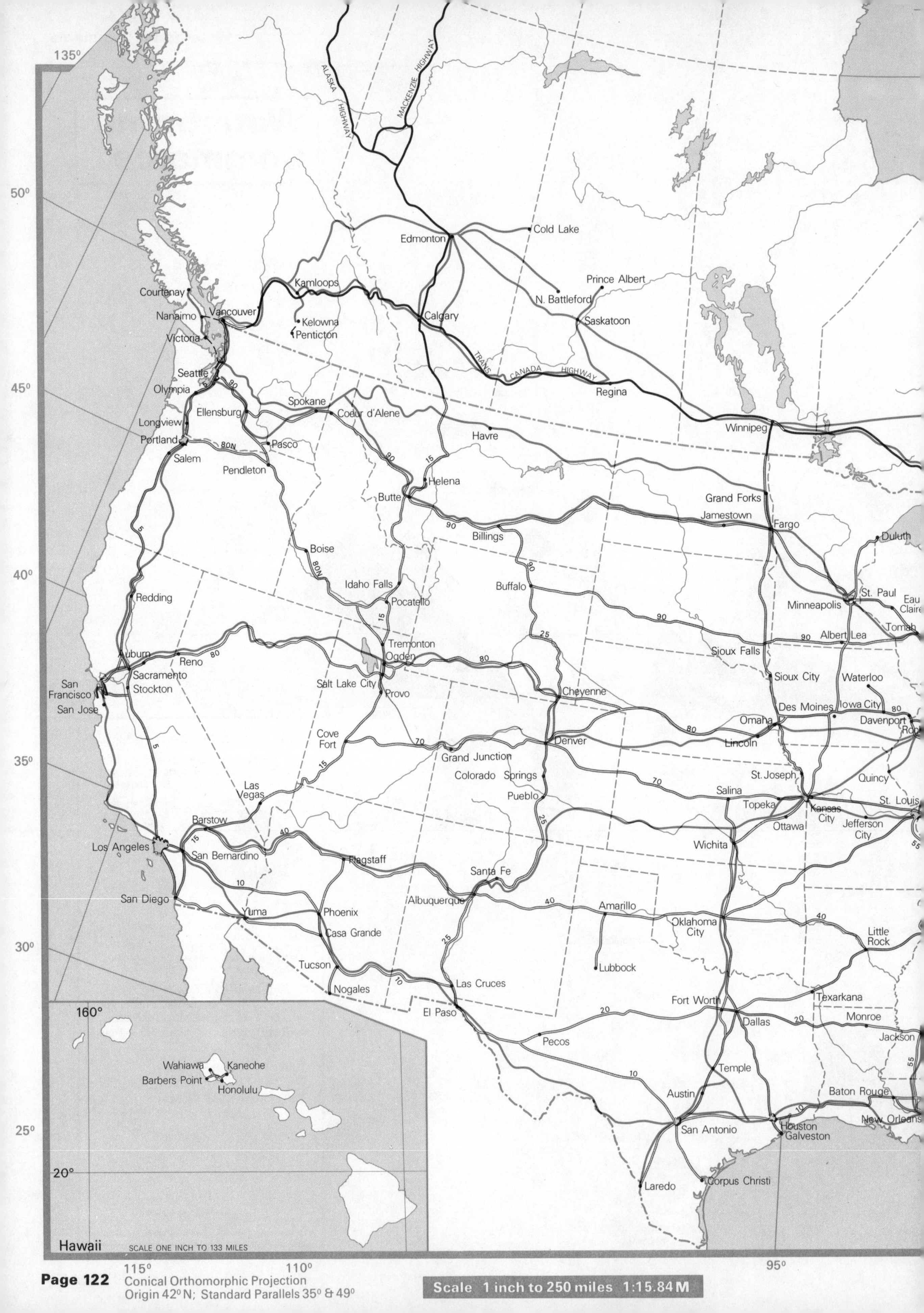

135°

50°

45°

40°

35°

30°

25°

ALASKA HIGHWAY

MACKENZIE HIGHWAY

Cold Lake

Edmonton

Prince Albert

N. Battleford

Kamloops

Courtenay

Nanaimo

Vancouver

Kelowna

Penticton

Calgary

Saskatoon

Victoria

Seattle

Olympia

Spokane

90

Coeur d'Alene

TRANS CANADA HIGHWAY

Regina

Winnipeg

Longview

Ellensburg

Havre

Grand Forks

Jamestown

Fargo

Portland

80N

Pasco

Duluth

Salem

Pendleton

80

Helena

15

Butte

90

Billings

St. Paul

Eau Claire

Boise

Buffalo

Minneapolis

Tomah

Redding

Idaho Falls

80N

Pocatello

Sioux Falls

Albert Lea

90

Tremonton

Ogden

15

Auburn

Reno

80

Salt Lake City

Provo

80

Cheyenne

Sioux City

Waterloo

Sacramento

Stockton

San Francisco

San Jose

Cove Fort

70

Grand Junction

Denver

80

Des Moines

Omaha

Lincoln

Iowa City

Davenport

80

25

Colorado Springs

Pueblo

St. Joseph

Salina

Topeka

Quincy

St. Louis

Kansas City

55

Las Vegas

15

Barstow

40

San Bernardino

Flagstaff

Santa Fe

70

Ottawa

Jefferson City

Los Angeles

15

10

Wichita

San Diego

Yuma

Phoenix

Albuquerque

40

Amarillo

Oklahoma City

Little Rock

40

Casa Grande

25

Tucson

Nogales

10

Las Cruces

Lubbock

El Paso

Fort Worth

Texarkana

20

Monroe

Pecos

Dallas

20

Jackson

55

10

Temple

Baton Rouge

10

Austin

New Orleans

25

San Antonio

Houston

Galveston

Laredo

Corpus Christi

115°

110°

95°

160°

Wahiawa

Kaneohe

Barbers Point

Honolulu

20°

Hawaii

SCALE ONE INCH TO 133 MILES

Page 122

Conical Orthomorphic Projection
Origin 42° N; Standard Parallels 35° & 49°

Scale 1 inch to 250 miles 1:15.84 M

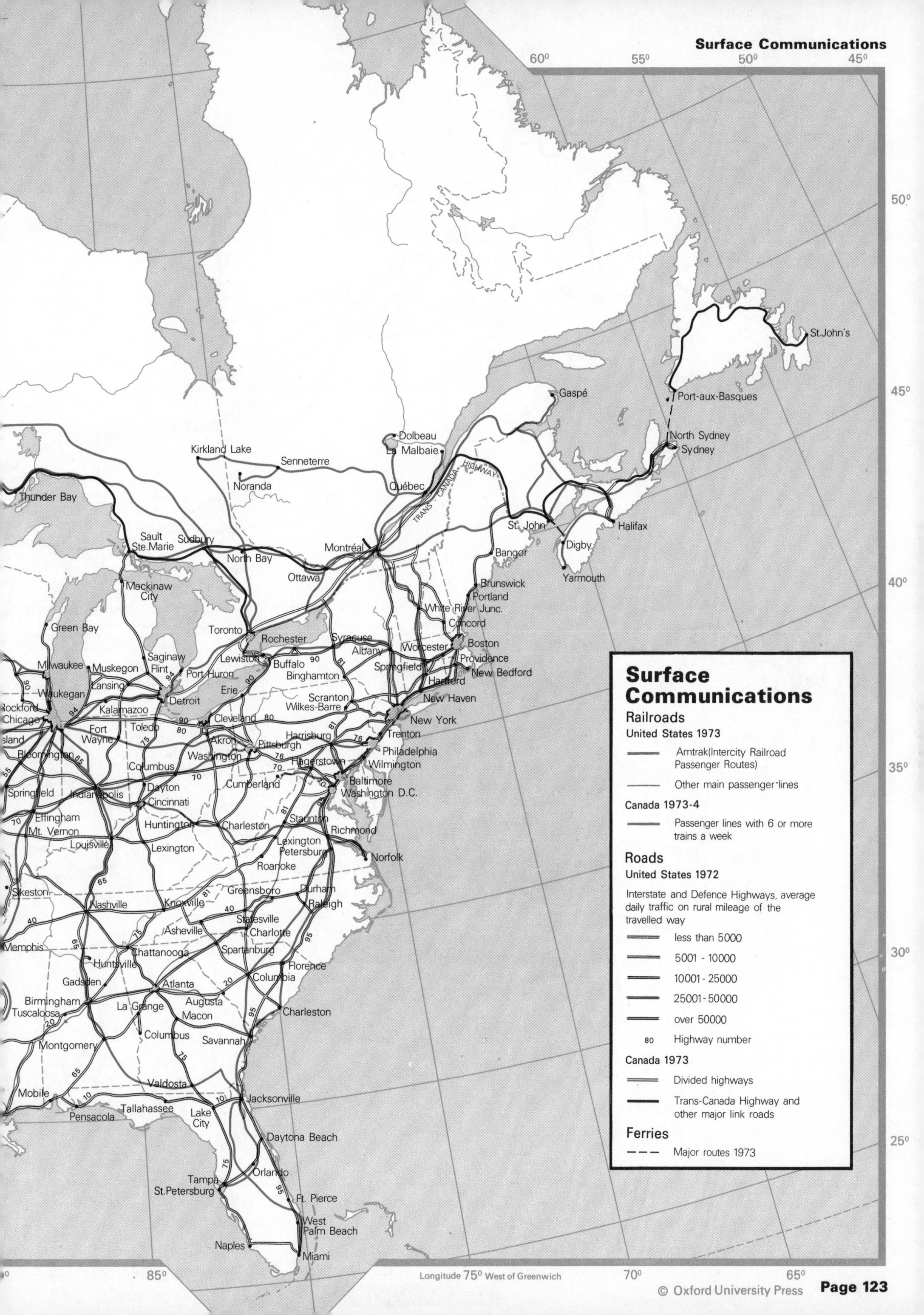
Surface Communications
Railroads
United States 1973
Amtrak(Intercity Railroad Passenger Routes)
Other main passenger lines
Canada 1973-4
Passenger lines with 6 or more trains a week
Roads
United States 1972
Interstate and Defence Highways, average daily traffic on rural mileage of the travelled way
less than 5000
5001 - 10000
10001 - 25000
25001 - 50000
over 50000
80
Highway number
Canada 1973
Divided highways
Trans-Canada Highway and other major link roads
Ferries
Major routes 1973
60⁰
55⁰
50⁰
45⁰
50⁰
45⁰
40⁰
35⁰
30⁰
25⁰
85⁰
Longitude 75⁰ West of Greenwich
70⁰
65⁰
St.John's
Port-aux-Basques
North Sydney
Sydney
Gaspé
Dolbeau
La Malbaie
Québec
TRANS - CANADA HIGHWAY
Kirkland Lake
Senneterre
Noranda
Thunder Bay
Sault Ste.Marie
Sudbury
North Bay
Montréal
Ottawa
St. John
Halifax
Digby
Yarmouth
Bangor
Brunswick
Portland
White River Junc.
Concord
Boston
Worcester
Providence
New Bedford
Hartford
Springfield
Albany
Syracuse
New Haven
New York
Trenton
Philadelphia
Wilmington
Baltimore
Washington D.C.
Mackinaw City
Green Bay
Toronto
Rochester
Lewiston
Buffalo
Binghamton
Scranton
Wilkes-Barre
Harrisburg
Pittsburgh
Hagerstown
Cumberland
Milwaukee
Muskegon
Saginaw
Flint
Port Huron
Lansing
Waukegan
Detroit
Erie
Kalamazoo
Rockford
Chicago
Toledo
Cleveland
Akron
Fort Wayne
Bloomington
Columbus
Washington
Springfield
Indianapolis
Dayton
Cincinnati
Effingham
Mt. Vernon
Huntington
Charleston
Staunton
Richmond
Louisville
Lexington
Lexington
Petersburg
Norfolk
Roanoke
Sikeston
Greensboro
Durham
Raleigh
Nashville
Knoxville
Statesville
Asheville
Charlotte
Memphis
Chattanooga
Spartanburg
Huntsville
Florence
Columbia
Gadsden
Atlanta
Birmingham
Tuscaloosa
La Grange
Augusta
Macon
Charleston
Columbus
Savannah
Montgomery
Valdosta
Mobile
Jacksonville
Tallahassee
Pensacola
Lake City
Daytona Beach
Orlando
Tampa
St.Petersburg
Ft. Pierce
West Palm Beach
Naples
Miami

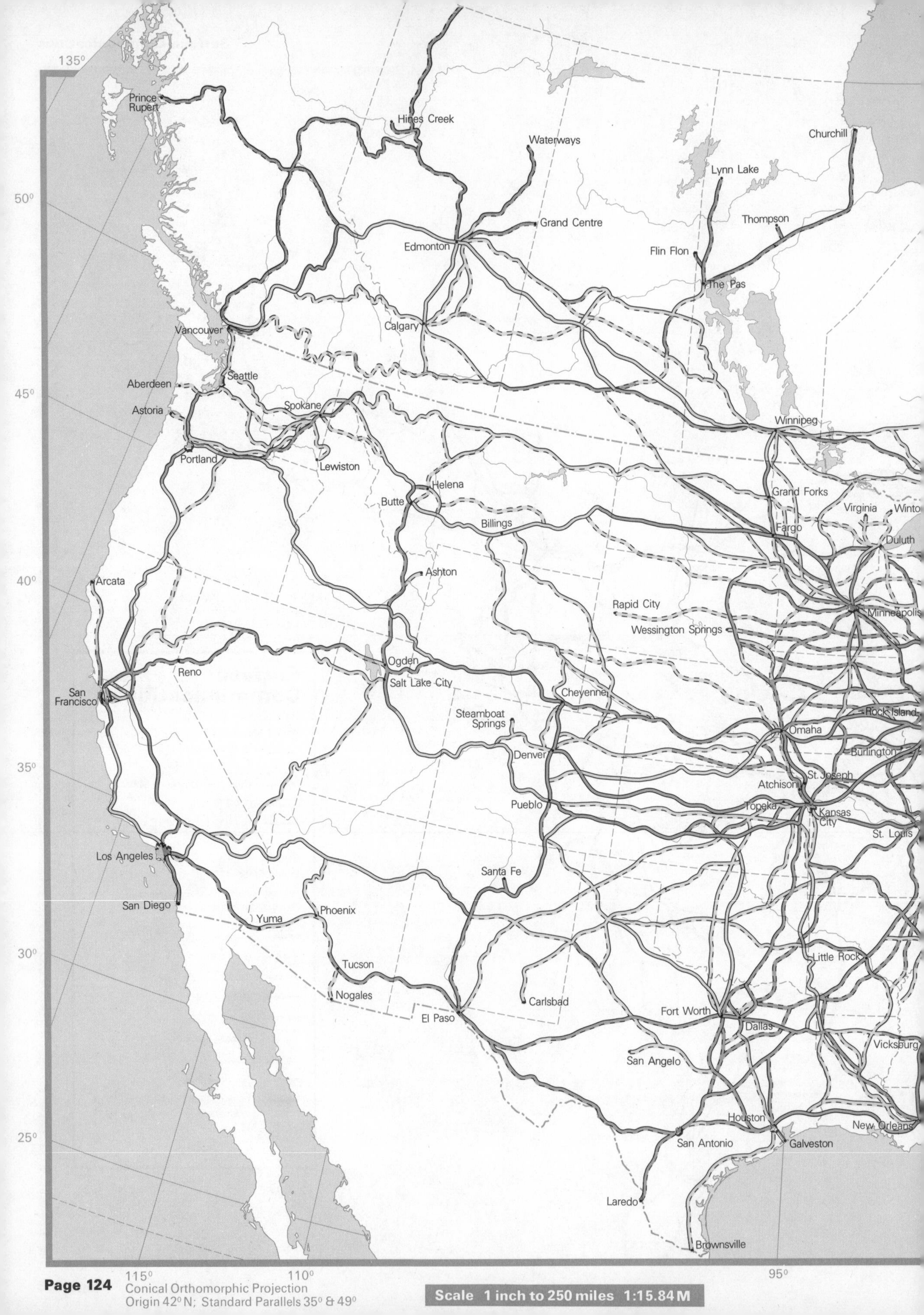

Conical Orthomorphic Projection
Origin 42° N; Standard Parallels 35° & 49°

Scale 1 inch to 250 miles 1:15.84 M

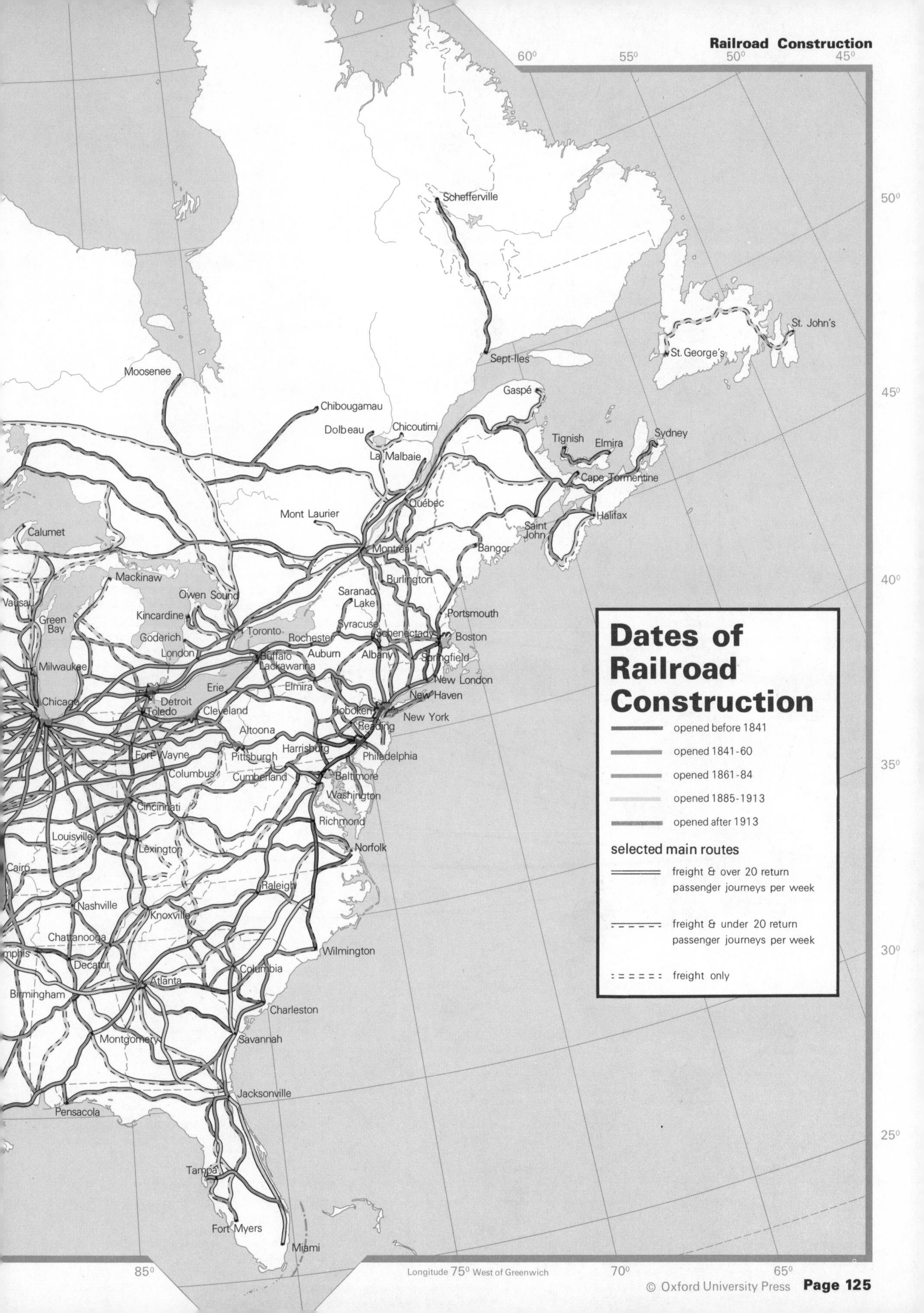

60⁰   55⁰   50⁰   45⁰

50⁰

Schefferville

45⁰

Moosenee

Sept-Iles

Chibougamau

Gaspé

Dolbeau   Chicoutimi

La Malbaie

St. John's

St. George's

Tignish   Elmira   Sydney

Cape Tormentine

Calumet

Mont Laurier

Québec

Halifax

40⁰

Mackinaw

Owen Sound

Saint John

Bangor

Kincardine

Montréal

Burlington

Wausau

Green Bay

Goderich

London

Toronto

Rochester

Saranac Lake

Syracuse

Schenectady

Portsmouth

Boston

Milwaukee

Buffalo

Auburn

Albany

Springfield

Lackawanna

New London

Chicago

Erie

Elmira

New Haven

Detroit

Cleveland

Hoboken

New York

Toledo

Altoona

Reading

Fort Wayne

Pittsburgh

Harrisburg

Philadelphia

35⁰

Columbus

Cumberland

Baltimore

Cincinnati

Washington

Louisville

Lexington

Richmond

Cairo

Norfolk

Nashville

Knoxville

Raleigh

Chattanooga

mphis

Decatur

Wilmington

Atlanta

Columbia

Birmingham

30⁰

Montgomery

Charleston

Savannah

Jacksonville

Pensacola

25⁰

Tampa

Fort Myers

Miami

Dates of Railroad Construction

— opened before 1841

— opened 1841-60

— opened 1861-84

— opened 1885-1913

— opened after 1913

selected main routes

═══ freight & over 20 return passenger journeys per week

--- freight & under 20 return passenger journeys per week

· · · · · freight only

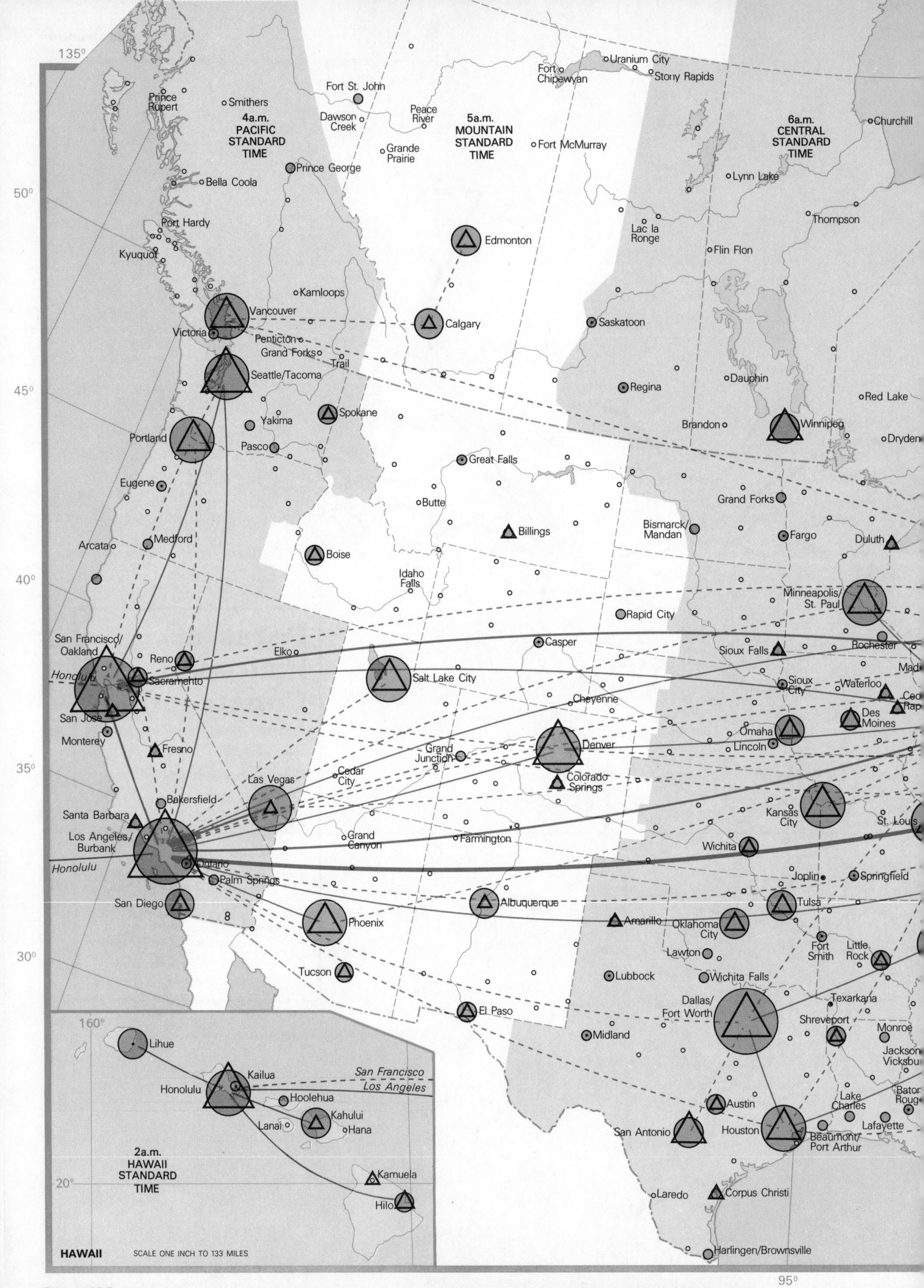

135°

50°

45°

40°

35°

30°

Prince
Rupert

Smithers

Fort St. John

Uranium City

Fort
Chipewyan

Stony Rapids

Churchill

4 a.m.
PACIFIC
STANDARD
TIME

Dawson
Creek

Peace
River

5 a.m.
MOUNTAIN
STANDARD
TIME

Lynn Lake

6 a.m.
CENTRAL
STANDARD
TIME

Grande
Prairie

Fort McMurray

Lac la
Ronge

Thompson

Bella Coola

Prince George

Edmonton

Flin Flon

Port Hardy

Kamloops

Kyuquot

Saskatoon

Red Lake

Vancouver

Victoria

Calgary

Regina

Dauphin

Dryden

Penticton
Grand Forks

Trail

Brandon

Winnipeg

Seattle/Tacoma

Spokane

Great Falls

Grand Forks

Portland

Yakima

Duluth

Pasco

Bismarck
Mandan

Fargo

Eugene

Butte

Arcata

Medford

Billings

Rapid City

Minneapolis/
St. Paul

Boise

Rochester

Idaho
Falls

Casper

Mad

San Francisco/
Oakland

Reno

Elko

Salt Lake City

Sioux Falls

Honolulu

Sacramento

Sioux
City

Waterloo

Cheyenne

Ceo
Rap

San Jose

Des
Moines

Monterey

Fresno

Grand
Junction

Denver

Omaha

Lincoln

Cedar
City

Colorado
Springs

Las Vegas

Kansas
City

St. Louis

Santa Barbara

Bakersfield

Grand
Canyon

Farmington

Wichita

Los Angeles/
Burbank

Joplin

Springfield

Honolulu

Ontario

Palm Springs

Tulsa

San Diego

8

Albuquerque

Amarillo

Oklahoma
City

Phoenix

Lawton

Little
Rock

Fort
Smith

Tucson

Lubbock

Wichita Falls

El Paso

Dallas/
Fort Worth

Texarkana

Midland

Shreveport

Monroe

Jackson
Vicksbu

160°

Lihue

Kailua

San Francisco
Los Angeles

Austin

Lake
Charles

Bator
Roug

Honolulu

Hoolehua

Lanai

Kahului

Hana

San Antonio

Houston

Beaumont/
Port Arthur

Lafayette

2 a.m.
HAWAII
STANDARD
TIME

Kamuela

20°

Hilo

Laredo

Corpus Christi

HAWAII

SCALE ONE INCH TO 133 MILES

Harlingen/Brownsville

95°

Scale 1 inch to 250 miles 1:15.84 M

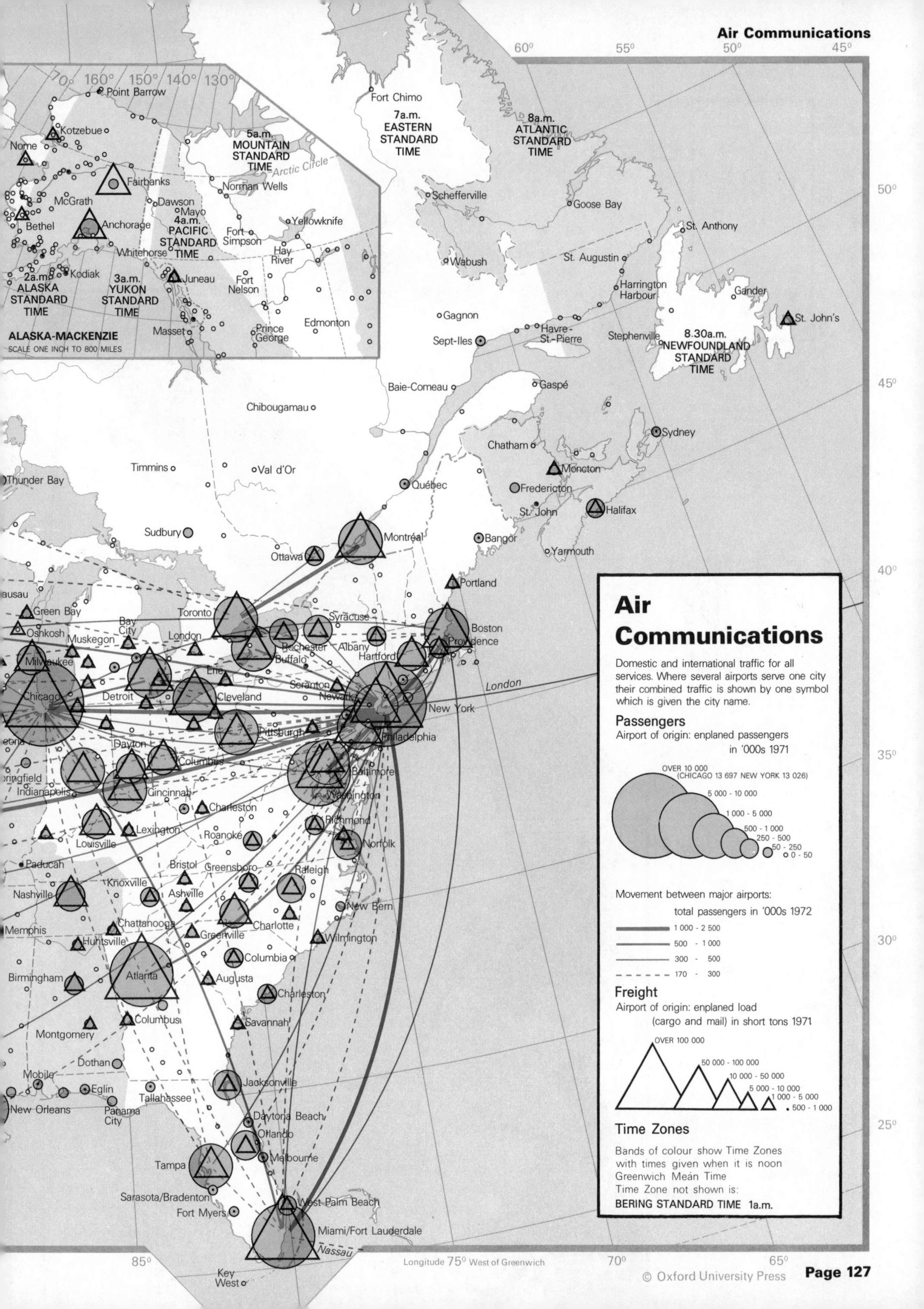

ALASKA-MACKENZIE
SCALE ONE INCH TO 800 MILES
Point Barrow
Kotzebue
Nome
Fairbanks
McGrath
Bethel
Anchorage
Dawson
Mayo
Whitehorse
Kodiak
Juneau
Masset
Norman Wells
Yellowknife
Fort Simpson
Hay River
Fort Nelson
Prince George
Edmonton
Arctic Circle
2a.m. ALASKA STANDARD TIME
3a.m. YUKON STANDARD TIME
4a.m. PACIFIC STANDARD TIME
5a.m. MOUNTAIN STANDARD TIME
7a.m. EASTERN STANDARD TIME
8a.m. ATLANTIC STANDARD TIME
8.30a.m. NEWFOUNDLAND STANDARD TIME
Fort Chimo
Schefferville
Goose Bay
St. Anthony
Wabush
St. Augustin
Harrington Harbour
Gander
St. John's
Gagnon
Sept-Iles
Havre-St.-Pierre
Stephenville
Baie-Comeau
Gaspé
Chibougamau
Sydney
Chatham
Timmins
Val d'Or
Thunder Bay
Québec
Moncton
Fredericton
St. John
Halifax
Sudbury
Montréal
Bangor
Yarmouth
Ottawa
Portland
Green Bay
Toronto
Syracuse
Boston
Oshkosh
Bay City
London
Muskegon
Rochester
Albany
Providence
Milwaukee
Buffalo
Hartford
Erie
Chicago
Detroit
Cleveland
Scranton
Newark
New York
London
Pittsburgh
Philadelphia
Dayton
Columbus
Baltimore
Indianapolis
Cincinnati
Washington
Charleston
Richmond
Lexington
Roanoke
Louisville
Norfolk
Paducah
Bristol
Greensboro
Raleigh
Knoxville
Ashville
Nashville
New Bern
Charlotte
Memphis
Chattanooga
Greenville
Wilmington
Huntsville
Columbia
Birmingham
Atlanta
Augusta
Charleston
Columbus
Savannah
Montgomery
Dothan
Jacksonville
Mobile
Eglin
Tallahassee
New Orleans
Panama City
Daytona Beach
Orlando
Melbourne
Tampa
Sarasota/Bradenton
West Palm Beach
Fort Myers
Miami/Fort Lauderdale
Nassau
Key West
60°
55°
50°
45°
40°
35°
30°
25°
85°
Longitude 75° West of Greenwich
70°
65°
Air Communications
Domestic and international traffic for all services. Where several airports serve one city their combined traffic is shown by one symbol which is given the city name.
Passengers
Airport of origin: enplaned passengers in '000s 1971
OVER 10 000 (CHICAGO 13 697 NEW YORK 13 026)
5 000 - 10 000
1 000 - 5 000
500 - 1 000
250 - 500
50 - 250
0 - 50
Movement between major airports: total passengers in '000s 1972
1 000 - 2 500
500 - 1 000
300 - 500
170 - 300
Freight
Airport of origin: enplaned load (cargo and mail) in short tons 1971
OVER 100 000
50 000 - 100 000
10 000 - 50 000
5 000 - 10 000
1 000 - 5 000
500 - 1 000
Time Zones
Bands of colour show Time Zones with times given when it is noon Greenwich Mean Time
Time Zone not shown is:
BERING STANDARD TIME 1a.m.

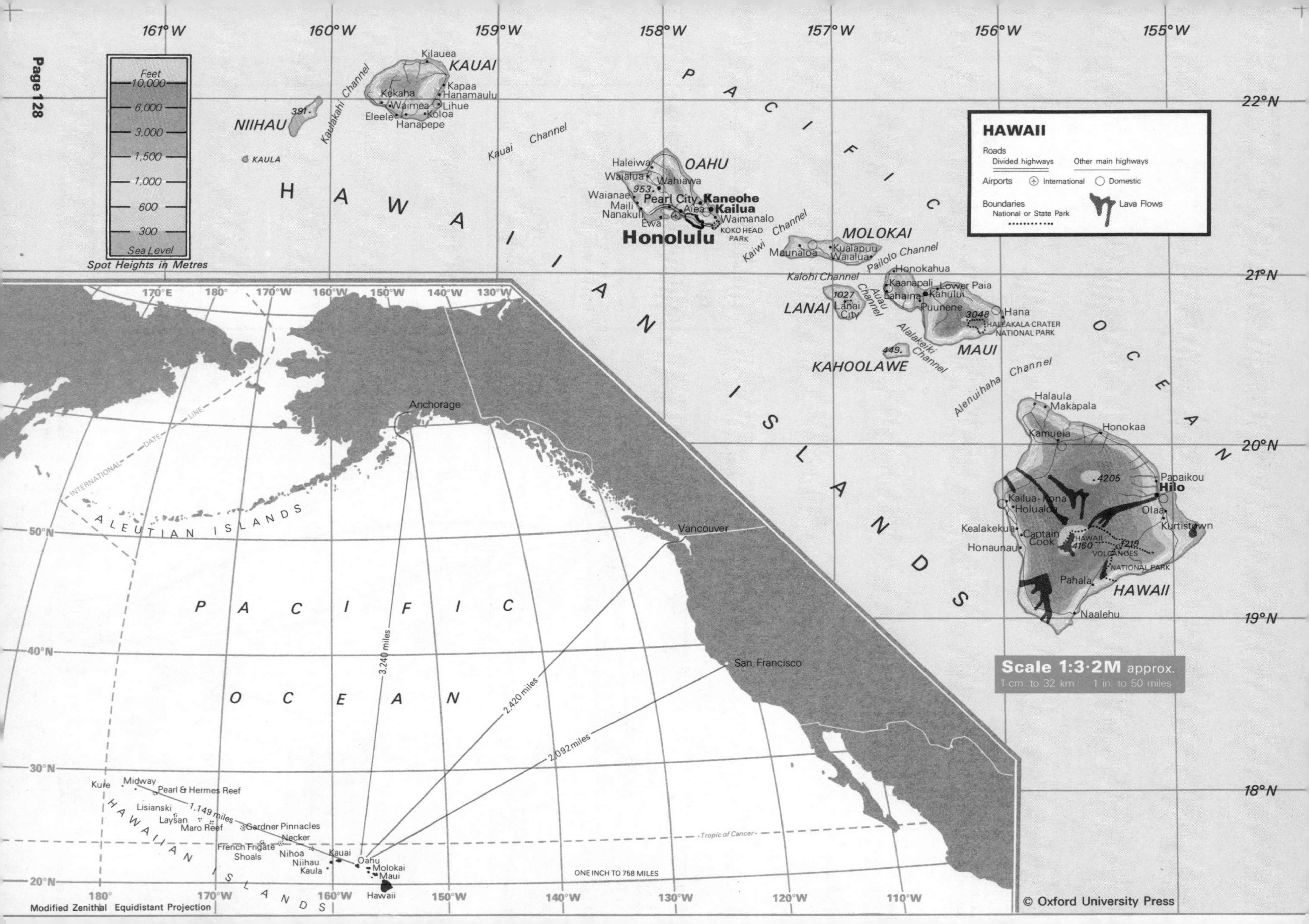

HAWAII
Roads
Divided highways
Other main highways
Airports
International
Domestic
Boundaries
National or State Park
Lava Flows
Feet
10,000
6,000
3,000
1,500
1,000
600
300
Sea Level
Spot Heights in Metres
161°W
160°W
159°W
158°W
157°W
156°W
155°W
22°N
21°N
20°N
19°N
18°N
P A C I F I C O C E A N
H A W A I I A N I S L A N D S
KAUAI
Kilauea
Kapaa
Hanamaulu
Lihue
Koloa
Hanapepe
Kekaha
Waimea
Eleele
NIIHAU
391
KAULA
Kaulakahi Channel
Kauai Channel
OAHU
Haleiwa
Waialua
Wahiawa
953
Waianae
Maili
Nanakuli
Ewa
Pearl City
Aiea
Kaneohe
Kailua
Waimanalo
KOKO HEAD PARK
Honolulu
Kaiwi Channel
MOLOKAI
Maunaloa
Kualapuu
Waialua
Pailolo Channel
Kalohi Channel
LANAI
1027
Lanai City
Auau Channel
Honokahua
Kaanapali
Lahaina
Lower Paia
Kahului
Puunene
3048
Hana
HALEAKALA CRATER NATIONAL PARK
MAUI
Alalakeiki Channel
449
KAHOOLAWE
Alenuihaha Channel
Halaula
Makapala
Honokaa
Kamuela
4205
Papaikou
Hilo
Kailua-Kona
Holualoa
Olaa
Kurtistown
Kealakekua
Captain Cook
Honaunau
HAWAII
4160
1219
VOLCANOES
NATIONAL PARK
Pahala
HAWAII
Naalehu
Scale 1:3·2M approx.
1 cm. to 32 km : 1 in. to 50 miles
170°E
180°
170°W
160°W
150°W
140°W
130°W
120°W
110°W
50°N
40°N
30°N
20°N
INTERNATIONAL DATE LINE
ALEUTIAN ISLANDS
Anchorage
Vancouver
San Francisco
P A C I F I C
O C E A N
3,240 miles
2,420 miles
2,092 miles
1,149 miles
Kure
Midway
Pearl & Hermes Reef
Lisianski
Laysan
Maro Reef
Gardner Pinnacles
Necker
French Frigate Shoals
Nihoa
Niihau
Kaula
Kauai
Oahu
Molokai
Maui
Hawaii
Tropic of Cancer
ONE INCH TO 758 MILES
HAWAIIAN ISLANDS
Modified Zenithal Equidistant Projection

Gazetteer of the United States and Canada

Coordinates are given to the nearest degree, plus or minus, so that 47° 19′N 94° 47′W is read as 47N 95W
Urban plan references are given to the nearest ¼ degree

Name	Page	N	W
Abbeville: Alabama	27	32	85
Abbeville: Georgia	24	32	83
Abbeville: Louisiana	26	30	92
Abbeville: South Carolina	24	34	82
Abbotsford: British Columbia	38	49	122
Aberdeen: Maryland	17	40	76
Aberdeen: Mississippi	27	34	89
Aberdeen: North Carolina	24	35	79
Aberdeen: South Dakota	28	45	99
Aberdeen: Washington	39	47	124
Aberdeen L.: N.W.T.	44	65	99
Abert, L.: Oregon	36	43	120
Abilene: Kansas	28	39	97
Abilene: Texas	29	32	100
Abingdon: Virginia	16	37	82
Abington: Massachusetts	15	42	71
Abington: Pennsylvania	2	40	75¼
Abitibi: r. Ontario	11	50	82
Abitibi, L.: Ontario	11	49	80
Abloviak Fiord: Québec	45	60	65
Absaroka Ra.: Mont./Wyo.	28	45	110
Absecon: New Jersey	15	39	74
Academy: California	37	37	120
Acadia Nat. Park: Maine	11	44	68
Accotink: Virginia	17	39	77
Achille: Oklahoma	26	34	96
Acland Bay: N.W.T.	44	72	101
Acton: California	35	34	118
Acton: Ontario	18	44	80
Acton Vale: Québec	13	46	73
Acworth: Georgia	24	34	85
Ada: Ohio	19	41	84
Ada: Oklahoma	26	35	97
Adair, C.: N.W.T.	45	72	71
Adairsville: Georgia	24	34	85
Adak: Alaska	46	52	177
Adams: Massachusetts	15	43	73
Adams: New York	12	44	76
Adams: Wisconsin	20	44	90
Adams City: Colorado	3	39¾	105
Adams, L.: British Columbia	38	51	120
Adams, Mt.: Washington	39	46	121
Adams Sound: N.W.T.	45	73	85
Addison: New York	14	42	77
Addyston: Ohio	10	39	85
Adel: Georgia	25	31	83
Adel: Oregon	36	42	120
Adelaide Penin.: N.W.T.	44	68	98
Adelanto: California	35	35	117
Adin: California	36	41	121
Adirondack Forest Preserve: New York	13	44	74
Adirondack Mts.: New York	13	44	74
Admiralty Inlet: N.W.T.	45	73	86
Admiralty I.: N.W.T.	44	70	101
Adrian: Michigan	21	42	84
Afognak: & i. Alaska	43	58	153
Agassiz: British Columbia	38	49	122
Agattu I.: Alaska	60	52	174
Agawam: Massachusetts	15	42	73
Ager: California	36	42	122
Agness: Oregon	36	43	124
Aguadilla: Puerto Rico	27	18	67
Agua Fria: r., Arizona	33	34	112
Aguanga: California	35	33	117
Aguanus: r., Québec	9	51	62
Agu Bay: N.W.T.	45	70	88
Agujereada, Punta: Puerto Rico.	27	19	67
Ahoskie: North Carolina	24	36	77
Aiea: Hawaii	128	21	158
Aiken: South Carolina	24	34	82
Aillik: Newfoundland	9	55	59
Air Force I.: N.W.T.	45	68	74
Aishihik: Yukon	40	62	138
Aishihik, L.: Yukon	40	61	137
Ajax: Ontario	12	44	79
Ajo: Arizona	33	32	113
Akhiok: Alaska	43	57	154
Akiachak: Alaska	43	61	162
Akiak: Alaska	43	61	161
Akimiski I.: N.W.T.	8	53	81
Aklavik: N.W.T.	44	68	135
Akpatok I.: N.W.T.	45	61	68
Akron: Ohio	19	41	82
Akron: Pennsylvania	14	40	76
Akulurak: Alaska	42	63	165
Akutan: Alaska	43	54	166
ALABAMA	27	—	—
Alabama: r., Albama	27	31	88
Alachua: Florida	25	30	83
Alakanuk: Alaska	42	63	165
Alalakeiki Ch.: Hawaii	128	21	157
Alameda: California	6	37¾	122¼
Alameda Creek: California	6	37½	122
Alamo: California	6	37¾	122
Alamo: Tennessee	27	36	89
Alamo: r., California	35	33	115
Alamogordo: New Mexico	29	33	106
Alamosa: Colorado	28	33	106
ALASKA	42/43	—	—
Alaska, Gulf of	43	59	145
Alaska Peninsula	43	56	159
Alaska Range	42/43	62	152
Alatna: Alaska	42	67	153
Alcatraz Is.: California	6	37¾	122¼
Albany: California	6	38	122¼
Albany: Georgia	24	32	84
Albany: Indiana	21	40	85
Albany: New York	15	43	74
Albany: Oregon	39	45	123
Albemarle: North Carolina	24	35	80
ALBERTA	30	—	—
Albert Edward Bay: N.W.T.	44	70	102
Albert Falls: dam, Idaho	32	48	117
Albert Lea: Minnesota	10	44	93
Albertville: Alabama	27	34	86
Albion: California	37	39	124
Albion: Indiana	21	41	85
Albion: Michigan	21	42	85
Albion: New York	12	43	78
Albion: Pennsylvania	19	42	80
Albreda: British Columba	41	53	119
Albuquerque: New Mexico	29	35	107
Alcoa: Tennessee	24	36	84
Alden: New York	14	43	79
Aldine: Texas	3	30	95½
Aldergrove: British Columbia	38	49	122
Alderpoint: California	36	40	124
Aleknagik: & lake, Alaska	43	59	159
Alenuihaha Ch.: Hawaii	128	20	156
Alert: Northwest Territories	62	83	62
Alert Bay: B.C.	41	51	127
Aleutian Islands	60	53	174
Aleutian Range: Alaska	43	58	155
Alexander Arch.: Alaska	40/41	57	136
Alexander City: Alabama	27	33	86
Alexandra Falls: sett., N.W.T.	30	60	116
Alexandria: Indiana	21	40	86
Alexandria: Louisiana	26	31	92
Alexandria: Ontario	13	45	75
Alexandria: Virginia	17	39	77
Alexandria City: Virginia	2	38¾	77
Algiers: Louisiana	3	30	90
Algoma: Wisconsin	20	45	87
Algonac: Michigan	19	43	83
Algonquin Prov. Park: Ontario	12	46	78
Alhambra: California	7	34	118¼
Alhambra: r., California	6	38	122
Alice: Texas	22	28	98
Aliquippa: Pennsylvania	19	41	80
Alisal: California	37	37	122
Alison Park: sett., Pennsylvania.	5	40½	80
Alix: Alberta	30	52	113
Alkali L.: Nevada	36	42	120
Allakaket: Alaska	42	67	153
Allard, Lac: Québec	9	51	64
Allatoona L.: Georgia	24	34	85
Allegan: Michigan	21	43	86
Allegany: & State Park, N.Y.	14	42	79
Allegheny: r., Pa./New York	11	42	79
Allegheny County Park: Pa.	5	40½	80
Allen: Oklahoma	26	35	96
Allendale: South Carolina	24	33	81
Allen Park: Michigan	5	42¼	83¼
Allens Mills: Pennsylvania	14	41	79
Allentown: Pennsylvania	14	41	76
Alliance: Nebraska	28	42	103
Alliance: Ohio	19	41	81
Allison: Pennsylvania	16	40	80
Allison Park: Pennsylvania	19	41	80
Alloy: West Virginia	16	38	81
Alma: Arkansas	26	35	94
Alma: Georgia	24	32	82
Alma: Michigan	20	43	85
Alma: Québec	8	49	72
Almanor: & lake & dam, Calif.	36	40	121
Almaville: Québec	13	47	73
Almont: Michigan	19	43	83
Almonte: Ontario	12	45	76
Alpaugh: California	34	36	119
Alpena: Michigan	18	45	83
Alpine: California	35	33	117
Alpine: Texas	29	30	104
Alsask: Saskatchewan	30	51	110
Alsek: r., Yukon/B.C.	40	60	138
Altadena: California	7	34¼	118¼
Altamaha: r., Georgia	34	32	82
Altamont: California	37	38	122
Altamont: New York	15	43	74
Altamont: Oregon	36	42	122
Altavista: Virginia	16	37	79
Alto: Texas	26	32	95
Alton: Illinois	10	39	90
Altoona: Alabama	27	34	86
Altoona: Pennsylvania	14	41	78
Alturas: California	36	42	121
Altus: Oklahoma	29	35	99
Alva: Kentucky	24	37	83
Alva: Oklahoma	29	37	99
Alvardo: California	6	37½	122
Alvarado: Texas	26	32	97
Alvin: Texas	26	29	95
Alymer, L.: Québec	12	46	71
Amadjuak L.: N.W.T.	45	65	71
Amado: Arizona	33	32	111
Amagansett: New York	15	41	72
Amarillo: Texas	29	35	102
Amasa: Michigan	20	46	88
Ambler: Alaska	42	67	158
Amboy: California	35	35	116
Amboy: Illinois	21	42	89
Ambridge: Pennsylvania	19	41	80
Amelia: Virginia	17	37	78
American Falls Res.: & dam, Idaho	32	43	113
American Fork: Utah	33	40	112
Americus: Georgia	24	32	84
Amery: Manitoba	31	57	94
Ames: Iowa	10	42	94
Amesbury: Massachusetts	15	43	71
Amherst: Massachusetts	15	42	73
Amherst: Nova Scotia	9	46	64
Amherst: Ohio	19	41	82
Amherst: Virginia	16	38	79
Amherstburg: Ontario	19	42	83
Amherst I.: Ontario	12	44	77
Amherst Junction: Wisconsin	20	44	89
Amisk L.: Saskatchewan	30	54	102
Amite: Louisiana	27	31	91
Amitoke Peninsula: N.W.T.	45	68	82
Amory: Mississippi	27	34	89
Amos: Québec	8	48	78
Amsterdam: New York	15	43	74
Amsterdam: Ohio	19	40	81
Amundsen Gulf: N.W.T.	44	70	124
Anacapa I.: California	34	34	119
Anaconda: Montana	32	46	113
Anacortes: Washington	38	49	123
Anacostia: r., D.C./Maryland	2	38¾	77
Anaheim: California	7	33¾	117¾
Anahuac: Texas	26	30	95
Anaktuvuk Pass: Alaska	42	68	152
Ancaster: Ontario	19	43	80
Anchorage: Alaska	43	61	150
Anchor Bay: Michigan	5	42¾	82¾
Anchor Point: sett., Alaska	43	60	152¾
Andalusia: Alabama	27	31	87
Anderson: California	36	40	122
Anderson: Indiana	21	40	86
Anderson: South Carolina	24	35	83
Anderson: r., N.W.T.	44	69	128
Anderson L.: B.C.	38	51	122
Andover: Massachusetts	15	43	71
Andover: New York	14	42	78
Andover: Ohio	19	42	81
Andreanof Is.: Alaska	60	52	175
Andrew Gordon Bay: N.W.T.	45	64	76
Andrews: Indiana	21	41	86
Andrews: North Carolina	24	35	84
Andrews: Oregon	36	42	119
Andrews: South Carolina	24	33	80
Androscoggin: r., N.H./Maine	9	45	71
Angel Is.: & State Park, Calif.	6	37¾	122¼
Angeles National Forest: Calif.	7	34¼	118
Angelina: r., Texas	26	32	95
Angels Camp: California	37	38	121
Angier: North Carolina	24	36	79
Angijak I.: N.W.T.	45	66	62
Angikuni L.: N.W.T.	44	62	100
Angleton: Texas	26	29	95
Angola: Indiana	21	42	85
Angola: New York	19	43	79
Angoon: Alaska	40	58	135
Aniak: Alaska	43	62	160
Animas: r., Colo./New Mexico	28	37	108
Anita: Pennsylvania	19	41	79
Aniwa: Wisconsin	20	45	89
Anmoore: West Virginia	16	39	80
Anna: Ohio	19	40	84
Annacis Island: British Columbia	6	49	123
Annandale: Virginia	2	38¾	77¼
Annapolis: Maryland	17	39	77
Annapolis Royal: Nova Scotia	9	45	66
Ann Arbor: Michigan	19	42	84
Ann, C.: Massachusetts	15	43	71
Annville: Pennsylvania	14	40	77
Anoka: Minnesota	3	45	93
Ansted: West Virginia	16	38	81
Anthony: Kansas	29	37	98
Anthony Chabot Regional Park: California	6	37¾	122
Anticosti I.: Québec	9	49	63
Antigo: Wisconsin	20	45	89
Antioch: California	37	38	122
Antlers: Oklahoma	26	34	96

	Page	N	W
Antwerp: New York	12	44	76
Antwerp: Ohio	21	41	85
Anvik: Alaska	42	63	160
Anvil Mts.: Yukon	40	62	133
Anza: California	35	34	117
Anza-Borrego Desert State Park: California	35	33	116
Apalachee Bay: Florida	25	30	84
Apalachia: *dam*, N. Carolina	24	35	84
Apalachicola: *& r.*, Florida	27	30	85
Apex: North Carolina	24	36	79
Apollo: Pennsylvania	19	41	80
Apopka: Florida	25	29	82
Apostle Is.: Wisconsin	10	47	91
Appalachia: Virginia	16	37	83
Appalachian Mountains	23	—	—
Applegate: California	37	39	121
Applegate: *& r.*, Oregon	36	42	123
Appleton: Wisconsin	20	44	88
Appomattox: Virginia	17	37	79
Appomattox: *r.*, Virginia	17	37	78
Appomattox: *r.*, Virginia	17	37	78
Aptos: California	37	37	122
Aransas Pass: Texas	22	28	97
Arbuckle: California	37	39	122
Arcade: New York	14	43	78
Arcadia: Florida	25	27	82
Arcadia: California	7	34¼	118
Arcadia: Louisiana	26	33	93
Arcanum: Ohio	21	40	85
Arcata: California	36	41	124
Archbold: Ohio	19	42	84
Arch Cape: *sett.*, Oregon	39	46	124
Archdale: North Carolina	24	36	80
Arches Nat. Mon.: Utah	33	39	110
Arcola: Illinois	21	40	88
Arcola: Saskatchewan	30	50	102
Arctic Village: Alaska	42	68	146
Arctic Red: *r.*, N.W.T.	44	66	132
Arctic Red River: *sett.*, N.W.T.	44	67	134
Arden: Nevada	35	36	115
Ardmore: Oklahoma	26	34	97
Ardnore: Pennsylvania	2	40	75¼
Arecibo: Puerto Rico	27	28	67
Arena Point: California	37	39	124
Argonne Forest: Illinois	4	41¾	88
Argos: Indiana	21	41	86
Arguello, Point: California	34	35	121
Arichat: Nova Scotia	9	46	61
Aristazabal I.: B.C.	41	53	129
ARIZONA	33	—	—
Arkabutla Res.: Mississippi	27	35	90
Arkadelphia: Arkansas	26	34	93
ARKANSAS	26	—	—
Arkansas: *r.*	22	34	91
Arkansas City: Arkansas	26	34	91
Arkansas City: Kansas	29	37	97
Arkville: New York	15	42	75
Arlington: Georgia	24	31	85
Arlington: Massachusetts	2	42½	71¼
Arlington: Virginia	17	39	77
Arlington: Washington	38	48	122
Arlington Heights: Illinois	21	42	88
Armand (Payne): *r.*, Québec	45	60	72
Armonk: New York	15	41	74
Armstrong: British Columbia	38	50	119
Armstrong: Ontario	10	50	89
Arnold: California	37	38	120
Arnold Res.: California	7	34	117¾
Arnprior: Ontario	12	45	76
Aroostook: *r.*, Maine	8	46	67
Arrowhead: British Columbia	41	51	118
Arrowrock Res.: Idaho	32	44	116
Arroyo Grande: California	34	35	121
Artesia: New Mexico	29	22	104
Arthabaska: Québec	13	46	72
Arthur: Illinois	21	40	88
Arthur: Ontario	18	44	81
Artillery L.: N.W.T.	44	63	108
Artois: California	37	40	122
Arvada: Colorado	3	39¾	105
Arvida: Québec	8	48	71
Arvin: California	35	35	119
Asbestos: Québec	13	46	72
Asbury Park: New Jersey	15	40	74
Ashburn: Georgia	24	32	84
Ashburnham: Massachusetts	15	43	72
Ashcroft: British Columbia	38	51	121
Ashdown: Arkansas	26	34	94
Asheboro: North Carolina	24	36	80
Asheville: North Carolina	24	36	83
Asheweig: *r.*, Ontario	31	53	89
Ashford: Alabama	27	31	85
Ashland: Kentucky	16	38	83
Ashland: Massachusetts	15	42	72
Ashland: New Hampshire	13	44	72
Ashland: Ohio	19	41	82
Ashland: Oregon	36	42	123
Ashland: Pennsylvania	14	41	76
Ashland: Virginia	17	38	77
Ashland: Wisconsin	10	47	91
Ashland, Mt.: Oregon	36	42	123
Ashley: Pennsylvania	14	41	76
Ashokan Res.: New York	15	42	74
Ashtabula: Ohio	19	42	81
Ashton: Idaho	32	44	111
Ashuanipi L.: Newfoundland	9	53	66

	Page	N	W
Aspen: Colorado	28	39	107
Assiniboine: *r.*, Manitoba	31	50	101
Assinica L.: Québec	8	50	75
Assumption: Alberta	30	59	119
Asti: California	37	39	123
Aston Bay: N.W.T.	44/45	74	95
Astray: Newfoundland	9	55	67
Atascadero: California	34	35	121
Atchafalaya: *r.*, Louisiana	26	31	92
Atchafalaya Bay: Louisiana	26	29	91
Atchison: Kansas	28	40	95
Atco: Georgia	27	34	85
Atco: New Jersey	14	40	75
Athabasca: Alberta	30	55	113
Athabasca: *r.*, Alberta	30	56	113
Athabasca, L.: Alta./Sask.	30	59	110
Athens: Alabama	27	35	87
Athens: Georgia	24	34	83
Athens: Illinois	21	40	90
Athens: New York	15	42	74
Athens: Ohio	16	39	82
Athens: Tennessee	24	35	85
Athens: Texas	26	32	96
Atherton: California	6	37½	122¼
Athlone: California	37	37	120
Athol: Massachusetts	15	43	72
Atikameg: Alberta	30	56	116
Atikokan: Ontario	10	49	92
Atikonak L.: Newfoundland	9	53	65
Atikup: Ontario	31	53	91
Atka I.: Alaska	60	52	174
Atkinson, Point: B.C.	6	49¼	123¼
Atlanta: Georgia	24	34	84
Atlanta: Texas	26	33	94
Atlantic City: New Jersey	15	39	74
Atlas: Michigan	19	43	84
Atlin I.: *& L.* British Columbia	40	60	134
Atmore: Alabama	27	31	88
Atoka: Oklahoma	26	34	96
Atoka Res.: Oklahoma	26	34	96
Attalla: Alabama	27	34	86
Attawapiskat: Ontario	8	53	83
Attawapiskat: *r.*, Ontario	8	53	84
Attawapiskat L.: Ontario	31	52	88
Attica: Indiana	21	40	87
Attica: New York	14	43	78
Attikamagen L.: Newfoundland	9	55	67
Attleboro: Massachusetts	15	42	71
Attu I.: Alaska	60	53	173
Atwater: California	37	37	121
Auau Ch.: Hawaii	128	21	157
Auberry: California	37	37	119
Auburn: Alabama	27	33	86
Auburn: California	37	39	121
Auburn: Indiana	21	41	85
Auburn: Maine	11	44	70
Auburn: Nebraska	28	40	96
Auburn: New York	14	43	77
Auburn: Washington	39	47	122
Auburndale: Florida	25	28	82
Auden: Ontario	10	50	88
Audubon Park: Louisiana	3	30	90
Au Fer, Pt.: Louisiana	26	29	91
Auglaize: *r.*, Ohio	19	41	84
Au Gres: Michigan	18	44	84
Augusta: Arkansas	26	35	91
Augusta: Georgia	24	33	82
Augusta: Kansas	29	38	97
Augusta: Maine	11	44	70
Augustine I: Alaska	43	59	153
Auke Bay: *sett.*, Alaska	40	58	135
Aulander: North Carolina	24	36	77
Aurora: Colorado	3	39¾	104¾
Aurora: Illinois	21	42	88
Aurora: Nebraska	28	41	98
Aurora: North Carolina	24	35	77
Aurora: Ontario	12	44	79
Au Sable: *r.*, Michigan	18	45	84
Ausable: *r.*, New York	13	44	74
Au Sable Forks: New York	13	44	74
Au Sable Point: Michigan	18	44	83
Austell: Georgia	27	34	85
Austin: Minnesota	10	44	93
Austin: Nevada	33	39	117
Austin: Pennsylvania	14	42	78
Austin: Texas	29	30	98
Austinburg: Ohio	19	42	81
Austinville: Virginia	16	37	81
Aux Barques, Pointe: Michigan	18	44	83
aux Feuilles (Leaf): *r.*, Québec	45	58	73
aux Feuilles, L. (Leaf Inlet): Québec	45	59	70
aux Outardes: *r.*, Québec	8	50	69
Avalon: California	35	33	118
Avalon: New Jersey	15	39	75
Avalon Penin.: Newfoundland	9	47	53
Avawatz Mts.: California	35	36	116
Avella: Pennsylvania	19	40	80
Avenal: California	34	36	120
Averill Park: New York	15	43	74
Avis: Pennsylvania	14	41	77
Avola: British Columbia	41	52	119
Avon: Connecticut	15	42	73
Avon: New York	14	43	78
Avondale: Louisiana	3	30	90
Avondale: Rhode Island	15	41	72
Avon Park: Florida	25	28	82

	Page	N	W
Awuna: *r.*, Alaska	42	69	157
Ayden: North Carolina	24	35	77
Ayer: Massachusetts	15	43	72
Aylmer: Québec	12	45	76
Aylmer West: Ontario	19	43	81
Azalea: Oregon	36	43	123
Azicoos L.: Maine	13	45	71
Aztec: New Mexico	29	37	108
Azusa: California	7	34¼	118
Babcock State Park: W.Va.	16	38	81
Babine Lake: B.C.	41	55	126
Babson Park: Florida	25	28	82
Bachelor Lake: Québec	8	50	77
Back: *r.*, Northwest Territories	44	66	96
Backbone Ranges: N.W.T.	40	63	128
Bad: *r.*, South Dakota	28	44	101
Bad Axe: Michigan	18	44	83
Baden: Ontario	18	43	81
Badin: North Carolina	24	35	80
Badlands Nat. Mon.: S.D.	28	44	102
Baffin Bay: Greenland/Canada	61	73	67
Baffin Bay: Texas	22	27	98
Baffin I.: N.W.T.	45	68	71
Baffin Island N.P.: N.W.T.	45	67	66
Bagby: California	37	38	120
Bagdad: Arizona	33	35	113
Bagdad: California	35	35	116
Bagnell: *dam*, Missouri	10	38	93
Bagotville: Québec	8	48	71
Bahia Mayagüez: Puerto Rico	27	18	67
Baie-Comeau: Québec	9	49	68
Baie Verte: *town*, Newfoundland	9	50	56
Baillie: *r.*, N.W.T.	44	65	106
Baillie Is.: N.W.T.	44	71	128
Bainbridge: Georgia	25	31	85
Bainbridge: New York	14	42	76
Bainbridge Island: Washington	6	47¾	122½
Baird Inlet: Alaska	43	61	164
Baird Mts.: Alaska	42	68	160
Baird Penin.: N.W.T.	45	69	76
Baker: California	35	35	116
Baker: Montana	28	46	104
Baker: Oregon	32	45	118
Baker L.: N.W.T.	44/45	64	96
Baker Lake: *sett.*, N.W.T.	44	64	96
Baker, Mt.: Washington	38	49	122
Bakers Dozen Is.: N.W.T.	8	57	79
Bakersfield: California	34	35	119
Bald Eagle, L.: Minnesota	3	45	93
Bald Knob: Arkansas	26	35	92
Baldwin: Florida	25	30	82
Baldwin Park: *town*, California	7	34	118
Baldwinsville: New York	12	43	76
Baldwyn: Mississippi	27	35	89
Ballston Spa: New York	13	43	74
Balsam L.: Ontario	12	45	79
Baltimore: Maryland	17	39	77
Baltimore: Ohio	16	40	83
Bamberg: South Carolina	24	33	81
Bamberton: British Columbia	38	49	124
Bamfield: British Columbia	38	49	125
Bancroft: Ontario	12	45	78
Bandelier Nat. Mon.: N. Mex.	29	36	106
Banff: Alberta	30	51	116
Banff Nat. Park: Alberta	30	52	116
Bangor: Maine	9	45	69
Bangor: Pennsylvania	14	41	75
Banks: Oregon	39	46	123
Banks I.: British Columbia	41	53	130
Banks I.: N.W.T.	44	73	121
Banks L.: Washington	39	48	119
Banning: California	35	34	117
Baraboo: *& range*, Wisconsin	20	43	90
Baranof I.: Alaska	40/41	57	136
Barataria Bay: Louisiana	27	29	90
Barboursville: West Virginia	16	38	82
Barco: North Carolina	17	36	74
Barge Canal: New York	12	43	78
Baring, C.: N.W.T.	44	70	118
Baring Chan.: N.W.T.	44	74	99
Barkerville: British Columbia	41	53	122
Barkley, L.: Kentucky	23	37	88
Barkley Sound: B.C.	38	49	125
Barnesboro: Pennsylvania	14	41	79
Barnesville: Georgia	24	33	84
Barnesville: Ohio	16	40	81
Barnstable: Massachusetts	15	42	70
Barnwell: South Carolina	24	33	81
Barraute: Québec	8	48	77
Barre: Vermont	13	44	73
Barren Is.: Alaska	43	59	152
Barrett: California	35	33	117
Barrhead: Alberta	30	54	114
Barrie: Ontario	12	44	80
Barrington: Illinois	21	42	88
Barrington: Rhode Island	15	42	71
Barrow: Alaska	42	71	157
Barrow, Point: Alaska	42	71	156
Barrow Strait: N.W.T.	45	74	93
Barstow: California	35	35	117
Barter I.: *sett.*, Alaska	42	70	144
Bartholemew Bayou: *r.*, Ark.	26	34	92
Bartle: California	36	41	122
Bartlesville: Oklahoma	29	37	96
Bartlett: California	35	36	118
Barton: Vermont	13	45	72

	Page	N	W
Bartow: Florida	**25**	28	82
Basile: Louisiana	**26**	30	93
Baskatong L.: Québec	**13**	47	75
Baskatong Res.: Québec	**12**	47	76
Bassona: Alberta	**30**	51	112
Bassets: California	**37**	40	121
Bassett: Virginia	**16**	37	80
Bass L.: Indiana	**21**	41	87
Bass Lake: *sett.*, California	**37**	37	120
Bastrop: Louisiana	**26**	33	92
Batavia: Illinois	**21**	42	88
Batavia: New York	**12**	43	78
Batesburg: South Carolina	**24**	34	82
Batesville: Arkansas	**26**	36	92
Batesville: Mississippi	**27**	34	90
Bath: New York	**14**	42	77
Bath: Pennsylvania	**14**	41	75
Bathurst: New Brunswick	**9**	48	66
Bathurst, C.: N.W.T.	**44**	71	128
Bathurst Inlet: N.W.T.	**44**	67	108
Bathurst Island: N.W.T.	**61**	76	100
Batiscan: *r.*, Québec	**13**	47	72
Baton Rouge: Louisiana	**26**	30	91
Battle: *r.*, Alta./Sask.	**30**	52	112
Battle Creek: *town*, Michigan	**21**	42	85
Battle Harbour: Newfoundland	**9**	52	56
Battle Mountain: Nevada	**33**	41	117
Batty Bay: N.W.T.	**45**	73	91
Baumstown: Pennsylvania	**14**	40	76
Bauxite: Arkansas	**26**	35	93
Baxley: Georgia	**24**	32	82
Baxter: California	**35**	35	116
Baxter State Park: Maine	**9**	46	69
Bayamon: Puerto Rico	**27**	18	66
Baybridge: Ohio	**19**	41	83
Bay City: Michigan	**20**	44	84
Bay City: Texas	**26**	29	96
Bay Minette: *town*, Alabama	**27**	31	88
Bayonne: New Jersey	**1**	40¾	74
Bayou: *r.*, Texas	**29**	32	99
Bayou La Batre: Alabama	**27**	30	88
Bayou Lafourche: *r.*, La.	**27**	29	90
Bayou Macon: *r.*, Louisiana	**26**	32	92
Bays Bayou: Texas	**3**	29¾	95½
Bay St. Louis: *town*, Miss.	**27**	30	89
Bay Shore: New York	**15**	41	73
Bayside: California	**36**	41	124
Bay Springs: Mississippi	**27**	32	89
Baytown: Texas	**26**	30	95
Bay Village: Ohio	**19**	41	82
Beach Haven: New Jersey	**15**	40	74
Beachwood: New Jersey	**15**	40	74
Beacon: New York	**15**	42	74
Beacon Falls: *sett.*, Connecticut	**15**	41	73
Beaconsfield: Québec	**2**	45½	73¾
Beacon Station: California	**35**	35	116
Beamsville: Ontario	**19**	43	80
Bear Brook State Park: N.H.	**13**	43	71
Bear Creek: *sett.*, Yukon	**40**	64	139
Bear Creek: Colorado	**3**	39¾	105
Bear Creek: Yukon	**42**	64	139
Bearden: Arkansas	**26**	34	93
Bear I.: N.W.T.	**8**	54	81
Bear L.: Idaho/Utah	**32**	42	111
Bear Mtn.: New York	**15**	41	74
Bearskin Lake: *sett.*, Ontario	**31**	54	91
Beatrice: Nebraska	**28**	40	97
Beatton: *r.*, British Columbia	**40**	57	121
Beatty: Nevada	**34**	37	117
Beatty: Oregon	**36**	42	121
Beattyville: Québec	**8**	49	77
Beauceville: Québec	**13**	46	71
Beaufort: North Carolina	**24**	35	77
Beaufort: South Carolina	**24**	32	81
Beaufort Sea	**60**	73	136
Beauharnois: Québec	**13**	45	74
Beaumont: California	**35**	34	117
Beaumont: Texas	**26**	30	94
Beaver: Alaska	**42**	66	174
Beaver: *cr.*, Kansas	**28**	40	101
Beaver: *cr.*, Kentucky	**16**	38	83
Beaver: *r.*, Alta./Sask.	**30**	54	110
Beaver: *r.*, Pennsylvania	**19**	41	80
Beaver: *r.*, Yukon	**40**	60	126
Beaver Dam: Wisconsin	**20**	43	89
Beaverdell: British Columbia	**38**	49	119
Beaver Falls: *town*, Pa.	**19**	41	80
Beaverhead: *r.*, Montana	**32**	45	112
Beaverhill L.: Alberta	**30**	53	113
Beaver I.: Michigan	**20**	46	86
Beaverlodge: Alberta	**30**	55	119
Beavertown: Pennsylvania	**14**	41	77
Bécancour: Québec	**13**	46	72
Becharof L.: Alaska	**43**	58	156
Beckley: West Virginia	**16**	38	81
Beckmeyer: Illinois	**10**	39	89
Beckwourth: California	**36**	40	120
Bedford: Indiana	**10**	39	87
Bedford: Massachusetts	**2**	42½	71¼
Bedford: Ohio	**19**	41	82
Bedford: Pennsylvania	**14**	40	79
Bedford: Virginia	**16**	37	80
Beechers Corners: California	**35**	35	118
Beechey Point: *sett.*, Alaska	**42**	70	149
Beechwood: Michigan	**20**	46	89
Beegum: California	**36**	40	123
Beeville: Texas	**22**	28	98

	Page	N	W
Beggs: Oklahoma	**26**	36	96
Bel Air: Maryland	**17**	40	76
Belcher Is.: N.W.T.	**8**	56	79
Belden: California	**36**	40	121
Belding: Michigan	**20**	43	85
Belen: New Mexico	**29**	35	107
Belfry: Kentucky	**16**	38	82
Belhaven: North Carolina	**24**	36	77
Belington: West Virginia	**16**	39	80
Belkofski: Alaska	**43**	55	162
Bella Bella: British Columbia	**41**	52	128
Bella Coola: British Columbia	**41**	52	127
Bellaire: Texas	**3**	29¾	95¼
Bellaire: Ohio	**16**	40	81
Belle: West Virginia	**16**	38	82
Belledune: New Brunswick	**9**	48	66
Bellefontaine: Ohio	**19**	40	84
Bellefonte: Pennsylvania	**14**	41	78
Belle Fourche: South Dakota	**28**	45	104
Belle Fourche: *r.*, Wyo./S.D.	**28**	44	105
Belle Glade: Florida	**25**	27	81
Belle Isle: Michigan	**5**	42¼	83
Belle Isle: Newfoundland	**9**	52	55
Belle Isle, Str. of: Newfoundland	**9**	52	57
Belleoram: Newfoundland	**9**	48	55
Belle Plaine: Saskatchewan	**30**	50	105
Belle River: *sett.*, Ontario	**5**	42¼	82¾
Belleterre: Québec	**8**	47	79
Belle Vernon: Pennsylvania	**19**	40	80
Belleview: Florida	**25**	29	82
Belleville: Kansas	**28**	40	98
Belleville: Ontario	**12**	44	77
Belleville: Pennsylvania	**14**	41	78
Bellevue: Nebraska	**28**	41	96
Bellevue: Ohio	**19**	41	83
Bellevue: Pennsylvania	**5**	40½	80
Bellevue: Washington	**6**	47¾	122¼
Bellflower: California	**7**	33¾	118¼
Bellingham: Washington	**38**	49	122
Bell I.: Newfoundland	**9**	51	56
Bellota: California	**37**	38	121
Bellot Strait: N.W.T.	**45**	72	95
Bellows Falls: *town*, Vermont	**13**	43	72
Bell Penin.: N.W.T.	**45**	64	82
Bell Rock: N.W.T.	**30**	60	112
Belle Chase: Louisiana	**3**	29¾	90
Bells: Tennessee	**27**	36	89
Bells Station: California	**37**	37	121
Bellville: Ohio	**19**	41	83
Bellville: Texas	**26**	30	96
Bellwood: Illinois	**4**	41¾	87¾
Bellwood: Pennsylvania	**11**	41	78
Belmont: Massachuesetts	**2**	42½	71¼
Belmont: New York	**14**	42	78
Belmont: North Carolina	**24**	35	81
Belmont: California	**6**	37½	122¼
Belmont Harbor: Illinois	**4**	42	87½
Beloit: Kansas	**29**	39	98
Beloit: Wisconsin	**21**	43	89
Belpre: Ohio	**16**	39	82
Belton: South Carolina	**24**	35	83
Belton: *dam*, Texas	**29**	31	97
Beltsville: Maryland	**2**	39	76¾
Belvidere: Illinois	**21**	42	89
Belvidere: New Jersey	**14**	41	75
Belzoni: Mississippi	**27**	33	91
Bement: Illinois	**21**	40	89
Bemidji: Minnesota	**10**	47	95
Bemis: Tennessee	**27**	36	88
Bend: Oregon	**32**	44	121
Bendeleben Mts.: Alaska	**42**	65	163
Benicia: California	**37**	38	122
Bennett: British Columbia	**40**	60	135
Bennettsville: South Carolina	**24**	35	80
Bennington: Vermont	**13**	43	73
Bensenville: Illinois	**4**	42	88
Benson: Arizona	**33**	32	110
Benson: North Carolina	**24**	35	79
Benson Lake: *sett.*, B.C.	**41**	50	127
Benson Mines: New York	**13**	44	75
Benton: Arkansas	**26**	35	93
Benton: Louisiana	**26**	33	94
Benton: Wisconsin	**10**	42	90
Benton City: Washington	**39**	46	119
Benton Harbor: Michigan	**21**	42	86
Benwood: West Virginia	**16**	40	81
Beowawe: Nevada	**33**	41	116
Berea: Ohio	**19**	41	82
Berenda: California	**37**	37	120
Berens: *r.*, Manitoba	**31**	52	96
Berens River: *sett.*, Manitoba	**31**	52	97
Bergholz: Ohio	**19**	41	81
Bering Sea	**42/43**	59	165
Bering Strait	**42**	66	169
Berkeley: California	**6**	37¾	122¼
Berkeley: Illinois	**4**	42	88
Berkeley, C.: N.W.T.	**44**	74	101
Berkeley Springs: W. Va.	**17**	40	78
Berkley: Michigan	**5**	42½	83¼
Berlin: Maryland	**17**	38	75
Berlin: New Hampshire	**13**	44	71
Berlin: Ohio	**19**	41	82
Berlin: Pennsylvania	**14**	40	79
Berlin: Wisconsin	**20**	44	89
Berlinguet Inlet: N.W.T.	**45**	71	86
Berlin Heights: Ohio	**19**	41	83
Berlin Res.: Ohio	**19**	41	81

	Page	N	W
Bermen, L.: Québec	**8**	54	69
Bernalillo: New Mexico	**29**	35	107
Berne: Indiana	**21**	41	85
Bernice: Louisiana	**26**	33	93
Bernier Bay: N.W.T.	**45**	71	88
Berryessa, L.: California	**37**	39	122
Berryville: Virginia	**17**	39	78
Bersimis River: *sett.*, Québec	**8**	49	69
Berwick: Louisiana	**26**	30	91
Berwick: Pennsylvania	**14**	41	76
Berwyn: Illinois	**4**	41¾	87¾
Bessemer: Alabama	**27**	33	87
Bessemer: Pennsylvania	**19**	41	82
Bessemer City: North Carolina	**24**	35	81
Bessmay: Texas	**26**	30	94
Bethel: Alaska	**43**	61	162
Bethel: Connecticut	**15**	41	73
Bethel: Maine	**13**	44	71
Bethel Park: Pennsylvania	**19**	40	80
Bethesda: Maryland	**2**	39	77
Bethesda: Ohio	**5**	40¼	80
Bethlehem: New Hampshire	**13**	44	72
Bethlehem: Pennsylvania	**14**	41	75
Betsiamites: Québec	**8**	49	69
Betsiamites: *r.*, Québec	**8**	49	70
Betsie, Point: Michigan	**20**	45	86
Bettles: Alaska	**42**	67	152
Beverly: Massachusetts	**15**	43	71
Beverly: New Jersey	**14**	40	75
Beverly: Ohio	**16**	40	82
Beverly: Washington	**39**	47	120
Beverly Hills: California	**7**	34	118½
Beverly Hills: Michigan	**5**	42½	83¼
Beverly L.: N.W.T.	**44**	65	100
Biddeford: Maine	**11**	43	70
Bieber: California	**36**	41	121
Bienville, Lac: Québec	**8**	55	73
Big Bay de Noc: Michigan	**20**	46	87
Big Bear Lake: *sett.*, California	**35**	34	117
Big Beaver House: Ontario	**31**	53	90
Big Bend: California	**36**	41	122
Big Bend Nat. Park: Texas	**29**	29	104
Big Black: *r.*, Mississippi	**27**	32	91
Big Blue: *r.*, Nebraska/Kansas	**28**	41	97
Big Creek: *sett.*, California	**37**	37	119
Big Cypress Swamp: Florida	**25**	26	81
Big Dalton Res.: California	**7**	34¼	117¾
Big Delta: Alaska	**42**	64	146
Big Diomede: *i.*, Alaska	**42**	66	169
Big Falls: *sett.*, Minnesota	**10**	48	94
Big Fork: *r.*, Minnesota	**10**	48	94
Biggar: Saskatchewan	**30**	52	108
Big Hole: *r.*, Montana	**32**	46	113
Bighorn: *r.*, Wyo./Montana	**28**	45	108
Bighorn Mts.: Wyoming	**28**	44	107
Big I.: N.W.T.	**40**	61	117
Big I.: N.W.T.	**45**	63	71
Big Island: *sett.*, Virginia	**16**	38	79
Biglerville: Pennsylvania	**14**	40	77
Big Meadows: California	**37**	38	120
Big Pine: California	**35**	37	118
Big Rapids: Michigan	**20**	44	86
Big River: *sett.*, Saskatchewan	**30**	54	107
Big Sable Point: Michigan	**20**	44	87
Big Sage Res.: California	**36**	42	121
Big Sandy: *r.*, Tennessee	**27**	36	88
Big Sandy: *r.*, W.Va./Kentucky	**16**	38	83
Big Santa Anna Res.: California	**7**	34¼	118
Big Satilla: *cr.*, Georgia	**24**	32	82
Big Sioux: *r.*, South Dakota	**28**	44	97
Big Spring: Texas	**29**	32	102
Big Stone Gap: Virginia	**16**	37	83
Big Sunflower: *r.*, Mississippi	**27**	33	91
Big Sur: California	**34**	36	122
Big Timber: Montana	**32**	46	110
Big Trout L.: Ontario	**31**	54	90
Big Tujunga Res.: California	**7**	34¼	118¼
Big Valley: *sett.*, Alberta	**30**	52	113
Big Walnut: *r.*, Ohio	**16**	40	83
Big Wood: *r.*, Idaho	**32**	43	115
Billings: Montana	**28**	46	109
Biloxi: Mississippi	**27**	30	89
Bingham: Utah	**33**	41	112
Binghamton: New York	**14**	42	76
Birch Bay: Washington	**38**	49	123
Birch Island: *sett.*, B.C.	**41**	52	120
Birch Mts.: Alberta	**30**	58	113
Birmingham: Alabama	**27**	33	87
Birmingham: Michigan	**5**	42½	83¼
Birmingham: Ohio	**19**	41	82
Bisbee: Arizona	**33**	31	110
Biscayne Bay: Florida	**25**	26	80
Biscoe: North Carolina	**24**	35	80
Bishop: California	**33**	37	118
Bishop: Texas	**22**	28	98
Bishopville: South Carolina	**24**	34	80
Biskotasi L.: Ontario	**11**	47	82
Bismarck: North Dakota	**28**	47	101
Bissett: Manitoba	**31**	51	96
Bistcho L.: Alberta	**30**	60	119
Bistineau, L.: Louisiana	**26**	32	93
Bitteroot Range: Mont./Idaho	**32**	46	115
Bixby: Oklahoma	**26**	36	96
Bizard, Île: Québec	**2**	45½	74
Black: *r.*, Alaska	**42**	66	142
Black: *r.*, Arkansas	**22**	36	91
Black: *r.*, Michigan	**18**	43	83

	Page	N	W
Carnegie: Pennsylvania	5	40½	80
Carnwath: *r.*, N.W.T.	44	68	128
Caro: Michigan	18	43	83
Caroleen: North Carolina	24	35	82
Carpentersville: Illinois	21	42	88
Carpenterville: Oregon	36	42	124
Carpinteria: California	34	34	120
Carrabelle: Florida	25	30	85
Carrara: Nevada	35	37	117
Carrizo: *cr.*, California	35	33	116
Carrollton: Georgia	24	34	85
Carrollton: Ohio	19	41	81
Carrollton: Texas	26	33	97
Carrolltown: Pennsylvania	14	41	79
Carrot: *r.*, Saskatchewan	30	53	103
Carson: California	7	33¾	118¼
Carson: *r.*, Nevada	37	39	120
Carson City: Michigan	20	43	85
Carson City: Nevada	37	39	120
Carson Sink: Nevada	33	40	119
Cartago: California	35	36	118
Carteret: New Jersey	15	41	74
Cartersville: Georgia	24	34	85
Carthage: Indiana	21	40	86
Carthage: Missouri	10	37	94
Carthage: New York	12	44	76
Carthage: North Carolina	24	35	79
Carthage: Texas	26	32	94
Cartwright: Newfoundland	9	54	57
Cary: North Carolina	24	36	79
Caryville: Tennessee	24	36	84
Casa Grande: Arizona	33	33	112
Cashmere: Washington	39	48	120
Casitas Springs: California	34	34	119
Casmalia: California	34	35	121
Casper: Wyoming	28	43	106
Cass: *r.*, Michigan	18	43	83
Cass City: Michigan	18	44	83
Casselman: Ontario	13	45	75
Casselman: *r.*, Pa./Maryland	16	40	79
Cassiar: British Columbia	40	59	130
Cassiar Mts.: British Columbia	40	59	130
Cassopolis: Michigan	21	42	86
Castaic: California	35	35	119
Castella: California	36	41	122
Castile: New York	14	43	78
Castillo de San Marcos Nat. Mon.: Florida	25	30	81
Castlegar: British Columbia	41	49	118
Castle Rock: Washington	39	46	123
Castleton-on-Hudson: N.Y.	15	43	74
Castor: Alberta	30	52	112
Castro Valley: *town*, California	6	37¾	122
Castroville: California	37	37	122
Catahoula L.: Louisiana	26	32	92
Catawba Island: *sett.*, Ohio	19	42	83
Catawissa: Pennsylvania	14	41	76
Cathay: California	37	37	120
Cathlamet: Washington	39	46	123
Cat Island: Mississippi	27	30	89
Catlettsburg: Kentucky	16	38	83
Catlin: Illinois	21	40	88
Cataouatche, L.: Louisiana	3	29¾	90¼
Catskill: New York	15	42	74
Catskill Forest Preserve: N.Y.	15	42	75
Catskill Mtns.: New York	15	42	74
Cattaraugus: New York	19	42	79
Cattaraugus: *cr.*, New York	14	42	79
Caughnawaga: Québec	2	45½	73¾
Caumsett State Park: New York	1	41	73½
Cayey: Puerto Rico	27	18	66
Cayoosh Range: B.C.	38	50	122
Cayucos: California	34	35	121
Cayuga L.: New York	14	43	77
Cazenovia: New York	14	43	76
Cedar: *cr.*, North Dakota	28	46	102
Cedar: *r.*, Iowa	10	43	93
Cedar: *r.*, Washington	6	47½	122¼
Cedar Bluff: Virginia	16	37	82
Cedarburg: Wisconsin	20	43	88
Cedar City: Utah	33	38	113
Cedar Falls: *town*, Iowa	10	43	92
Cedar Grove: W. Va.	16	38	81
Cedar L.: Manitoba	31	53	100
Cedar Rapids: Iowa	10	42	92
Cedar Springs: Michigan	20	43	86
Cedartown: Georgia	27	34	85
Cedarville: California	36	42	120
Cedarville: New Jersey	14	39	75
Celeste: Texas	26	33	96
Celina: Ohio	21	41	85
Celina: Texas	26	33	97
Center: Connecticut	15	41	73
Center: Texas	26	32	94
Center Hill Res.: Tennessee	27	36	86
Center Line: Michigan	5	42½	83
Center Moriches: New York	15	41	73
Centerville: Indiana	21	40	85
Centerville: Iowa	10	41	93
Centerville: Tennessee	27	36	87
Centerville: Texas	26	31	96
Centerville, L.: Minnesota	3	45¼	93
Central: Alaska	42	66	145
Central: New Mexico	29	33	108
Central: South Carolina	24	35	83
Central City: Colorado	28	40	106
Central City: Pennsylvania	14	40	79

	Page	N	W
Centralia: Illinois	10	39	89
Centralia: Washington	39	47	123
Central Lake: *sett.*, Michigan	20	45	85
Central Park: British Columbia	6	49¼	123
Central Park: New York	1	40¾	74
Central Valley: *town*, California	36	41	122
Centre: Alabama	27	34	86
Centreville: Maryland	17	39	76
Centreville: Michigan	21	42	86
Centreville: Mississippi	26	31	91
Ceres: California	37	38	121
Cerro Gordo: Illinois	21	40	89
Chabot, L.: California	6	37¾	120
Chacahoula: Louisiana	27	30	91
Chaco Canyon Nat. Mon.: New Mexico	29	36	108
Chadbourn: North Carolina	24	34	79
Chadron: Nebraska	28	43	103
Chagrin Falls: *town*, Ohio	19	41	81
Chaleur, Baie de: Québec/N.B.	9	48	66
Chalkyitsik: Alaska	42	67	144
Chalmette: Louisiana	3	30	90
Chalmette Natural History Pk.: La.	3	30	90
Chamberlain: South Dakota	28	44	99
Chamberlain, L.: Maine	8	46	69
Chambersburg: Pennsylvania	14	40	78
Chamouchouane: *r.*, Québec	8	49	73
Champagne: Yukon	40	61	137
Champaign: Illinois	21	40	88
Champlain: New York	13	45	73
Champlain, L.: Vt./New York	13	45	73
Chandalar: Alaska	42	68	149
Chandalar: *r.*, Alaska	42	67	147
Chandeleur Is.: Louisiana	27	30	89
Chandeleur Sound: Louisiana	27	30	89
Chandler: Arizona	33	33	112
Chandler: Oklahoma	26	36	97
Chandler: Québec	9	48	65
Chandler: Texas	26	32	95
Chaniliut: Alaska	42	63	163
Channel Is. Nat. Mon.: Calif.	34	34	119
Channing: Michigan	20	46	88
Chantrey Inlet: N.W.T.	44	68	96
Chanute: Kansas	29	38	95
Chapais: Québec	8	50	75
Chapel Hill: *town*, N.C.	24	36	79
Chapleau: Ontario	10	48	83
Chapman, C.: N.W.T.	45	69	89
Chardon: Ohio	19	42	81
Chariton: *r.*, Iowa/Missouri	10	40	93
Charles: *r.*, Massachusetts	2	42¼	71
Charles City: Iowa	10	43	93
Charles I.: N.W.T.	45	63	75
Charles Lee Tilden Regional Park: California	6	38	122¼
Charleston: Arkansas	26	35	94
Charleston: Illinois	21	40	88
Charleston: Mississippi	27	34	90
Charleston: South Carolina	24	33	80
Charleston: Tennessee	24	35	85
Charleston: West Virginia	16	38	82
Charleston Park: Nevada	35	36	116
Charlestown: New Hampshire	13	43	72
Charles Town: West Virginia	17	39	78
Charlevoix: Michigan	20	45	85
Charlotte: Michigan	21	43	85
Charlotte: North Carolina	24	35	81
Charlotte Harbor: Florida	25	27	82
Charlottesville: Virginia	17	38	78
Charlottetown: P.E.I.	9	46	63
Charlton City: Massachusetts	15	42	72
Charlton Depot: N.W.T.	8	52	79
Charlton I.: N.W.T.	8	52	80
Chartiers Creek: Pennsylvania	5	40½	80
Chase: British Columbia	38	51	120
Chase City: Virginia	17	37	78
Chatanika: Alaska	42	65	147
Chatham: Massachusetts	15	42	70
Chatham: Michigan	20	46	87
Chatham: New York	15	42	74
Chatham: Ontario	19	42	82
Chatham: Virginia	16	37	79
Chatham Strait: Alaska	41	56	134
Chatsworth: Georgia	24	35	85
Chattahoochee: Florida	27	31	85
Chattahoochee: *r.*, Ga./Ala.	27	31	85
Chattanooga: Tennessee	27	35	85
Chatuge: *dam.*, N.C./Georgia	24	35	84
Chaudière: *r.*, Québec	13	47	71
Chauncey: Ohio	16	39	82
Chautauqua L.: New York	19	42	79
Chazy: New York	13	45	73
Cheaha Mount: Alabama	27	33	86
Cheat: *r.*, West Virginia	16	40	80
Cheatham: *dam*, Tennessee	23	36	87
Cheat Mtn.: West Virginia	16	39	80
Cheboygan: Michigan	20	46	84
Checotah: Oklahoma	26	35	96
Chefornak: Alaska	43	60	164
Chehalis: *& r.*, Washington	39	47	123
Chelan: Washington	39	48	120
Chelan L.: Washington	38/39	48	120
Chelsea: Massachusetts	2	42½	71
Chelsea: Michigan	21	42	84
Chemainus: British Columbia	38	49	124
Chenega: Alaska	43	60	148
Cheneyville: Louisiana	26	31	92

	Page	N	W
Chenik: Alaska	43	59	154
Chenoa: Illinois	21	41	89
Cheoah: *dam*, North Carolina	24	35	84
Cheraw: South Carolina	24	35	80
Cherikof I.: Alaska	43	56	156
Cherokee: Alabama	27	35	88
Cherokee: *dam*, Tennessee	24	36	83
Cherokees, L. of the: Okla.	29	37	95
Cherry Creek: Colorado	3	39¾	105
Cherry Creek Reservoir: Colo.	3	39¾	104¾
Cherry Hill: *sett.*, New Jersey	2	40	75
Cherry Hills Village: Colorado	3	39¾	105
Cherry Valley: *sett.*, New York	15	43	75
Chesaning: Michigan	20	43	84
Chesapeake: Ohio	16	38	82
Chesapeake: Virginia	17	37	76
Chesapeake: West Virginia	16	38	82
Chesapeake Bay: Md./Virginia	17	38	76
Cheshire: Connecticut	15	42	73
Cheshire: Massachusetts	15	43	73
Chester: California	36	40	121
Chester: Massachusetts	15	42	73
Chester: New York	15	41	74
Chester: Pennsylvania	2	39¾	75¼
Chester: South Carolina	24	35	81
Chester: Virginia	17	37	77
Chesterfield: South Carolina	24	35	80
Chesterfield Inlet: N.W.T.	45	63	92
Chesterfield Inlet: *sett.*, N.W.T.	45	63	91
Chesterland: Ohio	19	42	81
Chesterton: Indiana	21	42	87
Chestertown: Maryland	17	39	76
Chesterville: Ontario	13	45	75
Chestnut Hill: *sett.*, Pennsylvania	2	40	75¼
Chesuncook L.: Maine	8	46	69
Chevak: Alaska	43	62	166
Chevy Chase: Maryland	2	39	77
Cheyenne: Wyoming	28	41	105
Cheyenne: *r.*, South Dakota	28	44	102
Cheyenne Wells: Colorado	29	39	102
Chibougamau: Québec	8	50	74
Chicago: Illinois	21	42	88
Chicago Habor: Illinois	4	42	87½
Chicago Heights: Illinois	21	42	88
Chicago Sanitary and Ship Canal: Illinois	4	41¾	87¾
Chichagof I.: Alaska	40	58	136
Chickaloon: Alaska	43	62	148
Chickamauga L.: *& dam*, Tenn.	27	35	85
Chickasawhay: *r.*, Mississippi	27	31	89
Chickasha: Oklahoma	29	35	98
Chicken: Alaska	42	64	142
Chico: California	37	40	122
Chico: Washington	39	48	123
Chicopee: Massachusetts	15	43	73
Chicoutimi: Québec	8	48	71
Chief Joseph: *dam*, Wash.	39	48	120
Chignecto Bay: N.S./N.B.	9	46	65
Chignik: Alaska	43	56	158
Chignik Lagoon: *sett.*, Alaska	43	56	159
Chikaskia: *r.*, Kansas/Okla.	29	37	98
Chilcotin: *r.*, British Columbia	41	52	124
Childersburg: Alabama	27	33	86
Childress: Texas	29	34	100
Chilhowee: *dam*, Tennessee	24	35	84
Chilhowie: Virginia	16	37	82
Chilkoot: British Columbia	40	60	134
Chillicothe: Illinois	21	41	90
Chillicothe: Missouri	10	40	94
Chillicothe: Ohio	16	39	83
Chilliwack: British Columbia	38	49	122
Chiloquin: Oregon	36	43	122
Chilton: Wisconsin	20	44	88
China L.: California	35	36	118
China Lake: *sett.*, California	35	36	118
Chinchaga: *r.*, Alberta	30	58	119
Chincoteague: Virginia	17	38	75
Chincoteague B.: Maryland	17	38	75
Chiniak, C.: Alaska	43	58	152
Chino: California	7	34	117¾
Chipai L.: Ontario	31	53	88
Chipley: Florida	27	31	86
Chipola: *r.*, Fla./Alabama	27	31	85
Chippewa: *r.*, Michigan	20	44	84
Chippewa: *r.*, Wisconsin	10	45	91
Chippewa Falls: *town*, Wisconsin	10	45	91
Chistochina: Alaska	43	63	145
Chitina: Alaska	43	62	145
Chitina: *r.*, Alaska	43	61	144
Choate: British Columbia	38	49	121
Chocolate Mts.: California	35	33	115
Choctawhatchee: *r.*, Ala./Fla.	27	31	86
Cholame: California	34	36	120
Chomedey: Québec	2	45¼	73¾
Choptank: *r.*, Maryland	17	39	76
Chorkbak Inlet: N.W.T.	45	65	74
Chowan: *r.*, North Carolina	24	36	77
Chowchilla: California	37	37	120
Chrisman: Illinois	21	40	88
Christiana: Pennsylvania	14	40	76
Christian I.: Ontario	18	45	80
Christiansburg: Virginia	16	37	80
Christie Bay: N.W.T.	44	63	111
Christina: *r.*, Alberta	30	56	111
Chualar: California	37	37	122
Chubbuck: California	35	34	115
Chuckawalla Mts.: California	35	34	115

	Page	N	W
Coquille: Oregon	32	43	124
Coquitlam: British Columbia	6	49¼	122¾
Coquitlam: *r.*, British Columbia	6	49¼	122¾
Coral: Pennsylvania	19	41	79
Coral Gables: Florida	25	26	80
Coral Harbour: N.W.T.	45	64	83
Coral Rapids: Ontario	11	50	82
Coraopolis: Pennsylvania	19	41	80
Corbett Inlet: N.W.T.	45	62	92
Corcoran: California	34	36	120
Cordele: Georgia	24	32	84
Cordova: Alabama	27	34	87
Cordova: Alaska	43	60	146
Cordova: Illinois	10	42	90
Corinth: Mississippi	27	35	89
Corinth: New York	13	43	74
Cornelia: Georgia	24	35	84
Cornelius: North Carolina	24	35	81
Cornelius Grinnel B.: N.W.T.	45	63	65
Corner Brook: Newfoundland	9	49	58
Corning: California	36	40	122
Corning: New York	14	42	77
Corning: Ohio	16	40	82
Cornwall: Ontario	13	45	75
Cornwall: Pennsylvania	14	40	76
Cornwallis I.: N.W.T.	45	75	95
Corona: California	7	34	117¾
Coronado: California	35	33	117
Coronation G.: N.W.T.	44	68	113
Corpus Christi: *& bay*, Texas	22	28	97
Corrigan: Texas	26	31	95
Corry: Pennsylvania	19	42	80
Corsicana: Texas	26	32	96
Cortez: Colorado	29	37	109
Cortland: New York	14	43	76
Cortland: Ohio	19	41	81
Corunna: Michigan	20	43	84
Corvallis: Oregon	39	45	123
Coshocton: Ohio	19	40	82
Cosmopolis: Washington	39	47	124
Cotati: California	37	38	123
Cottage Grove: Oregon	32	44	123
Cottonport: Louisiana	26	31	92
Cotton Valley: *sett.*, La.	26	33	93
Cottonwood: California	36	40	122
Cotuit: Massachusetts	15	42	70
Cotulla: Texas	22	28	99
Coudersport: Pennsylvania	14	42	78
Coulee: *dam*, Washington	32	48	119
Coulee City: Washington	39	48	119
Coulee Dam Nat. Rec. Area: Washington	32	48	118
Coulonge: *r.*, Québec	12	46	77
Coulterville: California	37	38	120
Council Bluffs: Iowa	10	41	96
Courtenay: British Columbia	38	50	125
Courtland: California	37	38	122
Coushatta: Louisiana	26	32	93
Coutoleno: California	36	40	122
Covelo: California	36	40	123
Coventry: Connecticut	14	42	72
Coventry: Rhode Island	15	42	72
Covina: California	7	34	118
Covington: Georgia	24	34	84
Covington: Kentucky	10	39	85
Covington: Louisiana	27	31	90
Covington: Ohio	21	40	84
Covington: Pennsylvania	14	42	77
Covington: Tennessee	27	36	90
Covington: Virginia	16	38	80
Cowan: Tennessee	27	35	86
Cowanesque: *r.*, Pennsylvania	14	42	77
Cowansville: Québec	13	45	73
Coweta: Oklahoma	26	36	96
Cow Head L.: California	37	42	120
Cowichan L.: British Columbia	38	49	124
Cowlitz: *r.*, Washington	39	46	122
Cowpasture: *r.*, Virginia	16	38	79
Coxsackie: New York	15	42	74
Coyle: Washington	39	48	123
Coyote: California	37	37	122
Coyote Hills Regional Park: California	6	37½	120
Coyote L.: California	35	35	117
Cozad: Nebraska	28	41	100
Crab: *cr.*, Washington	39	47	120
Crabtree: Pennsylvania	19	40	79
Craig: Alaska	41	55	133
Craig: Colorado	28	41	108
Craig: *cr.*, Virginia	16	37	80
Craigsville: Virginia	16	38	79
Cranberry L.: New York	13	44	75
Cranberry Portage: Manitoba	31	55	101
Cranbrook: British Columbia	41	49	116
Crandon: Wisconsin	20	46	89
Crannell: California	36	41	124
Cranston: Rhode Island	15	42	71
Cranstown, C.: Greenland	45	71	55
Crater L.: Oregon	36	43	122
Crater Lake: *sett.*, Oregon	36	43	122
Crater Lake Nat. Park: Oregon	36	43	122
Crater Peak: California	36	41	122
Craters of the Moon Nat. Mon.: Idaho	32	43	114
Crauford, C.: N.W.T.	45	74	85
Crawfordsville: Indiana	21	40	87
Crawfordville: Georgia	24	34	83

	Page	N	W
Cree: *r.*, Saskatchewan	30	58	106
Creede: Colorado	29	38	107
Cree L.: Saskatchewan	30	58	107
Crescent Beach: *sett.*, S.C.	25	34	79
Crescent City: California	36	42	124
Crescent City: Florida	25	29	82
Crescent, L.: Washington	38	48	124
Crescent Mills: California	36	40	121
Cresson: Pennsylvania	14	40	79
Crestline: Ohio	19	41	83
Creston: British Columbia	41	49	117
Creston: Ohio	19	41	82
Crestview: California	37	38	119
Crestview: Florida	27	31	87
Creswell Bay: N.W.T.	45	73	94
Crete: Nebraska	28	41	97
Crewe: Virginia	17	37	78
Cripple Creek: *sett.*, Colorado	29	39	105
Crisfield: Maryland	17	38	76
Crivitz: Wisconsin	20	45	88
Crockett: Texas	26	31	95
Croker Bay: N.W.T.	45	75	83
Crooked Creek: *sett.*, Alaska	43	62	158
Crookston: Minnesota	10	48	97
Crooksville: Ohio	16	40	82
Crosby: Minnesota	10	46	94
Crosby: North Dakota	28	49	103
Cross City: Florida	25	30	83
Crossett: Arkansas	26	33	92
Cross L.: Manitoba	31	55	98
Cross Sound: Alaska	40	58	137
Crossville: Tennessee	27	36	85
Croswell: Michigan	19	43	83
Crowley: Louisiana	26	30	92
Crown Point: *town.*, Indiana	21	41	87
Crown Prince Frederick I.: Northwest Territories	45	70	87
Crowsnest Pass: Alta./B.C.	41	50	115
Crozet: Virginia	17	38	79
Crump L.: Oregon	36	42	120
Crystal: Minnesota	3	45	93¼
Crystal: Oregon	36	43	122
Crystal City: Missouri	10	38	90
Crystal City: Texas	22	29	100
Crystal Falls: *sett.*, Michigan	20	46	88
Crystal Lake: *town.* Illinois	21	42	88
Crystal Springs: Mississippi	27	32	90
Cuba: New York	14	42	78
Cuddeback L.: California	35	35	117
Culebra, I. de: Puerto Rico	27	18	65
Cull Cr.: California	6	37¾	120
Cullman: Alabama	27	34	87
Culpeper: Virginia	17	38	78
Culver: Indiana	21	41	86
Culver City: California	7	34	118½
Cumberland: British Columbia	38	50	125
Cumberland: Maryland	17	40	79
Cumberland: Kentucky	16	37	83
Cumberland: *r.*, Ky./Tenn.	23	37	86
Cumberland Gap: Tennessee	24	37	84
Cumberland Gap Nat'l Hist. Park: Kentucky	24	37	84
Cumberland, L.: Kentucky	23	37	85
Cumberland Mts.: Tenn./Ky.	23	36	84
Cumberland Plat.: Tennessee	24	36	85
Cumberland Sound: N.W.T.	45	65	65
Cummings: California	36	40	124
Cunningham Falls St. Park: Md.	17	40	77
Cunningham Landing: N.W.T.	30	60	112
Current: *r.*, Missouri	10	37	91
Curry: Alaska	43	63	150
Curtisville: Pennsylvania	19	41	80
Curwensville: Pennsylvania	14	41	79
Cushing: Oklahoma	26	36	97
Cushing: Texas	26	32	95
Custer: South Dakota	29	44	104
Cut Bank: Montana	28	49	112
Cuthbert: Georgia	27	32	85
Cutler: California	34	37	119
Cutler: Ontario	18	46	82
Cutler Park: Massachusetts	2	42¼	71¼
Cuyagoha: *r.*, Ohio	19	41	81
Cuyama: California	34	35	120
Cuyama: *r.*, California	34	35	120
Cuyamaca Res.: California	35	33	117
Cuyana Range: Minnesota	10	46	94
Cypress: Texas	3	30	95½
Cypress: *r.*, Texas/Louisiana	26	33	95
Cypress Hills: Alta./Sask.	30	50	110
Dade City: Florida	25	28	82
Dadeville: Alabama	27	33	86
Dahlgren: Virginia	17	38	77
Dahlonega: Georgia	24	35	84
Daingerfield: Texas	26	33	95
Dairy: Oregon	36	42	122
Daisetta: Texas	26	30	95
Dale: Oregon	39	45	119
Dale Hollow Res.: Tennessee	23	37	86
Dales: California	36	40	122
Daleville: Indiana	21	40	86
Dalhart: Texas	29	36	103
Dalhousie, C.: N.W.T.	44	70	130
Dallas: Georgia	27	34	85
Dallas: Oregon	39	45	123
Dallas: Pennsylvania	14	41	76
Dallas: Texas	26	33	97

	Page	N	W
Dallastown: Pennsylvania	14	40	77
Dalles, The: *dam*, Oregon	39	46	121
Dall I.: Alaska	41	55	133
Dall L.: Alaska	43	60	164
Dalton: Georgia	27	35	85
Dalton: Massachusetts	15	42	73
Dalton: Pennsylvania	14	42	76
Daly Bay: N.W.T.	45	64	90
Daly City: California	6	37¾	122½
Daly L.: Saskatchewan	30	57	106
Damascus: Maryland	17	39	77
Damascus: Virginia	16	37	82
Dam B. Res.: Texas	26	31	94
Dan: *r.*, Virginia/N.C.	16	37	79
Dana: California	36	41	122
Danbury: Connecticut	15	41	73
Danby: California	35	35	115
Danby L.: California	35	34	115
Danielson: Connecticut	15	42	72
Dannemora: New York	13	45	74
Dansville: New York	14	43	78
Dante: Virginia	16	37	82
Danvers: Massachusetts	15	43	71
Danville: Arkansas	26	35	93
Danville: Illinois	21	40	88
Danville: Indiana	21	40	87
Danville: Pennsylvania	14	41	77
Danville: Québec	13	46	72
Danville: Virginia	16	37	79
Darby: Pennsylvania	2	40	75¼
Darby: *cr.*, Ohio	16	40	83
Darby Mts.: Alaska	42	65	162
Dardanelle: Arkansas	26	35	93
Dardanelle Res.: Arkansas	26	35	93
Dardanelle: California	37	38	120
Darien: Connecticut	15	41	73
Darien: Georgia	25	31	81
Darlington: South Carolina	24	34	80
Darnley Bay: N.W.T.	44	70	124
Darrington: Washington	38	48	122
Dartmouth: Nova Scotia	9	45	64
Darwin: California	35	36	118
Dauphin: Manitoba	31	51	100
Dauphin I.: Alabama	27	30	88
Dauphin L.: Manitoba	31	51	100
Davenport: California	37	37	122
Davenport: Florida	25	28	81
Davenport: Iowa	10	42	91
Davenport: Oklahoma	26	36	97
Davidson: North Carolina	24	36	81
Davidson Mts.: Alaska	42	69	142
Davis: California	37	39	122
Davis: Oklahoma	26	35	97
Davis: West Virginia	16	39	79
Davis: *dam*, Nevada/Arizona	33	35	115
Davis Creek: *sett.*, California	36	42	120
Davis Inlet: *sett.*, Newfoundland	9	56	61
Davis, Mt.: Pennsylvania	16	40	79
Davison: Michigan	19	43	84
Davis Strait: Greenland/Canada	45	67	58
Davy: West Virginia	16	38	82
Dawson: Georgia	24	32	84
Dawson: Texas	26	32	97
Dawson: Yukon	40	64	129
Dawson Creek: B.C.	41	46	120
Dawson Inlet: N.W.T.	45	62	93
Dawson Landing: N.W.T.	30	61	114
Dawson Range: Yukon	40	63	139
Day: California	36	41	121
Dayton: New York	19	42	79
Dayton: Ohio	21	40	84
Dayton: Oregon	39	45	123
Dayton: Tennessee	27	36	85
Dayton: Texas	26	30	95
Dayton: Washington	32	46	118
Daytona Beach: *town*, Florida	25	29	81
Dedman L.: California	35	34	116
Deadwood: South Dakota	28	44	104
Dean Ch.: British Columbia	41	53	127
Deans Dundas Bay: N.W.T.	44	72	118
Dearborn: Michigan	5	42¼	83¼
Dearborn Heights: *town*, Mich.	5	42¼	83¼
Deas Is.: British Columbia	6	49	123
Dease Arm: Great Bear L., N.W.T.	40	67	120
Dease Inlet: Alaska	42	71	156
Dease L.: British Columbia	40	59	130
Dease Lake: *sett.*, B.C.	40	58	130
Dease Strait: N.W.T.	44	69	108
Death Valley: California	35	37	117
Death Valley Jct.: California	35	36	116
Death Valley Nat. Mon.: Calif.	35	36	117
Decatur: Alabama	27	35	87
Decatur: Georgia	24	34	84
Decatur: Illinois	21	40	89
Decatur: Indiana	21	41	85
Decatur: Michigan	21	42	86
Decherd: Tennessee	27	35	86
Decorah: Iowa	10	43	92
Dedham: Massachusetts	2	42¼	71¼
Dedrick: California	36	41	123
Deep Creek L. Maryland	16	39	79
Deep Cove: British Columbia	6	49¼	123
Deep River: *town*, Ontario	12	46	78
Deer: *cr.*, California	36	40	122
Deerfield: Illinois	4	42¼	88
Deerfield: Massachusetts	15	43	73

	Page	N	W
East Liverpool: Ohio	19	41	81
East Longmeadow: Mass	15	42	73
East Los Angeles: California	7	34	118¼
Eastmain: Québec	8	52	79
Eastmain: *r.*, Québec	8	52	76
Eastman: Georgia	24	32	83
Easton: Maryland	17	39	76
Easton: Pennsylvania	14	41	75
East Palestine: Ohio	19	41	81
East Park Res.: California	37	39	122
East Pepperell: Massachusetts	15	43	72
Eastport: Maine	11	45	67
East Quoque: New York	15	41	73
East Rochester: New Hampshire	13	43	71
East Rochester: New York	12	43	78
East St. Louis: Illinois	10	39	90
East Syracuse: New York	12	43	76
East Walker: *r.*, Nevada	37	39	119
East York: Ontario	5	43¾	79¼
Eaton: Indiana	21	40	85
Eaton Rapids: Michigan	21	43	85
Eatonton: Georgia	24	33	83
Eatonville: Washington	39	47	122
Eaton Wash Reservoir: Calif.	7	34¼	118
Eau Claire: Wisconsin	10	45	92
Eau Claire: *r.*, Wisconsin	20	45	89
Ebensburg: Pennsylvania	14	40	79
Eckerman: Michigan	20	46	85
Eclipse Sound: N.W.T.	45	73	79
E. C. Manning Prov. Park: B.C.	38	49	121
Ecorse: Michigan	5	42¼	83
Eddington: Pennsylvania	14	40	75
Edehon L.: N.W.T.	31	60	97
Eden: New York	19	43	79
Edenton: North Carolina	24	36	77
Edgartown: Massachusetts	15	41	71
Edgefield: South Carolina	24	34	82
Edgell I.: N.W.T.	45	62	65
Edgemont: California	35	34	117
Edgemont: South Dakota	28	43	104
Edgerton: Ohio	21	41	85
Edgewater: Colorado	3	39¾	105
Edgewater: Florida	25	29	81
Edina: Minnesota	3	44¾	93¼
Edinboro: Pennsylvania	19	42	80
Edinburg: Illinois	21	40	89
Edison: California	35	35	119
Edison: Georgia	27	32	85
Edisto: *r.*, South Carolina	24	33	81
Edmond: Oklahoma	26	36	98
Edmonds: Washington	39	48	122
Edmonton: Alberta	30	54	113
Edmundston: New Brunswick	9	47	68
Edna: Texas	26	29	97
Edna Bay: *sett.*, Alaska	41	56	134
Edson: Alberta	30	54	116
Eduni, Mt.: N.W.T.	40	64	128
Edwards: California	35	35	118
Edwards: Mississippi	27	32	91
Edwards: New York	13	44	75
Edwards Plateau: Texas	29	31	100
Eek: Alaska	43	60	162
Eel: *r.*, California	36	40	123
Eel: *r.*, Indiana	21	41	86
Eganville: Ontario	12	46	77
Egegik: Alaska	43	58	157
Egg Harbor City: New Jersey	15	40	75
Eglinton, C.: N.W.T.	45	71	70
Eileen L.: N.W.T.	44	62	108
Ekka I.: N.W.T.	40	66	123
Ekuk: Alaska	43	59	159
Ekwok: Alaska	43	59	158
Elba: Alabama	27	31	86
Elbert, Mt.: Colorado	28	39	106
Elberton: Georgia	24	34	83
El Cajon: California	35	33	117
El Campo: Texas	26	29	96
El Centro: California	35	33	116
El Cerrito: California	6	38	122¼
Elcho: Wisconsin	20	45	89
El Dorado: Arkansas	26	33	93
El Dorado: Kansas	29	38	97
Eldorado: Saskatchewan	30	60	108
Eldred: Pennsylvania	14	42	78
Eleele: Hawaii	128	22	160
El Granada: California	6	37½	122½
Elephant Butte Res.: *& dam*, New Mexico	29	33	107
Elgin: Illinois	21	42	88
Elim: Alaska	42	65	162
Elitch Gardens: Colorado	3	39¾	105
Elizabeth: Louisiana	26	31	93
Elizabeth: New Jersey	1	40¾	74¼
Elizabeth City: North Carolina	17	36	76
Elizabeth Is.: Massachusetts	15	41	71
Elizabeth L.: *sett.*, California	35	35	118
Elizabethon: Tennessee	16	36	82
Elizabethtown: Kentucky	23	38	86
Elizabethtown: New York	13	44	74
Elizabethtown: North Carolina	24	35	79
Elizabethtown: Pennyslvania	14	40	77
Elizabethville: Pennsylvania	14	41	77
Eliza Powell Park: Michigan	5	42¼	83¼
Elk: California	37	39	124
Elk: *r.*, West Virginia	16	38	81
Elk City: Oklahoma	29	35	99
Elk Creek: *sett.*, California	37	40	123
Elk Falls: *sett.*, B.C.	38	50	125
Elk Grove: California	37	38	121
Elk Grove Village: Illinois	4	42	88
Elkhart: Indiana	21	42	86
Elkhorn: Wisconsin	21	43	89
Elkhorn: *r.*, Nebraska	28	42	97
Elkin: North Carolina	16	36	81
Elkins: West Virginia	16	39	80
Elk Island Nat. Park: Alberta	30	54	113
Elko: Nevada	33	41	116
Elk River: *sett.*, Idaho	32	47	116
Elkton: Maryland	17	40	76
Elkton: Virginia	17	38	79
Ellaville: Georgia	24	32	84
Ell Bay: N.W.T.	45	64	86
Ellensburg: Washington	39	47	121
Ellenville: New York	15	42	74
Ellesmore Island: N.W.T.	61	80	80
Ellice: *r.*, N.W.T.	44	66	105
Ellice I.: N.W.T.	44	69	136
Ellicott City: Maryland	17	39	77
Ellicottville: New York	19	42	79
Ellijay: Georgia	24	35	84
Elliott Bay: Washington	6	47½	122¼
Elliot Lake: *sett.*, Ontario	18	46	83
Ellisville: Mississippi	27	32	89
Elloree: South Carolina	24	34	81
Ellsworth: Maine	11	45	68
Ellsworth: Pennsylvania	19	40	80
Ellwood City: Pennsylvania	19	41	80
Elma: Washington	39	47	123
Elm City: North Carolina	24	36	78
Elmer: New Jersey	14	40	75
Elmhurst: Illinois	4	42	88
Elmira: California	37	38	122
Elmira: New York	14	42	77
Elmira: Ontario	18	44	81
Elmira Heights: New York	14	42	77
Elmore: Ohio	19	41	83
El Morro Nat. Mon.: N. Mex.	29	35	108
Elmsdale: Nova Scotia	9	45	64
Elmwood Park: *town*, Illinois	4	42	87¾
Elmwood Park: *town*, Michigan	5	42¼	83
El Nido: California	37	37	120
Elora: Ontario	18	44	80
Eloy: Arizona	33	33	112
El Paso: Illinois	21	41	89
El Paso: Texas	29	32	107
El Portal: California	37	38	120
Elrama: Pennsylvania	19	40	80
El Reno: Oklahoma	29	36	98
El Rio: California	34	34	119
Elsa: Yukon	40	64	135
Elsinore: California	35	34	117
Elton: Louisiana	26	30	93
El Toro: California	35	34	118
Elu Inlet: N.W.T.	44	68	106
Elvira, C.: N.W.T.	44	74	105
Elwood: Indiana	21	40	86
Ely: Minnesota	10	48	92
Ely: Nevada	33	39	115
Elyria: Ohio	19	41	82
Elysian Park: California	7	34¼	118¼
Emerson: Manitoba	31	49	97
Emeryville: California	6	37¾	122¼
Emigrant Gap: California	37	39	121
Emigrant Junction: California	35	36	117
Emlenton: Pennsylvania	19	41	80
Emmaus: Pennsylvania	14	41	76
Emmett: Idaho	32	44	117
Emmitsburg: Maryland	17	40	77
Emory Peak: Texas	29	29	103
Empire: Michigan	20	45	86
Empire: Nevada	36	41	119
Emporia: Kansas	29	38	96
Emporia: Virginia	17	37	78
Emporium: Pennsylvania	14	42	78
Empress: Alberta	30	51	110
Emsdale: Ontario	18	46	79
Encinitas: California	35	33	117
Encino Res.: California	7	34¼	118½
Endako: British Columbia	41	54	125
Enderby: British Columbia	41	51	119
Enderlin: North Dakota	28	47	98
Endicott: New York	14	42	76
Endicott Mts.: Alaska	42	67	153
Endwell: New York	14	42	76
Enfield: New Hampshire	13	44	72
Engineer: British Columbia	40	60	134
England: Arkansas	26	35	92
Englee: Newfoundland	9	51	56
Englewood: Colorado	3	39¾	105
Englewood: New Jersey	1	41	74
Englewood: Tennessee	24	35	85
English: *r.*, Ontario	10	50	95
English Bay: *sett.*, Alaska	43	59	152
English Bay: British Columbia	6	49¼	123¼
English Center: Pennsylvania	14	41	77
Enid: Oklahoma	29	36	98
Enid Res.: Mississippi	27	34	90
Ennadai: N.W.T.	31	61	101
Ennadai L.: N.W.T.	31	61	101
Ennis: Texas	26	32	97
Enoree: South Carolina	24	35	82
Enosburg Falls: *sett.*, Vermont	13	45	73
Enterprise: Alabama	27	31	86
Entiat: Washington	39	48	120
Entiat: *r.*, Washington	39	48	121
Entiat Mts.: Washington	38/39	48	121
Enumclaw: Washington	39	47	122
Ephrata: Pennsylvania	14	40	76
Ephrata: Washington	39	47	120
Erath: Louisiana	26	30	92
Erie: Pennsylvania	19	42	80
Erie, Lake	19	—	—
Erlandson L.: Québec	8	57	69
Erwin: North Carolina	24	35	79
Escalon: California	37	38	121
Escambia: *r.*, Florida	27	31	87
Escanaba: Michigan	20	46	87
Escanaba: *r.*, Michigan	20	46	87
Escondido: California	35	33	117
Eska: Alaska	43	62	149
Esker: Newfoundland	9	54	66
Eskimo Ls.: N.W.T.	44	69	132
Eskimo Point: *sett.*, N.W.T.	31	61	94
Espanola: Ontario	18	46	82
Esparto: California	37	39	122
Esquimalt: British Columbia	38	48	123
Essex: California	35	35	115
Essex: Connecticut	15	41	72
Essex: Maryland	17	39	76
Essex: Ontario	19	42	83
Essex: Vermont	13	45	73
Essondale: British Columbia	6	49¼	122¾
Estelle: Louisiana	3	29¾	90
Esterhazy: Saskatchewan	31	51	102
Esterto Bay: California	34	45	121
Estervan: Saskatchewan	30	49	103
Estherville: Iowa	10	43	95
Estill: South Carolina	24	33	81
Estrella: California	34	36	121
Etawney L.: Manitoba	31	58	97
Etna: Pennsylvania	5	40½	80
Etobicoke: Ontario	5	43¾	79¼
Etobicoke Creek: Ontario	5	43¾	79¾
Etowah: Tennessee	24	35	85
Ettersburg: California	36	40	124
Euclid: Ohio	19	42	82
Eudora: Arkansas	26	33	91
Eufaula: Alabama	27	32	85
Eufaula: Oklahoma	26	35	96
Eufaula L.: *& dam*, Oklahoma	26	35	96
Eugene: Oregon	32	44	123
Eunice: Louisiana	26	31	92
Eunice: New Mexico	29	32	103
Eupora: Mississippi.	27	34	89
Eureka: California	36	41	124
Eureka: Illinois	21	41	89
Eureka: Montana	32	49	115
Eureka: Nevada	33	40	116
Eureka: N.W.T.	61	80	86
Eureka: Utah	33	40	112
Eustis: Florida	25	29	82
Eutaw: Alabama	27	33	88
Eutsuk L.: British Columbia	41	53	127
Evans City: Pennsylvania	19	41	80
Evans, L.: Québec	8	51	77
Evans Strait: N.W.T.	45	63	82
Evanston: Illinois	4	42	87¾
Evanston: Wyoming	28	41	111
Evansville: Indiana	10	38	88
Evansville: Wisconsin	21	43	89
Evart: Michigan	20	44	85
Everett: Massachusetts	2	42½	71
Everett: Pennsylvania	14	40	78
Everett: Washington	39	48	122
Everett Mts.: N.W.T.	45	63	68
Everglades: Florida.	25	26	81
Everglades Nat. Park: Florida	25	25	81
Evergreen: Alabama	27	31	87
Evergreen Park: *town*, Illinois	4	47¾	87¾
Ewa: Hawaii	128	21	158
Exeter: California	34	36	119
Exeter: New Hampshire	15	43	71
Exeter: Ontario	18	43	82
Exeter Bay: N.W.T.	45	67	62
Exeter Sound: N.W.T.	45	66	62
Exmore: Virginia	17	38	76
Export: Pennsylvania	19	40	80
Exshaw: Alberta	30	51	115
Exton: Pennsylvania	14	40	76
Fabens: Texas	29	31	106
Faber L.: N.W.T.	40	64	117
Faden: Newfoundland	9	54	67
Fairbanks: Alaska	42	65	148
Fairbanks: Texas	3	30	95½
Fairborn: Ohio	21	40	84
Fairburn: Georgia	24	34	85
Fairbury: Illinois	21	41	89
Fairbury: Nebraska	28	40	97
Fairchance: Pennsylvania	16	40	80
Fairfax: South Carolina	24	33	81
Fairfax City: Virginia	2	38¾	77¼
Fairfield: California	37	38	122
Fairfield: Illinois	4	42½	88
Fairfield: Texas	26	32	96
Fair Haven: Vermont	13	44	73
Fair Lawn: New Jersey	1	41	74
Fairless Hills: *town*, Pa.	14	40	75
Fairmont: Minnesota	10	44	94
Fairmont: North Carolina	24	35	79
Fairmont: West Virginia	16	39	80

	Page	N	W
Fairmount: Indiana.	21	40	86
Fairmount Park: Pennsylvania	2	40	75¼
Fair Ness: *cape*, N.W.T.	45	63	72
Fair Oaks: California	37	39	121
Fairplay: Colorado	28	39	106
Fairport: New York	12	43	77
Fairport Harbor: Ohio	19	42	81
Fairview: Alberta	30	56	118
Fairy Stone St. Park: Va.	16	37	80
Faith: South Dakota	28	45	102
Falconbridge: Ontario	18	47	81
Fallbrook: California	35	33	117
Fallon: Nevada	37	39	119
Fall River: *town*, Mass.	15	42	71
Fall River Mills: California	36	41	121
Falls Church City: Virginia	2	39	77¼
Falls City: Nebraska	28	40	96
Falls Creek: *sett.*, Pa.	14	41	79
Falls Creek N.P.: Tennessee	27	36	86
Falls Village: Connecticut	15	42	73
Falmouth: Massachusetts.	15	42	71
False Pass: Alaska	43	55	163
Familles, Bayou des: *cr.*, La.	3	29¾	90
Fannett: Texas	26	30	94
Farewell: Alaska	43	63	154
Fargo: North Dakota	28	47	97
Faribault: Minnesota	10	44	93
Faribault, Lac: Québec	45	59	72
Farmer's Canal: Colorado	3	39¾	105¼
Farmersville: Texas	26	33	96
Farmerville: Louisiana	26	33	92
Farmington: California	37	38	121
Farmington: Michigan	5	42½	83¼
Farmington: New Hampshire	13	43	71
Farmington: New Mexico	29	37	108
Farmington: *r.*, Connecticut	15	42	73
Farmville: North Carolina	24	36	78
Farmville: Virginia	17	37	78
Farnham: Québec	13	45	73
Farrell: Pennsylvania	19	41	81
Favourable Lake: *sett.*, Ontario	31	53	94
Fayette: Alabama	27	34	88
Fayette: Mississippi	26	32	91
Fayette: Ohio	19	42	84
Fayetteville: Arkansas	26	36	94
Fayetteville: New York	12	43	76
Fayetteville: North Carolina	24	35	79
Fayetteville: Tennessee	27	35	87
Fawn: *r.*, Ontario	31	54	89
Fawnskin: California	35	34	117
Fear, C.: North Carolina	24	34	78
Feather: *r.*, California	37	39	122
Featherly Regional Park: Calif.	7	33¾	117¾
Federalsburg: Maryland	17	39	76
Felix, C.: N.W.T.	44	70	98
Fellows: California	34	35	120
Felton: California	37	37	122
Fenner: California	35	35	115
Fenton: Michigan	19	43	84
Fergus: Ontario	18	44	80
Fergus Falls: *town*, Minnesota	10	46	96
Ferguson L.: N.W.T.	44	70	105
Ferndale: Michigan	5	42½	83¼
Ferndale: Washington	38	49	123
Fernie: British Columbia	41	50	115
Fernley: Nevada	37	40	119
Ferrels Bridge Res.: Texas	26	33	95
Ferriday: Louisiana	26	32	92
Field: Alberta	30	51	116
Fieldale: Virginia	16	37	80
Fieldbrook: California	36	41	124
Fields: Oregon	36	42	119
Fighting Is.: Ontario	5	42¼	83
Filbert: West Virginia	16	37	82
Fillmore: California	35	34	119
Finch: Ontario	13	45	75
Findlay: Ohio	19	41	84
Finlay: *r.*, British Columbia	41	56	124
Finlay Forks: British Columbia	41	56	124
Finnie Bay: N.W.T.	45	65	78
Firebaugh: California	37	37	120
Fire Island Nat. Seashore: N.Y.	15	41	73
Firth: *r.*, Yukon	42	69	140
Fish Camp: California	37	37	120
Fisher Strait: N.W.T.	45	63	84
Fishkill: New York	15	42	74
Fish Rock: California	37	39	124
Fitchburg: Massachusetts	15	43	72
Fitzgerald: Georgia	24	32	83
Fitzgerald Bay: N.W.T.	45	72	90
Fitzwilliam I.: Ontario	18	45	82
Flagstaff: Arizona	33	35	112
Flambeau: *r.*, Wisconsin	10	46	91
Flaming Gorge Reservoir: Wyoming/Utah	28	41	110
Flanigan: Nevada	36	40	120
Flat: Alaska	43	62	158
Flat: *r.*, N.W.T.	40	62	126
Flathead: *r.*, B.C./Montana	32	49	114
Flathead L.: Montana	32	48	114
Flatonia: Texas	26	30	97
Flat Rock: Michigan	19	42	83
Flat Rock: Ohio	19	41	83
Flattery, C.: Washington	38	48	125
Fleetwood: Pennsylvania	14	40	76
Flemington: New Jersey	14	41	75
Fletcher Pond: Michigan	18	45	84
Flin Flon: Manitoba	31	55	102
Flinn Springs: California	35	33	117
Flint: Michigan	19	43	84
Flint: *r.*, Georgia	25	31	85
Flint: *r.*, Michigan	19	43	83
Flint L.: N.W.T.	45	69	74
Flora: Indiana	21	41	87
Florala: Alabama	27	31	86
Florence: Alabama	27	35	88
Florence: Arizona	33	33	111
Florence: Colorado	29	38	105
Florence: South Carolina	24	34	80
Florence: Wisconsin	20	46	88
Florence L.: California	37	37	119
FLORIDA	25	—	—
Florida Bay	25	25	81
Florida Keys: *is.*, Florida	25	25	81
Florida, Straits of	25	25	80
Florin: Pennsylvania	14	40	77
Flowers Cove: Newfoundland	9	51	57
Flushing: Michigan	19	43	84
Flushing: Ohio	19	40	81
Flying Cloud: Minnesota	3	44¾	93¼
F. M. Kerr: *dam*, Montana	32	48	114
Fogo I.: Newfoundland	9	50	54
Foley I.: N.W.T.	45	69	75
Folkston: Georgia	25	31	82
Follansbee: West Virginia	16	40	81
Folsom: *& dam*, California	37	39	121
Fonda: New York	15	43	74
Fond-du-Lac: Saskatchewan	30	59	107
Fond du Lac: Wisconsin	20	44	88
Fond-du-Lac: *r.*, Saskatchewan	30	59	106
Fontana: California	35	34	117
Fontana L.: *& dam*, N.C.	24	35	84
Fontas: *r.*, British Columbia	40	58	121
Ford: Washington	32	48	118
Ford: *r.*, Michigan	20	46	87
Ford City: California	34	35	119
Ford City: Pennsylvania	19	41	80
Fordwick: Virginia	16	38	79
Fordyce: Arkansas	26	34	92
Foreman: Arkansas	26	34	94
Forest: Mississippi	27	32	89
Forest: Ohio	19	41	84
Forest: Ontario	19	43	82
Forest City: North Carolina	24	35	82
Forest City: Pennsylvania	14	42	75
Forest Glen: California	36	40	123
Forest Grove: Oregon	39	46	123
Foresthill: California	37	39	121
Forest Hill: Ontario	5	43¾	79½
Forest Park: New York	1	40¾	73¾
Forest Ranch: California	36	40	122
Forestville: Québec	8	49	69
Forked Deer: *r.*, Tennessee	27	36	89
Forks: Washington	38	48	124
Forney: Texas	26	33	96
Forrest: Illinois	21	41	88
Forrest City: Arkansas	27	35	91
Forreston: Illinois	21	42	90
Forsyth: Georgia	24	33	84
Forsyth: Montana	28	46	107
Fort Albany: Ontario	8	52	82
Fort Ann: New York	13	43	74
Fort Atkinson: Wisconsin	20	43	89
Fort Bidwell: California	36	42	120
Fort Bragg: California	37	39	124
Fort Bragg: North Carolina	24	35	79
Fort Chimo: Québec	45	58	68
Fort Chipewyan: Alberta	30	59	111
Fort Collins: Colorado	28	41	105
Fort Covington: New York	13	45	75
Fort Dick: California	36	42	124
Fort Dix: New Jersey	15	40	75
Fort Dodge: Iowa	10	43	94
Fort Edward: New York	13	43	74
Fort Erie: Ontario	19	43	79
Fort Eustis: Virginia	17	37	77
Fort Fitzgerald: Alberta	30	60	112
Fort Frances: Ontario	10	49	93
Fort Franklin: N.W.T.	40	65	124
Fort Fraser: British Columbia	41	54	125
Fort Gaines: Georgia	27	32	85
Fort George: Québec	8	54	79
Fort George: *r.*, Québec	8	54	77
Fort Gibson: Oklahoma	26	36	95
Fort Gibson: *dam*, Oklahoma	26	36	95
Fort Good Hope: N.W.T.	40	66	129
Fort Greely: Alaska	42	64	146
Fort Hall: Idaho	32	43	112
Fort Jones: California	36	42	123
Fort Klamath: Oregon	36	43	122
Fort Laramie: *& Nat. Hist. Site*, Wyoming	28	42	104
Fort Lauderdale: Florida	25	26	80
Fort Liard: N.W.T.	40	60	123
Fort Loramie: Ohio	19	40	84
Fort McKenzie: Québec	8	57	69
Fort Macleod: Alberta	30	50	113
Fort McMurray: Alberta	30	57	111
Fort McPherson: N.W.T.	44	67	135
Ford Madison: Iowa	10	41	91
Fort Mantanzas Nat. Mon.: Florida	25	30	81
Fort Meade: Florida	25	28	82
Fort Mill: South Carolina	24	35	81
Fort Morgan: Colorado	28	30	104
Fort Myers: Florida	25	27	82
Fort Nelson: British Columbia	40	59	123
Fort Nelson: *r.*, B.C.	40	59	124
Fort Norman: N.W.T.	40	65	125
Fort Payne: Alabama	27	34	86
Fort Peck Res.: *& dam*, Montana	28	48	107
Fort P. Henry: *dam*, Tennessee	24	36	82
Fort Pierce: Florida	25	27	80
Fort Pierre: South Dakota	28	44	100
Fort Plain: New York	15	43	75
Fort Providence: N.W.T.	40	61	118
Fort Pulaski Nat. Mon.: Ga.	24	32	81
Fort Qu' Appelle: Saskatchewan	30	51	104
Fort Randall: Alaska	43	55	163
Fort Randall: *dam*, S.D.	28	43	99
Fort Recovery: Ohio	21	40	85
Fort Reliance: N.W.T.	44	63	109
Fort Resolution: N.W.T.	30	61	114
Fort Ross: California	37	39	123
Fort Rupert *see* Rupert House			
Fort St. James: B.C.	41	54	124
Fort St. John: B.C.	30	56	121
Fort Saskatchewan: Alberta	30	54	113
Fort Scott: Kansas	29	38	95
Fork Selkirk: Yukon	40	63	137
Fort Severn: Ontario	31	56	88
Fort Seward: California	36	40	124
Fort Simpson: N.W.T.	40	62	121
Fort Smith: Arkansas	26	35	94
Fort Smith: N.W.T.	30	60	112
Fort Snelling State Park: Minn.	3	44¾	93¼
Fort Stockton: Texas	29	31	103
Fort Sumner: New Mexico	29	34	104
Fort Sumter Nat. Mon.: S.C.	24	33	80
Fortuna: California	36	41	124
Fortuna Ledge: Alaska	43	62	162
Fortune B.: Newfoundland	9	47	56
Fort Valley: *town*, Georgia	24	33	84
Fort Vermilion: Alberta	30	58	116
Fortville: Indiana	21	40	86
Fort Walton Beach: *town*, Fla.	27	30	87
Fort Washington: Pa.	14	40	75
Fort Wayne: Indiana	21	41	85
Fort White: Florida	25	30	83
Fort Whyte: Manitoba	31	50	98
Fort William (*now* Thunder Bay): Ontario	10	48	89
Fort Worth: Texas	29	33	97
Forty Mile: Yukon	40	64	141
Forty Mile: *r.*, Alaska/Yukon	42	64	142
Fort Yukon: Alaska	42	67	145
Fosser: *r.*, Saskatchewan	30	56	106
Fossil: Oregon	39	45	120
Foster City: California	6	37½	122¼
Fostoria: Ohio	19	41	83
Fountain Inn: South Carolina	24	35	82
Fowler: Indiana	21	41	87
Fowlerville: Michigan	21	43	84
Fox: *r.*, Wisconsin	20	44	88
Fox: *r.*, Wisconsin/Illinois	21	42	89
Foxboro (Foxborough): Mass.	19	42	71
Foxburg: Pennsylvania	15	41	80
Foxe Basin: N.W.T.	45	67	79
Foxe Channel: N.W.T.	45	65	80
Foxe Penninsula: N.W.T.	45	65	77
Fox L.: Illinois	21	42	88
Fox Lake: *sett.*, Wisconsin	20	44	89
Framingham: Massachusetts	15	42	71
Frances L.: Yukon	40	61	129
Francesville: Indiana	21	41	87
Frances, L.: New Hampshire	13	45	71
Francis Case, L.: S.D.	28	44	99
François L.: British Columbia	41	54	126
Frankford: Ontario	12	44	78
Frankford: Pennsylvania	2	40	75
Frankfort: Indiana	21	40	87
Frankfort: Kentucky	23	38	85
Frankfort: Michigan	20	45	86
Franklin: Indiana	21	39	86
Franklin: Louisiana	26	30	92
Franklin: Massachusetts	15	42	71
Franklin: Michigan	5	42½	83¼
Franklin: New Hampshire	13	43	72
Franklin: New Jersey	15	41	75
Franklin: New York	14	42	75
Franklin: North Carolina	24	35	83
Franklin: Ohio	21	40	84
Franklin: Pennsylvania	19	41	80
Franklin: Tennessee	27	36	87
Franklin: Texas	26	31	97
Franklin: Virginia	17	37	77
Franklin Bay: N.W.T.	44	70	129
Franklin Bay: N.W.T.	45	69	85
Franklin Canyon Res.: Calif.	7	34	118½
Franklin D. Roosevelt L.: Wash.	32	48	118
Franklin, District of: N.W.T.	44/45	—	—
Franklin L.: N.W.T.	44	67	96
Franklin Mts.: N.W.T.	40	63	123
Franklin Park: *town*, Illinois	4	42	87¾
Franklin Park: Massachusetts	2	42¼	71
Franklin Strait: N.W.T.	44	71	97
Franklinton: Louisiana	27	31	90
Franklinton: North Carolina	24	36	78
Franklinville: New York	14	42	78
Franklinville: North Carolina	24	36	80
Frankston: Texas	26	32	96

	Page	N	W
Frankton: Indiana	**21**	40	86
Franktown: Nevada	**37**	39	120
Fraser: Michigan	**5**	42½	83
Fraser: *r.*, British Columbia	**41**	51	122
Fraser: *r.*, Newfoundland	**9**	57	64
Frederick: Maryland	**17**	39	77
Frederick: Oklahoma	**29**	34	99
Fredericksburg: Virginia	**17**	38	78
Fredericktown: Missouri	**10**	38	90
Fredericktown: Ohio	**19**	40	83
Fredericton: New Brunswick	**9**	46	67
Fredonia: New York	**19**	42	79
Fredrikshald Bay: N.W.T.	**44**	71	104
Freehold: New Jersey	**15**	40	74
Freeland: Michigan	**20**	44	84
Freeland: Pennsylvania	**14**	41	76
Freels, C.: Newfoundland	**9**	49	53
Freeman: Wisconsin	**20**	45	89
Freeport: Illinois	**21**	42	90
Freeport: New York	**1**	40¾	73½
Freeport: Pennsylvania	**19**	41	80
Freeport: Texas	**26**	29	95
Fremont: Michigan	**20**	43	86
Fremont: Nebraska	**28**	41	97
Fremont: North Carolina	**24**	36	78
Fremont: Ohio	**19**	41	83
French: *cr.*, Pennsylvania	**9**	42	80
French Broad: *r.*, N.C./Tenn.	**24**	36	83
French Camp: California	**37**	38	121
French Frigate Shoals: *is.*, Hawaii	**128**	24	167
Frenchglen: Oregon	**36**	43	119
French Gulch: California	**36**	41	123
Frenchman: *cr.*, Colo./Nebraska	**28**	41	102
Frenchman Flat: *dry lake*, Nev.	**35**	37	116
Frenchtown: New Jersey	**14**	41	75
Fresh Pond: Massachusetts	**2**	42½	71
Fresno: California	**37**	37	120
Fresno: *r.*, California	**37**	37	120
Frewsburg: New York	**19**	42	79
Friant: California	**37**	37	120
Friars Point: *sett.*, Mississippi	**27**	34	91
Friday Harbor: Washington	**38**	49	123
Fridley: Minnesota	**3**	45	93¼
Friedens: Pennsylvania	**17**	40	79
Friendship: New York	**14**	42	78
Friendsville: Maryland	**16**	40	79
Fries: Virginia	**16**	37	81
Frio: *r.*, Texas	**22**	29	99
Frobisher Bay: N.W.T.	**45**	63	67
Frobisher Bay: *sett.*, N.W.T.	**45**	64	69
Frobisher L.: Saskatchewan	**30**	56	108
Front Royal: Virginia	**17**	39	78
Frostburg: Maryland	**17**	40	79
Frostproof: Florida	**25**	28	82
Froze Strait: N.W.T.	**45**	66	85
Fruitland: Maryland	**17**	38	76
Fryeburg: Maine	**13**	44	71
Fulford Harbour: B.C.	**38**	49	123
Fullerton: California	**7**	34	117¾
Fullerton: Kentucky	**16**	39	83
Fullerton, C.: N.W.T.	**45**	64	89
Fullerton Res.: California	**7**	34	118
Fulton: Mississippi	**27**	34	88
Fulton: Missouri	**10**	39	92
Fulton: New York	**12**	43	76
Fultonville: New York	**15**	43	74
Fundy, Bay of: N.S./N.B.	**9**	45	66
Fundy Nat. Pk.: New Brunswick	**9**	46	65
Fury and Hecla Str.: N.W.T.	**45**	70	85
Gabriel Str.: N.W.T.	**45**	62	66
Gadsden: Alabama	**27**	34	86
Gaffney: South Carolina	**24**	35	82
Gages Lake: Illinois	**4**	42½	88
Gagnon: Québec	**9**	52	68
Gainesville: Florida	**25**	30	82
Gainesville: Georgia	**24**	34	84
Gainesville: Texas	**26**	34	97
Gaithersburg: Maryland	**17**	39	77
Gakona: Alaska	**43**	62	145
Galax: Virginia	**16**	37	81
Galena: Alaska	**42**	60	157
Galena: Illinois	**10**	42	90
Galena: Kansas	**28**	37	95
Galena Park: *sett.*, Texas	**3**	29¾	95¼
Galesburg: Illinois	**10**	41	90
Galeton: Pennsylvania	**14**	42	78
Galiano I.: B.C.	**38**	49	123
Galice: Oregon	**36**	43	124
Galion: Ohio	**19**	41	83
Gallatin: Tennessee	**23**	36	87
Gallatin: *r.*, Montana	**28**	45	111
Gallipolis: Ohio	**16**	39	82
Gallitzin: Pennsylvania	**14**	41	79
Galloo I.: New York	**12**	44	76
Galloway: Wisconsin	**20**	45	89
Gallup: New Mexico	**29**	36	109
Galt: California	**37**	38	121
Galt: Ontario	**18**	43	80
Galveston: Texas	**26**	39	95
Galveston Bay: Texas	**26**	30	95
Gambell: Alaska	**60**	64	172
Gambier I.: B.C.	**38**	49	123
Ganado St. Park: Texas	**26**	29	97
Gananoque: Ontario	**12**	44	76
Gander: *& r.*, Newfoundland	**9**	49	55
Gannett Peak: Wyoming	**28**	43	110
Garberville: California	**36**	30	124
Gardena: California	**7**	34	118¼
Garden City: Kansas	**29**	38	101
Garden City: Michigan	**5**	42½	83½
Garden City: New York	**1**	40¾	73¾
Garden City: South Carolina	**24**	34	79
Garden Grove: California	**7**	33¾	118
Garden I.: Michigan	**20**	46	86
Garden State Parkway: N.J.	**15**	40	74
Gardiner: Washington	**38**	48	123
Gardner: Illinois	**21**	41	88
Gardner: Massachusetts	**15**	43	72
Gardner Canal: B.C.	**41**	53	128
Gardner Pinnacles: *rocks*, Hawaii	**128**	25	168
Gardnerville: Nevada	**37**	39	120
Garfield: New Jersey	**1**	40¾	74
Garfield: Utah	**33**	41	112
Garibaldi: Oregon	**39**	46	124
Garibaldi Prov. Park: B.C.	**38**	50	123
Garland: Texas	**26**	33	97
Garnet Bay: N.W.T.	**45**	65	75
Garnett: Kansas	**29**	38	95
Garnier Bay: N.W.T.	**45**	74	92
Garrettsville: Ohio	**19**	41	81
Garrett: Indiana	**21**	41	85
Garrison: Montana	**32**	47	113
Garry Bay: N.W.T.	**45**	69	85
Garry L.: N.W.T.	**44**	66	100
Gary: Indiana	**4**	41½	87½
Gas City: Indiana	**21**	40	86
Gasconade: *r.*, Missouri	**10**	38	92
Gas Hills: Wyoming	**28**	44	109
Gaspé: Québec	**9**	49	65
Gaspé Passage: Québec	**9**	49	65
Gaspé Penin.: Québec	**9**	49	66
Gaspesian Prov. Park: Québec	**9**	49	66
Gassaway: West Virginia	**16**	39	81
Gaston, L.: Virginia	**17**	37	78
Gastonia: North Carolina	**24**	35	81
Gate City: Virginia	**16**	37	83
Gateshead I.: N.W.T.	**44**	71	100
Gatineau: *r.*, Québec	**8**	46	76
Gatineau Park: Ontario	**12**	45	76
Gatlinburg: Tennessee	**24**	36	83
Gauer L.: Manitoba	**31**	57	98
Gaukler Point: Michigan	**5**	42½	82¾
Gauley: *r.*, West Virginia	**16**	38	80
Gauley Bridge: W. Va.	**16**	38	81
Gaviota: California	**34**	34	120
Gearhart Mt.: Oregon	**36**	43	121
Geikie: *r.*, Saskatchewan	**30**	58	104
Geismar: Louisiana	**26**	30	91
Genesee: California	**36**	40	121
Geneva: Alabama	**27**	31	86
Geneva: Illinois	**21**	42	88
Geneva: Indiana	**21**	41	85
Geneva: New York	**14**	43	77
Geneva: Ohio	**19**	42	81
Geneva: Utah	**33**	40	112
Geneva, L.: Wisconsin	**21**	43	88
Geneva-on-the-Lake: Ohio	**19**	42	81
Genoa: Nevada	**37**	39	120
Genoa: Ohio	**19**	42	83
Gentilly: Louisiana	**3**	30	90
George: *r.*, Québec	**9**	57	65
George, L.: Florida	**25**	29	82
George, L.: New York	**13**	44	74
George River (Port-Nouveau-Québec): *sett.*, Québec	**45**	58	65
Georgetown: California	**37**	39	121
Georgetown: Connecticut	**15**	41	73
Georgetown: Delaware	**17**	39	75
Georgetown: Idaho	**32**	42	111
Georgetown: Illinois	**21**	40	88
Georgetown: Massachusetts	**15**	43	71
Georgetown: Ontario	**12**	44	80
Georgetown: South Carolina	**24**	33	79
GEORGIA	**24/25**	—	—
Georgiana: Alabama	**27**	32	87
Georgian Bay: Ontario	**18**	45	81
Georgian Bay Islands Nat. Pk.: Ontario	**18**	45	82
Georgia, Strait of: B.C.	**38**	49	124
Geraldton: Ontario	**10**	40	87
Gerber: California	**36**	40	122
Gerber Res.: Oregon	**36**	42	121
Gerdine, Mt.: Alaska	**43**	62	153
Gering: Nebraska	**28**	42	104
Gerlach: Nevada	**36**	41	119
Germantown: Ohio	**21**	40	84
Germantown: Pennsylvania	**2**	40	75¼
Gethsémani: Québec	**9**	50	61
Gettysburg: Pennsylvania	**14**	40	77
Geyserville: California	**37**	39	123
Gibbs Fiord: N.W.T.	**45**	71	72
Gibbstown: New Jersey	**14**	40	75
Gibsland: Louisiana	**26**	33	93
Gibson: California	**36**	41	122
Gibsonburg: Ohio	**19**	41	83
Gibson City: Illinois	**21**	40	88
Gibsonia: Pennsylvania	**5**	40¾	80
Gibsonville: North Carolina	**24**	36	80
Giddings: Texas	**26**	30	97
Gifford: *r.*, N.W.T.	**45**	71	83
Gifford Fiord: N.W.T.	**45**	70	82
Gig Harbor: Washington	**39**	47	123
Gila: *r.*, Arizona	**33**	33	109
Gila Bend: Arizona	**33**	33	113
Gila Cliff Dwellings Nat. Mon.: New Mexico	**29**	33	108
Gilbert, Mt.: B.C.	**38**	51	124
Gilbertville: Massachusetts	**15**	42	72
Gilford Park: New Jersey	**15**	40	74
Gillam: Manitoba	**31**	56	95
Gillett: Arkansas	**26**	34	91
Gillett: Wisconsin	**20**	45	88
Gillette: Wyoming	**28**	44	106
Gillian L.: N.W.T.	**45**	70	75
Gilman: Illinois	**21**	41	88
Gilmer: Texas	**26**	33	95
Gilroy: California	**37**	37	122
Gilroy Hot Springs: California	**37**	37	121
Girard: Ohio	**19**	41	81
Girard: Pennsylvania	**19**	42	80
Girdwood: Alaska	**43**	61	149
Giscome: British Columbia	**41**	54	122
Gjoa Haven: N.W.T.	**44**	69	96
Glace Bay: *town*, Nova Scotia	**9**	46	60
Glacier: British Columbia	**41**	51	118
Glacier Bay N.M.: Alaska	**40**	59	136
Glacier Creek: *sett.*, Yukon	**40**	64	141
Glacier National Park: B.C.	**41**	53	120
Glacier International Peace Park: Montana	**32**	49	114
Glacier Peak: Washington	**38**	48	121
Glacier View: *dam*, Montana	**32**	49	114
Gladewater: Texas	**26**	33	95
Gladstone: Michigan	**20**	46	87
Gladstone: Oregon	**39**	45	123
Gladwin: Michigan	**20**	44	84
Glamis: California	**35**	30	115
Glasgow: Kentucky	**23**	37	86
Glasgow: Montana	**28**	48	107
Glassboro: New Jersey	**14**	40	75
Glassmere: Pennsylvania	**19**	41	80
Glastonbury: Connecticut	**15**	42	73
Gleichen: Alberta	**30**	51	113
Glenbrook: Nevada	**37**	39	120
Glen Burnie: Maryland	**17**	39	77
Glen Canyon: *dam*, Arizona	**33**	37	111
Glencoe: Illinois	**4**	42½	87¾
Glencoe: Minnesota	**10**	45	94
Glen Cove: New York	**1**	40¾	73¾
Glendale: Arizona	**33**	34	112
Glendale: California	**7**	34¼	118¼
Glendale: Colorado	**3**	39¾	105
Glendive: Montana	**28**	47	105
Glendora: California	**7**	34	117¾
Glen Ellen: California	**37**	38	123
Glen Ellyn: Illinois	**4**	42	88
Glen Lyon: Pennsylvania	**14**	41	76
Glenmora: Louisiana	**26**	31	93
Glenn: California	**37**	40	122
Glennallen: Alaska	**43**	62	146
Glennville: Georgia	**24**	32	82
Glen Ridge: New Jersey	**1**	40¾	74¼
Glen Rock: Pennsylvania	**14**	40	77
Glens Fall: *town*, N.Y.	**13**	43	74
Glenshaw: Pennsylvania	**5**	40½	80
Glenview: Illinois	**4**	42	87¾
Glenville: Pennsylvania	**14**	40	77
Glenville: West Virginia	**16**	39	81
Glenwood: Minnesota	**10**	46	95
Glenwood Springs: Colorado	**28**	40	107
Globe: Arizona	**33**	33	111
Gloster: Mississippi	**26**	31	91
Gloucester: Massachusetts	**15**	43	71
Gloucester: Virginia	**17**	37	77
Gloucester: Ohio	**16**	39	82
Gloucester City: New Jersey	**2**	40	75
Gloversville: New York	**13**	43	74
Gnadenhutten: Ohio	**19**	40	81
Goat I.: British Columbia	**38**	50	124
Goderich: Ontario	**18**	44	82
Godhavn: Greenland	**45**	69	54
Gods: *r.*, Manitoba	**31**	55	93
Gods L.: Manitoba	**31**	55	94
Gods Mercy, Bay of: N.W.T.	**45**	64	86
Goffs: California	**35**	35	115
Goffstown: New Hampshire	**13**	43	72
Gold Beach: Oregon	**36**	42	124
Golden: British Columbia	**32**	51	117
Golden: Colorado	**28**	40	105
Goldendale: Washington	**39**	46	121
Golden Ears Prov. Park: B.C.	**38**	50	122
Golden Gate: *str.*, California	**6**	37¾	122½
Golden Gate Nat. Recreation Area: California	**6**	37¾	122½
Golden Gate Park: California	**6**	37¾	122½
Golden Valley: Minnesota	**3**	45	93¼
Gold Hill: *sett.*, Oregon	**32**	42	123
Gold Mt.: Washington	**39**	48	123
Goldpines: Ontario	**10**	51	93
Goldsboro: North Carolina	**24**	35	78
Goldstone L.: California	**35**	35	117
Goleta: California	**34**	34	120
Golovin: Alaska	**42**	65	163
Gonzales: California	**37**	37	121
Gooding: Idaho	**32**	43	115
Goodland: Kansas	**28**	39	102
Goodman: Wisconsin	**20**	46	88
Goodnews (Mumtrak): *sett.*, Alaska	**43**	59	162

Name	Page	N	W
Goodsprings: Nevada	35	36	115
Goose: *r.*	32	42	114
Goose: *r.*, North Dakota	28	47	97
Goose Bay: *town*, Alaska	43	61	150
Goose Bay: *town*, Newfoundland	9	53	60
Goose L.: Oregon/California	36	42	120
Gorda: California	34	36	121
Gorda, Punta: *cape*, California	36	40	124
Gordon: Alaska	42	70	141
Gordon: Georgia	24	33	83
Gordon: Pennsylvania	14	41	76
Gordon Lake: *sett.*, Manitoba	31	49	100
Gordonsville: Virginia	17	38	78
Gore Bay: *town*, Ontario	18	46	82
Gorham: New Hampshire	13	44	71
Gorham: New York	14	43	77
Gorman: California	35	35	119
Goshen: California	34	36	119
Goshen: Indiana	21	42	86
Goshen: New York	15	41	74
Gothenburg: Nebraska	28	41	100
Gouin Reservoir: Québec	8	49	75
Gould: Arkansas	26	34	92
Gould City: Michigan	20	46	86
Gouverneur: New York	13	44	75
Gowanda: New York	19	42	79
Gowganda: Ontario	11	48	81
Graceville: Florida	27	31	86
Grafton: New Hampshire	13	44	72
Grafton: North Dakota	28	48	97
Grafton: Ohio	19	41	82
Grafton: West Virginia	16	39	80
Graham: Texas	29	33	99
Graham: West Virginia	16	39	82
Graham I.: B.C.	41	53	132
Graham Moore, C.: N.W.T.	45	73	76
Gramercy: Louisiana	27	30	91
Granby: Connecticut	15	42	73
Granby: Québec	13	45	73
Granby: *r.*, B.C.	41	50	119
Grand: *r.*, Michigan	20	43	85
Grand: *r.*, Missouri	10	40	94
Grand: *r.*, Ohio	19	42	81
Grand: *r.*, Ontario	18	43	80
Grand: *r.*, South Dakota	28	46	102
Grand Bank: *town*, Newfoundland	9	47	56
Grand Blanc: Michigan	19	43	84
Grand Calumet: Ontario	12	46	77
Grand Canyon: Arizona	33	36	113
Grand Canyon: *sett.*, Arizona	33	36	112
Grand Canyon Nat. Park: Ariz.	33	36	112
Grand Centre: Alberta	30	54	110
Grand Coulee: *dam*, Washington	38	48	119
Grand Calumet: Québec	12	46	77
Grande Prairie: Alberta	30	55	119
Grand Ronde: *r.*, Oregon	32	46	118
Grand Falls: *town*, N.B.	9	47	68
Grand Falls: *town*, Nfld.	9	49	56
Grand Forks: British Columbia	41	49	119
Grand Forks: North Dakota	10	48	97
Grand Gorge: New York	15	42	75
Grand Haven: Michigan	20	43	86
Grandin, L.: N.W.T.	40	64	119
Grand I.: Louisiana	27	29	90
Grand Island: *town*, Nebraska	28	41	98
Grand Junction: Colorado	29	39	109
Grand L.: Louisiana	26	30	91
Grand L.: Louisiana	26	30	93
Grand L.: Newfoundland	9	49	58
Grand L.: Ohio	21	41	85
Grand Ledge: Michigan	21	43	85
Grand Manan I.: N.B.	9	45	67
Grand'Mère: Québec	13	47	73
Grand Prairie: Texas	26	33	97
Grand Rapids: Manitoba	31	53	99
Grand Rapids: Michigan	20	43	86
Grand Rapids: Minnesota	10	47	94
Grand Saline: Texas	26	33	96
Grand Teton Nat. Park: Wyo.	28	44	111
Grand Traverse Bay: Michigan	20	45	86
Grandview: Manitoba	31	51	101
Grandview: Texas	26	32	97
Grandview: Washington	39	46	120
Grandville: Michigan	20	43	86
Granger: Washington	39	46	120
Grangeville: Idaho	32	46	116
Granite Falls: *sett.*, N.C.	24	36	81
Granite Mts.: California	35	34	115
Granite Mts.: California	35	35	116
Granite Peak: Montana	28	45	110
Granite Range: Nevada	36	41	120
Graniteville: California	37	39	121
Graniteville: South Carolina	24	34	82
Gran Quivira Nat. Mon.: New Mexico	29	34	106
Grant Park: Illinois	4	41¾	87½
Grant Point: N.W.T.	44	68	98
Grants: New Mexico	29	35	108
Grants Pass: Oregon	36	42	123
Grantsville: Maryland	16	40	79
Grant Town: West Virginia	16	40	80
Granville: New York	13	43	73
Granville: Ohio	16	40	83
Granville: Pennsylvania	14	41	78
Granville L.: Manitoba	31	56	100
Grapeland: Texas	26	32	96
Grapevine: California	35	35	119
Grass: *r.*, Manitoba	31	55	98
Grassflat: Pennsylvania	14	41	78
Grass Lake: *sett.*, California	36	42	122
Grass Narrows: Ontario	10	50	94
Grass Valley: *town*, California	37	39	121
Gravelbourg: Saskatchewan	30	50	107
Gravell Point: N.W.T.	45	67	77
Grayling: Michigan	20	45	85
Grays Harbor: Washington	39	47	124
Grayslake: Illinois	4	42½	88
Grayson: Kentucky	16	38	83
Great Barrington: Massachusetts	15	42	73
Great Basin	33	40	116
Great Bear L.: N.W.T.	40	66	121
Great Bend: Kansas	29	38	99
Great Cacapon: W. Va.	17	40	78
Great Central: British Columbia	43	49	125
Great Central L.: B.C.	38	49	125
Great Falls: *sett.*, S.C.	24	35	81
Great Falls: *town*, Montana	28	48	111
Great Falls of the Potomac: Maryland	2	39	77¼
Great Kills Park: New York	1	40½	74
Great Meadows Nat. Wild Life Refuge: Massachusetts	2	42½	71¼
Great Neck: New York	1	40¾	73¾
Great Salt L.: Utah	33	41	113
Great Salt Lake Desert: Utah	33	41	113
Great Sand Dunes Nat. Mon.: Colorado	28	38	106
Great Slave L.: N.W.T.	44	61	114
Great Smoky Mts. Nat. Park: Tennessee/North Carolina	24	36	83
Great South Bay: New York	1	40¾	74¼
Great Whale: *r.*, Québec	8	55	76
Great Whale River: *sett.*, Qué.	8	55	78
Greely: Colorado	28	40	105
Green: *r.*, Illinois	21	42	89
Green: *r.*, Kentucky	23	38	87
Green: *r.*, Wyoming/Utah	28	40	110
Greenbackville: Virginia	17	38	75
Greenbank: Washington	38	48	123
Green Bay: Wis./Michigan	20	45	87
Green Bay: *town*, Wisconsin	20	45	88
Greenbelt: *sett. and park*, Md.	2	39	77
Greenbrier: *r.*, West Virginia	16	38	80
Greencastle: Indiana	21	40	87
Greencastle: Pennsylvania	14	40	78
Green Cove Springs: Florida	25	30	82
Greene: New York	14	42	76
Greeneville: Tennessee	16	36	83
Greenfield: California	34	35	119
Greenfield: California	34	36	121
Greenfield: Indiana	21	40	86
Greenfield: Massachusetts	15	43	73
Greenfield: Ohio	16	39	83
Greenfield: Tennessee	22	36	89
Green L.: Washington	6	47¾	122¼
Green L.: Wisconsin	20	44	89
Green Mts.: Vermont	13	44	73
Greenpark: Pennsylvania	14	40	77
Greenport: New York	15	41	72
Green River: Wyoming	28	42	109
Greens Bayou: Texas	3	29¾	95¼
Greensboro: Alabama	27	33	88
Greensboro: Georgia	24	34	83
Greensboro: Maryland	17	39	76
Greensboro: North Carolina	24	36	80
Greensburg: Pennsylvania	19	40	80
Green Springs: Ohio	19	41	83
Greentown: Indiana	21	40	86
Greenview: California	36	42	123
Greenville: Alabama	27	32	87
Greenville: California	36	40	121
Greenville: Florida	25	30	84
Greenville: Michigan	20	43	85
Greenville: Mississippi	27	33	91
Greenville: New Hampshire	13	43	72
Greenville: North Carolina	24	36	77
Greenville: Ohio	21	40	85
Greenville: Pennsylvania	19	41	80
Greenville: South Carolina	24	35	82
Greenville: Texas	26	33	96
Greenwich: Connecticut	1	41	73½
Greenwich: New Jersey	14	39	75
Greenwich: New York	13	43	74
Greenwich: Ohio	19	41	83
Greenwood: British Columbia	41	49	119
Greenwood: Indiana	21	40	86
Greenwood: Mississippi	27	34	90
Greenwood: New York	15	41	74
Greenwood: South Carolina	24	34	82
Greenwood Village: Colorado	3	39½	105
Greer: South Carolina	24	35	82
Greer's Ferry Res.: *& dam*, Ark.	26	36	92
Greeson, L.: Arkansas	26	34	94
Grenada: California	36	42	123
Grenada: Mississippi	27	34	90
Grenada Res.: Mississippi	27	34	90
Gresham: Oregon	39	46	122
Gretna: Louisiana	3	30	90
Gridley: California	37	39	122
Griffin: Georgia	24	33	84
Griffith: Indiana	21	42	87
Griffith I.: N.W.T.	45	75	96
Griffith Park: California	7	34¼	118¼
Grimsby: *sett.*, Ontario	19	43	80
Grimshaw: Alberta	30	56	118
Grinnell Ice Cap: N.W.T.	45	62	67
Grise Fiord: *sett.*, N.W.T.	61	76	83
Groais I.: Newfoundland	9	51	55
Groesbeck: Texas	26	32	97
Grosse Point: Michigan	5	42½	83
Grosse Pointe: *sett.*, Michigan	5	42½	83
Grosse Pointe Park: *sett.*, Mich.	5	42½	83
Grosse Pointe Shores: *sett.*, Mich.	5	42½	83
Groswater Bay: Newfoundland	9	54	58
Groton: Connecticut	15	41	72
Groton: New York	14	43	76
Grottoes: Virginia	17	38	79
Groundhog: *r.*, Ontario	11	49	82
Grove City: Ohio	16	40	83
Grove City: Pennsylvania	19	41	80
Groveland: California	37	38	120
Groveport: Ohio	16	40	83
Grover City: California	34	35	121
Groveton: New Hampshire	13	45	72
Groveton: Texas	26	31	95
Grundy: Virginia	16	37	82
Grundy Lake Prov. Park: Ont.	18	46	81
Guadalupe: California	34	35	121
Guadalupe: *r.*, Texas	22	29	97
Gualala: California	37	39	124
Guano L.: Oregon	36	42	120
Guayama: Puerto Rico	27	18	66
Guelph: Ontario	18	44	80
Gueydan: Louisiana	26	30	93
Guilford: Connecticut	15	41	73
Guin: Alabama	27	34	88
Gulfport: Mississippi	27	30	89
Gulkana: Alaska	43	62	145
Gulliver: Michigan	20	46	86
Gunisao: *r.*, Manitoba	31	53	97
Gunnar: Saskatchewan	30	59	109
Gunnison: *& r.*, Colorado	29	39	107
Guntersville: *& lake & dam*, Ala.	27	34	86
Gurdon: Arkansas	26	34	93
Gustavus: Alaska	40	58	136
Gustine: California	37	37	121
Guthrie: Oklahoma	26	36	97
Guyandot: *r.*, West Virginia	16	38	82
Guymon: Oklahoma	29	37	102
Guyton: Georgia	24	32	81
Gwinn: Michigan	20	46	87
Gypsum Point: N.W.T.	40	62	115
Gypsumville: Manitoba	31	52	99
Gyrfalcon Is.: N.W.T.	45	59	69
Habay: Alberta	30	59	119
Hackamore: California	36	42	121
Hackberry: Louisiana	26	30	93
Hackensack: New Jersey	1	41	74
Hackensack: *r.*, New Jersey	1	40¾	74
Hackettstown: New Jersey	14	41	75
Haddam: Connecticut	15	41	73
Haddock: Georgia	24	33	83
Haddonfield: New Jersey	2	40	75
Hadley: Pennsylvania	19	41	80
Hadley Bay: N.W.T.	44	72	108
Hagaman: New York	15	43	74
Hagemeister I.: Alaska	43	58	161
Hagerstown: Indiana	21	40	85
Hagerstown: Maryland	17	40	78
Hagersville: Ontario	19	43	80
Hahira: Georgia	25	31	83
Haines: Alaska	40	59	135
Haines City: Florida	25	28	82
Haines Junction: Yukon	40	61	137
Haiwee: *& Res.*, California	35	36	118
Halaula: Hawaii	128	20	156
Haleakala Crater N. P.: Hawaii	128	20	156
Haleiwa: Hawaii	128	22	156
Hales Bar: *dam*, Tennessee	27	35	85
Haley: Ontario	12	46	77
Haleyville: Alabama	27	34	88
Half Moon Bay: *& sett.*, California	6	37½	122½
Halfway: *r.*, British Columbia	41	57	123
Haliburton: Ontario	12	45	79
Halifax: North Carolina	24	36	78
Halifax: Nova Scotia	9	45	64
Halifax: Pennsylvania	14	40	77
Halkett, C.: Alaska	42	71	152
Hallettsville: Texas	26	29	97
Hall L.: N.W.T.	45	69	82
Hall Lake: *sett.*, N.W.T.	45	69	81
Hall Penin.: N.W.T.	45	64	67
Halls: Tennessee	27	36	89
Halls Bayou: Texas	3	29¾	95¼
Halls Flat: California	36	41	121
Hallstead: Pennsylvania	14	42	76
Hallsville: Texas	26	33	95
Hamburg: Arkansas	26	33	92
Hamburg: California	36	42	123
Hamburg: New Jersey	15	41	75
Hamburg: New York	19	43	79
Hamburg: Pennsylvania	14	41	76
Hamilton: Alabama	27	34	88
Hamilton: Alaska	42	63	164
Hamilton: Indiana	21	42	85
Hamilton: New York	14	43	76
Hamilton: Ohio	10	39	85
Hamilton: Ontario	19	43	80
Hamilton City: California	37	40	122
Hamilton Inlet: Newfoundland	9	54	59

	Page	N	W
Honeydew: California	**36**	40	124
Honey Grove: Pennsylvania	**14**	40	78
Honey Grove: Texas	**26**	34	96
Honey L.: California	**36**	40	120
Honokaa: Hawaii	**128**	20	155
Honokahua: Hawaii	**128**	21	157
Honolulu: Hawaii	**128**	21	158
Hood: *r.*, N.W.T.	**44**	67	110
Hood Canal: Washington	**39**	47	123
Hood, Mt.: Oregon	**39**	45	122
Hood River: *town*, Oregon	**39**	46	122
Hoonah: Alaska	**40**	58	135
Hoopa: California	**36**	41	124
Hooper Bay: *sett.*, Alaska	**43**	61	166
Hoopeston: Illinois	**21**	40	88
Hoosic: *r.*	**15**	43	73
Hoosick Falls: *town*, New York	**15**	43	73
Hoover: *dam*, Arizona/Nevada	**33**	36	115
Hoover Res.: Ohio	**19**	40	83
Hooversville: Pennsylvania	**14**	40	79
Hope: Alaska	**43**	61	150
Hope: Arkansas	**26**	34	94
Hope: British Columbia	**38**	49	121
Hopedale: Newfoundland	**9**	56	60
Hope, Point: Alaska	**42**	68	167
Hopes Advance Bay: Québec	**45**	59	70
Hopes Advance, C.: N.W.T.	**45**	61	70
Hopewell: New Jersey	**15**	40	75
Hopewell: Virginia	**17**	37	77
Hopewell Is.: N.W.T.	**45**	59	78
Hopkins: Minnesota	**3**	45	93¼
Hopkinsville: Kentucky	**23**	37	88
Hopland: California	**37**	39	123
Hopwood: Pennsylvania	**16**	40	80
Hoquiam: Washington	**39**	47	124
Horatio: Arkansas	**26**	34	94
Horicon: Wisconsin	**20**	43	89
Horn: *r.*, N.W.T.	**40**	62	118
Hornbrook: California	**36**	42	123
Hornby Bay: N.W.T.	**40**	66	118
Hornby I.: British Columbia	**38**	50	125
Hornell: New York	**14**	42	78
Horn I.: Mississippi	**27**	30	89
Horn Mts.: N.W.T.	**40**	62	120
Horse Creek: *sett.*, California	**36**	42	123
Horseheads: New York	**14**	42	77
Horse Heaven Hills: Wash.	**39**	46	120
Horse Is.: Newfoundland	**9**	50	56
Horse L.: California	**36**	41	121
Horseshoe Bay: *sett.*, B.C.	**38**	49	123
Horton: *r.*, N.W.T.	**44**	68	123
Horton L.: N.W.T.	**44**	68	122
Hortonville: Wisconsin	**20**	44	89
Hotham Inlet: Alaska	**42**	67	162
Hot Springs: *& Nat. Park*, Ark.	**26**	35	93
Hot Springs: South Dakota	**28**	43	103
Hot Springs: Virginia	**16**	38	80
Hottah L.: N.W.T.	**40**	65	118
Houghton: Washington	**6**	47¾	122¼
Houghton L.: Michigan	**20**	44	85
Houma: Louisiana	**27**	30	91
Housatonic: *r.*, Mass./Conn.	**15**	42	73
Houston: Mississippi	**27**	34	89
Houston: Pennsylvania	**19**	40	80
Houston: Texas	**26**	30	95
Houston Ship Channel: Texas	**3**	29¾	95¼
Houtzdale: Pennsylvania	**14**	41	78
Howell: Michigan	**21**	43	84
Hoxie: Arkansas	**26**	36	91
Hubbard: Ohio	**19**	41	81
Hubbard: Texas	**26**	32	97
Hubbard L.: Michigan	**18**	45	84
Hubbell: Wisconsin	**10**	47	88
Huddart Park: California	**6**	37½	122¼
Hudson: Massachusetts	**15**	42	72
Hudson: Michigan	**21**	42	84
Hudson: New York	**15**	42	74
Hudson: Ohio	**19**	41	81
Hudson: Ontario	**10**	50	92
Hudson: *r.*, New York	**11**	42	74
Hudson Bay: N.W.T.	**45**	60	87
Hudson Bay: *town*, Sask.	**30**	53	102
Hudson Falls: *town*, New York	**13**	43	74
Hudson Hope: British Columbia	**41**	56	122
Hudson Strait: N.W.T./Québec.	**45**	63	73
Hughes: Alaska	**42**	66	154
Hughesville: Maryland	**17**	39	77
Hughesville: Pennsylvania	**14**	41	77
Hugo: Oklahoma	**26**	34	96
Hugo: Oregon	**36**	43	123
Hall: Massachusetts	**2**	42¼	71
Hull: Québec	**12**	45	76
Hullville: California	**37**	39	123
Humacao: Puerto Rico	**27**	18	66
Humber: *r.*, Ontario	**5**	43¾	79½
Humber Bay.: Ontario	**5**	43½	79½
Humboldt: Arizona	**33**	35	110
Humboldt: Saskatchewan	**30**	52	105
Humboldt: Tennessee	**27**	36	89
Humboldt: *r.*, Nevada	**33**	40	118
Hummels Wharf: Pennsylvania.	**14**	41	77
Humptulips: Washington	**39**	47	124
Hungry Horse: *res & dam*, Montana	**32**	48	114
Hungry Mother State Park: Va.	**16**	37	81
Hunter: New York	**15**	42	74
Hunters Point: California	**6**	37¾	122¼

	Page	N	W
Hunting Bayou: Texas	**3**	29¾	95¼
Huntingdon: Pennsylvania	**14**	41	78
Huntingdon: Québec	**13**	45	74
Huntingdon: Tennessee	**27**	36	88
Huntingdon I.: Newfoundland	**9**	54	57
Huntington: Indiana	**21**	41	86
Huntington: Massachusetts	**15**	42	73
Huntington: New York	**1**	41	73½
Huntington: Texas	**26**	31	95
Huntington: West Virginia	**16**	38	82
Huntington Beach: *town*, Calif.	**7**	33¾	118
Huntsville: Alabama	**27**	35	87
Huntsville: Arkansas	**26**	36	94
Huntsville: Ontario	**12**	45	79
Huntsville: Texas	**26**	31	96
Hurd, C.: Ontario	**18**	45	82
Hurley: New Mexico	**29**	33	108
Hurlock: Maryland	**17**	39	76
Huron: California	**34**	36	120
Huron: Ohio	**19**	41	83
Huron: South Dakota	**28**	44	98
Huron: *r.*, Michigan	**19**	42	83
Huron: *r.*, Ohio	**19**	41	83
Huron, Lake	**18**	—	—
Huron, Point: Michigan	**5**	42½	82¾
Hurricane: Alaska	**42**	63	150
Hurricane: *cr.*, Arkansas	**26**	34	92
Hurtsboro: Alabama	**27**	32	85
Huslia: Alaska	**42**	66	157
Hutchinson: Kansas	**29**	38	98
Huttig: Arkansas	**26**	33	92
Hyampom: California	**36**	41	123
Hyannis: Massachusetts	**15**	42	70
Hyattsville: Washington, D.C.	**2**	39	77
Hyadburg: Alaska	**41**	55	133
Hyde Park: New York	**15**	42	74
Hyde Park: Vermont	**13**	45	73
Hyder: Alaska	**41**	56	130
Hydesville: California	**36**	41	124
Hyland: *r.*, Yukon	**40**	61	129
Hyndman: Pennsylvania	**14**	40	79
Iberville: Québec	**13**	45	73
Ice Harbor: *dam*, Wash.	**32**	46	119
Ickesburg: Pennsylvania	**14**	40	77
Icy B.: Alaska	**43**	60	141
Idabel: Oklahoma	**26**	34	95
IDAHO	**32**	—	—
Idaho Falls: *town*, Idaho	**32**	44	112
Idria: California	**34**	36	121
Igiugig: Alaska	**43**	59	156
Igloolik: N.W.T.	**45**	69	82
Igo: California	**36**	41	123
Ikatan: Alaska	**43**	55	163
Ikpikpuk: *r.*, Alaska	**42**	70	155
Ile-à-la-Crosse: Saskatchewan	**30**	55	108
Ile-à-la-Crosse, Lac: Sask.	**30**	56	108
Iliamna L.: Alaska	**43**	60	155
Ilion: New York	**14**	43	75
ILLINOIS	**10**	—	—
Illinois: *r.*, Illinois	**21**	41	90
Illinois: *r.*, Oregon	**36**	42	124
Ilinois and Mich. Canal: Illinois	**4**	41¾	87¾
Ilwaco: Washington	**39**	46	124
Imlay City: Michigan	**19**	43	83
Immokalee: Florida	**25**	26	81
Imperial: California	**35**	33	116
Imperial: Pennsylvania	**19**	40	80
Imperial: *dam*, Calif./Arizona	**33**	33	115
Imperial Beach: *town*, Calif.	**35**	33	117
Imperial Valley: California	**35**	33	115
Imuruk L.: Alaska	**42**	66	163
Independence: California	**35**	37	118
Independence: Kansas	**29**	37	96
Independence: Louisiana	**27**	31	91
Independence: Oregon	**39**	45	123
Indian: *r.*, New York	**12**	44	76
INDIANA	**10**	—	—
Indiana: Pennsylvania	**19**	41	79
Indiana E.-W. Toll Road: Ind.	**21**	42	86
Indiana Harbor: Indiana	**4**	41½	87½
Indianapolis: Indiana	**21**	40	86
Indian Arm: *bay*, B.C.	**6**	49¼	122¾
Indian Cabins: Alberta	**30**	60	117
Indian Creek: Illinois	**4**	42¼	88
Indian Head: Pennsylvania	**16**	40	79
Indian House L.: Québec	**9**	56	65
Indian L.: New York	**13**	44	74
Indian L.: Ohio	**19**	40	84
Indianola: Mississippi	**24**	33	91
Indian River Bay: Delaware	**17**	39	75
Indian Springs: Nevada	**35**	37	116
Indio: California	**35**	34	116
Ingersoll: Ontario	**19**	43	81
Inglewood: California	**7**	34	118¼
Ingot: California	**36**	41	122
Inkom: Idaho	**32**	43	112
Inkster: Michigan	**5**	42¼	83¼
Inman: South Carolina	**24**	35	82
Innerkip: Ontario	**19**	43	81
Innisfail: Alberta	**30**	52	114
Inspiration: Arizona	**33**	33	111
Institute: West Virginia	**16**	38	82
Interlochen: Michigan	**20**	45	86
International Falls: *town*, Minn.	**10**	49	93
Intracoastal Waterway	**26**	—	—
Inugsuin Fiord: N.W.T.	**45**	70	69

	Page	N	W
Inuvik: Northwest Territories	**44**	68	134
Invermere: British Columbia	**41**	51	116
Inverness: California	**37**	38	123
Inverness: Florida	**25**	29	82
Inverness: Nova Scotia	**9**	46	61
Inyokern: California	**35**	36	118
Inyo Range: California	**35**	37	118
Ioco: British Columbia	**6**	49¼	122¾
Iola: Kansas	**29**	38	95
Iola: Wisconsin	**20**	45	89
Ione: California	**37**	38	121
Ionia: Michigan	**20**	43	85
Iota: Louisiana	**26**	30	93
IOWA	**10**	—	—
Iowa: *r.*, Iowa	**10**	43	94
Iowa City: Iowa	**10**	42	92
Ipperwash Prov. Park: Ontario	**19**	43	82
Ipswich: Massachusetts	**15**	43	71
Irish Hills: Michigan	**19**	43	84
Irondequoit: New York	**12**	43	78
Iron Mtn.: Idaho	**32**	43	117
Iron Mountain: *town*, Michigan	**20**	46	88
Iron Mountain: *sett.*, Missouri	**10**	38	91
Iron Mts.: Va./Tennessee	**16**	37	81
Iron River: *town*, Michigan	**20**	46	89
Iron Springs: Utah	**33**	38	113
Ironton: Ohio	**16**	39	83
Ironton: Utah	**33**	40	112
Ironwood: Michigan	**10**	46	90
Iroquis: Ontario	**13**	45	75
Iroquis: *r*, Illinois/Indiana	**21**	41	87
Irvine: Pennsylvania	**19**	42	79
Irvines Landing: B.C.	**38**	50	124
Irvington: New Jersey	**1**	40¾	74¼
Isabella: Michigan	**20**	46	87
Isabella Bay: N.W.T.	**45**	70	68
Isabella Res.: California	**35**	36	118
Isachsen: Northwest Territories.	**61**	79	104
Ishpeming: Michigan	**10**	46	88
Iskut: *r.*, British Columbia	**41**	57	131
Island Beach State Park: N.J.	**15**	40	74
Island Falls: *sett.*, Ontario	**11**	50	81
Island L.: Manitoba	**31**	54	95
Island Mountain: *sett.*, Calif.	**36**	40	124
Island Pond: Vermont	**13**	45	72
Islands, Bay of: Newfoundland	**9**	49	58
Islands, Bay of: Ontario	**18**	46	82
Isle Royale Nat. Park: Michigan.	**10**	48	89
Iselton: California	**37**	38	122
Islington: Ontario	**5**	43¾	79½
Issaquah: Washington	**39**	48	122
Italy: Texas	**26**	32	97
Itasca: Illinois	**4**	42	88
Itasca: Texas	**26**	32	97
Itchen L.: N.W.T.	**40**	65	113
Ithaca: New York	**14**	42	77
Itta Bena: Mississippi	**27**	34	90
Iuka: Mississippi	**27**	35	88
Ivanof Bay: *town*, Alaska	**43**	56	159
Ivanpah: California	**35**	35	115
Ivishak: *r.*, Alaska	**42**	69	149
Ivoryton: Connecticut	**15**	41	72
Ivugivik: Québec	**45**	62	78
Jacinto City: Texas	**3**	29¾	95¼
Jackfish River: *sett.*, Alberta	**30**	59	113
Jackrabbit: Nevada	**33**	38	115
Jacks Mtn.: Pennsylvania	**14**	40	78
Jackson: Alabama	**27**	32	88
Jackson: California	**37**	38	121
Jackson: Georgia	**24**	33	84
Jackson: Louisiana	**26**	31	91
Jackson: Michigan	**21**	42	84
Jackson: Mississippi	**27**	32	90
Jackson: North Carolina	**17**	36	77
Jackson: Ohio	**16**	39	83
Jackson: Tennessee	**27**	36	89
Jackson: Wyoming	**28**	43	111
Jackson: *r.*, Virginia	**16**	38	80
Jackson Creek: *sett.*, Nevada	**33**	41	119
Jackson Park: Illinois	**4**	41¾	87½
Jacksonville: Alabama	**27**	34	86
Jacksonville: Arkansas	**26**	35	92
Jacksonville: Florida	**25**	30	82
Jacksonville: Illinois	**10**	40	90
Jacksonville: North Carolina	**24**	35	77
Jacksonville: Oregon	**36**	42	123
Jacksonville: Texas	**26**	32	95
Jacksonville Beach: *town*, Fla.	**25**	30	81
Jacques Cartier: Québec	**2**	45½	73½
Jacques Cartier Passage: Québec	**9**	50	63
Jacumba: California	**35**	33	116
Jaffrey: New Hampshire	**13**	43	72
Jal: New Mexico	**29**	32	103
Jalama: California	**34**	35	121
Jamaica Bay: New York	**1**	40¾	73¾
Jamaica Bay Wildlife Refuge: New York	**1**	40½	73¾
James: *r.*, N.D./S.D.	**28**	44	98
James: *r.*, Virginia	**17**	37	77
James Bay: Ontario/Québec	**8**	54	81
Jamesburg: New Jersey	**15**	40	74
James Ross Strait: N.W.T.	**44**	69	96
Jamestown: California	**37**	38	120
Jamestown: New York	**19**	42	79
Jamestown: North Dakota	**28**	47	99
Jamestown: Rhode Island	**15**	42	71

	Page	N	W
Jamestown: Tennessee	**24**	36	85
Jamul: California	**35**	33	117
Janesville: California	**36**	40	121
Janesville: Wisconsin	**21**	43	89
Jasper: Alabama	**27**	34	87
Jasper: Alberta	**30**	53	118
Jasper: Florida	**25**	31	83
Jasper: Georgia	**24**	34	84
Jasper: Tennessee	**27**	35	86
Jasper: Texas	**26**	31	94
Jasper Nat. Park: Alberta	**30**	53	118
Jean: Nevada	**35**	36	115
Jeanerette: Louisiana	**26**	30	92
Jeannette: Pennsylvania	**19**	40	80
Jeannine, Lac: Québec	**9**	68	53
Jefferson: Georgia	**24**	34	84
Jefferson: North Carolina	**26**	36	81
Jefferson: Ohio	**19**	42	81
Jefferson: Texas	**26**	33	94
Jefferson: *r.*, Montana	**32**	46	112
Jefferson City: Missouri	**10**	39	92
Jefferson City: Montana	**28**	46	112
Jefferson City: Tennessee	**24**	36	84
Jefferson, Mt.: Oregon	**39**	41	122
Jeffersonville: India	**10**	40	87
Jelly: California	**36**	40	122
Jena: Louisiana	**26**	32	92
Jenkins: Kentucky	**16**	37	83
Jenkintown: Pennsylvania	**2**	40	75¼
Jenner: California	**37**	38	123
Jenners: Pennsylvania	**19**	40	79
Jennings: Louisiana	**26**	30	93
Jenny Lind I.: N.W.T.	**44**	69	102
Jens Munk I.: N.W.T.	**45**	70	80
Jerome: Idaho	**32**	43	115
Jerome: Pennsylvania	**17**	40	79
Jersey City: New Jersey	**1**	40¾	74
Jersey Shore: Pennsylvania	**14**	41	77
Jervis Inlet: British Columba	**38**	50	124
Jesup: Georgia	**24**	32	82
Jésus, Île: Québec	**2**	45½	73¾
Jewett: Ohio	**19**	40	81
Jewett City: Connecticut	**15**	42	72
J. F. Kennedy Space Center: Fla.	**25**	29	81
Jim Thorpe: Pennsylvania	**14**	41	76
Joe W. Brown Memorial Park: La.	**3**	30	90
Johannesburg: California	**35**	35	118
John Day: *dam*, Wash./Oregon	**39**	46	121
John Day: *r.*, Oregon	**32**	45	120
John Hendry Park: B.C.	**6**	49¼	123
John H. Kerr Res.: Virginia	**17**	37	78
John Sevier: Tennessee	**24**	36	83
Johnsonburg: Pennsylvania	**14**	41	79
Johnson City: New York	**14**	42	76
Johnson City: Tennessee	**16**	36	82
Johnsons Crossing: Yukon	**40**	60	133
Johnston: South Carolina	**24**	34	82
Johnstown: New York	**13**	43	74
Johnstown: Ohio	**19**	40	83
Johnstown: Pennsylvania	**14**	40	79
Joliet: Illinois	**4**	41½	88
Joliette: Québec	**13**	46	73
Jolon: California	**34**	36	121
Jones Beach State Park: N.Y.	**1**	40½	73½
Jonesboro: Arkansas	**27**	36	91
Jonesboro: Indiana	**21**	40	86
Jonesboro: Louisiana	**26**	32	93
Jonesboro: Tennessee	**16**	36	82
Jones, C.: Québec	**8**	44	80
Jones Mill: Arkansas	**26**	34	93
Jones Sound: N.W.T.	**61**	76	85
Jonesville: Michigan	**21**	42	85
Jonesville: South Carolina	**24**	35	82
Jonquière: Québec	**8**	48	71
Joplin: Missouri	**10**	37	95
Jordan: New York	**12**	43	77
Joseph, Lac: Newfoundland	**9**	53	65
Joshua Tree: California	**35**	34	116
Joshua Tree Nat. Mon.: Calif.	**35**	34	116
Juan de Fuca, Str. of: British Columbia/Washington	**38**	48	124
Judith Gap: Montana	**28**	47	110
Judith Point: Rhode Island	**15**	41	71
Julian: California	**35**	33	117
Junction City: Kansas	**28**	39	97
Junction City: Ohio	**16**	40	82
Junction City: Wisconsin	**20**	45	90
Juneau: Alaska	**40**	58	134
June Lake: *sett.*, California	**37**	38	119
Juniata: *r.*, Pennsylvania	**14**	41	78
Juniata R., Raystown Br.: Pa.	**14**	40	78
Junipero Serra Peak: California	**34**	36	121
Kaanapali: Hawaii	**128**	21	157
Kaguyak: Alaska	**43**	57	154
Kahoolawe: *i.*, Hawaii	**128**	21	157
Kahului: Hawaii	**128**	21	156
Kailua: Hawaii	**128**	21	158
Kailua-Kona: Hawaii	**128**	20	156
Kaiwi Ch.: Hawaii	**128**	21	157
Kakagi L.: Ontario	**10**	49	94
Kake: Alaska	**41**	57	134
Kakhonak Bay: *sett.*, Alaska	**43**	59	155
Kakisa L.: N.W.T.	**40**	61	118
Kaktovik: Alaska	**42**	70	144
Kalama: Washington	**39**	46	123
Kalamazoo: Michigan	**21**	42	86

	Page	N	W
Kalamazoo: *r.*, Michigan	**21**	43	86
Kaleva: Michigan	**20**	44	86
Kalispell: Montana	**32**	48	114
Kalkaska: Michigan	**20**	45	85
Kalohi Ch.: Hawaii	**128**	21	157
Kalskag: Alaska	**43**	61	160
Kaltag: Alaska	**42**	64	159
Kamilukuak L.: N.W.T.	**44**	62	102
Kaminak L.: N.W.T.	**45**	62	94
Kaminuriak L.: N.W.T.	**44**	63	96
Kamloops: British Columbia	**38**	51	120
Kamloops L.: B.C.	**38**	51	121
Kamuela: Hawaii	**128**	20	156
Kanaaupscow: Québec	**8**	54	77
Kanaaupscow: *r.*, Québec	**8**	54	74
Kanairiktok: *r.*, Newfoundland	**9**	55	62
Kanawha: *r.*, West Virginia	**16**	39	82
Kane: Pennsylvania	**14**	42	79
Kaneohe: Hawaii	**128**	21	158
Kaniapiskau: *r.*, Québec	**8**	55	69
Kaniapiskau L.: Québec	**8**	54	70
Kankakee: *& r.*, Illinois	**21**	41	88
Kannapolis: North Carolina	**24**	36	81
Kanopolis: Kansas	**29**	39	98
KANSAS	**29**	—	—
Kansas: *r.*, Kansas	**29**	39	96
Kansas City: Kansas	**28**	39	95
Kansas City: Missouri	**10**	39	95
Kansas Turnpike: Kansas	**28**	38	97
Kantishna: *r.*, Alaska	**42**	64	150
Kapaa: Hawaii	**128**	22	159
Kapiskau: Ontario	**8**	53	82
Kapiskau: *r.*, Ontario	**8**	52	84
Kaplan: Louisiana	**26**	30	92
Kapuskasing: Ontario	**11**	49	82
Kapuskasing: *r.*, Ontario	**11**	49	83
Karluk: Alaska	**43**	58	155
Karrats Fiord: Greenland	**45**	71	54
Kasaan: Alaska	**41**	56	132
Kasba L.: N.W.T.	**30/31**	62	102
Kashabowie: Ontario	**10**	49	90
Kasiglook: Alaska	**43**	61	163
Kasilof: Alaska	**43**	60	151
Kaskaskia: *r.*, Illinois	**10**	39	89
Kaskattama: *r.*, Manitoba	**31**	56	91
Kaslo: British Columbia	**41**	50	117
Katahdin, Mt.: Maine	**8**	46	69
Katalla: Alaska	**43**	60	145
Katmai Nat. Mon.: Alaska	**43**	58	155
Katonah: New York	**15**	41	74
Kauai: Hawaii	**128**	22	160
Kauai Ch.: Hawaii	**128**	22	159
Kaufman: Texas	**26**	33	96
Kaukauna: Wisconsin	**20**	44	88
Kaula: *i.*, Hawaii	**128**	22	161
Kaulakahi Ch.: Hawaii	**128**	22	160
Kayak I.: Alaska	**43**	60	145
Kazan: *r.*, N.W.T.	**44**	62	101
Kealakekua: Hawaii	**128**	20	156
Keansburg: New Jersey	**15**	40	74
Keaney: Nebraska	**28**	41	99
Kearns: Utah	**33**	41	112
Kechika: *r.*, B.C.	**40**	49	127
Keddie: California	**36**	40	121
Keefers: British Columbia	**38**	50	122
Keele: *r.*, N.W.T.	**40**	64	127
Keele Park: Yukon	**40**	63	130
Keeler: California	**35**	37	118
Keene: California	**35**	35	119
Keene: New Hampshire	**13**	43	72
Keeseville: New York	**13**	45	74
Keetley: Utah	**33**	41	111
Keewatin: Ontario	**10**	50	95
Keewatin, District of: N.W.T.	**44/45**	64	97
Keg River: Alberta	**30**	58	118
Keith Arm: Great Bear L., Northwest Territories	**40**	65	122
Kekaha: Hawaii	**128**	22	160
Kekertaluk: N.W.T.	**45**	68	67
Keller L.: Northwest Territories	**40**	64	122
Kellett, C.: N.W.T.	**44**	72	126
Kelleys Island: *sett.*, Ohio	**19**	42	83
Kellogg: Idaho	**32**	48	116
Kelowna: British Columbia	**38**	50	119
Kelseyville: California	**37**	39	123
Kelso: California	**35**	35	116
Kelso: Washington	**39**	46	123
Kemano: British Columbia	**41**	54	128
Kemp: Texas	**26**	32	96
Kempt L.: Québec	**8**	47	74
Kemptville: Ontario	**12**	45	76
Kenai: Alaska	**43**	61	151
Kenai Mts.: Alaska	**43**	60	150
Kenbridge: Virginia	**17**	37	78
Kendall, C.: N.W.T.	**45**	64	87
Kendallville: Indiana	**21**	41	85
Kenly: North Carolina	**24**	36	78
Kenmare: North Dakota	**28**	49	102
Kennebec: *r.*, Maine	**11**	45	70
Kennebunkport: Maine	**15**	43	70
Kennedy L.: British Columbia	**38**	49	126
Kennedy Meadow: California	**37**	33	120
Kennett: Missouri	**10**	36	90
Kennewick: Washington	**39**	46	119
Kennydale: Washington	**6**	47½	122¼
Keno: Oregon	**36**	42	122
Kenogami: Québec	**8**	48	71

	Page	N	W
Kenogami: *r.*, Ontario	**10**	50	86
Keno Hill: Yukon	**40**	64	135
Kenora: Ontario	**10**	50	94
Kenosha: Wisconsin	**21**	43	88
Kensington: Maryland	**2**	39	77
Kensington: Pennsylvania	**2**	40	75
Kent: Connecticut	**15**	42	73
Kent: Washington	**39**	47	122
Kent I.: Maryland	**17**	39	76
Kentland: Indiana	**21**	41	87
Kenton: Ohio	**19**	41	84
Kent Peninsula: N.W.T.	**44**	68	107
KENTUCKY	**23**	—	—
Kentucky: *r.*, Kentucky	**23**	38	85
Kentucky L.: Ky./Tennessee	**23**	36	88
Kentucky Turnpike & Pkwy.: Ky.	**23**	38	86
Kentwood: Louisiana	**27**	31	91
Kenwood: California	**37**	38	123
Keokuk: Iowa	**10**	40	91
Kerby: Oregon	**36**	42	124
Keremeos: British Columbia	**38**	40	120
Kerens: Texas	**26**	32	96
Kerman: California	**37**	37	120
Kermit: Texas	**29**	32	103
Kern: *r.*, California	**35**	36	118
Kernville: California	**35**	36	118
Kerrville: Texas	**29**	30	99
Kershaw: South Carolina	**24**	35	81
Kesagami L.: Ontario	**11**	50	80
Ketchikan: Alaska	**41**	55	132
Kettleman City: California	**34**	36	120
Kettlestone Bay: Québec	**45**	62	78
Keuka L.: New York	**14**	42	77
Kewanee: Illinois	**10**	41	90
Kewaunee: Wisconsin	**20**	44	88
Keweenaw Penin.: Michigan	**10**	47	89
Key Largo: *i.*, Florida	**25**	25	80
Keyser: West Virginia	**17**	39	79
Keystone: California	**37**	38	121
Keystone: South Dakota	**29**	44	103
Keystone: West Virginia	**16**	37	81
Keystone Res.: *& dam*, Oklahoma	**29**	36	96
Keysville: Virginia	**17**	37	79
Key West: Florida	**25**	25	82
Kezar Falls: *sett.*, Maine	**13**	44	71
Kiamichi: *r.*, Oklahoma	**26**	35	95
Kiana: Alaska	**42**	67	161
Kicking Horse P.: B.C./Alberta	**41**	51	116
Kiglapait, C.: Newfoundland	**9**	57	61
Kigluaik Mts.: Alaska	**42**	65	165
Kikerk L.: N.W.T.	**44**	67	113
Kikitat: *r.*, Washington	**39**	46	121
Kikkertorsoak I.: Québec	**45**	59	66
Kilauea: Hawaii	**128**	22	159
Kilbuck Mts.: Alaska	**43**	61	160
Kilgore: Texas	**26**	32	95
Killarney: Manitoba	**31**	49	100
Killarney Prov. Park: Ontario	**18**	46	81
Killbuck: *r.*, Ohio	**19**	41	82
Killeen: Texas	**29**	31	98
Kimakto Penin.: N.W.T.	**45**	70	88
Kimball: Nebraska	**28**	41	104
Kimbasket, L.: British Columbia	**41**	52	118
Kimberley: British Columbia	**41**	49	116
Kimberly: Oregon	**39**	45	120
Kincaid: Illinois	**21**	40	89
Kincaid: West Virginia	**16**	38	81
Kincardine: Ontario	**18**	44	82
Kinder: Louisiana	**26**	30	93
King City: California	**34**	36	121
King Cove: Alaska	**43**	55	162
King George Is.: N.W.T.	**8**	57	79
King Island: Alaska	**42**	65	168
Kingman: Arizona	**33**	35	114
Kingman: Kansas	**29**	38	98
King of Prussia: Pennsylvania	**2**	40	75¼
Kings: *r.*, California	**34**	36	120
King Salmon: Alaska	**43**	59	157
Kingsburg: California	**37**	37	120
Kings Canyon Nat. Park: Calif.	**35**	37	119
Kingsford: Michigan	**20**	46	88
Kingsley: *dam*, Nebraska	**28**	41	102
Kings Mtn.: *town*, N.C.	**24**	35	81
Kingsport: Tennessee	**16**	37	83
Kingston: New York	**15**	42	74
Kingston: Ontario	**12**	44	77
Kingston: Pennsylvania	**14**	41	76
Kingston: Tennessee	**24**	36	85
Kingston: Washington	**39**	48	123
Kingstree: South Carolina	**24**	34	80
Kingsville: Ontario	**19**	42	83
Kingsville: Texas	**22**	28	98
King William I.: N.W.T.	**44**	69	97
Kingwood: West Virginia	**16**	39	80
Kinsman: Ohio	**19**	41	81
Kinston: North Carolina	**24**	35	78
Kinuso: Alberta	**30**	55	115
Kinyon: California	**36**	41	122
Kinzua: Pennsylvania	**14**	42	79
Kipawa L.: Québec	**8**	47	79
Kipawa Reserve Prov. Park: Ont.	**12**	47	79
Kipling: Saskatchewan	**30**	50	103
Kipnuk: Alaska	**43**	60	164
Kippokok: Newfoundland	**9**	55	60
Kiptopeke: Virginia	**17**	37	76
Kirbyville: Texas	**26**	31	94
Kirk: Oregon	**36**	43	122

	Page	N	W
Kirkland: Washington	6	47¾	122¼
Kirkland Lake: *town*, Ontario	11	48	80
Kirksville: Missouri	10	40	93
Kirkwood: California	36	40	122
Kissimmee: Florida	25	28	81
Kissimmee: *r.*, Florida	25	27	81
Kississing L.: Manitoba	31	55	101
Kit Carson: California	37	39	120
Kitchener: Ontario	18	43	81
Kitimat: British Columbia	41	54	129
Kittanning: Pennsylvania	19	41	80
Kittery: Maine	15	43	71
Kivalina: Alaska	42	68	165
Kivitoo: N.W.T.	45	68	65
Kiwalik: Alaska	42	66	162
Klamath: California	36	42	124
Klamath: *r.*, California	36	41	124
Klamath Falls: *town*, Oregon	36	42	122
Klamath Falls Junction: Oregon	36	42	123
Klamath Marsh: Oregon	36	43	122
Klamath Mts.: California	36	41	123
Klawock: Alaska	41	56	133
Klemtu: British Columbia	41	53	129
Klickitat: *r.*, Washington	39	46	121
Klondike: California	35	35	116
Klondike: *r.*, Yukon	40	64	138
Kluane: Yukon	40	61	138
Kluane L.: Yukon	40	61	139
Kluane National Park: Yukon	40	60	139
Klukwan: Alaska	40	59	136
Knee L.: Manitoba	31	55	95
Knife: *r.*, North Dakota	28	47	102
Knight Inlet: B.C.	41	51	125
Knights Landing: California	37	39	122
Knightstown: Indiana	21	40	86
Knobley Mtn.: West Virginia	16	39	79
Knowlton: Québec	13	45	73
Knox: Indiana	21	41	87
Knox: Pennsylvania	19	41	80
Knox, C.: British Columbia	41	54	133
Knoxville: Tennessee	24	36	84
Koartak: Québec	45	61	70
Kobuk: Alaska	42	67	157
Kobuk: *r.*, Alaska	42	67	159
Koch I.: N.W.T.	45	70	78
Kodiak: Alaska	43	58	153
Kodiak Is.: Alaska	43	57	153
Kogaluk: *r.*, Québec	45	59	77
Kogaluk Bay: Québec	45	59	78
Kohler: Wisconsin	20	44	88
Koko Head Pk.: Hawaii	128	21	158
Kokolik: *r.*, Alaska	42	69	162
Kokomo: Indiana	21	41	86
Kokrines: Alaska	42	65	155
Kokrines Hills: Alaska	42	65	154
Koksoak: *r.*, Québec	45	58	69
Koliganek: Alaska	43	60	157
Koloa: Hawaii	128	22	159
Konawa: Oklahoma	26	35	97
Kootenai: *r.*, Idaho/Montana	32	49	115
Kootenai Falls: *dam*, Montana	32	49	116
Kootenay: *r.*, British Columbia	41	50	116
Kootenay L.: British Columbia	41	50	117
Kootenay National Park: B.C.	30	51	116
Koppel: Pennsylvania	19	41	80
Koraluk: *r.*, Newfoundland	9	56	63
Kosciusko: Mississippi	26	33	90
Koshkonong L.: Wisconsin	21	43	89
Kosmosdale: Kentucky	23	38	86
Kotcho L.: B.C.	30	59	121
Kotlik: Alaska	42	63	164
Kotzebue: Alaska	42	67	163
Kotzebue Sound: Alaska	42	67	163
Koukdjuak: *r.*, N.W.T.	45	67	72
Kountze: Texas	26	30	94
Kovik Bay: Québec	45	62	78
Koyuk: *& r.*, Alaska	42	65	161
Koyukuk: Alaska	42	65	158
Koyukuk: *r.*, Alaska	42	66	157
Krusenstern, C.: Alaska	42	67	164
Kruzof I.: Alaska	40	57	136
Kualapuu: Hawaii	128	21	157
Kugmallit Bay: N.W.T.	44	70	133
Kulik Lodge: Alaska	43	59	155
Kunghit I.: British Columbia	41	52	131
Kuparuk: *r.*, Alaska	42	70	149
Kure: *i.*, Hawaii	128	29	178
Kurtistown: Hawaii	128	20	155
Kusawa L.: Yukon	40	60	136
Kuskokwim: *r.*, Alaska	42	62	156
Kuskokwim Bay: Alaska	43	59	163
Kuskokwim Mts.: Alaska	42/43	62	157
Kuskokwim North Fork: *r.*, Alaska	42	64	153
Kwethluk: Alaska	43	61	162
Kwigillingok: Alaska	43	60	165
Kwiguk: Alaska	42	63	165
Kyburz: California	37	39	120
La Belle: Florida	25	27	81
Labelle: Québec	13	46	75
Laberge L.: Yukon	40	61	135
Labrador: *district*, Newfoundland	9	—	—
Labrador City: Newfoundland	8	53	67
La Canada: California	7	34¼	118¼
Lachine: Québec	2	45½	73¾
Lachute: Québec	13	46	74

	Page	N	W
Lac La Biche: *town*, Alberta	30	55	112
Lac la Hache: B.C.	41	52	121
Lac la Ronge: *sett., and Prov. Park*, Sask.	30	55	104
Lac-Mégantic: Québec	13	46	71
Lacolle: Québec	13	45	73
Lacombe: Alberta	30	53	114
Lacombe: Louisiana	27	30	90
Lacon: Illinois	21	41	89
Laconia: New Hampshire	13	44	71
Lacoochee: Florida	25	28	82
Lacorne: Québec	8	48	78
La Crosse: Wisconsin	10	44	91
Ladner: British Columbia	38	49	123
Ladonia: Texas	26	33	96
Ladysmith: British Columbia	38	49	124
Lafayette: Alabama	27	33	85
Lafayette: *& res.*, California	6	38	120
La Fayette: Georgia	27	35	85
Lafayette: Indiana	21	40	87
Lafayette: Louisiana	26	30	92
Lafayette, Mt.: N.H.	13	44	72
La Follete: Tennessee	24	36	84
La Grand: Oregon	32	45	118
La Grange: Georgia	27	33	85
La Grange: Illinois	4	41¾	87¾
Lagrange: Indiana	21	42	85
La Grange: North Carolina	24	35	78
La Grange: Texas	26	30	97
Laguna Beach: *town*, California	35	34	118
Lahontan Res.: Nevada	37	39	119
La Jolla: California	35	33	117
La Junta: Colorado	29	38	104
Lake Alpine: *sett.*, California	37	38	120
Lake Ariel: *sett.*, Pennsylvania	14	41	75
Lake Arthur: *town*, Louisiana	26	30	93
Lake Bluff: *sett.*, Illinois	4	42¼	87¾
Lake Borgne Canal: Louisiana	3	30	90
Lake Calumet Harbor: Illinois	4	43¾	87½
Lake Charles: *town*, Louisiana	26	30	93
Lake City: *town*, Florida	25	30	83
Lake City: *sett.*, Seattle	6	47¾	122¼
Lake City: *town*, South Carolina	24	34	80
Lake City: *sett.*, Tennessee	24	36	84
Lake Cowichan: *sett.*, B.C.	38	49	124
Lake Delton: *sett.*, Wisconsin	20	44	90
Lakefield: Ontario	12	44	78
Lake Forest: *town*, Illinois	21	42	88
Lake George: *sett.*, Colorado	28	39	105
Lake George: *sett.*, Michigan	20	44	85
Lake George: *sett.*, New York	13	43	74
La Habra: California	7	34	118
Lake Habour: *sett.*, N.W.T.	45	63	70
Lake Hills: *sett.*, Washington	6	47½	122¼
Lake Hughes: *sett.*, California	35	35	118
Lakehurst: New Jersey	15	40	74
Lake Isabella: *sett.*, California	35	36	118
Lake Jackson: *town*, Texas	26	29	95
Lakeland: Florida	25	28	82
Lakeland: Georgia	25	31	83
Lake Louise: *sett.*, Alberta	30	51	116
Lake Luzerne: *sett.*, New York	13	43	74
Lake Mead Nat. Rec. Area: Arizona/Nevada	33	36	114
Lake Mills: *town*, Wisconsin	20	43	89
Lake Minchumina: *sett.*, Alaska	42	64	152
Lake Odessa: *sett.*, Michigan	21	43	85
Lake Orion: *town*, Michigan	19	43	83
Lake Oswego: *sett.*, Oregon	36	45	123
Lake Park: *town*, Florida	25	27	80
Lake Placid: *town*, New York	13	44	74
Lakeport: California	37	39	123
Lake Providence: *town*, La.	26	33	91
Lake River: *town*, Ontario	8	55	83
Lakeshore: California	37	37	119
Lakeside: California	35	33	117
Lakeside: Michigan	21	42	87
Lakeview: California	35	34	117
Lakeview: Oregon	36	42	120
Lake Village: *town*, Arkansas	26	33	91
Lakeville: Connecticut	15	42	73
Lake Wales: *town*, Florida	25	28	82
Lakewood: California	7	33¾	118
Lakewood: Colorado	3	39¾	105
Lakewood: New Jersey	15	40	74
Lakewood: New York	19	42	79
Lakewood: Wisconsin	20	45	89
Lake Worth: *town*, Florida	25	27	80
Lake Zurich: *town*, Illinois	4	42¼	88
La Loche: Saskatchewan	30	57	109
La Loche Lac: Saskatchewan	30	57	110
La Malbaie: Québec	8	48	70
Lamar: Colorado	29	38	103
Lamar: South Carolina	24	34	80
La Martre, Lac: N.W.T.	40	63	118
Lambert: Mississippi	27	34	90
Lambertville: New Jersey	14	40	75
Lambertville: Pennsylvania	14	40	75
Lambton, C.: N.W.T.	44	71	123
Lame Deer: Montana	28	46	107
La Mesa: California	35	33	117
Lamesa: Texas	29	33	102
Lamoille: *r.*, Vermont	13	45	73
Lamont: California	35	35	119
Lahaina: Hawaii	128	21	157
Lanai: *i.*, Hawaii	128	21	157
Lanai City: Hawaii	128	21	157

	Page	N	W
Lanark: Illinois	21	42	90
Lanark: Ontario	12	45	76
Lancaster: California	35	35	118
Lancaster: New Brunswick	9	45	66
Lancaster: New Hampshire	13	44	72
Lancaster: New York	14	43	79
Lancaster: Ohio	16	40	83
Lancaster: Pennsylvania	14	40	76
Lancaster: South Carolina	24	35	81
Lancaster: Texas	26	33	97
Lancaster Sound: N.W.T.	45	74	85
Lander: Wyoming	28	43	109
Landisville: Pennsylvania	14	40	76
Landrum: South Carolina	24	35	82
Lanett: Alabama	27	33	85
Langell Valley: *sett.*, Oregon	36	42	121
Langeloth: Pennsylvania	19	40	80
Langhorne: Pennsylvania	14	40	75
L'Anguille: *r.*, Arkansas	27	35	91
Lanigan: Saskatchewan	30	52	105
Lansdale: Pennsylvania	14	40	75
Lansdowne House: Ontario	31	52	88
Lansing: Illinois	4	41½	87½
Lansing: Michigan	21	43	86
Laona: Wisconsin	20	46	89
La Panza: California	34	35	120
Lapeer: Michigan	19	43	83
La Poile B.: Newfoundland	9	48	59
La Porte: California	37	40	121
La Porte: Indiana	21	42	87
La Porte: Texas	26	30	95
La Potherie, Lac: Québec	45	59	72
La Prairie: Québec	2	45¼	73½
La Puente: California	7	34	118
La Quinta: Texas	22	28	98
Laramie: Wyoming	28	41	106
Laramie: *r.*, Wyoming	28	41	105
Larch: *r.*, Québec	8	57	72
Larder Lake: *sett.*, Ontario	11	48	80
Laredo: Texas	22	28	99
Larned: Kansas	29	38	99
La Ronge: Saskatchewan	30	55	105
La Ronge, Lac: Saskatchewan	31	55	105
Larsen Bay: *sett.*, Alaska	43	58	154
La Salle: Illinois	21	41	89
La Salle: Ontario	5	42¼	83
La Salle: Québec	2	45½	78½
Las Animas: Colorado	29	38	103
Las Cruces: California	34	35	120
Las Cruces: New Mexico	29	32	107
Las Plumas: California	37	40	121
Lasqueti I.: British Columbia	38	49	124
Lassen Peak: California	36	41	122
Lassen Volcanic Nat. Park: Calif.	36	40	122
L'Assomption: Québec	13	46	73
Last Mountain L.: Sask.	30	51	105
Las Vegas: Nevada	35	36	115
Las Vegas: New Mexico	29	36	105
Lathrop: California	37	38	121
Lathrop: Michigan	20	46	87
Lathrop Wells: Nevada	35	37	116
Latrobe: Pennsylvania	19	40	79
Latta: South Carolina	24	34	79
La Tuque: Québec	8	47	73
Laurel: Delaware	17	39	76
Laurel: Maryland	17	39	77
Laurel: Mississippi	27	32	89
Laurel: Montana	28	46	109
Laureldale: Pennsylvania	14	40	76
Laurel Ridge: West Virginia	16	49	80
Laurens: South Carolina	24	34	82
Laurentides Prov. Park: Québec	8	48	72
Laurinburg: North Carolina	24	35	79
Lauzon: Québec	13	47	71
Lava Beds Nat. Mon.: Calif.	36	42	122
Laval-des-Rapides: Québec	2	45½	73¾
La Verendrye Prov. Park: Qué.	8	47	77
La Verne: California	35	34	118
Lavonia: Georgia	24	34	83
Lavon Res.: Texas	26	33	96
Lawrence: Indiana	21	40	86
Lawrence: Kansas	28	39	95
Lawrence: Massachusetts	15	43	71
Lawrenceburg: Tennessee	27	35	87
Lawrenceville: Georgia	24	34	84
Lawrenceville: Virginia	17	37	78
Lawton: Oklahoma	29	35	98
Laysan: *i.*, Hawaii	128	26	172
Laytonville: California	37	40	123
Lead: South Dakota	28	44	104
Leadville: Colorado	28	39	106
Leaf: *r.*, Mississippi	27	32	89
Leaf (aux Feuilles): *r.*, Québec	45	58	73
Leaf Inlet (aux Feuilles): Québec	45	59	70
Leaksville: North Carolina	16	36	80
Leamington: Ontario	19	42	83
Leaside: Ontario	5	43¾	79¼
Leavenworth: Kansas	28	39	95
Leavenworth: Washington	39	48	121
Lebanon: Indiana	21	40	87
Lebanon: New Hampshire	13	44	72
Lebanon: Oregon	32	45	123
Lebanon: Pennsylvania	14	40	76
Lebanon: Tennessee	23	36	86
Lebec: California	35	35	119
Lecompte: Louisiana	26	31	92
Leduc: Alberta	30	53	114

	Page	N	W
Lee: Massachusetts	**15**	42	73
Leechburg: Pennsylvania	**19**	41	80
Leeds: Alabama	**27**	34	87
Leeds: North Dakota	**28**	48	100
Leesburg: Florida	**25**	29	82
Leesburg: Virginia	**17**	39	78
Leesville: California	**37**	39	122
Leesville: Louisiana	**26**	31	93
Leetonia: Ohio	**19**	41	81
Leetsdale: Pennsylvania	**19**	41	80
Lee Vining: California	**37**	38	119
Le Feuvre Inlet: N.W.T.	**44**	72	97
Leggett: California	**36**	40	124
Le Grand: California	**37**	37	120
Lehighton: Pennsylvania	**14**	41	76
Leipsic: Ohio	**19**	41	84
Lekington: Massachusetts	**2**	42½	71¼
Leland: Mississippi	**27**	33	91
Lemieux Is.: N.W.T.	**45**	64	65
Lemon Fair: *r.*, Vermont	**13**	44	73
Lemont: Illinois	**4**	41¾	88
Lemoore: California	**34**	36	120
Lena: Illinois	**21**	42	90
Lennoxville: Québec	**13**	45	72
Lenoir: North Carolina	**24**	36	82
Lenoir City: Tennessee	**24**	36	84
Lenox: Massachusetts	**15**	42	73
Lenwood: California	**35**	35	117
Lenz: Oregon	**36**	43	122
Leominster: Massachusetts	**15**	43	72
Leon: *r.*, Texas	**29**	32	98
Leonard: Texas	**26**	33	96
Leonardtown: Maryland	**17**	38	77
Leopold I.: N.W.T.	**45**	65	63
Lepelle: *r.*, Québec	**45**	60	73
L'Epiphanie: Québec	**13**	46	73
Le Roy: Illinois	**21**	40	89
Le Roy: Michigan	**20**	44	85
Le Roy: New York	**14**	43	78
Lery L.: Louisiana	**3**	39¾	90
Leslie: Michigan	**21**	42	84
Lesser Slave L.: Alberta	**30**	56	117
Lester: West Virginia	**16**	38	81
Letchworth State Park: N.Y.	**14**	43	78
Lethbridge: Alberta	**30**	50	113
Letty Harbour: N.W.T.	**44**	70	124
Levelland: Texas	**29**	34	102
Levelock: Alaska	**43**	59	157
Lévis: Québec	**13**	47	71
Levisa Fork: *r.*, Kentucky	**16**	38	83
Levittown: New York	**1**	40¾	73½
Levittown: Pennsylvania	**14**	40	75
Lewes: Delaware	**17**	39	75
Lewis: *r.*, Washington	**39**	46	122
Lewisburg: Ohio	**21**	40	85
Lewisburg: Pennsylvania	**14**	41	77
Lewisburg: Tennessee	**27**	35	87
Lewisburg: West Virginia	**16**	38	80
Lewis Smith Res.: Alabama	**27**	34	87
Lewiston: California	**36**	41	123
Lewiston: Idaho	**32**	46	117
Lewiston: Maine	**11**	44	70
Lewiston: New York	**19**	43	79
Lewistown: Montana	**28**	47	109
Lewistown: Pennsylvania	**14**	41	78
Lewisville: Arkansas	**26**	33	94
Lewisville: Texas	**26**	33	97
Lewisville: *dam*, Texas	**26**	33	97
Lexington: Illinois	**21**	41	89
Lexington: Kentucky	**23**	38	85
Lexington: Massachusetts	**15**	42	71
Lexington: Mississippi	**27**	33	90
Lexington: Nebraska	**28**	41	100
Lexington: North Carolina	**24**	36	80
Lexington: Oklahoma	**26**	35	97
Lexington: Tennessee	**27**	36	88
Lexington: Virginia	**16**	38	79
Lexington Park: Maryland	**17**	38	76
Leyson Point: N.W.T.	**45**	63	81
Liard: *r.*, B.C./N.W.T.	**40**	61	122
Liard Range: N.W.T.	**40**	61	124
Libby: Montana	**32**	48	116
Liberal: Kansas	**29**	37	101
Liberty: Indiana	**21**	40	85
Liberty: New York	**15**	42	75
Liberty: North Carolina	**24**	36	80
Liberty: Pennsylvania	**14**	42	77
Liberty: South Carolina	**24**	35	83
Liberty: Texas	**26**	30	95
Liberty Inlet: Washington	**6**	47¾	122½
Libertyville: Illinois	**4**	42¼	88
Licking: *r.*, Kentucky	**23**	39	84
Licking: *r.*, Ohio	**16**	40	83
Lievre, R. du: Québec	**13**	47	75
Lignite: Alaska	**42**	64	149
Ligonier: Indiana	**21**	41	86
Ligonier: Pennsylvania	**19**	40	79
Lihue: Hawaii	**128**	22	159
Likely: California	**36**	41	121
Lillington: North Carolina	**24**	35	79
Lillooet: British Columbia	**38**	51	122
Lillooet: *r.*, British Columbia	**38**	50	122
Lillooet L.: British Columbia	**38**	50	123
Lilly: Pennsylvania	**14**	40	79
Lima: New York	**14**	43	78
Lima: Ohio	**19**	41	84
Lime: Oregon	**32**	44	117

	Page	N	W
Limon: Colorado	**28**	39	104
Lincoln: California	**37**	39	121
Lincoln: Illinois	**21**	40	89
Lincoln: Massachusetts	**2**	42½	71¼
Lincoln: Nebraska	**28**	41	97
Lincoln: New Hampshire	**13**	44	72
Lincoln Beach: *sett.*, Oregon	**39**	45	124
Lincoln Park: *sett.*, Illinois	**4**	42	87½
Lincoln Park: *sett.*, Michigan	**5**	42¼	83¼
Lincoln Sea: Greenland	**61**	84	52
Lincolnton: Georgia	**24**	34	82
Lincolnton: North Carolina	**24**	35	81
Lincolnwood: Illinois	**4**	42	87¾
Lindale: Georgia	**27**	34	85
Lindale: Texas	**26**	33	95
Linda Mar: California	**6**	37½	122½
Lindbergh: Alberta	**30**	54	111
Linden: California	**37**	38	121
Linden: New Jersey	**15**	41	74
Linden: Texas	**26**	33	94
Lindsay: California	**34**	36	119
Lindsay: Ontario	**12**	44	79
Linesville: Pennsylvania	**19**	42	80
Lineville: Alabama	**27**	33	86
Linton: North Dakota	**28**	46	100
Linwood: New Jersey	**15**	39	75
Linwood: Ontario	**18**	44	81
Lisbon: New Hampshire	**13**	44	72
Lisbon: Ohio	**19**	41	81
Lisburne, C.: Alaska	**42**	69	166
Lisianski: *i.*, Hawaii	**128**	26	174
Lisle: Illinois	**4**	41¾	88
Listerhill: Alabama	**27**	35	88
Listowel: Ontario	**18**	44	81
Litchfield: California	**36**	40	120
Litchfield: Connecticut	**15**	42	73
Lithonia: Georgia	**24**	34	84
Lititz: Pennsylvania	**14**	40	76
Little: *r.*, Okla./Arkansas	**26**	34	95
Little: *r.*, Virginia	**16**	37	80
Little Bay: Newfoundland	**9**	50	56
Little Beaver: *r.*, Ohio	**19**	41	81
Little Black: *r.*, Alaska	**42**	66	143
Little Blue: *r.*, Nebr./Kansas	**28**	40	98
Little Calumet: *r.*, Indiana	**4**	41½	87½
Little Chicago: N.W.T.	**44**	67	130
Little Colorado: *r.*, Arizona	**33**	35	110
Little Current: Ontario	**18**	46	82
Little Current: *r.*, Ontario	**10**	51	86
Little Deer Creek: Pennsylvania	**5**	40½	79¾
Little Diomede: *i.*, Alaska	**42**	66	169
Little Falls: *town*, Minnesota	**10**	46	94
Little Falls: *town*, New York	**13**	43	75
Littlefield: Texas	**29**	34	102
Little Goose: *dam*, Washington	**32**	47	118
Little Grand Rapids: Manitoba	**31**	52	95
Little Kanawha: *r.*, W. Va.	**16**	39	81
Little Lake: *sett.*, California	**35**	36	118
Little Longlac: Ontario	**10**	50	87
Little Mecatina: *r.*, Nfld./Québec	**9**	52	62
Little Mecatina I.: Québec	**9**	51	59
Little Missouri: *r.*	**28**	46	104
Little Missouri: *r.*, Arkansas	**26**	34	93
Little Red: *r.*, Arkansas	**26**	35	92
Little Rock: Arkansas	**26**	35	92
Littlerock: California	**35**	35	118
Little Sable Point: Michigan	**20**	44	87
Little Sandy: *r.*, Kentucky	**16**	38	83
Little Sioux: *r.*, Iowa	**10**	42	96
Little Smoky: *r.*, Alberta	**30**	55	122
Little Snake: *r.*, Colorado	**28**	41	108
Littlestown: Pennsylvania	**14**	40	77
Littleton: Colorado	**3**	39½	105
Littleton: New Hampshire	**13**	44	72
Littleton: North Carolina	**17**	36	78
Little Traverse Bay: Michigan	**20**	45	85
Little Valley: *sett.*, New York	**19**	42	79
Little White Oak Bayou: Texas	**3**	29¾	95¼
Little Whale: *r.*, Québec	**8**	56	76
Livengood: Alaska	**42**	66	149
Live Oak: California	**37**	39	122
Live Oak: Florida	**25**	30	83
Livermore: California	**37**	38	122
Liverpool: New York	**12**	43	76
Liverpool: Nova Scotia	**9**	44	65
Liverpool Bay: N.W.T.	**44**	70	129
Liverpool, C.: N.W.T.	**45**	74	78
Livingston: Alabama	**27**	33	88
Livingston: California	**37**	37	121
Livingston: Montana	**28**	46	111
Livingston: Newfoundland	**9**	54	66
Livingston: New Jersey	**15**	41	74
Livingston: Tennessee	**23**	36	85
Livingston: Texas	**26**	31	95
Livingstone Creek: *sett.*, Yukon	**40**	61	134
Llano: *& r.*, Texas	**29**	31	99
Llano Estacado: *plateau*, New Mexico/Texas	**29**	33	103
Lloydminster: Alta./Sask.	**30**	53	110
Lobstick L.: Newfoundland	**9**	54	65
Lockeford: California	**37**	38	121
Lockhart: Alabama	**27**	31	86
Lockhart: South Carolina	**24**	35	81
Lock Haven: Pennsylvania	**14**	41	77
Lockport: Illinois	**4**	41½	88
Lockport: Louisiana	**27**	30	91
Lockport: New York	**19**	43	79

	Page	N	W
Lockwood: California	**34**	36	121
Lodi: California	**37**	38	121
Lodi: Ohio	**19**	41	82
Lodi: Wisconsin	**20**	43	90
Lodoga: California	**37**	39	122
Logan: Ohio	**16**	40	82
Logan: Utah	**33**	42	112
Logan: West Virginia	**16**	38	82
Logan, Mt.: Yukon	**40**	61	140
Logan Mts.: Yukon/N.W.T.	**40**	62	128
Logansport: Indiana	**21**	41	86
Logansport: Louisiana	**26**	32	94
Loks Land: *i.* N.W.T.	**45**	62	65
Loleta: California	**36**	41	124
Loma Linda: California	**35**	34	117
Lombard: Illinois	**4**	42	88
Lomond: California	**37**	39	123
Lompoc: California	**34**	35	120
Lonaconing: Maryland	**17**	40	79
London: Ontario	**19**	43	81
Londonderry: Vermont	**13**	43	73
Lonely I.: Ontario	**18**	46	81
Lone Pine: California	**35**	37	118
Lone Star: Texas	**26**	33	95
Long: Alaska	**42**	64	156
Long Barn: California	**37**	38	120
Long Bay: *sett.*, South Carolina	**24**	33	79
Long Beach: *town*, California	**7**	33¾	118¼
Long Beach: *town*, New York	**1**	40½	73¾
Long Branch: New Jersey	**15**	40	74
Long Branch: Ontario	**5**	43½	79½
Long I.: New York	**15**	41	73
Long Island: Massachusetts	**2**	42¼	71
Long I.: N.W.T.	**8**	55	80
Long Island Sound: Conn./N.Y.	**1**	41	73½
Longlac: Ontario	**10**	50	87
Long L.: British Columbia	**38**	50	119
Long Meadow Lake: Minnesota	**3**	44¾	93¼
Long Lake: *sett.*, Wisconsin	**20**	46	89
Longmont: Colorado	**28**	40	105
Long Point: *sett.*, Texas	**26**	30	96
Long Range: Newfoundland	**9**	50	57
Longueuil: Québec	**2**	45½	73½
Longvale: California	**37**	40	123
Longview: Texas	**26**	33	95
Longview: Washington	**39**	46	123
Longwood: Florida	**25**	29	81
Lonoke: Arkansas	**26**	35	92
Lookout: California	**36**	41	121
Lookout Point: Maryland	**17**	38	76
Lookout Ridge: Alaska	**42**	69	157
Lorain: Ohio	**19**	41	82
Lord Mayor Bay: N.W.T.	**45**	70	92
Lordsburg: New Mexico	**29**	32	109
Loretteville: Québec	**13**	47	71
L'Orignal: Ontario	**13**	46	75
Los Alamos: California	**34**	35	120
Los Alamos: New Mexico	**29**	36	106
Los Altos: California	**6**	37½	122
Los Angeles: California	**35**	34	118
Los Angeles: *r.*, California	**7**	33¾	118¼
Los Angeles Aq.: California	**35**	35	118
Los Angeles County Fairgrounds: California	**7**	34	117¾
Los Banos: California	**37**	37	121
Los Gatos: California	**37**	37	122
Los Molinos: California	**36**	40	122
Los Olivos: California	**34**	35	120
Lost: *r.*, West Virginia	**17**	39	79
Lost Hills: *sett.*, California	**34**	36	120
Lost River State Park: W. Va.	**17**	39	79
Lothair: Kentucky	**16**	37	83
Loudon: Tennessee	**24**	36	84
Loudonville: Ohio	**19**	41	82
Louisa: Kentucky	**16**	38	83
Louisa: Virginia	**17**	38	78
Louisburg: North Carolina	**24**	36	78
Louise I.: British Columbia	**41**	53	132
LOUISIANA	**26/27**	—	—
Louisiana: Missouri	**10**	39	91
Louisville: Georgia	**24**	33	82
Louisville: Kentucky	**23**	38	86
Louisville: Mississippi	**27**	33	89
Louisville: Nebraska	**28**	41	96
Louisville: Ohio	**19**	41	81
Loup: *r.*, Nebraska	**28**	41	98
Loup City: Nebraska	**28**	41	99
Loveland: Colorado	**28**	40	105
Lovelock: Nevada	**33**	40	118
Lovington: Illinois	**21**	40	89
Lovington: New Mexico	**29**	33	103
Low, C.: Northwest Territories	**45**	63	85
Lowell: Massachusetts	**15**	43	71
Lowell: Michigan	**20**	43	85
Lowellville: Ohio	**19**	41	81
Lower Arrow L.: B.C.	**41**	50	118
Lower Crystal Springs Res.: Calif.	**6**	37½	122¼
Lower Granite: *dam*, Wash.	**32**	47	117
Lower Huron Metropolitan Park: Michigan	**5**	42¼	83¾
Lower Kalskag: Alaska	**43**	61	160
Lower Laberge: Yukon	**40**	61	135
Lower L.: California	**36**	41	120
Lower Lake: *sett.*, California	**37**	39	123
Lower Monument: *dam*, Mont.	**32**	47	119
Lower New York Bay: New York	**1**	40½	74
Lower Paia: Hawaii	**128**	21	156

	Page	N	W
Lower Post: B.C.	40	60	129
Lower Red L.: Minnesota	10	48	95
Lower Rouge: *r.*, Michigan	5	42¼	83½
Lowther I.: N.W.T.	44	75	98
Lowville: New York	12	44	76
Loyalsock: *cr.*, Pennsylvania	14	41	77
Loyalton: California	37	40	120
Lubbock: Texas	29	34	102
Lucas Channel: Ontario	18	45	82
Lucerne: California	37	39	123
Lucerne L.: California	35	35	117
Lucerne Valley: *sett.*, California	35	34	117
Lucia: California	34	36	122
Lucin: Utah	33	41	114
Lucknow: Ontario	18	44	82
Lucyville: Newfoundland	9	55	58
Ludington: *& St. Park*, Michigan	20	44	86
Ludlow: California	35	35	116
Ludlow: Vermont	13	43	73
Ludlowville: New York	14	43	77
Ludowici: Georgia	24	32	82
Lufkin: Texas	26	31	95
Lukens Mount: California	7	34¼	118¼
Lulu Island: British Columbia	6	49	123
Lumber City: Georgia	24	32	83
Lumberport: West Virginia	16	39	80
Lumberton: Mississippi	27	31	89
Lumberton: North Carolina	24	35	79
Lumby: British Columbia	41	50	119
Lumpkin: Georgia	27	32	85
Lund: British Columbia	43	50	125
Luray: Virginia	17	39	78
Lutcher: Louisiana	27	30	91
Luverne: Alabama	27	32	86
Lyell I.: British Columbia	41	53	131
Lykens: Pennsylvania	14	41	77
Lyles Wrigley: Tennessee	22	36	87
Lynch: Kentucky	16	37	83
Lynchburg: Virginia	16	37	79
Lynden: Washington	38	49	122
Lyndonville: New York	12	43	78
Lyndonville: Vermont	13	45	72
Lynn: Indiana	21	40	85
Lynn: Massachusetts	2	42½	71
Lynn Canyon Park: B.C.	6	49¼	123
Lynn Haven: Florida	27	30	86
Lynn Woods Res.: Massachusetts	2	42½	71
Lynn Lake: *sett.*, Manitoba	31	57	101
Lynx L.: N.W.T.	44	62	106
Lyon, C.: N.W.T.	44	70	123
Lyon Inlet: N.W.T.	45	66	84
Lyon Mountain: *sett.*, N.Y.	13	45	74
Lyons: Georgia	24	32	82
Lyons: Illinois	4	41¾	87¾
Lyons: Kansas	29	38	98
Lyons: New York	12	43	77
Lyons Falls: *sett.*, New York	13	44	75
Lytton: British Columbia	38	50	122
Lytton: California	37	39	123
Mabank: Texas	26	32	96
Mabton: Washington	39	46	120
McAdoo: Pennsylvania	14	41	76
McAlester: Oklahoma	26	35	96
McAllen: Texas	22	26	98
MacAlpine L.: N.W.T.	44	66	103
McArthur: Ohio	16	39	82
McBee: South Carolina	24	34	80
McBeth Fiord: N.W.T.	45	70	69
McBride: British Columbia	41	53	120
McCarthy: Alaska	43	61	143
McClean: Virginia	2	39	77¼
McCleary: Washington	39	47	123
McCloud: California	36	41	122
McCloud: *r.*, California	36	41	122
McClure L.: California	37	38	120
McColl: South Carolina	24	35	80
McComb: Mississippi	27	31	90
McComb: Ohio	19	41	84
McConnellsburg: Pennsylvania	14	40	78
McConnelsville: Ohio	16	40	82
McCook: Nebraska	28	40	101
McCormick: South Carolina	24	34	82
McDermitt: Nevada	33	42	118
Macdoel: California	36	42	122
McDonald: Pennsylvania	19	40	80
McDonough: Georgia	24	33	84
Macdougall L.: N.W.T.	44	66	99
MacFarlane: *r.*, Saskatchewan	30	58	108
McGee Bend: *dam*, Texas	26	31	94
McGehee: Arkansas	26	34	91
McGill: Nevada	33	39	115
McGrath: Alaska	42	63	156
McGraw: New York	14	43	76
McGregor: *r.*, B.C.	41	54	122
McHenry: Illinois	21	42	88
McIntosh: Alabama	27	31	88
McIntosh: South Dakota	28	46	101
Mackay L.: N.W.T.	44	64	111
McKeansburg: Pennsylvania	14	41	76
McKeesport: Pennsylvania	5	40¼	79¾
McKees Rocks: *sett.*, Pa.	5	40½	80
Mackenzie: British Columbia	41	55	123
McKenzie: Tennessee	27	36	89
Mackenzie: *r.*, N.W.T.	44	67	132
Mackenzie Bay: Yukon	44	69	137
Mackenzie, District of: N.W.T.	44	64	117

	Page	N	W
Mackenzie Mts.: Yukon/N.W.T.	40	64	130
Mackinac I.: Michigan	20	46	85
Mackinac, Straits of: Michigan	20	46	85
Mackinaw: *r.*, Illinois	21	41	89
Mackinaw City: Michigan	20	46	85
McKinley Bay: N.W.T.	44	70	131
McKinley, Mt.: Alaska	42	63	151
McKinley Park: Alaska	42	64	149
McKinney: Texas	26	33	97
McKittrick: California	34	35	120
McKnight: Pennsylvania	5	40½	80
McLennan: Alberta	30	56	117
McLeod: *r.*, Alberta	30	54	117
McLeod Bay: N.W.T.	44	63	110
McLeod Lake: *town*, B.C.	41	55	123
M'Clintock: Manitoba	31	58	94
M'Clintock Chan.: N.W.T.	44	72	102
McLoughlin Bay: N.W.T.	44	68	100
McLoughlin, Mt.: Oregon	36	42	122
M'Clure Strait: N.W.T.	46	75	120
McMillan: Michigan	20	46	86
Macmillan: *r.*, Yukon	40	63	135
McMinnville: Oregon	39	45	123
McMinnville: Tennessee	27	36	86
McMurray *see* Fort McMurray: Alberta	30	57	111
McNary: *dam*, Wash./Oregon	39	46	119
Macomb: Illinois	10	40	91
Macon: Georgia	24	33	84
Macon: Mississippi	27	33	89
McPherson: Kansas	29	38	98
McRae: Georgia	24	32	83
MacRae: Yukon	40	61	135
McTavish Arm: Great Bear L.: N.W.T.	40	66	119
McVicar Arm: Great Bear L.: N.W.T.	40	65	120
Mad: *r.*, California	36	41	124
Madawaska: *r.*, Ontario	12	45	77
Madeline: California	36	41	120
Madera: California	34	37	120
Madill: Oklahoma	26	34	97
Madison: Connecticut	15	41	73
Madison: Florida	25	30	84
Madison: Georgia	24	34	84
Madison: Indiana	10	39	85
Madison: North Carolina	16	36	80
Madison: Ohio	19	42	81
Madison: South Dakota	28	44	97
Madison: West Virginia	16	38	82
Madison: Wisconsin	20	43	89
Madison: *r.*, Montana	28	45	112
Madison Heights: *sett.*, Michigan	5	42½	83
Madisonville: Kentucky	23	37	88
Madisonville: Louisiana	27	30	90
Madisonville: Tennessee	24	36	84
Madisonville: Texas	26	31	96
Madras: Oregon	39	45	121
Madre, Laguna: Texas	22	27	97
Madrid: New York	13	45	75
Madrone: California	37	37	122
Madsen: Ontario	31	51	94
Magalia: California	36	40	122
Magazine Mt.: Arkansas	26	35	94
Magdalen Is.: Québec	9	47	62
Magee: Mississippi	27	32	90
Magnetawan: Ontario	18	46	80
Magnolia: Arkansas	26	33	93
Magnolia: Mississippi	27	31	91
Magnolia: North Carolina	24	35	78
Magog: Québec	13	45	72
Magpie L.: Québec	9	51	65
Maguse L.: N.W.T.	31	62	95
Maguse River: *sett.*, N.W.T.	31	61	94
Mahonoy City: Pennsylvania	14	41	76
Mahoning Creek Res.: Pa.	19	41	79
Mahood Creek: British Columbia	6	49	122¾
Mahwah: New Jersey	15	41	74
Maiden: North Carolina	24	36	81
Maidstone: Ontario	5	42¼	83
Maili: Hawaii	128	21	158
MAINE	8/9	—	—
Maine, Gulf of	11	43	70
Maitland: Ontario	12	45	76
Makapala: Hawaii	128	20	156
Makkovik: Newfoundland	9	55	59
Malaga: New Jersey	14	40	75
Malakoff: Texas	26	32	96
Mala Pascua, Cabo: Puerto Rico	17	18	66
Malartic: Québec	8	48	78
Malden: Massachusetts	2	42½	71
Malheur L.: Oregon	32	43	119
Mallory: West Virginia	16	38	82
Malone: New York	13	45	74
Malta: Montana	28	48	108
Malvern: Arkansas	26	34	93
Malvern: Ohio	19	41	81
Malvern: Pennsylvania	14	40	76
Mamaroneck: New York	1	41	73¾
Mammoth Caves Nat. Park: Ky.	23	37	86
Mammoth Lakes: *sett.*, Calif.	37	38	119
Mamou: Louisiana	26	32	92
Man: West Virginia	16	38	82
Manasquan: New Jersey	15	40	74
Manassas: Virginia	17	39	78
Manati: Puerto Rico	27	18	66
Manawa: Wisconsin	20	44	89

	Page	N	W
Manayunk: Pennsylvania	2	40	75¼
Mancelona: Michigan	20	45	85
Manchester: California	37	39	124
Manchester: Connecticut	15	42	73
Manchester: Georgia	24	33	85
Manchester: Massachusetts	15	43	71
Manchester: Michigan	21	42	84
Manchester: New Hampshire	13	43	71
Manchester: New York	14	43	77
Manchester: Pennsylvania	14	40	77
Manchester: Tennessee	27	35	86
Mandan: North Dakota	28	47	101
Mandeville: Louisiana	27	30	90
Mangum: Oklahoma	29	35	100
Manhattan: Kansas	28	39	97
Manhattan: New York	1	40¾	74
Manhattan Beach: *sett.*, Calif.	7	33¾	118½
Manheim: Pennsylvania	14	40	76
Manicouagan: *r.*, Québec	8	50	69
Manicouagan L.: *& dam*, Québec	8	52	69
Manicouagan Penin.: Québec	9	49	69
Manistee: *& r.*, Michigan	20	44	86
Manistique: Michigan	20	46	86
MANITOBA	31	—	—
Manitoba, Lake: Manitoba	31	51	99
Manitou I.: Michigan	10	47	88
Manitoulin I.: Ontario	18	46	82
Manitouwadge: Ontario	10	49	86
Manitowoc: Wisconsin	20	44	88
Maniwaki: Québec	12	46	76
Manix: California	35	35	117
Mankato: Minnesota	10	44	94
Manley Hot Springs: Alaska	42	65	151
Manlius: New York	14	43	76
Manning: South Carolina	24	34	80
Mannington: West Virginia	16	40	80
Manouane L.: Québec	8	51	71
Manse: Nevada	35	36	116
Mansel I.: N.W.T.	45	62	80
Mansfield: Georgia	24	34	84
Mansfield: Louisiana	26	32	94
Mansfield: Massachusetts	15	42	71
Mansfield: Ohio	19	41	83
Mansfield: Pennsylvania	14	42	77
Mansfield: Washington	39	48	120
Mansfield, Mt.: Vermont	13	45	73
Mansura: Louisiana	26	31	92
Manteca: California	37	38	121
Manteno: Illinois	21	41	88
Manton: Michigan	20	44	85
Mantua: Ohio	19	41	81
Manville: New Jersey	15	41	75
Many: Louisiana	26	32	93
Maple: Ontario	5	43¾	79½
Maple: *r.*, Michigan	20	43	85
Maple Creek: *town*, Sask.	30	50	109
Maple Shade: New Jersey	2	40	75
Maplewood: Minnesota	3	45	93
Marathon: Ontario	10	49	86
Marblehead: Massachusetts	2	42½	69¾
Marblehead: Ohio	19	42	83
Marble I.: N.W.T.	45	63	91
Marcellus: New York	14	43	76
Marcy, Mount: New York	13	44	74
Marengo: Illinois	21	42	89
Marfa: Texas	29	30	104
Margaret, C.: N.W.T.	45	70	92
Marian L.: N.W.T.	40	63	116
Marianna: Arkansas	27	35	91
Marianna: Florida	27	31	85
Maria Portage: Manitoba	31	54	95
Marias: *r.*, Montana	28	48	111
Maricopa: California	34	35	119
Marietta: Georgia	24	34	85
Marietta: Ohio	16	39	81
Marietta: Oklahoma	26	34	97
Marietta: Pennsylvania	14	40	77
Marieville: Québec	13	45	73
Marina: California	37	37	122
Marina del Rey: California	7	34	118½
Marine City: Michigan	19	43	83
Marinette: Wisconsin	20	45	88
Marin Pen.: California	6	37¾	122½
Marion: Alabama	27	33	87
Marion: Indiana	21	41	86
Marion: Iowa	10	42	92
Marion: Massachusetts	15	42	71
Marion: New York	12	43	77
Marion: North Carolina	24	36	82
Marion: Ohio	19	41	83
Marion: South Carolina	24	34	79
Marion: Virginia	16	37	82
Marion: Wisconsin	20	45	89
Marion, L.: South Carolina	24	34	80
Mariposa: California	37	38	120
Mark Tree: Arkansas	27	36	90
Markesan: Wisconsin	20	44	89
Markham: Ontario	5	43¾	79¼
Markham Bay: N.W.T.	45	63	72
Markleeville: California	37	39	120
Marks: Mississippi	27	34	90
Marksville: Louisiana	26	31	92
Marlboro: Massachusetts	15	42	72
Marlboro: New Hampshire	13	43	72
Marlboro: New York	15	42	74
Marlin: Texas	26	31	97
Marlinton: West Virginia	16	38	80

	Page	N	W
Marmet: West Virginia	16	38	82
Marmora: Ontario	12	44	78
Marmot Is.: Alaska	43	58	152
Maro Reef: Hawaii	128	25	171
Marquette: Michigan	10	47	87
Marquette Park: Illinois	4	41¾	87¾
Marrero: Louisiana	3	30	90
Mars: Pennsylvania	19	41	80
Marseilles: Illinois	21	41	89
Marshall: California	37	38	123
Marshall: Michigan	21	42	85
Marshall: Texas	26	33	94
Marshall Ford: *dam*, Texas	29	30	98
Marshalltown: Iowa	10	42	93
Marshallville: Georgia	24	32	84
Marsh I.: Louisiana	26	30	92
Marshville: North Carolina	24	35	80
Marsoui: Québec	9	49	66
Marston Lake: Colorado	3	39½	105
Mart: Texas	26	32	97
Martha's Vineyard: *i.*, Mass.	15	41	71
Martin: Texas	26	31	97
Martinez: California	37	38	122
Martin L.: & *dam*, Alabama	27	33	86
Martins Beach: *sett.*, California	37	37	122
Martinsburg: Pennsylvania	14	40	78
Martinsburg: West Virginia	17	39	78
Martins Ferry: Ohio	16	40	81
Martinsville: Virginia	16	37	80
Marvell: Arkansas	27	35	91
Mary Jones B.: N.W.T.	45	70	92
MARYLAND	17	—	—
Maryneal: Texas	29	32	100
Mary's Harbour: Newfoundland	9	52	56
Marysville: California	37	39	122
Marysville: Michigan	19	43	82
Marysville: Ohio	19	40	83
Marysville: Pennsylvania	14	40	77
Marysville: Washington	38	48	122
Maryville: Tennessee	24	36	84
Mason: Michigan	21	43	84
Mason: Nevada	37	39	119
Mason City: Illinois	21	40	90
Mason City: Iowa	10	43	93
Masontown: Pennsylvania	16	40	80
Masontown: West Virginia	16	40	80
Massabesic L.: New Hampshire	13	43	71
MASSACHUSETTS	15	—	—
Massachusetts Bay	15	42	71
Massachusetts Turnpike	15	42	73
Massack: California	36	40	121
Massacre L.: Nevada	36	42	120
Massena: New York	13	45	75
Masset: British Columbia	41	45	132
Massillon: Ohio	19	41	82
Masson: Québec	13	46	75
Mastic Beach: *town*, N.Y.	15	41	73
Matagami: Québec	8	50	78
Matagami, L.: Québec	8	50	78
Matagorda Bay: Texas	22	28	96
Matagorda I.: Texas	22	28	97
Matane: Québec	9	49	68
Matanuska: Alaska	43	62	149
Matawan: New Jersey	15	40	74
Mather: California	37	38	120
Mather: Pennsylvania	16	40	80
Matheson: Ontario	11	49	80
Matoake: West Virginia	16	37	81
Mattagami: *r.*, Ontario	11	50	82
Mattaponi: *r.*, Virginia	17	38	77
Mattawa: Ontario	12	46	79
Mattawin: *r.*, Québec	13	47	73
Mattawin Res.: Québec	13	47	74
Mattituck: New York	15	41	73
Mattoon: Illinois	21	39	88
Maud: Oklahoma	26	35	97
Maui: *i.*, Hawaii	128	21	156
Maumee: Ohio	19	42	84
Maumee: *r.*, Ohio/Indiana	19	41	84
Maunaloa: Hawaii	128	21	157
Maunoir, L.: N.W.T.	44	68	126
Maupin: Oregon	39	45	121
Maurepas, L.: Louisiana	27	30	91
Maxinkuckee, L.: Indiana	21	41	86
Maxton: North Carolina	24	35	79
Maxwell: California	37	39	122
Maxwell Bay: N.W.T.	45	75	89
Mayagüez: Puerto Rico	27	18	67
Maybeury: West Virginia	16	37	81
Mayfield: Kentucky	22	37	89
Mayfield Res.: Washington	39	47	123
Maynard: Massachusetts	15	42	71
Maynard: Washington	38	48	123
Mayo: Florida	25	30	83
Mayo: Yukon	40	64	136
Mayo L.: Yukon	40	64	135
Mayo Landing: Yukon	40	64	136
Mayville: New York	19	42	80
Mayville: Wisconsin	20	44	89
Maywood: Illinois	4	41¾	87¾
Mead: Washington	32	48	117
Meade: *r.*, Alaska	42	70	157
Meade River: *sett.*, Alaska	42	70	157
Mead, L.: Nevada	35	36	115
Meadowbrook: West Virginia	16	39	80
Meadow Lake Prov. Park: Sask.	30	55	109
Meadow Lands: Pennsylvania	19	40	80

	Page	N	W
Meadville: Mississippi	27	31	91
Meadville: Pennsylvania	19	42	80
Mealy Mts.: Newfoundland	9	54	59
Meander River: *sett.*, Alberta	30	59	118
Meares, C.: Oregon	39	46	124
Mebane: North Carolina	24	36	79
Mecca: California	35	34	116
Mechanicsburg: Ohio	19	40	84
Mechanicsburg: Pennsylvania	14	40	77
Medfield: Massachusetts	2	42½	71
Medford: New Jersey	15	40	75
Medford: Oklahoma	29	37	98
Medford: Oregon	36	42	123
Medford Station: New York	15	41	73
Medfra: Alaska	42	63	155
Medicine Hat: Alberta	30	50	111
Medicine Lake: Minnesota	3	45	93½
Medina: New York	12	43	78
Medway: Massachusetts	15	42	71
Medway: Ohio	21	40	84
Meelpaeg L.: Newfoundland	9	48	58
Megantic Mtn.: Québec	13	45	71
Meherrin: *r.*, Virginia	17	37	78
Meigs: Georgia	25	31	84
Meiners Oaks: California	34	34	119
Mekoryuk: Alaska	43	60	116
Melbourne: Florida	25	28	81
Melbourne I.: N.W.T.	44	68	105
Melfort: Saskatchewan	30	53	105
Melones: California	37	38	120
Melones Res.: California	37	38	121
Melrose: Massachusetts	2	42½	71
Melrose: Montana	32	36	113
Melrose Park: *town*, Illinois	4	42	87¾
Melton Hill: *dam*, Tennessee	24	36	84
Melville: Louisiana	26	31	92
Melville: Saskatchewan	30	51	103
Melville Bay: Greenland	61	75	63
Melville Hills: N.W.T.	44	69	122
Melville, L.: Newfoundland	9	54	60
Melville Penin.: N.W.T.	45	68	84
Melville Sound: N.W.T.	44	68	108
Melvindale: Michigan	5	42¼	83¼
Memorial Park: Texas	3	29¾	95¾
Memphis: Tennessee	27	35	90
Memphremagog, L.: Québec	13	45	72
Mena: Arkansas	26	35	94
Menash: Wisconsin	20	44	88
Mendenhall: Mississippi	27	32	90
Mendenhall, C.: Alaska	43	60	166
Mendham: New Jersey	15	41	75
Mendocino: California	37	39	124
Mendota: California	37	37	120
Mendota: Illinois	21	42	89
Mendota: Minnesota	3	44¾	93¼
Mendota, L.: Wisconsin	20	43	89
Menihek: Newfoundland	9	54	67
Menihek Lakes: Newfoundland	9	54	67
Menlo Park: *sett.*, California	6	37½	122¼
Menominee: Michigan	20	45	88
Menominee: *r.*, Mich./Wis.	20	45	88
Menomonee Falls: *town*, Wis.	20	43	88
Mentasta: Alaska	42	63	144
Mentone: California	25	34	117
Mentor-on-the-Lake: Ohio	19	42	81
Meramec: *r.*, Missouri	10	38	91
Merced: California	37	37	120
Merced: *r.*, California	37	37	121
Merced, L.: California	6	37¾	122½
Mercer: Pennsylvania	19	41	80
Mercer: Wisconsin	20	46	90
Mercer Island: Washington	6	47½	122¼
Mercersburg: Pennsylvania	14	40	78
Merchants Bay: N.W.T.	45	67	63
Meredith: New Hampshire	13	44	72
Meriden: Connecticut	15	42	73
Meridian: California	37	39	122
Meridian: Mississippi	27	32	89
Meridan: Pennsylvania	19	41	80
Merrill: Oregon	36	42	122
Merrill: Wisconsin	20	45	90
Merrimack: *r.*, N.H.	13	43	72
Merritt: British Columbia	38	50	121
Merrit, L.: California	6	37¾	122¼
Merryville: Louisiana	26	31	94
Merwin, L.: *& Res.*, Washington	39	46	122
Mesa: Arizona	33	33	112
Mesabi Range: Minnesota	10	47	93
Mesa Grande: California	35	33	117
Mesa Verde Nat Park: Colo.	29	37	108
Mesgouez L.: Québec	8	51	75
Meshik: Alaska	43	57	159
Mesick: Michigan	20	44	86
Mesquite: Texas	26	33	97
Mesquite L.: California	35	36	116
Metairie: Louisiana	3	30	90¼
Metaline: Washington	32	49	118
Metchosin: British Columbia	38	48	124
Methow: *r.*, Washington	38	48	120
Methuen: Massachusetts	15	43	71
Metlakatla: Alaska	41	55	132
Mexia: Texas	26	32	97
Mexican Hat: Utah	33	37	110
Mexico: Missouri	10	39	92
Mexico: New York	12	43	76
Meyersdale: Pennsylvania	16	40	79
Miami: Arizona	33	33	111

	Page	N	W
Miami: Florida	25	26	80
Miami: Oklahoma	29	37	95
Miami: *r.*, Ohio	19	40	84
Miami Beach: *town*, Florida	25	26	80
Miami Canal: Florida	25	26	81
Miamisburg: Ohio	21	40	84
Mica: *cr.*, British Columbia	41	52	119
Michelsen, C.: N.W.T.	44	71	103
Michelson, Mt.: Alaska	42	69	144
MICHIGAN	10	44	85
Michigan City: Indiana	21	42	87
Michigan, Lake	20/21	—	—
Michikamau L.: Newfoundland	9	54	64
Michipicoten Harbour: Ontario	10	48	85
Michoud: Louisiana	3	30	90
Middleboro: Massachusetts	15	42	71
Middleburg: New York	15	43	74
Middleburg: Pennsylvania	14	41	77
Middlebury: Vermont	13	44	73
Middlefield: Ohio	19	41	81
Middle Fork: *r.*, Calif.	36/37	40	121
Middle Fork: *r.*, Illinois	21	40	88
Middle Fork: *r.*, Virginia	16	37	82
Middle Granville: New York	13	43	73
Middle L.: California	36	41	120
Middleport: New York	12	43	78
Middleport: Ohio	16	39	82
Middle Rouge: *r.*, Michigan	5	42¼	83¼
Middlesboro: Kentucky	24	37	84
Middlesex Falls Res.: Mass.	2	42½	71
Middleton: Wisconsin	20	43	90
Middleton I.: Alaska	43	59	146
Middletown: California	37	39	123
Middletown: Connecticut	15	42	73
Middletown: Delaware	17	39	76
Middletown: Indiana	21	40	86
Middletown: New York	15	41	74
Middletown: Ohio	21	40	84
Middletown: Pennsylvania	14	40	77
Mid Island: *cr.*, West Virginia	16	39	81
Midland: Maryland	17	40	79
Midland: Michigan	20	44	84
Midland: Ontario	18	45	80
Midland: Oregon	36	42	122
Midland: Pennsylvania	19	41	80
Midland: Texas	29	32	102
Midland City: Alabama	27	31	85
Midlothian: Texas	26	32	97
Mid Loup: *r.*, Nebraska	28	42	100
Midpines: California	37	38	120
Midway: British Columbia	41	49	119
Midway: *is.*, Hawaii	128	20	177
Midway Park: North Carolina	24	35	77
Midwest: Wyoming	28	43	106
Mifflinburg: Pennsylvania	14	41	77
Milagra Valley: California	6	37½	122½
Milan: Michigan	19	42	84
Milan: Ohio	19	41	83
Milan: Tennessee	27	36	89
Milbank: South Dakota	28	45	97
Miles City: Montana	28	46	106
Milford: Connecticut	15	41	73
Milford: Delaware	17	39	75
Milford: Illinois	21	41	88
Milford: Massachusetts	15	42	72
Milford: New Hampshire	13	43	72
Milford: Pennsylvania	14	41	75
Milk: *r.*, Alberta/Montana	28	49	109
Mill: *cr.*, California	36	40	122
Millbrae: California	6	37½	122¼
Millbury: Massachusetts	15	42	72
Mill City: Nevada	33	41	118
Mill City: Oregon	39	45	122
Mill Creek: *sett.*, California	36	40	122
Milledgeville: Georgia	24	33	83
Milledgeville: Illinois	21	42	90
Mille Îles: *r.*, Québec	2	45¾	73¾
Mille Lacs L.: Minnesota	10	46	94
Millen: Georgia	24	33	82
Millersburg: Ohio	19	41	82
Millers Falls: *sett.*, Mass.	15	43	73
Millersville: Pennsylvania	14	40	76
Millerton: New York	15	42	74
Mill Hall: Pennsylvania	14	41	78
Millington: Michigan	19	43	84
Millinocket: Maine	8	46	69
Millis: Massachusetts	15	42	71
Mill I.: N.W.T.	45	64	78
Millsaps: California	37	40	123
Millsboro: Pennsylvania	16	40	80
Mills L.: Northwest Territories	40	61	119
Mill Valley: *town*, California	6	38	122½
Millville: New Jersey	14	39	75
Milne Inlet: N.W.T.	45	72	81
Milpitas: California	37	37	122
Milroy: Pennsylvania	14	41	78
Milton: Delaware	17	39	75
Milton: Florida	27	31	87
Milton: Massachusetts	2	42½	71
Milton Ontario	12	44	80
Milton: Pennsylvania	14	41	77
Milton: Vermont	13	45	73
Milton: Washington	39	47	122
Milton-Freewater: Oregon	32	46	118
Milwaukee: Wisconsin	20	43	88
Mimico: Ontario	5	43½	79½
Mina: California	36	40	123

	Page	N	W
Minas Channel: Nova Scotia	**9**	45	65
Minden: Louisiana	**26**	33	93
Minden: Nevada	**37**	39	120
Mine Centre: Ontario	**10**	49	93
Mineola: Texas	**26**	33	96
Mineral: California	**36**	40	122
Mineral: Virginia	**17**	38	78
Mineral City: Ohio	**19**	41	81
Mineral Ridge: *sett.*, Ohio	**19**	41	81
Mineral Wells: Texas	**29**	33	98
Minersville: Pennsylvania.	**14**	41	76
Minerva: Ohio	**19**	41	81
Mineville: New York	**13**	44	74
Mingan: Québec	**9**	50	64
Mingo Junction: Ohio	**19**	40	81
Minneapolis: Minnesota	**10**	45	93
Minnedosa: Manitoba	**31**	50	100
Minnehaha Cr.: Minnesota	**3**	44¾	93¼
Minnehaha Park: Minnesota	**3**	44¾	93¼
MINNESOTA	**10**	—	—
Minnesota: *r.*, Minnesota	**10**	45	95
Minnesota: Minnesota	**3**	45	93½
Minnetonka: Minnesota	**3**	45	93½
Minocqua: Wisconsin	**20**	46	90
Minonk: Illinois	**21**	41	89
Minot: North Dakota	**28**	48	101
Minster: Ohio	**19**	40	84
Minto: Alaska	**42**	65	149
Minto: Yukon	**40**	63	137
Minto Head: N.W.T.	**44**	73	103
Minto Inlet: N.W.T.	**44**	71	117
Minto L.: Québec	**8**	57	75
Minton: Saskatchewan	**30**	49	105
Minute Man N.Hist. P.: Mass.	**2**	42½	71¼
Miquelon: *i.*	**9**	47	56
Mirage L.: California	**35**	35	118
Mishawaka: Indiana	**21**	42	86
Missanabie: Ontario	**10**	48	84
Missinaibi: *r.*, Ontario	**11**	50	83
Mission City: British Columbia	**38**	49	122
Missisa L.: Ontario	**31**	52	85
Missisquoi: *r.*, Vermont	**13**	45	73
Mississagi: *r.*, Ontario	**10**	47	83
Mississagi Prov. Park: Ont.	**18**	47	83
Mississauga: Ontario	**12**	44	80
Mississinewa: *r.*, Indiana	**21**	40	85
MISSISSIPPI	**27**	—	—
Mississippi: *r.*,	**22**	31	92
Mississippi Sound	**27**	30	89
Missoula: Montana	**32**	47	114
MISSOURI	**10**	38	92
Missouri: *r.*	**28**	39	94
Missouri City: Texas	**26**	30	96
Mist: Oregon	**39**	46	123
Mistassibi: *r.*, Québec	**8**	49	72
Mistassini L.: Québec	**8**	51	74
Mistassini Post: Québec	**8**	50	74
Mitchell: Ontario	**18**	43	81
Mitchell: South Dakota	**28**	44	98
Mitchell, Mt.: North Carolina	**24**	36	82
Moab: Utah	**33**	39	110
Moberley: Missouri	**10**	39	92
Mobile: Alabama	**27**	31	88
Mobile Bay: Alabama	**27**	30	88
Mobridge: South Dakota	**28**	46	100
Mocksville: North Carolina	**24**	36	81
Moclips: Washington	**39**	47	124
Modesto: California	**37**	38	121
Mogollon Plateau: Arizona	**33**	35	111
Mohawk: *r.*, New York	**15**	43	75
Mohican: *r.*, Ohio	**19**	40	82
Moira: New York	**13**	45	75
Moisie: Québec	**9**	50	66
Moisie: *r.*, Québec	**9**	51	66
Mojave: California	**35**	35	118
Mojave: *r.*, California	**35**	35	117
Mojave Desert: California	**35**	35	117
Mokelumne: *r.*, California	**37**	38	120
Mokelumne Aqueduct: Calif.	**6**	38	122
Mokelumne Hill: *sett.*, Calif.	**37**	38	121
Molalla: Oregon	**39**	38	123
Molokai: *i.*, Hawaii	**128**	21	157
Molson L.: Manitoba	**31**	54	97
Momence: Illinois	**21**	41	88
Mona, Isla: Puerto Rico	**27**	18	68
Moncton: New Brunswick	**9**	46	65
Monessen: Pennsylvania	**19**	40	80
Monmouth: Illinois	**10**	41	91
Monmouth: Oregon	**39**	45	123
Monocacy: *r.*, Maryland	**17**	40	77
Mono L.: California	**37**	38	119
Mono Lake: *sett.*, California	**37**	38	119
Monomoy I.: Massachusetts	**15**	42	70
Monon: Indiana	**21**	41	87
Monongahela: Pennsylvania	**19**	40	80
Monongahela: *r.*, W. Va./Pa.	**16**	40	80
Monroe: California	**36**	40	124
Monroe: Georgia	**24**	34	84
Monroe: Louisiana	**26**	33	92
Monroe: Michigan	**19**	42	83
Monroe: New York	**15**	41	74
Monroe: North Carolina	**24**	35	81
Monroe: Washington	**39**	48	122
Monroe: Wisconsin	**21**	43	90
Monroeville: Alabama	**27**	32	87
Monroeville: Indiana	**21**	41	85
Monroeville: Ohio	**19**	41	83

	Page	N	W
Monroeville: Pennsylvania	**19**	40	80
Montague: California	**36**	42	123
Montague: Michigan	**20**	43	86
Montague I.: Alaska	**43**	60	148
MONTANA	**28**	—	—
Montana: Alaska	**43**	62	150
Montara: California	**6**	37½	122½
Montara Mtn.: California	**6**	37½	122½
Montara Pt.: California	**6**	37½	122½
Montauk: New York	**15**	41	72
Montauk Point: New York	**15**	41	72
Mont Belvieu: Texas	**26**	30	95
Montclair: New Jersey	**1**	40¾	74¼
Mont Clare: *sett.*, Pennsylvania	**14**	40	76
Monteagle: Tennessee	**27**	35	86
Montebello: California	**7**	34	118
Montebello: Québec	**13**	46	75
Montello: Wisconsin	**20**	44	89
Monterey: California	**37**	37	122
Monterey Bay: California	**37**	37	122
Monterey Park: *town*, California	**7**	34	118
Monte Rio: California	**37**	38	123
Montesano: Washington	**39**	47	124
Monte Vista: Colorado	**28**	38	106
Montezuma: Georgia	**24**	32	84
Montezuma: Indiana	**21**	40	87
Montgomery: Alabama	**27**	32	86
Montgomery: California	**36**	31	122
Montgomery: New York	**15**	42	74
Montgomery: Pennsylvania	**14**	41	77
Montgomery: West Virginia	**16**	38	81
Monticello: Arkansas	**26**	34	92
Monticello: Florida	**25**	31	84
Monticello: Georgia	**24**	33	84
Monticello: Illinois	**21**	40	89
Monticello: Indiana	**21**	41	87
Monticello: Mississippi	**27**	32	90
Monticello: New York	**15**	42	75
Mont-Joli: *town*, Québec	**9**	49	68
Mont-Laurier: *town*, Québec	**13**	47	76
Mont-Louis: *sett.*, Québec	**9**	49	66
Mont-Royal: *sett.*, Québec	**2**	45½	73½
Montmagny: Québec	**8**	47	71
Montmorency: Québec	**13**	47	71
Montour Falls: *sett.*, New York	**14**	42	77
Montpelier: Idaho	**32**	42	111
Montpelier: Indiana	**21**	41	85
Montpelier: Ohio	**21**	42	85
Montpelier: Vermont	**13**	44	73
Montréal: Québec	**13**	46	74
Montreal: *r.*, Ontario	**10**	47	84
Montréal Est: Québec	**2**	45½	73½
Montréal, Île de: Québec	**2**	45½	73½
Montreal L.: Saskatchewan	**30**	54	106
Montréal Nord: Québec	**2**	45½	73½
Montrose: Colorado	**28**	38	108
Montrose: Pennsylvania	**14**	42	76
Montrose-Wilson Beach: Illinois	**4**	42	87½
Mont Tremblant Prov. Park: Qué.	**13**	47	74
Moodus: Connecticut	**15**	42	72
Moorefield: & *r.*, West Virginia	**17**	39	79
Moorestown: New Jersey	**14**	40	75
Mooresville: North Carolina	**24**	36	81
Moorhead: Minnesota	**10**	47	97
Moorhead: Mississippi	**27**	33	91
Moorpark: California	**35**	34	119
Moose: *r.*, Ontario	**11**	51	81
Moosehead L.: Maine	**8**	46	70
Moose Jaw: Saskatchewan	**30**	50	106
Moose L.: Manitoba	**31**	54	100
Moose Pass: Alaska	**43**	60	149
Moosonee: Ontario	**11**	51	81
Moosup: Connecticut	**15**	42	72
Mora: Washington	**38**	48	125
Mora: *r.*, New Mexico	**29**	36	105
Moraga: California	**6**	37¾	122¼
Moravia: New York	**14**	43	76
Morden: Manitoba	**31**	49	98
Moreau: *r.*, South Dakota	**28**	45	102
Morehead City: North Carolina	**24**	35	77
Morena Res.: California	**35**	33	116
Morenci: Arizona	**33**	33	109
Morenci: Michigan	**21**	42	84
Moresby I.: British Columbia	**41**	52	132
Morgan City: Louisiana	**26**	30	91
Morgan Hill: *town*, California	**37**	37	122
Morganton: North Carolina	**24**	36	82
Morgantown: West Virginia	**16**	40	80
Morice L.: British Columbia	**41**	54	128
Morley River: *sett.*, Yukon	**40**	60	133
Moro: Oregon	**39**	46	121
Morocco: Indiana	**21**	41	87
Morrilton: Arkansas	**26**	35	93
Morris: Illinois	**21**	41	88
Morris: Manitoba	**31**	49	97
Morris: Oklahoma	**26**	36	96
Morris Res.: California	**7**	34¼	117¾
Morrisburg: Ontario	**13**	45	75
Morrison: Pennsylvania	**14**	42	79
Morristown: New Jersey	**1**	40¾	74½
Morristown: New York	**12**	45	76
Morristown: Tennessee	**24**	36	83
Morrisville: New York	**14**	43	76
Morrisville: Pennsylvania	**15**	40	75
Morrisville: Vermont	**13**	45	73
Morro Bay: *town*, California	**34**	35	121
Morrow Mtn.: North Carolina	**24**	35	80

	Page	N	W
Morton: Illinois	**21**	41	89
Morton: Washington	**39**	47	122
Morton Grove: Illinois	**4**	42	87¾
Moscow: Idaho	**32**	47	117
Moscow: Pennsylvania	**14**	41	76
Moses Lake: *town*, Washington	**39**	47	119
Moses Point: *sett.*, Alaska	**42**	65	162
Moshannon: Pennsylvania	**14**	41	78
Mosinee: Wisconsin	**20**	45	90
Mosquito Creek Res.: Ohio	**19**	41	81
Moss Beach: *sett.*, California	**6**	37½	122½
Moss Point: *town*, Mississippi	**27**	30	89
Mossy: West Virginia	**16**	38	81
Mosting, C.: Greenland	**47**	64	41
Mould Bay: *sett.*, N.W.T.	**60**	76	119
Moultrie: Georgia	**25**	31	84
Moultrie L.: South Carolina	**24**	33	80
Mound Bayou: Mississippi	**27**	34	91
Moundsville: West Virginia	**16**	40	81
Mountain: Wisconsin	**20**	45	88
Mountain: *r.*, N.W.T.	**40**	65	129
Mountainair: New Mexico	**29**	35	106
Mountain Center: California	**35**	34	117
Mountain City: Tennessee	**16**	36	82
Mountain Home: Idaho	**32**	43	116
Mountain Parkway: Kentucky	**23**	37	83
Mountain Point: *sett.*, Alaska	**41**	55	132
Mountain Sheep: *dam*, Oregon/Idaho	**32**	46	117
Mountain Spring: California	**35**	33	116
Mountaintop: Pennsylvania	**14**	41	76
Mountain View: Alaska	**43**	61	150
Mountain View: California	**6**	37½	122
Mountain Village: Alaska	**43**	62	164
Mount Airy: *sett.*, Maryland	**17**	39	77
Mount Airy: *town*, N.C.	**16**	37	81
Mount Angel: *sett.*, Oregon	**39**	45	123
Mount Assiniboine Prov. Park: British Columbia	**30**	50	116
Mount Bullion: *sett.*, California	**37**	38	120
Mount Burke: British Columbia	**6**	49¼	122¾
Mount Carmel: *town*, Pa.	**14**	41	76
Mount Clare: *sett.* West Virginia	**16**	39	80
Mount Clemens: *town*, Mich.	**19**	43	83
Mount Desert I.: Maine	**9**	44	68
Mount Dora: *town*, Florida	**25**	29	82
Mount Eden: California	**6**	37¾	122
Mount Edgecumbe: *sett.*, Alaska	**41**	57	135
Mount Forest: *town*, Ontario	**18**	44	81
Mount Gilead: *sett.*, N.C.	**24**	35	80
Mount Gilead: *town*, Ohio	**19**	41	83
Mount Holly: *town*, New Jersey	**15**	40	75
Mount Holly Springs: *sett.*, Pa.	**14**	40	77
Mount Hope: *sett.*, W. Va.	**16**	38	81
Mount Horeb: *sett.*, Wisconsin	**20**	43	90
Mount Jewett: *sett.*, Pa.	**14**	42	79
Mount Kisco: *town*, New York	**15**	41	74
Mountlake Terrace: Washington	**6**	47¾	122¼
Mount Lebanon: Pennsylvania	**5**	40¼	80
Mount McKinley Nat. Park: Alaska	**42**	63	150
Mount Meadows Res.: Calif.	**36**	40	121
Mount Morris: *town*, Illinois	**21**	42	89
Mount Morris: *town*, New York	**14**	43	78
Mount Olive: *town*, N.C.	**24**	35	78
Mount Pleasant: *town*, Mich.	**20**	44	85
Mount Pleasant: *town*, Pa.	**19**	40	80
Mount Pleasant: *town*, Tenn.	**27**	36	87
Mount Pleasant: *town*, Texas	**26**	33	95
Mount Prospect: *town*, Illinois	**4**	42	88
Mount Pulaski: *sett.*, Illinois	**21**	40	89
Mount Rainier Nat. Park: Wash.	**39**	47	122
Mount Revelstoke Nat. Park: B.C.	**41**	51	118
Mount Rushmore Nat. Memorial: South Dakota	**28**	44	103
Mount Savage: *sett.*, Md.	**17**	40	79
Mount Seymour Prov. Park: B.C.	**6**	49¼	123
Mount Shasta: *sett.*, California	**36**	41	122
Mount Sterling: Ohio	**16**	40	83
Mount Union: *town*, Pa.	**14**	40	78
Mount Vernon: *sett.*, Georgia	**24**	32	83
Mount Vernon: *sett.*, Indiana	**10**	38	88
Mount Vernon: *sett.*, Texas	**26**	33	95
Mount Vernon: *town*, Illinois	**10**	38	89
Mount Vernon: *town*, New York	**1**	41	73¾
Mount Vernon: *town*, Ohio	**19**	40	82
Mount Vernon: *town*, Wash.	**38**	48	122
Mount Victory: *sett.*, Ohio	**19**	41	84
Moweagua: Illinois	**21**	40	89
Mud L.: Nevada	**36**	41	119
Mud L.: Nevada	**36**	42	120
Muir: Michigan	**20**	43	85
Mukilteo: Washington	**39**	48	122
Mukwonago: Wisconsin	**21**	43	88
Mulberry: Florida	**25**	28	82
Mulberry: Indiana	**21**	40	87
Mulchatna: *r.*, Alaska	**43**	60	156
Muleshoe: Texas	**29**	34	103
Mulgrave: Nova Scotia	**9**	46	61
Mulgrave Hills: Alaska	**42**	68	163
Mullens: West Virginia	**16**	38	81
Mullett L.: Michigan	**20**	45	85
Mullica: *r.*, New Jersey	**15**	40	75
Mullins: South Carolina	**24**	34	79
Muncho Lake: *sett.*, B.C.	**40**	59	126
Muncie: Indiana	**21**	40	85
Muncy: Pennsylvania	**14**	41	77

	Page	N	W
Noranda: Québec	**8**	48	79
Norco: California	**35**	34	118
Norco: Louisiana	**27**	30	90
Nordyke: Nevada	**37**	39	119
Norfolk: Arkansas	**26**	36	92
Norfolk: Nebraska	**28**	42	97
Norfolk: New York	**13**	45	75
Norfolk: Virginia	**17**	37	76
Norfolk, L.: Arkansas	**10**	36	92
Norfork: *dam*, Arkansas	**22**	37	92
Normal: Illinois	**21**	40	89
Norman: Oklahoma	**26**	35	97
Normangee: Texas	**26**	31	96
Norman Wells: N.W.T.	**40**	65	127
Normetal: Québec	**8**	49	80
Norris, L.: *& dam*, Tennessee	**24**	36	84
Norristown: Pennsylvania	**2**	40	75¼
North: South Carolina	**24**	34	81
North: *r.*, Newfoundland	**9**	57	63
North: *r.*, Virginia	**16**	38	79
North Adams: Massachusetts	**15**	43	73
Northampton: Massachusetts	**15**	42	73
North Anna: *r.*, Virginia	**17**	38	78
North Arm: *r.*, B.C.	**6**	49¼	123
North Attleboro: Massachusetts	**15**	42	71
North Augusta: South Carolina	**24**	34	82
North Battleford: Saskatchewan	**30**	53	108
North Bay: *town*, Ontario	**18**	46	79
North Bend: Oregon	**32**	43	124
North Bend: Pennsylvania	**14**	41	78
North Bennington: Vermont	**13**	43	73
North Bergen: New Jersey	**1**	40¾	74
North Berwick: Maine	**15**	43	71
North Billerica: Massachusetts	**15**	43	71
North Brook: Illinois	**4**	42¼	87¾
North Brookfield: Massachusetts	**15**	42	72
North Canadian: *r.*, Oklahoma	**29**	37	103
North, C.: Nova Scotia	**9**	47	60
North Caribou L.: Ontario	**31**	53	91
NORTH CAROLINA	**24**	—	—
North Cascades Nat. Park: Washington	**32**	49	121
North Channel: Ontario	**18**	46	83
North Chelmsford: Mass.	**15**	43	71
North Chicago: Illinois	**4**	42¼	87¾
North Collins: New York	**19**	43	79
NORTH DAKOTA	**28**	—	—
North East: Pennsylvania	**19**	42	80
Northeast, C.: Alaska	**42**	63	169
North Easton: Massachusetts	**15**	42	71
Northern Indian L.: Manitoba	**31**	57	98
Northfield: Massachusetts	**15**	43	72
Northfield: Minnesota	**10**	44	93
Northfield: Ohio	**19**	41	82
Northfield: Vermont	**13**	44	73
North Forest: *sett.*, Texas	**3**	30	95¼
North Fork: California	**37**	37	120
North Fork: *r.*, Kansas	**28**	40	100
North Fork: *r.*, Virginia	**16**	37	82
North Fork American: *r.*, Calif.	**37**	39	121
Northgate: Saskatchewan	**30**	49	102
Northglenn: Colorado	**3**	40	105
North Grosvenor Dale: Conn.	**15**	42	72
North Haven: Connecticut	**15**	41	73
North Hollywood: California	**7**	34¼	118½
North Judson: Indiana	**21**	41	87
North Knife L.: Manitoba	**31**	58	97
Northlake: Illinois	**4**	42	88
Northland: Michigan	**20**	46	88
North Las Vegas: Nevada	**35**	36	115
North Lewisburg: Ohio	**19**	40	84
North Liberty: Indiana	**21**	42	86
North Little Rock: Arkansas	**26**	35	92
North Loup: *r.*, Nebraska	**28**	42	99
North Manchester: Indiana	**21**	41	86
North Manitou I.: Michigan	**20**	45	86
North Mtn.: West Virginia	**17**	39	79
North Oaks: *sett.*, Minnesota	**3**	45	93¼
North Olmstead: Ohio	**19**	41	82
North Oxford: Massachusetts	**15**	42	72
North Park: Pennsylvania	**5**	40¾	80
North Platte: Nebraska	**28**	41	101
North Platte: *r.*, Wyo./Nebr.	**28**	41	103
North Point: Michigan	**18**	45	83
North Point: P.E.I.	**9**	47	64
Northport: Michigan	**20**	45	86
Northport: New York	**15**	41	73
North Richland: Washington	**39**	46	119
North Ridgeville: Ohio	**19**	41	82
North Rose: New York	**12**	43	77
North Royalton: Ohio	**19**	41	82
North San Juan: California	**37**	39	121
North Saskatchewan: *r.*, Alberta/Saskatchewan	**30**	53	107
North Syracuse: New York	**12**	43	76
North Thompson: *r.*, B.C.	**38**	51	120
North Troy: Vermont	**13**	45	72
Northumberland: Pennsylvania	**14**	41	77
Northumberland Strait	**9**	46	63
North Vancouver: B.C.	**6**	49¾	122¾
Northville: Michigan	**5**	42½	83¾
Northville: New York	**13**	43	74
Northway: Alaska	**42**	63	142
North West River: *sett.*, Nfld.	**9**	54	60
NORTHWEST TERRITORIES	**44/45**	—	—
North Wilkesboro: N.C.	**24**	36	81

	Page	N	W
North York: Ontario	**5**	43¾	79½
Norton: Virginia	**16**	37	83
Norton Bay: Alaska	**42**	65	161
Norton Sound: Alaska	**42**	64	164
Norwalk: California	**7**	34	118
Norwalk: Connecticut	**15**	41	73
Norwalk: Ohio	**19**	41	83
Norway: Michigan	**20**	46	88
Norway Bay: N.W.T.	**44**	71	105
Norway House: Manitoba	**31**	54	98
Norwich: Connecticut	**15**	42	72
Norwich: New York	**14**	43	76
Norwich: Ontario	**19**	43	81
Norwood: Massachusetts	**15**	42	71
Norwood: New York	**13**	45	75
Norwood: North Carolina	**24**	35	80
Notikewin: *r.*, Alberta	**30**	57	118
Notleys Ldg.: California	**34**	36	122
Notre Dame Bay: Newfoundland	**9**	50	55
Notre Dame Mts.; Québec	**9**	48	67
Nottawasaga Bay: Ontario	**18**	45	80
Nottaway: *r.*, Québec	**8**	51	78
Nottely: *dam.*, Tennessee	**24**	35	84
Nottingham I.: N.W.T.	**45**	63	78
Nottingham Island: *sett.*, N.W.T.	**45**	63	78
Nottoway: *r.*, Virginia	**17**	37	78
Nouvelle France, C. de la (C. Weggs): Québec	**45**	62	74
NOVA SCOTIA	**9**	—	—
Novato: California	**37**	38	123
Nova Zembla I.: N.W.T.	**45**	72	75
Noxon Rapids: *dam*, Montana	**32**	48	116
Noxubee: *r.*, Mississippi	**27**	33	89
Noyo: California	**37**	39	124
Nubieber: California	**36**	41	121
Nueces: *r.*, Texas	**22**	28	98
Nueltin L.: N.W.T.	**31**	60	99
Nulato: Alaska	**42**	65	158
Nunaksaluk I.: Newfoundland	**9**	56	60
Nunapitchuk: Alaska	**43**	61	163
Nunda: New York	**14**	43	78
Nunivak I.: Alaska	**43**	60	166
Nushagak: Alaska	**43**	59	158
Nushagak: *r.*, Alaska	**43**	59	157
Nushagak Pen.: Alaska	**43**	58	159
Nuyakuk L.: Alaska	**43**	60	158
Nyac: Alaska	**43**	61	160
Nye: Montana	**28**	45	110
Nyssa: Oregon	**32**	44	117
Oahe: *dam*, South Dakota	**28**	44	100
Oahe Res.: South Dakota	**28**	45	100
Oahu: *i.*, Hawaii	**128**	21	158
Oak Bluffs: Massachusetts	**15**	41	71
Oakdale: California	**37**	38	121
Oakdale: Louisiana	**26**	31	93
Oakes: North Dakota	**28**	46	98
Oakfield: New York	**12**	43	78
Oakford: Pennsylvania	**14**	40	75
Oak Grove: Louisiana	**26**	33	91
Oak Harbor: Ohio	**19**	42	83
Oak Harbor: Washington	**38**	48	123
Oak Hill: *sett.*, Ohio	**16**	39	83
Oak Hill: West Virginia	**16**	38	81
Oakhurst: California	**37**	37	120
Oakland: California	**6**	37¾	122¼
Oakland: Illinois	**21**	40	88
Oakland: Maryland	**16**	39	79
Oakland Inner Harbor: California	**6**	37¾	122¼
Oak Lawn: Illinois	**4**	41¾	87¾
Oakley: California	**37**	38	122
Oakmont: Pennsylvania	**19**	41	80
Oak Park: Illinois	**4**	42	87¾
Oak Park: *sett*, Michigan	**5**	42½	83
Oak Ridge: *town*, Tennessee	**24**	36	84
Oak Run: California	**36**	41	122
Oak Street Beach: Illinois	**4**	42	87½
Oak View: California	**34**	34	119
Oakville: Connecticut	**15**	42	73
Oakville: Ontario	**12**	43	80
Oakwood: Ohio	**21**	40	84
Oakwood: Texas	**26**	32	96
Oba: Ontario	**10**	49	84
Oban: Saskatchewan	**30**	52	108
Oberlin: Louisiana	**26**	31	93
Oberlin: Ohio	**19**	41	82
Obion: *r.*, Tennessee	**27**	36	90
Ocala: Florida	**25**	29	82
Ocean City: Maryland	**17**	38	75
Ocean City: New Jersey	**15**	39	75
Ocean City: Washington	**39**	47	124
Ocean Falls: *sett.*, B.C.	**41**	52	128
Oceanlake: Oregon	**32**	45	124
Ocean Park: Washington	**39**	46	124
Oceanport: New Jersey	**15**	40	74
Oceanside: California	**35**	33	117
Ocean Springs: Mississippi	**27**	30	89
Ocean View: Delaware	**17**	39	75
Ochlocknee: *r.*, Ga./Florida	**25**	31	84
Ocilla: Georgia	**24**	32	83
Ocmuglee: *r.*, Georgia	**24**	32	83
Ocoees: *dams*, Tennessee	**24**	35	84
Oconee: *r.*, Georgia	**24**	32	82
Oconomowoc: Wisconsin	**20**	43	89
Oconto: Wisconsin	**20**	45	88
Oconto Falls: *sett.*, Wisconsin	**20**	45	88
Ocotillo: Cailfornia	**35**	33	116

	Page	N	W
Odell: Illinois	**21**	41	89
Odenton: Maryland	**17**	39	77
Odessa: Texas	**29**	32	102
Ogallala: Nebraska	**28**	41	102
Ogden: Utah	**33**	41	112
Ogdensburg: New York	**13**	45	76
Ogeechee: *r.*, Georgia	**24**	33	82
Ogilvie Mts : Yukon	**40**	65	138
Oglesby: Illinois	**21**	41	89
Ogoki: Ontario	**31**	52	86
Ogoki: *r.*, Ontario	**31**	51	88
Ogunquit: Maine	**15**	43	71
OHIO	**10/11**	—	—
Ohio: *r.*	**10/11**	37	89
Ohio Turnpike	**21**	42	84
Oil City: California	**35**	35	119
Oil City: Louisiana	**26**	33	94
Oil City: Pennsylvania	**19**	41	80
Oildale: California	**34**	34	119
Ojai: California	**34**	34	119
Ojibway: Ontario	**19**	42	83
Okanagan L.: British Columbia	**38**	50	120
Okanogan: Washington	**38**	48	120
Okanogan: *r.*, Washington	**38**	47	119
Okanogan Range: B.C.	**38**	49	120
Okay: Oklahoma	**27**	36	95
Okeechobee: Florida	**25**	27	81
Okeechobee, L.: Florida	**25**	27	81
Okefenokee Swamp: Georgia	**25**	31	82
Okemah: Oklahoma	**26**	35	96
OKLAHOMA	**29**	—	—
Oklahoma City: Oklahoma	**26**	35	98
Oklawaha: *r.*, Florida	**25**	29	82
Okmuglee: Oklahoma	**26**	36	96
Okolona: Mississippi	**27**	34	89
Okotoks: Alberta	**30**	51	114
Ola: Arkansas	**26**	35	93
Olaa: Hawaii	**128**	20	155
Olancha: California	**35**	36	118
Old Bridge: New Jersey	**15**	40	74
Old Crow: *& r.*, Yukon	**42**	68	140
Old Factory: Québec	**8**	53	79
Old Forge: New York	**13**	44	75
Old Forge: Pennsylvania	**14**	41	76
Old Fort: Pennsylvania	**14**	41	78
Old Harbor: Alaska	**43**	57	153
Old Harbor: *bay*, Mass.	**2**	42¼	71
Old Hickory: Tennessee	**23**	36	87
Oldman: *r.*, Alberta	**30**	50	113
Olds: Alberta	**30**	52	114
Old Saybrook: Connecticut	**15**	41	72
Old Wives L.: Saskatchewan	**30**	50	106
Olean: New York	**14**	42	78
Olene: Oregon	**36**	42	122
Olentangy: *r.*, Ohio	**19**	40	83
Olive Hill: Kentucky	**16**	38	83
Olivehurst: California	**37**	39	122
Oliver: British Columbia	**38**	49	120
Oliver Springs: Tennessee	**24**	36	84
Olmstead Falls: *sett.*, Ohio	**19**	41	82
Olympia: Washington	**39**	47	123
Olympic Mts.: Wash.	**38/39**	48	124
Olympic Nat. Park: Wash.	**38/39**	48	125
Olympus, Mt.: Washington	**39**	48	124
Omaha: Nebraska	**28**	41	96
Omak: Washington	**38**	48	120
Omineca: *r.*, British Columbia	**41**	56	126
Omineca Mts.: B.C.	**41**	56	126
Ommaney, C.: Alaska	**41**	56	135
Ommanney Bay: N.W.T.	**44**	73	101
Omro: Wisconsin	**20**	44	89
Onaway: Michigan	**20**	45	84
O'Neals: California	**37**	37	120
Oneida: New York	**12**	43	76
Oneida: Tennessee	**24**	37	85
Oneida L.: New York	**12**	43	76
O'Neill: Nebraska	**28**	42	99
Oneonta: Alabama	**27**	34	86
Ono: California	**36**	40	123
Onslow Bay: *sett.*, N.C.	**24**	34	77
ONTARIO	**10/11**	—	—
Ontario: California	**7**	34	117¾
Ontario: Ohio	**19**	41	83
Ontario: Oregon	**32**	44	117
Ontario, Lake	**12**	—	—
Onyx: California	**35**	36	118
Oolagah Res.: *& dam*, Oklahoma	**29**	36	96
Ootsa L.: British Columbia	**41**	54	126
Opasquia: Ontario	**31**	53	94
Opelika: Alabama	**27**	33	85
Opelousas: Louisiana	**26**	31	92
Ophir: Alaska	**42**	63	157
Ophir: Colorado	**29**	38	108
Ophir: Oregon	**36**	43	124
Ophir: Utah	**33**	41	112
Opinaca: *r.*, Québec	**8**	52	78
Opiscoteo L.: Québec	**9**	53	68
Opp: Alabama	**27**	31	86
Oradell Res:. New Jersey	**1**	41	74
Orange: California	**7**	33¾	117¾
Orange: Massachusetts	**15**	43	72
Orange: New Jersey	**1**	40¾	74¼
Orange: Texas	**26**	30	94
Orange: Virginia	**17**	38	78
Orangeburg: South Carolina	**24**	33	81
Orange City: Florida	**25**	29	81

	Page	N	W
Orange Grove: California	**34**	37	119
Orangeville: Ontario	**18**	44	80
Orchard Beach: *sett.*, Maryland	**17**	39	77
Orchard City: Texas	**26**	30	96
Orcutt: California	**34**	35	120
Ord Mt.: California	**35**	35	117
OREGON	**32**	—	—
Oregon: Illinois	**21**	42	89
Oregon: Ohio	**19**	42	83
Oregon: Wisconsin	**20**	43	89
Oregon Caves Nat. Mon.: Oregon	**36**	42	123
Oregon City: Oregon	**39**	45	123
Orem: Utah	**33**	40	112
Organ Pipe Cactus Nat. Mon.: Arizona	**33**	32	113
Orick: California	**36**	41	124
Orient: New York	**15**	41	72
Oriental: North Carolina	**24**	35	77
Orillia: Ontario	**12**	45	79
Orinda: California	**6**	38	122¼
Oriskany: New York	**13**	43	75
Orland: California	**36**	40	122
Orlando: Florida	**25**	29	81
Orleans: California	**36**	41	124
Orleans: Massachusetts	**15**	42	70
Orleans: Vermont	**13**	45	72
Orleans, Île d': Québec	**13**	47	71
Ormond Beach: *town*, Florida	**25**	29	81
Ormstown: Québec	**13**	45	74
Orofino: Idaho	**32**	47	116
Oro Grande: California	**35**	35	117
Oromocto: New Brunswick	**9**	46	66
Oroville: California	**37**	40	122
Oroville: Washington	**38**	49	119
Oroville: *dam*, California	**37**	40	121
Orrville: Ohio	**19**	41	82
Orsainville: Québec	**13**	47	71
Osage: Oklahoma	**29**	36	96
Oscarville: Alaska	**43**	61	162
Osceola: Arkansas	**27**	36	90
Osceola Mills: Pennsylvania	**14**	41	78
Oshawa: Ontario	**12**	44	79
Oshkosh: Wisconsin	**20**	44	89
Oskaloosa: Iowa	**10**	41	93
Osketaneo: Québec	**8**	48	75
Ossining: New York	**15**	41	74
Ossipee L.: New Hampshire	**13**	44	71
Oswegatchie: *r.*, New York	**13**	44	75
Oswego: New York	**12**	43	77
Oswego: *r.*, New York	**12**	43	76
Osyka: Mississippi	**27**	31	90
Othello: Washington	**39**	47	119
Otish Mts.: Québec	**8**	53	71
Otoskwin: *r.*, Ontario	**31**	52	89
Otsego: Michigan	**21**	42	86
Otsego L.: New York	**14**	43	75
Ottawa: Illinois	**21**	41	89
Ottawa: Kansas	**28**	39	95
Ottawa: Ohio	**19**	41	84
Ottawa: Ontario	**12**	45	76
Ottawa: *r.*, Ontario/Québec	**12**	46	77
Ottawa Is.: N.W.T.	**45**	59	80
Otter: *cr.*, Vermont	**13**	44	73
Otter L.: Saskatchewan	**31**	56	105
Ottumwa: Iowa	**10**	41	92
Ouachita: *r.*, Arkansas/La.	**26**	33	93
Ouachita, L.: Arkansas	**26**	35	93
Ouachita Mts.: Okla./Ark.	**26**	35	94
Ouray: Colorado	**29**	38	108
Outer I.: Québec	**9**	51	58
Outlook: Saskatchewan	**30**	52	107
Outremont: Québec	**2**	45½	73¾
Ouzinkie: Alaska	**43**	58	153
Overton: Texas	**26**	32	95
Ovid: Michigan	**20**	43	84
Oviedo: Florida	**25**	29	81
Owasco L.: New York	**14**	43	77
Owasso, L.: Minnesota	**3**	45	93¼
Owatonna: Minnesota	**10**	44	93
Owego: New York	**14**	42	76
Owensboro: Kentucky	**23**	38	87
Owens L.: California	**35**	36	118
Owen Sound: *town*, Ontario	**18**	45	81
Owenyo: California	**35**	37	118
Owl: *r.*, Manitoba	**31**	47	94
Owosso: Michigan	**20**	43	84
Owyhee: *r.*, Oregon	**32**	43	117
Owyhee Res.: *& dam*, Oregon	**32**	43	117
Oxbow: *dam*, Oregon/Idaho	**32**	45	117
Oxford: Maryland	**17**	39	76
Oxford: Michigan	**19**	43	83
Oxford: Mississippi	**27**	34	90
Oxford: New York	**14**	42	76
Oxford: North Carolina	**17**	36	79
Oxford: Ohio	**21**	40	85
Oxford: Pennsylvania	**14**	40	76
Oxford House: Manitoba	**31**	55	95
Oxford L.: Manitoba	**31**	55	96
Oxnard: California	**34**	34	119
Oyster Point: California	**6**	37¾	122¼
Ozark: Alabama	**27**	31	86
Ozark: Arkansas	**26**	35	94
Ozark Plateau	**10**	37	93
Ozarks, L. of the: Missouri	**10**	38	93
Ozette: Washington	**38**	48	125
Ozette L.: Washington	**38**	48	125

	Page	N	W
Pacific: California	**37**	39	121
Pacifica: California	**6**	37¾	122½
Pacific City: Oregon	**32**	45	124
Pacific Grove: California	**37**	37	122
Packs Harbour: Newfoundland	**9**	54	57
Pacolet: *r.*, South Carolina	**24**	35	82
Pacolet Mills: South Carolina	**24**	35	82
Paden City: West Virginia	**16**	40	81
Padlei: Northwest Territories	**31**	62	97
Padloping: Northwest Territories	**45**	67	63
Padre I.: Texas	**22**	27	97
Padre Island Nat. Seashore: Texas	**22**	27	97
Paducah: Kentucky	**22**	37	89
Page: Arizona	**33**	37	111
Pageland: South Carolina	**24**	35	80
Pagwa River: *sett.*, Ontario	**10**	50	85
Pahala: Hawaii	**128**	19	155
Pahrump: Nevada	**35**	36	116
Pahute Peak: Nevada	**36**	41	119
Pailolo Ch.: Hawaii	**128**	21	157
Paimiut: Alaska	**43**	62	160
Painesville: Ohio	**19**	42	81
Paintsville: Kentucky	**16**	38	83
Paisley: Oregon	**36**	43	121
Pala: California	**35**	33	117
Palatine: Illinois	**4**	42	88
Palatka: Florida	**25**	30	82
Palen L.: California	**35**	34	115
Palermo: California	**37**	39	122
Palestine: Texas	**26**	32	96
Palisade: Nevada	**33**	41	116
Palisades: *dam*, Idaho	**32**	43	111
Palm Beach: Florida	**25**	27	80
Palmdale: California	**35**	35	118
Palm Desert: California	**35**	34	116
Palmer: Alaska	**43**	62	149
Palmer: Massachusetts	**15**	42	72
Palmer: Texas	**26**	32	97
Palmerston: Ontario	**18**	44	81
Palmerton: Pennsylvania	**14**	41	76
Palmetto: Florida	**25**	28	83
Palm Springs: California	**35**	34	117
Palmyra: New Jersey	**2**	40	75
Palmyra: New York	**12**	43	77
Palmyra: Pennsylvania	**14**	40	77
Palmyra: Virginia	**17**	38	78
Palo Alto: California	**6**	37½	122¼
Palos Verdes Hills: California	**7**	33¾	118¼
Palouse Hills: Washington	**32**	47	117
Palo Verde: California	**33**	33	115
Pamlico: *r.*, North Carolina	**24**	35	77
Pampa: Texas	**29**	36	101
Pamunkey: *r.*, Virginia	**17**	38	77
Panama City: Florida	**27**	30	86
Panamint Range: California	**35**	36	117
Pangnirtung: N.W.T.	**45**	66	66
Panguitch: Utah	**33**	38	112
Panoche: California	**37**	37	121
Papaikou: Hawaii	**128**	20	155
Paradise: California	**37**	40	122
Paradise: Kentucky	**23**	37	87
Paragould: Arkansas	**27**	36	91
Paramus: New Jersey	**1**	41	74
Parent: Québec	**8**	48	75
Paris: Arkansas	**26**	35	94
Paris: Illinois	**21**	40	88
Paris: Ontario	**19**	43	80
Paris: Texas	**26**	34	96
Park City: Utah	**33**	41	112
Parker: Pennsylvania	**19**	41	80
Parker: *dam*, Arizona/California	**33**	34	115
Parkersburg: West Virginia	**16**	39	82
Parkesburg: Pennsylvania	**14**	40	76
Parkfield: California	**34**	36	120
Park Range: Colorado	**28**	40	107
Park Rapids: Minnesota	**10**	47	95
Park Ridge: Illinois	**4**	42	87¾
Parksley: Virginia	**17**	38	76
Parksville: British Columbia	**38**	49	124
Park Village: California	**35**	36	117
Parma: Ohio	**19**	41	82
Parrish: Alabama	**27**	34	87
Parry, C.: Northwest Territories	**44**	70	125
Parry Sound: *town*, Ontario	**18**	45	80
Parsnip: *r.*, British Columbia	**41**	56	124
Parson: Kansas	**29**	37	95
Parsons: Tennessee	**27**	36	88
Parsons: West Virginia	**16**	39	80
Pasadena: California	**7**	34¼	118¼
Pasadena: Texas	**26**	30	95
Pasagoula: Mississippi	**27**	30	89
Pasco: Washington	**39**	46	119
Pascoag: Rhode Island	**15**	42	72
Paskenta: California	**36**	40	123
Pasley Bay: N.W.T.	**44**	71	96
Paso Robles: California	**34**	36	121
Pasquia Hills: Saskatchewan	**30**	53	103
Passaic: New Jersey	**1**	40¾	74¼
Passamaquoddy Bay: N.B.	**9**	45	67
Pass Christian: Mississippi	**27**	30	89
Patapsco Res.: Maryland	**17**	39	77
Patchogue: New York	**15**	41	73
Paterson: New Jersey	**1**	41	73
Paterson: Washington	**39**	46	120
Pathfinder Res.: *& dam* Wyo.	**28**	42	107
Patience L.: Saskatchewan	**32**	52	106
Patterson: California	**37**	37	121

	Page	N	W
Patterson: Louisiana	**26**	30	91
Patterson Point: Michigan	**20**	46	86
Patton: Pennsylvania	**14**	41	79
Patuxent: *r.*, Maryland	**17**	38	77
Paulatuk: N.W.T.	**44**	69	124
Paulding: Ohio	**21**	41	85
Paul I.: Newfoundland	**9**	56	62
Pauloff Harbor: Alaska	**43**	54	163
Paulsboro: New Jersey	**14**	40	75
Pauls Valley: *town*, Oklahoma	**26**	35	97
Pawling: New York	**15**	42	74
Paw Paw: Michigan	**21**	42	86
Pawtucket: Rhode Island	**15**	42	71
Paxton: Illinois	**21**	40	88
Payette: Idaho	**32**	44	117
Payette: *r.*, Idaho	**32**	44	116
Payne: Ohio	**21**	41	85
Payne (Amand): *r.*, Québec	**45**	60	72
Payne Bay: Québec	**45**	60	70
Payne L.: Québec	**45**	59	74
Paynes Creek: *sett.*, California	**36**	40	122
Payson: Alaska	**42**	62	145
Pea: *r.*, Alabama	**27**	32	86
Peace: *r.*, B.C./Alberta	**30**	59	114
Peace: *r.*, Florida	**25**	27	82
Peace River: *town*, Alberta	**30**	56	117
Peale, Mt.: Utah	**33**	38	109
Peanut: California	**36**	40	123
Pearblossom: California	**35**	35	118
Pearford: Texas	**3**	29½	95¼
Pearisburg: Virginia	**16**	37	81
Pearl: *r.*, Miss./Louisiana	**27**	31	90
Pearl City: Hawaii	**128**	21	158
Pearl & Hermes Reef: Hawaii	**128**	28	176
Pearl River: *sett.*, New York	**15**	41	74
Pearsall: Texas	**22**	29	99
Pearson: Georgia	**25**	31	83
Pease: *r.*, Texas	**29**	34	100
Pebble Beach: *sett.*, California	**37**	37	122
Pecatonica: Illinois	**21**	42	89
Peche Is.: Ontario	**5**	42¼	83
Peck: Oregon	**36**	43	124
Peckville: Pennsylvania	**14**	41	76
Pecos: Texas	**29**	31	104
Pecos: *r.*, N. Mex./Texas	**29**	31	102
Peddocks I.: Massachusetts	**2**	42¼	71
Pedro Bay: *town*, Alaska	**43**	60	154
Pee Dee: *r.*, S.C./N.C.	**24**	34	79
Peekskill: New York	**15**	41	74
Peel: *r.*, Yukon/N.W.T.	**40**	67	135
Peel Plateau: Yukon/N.W.T.	**40**	67	134
Peel Point: N.W.T.	**44**	74	115
Peel Sound: N.W.T.	**44/45**	73	97
Pekin: Illinois	**21**	41	90
Pelahatchie: Mississippi	**27**	32	90
Pelee I.: Ontario	**19**	42	83
Pelham: Georgia	**25**	31	84
Pelham Bay Park: New York	**1**	40¾	13¾
Pelican: Alaska	**40**	58	136
Pelican Narrows: Saskatchewan	**30**	55	103
Pellston: Michigan	**20**	46	85
Pelly: *r.*, Yukon	**40**	62	134
Pelly Bay: N.W.T.	**45**	69	90
Pelly Bay: *sett.*, N.W.T.	**45**	68	89
Pelly Crossing: Yukon	**40**	63	137
Pelly L.: N.W.T.	**44**	66	102
Pelly Mts.: Yukon	**40**	62	133
Pelzer: South Carolina	**24**	35	82
Pemberville: Ohio	**19**	41	83
Pembina: *r.*, Alberta	**30**	53	115
Pembina: *r.*, N.D./Manitoba	**28**	49	98
Pembine: Wisconsin	**20**	46	88
Pembroke: Georgia	**24**	32	82
Pembroke: Ontario	**12**	46	77
Pembroke, C.: N.W.T.	**45**	63	82
Penacook: New Hampshire	**13**	43	72
Pen Argyl: Pennsylvania	**14**	41	75
Penasco: *r.*, New Mexico	**29**	33	105
Pendleton: Indiana	**21**	40	86
Pendleton: Oregon	**39**	46	119
Pendleton: South Carolina	**24**	35	83
Pend Oreille L.: Idaho	**32**	48	116
Pentanguishene: Ontario	**18**	45	80
Penfield: New York	**12**	43	77
Peninsula: Ohio	**19**	41	82
Peninsula Point: Michigan	**20**	46	87
Pennask L.: British Columbia	**38**	50	120
Penn Hills: Pennsylvania	**5**	40½	79¾
Pennington: New Jersey	**14**	40	75
Pennington Gap: Virginia	**24**	37	83
Penn Park: Pennsylvania	**2**	40	75
Pennsauken: New Jersey	**2**	40	75
Pennsboro: West Virginia	**16**	39	81
Pennsburg: Pennsylvania	**14**	40	75
Penns Grove: New Jersey	**14**	40	75
Pennsville: New Jersey	**14**	40	76
PENNSYLVANIA	**11**	—	—
Pennsylvania Turnpike N.E. Extension: Pennsylvania	**14**	41	76
Pennsylvania Turnpike	**14**	40	78
Penn Yan: New York	**14**	43	77
Penny Highland: N.W.T.	**45**	67	66
Penobscot: *r.*, Maine	**11**	45	69
Penobscot Bay: Maine	**11**	44	69
Penoyar: California	**36**	42	122
Pensacola: Florida	**27**	30	87
Pensacola: *dam*, Oklahoma	**29**	36	96

Place	Page	N	W
Penticton: British Columbia	38	49	120
Pentwater: Michigan	20	44	86
Pentz: California	37	40	122
Peoria: Illinois	21	41	90
Peotone: Illinois	21	41	88
Pepperwood: California	36	40	124
Pere Marquette: *r.*, Michigan	20	44	86
Perez: California	36	42	121
Péribonca: *r.*, Québec	8	49	71
Perkasie: Pennsylvania	14	40	75
Perris: California	35	34	117
Perry: Florida	25	30	84
Perry: Georgia	24	32	84
Perry: Michigan	21	43	84
Perry River: *sett.*, N.W.T.	44	68	102
Perrysburg: Ohio	19	42	84
Perryton: Texas	29	36	101
Perryville: Alaska	43	56	159
Perth: Ontario	12	45	76
Perth Amboy: New Jersey	1	40½	74
Peru: Illinois	21	41	89
Peru: Indiana	21	41	86
Pescadero: California	37	37	122
Peshtigo: *& r.*, Wisconsin	20	45	88
Petaluma: California	37	38	123
Petenwell Res.: Wisconsin	20	44	90
Peterborough: New Hampshire	13	43	72
Peterborough: Ontario	12	44	78
Peter Pond L.: Saskatchewan	30	56	109
Peters: California	37	38	121
Peters Canon Res.: California	7	33¾	117¾
Petersburg: Alaska	41	57	133
Petersburg: Michigan	19	42	84
Petersburg: Virginia	17	37	77
Petersburg: West Virginia	16	39	79
Peters Mt.: West Virginia	16	38	81
Petit Bois I.: Mississippi	27	30	88
Petitot: *r.*, B.C./Alberta	40	60	121
Petitskapau L.: Newfoundland	9	55	67
Petoskey: Michigan	20	45	85
Petrified Forest Nat. Park: Ariz.	33	35	110
Petrolia: California	36	40	124
Pewamo: Michigan	20	43	85
Phelan: California	35	34	118
Phelps: New York	14	43	77
Phenix City: Alabama	27	32	85
Philadelphia: Mississippi	27	33	89
Philadelphia: New York	12	44	76
Philadelphia: Pennsylvania	14	40	75
Philipsburg: Montana	32	46	113
Philipsburg: Pennsylvania	14	41	78
Philip Smith Mts.: Alaska	42	68	147
Phillips: California	37	39	120
Phillipsburg: Kansas	28	40	99
Phillipsburg: New Jersey	14	41	75
Philmont: New York	15	42	74
Philo: California	37	39	123
Philo: Ohio	16	40	82
Philpott Res.: Virginia	16	37	80
Phoenix: Arizona	33	34	112
Phoenix: New York	12	43	76
Phoenix: Oregon	36	42	123
Phoenixville: Pennsylvania	14	40	76
Picayune: Mississippi	27	31	90
Pickens: South Carolina	24	35	83
Pickle Crow: Ontario	31	52	90
Pickwick L.: Miss./Alabama	27	35	88
Pickwick Landing: *dam*, Tenn.	27	35	88
Picton: Ontario	12	44	77
Piedmont: Alabama	27	34	86
Piedmont: California	6	37¾	122¼
Piedmont: South Carolina	24	35	82
Piedmont: West Virginia	16	39	79
Piedmont Res.: Ohio	19	40	81
Piedras Blancas Point: Calif.	34	36	121
Pierrefonds: Québec	2	42½	73¾
Pierce: Florida	25	28	82
Piercy: California	36	40	124
Pierre: South Dakota	28	44	100
Pierreville: Québec	13	46	73
Pigeon: Michigan	18	44	83
Pigeon: *r.*, Minnesota	10	48	90
Pigeon Point: California	37	37	122
Pigs Eye, L.: Minnesota	3	45	93
Pikangikum L.: Ontario	31	52	94
Pikes Peak: Colorado	28	39	105
Pikeville: Kentucky	16	37	83
Pilarcitos Lake: California	6	37½	122½
Pillar Pt.: California	6	37½	122½
Pillsbury, L.: California	37	39	123
Pilot Mountain: *sett.*, N.C.	16	37	81
Pilot Point: Alaska	43	58	158
Pilot Point: *sett.*, Texas	26	33	97
Pilot Rock: *sett.*, Oregon	39	45	119
Pilot Station: Alaska	43	62	163
Pilottown: Louisiana	27	29	89
Pima: Arizona	33	33	110
Pincher Creek: *town*, Alberta	30	50	114
Pinconning: Michigan	20	44	84
Pine: *cr.*, Pennsylvania	14	41	77
Pine: *r.*, British Columbia	41	56	122
Pine: *r.*, Michigan	20	43	84
Pine Bluff: Arkansas	26	34	92
Pine Camp: New York	12	44	76
Pine Creek Res.: Oklahoma	26	34	95
Pinecrest: California	37	38	120
Pinedale: California	37	37	120

Place	Page	N	W
Pine Falls: *sett.*, Manitoba	31	51	96
Pine Flat Res.: *& dam*, Calif.	34	37	119
Pine Forest Mts.: Nevada	36	42	119
Pine Grove: Pennsylvania	14	41	76
Pinehouse L.: Saskatchewan	30	56	107
Pinehurst: North Carolina	24	35	79
Pinehurst: Oregon	36	42	122
Pine Island Sound: Florida	25	27	82
Pineland: Texas	26	31	94
Pine Pass: British Columbia	41	55	122
Pine Plains: New York	15	42	74
Pine Point: N.W.T.	30	61	114
Pint Point: *sett.*, N.W.T.	30	61	114
Pine Valley: *sett.*, California	35	33	117
Pineville: Kentucky	24	37	84
Pinnacles Nat. Mon.: California	34	37	121
Pinopolis: *dam*, South Carolina	24	33	80
Pinos, Mt.: California	34	35	119
Pinto: Maryland	17	40	79
Pioche: Nevada	33	38	115
Pioneer: California	37	38	121
Pipestone: *r.*, Ontario	31	52	91
Pipmuacan L.: Québec	8	50	70
Piqua: Ohio	19	40	84
Piru: California	35	34	119
Piru: *cr.*, California	35	35	119
Pismo Beach: *sett.*, California	34	35	121
Pistol River: *sett.*, Oregon	36	42	124
Pit: *r.* California	36	41	121
Pitkas Point: *sett.*, Alaska	43	62	163
Pitman: New Jersey	14	40	75
Pitt I.: British Columbia	41	54	130
Pitt River: *r.*, B.C.	6	49¼	122¾
Pittsboro: North Carolina	24	36	79
Pittsburg: California	37	38	122
Pittsburg: Kansas	29	37	95
Pittsburg: Texas	26	33	95
Pittsburgh: Pennsylvania	19	40	80
Pittsfield: Massachusetts	15	42	73
Pittsfield: New Hampshire	13	43	71
Pittsford: New York	12	43	78
Pittston: Pennsylvania	14	41	76
Pixley: California	34	36	119
Placentia: Newfoundland	9	47	54
Placentia B.: Newfoundland	9	48	54
Placerville: California	37	39	121
Plain City: Ohio	19	40	83
Plain Dealing: Louisiana	26	33	94
Plainfield: Connecticut	15	42	72
Plainfield: Illinois	21	42	88
Plainfield: New Jersey	1	40½	74½
Plainfield: Wisconsin	20	44	90
Plainview: Arkansas	26	35	93
Plainview: Texas	29	34	102
Plainville: Connecticut	15	42	73
Plainwell: Michigan	21	42	86
Planada: California	37	37	120
Plano: Illinois	21	42	89
Plano: Texas	26	33	97
Plant City: Florida	25	28	82
Plaquemine: Louisiana	26	30	91
Plaster City: California	35	33	116
Platinum: Alaska	43	59	162
Platte: *r.*, Nebraska	28	41	100
Platt National Park: Oklahoma	26	34	97
Plattsburgh: New York	13	45	73
Plattsmouth: Nebraska	28	41	96
Playgreen L.: Manitoba	31	54	98
Pleasant Gap: Pennsylvania	14	41	78
Pleasant Grove: California	37	39	121
Pleasant Hill: *town*, California	6	38	122
Pleasant Hills: Pennsylvania	5	40¼	80
Pleasanton: California	37	38	122
Pleasanton: Texas	22	29	99
Pleasantville: New Jersey	15	39	75
Pleasantville: New York	15	41	74
Plentywood: Montana	28	49	105
Plessisville: Québec	13	46	72
Pletipi L.: Québec	8	52	70
Plover: Wisconsin	20	44	90
Plush: Oregon	36	42	120
Plymouth: California	37	38	121
Plymouth: Indiana	21	41	86
Plymouth: Massachusetts	15	42	71
Plymouth: Michigan	5	42¼	83¾
Plymouth: Minnesota	3	45	93¼
Plymouth: New Hampshire	13	44	72
Plymouth: North Carolina	24	36	77
Plymouth: Ohio	19	41	83
Plymouth: Washington	39	46	119
Plymouth: Wisconsin	20	44	88
Pocatello: Idaho	32	43	112
Pocohontas: Virginia	17	37	78
Pocomoke: *r.*, Maryland	17	38	75
Pocomoke City: Maryland	17	38	76
Point Arena: *sett.*, California	37	39	124
Point Comfort: *sett.*, Texas	22	29	97
Pointe-aux-Trembles: *sett.*, Qué.	2	45¾	73½
Pointe-Claire: *town*, Québec	2	45½	73¾
Point Hope: *sett.*, Alaska	42	68	167
Point L.: Northwest Territories	40	65	113
Point Lay: *sett.*, Alaska	42	70	163
Point Pelee Nat. Pk.: Ontario	19	42	82
Point Pleasant: *town*, N.J.	15	40	74
Point Pleasant: *town*, W. Va.	16	39	82
Point Reyes Nat. Seashore: Calif.	37	38	123
Poisson Blanc, L.: Québec	12	46	76

Place	Page	N	W
Poland: Ohio	19	41	81
Polk: Pennsylvania	19	41	80
Polo: Illinois	21	42	90
Pomeroy: Ohio	16	39	82
Pomona: California	7	34	117¾
Pompano Beach: *town*, Florida	25	26	80
Pompton Lakes: New Jersey	1	41	74¼
Ponca City: Oklahoma	29	37	97
Ponce: Puerto Rico	27	18	67
Ponchatoula: Louisiana	27	30	90
Pond Fork: *r.*, West Virginia	16	38	82
Pond Inlet: N.W.T.	45	73	77
Pond Inlet: *sett.*, N.W.T.	45	73	78
Pondosa: California	36	41	122
Ponoka: Alberta	30	53	114
Pontchartrain, L.: Louisiana	27	30	90
Pontiac: Illinois	21	41	89
Pontiac: Michigan	19	43	83
Pontotoc: Mississippi	27	34	89
Pont-Rouge: Québec	13	47	72
Pont-Viau: *sett.*, Québec	2	45½	73¾
Poorman: Alaska	42	64	156
Pope: California	35	33	116
Poplar: *r.*, Manitoba	31	53	97
Poplar Bluff: Missouri	10	37	90
Porcher I.: B.C.	41	54	131
Porcupine: Ontario	11	49	81
Porcupine: *r.*, Yukon/Alaska	42	67	143
Portage: Alaska	43	61	149
Portage: Pennsylvania	14	40	79
Portage: Wisconsin	20	44	89
Portage-la-Prairie: Manitoba	31	50	98
Port Alberni: British Columbia	38	49	125
Portales: New Mexico	29	34	103
Port Alexander: Alaska	41	56	135
Port Alice: British Columbia	41	50	127
Port Allegany: Pennsylvania	14	42	78
Port Angeles: Washington	38	48	123
Port Arthur (*now* Thunder Bay): Ontario	10	48	89
Port Arthur: Texas	26	30	94
Port Austin: Michigan	18	44	83
Port-aux-Basques: Nfld.	9	48	59
Port Barre: Louisiana	26	31	92
Port Blandford: Newfoundland	9	48	54
Port Burwell: *bay*, Québec	45	60	65
Port Burwell: Ontario	19	43	81
Port Byron: New York	12	43	77
Port Cartier: Québec	9	50	67
Port Chester: New York	1	41	73¾
Port Chicago: California	37	38	122
Port Chilkoot: Alaska	40	59	135
Port Clarence: *bay*, Alaska	42	65	166
Port Clinton: Ohio	19	42	83
Port Colborne: Ontario	19	43	79
Port Coquitlam: B.C.	6	49¼	122¾
Port Credit: Ontario	5	43½	79½
Port Dalhousie: Ontario	19	43	79
Port Deposit: Maryland	17	40	76
Port Dover: Ontario	19	43	80
Port Edward: British Columbia	41	54	130
Port Edwards: Wisconsin	20	44	90
Portersville: Pennsylvania	19	41	80
Porterville: California	34	36	119
Port Everglades: Florida	25	26	80
Port Gibson: Mississippi	26	32	91
Port Henry: New York	13	44	73
Port Graham: Alaska	43	59	152
Port Hardy: British Columbia	41	51	128
Port Harrison: Québec	45	58	78
Port Heiden: Alaska	43	57	159
Port Hope: Ontario	12	44	78
Port Huron: Michigan	19	43	82
Port Jefferson: New York	15	41	73
Port Jervis: New York	15	41	75
Portland: Connecticut	15	42	73
Portland: Indiana	21	40	85
Portland: Maine	11	44	70
Portland: Michigan	21	43	85
Portland: Oregon	39	46	123
Port Logan: N.W.T.	45	72	93
Port Madison: *and bay*, Wash.	6	47¾	122½
Port Maitland: Ontario	19	43	80
Port Marion: Pennsylvania	16	40	80
Port Mellon: British Columbia	38	50	123
Port Menier: Québec	9	50	64
Port Moller: Alaska	43	56	161
Port Monmouth: New Jersey	14	40	74
Port Moody: British Columbia	6	49¼	122¾
Port Neches: Texas	26	30	94
Port Nelson: Manitoba	31	57	93
Portneuf: Québec	13	47	72
Port Norris: New Jersey	14	39	75
Port-Nouveau-Québec (George River): *sett.*, Québec	45	58	65
Portola: California	36	40	120
Port Orchard: *& chan.*, Wash.	6	47½	122¾
Port Radium: N.W.T.	40	66	118
Port Renfrew: B.C.	38	49	124
Port Rowan: Ontario	1	43	80
Port Royal: Virginia	17	38	77
Port St. Joe: Florida	27	30	85
Port San Luis Obispo: Calif.	34	35	121
Port Saunders: Newfoundland	9	51	57
Port Simpson: British Columbia	41	55	130
Portsmouth: New Hampshire	15	43	71
Portsmouth: Ohio	16	39	83

	Page	N	W
Portsmouth: Virginia	**17**	37	76
Port Stanley: Ontario	**19**	43	81
Port Sulphur: Louisiana	**27**	29	90
Port Townsend: Washington	**38**	48	123
Portville: New York	**14**	42	78
Port Washington: New York	**1**	40¾	73¾
Port Washington: Wisconsin	**20**	43	88
Port Weller: Ontario	**19**	43	79
Poste-de-la-Baleine *see* Great Whale River: *sett.*, Qué.	**8**	55	78
Postville: Newfoundland	**9**	55	60
Poteau: Oklahoma	**26**	35	95
Poteau: *r.*, Ark./Oklahoma	**26**	35	94
Poteet: Texas	**22**	29	99
Potholes Res.: Washington	**39**	47	119
Potomac: *r.*	**17**	39	78
Potomac R., N.Br.: W. Va./Md.	**16**	39	79
Potomac R., S. Br.: W. Va.	**17**	39	79
Potsdam: New York	**13**	45	75
Pottstown: Pennsylvania	**14**	40	76
Potwin: Kansas	**29**	38	97
Poughkeepsie: New York	**15**	42	74
Poulsbo: Washington	**6**	47¾	122¾
Poultney: Vermont	**13**	44	73
Pound: Wisconsin	**20**	45	88
Povungnituk: Québec	**45**	60	77
Povungnituk: *r.*, Québec	**45**	60	76
Poway: California	**35**	33	117
Powder: *r.*, Wyoming/Montana	**28**	45	106
Powell: Wisconsin	**20**	46	90
Powell: Wyoming	**28**	45	109
Powell, L.: Arizona/Utah	**33**	37	112
Powell River: *sett.*, B.C.	**38**	50	125
Powellton: West Virginia	**16**	38	81
Powers: Michigan	**20**	46	88
Powers: Oregon	**36**	43	124
Powhatan Point: *sett.*, Ohio	**16**	40	81
Poygan, L.: Wisconsin	**20**	44	89
Prado Flood Control Basin: Calif.	**7**	34	117¾
Prague: Oklahoma	**26**	35	97
Prairies, des: *r.*, Québec	**2**	45½	73½
Prairie Dog Town Fork: *r.*, Texas	**29**	35	101
Prairie du Sac: Wisconsin	**20**	43	90
Prairie Grove: Arkansas	**26**	36	94
Prather: California	**37**	37	120
Pratt: Kansas	**29**	38	99
Prattville: Alabama	**27**	32	87
Preeceville: Saskatchewan	**30**	52	103
Preissac, L.: Québec	**8**	48	78
Prescot I.: N.W.T.	**44**	73	97
Prescott: Arizona	**33**	35	112
Prescott: Arkansas	**26**	34	93
Prescott: Ontario	**12**	45	76
Presidio: California	**6**	37¾	122½
Presque Isle: Maine.	**9**	47	68
Presque Isle State Park: Pa.	**19**	42	80
Press Park: Louisiana	**3**	30	90
Preston: Idaho	**32**	42	112
Preston: Ontario	**18**	43	80
Prestonburg: Kentucky	**16**	38	83
Prettyboy Res.: Maryland	**17**	40	77
Price: Utah	**33**	40	111
Prichard:Alabama	**27**	31	88
Priest Rapids: *dam.* Wash.	**39**	47	120
Primrose L.: Saskatchewan	**30**	55	110
Prince Albert: Saskatchewan	**30**	53	106
Prince Albert Hills: N.W.T.	**45**	68	85
Prince Albert National Park: Saskatchewan	**30**	54	106
Prince Albert Penin.: N.W.T.	**44**	72	117
Prince Albert Sound: N.W.T.	**44**	70	115
Prince Charles I.: N.W.T.	**45**	68	76
PRINCE EDWARD ISLAND	**9**	—	—
Prince Edward Island Nat. Park	**9**	46	63
Prince George: B.C.	**41**	54	123
Prince Leopold I.: N.W.T.	**45**	74	90
Prince of Wales, C.: Québec	**45**	62	72
Prince of Wales I.: Alaska	**41**	56	133
Prince of Wales I.: N.W.T.	**44**	73	100
Prince of Wales Strait: N.W.T.	**44**	73	118
Prince Regent Inlet: N.W.T.	**45**	73	90
Prince Rupert: B.C.	**41**	54	130
Princess Anne: Maryland.	**17**	38	76
Princess Royal I.: B.C.	**41**	53	129
Princeton: British Columbia	**38**	49	121
Princeton: Illinois	**21**	41	89
Princeton: New Jersey	**15**	40	75
Princeton: West Virginia	**16**	37	81
Prince William Sound: Alaska	**43**	61	147
Prineville: Oregon	**32**	44	121
Proberta: California	**36**	40	122
Proctor: British Columbia	**41**	50	117
Proctor: Vermont	**13**	44	73
Prophet: *r.*, British Columbia	**40**	58	123
Prospect: Ohio	**19**	40	83
Prospect: Oregon	**36**	43	123
Prospect: Pennsylvania	**19**	41	80
Prospect Heights: *town*, Illinois	**4**	42	88
Prospect Park: *town*, New York	**1**	40¾	74
Prosser: Washington	**39**	46	120
Proven: Greenland	**45**	73	56
Providence: Rhode Island	**15**	42	71
Provincetown: Massachusetts	**15**	42	70
Provo: Utah	**33**	40	112
Provost: Alberta	**30**	52	110
Prudhoe B.: & *sett.*, Alaska	**42**	70	148
Prunedale: California	**37**	37	122

	Page	N	W
Puce: Ontario	**5**	42¼	82¾
Puckaway, L.: Wisconsin	**20**	44	89
Pueblo: Colorado	**29**	38	105
Puerco: *r.*, New Mexico/Arizona	**29**	35	109
Puget Sound: Washington	**38/39**	48	122
Pulaski: New York	**12**	44	76
Pulaski: Pennsylvania	**19**	41	80
Pulaski: Tennessee.	**27**	35	87
Pulaski: Virginia	**16**	37	81
Pulaski: Wisconsin	**20**	45	88
Pulga: California	**36**	40	121
Pulgas Ridge: California	**6**	37½	122¼
Pullman: Washington	**32**	47	117
Punta Gorda: Florida	**25**	27	82
Punxsutawney: Pennsylvania	**14**	41	79
Purcellville: Virginia	**17**	39	78
Purvis: Mississippi	**27**	31	89
Putnam: Connecticut	**15**	42	72
Puunene: Hawaii	**128**	21	156
Putunia: Québec	**45**	62	74
Puyallup: Washington	**39**	47	122
Pymantuning Res.: Pennsylvania.	**19**	42	80
Pyramid: Nevada	**36**	40	120
Pyramid L.: Nevada	**36**	40	120
Quabbin Res.: Massachusetts	**15**	42	72
Quadra I.: British Columbia	**38**	50	125
Quail Mts.: California	**35**	36	117
Quakertow: Pennsylvania.	**14**	40	75
Quantico: Virginia	**17**	39	77
Qu'Appelle: *r. & dam*, Saskatchewan	**31**	51	102
Quarryville: Pennsylvania	**14**	40	76
Quartz Hill: *town*, California	**35**	35	118
Quartz Mountain: *sett.*, Oregon	**36**	42	121
QUÉBEC	**8**	—	—
Québec: Québec	**13**	47	71
Queen Charlotte: B.C.	**41**	53	132
Queen Charlotte Is.: B.C..	**41**	53	132
Queen Charlotte Sound: B.C.	**41**	51	130
Queen Charlotte Str.: B.C.	**41**	51	128
Queen Elizabeth Park: B.C.	**6**	49¼	123
Queen Maud G.: Northwest Territories	**44**	68	103
Queens: New York	**1**	40¾	74
Queenstown: Maryland	**17**	39	76
Queets: Washington	**39**	48	124
Quesnel: British Columbia	**41**	53	123
Quesnel L.: British Columbia	**41**	52	121
Questa: New Mexico	**29**	37	106
Quetico Prov. Park: Ontario	**10**	48	92
Quibell: Ontario	**10**	50	93
Quilcene: Washington	**39**	48	123
Quill Lakes: Saskatchewan	**31**	52	104
Quinault: *r.*, Washington	**39**	48	124
Quinault, L.: Washington.	**39**	47	124
Quincy: California	**36**	40	121
Quincy: Florida	**25**	31	85
Quincy: Illinois	**10**	40	91
Quincy: Massachusetts	**2**	42¼	71
Quincy: Michigan	**21**	42	85
Quincy: Washington	**39**	47	120
Quincy Bay: Massachusetts	**2**	42¼	71
Quinebaug: *r.*, Mass./Conn.	**15**	42	72
Quinhagak: Alaska	**43**	60	162
Quinton: Oklahoma	**26**	35	95
Quitman: Georgia	**25**	31	84
Quitman: Mississippi	**27**	32	89
Quitman: Texas	**26**	33	95
Quoich: *r.*, N.W.T.	**45**	65	95
Quorn: Ontario	**10**	49	91
Qutdligssat: Greenland	**45**	70	53
Raccoon: *r.*, Iowa	**10**	42	95
Raccoon: *r.*, Ohio	**16**	39	82
Raccoon Point: Louisiana	**26**	29	91
Race, C.: Newfoundland	**9**	47	53
Racine: Wisconsin	**21**	43	88
Radec: California	**35**	34	117
Radford: Virginia	**16**	37	81
Radisson: Saskatchewan	**30**	52	107
Radville: Saskatchewan	**30**	49	104
Rae: Northwest Territories	**40**	63	116
Rae: *r.*, Northwest Territories	**44**	68	116
Raeford: North Carolina	**24**	35	79
Rae Isthmus: N.W.T.	**45**	67	88
Rae Strait: N.W.T.	**45**	69	95
Ragland: Alabama	**27**	34	86
Rainbow: Alaska	**43**	61	150
Rainier: Oregon	**36**	46	123
Rainier, Mt.: Washington	**39**	47	122
Rainy: *r.*, Ontario/Manitoba	**10**	49	94
Rainy L.: Minn./Ontario	**10**	49	93
Rainy River: *town.* Ontario	**10**	49	95
Raisin: *r.*, Michigan	**19**	42	84
Raleigh: North Carolina	**24**	36	79
Ramona: California.	**35**	33	117
Rampart: Alaska	**42**	65	150
Ramsey: New Jersey	**15**	41	74
Rancheria: Yukon	**40**	60	131
Rancocas Creek: New Jersey	**2**	40	75
Rand: West Virginia	**16**	38	82
Randleman: North Carolina	**24**	36	80
Randolph: Massachusetts	**15**	42	71
Randolph: New York	**19**	42	79
Randolph: Utah	**33**	42	111

	Page	N	W
Randolph: Vermont	**13**	44	73
Randsburg: California	**35**	35	118
Rankin Inlet: N.W.T.	**45**	63	92
Rankin Inlet: *sett.*, N.W.T.	**45**	63	92
Rantoul: Illinois	**21**	40	88
Rapid City: South Dakota	**28**	44	103
Rapid River: *sett.*, Michigan	**20**	46	87
Rappahannock: *r.*, Virginia	**17**	38	77
Raquette: *r.*, New York	**13**	44	75
Raquette L.: New York	**13**	44	75
Rarden: Ohio	**16**	39	83
Raritan: r., New Jersey	**1**	40½	74¼
Raritan Bay: New Jersey	**1**	40½	74¼
Rat: *r.*, Manitoba	**31**	56	99
Rat Is.: Alaska	**60**	52	178E
Raton: New Mexico	**29**	37	104
Rat River: *sett.*, N.W.T.	**30**	61	113
Ratz, Mt.: British Columbia	**40**	57	132
Ravendale: California	**36**	41	120
Ravenna: California	**35**	34	118
Ravenswood: West Virginia	**16**	39	82
Rawdon: Québec	**13**	46	74
Rawlins: Wyoming	**28**	42	107
Ray: Arizona	**33**	33	111
Ray, C.: Newfoundland	**9**	48	59
Raymond: Alberta	**30**	50	113
Raymond: California	**37**	37	120
Raymond: Washington	**39**	47	124
Raymondville: Texas	**22**	27	98
Ray Mts.: Alaska	**42**	66	152
Rayne: Louisiana	**26**	30	92
Rayville: Louisiana	**26**	32	92
Reading: Massachusetts	**15**	43	71
Reading: Michigan	**21**	42	85
Reading: Pennsylvania	**14**	40	76
Read Island: *sett.*, N.W.T.	**44**	69	114
Red: *r.*	**22**	31	92
Red Bank: New Jersey	**15**	40	74
Red Bay: *sett.*, Alabama	**27**	34	88
Red Bluff: California	**36**	40	122
Redcliff: Colorado	**28**	40	106
Red Deer: Alberta	**30**	52	114
Red Deer: *r.*, Alberta	**30**	51	112
Red Deer: *r.*, Saskatchewan	**30**	53	103
Red Deer L.: Manitoba	**31**	53	101
Red Devil: Alaska	**43**	62	157
Redding: California	**36**	41	122
Redfield: South Dakota	**28**	45	99
Redkey: Indiana	**21**	40	85
Red Lake: *r.*, Minnesota	**10**	48	96
Red L.: Ontario	**31**	51	94
Redlands: California	**35**	34	117
Red Lion: Pennsylvania	**14**	40	77
Red Mesa: Arizona.	**33**	37	109
Redmond: Oregon	**32**	44	121
Redmond: Utah	**33**	39	112
Redmond: Washington	**6**	47¾	122
Red Mountain: *sett.*, California.	**35**	35	118
Redonda Is.: British Columbia	**38**	50	125
Redondo Beach: *town*, Calif.	**7**	33¾	118½
Redoubt Volcano: Alaska	**43**	61	153
Red River of the North	**10**	48	97
Red Springs: North Carolina	**24**	35	79
Redwater: Alberta	**30**	54	113
Redway: California.	**36**	40	124
Red Valley: *sett.*, California	**37**	39	123
Red Wing: Minnesota	**10**	45	93
Redwood: Mississippi	**27**	32	91
Redwood City: California	**6**	37½	122¼
Redwood Estates: California	**37**	37	122
Redwood Falls: *town*, Minn.	**10**	45	95
Redwood Regional Park: California	**6**	37¾	122¼
Reed City: Michigan	**20**	44	86
Reedley: California	**34**	37	119
Reeds Gap; Pennsylvania	**14**	40	78
Reedville: Virginia	**17**	38	76
Regina: Saskatchewan	**30**	51	105
Rehoboth Bay: Delaware	**17**	39	75
Rehoboth Beach: *sett*,. Del.	**17**	39	75
Reidsville: Georgia	**24**	32	82
Reidsville: North Carolina	**16**	36	80
Reindeer Depot: N.W.T.	**44**	69	134
Reindeer L.: Man./Sask.	**30/31**	58	102
Reindeer Station: Alaska	**42**	66	161
Reisterstown: Maryland	**17**	39	77
Reltier, L.: Minnesota	**3**	45½	93
Remington: Indiana	**21**	41	87
Renfrew: Ontario	**12**	45	77
Reno: Nevada	**37**	40	120
Reno: Pennsylvania	**19**	41	80
Renovo: Pennsylvania	**14**	41	78
Rensselaer: Indiana	**21**	41	87
Rensselaer: New York	**15**	43	74
Renton: Washington	**6**	47½	122¼
Republic: Washington	**32**	49	119
Republican:*r.*, Nebr./Kansas	**28**	40	98
Repulse Bay: *sett.*, N.W.T.	**45**	67	86
Requa: California	**36**	42	124
Reseda: California	**7**	39¼	118½
Reserve: Louisiana	**27**	30	91
Resolute: Northwest Territories	**45**	75	95
Resolution I.: N.W.T.	**45**	62	65
Resolution Island: *sett.*, N.W.T.	**45**	62	65
Retsof: New York	**14**	43	78
Reusens: Virginia	**16**	37	79
Revelstoke: British Columbia	**41**	51	118

	Page	N	W
Revere: Massachusetts	2	42½	71
Revere Beach: Massachusetts	2	42½	71
Rexburg: Idaho	32	44	112
Reyes, Point: California	37	38	123
Reynolds: Georgia	24	33	84
Reynoldsville: Pennsylvania	14	41	79
Rhinebeck: New York	15	42	74
Rhinelander: Wisconsin	20	46	89
RHODE ISLAND	15	—	—
Rice, L.: Minnesota	3	45¼	93¼
Rice L.: Ontario	12	44	78
Richard Collinson Inlet: N.W.T.	44	72	114
Richards L.: N.W.T.	44	69	135
Richardson: Texas	26	33	97
Richardson: *r.*, Alberta	30	58	111
Richardson I.: N.W.T.	40	66	118
Richardson Is.: N.W.T.	44	58	110
Richardson Mts.: Yukon	42	68	137
Richelieu: *r.*, Québec	13	46	73
Riche Point: Newfoundland	9	51	57
Richfield: Minnesota	3	35	93¼
Richfield: Utah	33	39	112
Richfield Springs: New York	14	43	75
Richford: Vermont	13	45	73
Richgrove: California	34	36	119
Richibucto: New Brunswick	9	47	65
Richland: Georgia	27	32	85
Richland: Washington	39	46	119
Richlands: Virginia	16	37	82
Richmond: British Columbia	6	49	123½
Richmond: California	6	38	122¼
Richmond: Indiana	21	40	85
Richmond: Kentucky	23	38	84
Richmond: Michigan	19	43	83
Richmond: New York	1	40½	74¼
Richmond: Pennsylvania	2	40	75
Richmond: Québec	13	46	72
Richmond: Texas	26	30	96
Richmond: Virginia	17	38	77
Richmond Beach: *sett.*, Wash.	6	47¾	122½
Richmond Gulf: Québec	8	56	76
Richmond Heights: *sett.*, Washington	6	47¾	122½
Richmond Hill: *town*, Ontario	6	43¾	79½
Rich Mt.: West Virginia	16	39	80
Rich Passage: Washington	6	47½	122½
Richton: Mississippi	27	31	89
Richwood: Ohio	19	40	83
Richwood: West Virginia	16	38	81
Rico: Colorado	29	38	108
Riddle: Oregon	32	43	123
Rideau: *r.*, Ontario	12	45	76
Rideau L.: Ontario	12	45	76
Ridgecrest: California	35	36	118
Ridgefield: Connecticut	15	41	74
Ridgeland: South Carolina	24	33	81
Ridgely: Maryland	17	39	76
Ridgetown: Ontario	19	42	82
Ridgeway: Ohio	19	41	84
Ridgway: Pennsylvania	14	41	79
Ridgewood: Illinois	4	41½	88
Ridgewood: New Jersey	1	41	74¼
Riding Mountain Nat. Park: Manitoba	31	51	100
Ridley Creek State Park: Pennsylvania	2	40	75¼
Rifle: Colorado	28	40	108
Rigaud: Québec	13	45	74
Rigolet: Newfoundland	9	54	59
Rillito: Arizona	33	32	111
Rimbey: Alberta	30	53	114
Rimouski: Québec	9	48	69
Rio Dell: California	36	41	124
Rio Grande: *r.*	29	30	105
Riondel: British Columbia	41	50	117
Rio Vista: California	37	38	122
Ripley: Mississippi	27	35	89
Ripley: New York	19	42	80
Ripley: Tennessee	27	36	90
Ripley: West Virginia	16	39	82
Ripon: California	37	38	121
Ripon: Wisconsin	20	44	89
Rison: Arkansas	26	34	92
Ritter, Mt.: California	37	38	119
Rittman: Ohio	19	41	82
Rivanna: *r.*, Virginia	17	38	78
Riverbank: California	37	38	121
Riverdale: New Jersey	15	41	74
River Forest: *town*, Illinois	4	42	87¾
Riverhead: New York	15	41	73
Riverhurst: Saskatchewan	30	51	107
River Jordan: *sett.*, B.C.	38	48	124
River Rouge: Michigan	5	42¼	83¼
River Rouge Park: Michigan	5	42¼	83¼
Riverside: California	35	34	117
Riverside: Illinois	4	41¾	87¾
Riverside: New Jersey	2	40	75
Riverside: Ontario	5	42¼	83
Rivers Inlet: B.C.	41	52	127
Riverton: Manitoba	31	51	97
Riverton: Wyoming	28	43	108
Riverton Heights: *sett.*, Wash.	6	47½	112¼
Rivesville: West Virginia	16	40	80
Rivière Bersimis: *sett.*, Québec	8	49	69
Rivière du Loup: Québec	9	48	70
Roanoke: Alabama	27	33	85
Roanoke: Illinois	21	41	89

	Page	N	W
Roanoke: Virginia	16	37	80
Roanoke: *r.*, Va./N.C.	16/17	37	79
Roanoke Rapids: N.C.	17	36	78
Roanoke Rapids L.: N.C.	17	37	78
Roaring Spring: Pennsylvania	14	40	78
Robbins: California	37	39	122
Robbinsdale: Minnesota	3	45	93¼
Robbinsville: New Jersey	15	40	75
Robersonville: North Carolina	24	36	77
Robert Brown, C.: N.W.T.	45	68	81
Robert, C.: Ontario	18	46	83
Roberval: Québec	8	49	72
Robesonia: Pennsylvania	14	40	76
Robinson: Pennsylvania	19	40	79
Robinson: Yukon	40	60	135
Robson, Mount: Alberta/B.C.	41	53	119
Robstown: Texas	22	28	98
Rochdale: Massachusetts	15	42	72
Rochelle: Georgia	24	32	83
Rochelle: Illinois	21	42	89
Rocher River: *sett.*, N.W.T.	30	61	113
Rochester: Indiana	21	41	86
Rochester: Michigan	19	43	83
Rochester: Minnesota	10	44	92
Rochester: New Hampshire	11	43	71
Rochester: New York	12	43	78
Rochester: Pennsylvania	19	41	80
Rock: *r.*, Illinois/Wisconsin	21	42	89
Rockaway: Oregon	39	46	124
Rockaway Beach: New York	1	40½	74
Rockaway Inlet: New York	1	40½	74
Rock Creek: *sett.*, B.C.	38	49	119
Rock Creek Park: D.C.	2	40	75¼
Rockdale: Texas	26	31	97
Rock Falls: *town*, Illinois	21	42	90
Rockford: Illinois	21	42	89
Rockford: Michigan	20	43	86
Rockford: Ohio	21	41	85
Rock Hill: *town*, S.C.	24	35	81
Rockingham: North Carolina	24	35	80
Rock Island: *dam*, Washington	39	47	120
Rock Island: *town*, Illinois	10	42	91
Rockland: Massachusetts	15	42	71
Rockland: Ontario	13	46	75
Rockland: *dam*, Texas	26	31	94
Rocklin: California	37	39	121
Rockmart: Georgia	27	34	85
Rockport: California	36	40	124
Rockport: Massachusetts	15	43	71
Rock Springs: Wyoming	28	42	109
Rockville: California	37	38	122
Rockville: Connecticut	15	42	72
Rockville: Indiana	21	40	87
Rockville: Maryland	17	39	77
Rockville Centre: New York	1	40¾	73¾
Rockwall: Texas	26	33	96
Rockwell: North Carolina	24	36	80
Rockwood: Maine	9	46	70
Rockwood: Pennsylvania	16	40	79
Rockwood: Tennessee	24	36	85
Rocky Ford: Colorado	29	38	104
Rocky Hill: *sett.*, Connecticut	15	42	73
Rocky Mount: *town*, N.C.	24	36	78
Rockymount: Virginia	16	37	80
Rocky Mountain Arsenal: Colo.	3	39¾	104¾
Rocky Mountain House: Alta.	30	52	115
Rocky Mt. Nat. Park: Colorado	28	40	106
Rocky Mountains	32	—	—
Rocky Point: *sett.*, New York	15	41	73
Rocky Reach: *dam*, Washington	39	48	120
Rodessa: Louisiana	26	33	94
Roebling: New Jersey	15	40	75
Roes Welcome Sound: N.W.T.	45	65	87
Roff: Oklahoma	26	35	97
Rogers City: Michigan	20	45	84
Rogers L.: California	35	35	118
Rogers, Mount: Virginia	16	37	82
Rogersville: Tennessee	24	36	83
Roggan River: *sett.*, Québec	8	54	79
Rogue: *r.*, Oregon	36	43	124
Rogue River: *sett.*, Oregon	36	42	123
Rojo, Cabo: Puerto Rico	27	18	67
Rolla: Missouri	10	38	92
Rolling Fork: Mississippi	27	33	91
Rolling Prairie: Indiana	21	42	87
Romain, C.: South Carolina	24	33	79
Romaine: *r.*, Québec	9	51	63
Romano, C.: Florida	25	26	82
Romanzof, C.: Alaska	43	62	166
Rome: Georgia	27	34	85
Rome: New York	13	43	75
Romeo: Michigan	19	43	83
Romney: West Virginia	17	39	79
Romulus: Michigan	19	42	83
Ronceverte: West Virginia	16	38	80
Rondeau Prov. Park: Ontario	19	42	82
Rondout Res.: New York	15	42	74
Ronkonkoma: New York	15	41	73
Roosevelt: *dam*, Arizona	33	34	111
Root Portage: Ontario	10	51	91
Rosamond: California	35	35	118
Rosamond L.: California	35	35	118
Roscoe: Pennsylvania	19	40	80
Roseau: *r.*, Minn./Manitoba	10	49	96
Roseboro: North Carolina	24	35	79
Rosebud: Texas	26	31	97
Roseburg: Oregon	32	42	123

	Page	N	W
Rosedale: Mississippi	27	34	91
Roselle: Illinois	4	42	88
Rosemead: California	7	34	118
Rosenberg: Texas	26	30	96
Rosetown: Saskatchewan	30	52	108
Roseville: California	37	39	121
Roseville: Michigan	5	42½	83
Roseville: Minnesota	3	45	93¼
Rosewood: California	36	40	123
Ross: *r.*, Yukon	40	62	131
Rossignol L.: Nova Scotia	9	44	65
Rossiter: Pennsylvania	14	41	79
Ross Barnet Res.: Mississippi	27	32	90
Ross L.: Washington	38	49	121
Rossland: British Columbia	41	49	118
Ross River: *sett.*, Yukon	40	62	132
Rossville: Georgia	27	35	85
Rossville: Illinois	21	40	88
Rosthern: Saskatchewan	30	53	106
Roswell: Georgia	24	34	84
Roswell: New Mexico	29	33	105
Rouge: *r.*, Michigan	5	42½	83¼
Rouge: *r.*, Ontario	5	43¾	79¼
Rouge: *r.*, Québec	13	46	75
Round Hill Park: Pennsylvania	5	40½	79¾
Round L.: Ontario	12	46	78
Round Mountain: *sett.*, Calif.	36	41	122
Roundup: Montana	28	46	109
Rouseville: Pennsylvania	19	41	80
Rouyn: Québec	8	48	79
Rowes Run: Pennsylvania	16	40	80
Rowland: North Carolina	24	35	79
Rowley I.: N.W.T.	45	69	79
Roxboro: North Carolina	17	36	79
Roxbury: Massachusetts	2	42¼	71
Roxbury: New York	15	42	75
Roxton: Texas	26	34	96
Royale, Isle: Michigan	10	48	89
Royal Oak: Michigan	5	42½	83¼
Royersford: Pennsylvania	14	40	76
Royston: Georgia	24	34	83
Rubicon: *r.*, California	37	39	121
Ruby: Alaska	42	65	156
Ruby Ranges: Yukon	40	61	138
Rugby: North Dakota	28	48	100
Ruggs: Oregon	39	45	120
Ruleville: Mississippi	27	34	91
Rum: *r.*, Minnesota	10	46	94
Rumsey: California	37	39	122
Rumson: New Jersey	15	40	74
Running Springs: California	35	34	117
Rupert: Idaho	32	43	114
Rupert: *r.*, Québec	8	51	78
Rupert House: Québec	8	52	79
Rural Valley: *sett.*, Pennsylvania	19	41	79
Rushville: Indiana	21	40	85
Rushville: New York	14	43	77
Rusk: Texas	26	32	95
Russells: Kansas	28	39	99
Russell: Kentucky	16	39	83
Russell: Manitoba	31	51	101
Russell Fork: *r.*, Kentucky	16	37	82
Russell Inlet: N.W.T.	44	70	130
Russell I.: N.W.T.	44	74	99
Russell Point: N.W.T.	44	74	115
Russellville: Alabama	27	35	88
Russellville: Arkansas	26	35	93
Russian: *r.*, California	37	39	123
Russian Mission: Alaska	43	62	161
Ruston: Louisiana	26	33	93
Ruth: California	36	40	123
Ruth: Nevada	33	39	115
Rutherfordton: North Carolina	24	35	82
Rutland: Vermont	13	44	73
Ryan: California	35	36	117
Ryde: California	37	38	122
Sabine: *r.*, Texas/Louisiana	26	31	94
Sable, C.: Florida	25	25	81
Sable, C.: Nova Scotia	9	43	66
Sable I.: Nova Scotia	9	44	60
Sacandaga Res.: New York	13	43	74
Sachigo: *r.*, Ontario	31	54	91
Sachs Harbour: N.W.T.	44	72	125
Sachs Harbour: *sett.*, N.W.T.	44	72	125
Sackets Habor: New York	12	44	76
Saco: Maine	11	44	70
Sacramento: *& r.*, California	37	39	122
Sacramento Mts.: New Mexico	29	33	105
Safford: Arizona	33	33	110
Sagamore: Massachusetts	15	42	71
Sage: California	35	34	117
Sage: Wyoming	28	42	111
Sag Harbor: New York	15	41	72
Saginaw: Michigan	20	43	84
Saginaw: *r.*, Michigan	20	44	84
Saginaw Bay: Michigan	18	44	83
Sagola: Michigan	20	46	88
Saguaro Nat. Mon.: Arizona	33	32	111
Saguenay: *r.*, Québec	8	48	70
St. Albans: Newfoundland	9	48	56
St. Albans: Vermont	13	45	73
St. Albans: West Virginia	16	38	82
St. Andrews Bay: Florida	27	30	86
Ste.-Anne-de-Bellevue: Québec	2	45½	74
St. Anthony: Idaho	32	44	112
St. Anthony: Newfoundland	9	51	56

	Page	N	W
Sir James McBrien, Mt.: N.W.T.	40	62	128
Siskiyou: Oregon	36	42	123
Siskiyou Mts.: Calif./Oregon	36	42	124
Sisquoc: *& r.*, California	34	35	120
Sisseton: South Dakota	28	46	97
Sitidgi L.: Northwest Territories	44	69	132
Sitka: Alaska	41	57	135
Sitkalidak I.: Alaska	43	57	153
Sitkinak Is.: Alaska	43	56	154
Skagit: *r.*, Washington/B.C.	38	49	122
Skagway: Alaska	40	59	135
Skal I.: Greenland	45	72	56
Skaneateles: *& lake*, New York	14	43	76
Skeena: British Columbia	41	54	130
Skeena: *r.*, British Columbia	41	54	129
Skeena Mts.: British Columbia	41	57	129
Skihist Mt.: British Columbia	38	50	122
Skokie: Illinois	21	42	88
Skokie: *r.*, Illinois	4	42¼	87¾
Skwentna: Alaska	43	62	151
Slate Is.: Ontario	10	49	87
Slatington: Pennsylvania	14	41	76
Slave: *r.*, Alta./N.W.T.	30	59	111
Sleeper Is.: N.W.T.	8	57	80
Sleetmute: Alaska	43	62	157
Slidell: Louisiana	27	30	90
Slippery Rock: Pennsylvania	19	41	80
Sloan: Nevada	35	36	115
Sloat: California	36	40	121
Slocan: British Columbia	41	50	117
Sloughouse: California	37	38	121
Smackover: Arkansas	26	33	93
Smethport: Pennsylvania	14	42	78
Smith: Alberta	30	55	114
Smith: Nevada	37	39	119
Smith: *r.*, California	36	42	124
Smith: *r.*, Montana	28	47	111
Smith Arm: Great Bear L., Northwest Territories	40	66	124
Smith Bay: Alaska	42	71	154
Smithers: British Columbia	41	55	127
Smithfield: North Carolina	24	36	78
Smithfield: Pennsylvania	16	40	80
Smithfield: Utah	33	42	112
Smithfield: Virginia	17	37	77
Smith I.: Maryland	17	38	76
Smith Mt. Res.: Virginia	16	37	79
Smith River: *sett.*, B.C.	40	60	126
Smith River: *sett.*, California	36	42	124
Smiths Falls: *town*, Ontario	12	45	76
Smithville: Tennessee	27	36	86
Smithville: Texas	26	30	97
Smoke Creek Desert: Nevada	36	41	120
Smoky: *r.*, Alberta	30	55	119
Smoky Falls: *sett.*, Ontario	11	50	82
Smoky Hill: *r.*, Colo./Kansas	29	39	101
Smyrna: Delaware	17	39	76
Snag: Yukon	40	62	140
Snake: *r.*, Idaho/Washington	32	46	117
Snake: *r.*, Yukon	40	65	133
Snare: *r.*, N.W.T.	40	64	115
Snare River: *sett.*, N.W.T.	44	63	116
Snoqualmie Pass: Washington	39	47	121
Snowbird L.: N.W.T.	30	61	103
Snowden: California	36	41	123
Snowdrift: N.W.T.	44	62	111
Snowdrift: *r.*, N.W.T.	44	62	109
Snow Hill: *sett.*, Maryland	17	38	75
Snow Hill: *sett.*, North Carolina	24	35	78
Snow Lake: *sett.*, Manitoba	31	55	100
Snow Mt.: California	37	39	123
Snyder: Texas	29	33	101
Soap Lake: *sett.*, Washington	39	47	119
Social Circle: Georgia	24	34	84
Socorro: New Mexico	29	34	107
Soda L.: California	35	35	116
Soda L.: California	34	35	120
Soda Springs: California	37	39	120
Soda Springs: Idaho	32	43	112
Soddy: Tennessee	27	35	85
Sodus: New York	12	43	77
Solana Beach: *sett.* California	35	33	117
Soldatna: Alaska	43	61	151
Soledad: California	34	36	121
Soleduck: *r.*, Washington	38	48	124
Solomon: Alaska	42	65	164
Solomon: *r.*, Kansas	29	39	99
Solon: Ohio	19	41	81
Solromar: California	35	34	119
Solvang: California	34	35	120
Somerset: Kentucky	23	37	85
Somerset: Massachusetts	15	42	71
Somerset: Ohio	16	40	82
Somerset: Pennsylvania	16	40	79
Somerset I.: N.W.T.	45	73	93
Somerset Res.: Vermont	13	43	73
Somers Point: *town*, N.J.	15	39	75
Somersville: Connecticut	15	42	73
Somersworth: New Hampshire	15	43	71
Somerville: Massachusetts	2	42½	71¼
Somerville: New Jersey	15	41	75
Somerville: Tennessee	27	35	89
Somerville: Texas	26	30	97
Somesbar: California	36	41	124
Sonoita: Arizona	33	32	113
Sonoma: California	37	38	122
Sonora: California	37	38	120

	Page	N	W
Sonora: Texas	29	31	101
Sooke: British Columbia	38	48	124
Soperton: Georgia	24	32	83
Sorel: Québec	13	46	73
Souderton: Pennsylvania	14	40	75
Sound View: Connecticut	15	41	72
Souris: Manitoba	31	50	100
Souris: Prince Edward Island	9	46	62
Souris: *r.*	30/31	49	104
Sour Lake: *sett.*, Texas	26	30	94
South Amherst: Ohio	19	41	82
Southampton: New York	15	41	72
Southampton: Ontario	18	44	81
Southampton, C.: N.W.T.	45	62	84
Southampton I.: N.W.T.	45	64	84
South Anna: *r.*, Virginia	17	38	78
South Aulatsivik I.: Nfld.	9	57	62
South Bay: N.W.T.	45	64	83
South Bend: Indiana	21	42	86
South Bend: Washington	39	47	124
South Berwick: Maine	15	43	71
South Bjerremark: Alaska	42	65	148
South Boston: Virginia	17	37	79
South Branch Mt.: West Virginia	17	39	79
Southbridge: Massachusetts	15	42	72
SOUTH CAROLINA	24	—	—
South Charleston: West Virginia	16	38	82
SOUTH DAKOTA	28	—	—
South Deerfield: Massachusetts	15	42	73
Southend: Saskatchewan	30	56	103
Southern Indian L.: Manitoba	31	57	99
Southern Pines: North Carolina	24	35	79
Southfield: Michigan	5	42½	83¼
South Fork: California	36	40	124
South Fork: Pennsylvania	14	40	79
South Fork: *r.*, California	35	36	118
South Fork: *r.*, W. Va.	16	39	81
South Fox I.: Michigan	20	45	86
South Gate: California	7	34	118¼
Southgate: *r.*, British Columbia	38	51	125
South Hadley: Massachusetts	15	42	73
South Haven: Michigan	21	42	86
South Henik L.: N.W.T.	31	61	97
South Hill: *town*, Virginia	17	37	78
South Holston L.: Tennessee	16	37	82
South Holston Res.: Tenn.	24	37	82
South Houston: Texas	3	29¾	95¼
South Indian Lake: *sett.*, Man.	31	57	99
South Lyon: Michigan	19	42	84
South Manitou I.: Michigan	20	45	86
South Milwaukee: Wisconsin	20	43	88
South Nahanni: N.W.T.	40	61	123
South Nahanni: *r.*, N.W.T.	40	62	126
South Naknek: Alaska	43	59	157
Southold: New York	15	41	72
South Park: Pennsylvania	5	40¼	80
Souh Pittsburg: Tennessee	27	35	86
South Platte: *r.*, Colo./Nebr.	28	41	103
South Point: Michigan	18	45	83
South Point: Ohio	16	38	83
Southport: South Carolina	24	34	78
South River: New Jersey	15	40	74
South San Francisco: Calif.	6	37½	122¼
South Saskatchewan: *r.*, Alberta/Saskatchewan	30	51	110
South Sioux City: Nebraska	28	42	96
South St. Paul: Minnesota	3	44¾	93¼
South Whitley: Indiana	21	41	86
Spangler: Pennsylvania	14	41	79
Spanish: *r.*, Ontario	11	47	82
Spanish Banks: *Hd.*, B.C.	6	49¼	123¼
Sparkman: Arkansas	26	34	93
Sparks: Nevada	37	40	120
Sparrows Point: *town*, Maryland	17	39	76
Sparta: Georgia	24	33	83
Sparta: Michigan	20	43	86
Sparta: Tennessee	27	36	85
Spartanburg: South Carolina	24	35	32
Spearfish: South Dakota	28	44	104
Speed: Indiana	10	38	86
Speedway: Indiana	21	40	86
Spenard: Alaska	43	61	150
Spence Bay: *sett.*, N.W.T.	45	70	94
Spencer: Iowa	10	43	95
Spencer: West Virginia	16	39	81
Spencerville: Ohio	19	41	84
Spences Bridge: B.C.	38	50	121
Spicer Is.: N.W.T.	45	68	79
Spindale: North Carolina	24	35	82
Spirit Lake: *sett.*, Washington	39	46	122
Spirit River: *town*, Alberta	30	56	119
Spiro: Oklahoma	26	35	95
Split L.: Manitoba	31	56	96
Split Lake: *sett.*, Manitoba	31	56	96
Spokane: Washington	32	48	117
Spot Pond: Massachusetts	2	42½	71
Spragge: Ontario	18	46	83
Sprague River: *sett.*, Oregon	36	42	122
Spray: Oregon	39	46	120
Spring: *r.*	29	37	95
Spring Branch: *sett.*, Texas	3	29¾	95½
Spring Creek: *sett.*, Pennsylvania	19	42	80
Springdale: Arkansas	26	36	94
Springdale: Nevada	35	37	117
Springfield: Colorado	29	37	103
Springfield: Georgia	24	32	81
Springfield: Illinois	10	40	90

	Page	N	W
Springfield: Massachusetts	15	42	73
Springfield: Missouri	10	37	93
Springfield: Ohio	21	40	84
Springfield: Oregon	32	44	123
Springfield: Pennsylvania	2	40	75¼
Springfield: Vermont	13	43	72
Springfield: Virginia	2	38¾	77¼
Springhill: Louisiana	26	33	93
Springhill: Nova Scotia	9	46	64
Spring Hope: North Carolina	24	36	78
Spring Lake: *sett.*, Michigan	20	43	86
Spring Lake: *sett.*, Minnesota	3	45	93¼
Spring Mts.: Nevada	35	36	116
Springton Res.: Pennsylvania	2	40	75¼
Spring Valley: *sett.*, California	35	33	117
Spring Valley: *town*, Illinois	21	41	89
Spring Valley: *town*, New York	15	41	74
Springville: New York	19	43	79
Springville: Utah	33	40	112
Sproat L.: British Columbia	38	49	125
Spruce Knob: *mt.*, W. Va.	16	39	80
Spruce Pine: North Carolina	24	36	82
Spy Pond: Massachusetts	2	42½	71¼
Squamish: *& r.*, B.C.	38	50	123
Stafford Springs: Connecticut	15	42	72
Stambaugh: Michigan	20	46	89
Stamford: Connecticut	15	41	74
Stamford: New York	15	42	75
Stamps: Arkansas	26	33	94
Standish: California	36	40	120
Standish: Michigan	20	44	84
Standley L.: Colorado	3	39¾	105¼
Stang, C.: Northwest Territories	44	71	104
Stanley Park: British Columbia	6	49¼	123
Stanley Mission: Saskatchewan	30	55	105
Stanton: Michigan	20	43	85
Stanton: Northwest Territories	44	70	129
Star City: Arkansas	26	34	92
Starke: Florida	25	30	82
Starkville: Mississippi	27	33	89
State College: Pennsylvania	14	41	78
Staten Island: New York	1	40½	74¼
Statesboro: Georgia	24	32	82
States Hot Springs: California	34	36	122
Statesville: North Carolina	24	36	81
Staunton: Virginia	16	38	79
Stave L.: British Columbia	38	49	122
Stayton: Oregon	39	45	123
Steam Boat: British Columbia	40	59	124
Steamboat: Nevada	37	39	120
Steamboat Springs: Colorado	28	41	108
Stebbins: Alaska	42	64	162
Steelton: Pennsylvania	14	40	77
Steensby Inlet: N.W.T.	45	70	79
Stefansson I.: N.W.T.	44	74	106
Steinbach: Manitoba	31	50	97
Stephens: Arkansas	26	33	93
Stephens City: Virginia	17	39	78
Stephenson: Michigan	20	45	88
Stephenville: Newfoundland	9	49	59
Sterling: Alaska	43	61	151
Sterling: Colorado	28	41	103
Sterling: Illinois	21	42	90
Sterling Heights: *town*, Michigan	5	42½	83
Sterlington: Louisiana	26	33	92
Stettler: Alberta	30	52	113
Steuben: Michigan	20	46	86
Steubenville: Ohio	19	40	81
Stevenson: Washington	39	46	122
Stevens Point: *town*, Wisconsin	20	45	90
Stevens Village: Alaska	42	66	149
Steveston: British Columbia	6	49	123¼
Stevinson: California	37	37	121
Stewart: British Columbia	41	56	130
Stewart: Nevada	37	39	120
Stewart: *r.*, Yukon	40	63	138
Stewart River: *sett.*, Yukon	40	63	139
Stewartstown: Pennsylvania	14	40	77
Stickney: Illinois	4	41¾	87¾
Stigler: Oklahoma	26	35	95
Stikine: *r.*, British Columbia	40	58	132
Stillwater: New York	15	43	74
Stillwater: Oklahoma	29	36	97
Stirling: Alberta	30	50	113
Stockbridge: Massachusetts	15	42	73
Stockbridge: Michigan	21	42	84
Stockton: California	37	38	121
Stockton: Utah	33	40	112
Stockton Plateau: Texas	29	31	102
Stoneboro: Pennsylvania	19	41	80
Stone Canyon Res.: California	7	34	118½
Stoneham: Massachusetts	2	42½	71
Stoneham: Pennsylvania	19	42	79
Stone Harbor: New Jersey	15	39	75
Stonewall: Mississippi	27	32	89
Stonington: Connecticut	15	41	72
Stonington: Illinois	21	40	89
Stony Brook: *town*, N.Y.	15	41	73
Stony Brook Reservation: Mass.	2	42¼	71¼
Stony Creek: *sett.*, Connecticut	15	41	73
Stony Creek: Illinois	4	41¾	87¾
Stony Creek: *sett.*, Virginia	17	37	77
Stonyford: California	37	39	123
Stony Gorge Res.: California	37	40	123
Stony I.: New York	12	44	76
Stony L.: Manitoba	31	59	98
Stony L.: Ontario	12	45	78

	Page	N	W
Stony Point: *sett.*, New York	**15**	41	74
Stony Point: *sett.*, N.C.	**24**	36	81
Stony Rapids: Saskatchewan	**30**	59	106
Stony River: *sett.*, Alaska	**43**	62	157
Stouffville: Ontario	**12**	44	79
Stoughton: Massachusetts	**15**	42	71
Stoughton: Wisconsin	**20**	43	89
Strasburg: Ohio	**19**	41	82
Strasburg: Pennsylvania	**14**	40	76
Strasburg: Virginia	**17**	39	78
Stratford: California	**34**	36	120
Stratford: Connecticut	**15**	41	73
Stratford: Oklahoma	**26**	35	97
Stratford: Ontario	**18**	43	81
Strathcona Prov. Park: B.C.	**41**	50	126
Strathmore: Alberta	**30**	51	113
Strathroy: Ontario	**19**	43	82
Strawberry Mt.: Oregon	**32**	44	119
Streator: Illinois	**21**	41	89
Streetsboro: Ohio	**19**	41	81
Strongsville: Ohio	**19**	41	82
Stroud: Oklahoma	**26**	36	97
Stroudsburg: Pennsylvania	**14**	41	75
Stryker: Ohio	**19**	42	84
Stuart: Florida	**25**	27	80
Stuart: *r.*, British Columbia	**41**	54	124
Stuart I.: Alaska	**42**	64	162
Stuart L.: British Columbia	**41**	54	125
Stump L.: British Columbia	**38**	50	120
Sturgeon: *r.*, Saskatchewan	**30**	53	107
Sturgeon Bank: B.C.	**6**	49	123¼
Sturgeon Bay: *town*, Wisconsin	**20**	45	87
Sturgeon Falls: *town*, Ontario	**18**	46	80
Sturgis: Michigan	**21**	42	85
Sturgis: South Dakota	**28**	44	104
Stuttgart: Arkansas	**26**	34	92
Success, L.: California	**35**	36	119
Sudbury: Ontario	**18**	47	81
Suffern: New York	**15**	41	74
Suffield: Connecticut	**15**	42	73
Suffolk: Virginia	**17**	37	77
Sugar: *cr.*, Indiana	**21**	40	87
Sugar: *r.*, Wisconsin	**21**	43	89
Sugar Creek: *town*, Missouri	**10**	39	94
Sugar Land: Texas	**26**	30	96
Sugluk: Québec	**45**	62	76
Suisun B.: California	**37**	38	122
Suisun City: California	**37**	38	122
Suitland: Maryland	**2**	38¾	76¾
Sulligent: Alabama	**27**	34	88
Sullivan: Illinois	**21**	40	89
Sullivan L.: Alberta	**30**	52	112
Sulphur: Louisiana	**26**	30	93
Sulphur: Nevada	**36**	41	119
Sulphur: Oklahoma	**26**	35	97
Sulphur: *r.*, Texas/Arkansas	**26**	33	95
Sulphur Springs: Texas	**26**	33	96
Sumiton: Alabama	**27**	34	87
Summer I.: Michigan	**20**	46	87
Summer Lake: Oregon	**36**	43	121
Summerland: British Columbia	**38**	50	120
Summerside: P.E.I.	**9**	46	64
Summerton: South Carolina	**24**	34	80
Summerville: Georgia	**27**	34	85
Summerville: Pennsylvania	**19**	41	79
Summerville: South Carolina	**24**	33	80
Summit: Alaska	**42**	63	149
Summit: California	**35**	34	117
Summit: Illinois	**4**	41¾	87¾
Summit: Mississippi	**27**	31	90
Summit: New Jersey	**1**	40¾	74¼
Summit Hill: *town*, Pennsylvania	**14**	41	76
Summit Lake: *sett.*, B.C.	**40**	59	125
Summitville: Indiana	**21**	40	86
Sumner: Washington	**39**	47	122
Sumner Lake: *sett.*, Oregon	**36**	43	121
Sumrall: Mississippi	**27**	31	90
Sumter: South Carolina	**24**	34	80
Sunapee L.: New Hampshire	**13**	43	72
Sunbright: Tennessee	**23**	36	85
Sunbury: North Carolina	**17**	36	77
Sunbury: Pennsylvania	**14**	41	77
Sun City: California	**34**	34	117
Suncook: New Hampshire	**13**	43	71
Sundre: Alberta	**30**	52	114
Sunland: California	**7**	34¼	118¼
Sunnyside: Washington	**39**	46	120
Sunnyvale: California	**37**	37	122
Sun Prairie: Wisconsin	**20**	43	89
Sunrise: Alaska	**43**	61	149
Sunrise: Wyoming	**28**	42	105
Sunshine State Parkway: Fla.	**25**	29	82
Suntrana: Alaska	**42**	64	149
Sun Valley: Idaho	**32**	44	114
Superior: Arizona	**33**	33	111
Superior: Nebraska	**28**	40	98
Superior: Wisconsin	**10**	47	92
Superior, Lake:	**10**	—	—
Surf: California	**34**	35	121
Sur, Pt.: California	**34**	36	122
Surgoinsville: Tennessee	**16**	36	83
Surprise: British Columbia	**40**	60	133
Surrey: British Columbia	**6**	49¼	122¾
Susan: *r.*, California	**36**	40	121
Susanville: California	**36**	40	121
Susitna: *r.*, Alaska	**42/43**	62	150
Susquehanna: Pennsylvania	**14**	42	76

	Page	N	W
Susquehanna: *r.*	**14**	40	76
Susquehanna R., W. Br.: Pa.	**14**	41	78
Sussex: New Brunswick	**9**	46	66
Sussex: New Jersey	**15**	41	75
Sutcliffe: Nevada	**36**	40	120
Sutter Creek: *sett.*, California	**37**	38	121
Sutton: Québec	**13**	45	73
Sutton: West Virginia	**16**	39	81
Sutwik I.: Alaska	**43**	57	157
Suwannee: *r.*, Florida	**25**	30	83
Swainsboro: Georgia	**24**	33	83
Swampscott: Massachusetts	**2**	42½	71
Swan Hills: Alberta	**30**	55	116
Swan L.: Manitoba	**31**	52	101
Swan River: *town*, Manitoba	**31**	52	101
Swanto: California	**37**	37	122
Swanton: Ohio	**19**	42	84
Swanton: Vermont	**13**	45	73
Swedeland: Pennsylvania	**14**	40	75
Swedesboro: New Jersey	**14**	40	75
Sweeny: Texas	**26**	29	96
Sweet Home: Oregon	**32**	44	123
Sweetwater: Nevada	**37**	38	119
Sweetwater: Tennessee	**24**	36	84
Sweetwater: Texas	**29**	32	100
Swift Res.: Washington	**39**	46	122
Swift Current: Saskatchewan	**30**	50	108
Swift River: *sett.*, Yukon	**40**	60	133
Swinburne, C.: N.W.T.	**44**	71	99
Sycamore: Illinois	**21**	42	89
Sycan Marsh: Oregon	**36**	43	121
Sydney: Nova Scotia	**9**	46	60
Sydney Mines: Nova Scotia	**9**	46	60
Sykesville: Pennsylvania	**14**	41	79
Sylacauga: Alabama	**27**	33	86
Sylva: North Carolina	**24**	35	83
Sylvania: Georgia	**24**	33	82
Sylvania: Ohio	**19**	42	84
Sylvester: Georgia	**24**	32	84
Symmes: *cr.*, Ohio	**16**	39	82
Syracuse: Indiana	**21**	41	86
Syracuse: New York	**12**	43	76
Taber: Alberta	**30**	50	112
Table Rock Res.: *& dam*, Mo.	**10**	37	93
Tabor City: North Carolina	**24**	34	79
Taché, L.: Northwest Territories	**40**	64	120
Tacoma: Washington	**39**	47	123
Taconite Harbor: Minnesota	**10**	47	91
Tadoule L.: Manitoba	**31**	59	98
Tadoussac: Québec	**8**	48	70
Taft: California	**34**	35	119
Tagish L.: Yukon	**40**	60	134
Tahiryuak L.: N.W.T.	**41**	71	112
Tahlequah: Oklahoma	**26**	36	95
Tahoe City: California	**37**	39	120
Tahoe L.: California/Nevada	**37**	39	120
Tahoe L.: Northwest Territories	**44**	70	109
Tahoe Pines: California	**37**	39	120
Tahoe Valley: *sett.*, California	**37**	39	120
Tahoe Vista: California	**37**	39	120
Taholah: Washington	**39**	47	124
Tahsis: British Columbia	**41**	50	127
Takilma: Oregon	**36**	42	124
Takiyuak L.: N.W.T.	**40**	66	113
Takla L.: British Columbia	**41**	55	126
Takotna: Alaska	**42**	63	156
Taku: British Columbia	**40**	60	134
Taku: *r.*, British Columbia	**40**	59	133
Talco: Texas	**26**	33	95
Talcottville: Connecticut	**15**	42	72
Talent: Oregon	**36**	42	123
Talihina: Oklahoma	**26**	35	95
Talkeetna: Alaska	**43**	62	150
Talkeetna Mts.: Alaska	**43**	62	148
Talladega: Alabama	**27**	33	86
Tallahassee: Florida	**25**	30	84
Tallahatchie: *r.*, Mississippi	**27**	34	90
Tallapoosa: Georgia	**27**	34	85
Tallapoosa: *r.*, Ala./Georgia	**27**	32	86
Tallassee: Alabama	**27**	33	86
Tallulah: Louisiana	**26**	32	91
Talmage: California	**37**	39	123
Talquin, L.: Florida	**25**	30	85
Taltson: *r.*, N.W.T.	**44**	61	111
Tamaqua: Pennsylvania	**14**	41	76
Tampa: Florida	**25**	28	83
Tampa Bay: Florida	**25**	28	83
Tanacross: Alaska	**42**	63	144
Tanana: Alaska	**42**	65	152
Tanana: *r.*, Alaska	**42**	64	147
Taneytown: Maryland	**17**	40	77
Tangier I.: Virginia	**17**	38	76
Tangier Sound: Maryland	**17**	38	76
Tannery: Kentucky	**16**	38	83
Tanunak: Alaska	**43**	61	165
Taos: New Mexico	**29**	26	106
Tappahannock: Virginia	**17**	38	77
Tappen: British Columbia	**38**	51	119
Tar: *r.*, North Carolina	**24**	36	78
Tarboro: North Carolina	**24**	36	78
Tarentum: Pennsylvania	**5**	40½	79¾
Tarpon Springs: Florida	**25**	28	83
Tarrytown: New York	**15**	41	74
Tassialuk L.: Québec	**45**	59	74
Tathlina L.: N.W.T.	**40**	60	118
Tatitlek: Alaska	**43**	61	147

	Page	N	W
Tatnam, C.: Manitoba	**31**	57	91
Taunton: Massachusetts	**15**	42	71
Tavani: Northwest Territories	**45**	62	93
Tavares: Florida	**25**	29	82
Taverner Bay: N.W.T.	**45**	67	73
Tavistock: Ontario	**19**	43	81
Tawakoni, L.: Texas	**25**	33	96
Tawas City: Michigan	**18**	44	84
Tawas Point: Michigan	**18**	44	83
Taylor Flats: British Columbia	**41**	56	121
Taylors: South Carolina	**24**	35	82
Taylorville: Illinois	**21**	40	89
Taylorsville: Mississippi	**27**	32	89
Taylorsville: North Carolina	**24**	36	81
Tazewell: Virginia	**16**	37	82
Tazin: *r.*, N.W.T./Sask.	**30**	60	110
Tazin L.: Saskatchewan	**30**	60	109
Teague: Texas	**26**	32	96
Tecopa: California	**35**	36	116
Tecumseh: Michigan	**21**	42	84
Tecumseh: Oklahoma	**26**	35	97
Tecumseh: Ontario	**5**	42¼	82¾
Tehachapi: California	**35**	35	118
Tehachapi Mts.: California	**35**	35	119
Tehama: California	**36**	40	122
Tehek L.: Northwest Territories	**45**	65	95
Tekonsha: Michigan	**21**	42	85
Telegraph Creek: *sett.*, B.C.	**40**	58	131
Telescope Peak: California	**35**	36	117
Teller: Alaska	**42**	65	166
Teller Mission: Alaska	**42**	65	166
Tellico Plains: Tennessee	**24**	35	84
Temecula: California	**35**	34	117
Temple: Pennsylvania	**14**	40	76
Temple: Texas	**29**	31	97
Temple City: California	**7**	34	118
Templeton: California	**34**	36	121
Tenakee Springs: Alaska	**40**	58	135
Tenkiller Ferry Res.: *& dam*, Oklahoma	**26**	36	95
Tennant: California	**36**	42	122
TENNESSEE	**22/23**	—	—
Tennessee: *r.*, Tennessee	**27**	35	88
Tennille: Georgia	**24**	33	83
Tensas: *r.*, Louisiana	**26**	32	91
Ten Thousand Is.: Florida	**25**	26	82
Termo: California	**36**	41	120
Terra Alta: West Virginia	**16**	39	80
Terra Bella: California	**34**	36	119
Terrace: British Columbia	**41**	55	129
Terra Nova Nat. Park: Nfld.	**9**	49	54
Terrebonne: Québec	**13**	46	74
Terre Haute: Indiana	**21**	39	87
Terrell: Texas	**26**	33	96
Terro Point: N.W.T.	**45**	64	81
Terry: Montana	**28**	47	105
Teshekpuk, L.: Alaska	**42**	70	154
Teslin: Yukon	**40**	60	133
Teslin: *r.*, Yukon/B.C.	**40**	61	134
Teslin L.: Yukon	**40**	63	133
Tessik L.: N.W.T.	**45**	65	75
Tetlin: Alaska	**42**	63	143
Tetlin Junction: Alaska	**42**	63	143
Texada I.: British Columbia	**38**	50	125
Texarkana: Texas/Arkansas	**26**	33	94
Texarkana: *dam*, Texas	**26**	33	94
TEXAS	**29**	—	—
Texas City: Texas	**26**	29	95
Taxoma, L.: Oklahoma	**26**	34	97
Tha-anne: *r.*, N.W.T.	**31**	61	96
Thames: *r.*, Connecticut	**15**	41	72
Thames: *r.*, Ontario	**19**	43	82
The Bronx: New York	**1**	40¾	74
Thelon: *r.*, N.W.T.	**44/45**	64	94
Thelon Game Sanctuary: N.W.T.	**44**	64	105
Theodore Roosevelt National Memorial Park: N.D.	**28**	47	104
The Pass: Manitoba	**31**	54	101
Theresa: New York	**12**	44	76
Thermal: California	**35**	34	116
Thermopolis: Wyoming	**28**	44	108
Thesiger Bay: N.W.T.	**44**	72	125
Thessalon: Ontario	**18**	46	84
Thetford Mines: Québec	**13**	46	71
Thibodaux: Louisiana	**27**	30	91
Thief River Falls: *town*, Minn.	**10**	48	96
Thiewiaza: *r.*, N.W.T.	**31**	61	98
Thistletown: Ontario	**12**	44	80
Thoa: *r.*, N.W.T.	**30**	61	108
Thomas: West Virginia	**16**	39	80
Thomaston: Connecticut	**15**	42	73
Thomaston: Georgia	**24**	33	84
Thomaston: Maine	**11**	44	69
Thomasville: Alabama	**27**	32	88
Thomasville: Georgia	**25**	31	84
Thomasville: North Carolina	**24**	36	80
Thom Bay: N.W.T.	**45**	70	92
Thom Bay: *sett.*, N.W.T.	**45**	70	93
Thompson: Manitoba	**31**	56	97
Thompson: Pennsylvania	**14**	42	76
Thompson: *r.*, Manitoba	**31**	56	97
Thompson I.: Massachussetts	**2**	42¼	71
Thompson Lake: *sett.*, N.W.T.	**44**	63	114
Thompson Landing: N.W.T.	**44**	63	111
Thompson Res.: California	**7**	34¼	117¾
Thompsonville: Connecticut	**15**	42	73
Thomsen: *r.*, N.W.T.	**44**	73	119

	Page	N	W
Thomson: Georgia	24	33	83
Thomson: New York	13	43	74
Thornhill: Ontario	5	43¾	79½
Thornhurst: Pennsylvania	14	41	76
Thornton: Colorado	3	39¾	105
Thornton: Rhode Island	15	42	72
Thorntown: Indiana	21	40	87
Thorpe L.: North Carolina	24	35	83
Thousand Oaks: California	35	34	119
Thousand Palms: California	35	34	116
Three Lakes: *sett.*, Wisconsin	20	46	89
Three Rivers: Massachusetts	15	42	72
Three Rivers: Michigan	21	42	86
Thunder Bay: Michigan	18	45	83
Thunder Bay: *town*, Ontario	10	48	89
Thunder Bay: Ontario	10	48	89
Thurmont: Maryland	17	40	77
Thurso: Québec	13	46	75
Thutade L.: British Columbia	41	57	127
Tiber: *dam*, Montana	28	48	111
Tiburon: California	6	38	122½
Ticonderoga: New York	13	44	73
Tidioute: Pennsylvania	19	42	79
Tieton Res.: Washington	39	47	121
Tiffin: Ohio	19	41	83
Tifton: Georgia	24	31	84
Tignish: Prince Edward Island	9	47	64
Tijeras: New Mexico	29	35	106
Tijuana: California	35	33	117
Tilbury Island: British Columbia	6	49	123
Tillamook: Oregon	39	45	124
Tillsonburg: Ontario	19	43	81
Tilly Foster: New York	15	41	74
Tilt Cove: Newfoundland	9	50	56
Tilton: New Hampshire	13	43	72
Tiltonsville: Ohio	19	40	81
Timagami: Ontario	11	47	80
Timbalier Bay: Louisiana	27	29	91
Timberville: Virginia	17	39	79
Timiskaming: Québec	8	47	79
Timiskaming, L.: Qué./Ontario	11	47	80
Timmins: Ontario	11	49	81
Timmonsville: South Carolina	24	34	80
Timpson: Texas	26	32	94
Tinicum Wildlife Preserve: Pa.	2	40	75¼
Tioga: *r.*, New York	14	42	77
Tionesta: California	36	42	121
Tionesta: Pennsylvania	19	42	80
Tioughnioga: *r.*, New York	14	42	76
Tipp City: Ohio	21	40	84
Tippecanoe: *r.*, Indiana	21	41	86
Tipton: California	34	36	119
Tipton: Indiana	21	40	86
Tisdale: Saskatchewan	30	53	104
Tishomingo: Oklahoma	26	34	97
Tittabawassee: *r.*, Michigan	20	44	84
Titusville: Florida	25	29	81
Titusville: Pennsylvania	19	42	80
Tiverton: Rhode Island	15	42	71
Toad Hotsprings: B.C.	40	59	125
Toad River: *sett.*, B.C.	40	59	125
Toba Inlet: British Columbia	38	50	125
Tobermory: Ontario	18	45	82
Tobin: California	36	40	121
Tobique: *r.*, New Brunswick	9	47	67
Toccoa: Georgia	24	35	83
Tofield: Alberta	30	53	113
Tofino: British Columbia	41	49	126
Tofty: Alaska	42	65	151
Togiak: Alaska	43	59	161
Tok Junction: Alaska	42	63	143
Toledo: Ohio	19	42	84
Toledo: Oregon	39	45	124
Toledo Bend Res.: La./Texas	26	31	94
Tollhouse: California	37	37	119
Tolono: Illinois	21	40	88
Tolovana: Alaska	42	65	150
Tomahawk: Wisconsin	20	45	90
Tomales: California	37	38	123
Tomball: Texas	26	30	96
Tombigbee: *r.*, Alabama	27	32	88
Tombstone: Arizona	33	32	110
Toms River: *town*, New Jersey	15	40	74
Tonasket: Washington	38	49	119
Tonawanda: New York	19	43	79
Tongue: *r.*, Montana	28	46	106
Tonopah: Nevada	33	38	117
Tooele: Utah	33	41	112
Topaz L.: California/Nevada	37	39	120
Topeka: Kansas	28	39	96
Toppenish: Washington	39	46	120
Topton: Pennsylvania	14	41	76
Torch: *r.*, Saskatchewan	30	54	105
Toronto: Ohio	16	40	81
Toronto: Ontario	12	44	79
Torrance: California	7	33¼	118¼
Torrington: Connecticut	15	42	73
Torrington: Wyoming	28	42	104
Toulnustouc: *r.*, Québec	9	50	68
Towanda: Pennsylvania	14	42	76
Tower City: Pennsylvania	14	41	77
Towson: Maryland	17	39	77
Toy: Nevada	36	40	119
Tracadie: New Brunswick	9	48	65
Tracy: California	37	38	121
Tracy: Québec	13	46	73
Tracy City: Tennessee	27	35	86
Trail: British Columbia	41	49	118
Trail: Oregon	36	43	123
Tramping L.: Saskatchewan	30	52	109
Tranquillity: California	37	37	120
Trans Canada Highway	38	50	121
Transcona: Manitoba	31	50	97
Trapanege Plateau: B.C.	38	50	120
Traverse City: Michigan	20	45	86
Trego: Nevada	36	41	119
Tremblant, Mt.: Québec	13	46	75
Tremont: Pennsylvania	14	41	76
Trenary: Michigan	20	46	87
Trent: *r.*, Ontario	12	44	78
Trente-et-un-Milles, Lac: Qué.	12	46	76
Trenton: Michigan	19	42	83
Trenton: Missouri	10	40	94
Trenton: New Jersey	15	40	75
Trenton: Nova Scotia	9	46	63
Trenton: Ontario	12	44	78
Trenton: Tennessee	27	36	89
Trevorton: Pennsylvania	14	41	77
Triangle: Virginia	17	39	77
Trident: Montana	28	46	111
Trilby: Ohio	19	42	84
Trinidad: California	36	41	124
Trinidad: Colorado	29	37	105
Trinity: Newfoundland	9	48	53
Trinity: Texas	26	31	95
Trinity: *dam*, California	36	41	123
Trinity: *r.*, California	36	41	124
Trinity: *r.*, Texas	26	31	96
Trinity B.: Newfoundland	9	48	54
Trinity Is.: Alaska	43	56	154
Trion: Georgia	27	35	85
Trois-Rivières: Québec	13	46	73
Trombly: Michigan	20	46	87
Trona: California	35	36	117
Troup: Texas	26	32	95
Trout: *r.*, N.W.T.	40	61	120
Trout L.: Northwest Territories	40	61	121
Trout L.: Ontario	31	51	93
Troy: Alabama	27	32	86
Troy: Michigan	5	42½	83¼
Troy: New Hampshire	13	43	72
Troy: New York	15	43	74
Troy: North Carolina	24	35	80
Troy: Ohio	19	40	84
Troy: Pennsylvania	14	42	77
Truckee: California	37	39	120
Truckee: *r.*, Nevada/California	37	40	119
Trumann: Arkansas	27	36	91
Trumansburg: New York	14	43	77
Truro: Nova Scotia	9	45	63
Truth or Consequences: N. Mex.	29	33	107
Tsala Apopka, L.: Florida	25	29	82
Tuba City: Arizona	33	36	111
Tuckerton: New Jersey	15	40	74
Tucson: Arizona	33	32	111
Tucumcari: New Mexico	29	35	104
Tudor: California	37	39	122
Tudor, L.: Québec	9	56	66
Tug Fork: *r.*, Ky./W. Va.	16	38	82
Tug Hill Plat.: New York	12	44	76
Tugidak L.: Alaska	43	56	155
Tujunga: California	7	34¼	118¼
Tuktoyaktuk: N.W.T.	44	69	133
Tulare: California	34	36	119
Tulare Lake Area: California	34	36	120
Tularosa: New Mexico	29	33	106
Tule Lake: California	36	42	122
Tulelake: *sett.*, California	36	42	122
Tule L. Res.: California	36	41	120
Tulia: Texas	29	35	102
Tullahoma: Tennessee	27	35	86
Tulsa: Oklahoma	29	36	96
Tulsequah: British Columbia	40	59	134
Tuluksak: Alaska	43	61	161
Tumacacori Nat. Mon.: Ariz.	33	32	111
Tumwater: Washington	39	47	123
Tunica: Mississippi	27	35	90
Tunkhannock: Pennsylvania	14	42	76
Tunungayualuk I.: Nfld.	9	56	61
Tuolumne: California	37	38	120
Tuolumne: *r.*, California	37	38	120
Tupelo: Mississippi	27	34	89
Tupper Lake: *town*, New York	13	44	74
Turkey: *r.*, Iowa	10	43	91
Turlock: California	37	37	121
Turnagain: *r.*, British Columbia	40	59	128
Turner L.: Saskatchewan	30	57	108
Turner Turnpike: Oklahoma	29	36	97
Turner Valley: *sett.*, Alberta	30	51	114
Turtle Creek Res.: Kansas	28	39	97
Turtle, L.: Minnesota	3	45	93¼
Tuscaloosa: Albama	27	33	88
Tuscarawas: *r.*, Ohio	19	40	82
Tuscola: Illinois	21	40	88
Tuscumbia: Alabama	27	35	88
Tuskegee: Alabama	27	32	86
Tuttle: California	37	37	120
Tuttle Creek Res.: *& dam*, Kansas	10	39	97
Tuya: *r.*, British Columbia	40	59	131
Tweedsmuir Prov. Park: B.C.	41	53	126
Twenty Mile House: Alaska	42	66	144
Twentynine Palms: California	35	34	116
Twillingate: Newfoundland	9	50	55
Twin Bridges: Montana	28	46	112
Twin City: Georgia	24	33	82
Twin Falls: Idaho	32	43	115
Twin Peaks: *mtn.*, California	6	37¾	122½
Twin Is.: Northwest Territories	8	53	80
Twisp: Washington	38	48	120
Twitya: *r.*, Northwest Territories	40	64	129
Two Harbors: Minnesota	10	47	92
Two Rivers: Wisconsin	20	44	88
Two Rivers Res.: N. Mex.	29	33	105
Tygart: *r.*, West Virginia	16	39	80
Tygart Lake State Park: West Virginia	16	39	80
Tygarts: *cr.*, Kentucky	16	39	83
Tyler: Texas	26	32	95
Tyler, L.: Texas	26	32	95
Tylertown: Mississippi	27	31	90
Tyner: Tennessee	27	35	85
Tyonek: Alaska	43	61	151
Tyrone: Pennsylvania	14	41	78
Ucluelet: British Columbia	38	49	126
Ugak Bay: Alaska	43	57	152
Ugashik: Alaska	43	58	157
Uhrichsville: Ohio	19	40	81
Uinta Mts.: Utah	33	41	110
Ukiah: California	37	39	123
Umanak: Greenland	45	71	52
Umanak Fiord: Greenland	45	71	53
Umatilla: Oregon	39	46	119
Umbagog L.: New Hampshire	13	45	71
Umiat: Alaska	42	69	153
Unadilla: Georgia	24	32	84
Unadilla: New York	14	42	75
Unalakleet: Alaska	42	64	161
Unalaska I.: Alaska	43	54	167
Ungava Bay: Québec	45	60	68
Ungava Penin.: Québec	45	61	75
Unicoi: Tennessee	16	36	82
Unimak I.: Alaska	43	55	164
Union: Mississippi	27	33	89
Union: New Jersey	1	40¾	74¼
Union: South Carolina	24	35	82
Union Bay: *sett.*, B.C.	38	50	125
Union Bay: Washington	6	47½	122¼
Union Beach: *town*, New Jersey	15	40	74
Union City: California	6	37½	122
Union City: Michigan	21	42	85
Union City: Ohio	21	40	85
Union City: Pennsylvania	19	42	80
Union City: Tennessee	22	36	89
Union Creek: *sett.*, Oregon	36	43	122
Union Gap: Washington	39	47	121
Union, Lake: Washington	6	47½	122¼
Union Point: *sett.*, Georgia	24	34	83
Union Springs: Alabama	27	32	86
Uniontown: Alabama	27	32	88
Uniontown: Pennsylvania	16	40	80
Unionville: Connecticut	15	42	73
Unionville: Ohio	19	42	81
Unionville: Ontario	5	45¾	79¼
United States Atomic Energy Commission Res. Hanford Project: Wash.	39	46	120
Unity: Saskatchewan	30	52	109
Upland: California	7	34	117¾
Upper Arrow L.: B.C.	41	51	118
Upper Crystal Springs Res.: California	6	37½	122¼
Upper Darby: Pennsylvania	2	40	75¼
Upper Klamath L.: Oregon	36	42	122
Upper Laberge: Yukon	40	61	135
Upper L.: California	36	42	120
Upper Lake: *sett.*, California	37	39	123
Upper Mattole: California	36	40	124
Upper New York Bay: N.Y.	1	40¾	74
Upper Red L.: Minnesota	10	48	95
Upper Rouge: *r.*, Michigan	5	42½	83¼
Upper Sandusky: Ohio	19	41	83
Upper San Leandro Res.: Calif.	6	37¾	122¼
Uranium City: Saskatchewan	30	60	109
Urbana: Illinois	21	40	88
Urbana: Ohio	19	40	84
UTAH	33	—	—
Utah L.: Utah	33	40	112
Ute: *cr.*, New Mexico	29	36	104
Utica: Michigan	19	43	83
Utica: New York	13	43	75
Utica: Ohio	19	40	82
Utica: Pennsylvania	19	41	80
Utikuma L.: Alberta	30	56	115
Utuado: Puerto Rico	27	18	67
Utukok: *r.*, Alaska	42	70	161
Uvalde: Texas	22	29	100
Uyak: Alaska	43	58	154
Vacaville: California	37	38	122
Valatie: New York	15	42	74
Valdese: North Carolina	24	36	82
Valdes I.: British Columbia	38	49	124
Valdez: Alaska	43	61	146
Val d'Or: Québec	8	48	78
Valdosta: Georgia	25	31	83
Valentine: Nebraska	28	43	101
Vallecito Mts.: California	35	33	116
Vallée-Jonction: Québec	13	46	71
Vallejo: California	37	38	122
Vallye City: North Dakota	28	47	98

Place	Page	N	W
Valley Falls: *sett.*, Oregon	**36**	42	120
Valleyfield: Québec	**13**	45	74
Valley Forge: Pennsylvania	**15**	40	75
Valley Forge S.P.: Pennsylvania	**2**	40	75½
Valley Springs: California	**37**	38	121
Valley Stream: New York	**1**	40¾	73¾
Valleyview: Alberta	**30**	55	117
Valley View: Pennsylvania	**14**	41	77
Val Marie: Saskatchewan	**30**	49	108
Valona: California	**37**	38	122
Valparaiso: Florida	**27**	31	87
Valparaiso: Indiana	**21**	41	87
Valsetz: Oregon	**39**	45	124
Van Alstyne: Texas	**26**	33	97
Vanburen: Ohio	**19**	41	84
Vanceboro: North Carolina	**24**	35	77
Vanceburg: Kentucky	**16**	39	83
Vancouver: British Columbia	**38**	49	123
Vancouver: Washington	**39**	46	123
Vancouver I.: British Columbia	**41**	50	127
Vandalia: Ohio	**21**	40	84
Vandergift: Pennsylvania	**19**	41	80
Vanderhoof: British Columbia	**41**	54	124
Van Etten: New York	**14**	42	77
Vankleek Hill: *town*, Ontario	**13**	46	75
Van Norman L.: California	**7**	34¼	118½
Van Nuys: California	**7**	34¼	118½
Vansittart I.: N.W.T.	**45**	66	84
Vantage: Washington	**39**	47	120
Van Wert: Ohio	**21**	41	85
Varennes: Québec	**13**	46	73
Varnville: South Carolina	**24**	33	81
Vashon Island: Washington	**6**	47½	122½
Vassar: Michigan	**18**	43	84
Veedersburg: Indiana	**21**	40	87
Vegreville: Alberta	**30**	54	112
Velasco: Texas	**26**	30	95
Venetie: Alaska	**42**	67	146
Venice: Florida	**25**	27	82
Venice: Louisiana	**27**	29	89
Venice: Pennsylvania	**19**	40	80
Ventucopa: California	**34**	35	119
Ventura: California	**34**	34	119
Verchères: Québec	**13**	46	73
Verde: *r.*, Arizona	**33**	34	112
Verdemont: California	**35**	34	117
Verdi: Nevada	**37**	40	120
Verdigris: *r.*, Kansas/Oklahoma	**29**	38	96
Verdun: Québec	**13**	45	74
Vergennes: Vermont	**13**	44	73
Vermilion: Alberta	**30**	53	111
Vermilion: Ohio	**19**	41	82
Vermilion: *r.*, Illinois	**21**	41	89
Vermilion Bay: Louisiana	**26**	30	92
Vermilion Chutes: Alberta	**30**	58	115
Vermilion L.: Minnesota	**10**	48	93
Vermilion Pass: Alta./B.C.	**41**	51	116
Vermilion Range: Minnesota	**10**	48	92
Vermillion: South Dakota	**28**	43	97
Vermillion: *r.*, South Dakota	**28**	44	97
VERMONT	**13**	—	—
Vernal: Utah	**33**	40	110
Vernalis: California	**37**	38	121
Vernon: Alabama	**27**	34	88
Vernon: British Columbia	**38**	50	119
Vernon: Nevada	**36**	40	119
Vernon: Texas	**29**	34	99
Vernonia: Oregon	**39**	46	123
Vero Beach: *town*, Florida	**25**	28	80
Verret, L.: Louisiana	**26**	30	91
Versailles: Ohio	**21**	40	84
Versailles: Pennsylvania	**19**	40	80
Vesuvius: Virginia	**16**	38	79
Vian: Oklahoma	**26**	35	95
Vicksburg: Michigan	**21**	42	86
Vicksburg: Mississippi	**27**	32	91
Victor: New York	**14**	43	77
Victoria: British Columbia	**38**	48	123
Victoria: Texas	**26**	29	97
Victoria: Virginia	**17**	37	78
Victoria I.: N.W.T.	**44**	71	110
Victoria Strait: N.W.T.	**44**	69	110
Victoriaville: Québec	**13**	46	72
Victorville: California	**35**	35	117
Vidalia: Georgia	**24**	32	82
Vidalia: Louisiana	**26**	32	91
Vienna: Georgia	**24**	32	84
Vienna: Maryland	**17**	38	76
Vienna: Virginia	**2**	39	77¼
Vienna: West Virginia	**16**	39	82
Vieques, I. de: Puerto Rico	**27**	17	65
Vieux Carre: Louisiana	**3**	30	90
Viking: Alberta	**30**	53	112
Villa Grove: Illinois	**21**	40	88
Villa Park Res.: California	**7**	33¾	117¾
Villa Rica: Georgia	**27**	34	85
Villas: New Jersey	**14**	39	75
Ville de Laval: Québec	**2**	45¾	73¾
Villeneuve: Québec	**8**	47	71
Ville Platte: Louisiana	**26**	31	92
Vina: California	**36**	40	122
Vincennes: Indiana	**10**	39	88
Vincent: California	**35**	35	118
Vineland: New Jersey	**14**	39	75
Vineyard Haven: Massachusetts	**15**	41	71
Vinton: California	**36**	40	120
Vinton: Louisiana	**26**	30	94
Vintondale: Pennsylvania	**19**	40	79
Viola: California	**36**	41	122
Virden: Manitoba	**31**	50	101
Virgilia: California	**36**	40	121
Virgin: *r.*, Utah/Nevada	**33**	37	114
VIRGINIA	**16/17**	—	—
Virginia: Minnesota	**10**	48	92
Virginia Beach: *town*, Virginia	**17**	37	76
Virginia City: Nevada	**37**	39	120
Virginia Falls: *sett.*, N.W.T.	**40**	62	126
Virginia Mts.: Nevada	**36**	40	120
Visalia: California	**34**	36	119
Viscount Melville Sd.: N.W.T.	**44**	74	108
Vista: California	**35**	33	117
Vivian: Louisiana	**26**	33	94
Volta: California	**37**	37	121
Vya: Nevada	**36**	42	120
Wabana: Newfoundland	**9**	48	53
Wabasca: Alberta	**30**	56	114
Wabasca: *r.*, Alberta	**30**	57	114
Wabash: Indiana	**21**	41	86
Wabash: *r.*, Indiana/Illinois	**10**	39	88
Wabowden: Manitoba	**31**	55	99
Wabuk Point: Ontario	**31**	55	85
Wabush: Newfoundland	**9**	53	67
Wabush, L.: Newfoundland	**9**	53	67
Wabuska: Nevada	**37**	39	119
Waccassa Bay: Florida	**25**	29	83
Wachusett Res.: Massachusetts	**15**	42	72
Waco: Texas	**26**	32	97
Waco, L.: Texas	**26**	32	97
Waddington: New York	**13**	45	75
Waddington, Mt.: B.C.	**41**	51	125
Wadena: Minnesota	**10**	46	95
Wadena: Saskatchewan	**30**	52	104
Wadesboro: North Carolina	**24**	35	80
Wadley: Georgia	**24**	33	82
Wadsworth: Nevada	**37**	40	119
Wadsworth: Ohio	**19**	41	82
Wager Bay: N.W.T.	**45**	66	89
Wager Bay: *sett.*, N.W.T.	**45**	66	91
Wagoner: Oklahoma	**26**	36	95
Wahiawa: Hawaii	**128**	21	158
Wahoo: Nebraska	**28**	41	97
Wahpeton: North Dakota	**28**	46	97
Waialua: Hawaii	**128**	21	157
Waialua: Hawaii	**128**	22	158
Waianae: Hawaii	**128**	21	158
Waimanalo: Hawaii	**128**	21	158
Waimea: Hawaii	**128**	22	160
Wainwright: Alaska	**42**	71	160
Wainwright: Alberta	**30**	53	111
Wakarusa: Indiana	**21**	42	86
Wakaw: Saskatchewan	**30**	53	106
Wakeeney: Kansas	**28**	39	100
Wakefield: Massachusetts	**2**	42½	71
Wakefield: Québec	**12**	46	76
Wakefield: Rhode Island	**15**	41	72
Wakefield: Virginia	**17**	37	77
Wake Forest: North Carolina	**24**	36	79
Wakeham Bay: *sett.*, Québec	**45**	62	72
Walden: New York	**15**	42	74
Walden Pond: Massachusetts	**2**	42½	71
Walden Pond Reservation: Mass.	**2**	42½	71¾
Waldo: Arkansas	**26**	33	93
Wales: Alaska	**42**	66	168
Wales I.: N.W.T.	**45**	68	87
Walhalla: South Carolina	**24**	35	83
Walker: California	**36**	42	123
Walker: *r.*, Nevada	**37**	39	119
Walker Bay: N.W.T.	**44**	72	118
Walker L.: Nevada	**37**	39	119
Walkerton: Indiana	**21**	41	86
Walkerton: Ontario	**18**	44	81
Wallace: North Carolina	**24**	35	78
Wallace: Ontario	**12**	45	78
Wallaceburg: Ontario	**19**	43	82
Walla Walla: Washington	**32**	46	118
Walled Lake: *town*, Michigan	**5**	42½	83¾
Walled, L.: Michigan	**5**	42½	83¾
Wallenpaupack, L.: Pa.	**14**	41	75
Wallingford: Connecticut	**15**	41	73
Wallkill: *r.*, New York	**15**	42	74
Walnut: Illinois	**21**	42	90
Walnut Cove: North Carolina	**16**	36	80
Walnut Creek: *town*, California	**6**	38	122
Walnut Ridge: *town*, Arkansas	**27**	36	91
Walsenburg: Colorado	**29**	38	105
Walsingham, C.: N.W.T.	**45**	66	62
Walter Bathurst, C.: N.W.T.	**45**	73	77
Walterboro: South Carolina	**24**	33	81
Waltham: Massachusetts	**2**	42½	71¼
Waltham: Ontario	**12**	46	77
Walton: Michigan	**20**	45	85
Walton: New York	**14**	42	75
Walton: Nova Scotia	**9**	45	64
Wanakah: New York	**19**	43	79
Wanapum: *dam*, Washington	**39**	47	120
Waneta: British Columbia	**41**	49	118
Wantagh: New York	**1**	40¾	73½
Wapakoneta: Ohio	**19**	41	84
Wapato: Washington	**39**	46	120
Wapiti: *r.*, B.C./Alberta	**30**	55	120
War: West Virginia	**16**	37	82
Warden: Washington	**39**	47	119
Ware: British Columbia	**41**	57	126
Ware: & *r.*, Massachusetts	**15**	42	72
Wareham: Massachusetts	**15**	42	71
Waring Mts.: Alaska	**42**	67	159
Warman: Saskatchewan	**30**	52	106
Warner Range: Oregon/Calif.	**36**	42	120
Warner Robins: Georgia	**24**	33	84
Warner Springs: California	**35**	33	117
Warner Valley: Oregon	**36**	42	120
Warren: Arizona	**33**	31	110
Warren: Arkansas	**26**	34	92
Warren: Idaho	**32**	45	116
Warren: Indiana	**21**	41	85
Warren: Massachusetts	**15**	42	72
Warren: Michigan	**5**	42½	83
Warren: Minnesota	**10**	48	97
Warren: Ohio	**19**	41	81
Warren: Pennsylvania	**19**	42	79
Warren: Rhode Island	**15**	42	71
Warren Landing: Manitoba	**31**	54	98
Warrensburg: New York	**13**	43	74
Warrenton: Georgia	**24**	33	83
Warrenton: North Carolina	**17**	36	78
Warrenton: Oregon	**39**	46	124
Warrenton: Virginia	**17**	39	78
Warrior: Alabama	**27**	34	87
Warroad: Minnesota	**10**	49	95
Warsaw: Indiana	**21**	41	86
Warsaw: New York	**14**	43	78
Warsaw: North Carolina	**24**	35	78
Warwick: New York	**15**	41	74
Warwick: Rhode Island	**15**	42	71
Warwick: Québec	**13**	46	72
Wascana: *cr.*, Saskatchewan	**30**	50	104
Wasco: California	**34**	36	119
Wasco: Oregon	**39**	46	121
Washburn L.: N.W.T.	**44**	70	108
WASHINGTON	**32**	—	—
Washington: Connecticut	**15**	42	73
Washington: D.C.	**17**	39	77
Washington: Georgia	**24**	34	83
Washington: Illinois	**21**	41	89
Washington: Indiana	**10**	39	87
Washington: Louisiana	**26**	31	92
Washington: New Jersey	**14**	41	75
Washington: North Carolina	**24**	36	77
Washington: Pennsylvania	**19**	40	80
Washington I.: Wisconsin	**20**	45	87
Washington, L.: Washington	**6**	47½	122¼
Washington, Mt.: N.H.	**13**	44	71
Washington Park: Illinois	**4**	41¾	87½
Washingtonville: Ohio	**19**	41	81
Washougal: Washington	**39**	46	122
Watauga: *dam*, Tennessee	**24**	36	82
Watauga: *r.*, Tennessee	**16**	36	82
Watauga L.: Tennessee	**16**	36	82
Waterbury: Connecticut	**15**	42	73
Waterbury: Vermont	**13**	44	73
Wateree: *r.*, South Carolina	**24**	34	81
Waterford: New York	**15**	43	74
Waterford: Ontario	**19**	43	80
Waterford: Pennsylvania	**19**	42	80
Waterhen L.: Manitoba	**31**	52	100
Waterloo: Iowa	**10**	43	92
Waterloo: New York	**14**	43	77
Waterloo: Québec	**13**	45	73
Water Mill: New York	**15**	41	72
Watersmeet: Michigan	**20**	46	89
Waterton Glacier International Peace Park: Alta./Mont.	**30**	49	114
Watertown: Massachusetts	**2**	42¼	71¼
Watertown: New York	**12**	44	76
Watertown: South Dakota	**28**	45	97
Watertown: Wisconsin	**20**	43	89
Watertown Lakes Nat. Park: Alberta	**30**	49	114
Water Valley: *town* Mississippi	**27**	34	90
Waterville: Maine	**11**	45	70
Waterville: New York	**14**	43	75
Waterville: Ohio	**19**	41	84
Waterville: Washington	**39**	48	120
Watervliet: New York	**15**	43	74
Waterways: Alberta	**30**	57	111
Wathaman: *r.*, Saskatchewan	**30**	57	104
Watkins Glen: New York	**14**	42	77
Watoga St. Park: West Virginia	**16**	38	80
Watseka: Illinois	**21**	41	88
Watson Lake: *town*, Yukon	**40**	60	129
Watsontown: Pennsylvania	**14**	41	77
Watsonville: California	**37**	37	122
Watts Bar: *dam*, Tennessee	**24**	36	85
Wauchula: Florida	**25**	28	82
Waukegan: Illinois	**4**	42¼	87¾
Waukesha: Wisconsin	**20**	43	88
Waupaca: Wisconsin	**20**	44	89
Waupun: Wisconsin	**20**	44	89
Wausau: Wisconsin	**20**	45	90
Wausaukee: Wisconsin	**20**	45	88
Wauseon: Ohio	**19**	42	84
Wautoma: Wisconsin	**20**	44	89
Waverly: New York	**14**	42	77
Waverly: Ohio	**16**	39	83
Waverly: Tennessee	**27**	36	88
Waverly: Virginia	**17**	37	77
Wawasee, L.: Indiana	**21**	41	86
Wawona: California	**37**	38	120
Waxahachie: Texas	**26**	32	97
Waycross: Georgia	**25**	31	82

	Page	N	W
Wayland: Kentucky	16	37	83
Wayland: Massachusetts	2	42¼	71¼
Wayland: Michigan	21	43	86
Wayland: New York	14	43	78
Waymart: Pennsylvania	14	42	75
Wayne: Michigan	5	42¼	83¾
Wayne: Nebraska	28	42	97
Wayne: New Jersey	1	41	74¼
Wayne: West Virginia	16	38	82
Waynesboro: Georgia	24	33	82
Waynesboro: Mississippi	27	32	89
Waynesboro: Pennsylvania	14	40	78
Waynesboro: Virginia	17	38	79
Waynesburg: Ohio	19	41	81
Waynesburg: Pennsylvania	16	40	80
Waynesville: North Carolina	24	36	83
Weatherly: Pennsylvania	14	41	76
Weaverville: California	36	41	123
Weber: *r.*, Utah	33	41	111
Webster: Massachusetts	15	42	72
Webster: New York	12	43	77
Webster: Texas	26	30	95
Wedderburn: Oregon	36	42	124
Weed: California	36	41	122
Weed Heights: Nevada	37	39	119
Weedsport: New York	12	43	77
Weeks: Nevada	37	39	119
Weeksbury: Kentucky	16	37	83
Weggs, C. (C. de la Nouvelle France): Québec	45	62	74
Weimar: California	37	39	121
Weimar: Texas	26	30	97
Weirton: West Virginia	16	40	81
Weiser: Idaho	32	44	117
Weiss Res.: Alabama	27	34	86
Weitchpec: California	36	41	124
Welch: West Virginia	16	37	82
Weldon: California	35	36	118
Weldon: North Carolina	17	36	78
Weleetka: Oklahoma	26	35	96
Welland: Ontario	19	43	79
Wellesley: Massachusetts	2	42¼	71¼
Wellfleet: Massachusetts	15	42	70
Wellington: Kansas	29	37	97
Wellington: Nevada	37	39	119
Wellington: Ohio	19	41	82
Wellington: Texas	29	35	100
Wellington: Virginia	17	39	77
Wells: British Columbia	41	53	122
Wells: Nevada	33	41	115
Wells: *dam*, Washington	39	48	120
Wellsboro: Pennsylvania	14	42	77
Wellsburg: New York	14	42	77
Wellsburg: West Virginia	16	40	81
Wells Gray Prov. Park: B.C.	41	52	120
Wellston: Ohio	16	39	83
Wellsville: New York	14	42	78
Wellsville: Ohio	19	41	81
Welsh: Louisiana	26	30	93
Wenatchee: Washington	39	47	120
Wenatchee Mts.: Washington	39	48	121
Wendel: California	36	40	120
Wendell: North Carolina	24	36	78
Wendover: Utah	33	41	114
Wenham: Massachusetts	15	43	71
Wenona: Illinois	21	41	89
Wenonah: New Jersey	14	40	75
Wernecke Mts.: Yukon	40	65	133
Wesson: Mississippi	27	32	90
West: Texas	26	32	97
West Alexandria: Ohio	21	40	85
West Allis: Wisconsin	20	43	88
West Bay: Florida	27	30	86
West Bay: Louisiana	27	29	89
West Bend: Wisconsin	20	43	88
West Blocton: Alabama	27	33	87
West Branch: Michigan	20	44	84
Westbrook: Connecticut	15	41	72
Westbury: New York	1	40¾	73½
West Canada: *cr.*, New York	13	43	75
West Carrollton: Ohio	21	40	84
West Carthage: New York	12	44	76
Westchester: Illinois	4	41¾	88
West Chester: Pennsylvania	14	40	76
West Chicago: Illinois	21	42	88
West Columbia: Texas	26	29	96
West Concord: Massachusetts	15	42	71
West Cote Blanche Bay: La.	26	30	92
West Covina: California	7	34	118
Westerly: Rhode Island	15	41	72
Westernport: Maryland	16	39	79
Western Springs: Illinois	4	41¾	87¾
Westerville: Ohio	19	40	83
Westfield: Indiana	21	40	86
Westfield: Massachusetts	15	42	73
Westfield: Texas	3	30	95½
Westfield: New York	19	42	80
Westfield: Pennsylvania	14	42	78
West Fork: *r.*, West Virginia	16	39	80
West Grove: Pennsylvania	14	40	76
West Helena: Arkansas	27	35	91
West Jefferson: Ohio	16	40	83
West Kentucky Turnpike: Ky.	23	37	87
West Lafayette: Ohio	19	40	82
Westlake: Ohio	19	41	82
West Lake: *sett.*, Washington	39	47	119
West Lebanon: New Hampshire	13	44	72

	Page	N	W
Westley: California	37	38	121
West Liberty: Ohio	19	40	84
Westlock: Alberta	30	54	114
West Memphis: Arkansas	27	35	90
West Middlesex: Pennsylvania	19	41	80
West Milton: Ohio	21	40	84
Westminster: California	7	33¾	118
Westminster: Colorado	3	33¾	105
Westminster: Maryland	17	40	77
Westminster: South Carolina	24	35	83
Westmorland: California	35	33	116
Westmount: Québec	2	45½	73½
Weston: Massachusetts	2	42¼	71¼
Weston: Ontario	5	43¾	79½
Weston: West Virginia	16	39	80
West Palm Beach: *town*, Florida	25	27	80
West Plains: Missouri	10	37	92
West Point: *sett.*, California	37	38	121
West Point: *sett.*, Virginia	17	38	77
West Point: *town*, Mississippi	27	34	89
West Point: *town*, Nebraska	28	42	97
Westport: California	37	40	124
Westport: Connecticut	15	41	73
Westport: Oregon	39	46	123
Westport: Washington	39	47	124
West Rutland: Vermont	13	44	73
West St. Paul: Minnesota	3	45	93¼
West Side: Oregon	36	42	121
West Stockbridge: Mass.	15	42	73
West Swanzey: New Hampshire	13	43	72
West Vancouver: B.C.	6	49¼	123¼
Westview: British Columbia	38	50	125
West View: Pennsylvania	5	49½	80
Westville: Illinois	21	40	88
Westville: New Jersey	14	40	75
WEST VIRGINIA	16/17	—	—
West Virginia Turnpike: W. Va.	16	38	81
West Warwick: Rhode Island	15	42	72
Westwego: Louisiana	3	30	90¼
Westwood: California	36	40	121
Wetaskiwin: Alberta	30	53	113
Wetumka: Oklahoma	26	35	96
Wetumpka: Alabama	27	33	86
Wevok: Alaska	42	69	166
Wewoka: Oklahoma	26	35	97
Weyauwega: Wisconsin	20	44	89
Weyburn: Saskatchewan	30	50	104
Weymouth: Massachusetts	2	42¼	71
Whale: *r.*, Québec	9	57	67
Whale Cove: N.W.T.	45	62	92
Wharton: Texas	26	29	96
Wharton L.: N.W.T.	44	64	100
Wheatland: California	37	39	121
Wheaton: Illinois	4	41¾	88
Wheaton: Maryland	2	30	77
Wheat Ridge: *sett.*, Colorado	3	39¾	105
Wheeler: *r.*, Québec	9	56	67
Wheeler L.: *& dam*, Alabama	27	35	87
Wheeler Ridge: *sett.*, California	35	35	119
Wheelersburg: Ohio	16	39	83
Wheeler Springs: California	34	35	119
Wheeling: West Virginia	16	40	81
Whidbey I.: Washington	38	48	123
Whiskeytown: California	36	41	123
Whispering Pines: California	37	39	123
Whitby: Ontario	12	44	79
White: *r.*, Arkansas	26	34	91
White: *r.*, Colorado	28	40	109
White: *r.*, Ontario	10	49	86
White: *r.*, South Dakota	28	44	100
White: *r.*, Vermont	13	44	73
White: *r.*, Yukon	40	63	140
White B.: Newfoundland	9	50	57
White Bear L.: Minnesota	3	45	93
White Center: Washington	6	47½	122¼
Whitecourt: Alberta	30	54	116
Whitefield: New Hampshire	13	44	72
Whitefish: Montana	32	48	114
Whitefish Bay: *sett.*, Wisconsin	20	43	88
Whitefish L.: N.W.T.	44	63	107
Whitegull L.: Québec	9	55	64
Whitehall: Michigan	20	43	86
Whitehall: Montana	28	46	112
Whitehall: New York	13	44	73
White Haven: Pennsylvania	14	41	76
White Hills: *sett.*, California	34	35	120
White Horse: California	36	41	121
Whitehorse: Yukon	40	61	135
White I.: N.W.T.	45	66	85
White L.: Louisiana	26	30	93
White Lake: *sett.*, New York	14	42	75
White Lake: *sett.*, Wisconsin	20	45	89
White Mountain: *sett.*, Alaska	42	65	163
White Mts.: Alaska	42	66	146
White Mts.: New Hampshire	13	44	71
White Oak Bayou: Texas	3	29¾	95½
White Pigeon: Michigan	21	42	86
White Pine: Michigan	10	47	90
White Plains: New York	15	41	74
White River Junction: Vermont	13	44	72
White Rock: British Columbia	38	49	123
White Salmon: Washington	39	46	121
White Sands: *& Nat. Mon. & Missile Ra.*, N. Mex	29	33	106
Whitesboro: New York	13	43	75
Whitesboro: Texas	26	34	97
Whitesburg: Kentucky	16	37	83

	Page	N	W
Whiteshell Prov. Park: Ontario	10	50	95
White Sulphur Springs: W. Va.	16	38	80
Whitesville: West Virginia	16	38	82
Whiteville: North Carolina	24	34	79
White Water: California	35	34	117
Whitewater: Wisconsin	21	43	89
Whitewright: Texas	26	34	96
Whiting: Indiana	4	41¾	87½
Whitman: Massacusetts	15	42	71
Whitmans Pond: Massachusetts	2	42¼	71
Whitmire: South Carolina	24	35	82
Whitney: Ontario	12	45	78
Whitney: Texas	26	32	97
Whitney, L.: *& dam*, Texas	26	32	97
Whitney, Mt.: California	35	37	118
Whitney Woods: Massachusetts	2	42¼	71
Whittier: Alaska	43	61	149
Whittier: California	7	34	118
Whittier Narrow Dam Reservoir Area: California	7	34	118
Whittle, C.: Québec	9	50	60
Whitwell: Tennessee	27	35	86
Wholdaia L.: N.W.T.	30	61	104
Wichita: Kansas	29	38	97
Wichita: *r.*, Texas	29	34	100
Wichita Falls: *town*, Texas	29	34	99
Wickenburg: Arizona	33	34	113
Widen: West Virginia	16	38	81
Widows Creek: *sett.*, Alabama	27	35	85
Wiest: California	35	33	115
Wiggins: Mississippi	27	31	89
Wilberforce Falls: *sett.*, N.W.T.	44	67	109
Wilburton: Oklahoma	26	35	95
Wildcat: *cr.*, California	6	38	122¼
Wildcat: *cr.*, Indiana	21	40	87
Wildomar: California	35	34	117
Wildwood: Florida	25	29	82
Wildwood: New Jersey	14	39	75
Wilkes-Barre: Pennsylvania	14	41	76
Wilkie: Saskatchewan	30	52	109
Wilkinsburg: Pennsylvania	5	40½	80
Willacoochee: Georgia	24	31	83
Willamette: *r.*, Oregon	32	45	123
Willamina: Oregon	39	45	124
Willapa Bay: Washington	39	47	124
Willapa Hills: Washington	39	46	123
Willard: Ohio	19	41	83
Willcox: Arizona	33	32	110
William D. Boyce Park: Pa.	5	40½	79¾
Williams: Arizona	33	35	112
Williams: California	37	39	122
Williamsburg: Michigan	20	45	85
Williamsburg: Pennsylvania	14	40	78
Williamsburg: Virginia	17	37	77
Williams Lake: *sett.*, B.C.	41	52	122
Williamson: New York	12	43	77
Williamson: West Virginia	16	38	82
Williamsport: Maryland	17	40	78
Williamsport: Pennsylvania	14	41	77
Williamston: Michigan	21	43	84
Williamston: North Carolina	24	36	77
Williamston: South Carolina	24	35	82
Williamstown: Massachusetts	15	43	73
Williamstown: New Jersey	14	40	75
Williamstown: Pennsylvania	14	41	77
Williamsville: New York	14	43	79
Willimantic: Connecticut	15	42	72
Willis: Texas	26	30	95
Williston: North Dakota	28	48	104
Williston: South Carolina	24	33	81
Williston, L.: B.C.	41	56	124
Willits: California	37	39	123
Willmar: Minnesota	10	45	95
Willoughby: Ohio	19	42	81
Willow: *cr.*, Oregon	39	46	120
Willow Bunch: Saskatchewan	30	49	106
Willow Creek: *sett.*, California	36	41	124
Willowdale: Ontario	5	43¾	79¼
Willow Grove: Pennsylvania	2	40¼	75
Willow L.: N.W.T.	40	62	119
Willowlake: *r.*, N.W.T.	40	63	122
Willow Run: Michigan	19	42	84
Willows: California	37	40	122
Will Rogers Turnpike: Okla.	29	37	95
Will Rogers S. Hist. Park: Calif.	7	34	118½
Wills: *cr.*, Ohio	19	40	82
Willsboro: New York	13	44	73
Wills Point: *sett.*, Texas	26	33	96
Wilmette: Illinois	4	42	87¾
Wilmington: Delaware	17	40	76
Wilmington: Massachusetts	15	43	71
Wilmington: North Carolina	24	34	78
Wilson: Arkansas	27	36	90
Wilson: New York	18	43	79
Wilson: North Carolina	24	36	78
Wilson: Oklahoma	26	34	97
Wilson: Ontario	18	43	79
Wilson, C.: N.W.T.	45	67	82
Wilson Creek: *sett.*, Washington	39	47	119
Wilson L.: *& dam*, Alabama	27	35	88
Wilton: Connecticut	15	41	73
Wilton: New Hampshire	13	43	72
Winamac: Indiana	21	41	87
Winchendon: Massachusetts	15	43	72
Winchester: California	35	34	117
Winchester: Indiana	21	40	85
Winchester: Kentucky	23	38	84

Addendum

Lists places named on thematic maps that are not shown on urban plans or topographic maps

	N	W
Big Sandy: *power stn.*, Ky.	38° 06′	82° 36′
Bigstone Creek: *sett.*, Alta.	49° 22′	116° 57′
Bird River: *sett.*, Man.	30° 31′	95° 17′
Bixby: Missouri	37° 39′	91° 07′
Black River Falls: *sett.*, Wis.	44° 16′	91° 00′
Blueberry: British Columbia	56° 44′	121° 48′
Blake Terrace: Atlantic Ocean	32° 00′	78° 00′
Boss: Missouri	37° 38′	91° 11′
Bowdoin: Montana	48° 23′	107° 36′
Bowron Prov. Park: B.C.	53° 10′	123° 00′
Brackenridge: Pennsylvania	40° 36′	79° 44′
Braeburn: Pennsylvania	47° 37′	79° 42′
Braithwaite: Louisiana	29° 51′	89° 56′
Brayton Point: *power stn.*, Massachusetts	41° 46′	71° 07′
Bridge River: *dam*, B.C.	50° 43′	122° 20′
Bridgeville: Pennsylvania	40° 21′	80° 07′
Brighton: Pennsylvania	40° 58′	74° 46′
Brilliant: British Columbia	49° 19′	117° 38′
Browns Bank: Atlantic O.	43° 00′	66° 00′
Bruce Lake: *sett.*, Ontario	50° 49′	92° 25′
Brunner Is.: *power stn.*, Pa.	40° 17′	76° 43′
Brunswick: Maine	43° 54′	69° 57′
Buhl: Minnesota	47° 30′	92° 46′
Bull Run: *power stn.*, Tenn.	36° 06′	84° 07′
Burgin: Utah	39° 56′	111° 37′
Burin: Newfoundland	47° 02′	55° 10′
Burke: Idaho	47° 31′	115° 48′
Burnham: Pennsylvania	40° 38′	77° 34′
Burns Habor: Indiana	41° 37′	87° 10′
Burnsville: N. Carolina	35° 03′	80° 21′
Burnt Mills: N. Carolina	36° 45′	76° 21′
Butler: Alabama	32° 05′	88° 13′
Buttle Lake: British Columbia	49° 52′	124° 48′
Cabrillo Nat. Mon.: Calif.	32° 38′	117° 14′
Cairo: Illinois	37° 00′	89° 10′
Calcite: Michigan	45° 24′	83° 47′
Calhoun: Tennessee	35° 17′	83° 45′
California, Gulf of: Mexico	27° 00′	111° 00′
Calumet: Michigan	47° 14′	88° 27′
Cameron: Louisiana	29° 47′	93° 19′
Cane Run: *power stn.*, Ky.	38° 14′	85° 45′
Canoga Park: *sett.*, Calif.	34° 07′	118° 37′
Cape Tormentine: *sett.*, N.B.	46° 08′	63° 47′
Caraquet: New Brunswick	47° 48′	64° 57′
Castle Hayne: N. Carolina	34° 21′	77° 54′
Catawba: S. Carolina	34° 51′	80° 54′
Catawba: *r.*, N.C./S.C.	34° 40′	80° 54′
Cave in Rock: *sett.*, Illinois	37° 28′	88° 09′
Cave Spring: Georgia	34° 06′	85° 20′
Cayce: S. Carolina	33° 58′	81° 03′
Cedar Springs: Georgia	31° 12′	85° 00′
Cessford: Alberta	51° 01′	111° 33′
Chamblee: Georgia	33° 53′	84° 18′
Chance: Yukon	66° 02′	138° 25′
Charleston Rise: Atlantic O.	30° 00′	75° 00′
Chatham: New Brunswick	47° 02′	65° 28′
Chauvin: Louisiana	29° 26′	90° 35′
Chesterfield: Virginia	37° 23′	77° 30′
Cheswick: Pennsylvania	40° 32′	79° 48′
Chetwynd: British Columbia	55° 40′	121° 30′
Chibougamau Prov. Park: Qué.	49° 30′	73° 30′
Chickamauga & Chattanooga N. Military Pk.: Ga./Tenn.	35° 00′	85° 20′
Chicoutimi Prov. Park: Qué.	49° 30′	70° 15′
Chileno Valley: California	38° 10′	122° 45′
Chino: Arizona	35° 20′	112° 56′
Chinook: Montana	48° 35′	109° 13′
Chisholm: Minnesota	47° 29′	92° 52′
Cimarron: Oklahoma	35° 22′	97° 48′
Clancy: Montana	46° 27′	111° 58′
Clarkdale: Georgia	33° 49′	84° 39′
Clarkesville: Georgia	34° 36′	83° 31′
Clatskanie: Oregon	46° 06′	123° 12′
Claverack: New York	42° 13′	73° 43′
Clayton: Idaho	45° 15′	114° 24′
Clear Creek: Yukon	63° 45′	137° 15′
Clearwater Prov. Park: Man.	54° 00′	101° 01′
Cleveland: Georgia	34° 35′	83° 45′
Clifty Creek: *power stn.*, Ind.	38° 44′	85° 22′
Clinton: Maine	44° 38′	69° 30′
Clinton Creek: *sett.*, Yukon	64° 28′	140° 31′
Coal Harbour: B.C.	50° 36′	127° 35′
Coalton: Kentucky	38° 23′	82° 47′
Coleraine: Minnesota	47° 16′	93° 26′
Collbran: Alabama	34° 22′	85° 46′
College Station: Texas	30° 36′	96° 20′
Colton: California	34° 04′	117° 56′
Come-by-Chance: Nfld.	47° 51′	53° 59′
Conda: Idaho	42° 44′	111° 33′
Contra Costa: *power stn.*, Calif.	38° 00′	121° 48′
Cooper: *power stn.*, Kentucky	36° 59′	84° 36′
Coosa Pines: Alabama	33° 27′	86° 06′
Copper Cities: Arizona	33° 24′	110° 52′
Copper Queen: Arizona	31° 26′	109° 55′
Cordero: Nevada	41° 58′	117° 44′
Corinna: Maine	44° 55′	69° 15′
Cornwall Is.: N.W.T.	77° 40′	95° 00′
Cove Fort: Utah	38° 36′	112° 20′
Croft: N. Carolina	35° 20′	80° 50′
Crossfield: Alberta	51° 04′	113° 52′
Crystal River: *power stn.*, Fla.	28° 54′	82° 38′
Cuba: New Mexico	35° 00′	107° 03′
Cumberland Hill: *town*, R.I.	42° 55′	71° 28′
Cumberland Pen.: N.W.T.	63° 00′	60° 00′
Curwood, Mt.: Michigan	46° 42′	88° 15′
Dandridge: Tennessee	36° 00′	83° 24′
Darwin Mtn.: Calif.	37° 11′	118° 42′
Deception Bay: *sett.*, Québec	62° 10′	74° 45′
Delway: N. Carolina	34° 51′	78° 17′
Denmark Strait: Atlantic O.	67° 00′	25° 00′
Depot Harbour: Ontario	49° 19′	80° 06′
Delta: Utah	39° 21′	112° 34′
Detroit: *dam*, Oregon	44° 44′	122° 14′
Detroit: *r.*, Mich./Ont.	42° 12′	83° 08′
Digby: Nova Scotia	44° 37′	65° 46′
Drake Point: *sett.*, N.W.T.	76° 20′	108° 02′
Dresden: Illinois	41° 21′	88° 26′
Dresden: New York	42° 41′	76° 57′
Dryden: Ontario	49° 47′	92° 49′
Duck Mtn. Prov. Park: Man.	51° 40′	101° 00′
Dulac: Louisiana	29° 23′	90° 42′
Eagle: Colorado	39° 39′	106° 49′
Eagle Mtn.: California	33° 50′	115° 30′
East Crossfield: Alberta	51° 04′	113° 50′
East Stroudsburg: Pa.	40° 58′	78° 12′
Eden: N. Carolina	36° 28′	79° 40′
Effingham: Illinois	39° 07′	88° 32′
Eglin: Florida	30° 33′	86° 31′
Eielson: Alaska	64° 40′	147° 04′
Ellef Ringnes Is.: N.W.T.	78° 30′	102° 30′
Elmira: Prince Edward Island	46° 27′	62° 04′
Elmsford: New York	41° 03′	73° 49′
El Segundo: California	33° 55′	118° 24′
Emperius: Colorado	37° 50′	107° 20′
Empire: Colorado	39° 45′	105° 41′
Empire: Louisiana	29° 23′	89° 35′
Etiwanda: California	34° 07′	117° 27′
Eveleth: Minnesota	47° 27′	92° 32′
Ewa Beach: *sett.*. Hawaii	21° 18′	158° 00′
Faeroe Iceland Rise: Atlantic Ocean	67° 00′	10° 00′
Fairfax: Alabama	32° 47′	85° 11′
Fairfield: Alabama	33° 29′	86° 59′
Falcon: *dam*, Texas	26° 32′	99° 10′
Falconer: New York	42° 06′	79° 12′
Falls City: Texas	29° 59′	98° 01′
Faraday Seamount Group: Atlantic Ocean	50° 00′	28° 00′
Faro: Yukon	63° 14′	33° 03′
F. C. Gannon: *power stn.*, Fla.	27° 57′	82° 27′
Fernandina Beach: Florida	30° 40′	81° 27′
Festus: Missouri	38° 13′	90° 23′
Feuilles *see* Leaf: *r.*, Qué.	57° 45′	73° 00′
Filer City: Michigan	44° 12′	86° 19′
Five Corners: New York	42° 07′	77° 50′
Flat River: *sett.*, Missouri	39° 51′	90° 31′
Flemish Cap: Atlantic Ocean	47° 00′	43° 00′
Fontana: Tennessee	35° 27′	83° 47′
Forest Lawn: Alberta	51° 02′	113° 58′
Fort Donelson Nat. Military Park: Tennessee	36° 30′	87° 52′
Fort Loudon: *dam*, Tennessee	35° 47′	84° 16′
Fortune: Newfoundland	47° 04′	55° 51′
Four Corners: *power stn.*, New Mexico	36° 44′	108° 12′
Fox Islands: Alaska	53° 30′	167° 00′
Franklin: Kentucky	36° 43′	86° 34′
Fraser Mills: B.C.	49° 19′	122° 52′
Fredericksburg & Spotsylvania N. Military Pk.: Va.	38° 18′	77° 27′
Gabbs: Nevada	38° 52′	117° 55′
Gardiner: *dam*, Saskatchewan	51° 31′	107° 13′
Georges Bank: Atlantic O.	43° 00′	67° 00′
Gettysburg Nat. Cemetery: Pa.	39° 49′	77° 14′
Gibbs Fracture Zone: Atlantic Ocean	50° 00′	35° 00′
Gibraltar: California	34° 45′	120° 50′
Gimli: Manitoba	50° 39′	97° 00′
Glen Canyon Nat. Rec. Area: Ariz./Utah	37° 00′	110° 00′
Glenwood: Alabama	31° 39′	86° 10′
Gloucester: Ontario	45° 27′	75° 23′
Glover: Missouri	37° 29′	90° 42′
Gorda Escarpment: Pacific O.	40° 00′	127° 00′
Gordon Lake: Ontario	50° 00′	93° 35′
Gordon M. Shrum: *dam*, B.C.	56° 01′	122° 12′
Grand Banks: Atlantic Ocean	46° 00′	57° 00′
Grande Baleine *see* Great Whale: *r.*, Québec	55° 00′	76° 30′
Granite City: Illinois	38° 42′	90° 08′
Great Falls: *dam*, Tennessee	35° 48′	85° 36′
Grindstone: Québec	47° 22′	61° 56′
Gros Morne Nat. Park: Nfld.	49° 31′	57° 50′
Guild: New Hampshire	43° 15′	72° 08′
Guilford: Maine	45° 10′	69° 23′
Guilford Courthouse Nat'l Hist. Park: N.C.	36° 06′	79° 48′
Gulf Islands N.P.: Fla./Miss.	30° 15′	88° 30′
Hamilton: Mississippi	33° 44′	88° 27′
Hamshire: Texas	20° 51′	94° 18′
Happy Valley: Newfoundland	53° 18′	60° 18′
Harborside: Maine	44° 18′	68° 48′
Harpers Ferry Nat'l Hist. Park: W. Va./Md.	39° 19′	77° 44′
Harbour Grace: Nfld.	47° 42′	53° 13′
Harllee Branch: *power stn.*, Ga.	33° 05′	83° 14′
Harmattan: Alberta	51° 46′	114° 30′
Hawesville: Kentucky	37° 53′	86° 47′
H. B. Robinson: *power stn.*, S. Carolina	34° 22′	80° 04′
Henderson Creek: Yukon	63° 20′	139° 53′
High Level: Alberta	58° 30′	117° 08′
Hilton Mines: Québec	45° 36′	76° 29′
Hogatza River: *sett.*, Alaska	66° 00′	155° 29′
Holyrood: Newfoundland	47° 24′	53° 10′
Hoolehua: Hawaii	21° 09′	157° 05′
Horseshoe Lake: *power stn.*, Oklahoma	35° 29′	97° 09′
Hoyt Lakes: *sett.*, Minnesota	47° 27′	91° 50′
Hugh Keenleyside: *dam*, B.C.	49° 20′	117° 33′
Hugoton: Kansas	37° 10′	101° 20′
Huguley: Alabama	32° 51′	85° 18′
Humboldt Bay: *power stn.*, Calif.	40° 46′	124° 09′
Huntington: Oregon	44° 21′	117° 15′
Hussar: Alberta	51° 03′	112° 41′
Indiantown: Florida	27° 01′	80° 28′
Intercoastal City: Louisiana	29° 43′	90° 59′
Ironton: Missouri	37° 36′	90° 37′
Iroquois Falls: *sett.*, Ontario	48° 46′	80° 40′
Isle-Maligne: Québec	48° 34′	71° 38′
Jefferson Nat. Expansion Mem. Nat'l Hist. Site: Mo.	38° 37′	90° 11′
Joanna: S. Carolina	34° 24′	81° 48′
Johnsonville: Tennessee	36° 03′	87° 58′
J. D. Rockefeller Parkway: Wyo.	41° 00′	110° 30′
Joppa: Illinois	37° 12′	88° 50′
Joutel: Québec	40° 28′	78° 20′
Jumping Pound: Alberta	51° 12′	114° 33′
Kamsack: Saskatchewan	51° 03′	101° 54′
Karnes City: Texas	28° 53′	97° 54′
Kayob South: Alberta	54° 12′	117° 08′
Kearny: New Jersey	40° 45′	74° 09′
Keewatin: Minnesota	47° 23′	93° 04′
Kejimkujik Nat. Park: N.S.	44° 25′	65° 20′
Kelly Lake: *sett.*, Minnesota	47° 24′	93° 00′
Kelsey: California	38° 46′	119° 51′
Kennesaw Mtn. Nat. Battlefield Park: Ga.	34° 01′	84° 36′
Kentucky: *dam*, Kentucky	37° 00′	88° 15′
Kettle Rapids: *dam*, Manitoba	56° 19′	94° 40′
King Christian Island: N.W.T.	77° 45′	102° 00′
Kinkaid: *power stn.*, Illinois	37° 46′	89° 19′
Kinsella: Alberta	53° 00′	111° 32′
Kitsault: British Columbia	55° 44′	129° 35′
Kodiak Station: Alaska	57° 53′	152° 29′
Krannert: Georgia	34° 17′	85° 10′
Kyuquot: British Columbia	50° 02′	127° 23′
Labadie: Missouri	38° 31′	90° 48′
La Blanca: Texas	26° 20′	98° 02′
Labrador Sea: Can./Greenland	58° 00′	55° 00′
Lac de Renzy: Québec	45° 33′	75° 38′
Lackawanna: New York	42° 49′	78° 49′
La Grand *see* Ft. George: *r.*, Québec	53° 30′	77° 00′
Laguna: New Mexico	35° 03′	107° 24′
Lake Meredith Nat. Rec. Area: Texas	35° 40′	101° 40′
Landis: N. Carolina	35° 33′	80° 36′
La Sal: Utah	38° 19′	109° 14′
La Saire: Québec	48° 48′	79° 12′
Lawrenceville: Illinois	38° 44′	87° 41′
Lehi: Utah	40° 23′	111° 51′
Lisbon Valley: Utah	38° 10′	109° 05′
Little Gypsy: *power stn.*, La.	30° 00′	90° 27′
Lone Pine Creek: *sett.*, Alta.	51° 43′	114° 00′
Longhurst: N. Carolina	36° 25′	78° 58′
Long Island: *sett.*, New York	40° 44′	73° 52′
Louiseville: Québec	46° 16′	72° 57′
Louvicourt: Québec	48° 05′	77° 40′
Lowell: Vermont	44° 48′	72° 27′
Lowman: Idaho	44° 04′	115° 37′
Lyon: Colorado	40° 13′	105° 16′
Mackenzie King Is.: N.W.T.	78° 50′	113° 00′
McLeansville: N. Carolina	36° 05′	79° 45′
Magma: Arizona	33° 08′	111° 29′
Maiden Rock: Montana	45° 41′	112° 43′
Maple Grove: Ohio	30° 23′	83° 07′
Mapleville: Rhode Island	41° 57′	71° 39′
Marquette Range: Michigan	46° 35′	87° 25′
Marystown: Newfoundland	47° 11′	55° 10′
Mascot: Tennessee	36° 03′	83° 45′
Maspeth: New York	40° 43′	73° 55′
Maxville: Montana	46° 22′	113° 12′
Melville Island: N.W.T.	75° 40′	111° 00′
Mendocino Seascarp: Pacific O.	46° 00′	135° 00′
Metaline Falls: *sett.*, Wash.	48° 51′	117° 22′
Metropolis: Illinois	37° 09′	88° 43′
Mexico: Kentucky	37° 12′	88° 06′
Mica: *dam*, British Columbia	53° 24′	118° 20′
Mid-Atlantic Ridge: Atlantic Ocean	35° 00′	35° 00′
Midvale: Utah	40° 36′	111° 54′
Milltown: New Jersey	40° 27′	74° 26′
Mineral Park: *sett.*, Arizona	35° 10′	114° 01′
Mineral Point: Wisconsin	42° 51′	90° 10′
Moline: Illinois	41° 30′	90° 30′
Montana City: Montana	46° 31′	111° 57′
Montecello: *dam*, California	38° 30′	122° 07′

Place	N	W
Moose Mtn.: *sett.*, Ontario	46° 45'	80° 59'
Moreland: Georgia	33° 17'	84° 46'
Morgantown: Pennsylvania	40° 09'	75° 53'
Mosby: Montana	46° 59'	107° 53'
Moss Landing: *sett.*, Calif.	36° 48'	121° 47'
Mossyrock: *dam*, Washington	46° 31'	122° 29'
Mountain Iron: *sett.*, Minn.	47° 31'	92° 37'
Mt. Edzia Prov. Park: B.C.	57° 30'	130° 45'
Mount Storm: *sett.*, W. Va.	39° 16'	79° 14'
Mullans: Idaho	47° 28'	115° 48'
Mumtrak *see* Goodnews: Alaska	59° 47	161° 35'
Muncho L. Prov. Park: B.C.	58° 50'	125° 45'
Muskegon Heights: *town*, Michigan	43° 11'	86° 15'
Murray Fracture Zone: Pacific Ocean	35° 00'	130° 00'
Nashwauk: Minnesota	47° 22'	93° 09'
Natchez Trace Parkway: Miss./Tenn./Ala.	35° 50'	88° 15'
Needham Heights: Mass.	42° 17'	71° 14'
Needville: Texas	29° 24'	94° 50'
Negaunee: Michigan	46° 30'	87° 36'
New Almaden: California	37° 12'	121° 47'
Newark: Texas	33° 00'	97° 29'
New Cornelia: Arizona	32° 23'	112° 53'
Newfoundland Basin: Atlantic Ocean	42° 00'	43° 00'
New Idria: California	36° 24'	120° 40'
New Madrid: Missouri	36° 34'	89° 32'
Newmarket: Tennessee	36° 06'	83° 36'
Newton: Massachusetts	42° 20'	71° 11'
Niagara Falls: Can./U.S.A.	43° 05'	79° 04'
Nickajack: *dam*, Tennessee	35° 00'	85° 42'
Nine Mile Pt.: *power stn.*, N.Y.	43° 23'	76° 44'
Niota: Tennessee	35° 30'	84° 32'
Nolichucky: *dam*, Tennessee	36° 05'	82° 52'
N. American Basin: Atlantic Ocean	33° 00'	60° 00'
N. Magnetic Pole 1970: N.W.T.	76° 02'	101° 00'
Northport: Alabama	33° 12'	87° 36'
North Sea	55° 00'	0° —
North Surrey: B.C.	49° 13'	122° 54'
North Tonawanda: N.Y.	43° 01'	78° 52'
Nunivak Nat. Wildlife Refuge: Alaska	60° 10'	166° 30'
Oak Creek: *power stn.*, Wis.	42° 52'	87° 54'
Oceanographer Fracture Zone: Atlantic Ocean	35° 00'	35° 00'
Octagon: Newfoundland	47° 34'	52° 40'
Olustee: Oklahoma	34° 33'	99° 25'
Orange City: Iowa	43° 00'	96° 03'
Orange Lake: *sett.*, New York	41° 30'	74° 06'
Osburn: Idaho	47° 30'	116° 00'
Oyster Creek: *power stn.*, N.J.	39° 50'	74° 11'
Ozark Nat. Scenic Riverway: Missouri	38° 10'	92° 40'
Pacific Crest Trail: Calif.-Wash.	—	—
Pacific Ocean	—	—
Palmer: Michigan	46° 26'	87° 35'
Patrick Air Force Base: Fla.	28° 13'	80° 47'
Payson: Arizona	34° 13'	111° 20'
Peachland: British Columbia	49° 46'	119° 44'
Pelton: *dam*, Oregon	44° 37'	121° 07'
Permanente: California	37° 04'	122° 00'
Petersburg Nat. Battlefield: Va.	37° 13'	77° 24'
Petit-Mécantina *see* Little Mecantina: *r.*, Qué.	52° 55'	61° 30'
Pharr: Texas	26° 11'	98° 11'
Philadelphia: Tennessee	35° 40'	84° 24'
Philip Sporn: *power stn.*, West Virginia	38° 56'	81° 56'
Phillipsdale: Rhode Island	41° 50'	71° 22'
P. H. Robinson: *power stn.*, Texas	29° 30'	94° 58'
Pickering: *power stn.*, Ontario	43° 52'	79° 02'
Pictou: Nova Scotia	45° 41'	62° 43'
Pinchi Lake: British Columbia	54° 30'	124° 20'
Pine Bend: Minnesota	44° 46'	93° 01'
Pine Creek: *sett.*, California	37° 10'	118° 38'
Plainview: New York	40° 46'	73° 28'
Platteville: Wisconsin	42° 44'	90° 28'
Plymouth Meeting: Pa.	40° 06'	75° 16'
Point Barrow: *sett.*, Alaska	70° 42'	156° 25'
Point Beach: *power stn.*, Wis.	44° 18'	87° 33'
Pointe-Noire: *sett.*, Québec	50° 10'	66° 27'
Point Tupper: *sett.*, N.S.	45° 36'	61° 20'
Port-Cartier-Sept-Iles Prov. Park Québec	50° 30'	67° 10'
Porterdale: Georgia	33° 36'	83° 54'
Port Hawkesbury: N.S.	45° 37'	61° 21'
Port Isabel: Texas	26° 04'	97° 12'
Port Manatee: Florida	27° 28'	82° 30'
Port Reading: New Jersey	40° 34'	74° 15'
Potosi: Missouri	37° 56'	90° 47'
Powder River Basin: Wyo.	43° 03'	106° 58'
Prince Patrick Is.: N.W.T.	76° 30'	119° 00'
Queensboro: British Columbia	49° 09'	122° 29'
Quirk Creek: *sett.*, Alberta	50° 50'	114° 10'
Radersburg: Montana	46° 11'	111° 37'
Ram River: *sett.*, Alberta	52° 07'	114° 50'
Ray Point: *sett.*, Texas	28° 30'	98° 13'
Red Bird: Nevada	40° 10'	118° 30'
Remac: British Columbia	49° 01'	117° 22'
Rexdale: Ontario	43° 43'	79° 35'
Reykjanes Ridge: Atlantic O.	60° 00'	27° 00'
Riceboro: Georgia	31° 44'	81° 26'
Riegelwood: N. Carolina	34° 22'	78° 14'
Rimouski Prov. Park: Qué	48° 00'	68° 10'
Robbins: N. Carolina	35° 25'	79° 34'
Robert E. Ginna: *power stn.*, New York	43° 15'	77° 16'
Robinson: Illinois	39° 00'	87° 44'
Rocanville: Saskatchewan	50° 22'	101° 45'
Rockall Bank: Atlantic Ocean	57° 00'	17° 00'
Rockfield: Kentucky	36° 46'	86° 36'
Rogers: Arkansas	36° 20'	94° 07'
Romulus: N.W.T.	79° 40'	84° 00'
Round Butte: *dam*, Oregon	44° 37'	121° 07'
Rowley: Utah	32° 43'	100° 54'
Sable Is. Bank: Atlantic O.	44° 00'	61° 00'
St. Andrews: New Brunswick	45° 05'	67° 03'
St. Charles: Québec	45° 41'	73° 10'
St. Jean, L. *see* St. John, L.: Québec	49° 25'	72° 30'
St. Marys: Georgia	30° 43'	81° 32'
St. Mary's: *r.*, Mich./Ont.	46° 10'	84° 00'
St. Paul Park: Minnesota	44° 50'	92° 59'
Sakakewa, L. *see* Garrison Res.: N.D.	47° 30'	102° 00'
Sand Lake: *sett.*, Alaska	60° 30'	148° 57'
Sand Lake: *sett.*, New York	42° 32'	73° 31'
Sandon: British Columbia	49° 58'	117° 14'
San Pedro: New Mexico	35° 58'	106° 20'
Sargasso Sea: Atlantic Ocean.	27° 00'	67° 00'
Sault Ste. Maire Canal: Ont.	46° 32'	84° 22'
Savannah Creek: *sett.*, Alberta	50° 20'	114° 38'
Schumacher: Ontario	48° 21'	81° 16'
Scottsville: Virginia	37° 48'	78° 29'
Secaucus: New Jersey	40° 48'	75° 50'
Seguin: Texas	29° 34'	97° 58'
Sequoyah: Oklahoma	36° 22'	95° 33'
Shallow Water: Kansas	38° 22'	100° 55'
Sharonville: Ohio	39° 16'	84° 24'
Sharpsville: Pennsylvania	41° 15'	80° 28'
Shawinigan Falls *see* Shawinigan: Québec	46° 33'	72° 45'
Shawmut: Alabama	32° 48'	85° 12'
Shirley Basin: Wyo.	42° 20'	106° 25'
Shoshone: *r.*, Washington	44° 48'	108° 10'
Shullsburg: Wisconsin	42° 34'	90° 15'
Sierrita: Arizona	32° 00'	112° 58'
Siloam Springs: *sett.*, Ala.	36° 11'	94° 32'
Sinclair: Wyoming	41° 46'	107° 06'
Sixtymile: *r.*, Yukon	63° 58'	140° 45'
Southeast Newfoundland Ridge: Atlantic Ocean	42° 00'	48° 00'
South Shore (Taylor): *sett.*, Kentucky	38° 43'	82° 59'
Spelter: W. Virginia	39° 21'	80° 20'
Spokane: *r.*, Idaho/Wash.	47° 54'	118° 20'
Spor Mountain: Utah	39° 50'	113° 15'
Spring City: Pennsylvania	40° 10'	75° 33'
Springfield: Tennessee	36° 30'	86° 53'
Springvale: Maine	43° 27'	70° 50'
Star: N. Carolina	35° 24'	79° 46'
Star Lake: *sett.*, New York	44° 10'	75° 04'
Steep Rock Lake: *sett.*, Ont.	48° 50'	91° 39'
Stellarton: Nova Scotia	45° 34'	62° 40'
Stevenson: Alabama	34° 52'	85° 50'
Stillwater Range: Nevada	39° 35'	118° 10'
Stone Mtn. Prov. Park: B.C.	58° 40'	124° 30'
Strachan: Alberta	52° 40'	115° 04'
Stratford Centre: Québec	45° 48'	71° 08'
Sturgeon Lake: *sett.*, Ontario	45° 27'	78° 42'
Sullivan: Missouri	38° 12'	91° 09'
Sverdrup Islands: N.W.T.	79° 30'	90° 00'
Sweetwater: *sett.*, Missouri	37° 10'	90° 50'
Swepsonville: N. Carolina	35° 58'	79° 23'
Taconite: Minnesota	47° 13'	93° 22'
Tanners Creek: *power stn.*, Ind.	39° 05'	84° 51'
Tasu Harbour: B.C.	52° 45'	132° 07'
Tempe: Arizona	33° 24'	111° 55'
Theodore: Alabama	30° 32'	88° 10'
Thomas H. Allen: *power stn.*, Tennessee	34° 07'	90° 03'
Three Rivers: *sett.*, Texas	28° 28'	98° 11'
Tilden Township: Michigan	46° 26'	87° 44'
Toglu: Northwest Territories	69° 20'	133° 10'
Tomah: Wisconsin	43° 59'	90° 30'
Townsville: N. Carolina	36° 29'	78° 25'
Trading House Cr.: *power stn.*, Texas	31° 33'	97° 09'
Treadway: Tennessee	36° 23'	83° 16'
Tremonton: Utah	41° 42'	112° 10'
Troy: Michigan	42° 36'	83° 09'
Tungsten: N.W.T.	63° 08'	128° 08'
Tungsten Queen: N. Carolina	36° 29'	78° 25'
Twin Buttes: *sett.*, Arizona	31° 52'	111° 03'
Tyrone: New Mexico	32° 40'	108° 22'
Uchi Lake: *sett.*, Ontario	51° 04'	92° 35'
Umpqua: *r.*, Oregon	43° 15'	122° 40'
Union Bridge: Maryland	39° 34'	77° 10'
Upper Fraser: B.C.	54° 07'	121° 56'
Uravan: Colorado	38° 22'	108° 44'
Valencia: New Mexico	34° 48'	106° 43'
Vallecitos: California	37° 20'	121° 53'
Valliant: Oklahoma	34° 01'	95° 07'
Vanadium: New Mexico	32° 47'	108° 05'
Vananda: British Columbia	49° 45'	124° 33'
Vancoram: Ohio	40° 20'	80° 31'
Vanscoy: Saskatchewan	52° 00'	106° 58'
Veta Grande: Nevada	39° 00'	119° 30'
Viburnum: Missouri	37° 43'	91° 08'
Viscount: Saskatchewan	51° 57'	105° 41'
W. A. C. Bennett: *dam*, B.C.	56° 10'	122° 29'
Wallace: Idaho	47° 28'	115° 56'
Walters: *dam*, N. Carolina	35° 46'	83° 06'
W. A. Parrish: *power stn.*, Texas	29° 34'	95° 45'
Waterton: Alberta	49° 08'	112° 44'
Watertown: Connecticut	41° 36'	73° 07'
Wattenberg: Colorado	40° 01'	104° 50'
Wawa: Ontario	48° 00'	84° 46'
Wax: Georgia	34° 08'	84° 59'
W. C. Beckjord: *power stn.*, Ohio	38° 57'	84° 17'
Welland Canal: Ontario	43° 00'	79° 30'
Wessington Springs: *sett.*, S. Dakota	44° 05'	98° 34'
Westbrook: Maine	43° 40'	70° 21'
West European Basin: Atlantic Ocean	46° 00'	15° 00'
West Fork: *r.*, Missouri	37° 25'	91° 00'
West Green: Georgia	31° 36'	82° 44'
West Homestead: Pennsylvania	40° 24'	79° 56'
West Monroe: Louisiana	32° 32'	92° 10'
West Point: Alabama	34° 17'	86° 57'
West Valley: New York	42° 26'	78° 37'
White Pine: Michigan	46° 45'	89° 35'
Whiteshell Prov. Park: Man.	50° 00'	95° 25'
White Springs: *sett.*, Florida	30° 20'	82° 45'
W. H. Sammis: *power stn.*, Ohio	40° 32'	80° 41'
Wilder: Kentucky	39° 05'	84° 30'
Willmore Wilderness Park: Alberta	53° 40'	119° 00'
Wilson: *dam*, Alabama	34° 45'	87° 40'
Wilson Spring: *sett.*, Ark.	34° 33'	93° 20'
Wilton: Iowa	41° 34'	91° 02'
Winborne: Alberta	51° 52'	113° 48'
Windsor: *dam*, Massachusetts	42° 18'	72° 21'
Winton: Minnesota	47° 55'	91° 48'
Woodlawn: N. Carolina	35° 47'	82° 02'
Wood River Junction: R.I.	41° 26'	71° 42'
Woodville: S. Carolina	34° 37'	82° 24'
Woodward: Alabama	33° 26'	86° 59'

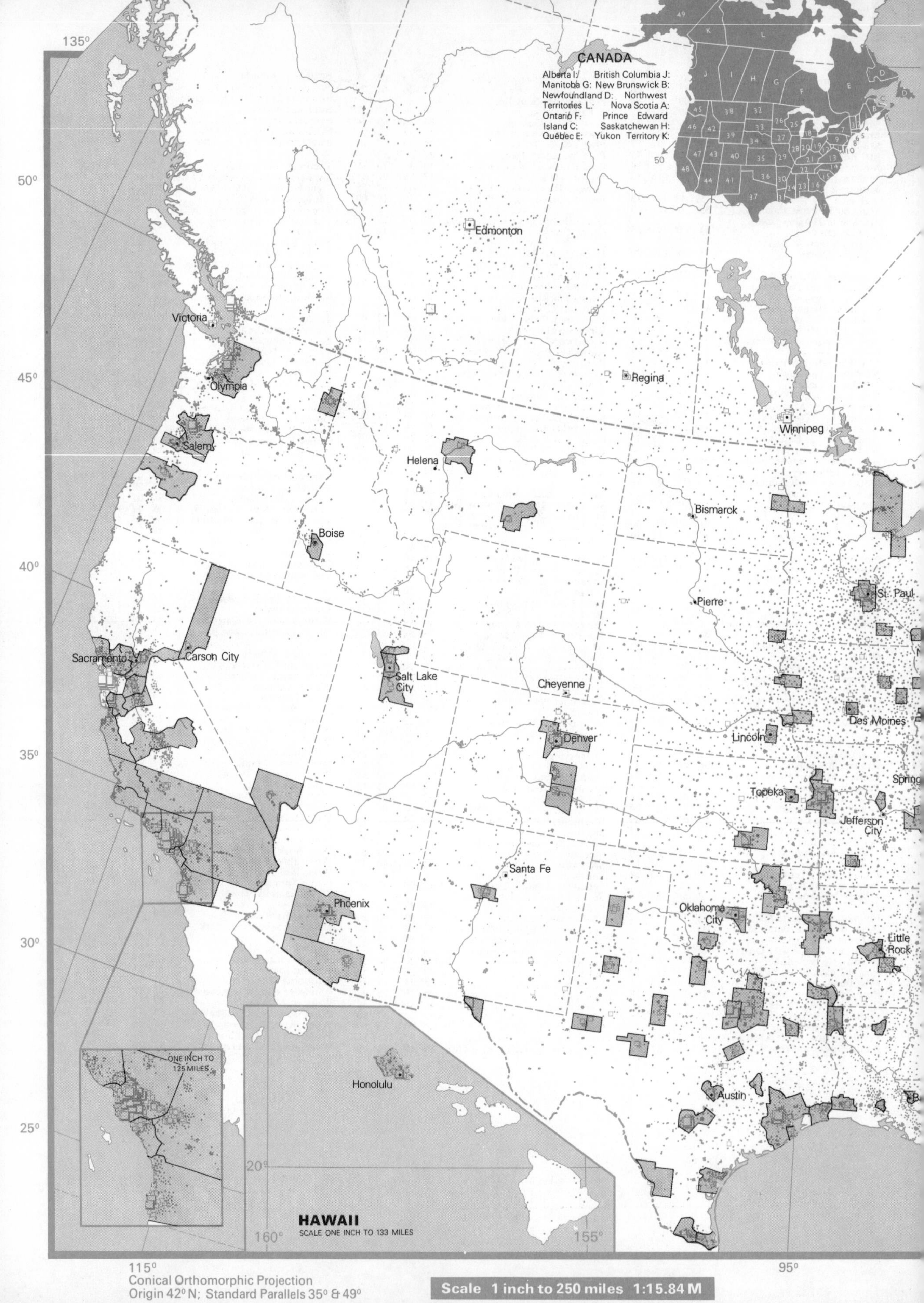

135°

50°

45°

40°

35°

30°

25°

20°

CANADA

Alberta I: British Columbia J:
Manitoba G: New Brunswick B:
Newfoundland D: Northwest
Territories L: Nova Scotia A:
Ontario F: Prince Edward
Island C: Saskatchewan H:
Québec E: Yukon Territory K:

Edmonton

Victoria

Olympia

Salem

Helena

Regina

Winnipeg

Boise

Bismarck

Sacramento   Carson City

Salt Lake
City

Pierre

St. Paul

Cheyenne

Des Moines

Denver

Lincoln

Santa Fe

Topeka

Jefferson
City

Spring

Phoenix

Oklahoma
City

Little
Rock

ONE INCH TO
125 MILES

Honolulu

Austin

20°

HAWAII
SCALE ONE INCH TO 133 MILES

160°

155°

115°
Conical Orthomorphic Projection
Origin 42° N; Standard Parallels 35° & 49°

95°

Scale   1 inch to 250 miles   1:15.84 M